THE AGING EXPERIENCE

THE AGING EXPERIENCE

An Introduction

to Social Gerontology

Russell A. Ward

DEPARTMENT OF SOCIOLOGY
STATE UNIVERSITY OF NEW YORK AT ALBANY

058912

J. B. Lippincott Company

New York   Hagerstown   Philadelphia   San Francisco

For Aunt Jessie

Sponsoring Editor: Dale Tharp
Project Editor: Claudia Kohner
Production Manager: Stefania J. Taflinska
Compositor: York Composition Co., Inc.
Printer and Binder: The Maple Press Company

The Aging Experience: An Introduction to Social Gerontology

Library of Congress Cataloging in Publication Data

Ward, Russel A.
    The aging experience.

    Includes bibliographies and index.
    1. Gerontology—United States.   I.   Title.
HO1064.U5W36   301.43'5'0973   78-27353
ISBN 0-397-47397-4

CONTENTS

PREFACE

The study of aging is a tremendously varied field. It is, of necessity, multidisciplinary, and this is both its strength and its weakness. The blending of many disciplines—sociology, psychology, economics, biology, and so on—reminds us that human behavior is multifaceted. No single approach can lay claim to possession of "truth." Gerontology has long benefitted from recognition of this fact. Yet the multiple "truths" of aging also make it an exceedingly complex topic, not easily grasped in its entirety.

This complexity makes writing a book about aging a difficult task best accomplished by narrowing the field to some degree. While this book is intended as an introduction to knowledge and issues in gerontology, its focus is clearly sociological—*social* gerontology. The emphasis is on the nature of the aging experience as it is shaped by the social context within which it occurs. Growing old is not and cannot be the same experience in different societies, or even in the same society at different times.

Chapter 1 is an introduction to the study of aging, its issues and concerns. Chapter 2 is intended to be a resource chapter, providing the "facts and figures" which can inform later discussions. Chapters 3, 4, and 5 present the major theoretical themes which should be referred to throughout the book. Chapter 3 discusses cross-cultural differences in aging, integrating them into a general model of age stratification. Chapters 4 and 5 consider the social-psychological consequences of aging: developmental changes over the life course, personality, and the impact of aging on the self. These chapters lay the foundation for the remainder of the book.

Chapters 6 through 12 each deal with particular substantive areas. Retirement and leisure are discussed in Chapters 6 and 7. Chapter 8 presents material on aging and the family, including marriage, widowhood, and extended family relationships. The community context of aging, encompassing problems of social integration and housing, is considered in Chapter 9. This is followed in Chapter 10 by a discussion of the politics of age and the potential for "senior power." Chapter 11 deals with service issues and Chapter 12 with the sociology of death and dying. Finally, Chapter 13 presents an overview and a look to the future of aging and of social gerontology.

This is not a "how to" book on aging, a road map to "golden aging." There are many ways to be happy in old age, just as there are many ways to be happy at any stage in the life course. It is hoped, however, that this book will inform readers about the factors which shape happiness and unhappiness in old age. This information can then perhaps be used to shape the reader's own aging experience, or that of others.

Inevitably, in a work of this scope, there are too many people who have contributed to adequately acknowledge each individually. While this book is not actually *for* older people, it is certainly *about* them, and a debt is owed to their willingness to be "studied." A more direct debt is owed to those researchers and thinkers who have contributed to the knowledge presented in this book.

Since the book flows from the intellectual and personal history of its author, other more direct contributions must be acknowledged. I would like to thank John DeLamater and David Mechanic for their contributions to my graduate training. Valuable suggestions and comments were made at various stages in writing the book by Susan Sherman, Art Richardson, Mark LaGory, and Arnold Foster. The publisher's reviewers also made many helpful suggestions. Students in my classes stimulated my thinking through their comments and questions. Kay Flanagan and Eileen Crary spent many hours typing and editing the manuscript, and Dorothy Hoffman did a marvelous job of copy editing. My editor, Dick Heffron, assisted in many ways, both large and small. A particular debt is owed Ron Farrell for his encouragement and support during this project. Finally, I would like to thank Marjorie and Matthew both for understanding the long hours I have put in on this book and for making everything I do so worthwhile.

1

Introduction to the Study of Aging

~~~~~~~~~~~~~~~~~~~~~~~~~~~~~~~

Aging and the aged have been subjects of interest throughout history. The sources of this interest vary from fascination with longevity and the dream of immortality, fear of the presumed "pathologies" of aging and the finality of death itself, conflict over the intergenerational transfer of power, to humanitarian concern over the circumstances of the aged. Concern with the aging experience is heightened by the aging of the population in the United States, which now includes 22 million people 65 years and older, more than 10 percent of the population. Old age thus presents both individuals and society with important challenges.

For the individual, there is the challenge of a greatly expanded life cycle, for most of us a span of 70 or 80 years. Thus, today's elderly are pioneers in a world where old age is no longer unusual. But how well will we use this additional time? Will we simply live out patterns established in adolescence and young adulthood, or will greater longevity cause us to reexamine the patterning of our lives? Since these and many other questions confront all whose old age lies ahead, the subject of aging is attracting increased interest among young people.

The growing number of older people also presents challenges to the larger society. On the one hand, the aged have greater need for many types of services. As we shall see, many older persons are plagued by poor health, poverty, inadequate housing, and related

1

problems. In addition, there is the question of the place of the aged in modern society, for the elderly have a right to meaningful roles and activities.

Scientific interest in aging has grown along with the aging of the population. This interest is still quite new, however, and knowledge in many areas remains limited. The study of aging is in a state of ferment as old ideas are displaced by new ones, a process repeated over and over. The future of the aging experience is itself a source of controversy. We will have ample opportunity as we proceed to see the extent to which the study of aging offers frontiers for new ideas.

Aging Themes in Literature

Long before aging aroused scientific interest, old age was a theme in the stories, myths, and cultures of societies. In her extensive review, Simone de Beauvoir (1972) notes that this theme occurs throughout history, and much of the treatment of aging is negative. For example, the Egyptian philosopher and poet, Ptah-hotep, wrote in 2500 B.C. that "old age is the worst of misfortunes that can afflict a man." Greek literature frequently reflected the conflict among generations, even among the gods; Zeus attacked his father and unseated the Titans, who were the "old" gods.

Plato and Aristotle both touched on the subject of age, though they came to rather different conclusions. Plato argued that the wisest men should serve as guardians of society, which implied a gerontocracy, since education would not bring its "full harvest" until the age of fifty. Aristotle, however, emphasized declines with old age and spoke much more positively about youth. This argument about the politics of age is still very much with us, of course.

Old age is also a theme in Shakespeare's sonnets and his play *King Lear*, one of the few great works in which the hero is an old man. It is not coincidental that *King Lear* is one of Shakespeare's tragedies, since the common treatment of old age through much of the literature reviewed by de Beauvoir depicts it as a time of misfortune and decline.

The myths and literature concerning aging present three prominent themes, all involving a search for prolonged life: the *antediluvian* theme, the *hyperborean* theme, and the *rejuvenation* theme (Birren and Clayton, 1975). The antediluvian theme involves belief in the greater longevity of earlier peoples (Gruman, 1966). Birren and Clayton note, for example, that according to the book of Genesis, Adam lived for 930 years and Noah for 950 years. The hyperborean theme "arises from the belief that in some distant place there is a culture or society whose people enjoy a remarkably long life" (Birren and Clayton, 1975:15). An interest in those who live beyond normal life spans remains strong, as evidenced by our fascination with such reputedly long-living people as the Abkhazians in the Soviet Union (see Chapter 3). Finally, the rejuvenation theme is found in many legends, such as the search for the "fountain of youth" by Juan Ponce de Leon, which resulted in the discovery of Florida. It is perhaps ironic that Florida still represents in many ways this search for eternal youth. Certainly this theme is still prominent in American culture, as even a casual look at current ads for skin cream and hair coloring suggest. The search for immortality has been a continuing theme in movies, including horror movies like "Frankenstein."

The Development of a Science of Aging

The scientific study of aging also has a long history (see Birren and Clayton, 1975). For example, Benjamin Franklin was interested in the aging process and, the possibility that in Frankensteinian fashion, lightning could resurrect the dead. However, Quetelet, a Belgian mathematician of the 1800s, is considered to be the first gerontologist, because of his statistical description of the distribution of traits by age. In the first large-scale survey related to aging, Sir Francis Galton demonstrated age differences in 17 different human abilities, such as visual accuracy and reaction time, through data collected from over 9,000 visitors to the International Health Exhibit in London in 1884.

Despite these early interests in old age, the scientific study of aging is a twentieth-century phenomenon. A number of studies in the early part of this century concerned biological aspects of aging and the inclusion of old age within developmental psychology (Birren and Clayton, 1975). G. Stanley Hall's *Senescence, the Second Half of Life* (1922) was an early classic. The perception of old age as a "social problem" had emerged by the 1930s, and there was growing recognition of the need for *collective* action on behalf of the aged (Maddox and Wiley, 1976). This was reflected in the passage of the Social Security Act of 1935.

It was during the post-World War II era, however, that gerontological research began to accelerate, coinciding with rising life expectancy and the growing size of the older population. A number of conferences on aging were held in the early 1940s, sponsored by such groups as the American Chemical Society and the National Institute of Health. It was also during this period that the Gerontological Society was formed and began publishing the *Journal of Gerontology*.

Early work in gerontology dealt largely with problems rather than with the aging process as a phenomenon. Psychology was the first discipline to approach aging as a process (Maddox and Wiley, 1976). Consideration of the social implications of the changing demographic structure of modern societies was stimulated by a Social Science Research Council research planning report (Pollak, 1948), and the late 1950s and early 1960s witnessed growing interest in the social processes associated with aging. The literature published on aging between 1950 and 1960 equaled that of the previous 115 years (Birren and Clayton, 1975). The White House Conferences on Aging in 1961 and 1971 gave further impetus to the study of aging, though there is some question whether the conferences themselves generated worthwhile information or policies.

However, there is no question that the last 20 years have seen an explosion of gerontological research. A recent attempt to create a definitive bibliography of biomedical and social science research for the years 1954 to 1974 yielded 50,000 titles (Woodruff, 1975). One recent issue of the *Journal of Gerontology*'s bimonthly bibliography of new publications in aging listed 687 new titles for a two-month period (Shock, 1976), and even this is not exhaustive (though no doubt exhausting). Another survey uncovered 152 doctoral dissertations on aging between 1972 and 1974 (Mueller, Moore, and Birren, 1975).

This knowledge explosion is typical of all scientific areas, and certainly contributes to feelings among researchers of being overwhelmed. It also has certain implications for a text such as this, which offers an introduction to the field.

First, in a book of limited scope, a comprehensive review of all the work in the field is not possible. The pace of knowledge growth suggests that this work is already obsolescent even as this passage is being read. It is our intention to introduce the "state of the art" as it currently exists, to review the important theoretical debates and empirical findings, and to highlight what seem to be the critical sociological issues of aging.

Second, the reader (and potential gerontologist?) should not feel overwhelmed by the weight of research findings. Most scientific fields today are bursting with new data and information. Yet there is still a great deal we do not know about aging and the aged, despite increasing interest in the field. Debates and uncertainties lend an air of excitement to a study of aging. And it should be noted that gerontology, perhaps more than most fields, has been characterized by attempts to bring order to the research explosion through the publication of bibliographies, such as those developed by the *Journal of Gerontology*, the Andrus Gerontology Center at the University of Southern California, and an "encyclopedia" of research findings through the mid-1960s (Riley and Foner, 1968). The recent publication of "The Handbooks of Aging Series" (Binstock and Shanas, 1976; Birren and Schaie, 1977; Finch and Hayflick, 1977) provides extremely valuable reviews of the field.

The Field of Social Gerontology

Before proceeding further, we should define the field and scope of this book. Gerontology is the study of aging. It includes all of the processes which are part of the aging experience, as well as those which intrude upon, and affect, that experience. Thus, gerontology is truly a multidisciplinary field which includes the medical researcher studying the causes of arteriosclerosis, the experimental psychologist studying the effect of the age of rats on learning, the sociologist studying the impact of modernization on the position of the aged, the economist studying social security systems, and the social worker studying the need for services.

The field of gerontology involves three major elements: biological, psychological, and social. The biological element concerns the impact of aging on physiology, cellular biology, and bodily systems. "Senescence," the deteriorative nature of biological aging, has been a major focus. There have been a number of theories about the nature of this process, and considerable research is still being done on the impact of aging on the organism. The biology of aging will not be emphasized in this book, however, except as it affects social aspects of aging. The health of older people, for example, is an important factor in the impact of aging on the individual self-image and personality and the reactions of society to aging and the aged.

The psychology of aging involves the psychological effects of aging on sensory processes (such as vision and hearing), perception, psychomotor performance, mental functioning (such as memory, learning, and intelligence), and so on. These aspects of aging will not be emphasized here, however, the biology and psychology of aging cannot simply be ignored in discussing the social aspects of aging. They may place very real constraints on the older person and have considerable consequences for the society as a whole. For example, the presumed conservatism of older people may be a function of their greater physical frailty and the uncertainty of their senses.

The focus of this book is on the social aspects of aging, the study of which is termed *social gerontology*. These social aspects may be divided into social-psychological and sociological elements. On the one hand, individuals do not age in a vacuum—they age within a social context which, to a large extent, determines their experience of aging. This social context encompasses the family or friends and peers at one level, and the society or culture at another level. The social framework determines the meaning of aging for the individual and whether aging will be primarily a positive or negative experience. On the other hand, the aging of individuals affects the social context in a variety of ways, whether one is concerned with a small family or a large society. For example, older individuals may have unique qualities which a society may or may not use to its advantage. Alternatively, the aged have certain handicaps which may or may not prove detrimental to a society.

Social gerontologists have a twofold task. First, we need to understand aging as an individual experience. What is it like to "be old"? How do people manage the possible accompaniments of aging—health problems, retirement, widowhood? We are still groping with answers to such questions. Social gerontology has been very useful in dispelling many of the myths about old age, but we are still trying to find the realities.

The second task is to understand the position of the aged in the political, economic, and social realms of each society. We know that older people encounter widely differing circumstances in different cultures. We can go back to Herodotus, the Greek historian, for accounts of this diversity.

> Herodotus tells us of some tribes who worshipped their elders as gods and of others who ate them. At one extreme were the Issedones, who gilded the heads of their aged parents and offered sacrifices before them. At the other were the people of Bactria, who disposed of their old folk by feeding them to flesh-eating dogs; or the ancient Sardinians, who hurled their elders from a high cliff and shouted with laughter as they fell on the rocks below. (Fischer, 1977:6)

Even in America, we have developed from a cult of old age among the Puritans to a cult of youth in contemporary society (Fischer, 1977). But we are only now beginning fully to appreciate the complex reasons for such differences.

There are many issues to be addressed by social gerontology. What is the place of older people in society, and how well are they integrated into modern cultures? How do we define and accordingly react to old age? What consequences does rising life expectancy have for both individuals and society? How is successful adaptation to aging achieved? How much conflict is there among different generations? What happens to people who retire or are widowed? How do the aged react to the prospect of death? What services do the elderly need and how are they best provided? These and many other questions form the subject matter of this book.

Social gerontology represents a truly interdisciplinary effort, as the review of doctoral dissertations noted earlier indicates. Among nonbiological subjects, the following disciplines were represented (in order of frequency): psychology, education, sociology, economics, language and literature, social work, anthropology, health sciences, nursing, business administration, music, speech pathology, statistics, geography, political science, theology, public administration, recreation, and engineering. Clearly there is plenty of room for everyone.

Why Study Aging?

The question—Why study aging?—may seem an odd one. But the reasons occasionally given for the need to study social gerontology can be misleading. First, old age as a developmental period of life is not completely distinct from other developmental periods, such as adolescence or middle age. Similar processes of socialization and adaptation are evident throughout the life cycle. Aging truly begins at birth, and it is unfortunate that old age is viewed as a separate period of an individual's life. There is increasing recognition that old age must be incorporated into the whole of developmental psychology (see, for example, Baltes and Schaie, 1973; Datan and Ginsberg, 1975).

Second, many people are drawn to the study of aging by a desire to help "all those poor old people." While this is certainly laudable, too heavy-emphasis on the problems of the aged may only contribute to stereotypes of old age as a period of unmitigated misfortune and unhappiness. Such stereotypes may generate negative attitudes toward aging, and the aged, resulting in denial of aging and withdrawal from the aged. It is true that older people encounter many problems—ill health, poverty, depression, feelings of uselessness—however, society itself often causes or exacerbates these problems.

These problems must be recognized and dealt with, but it must also be noted that our often irrational fear of aging and negative stereotypes about the aged are not based on a realistic picture of the "typical" older person (if there is such a thing). Most older people are *not* isolated from their families, are *not* in ill health or senile, and are *not* preoccupied with feelings of boredom and loneliness. We need to discard the stereotypes of old age as either gloom and misfortune or the serene "golden years." Both are true, and yet neither is true.

Finally, it must be recognized that people are not suddenly "reborn" on their sixty-fifth birthday. Older persons are not really so different from younger persons, and their difference may have very little to do with age itself. The best predictor of what a person will be like at age 65 is what he or she was like at age 45 or any other earlier age. The cheerful grandmother was probably a cheerful mother. The cranky retiree was probably a cranky worker. We are all prisoners of our pasts. And there is as much variety among older people as in other age groups.

Aging represents more than simple individual continuity, of course, or there would be no point to studying it. What makes aging interesting sociologically is that the individual ages *within a context*—a context which constrains the ability to maintain continuity. It is the existence of these constraints, and their more or less unique configuration, which allows one to treat old age as a distinct developmental period. The constraints are many, the most obvious, perhaps, being the biological decrements which accompany aging—increases in chronic illness and declining biological and psychological functioning. The social context of aging also creates constraints on personal continuity, through policies and institutional arrangements which affect the employment, health, housing, and other situations of the aged, and through social attitudes toward aging reflected in those policies. Individuals encounter change as they age, such as retirement and widowhood, and the meaning and impact of those changes are products of the social environment. Thus, aging is not a straight line extrapolation from earlier patterns of living, but must be seen in the following light:

> . . . to a great extent his last years depend upon those of his middle life. . . . Yet there is no inherent justice: Far from it. Illness and the social context may wreck the end of an active and open-hearted life. Earlier choice and present chance step in to give each old age its particular aspect. (de Beauvoir, 1972:505)

The Definition of Old Age

How do we determine whether someone is "young," "middle-aged," or "old"? Chronological age is certainly a basis for judgments about an individual's "stage of life." In some situations, society may define age in formal chronological terms, as with policies concerning eligibility for Social Security and compulsory retirement. Chronological age is at best a very rough indicator of what an individual is like, however, since it only partially reflects the biological, psychological, and sociological processes which truly define life stages. Indeed, it is unfortunate that we stereotype people according to age as much as we do.

Such categories as "middle age" and "old age" are social constructions, based on a wide variety of cues and standards which are socially defined. "Old age" may be defined functionally as a substantial change in an individual's capacity to contribute to the work and protection of the group. This functional capacity is determined by the socially perceived usefulness to the group of the qualities and abilities of its older members, and here cultural differences in the definition of age begin to emerge. For example, the skills of American older persons are often considered obsolete, and retirement is expected. Other cultures, such as the Abkhasians in the Soviet Union (Benet, 1974), have no concept of retirement, and the life cycle is viewed as a continuum, without the sharp transitions engendered by our retirement system.

All societies make distinctions about stages within the life cycle, however. Individuals encounter a series of changes which are linked to chronological age. The life course reflects the passage of individuals along a number of dimensions, including stages of work career and stages of family development (Clausen, 1972). The family cycle alone is comprised of a series of transitions: dating, young married couple, new parents, parents of adolescents, the "empty nest" when children leave, retirement of either or both spouses, widowhood, and possibly remarriage. Even this sequence of events is oversimplified. The study of life-cycle developmental stages is complicated by the fact that different life dimensions, such as work and family, may be synchronized in a variety of ways, as individuals enter and encounter transitions at different ages. Some persons marry at 18 and have three children by the time they are 23; others do not get married until they are 40. Some persons begin their employment career at 18, others at 25 or 30 (or, in the case of some housewives, even later). Career changes, divorce and remarriage, and other transitions further complicate the life course.

All is not chaos, however. Roles and statuses, and their sequences of occurrence, are age-graded in all societies and cultures.

> Age grade systems are expressions of the fact that all societies rationalize the passage of life time, divide life time into socially relevant units, and thus can be said to transform calendar time (or biological time) into social time . . . and duties, rights, and rewards are differentially distributed to age groups which themselves have been socially defined. (Neugarten and Datan, 1973: 58)

Thus, there are social expectations about age-appropriate behavior and the timing of events and transitions throughout the life cycle. The life course is an orderly sequence to the extent that social definitions of age are explicit and adhered to. This social definition of age varies among societies and constitutes a major way in which the social context shapes the aging experience. Social time results in an *age-stratification system*, according to which different age groups occupy different positions in the social structure, with associated rights, duties, rewards, and costs (Riley, Johnson, and Foner, 1972).

There have been numerous attempts to classify the "ages of adulthood" on the basis of life time and social time (Fry, 1976). Some of these represent attempts to define the stages of psychological development. Erikson (1950), for example, defines the following stages, each with its own type of "ego-identity crisis": early infancy, later infancy, early childhood, middle childhood, adolescence, early adulthood, middle adulthood, and late adulthood. It is interesting that such schemes typically show more stages during the first 20 years of life than during the later years. This may not be surprising for new parents, who feel that their child has a new developmental crisis every two months. But such schemes also reflect the fact that the latter half of the life cycle has only recently been of interest to development psychology. Indeed, it is only relatively recently that socialization has been considered relevant to the study of adulthood (Brim and Wheeler, 1966) and aging (Rosow, 1974).

There does seem to be substantial popular agreement on the definition of age categories, at least in Western societies. Neugarten and associates (1965) found that most middle-class respondents defined "young" as 18 to 24, "middle-aged" as 40 to 50, and "old" as 60 to 75, with some interesting sex differences. Women were considered "young" until 24, compared with 22 for men. On the other hand, women seem to age more quickly—they are "old" at 60, compared with 65 for men. These differences may reflect a narrower definition of women according to their physical characteristics.

There still is disagreement about the nature of age categories, however, even within one society. One study found that American respondents defined as few as two or as many as 15 age categories (Fry, 1976). The number of categories depended upon sex, socioeconomic status, and other respondent characteristics. This points out again that age is a social definition, shaped by the perceptions of the beholder.

To summarize, age is an ambiguous dimension. Chronological age tells us little about the individual, and age itself is a social construct. Many cues may be involved in feeling "old," from white hair and wrinkles to retirement or widowhood. To say that "you're only as old as you feel" is to recognize that age is more than a matter of years.

The Nature of Age Differences

While it is absurd to think that one can accurately predict social and psychological characteristics simply from an individual's age, it is equally absurd to deny the existence of age differences. For example, research studies indicate that older people may be more conservative, more cautious, less self-confident, less satisfied with life, and more religious (Riley and Foner, 1968). A primary task of social gerontology is to account for such differences and to specify the conditions under which they occur.

It must be stressed that age *differences* are not the same as age *changes*. This is a point which complicates both theory and research in aging and creates the potential for very misleading interpretations. This complication arises from the fact that age differences encountered in research may be the product of either "developmental time" or "historical time" (Bengtson, 1973).

Aging Effects

Developmental time refers to the changes in people as they grow older—they become more or less religious, more or less conservative, and so on. Thus, the person who is now 65 is in certain respects different from the same person 30 years earlier. These maturational or developmental changes may be termed *aging effects*, of which there are two types: *intrinsic* and *reactive*.

Intrinsic aging effects are changes which naturally accompany the aging process, regardless of social context. Reactive aging effects, on the other hand, are caused by social structure. It may be, for example, that there are intrinsic changes in brain functioning with age (Walker and Hertzog, 1975). Certainly biological changes seem to be essentially intrinsic aging effects. It should be recognized, however, that the extent to which older individuals are handicapped by biological change is reactive—it depends upon such aspects of the social context as the structure of available occupations and the network of supportive services. The concept of reactive aging effects implies that aging is different at different times, even in the same society.

It is often difficult, or even impossible, to make clear distinctions between intrinsic and reactive changes with age. Increasing religiosity may be viewed as an inevitable accompaniment of approaching death or as a consequence of the social conditions of aging and social definitions of death (as something to look forward to or avoid). There is a danger of ethnocentrism in social gerontology—of seeing the aging process in American society, for example, as being the same as in all societies. Purported intrinsic age changes must withstand the test of both cross-cultural and cross-time comparisons, which are still relatively infrequent. It is best to assume that all age changes are reactive—until proven otherwise. Certainly the essence of the approach taken in this book is that aging is a socially shaped experience.

One reason individuals change with age is that, as they grow through the life cycle, changes in roles and expected behaviors are inevitable (Clausen, 1972). The need to adjust to new experiences and life conditions, particularly at points of status and role transition, provides an impetus for personal change, even in identity. It is not surprising that those who are retired differ from those who work, or that those with children differ from those with none. The life course is itself affected by society, naturally. Retirement, for example, is a relatively new social institution, as is widespread college attendance. Additionally, the timing of events in the life cycle changes over the years. Industrialization has affected the timing of life events in both the family and economic spheres (Neugarten and Moore, 1968).

Cohort Effects

Historical time refers to the succession of generations. This implies that differences in age groups may be related to differences between generations rather than to the aging process. The term *cohort* means individuals born at the same time, and corresponds roughly to the concept of generations. Members of a cohort experience the same events at the same time in their life course. Mannheim (1952) suggests that one's generation locates an individual in the social structure. The similarity of experience creates the potential for a "generational consciousness." Thus, age groups differ in ways which are not attributable to aging, and cohort succession may create social change (Ryder, 1965).

That generations differ from one another and individuals are affected by historical events should not be surprising. Society can be thought of as a succession of cohorts flowing through time, each of which is shaped by a unique configuration of events. For example, persons born in 1890 grew up when frontier expansion was still a reality, encountered two world wars, went through the Great Depression during their middle (or working) years, and experienced the "future shock" of the 1970s at the end of their lives. Comparisons across generations indicate two major points about cohort analysis. First, events experienced by one cohort may not be encountered by another. Cohorts from 1890 and 1910 lived through a depression and global war; the 1950 cohort has not. Second, events may be experienced by different cohorts at different stages of the life cycle. What are the different consequences of the Depression for wage-earners (the 1890 cohort) and for children (the 1920 cohort)? How does the 1890 cohort react to the rush of the 1970s compared with the cohort born in 1950?

The shared experience of a cohort will shape the norms, values, attitudes, and behaviors of its members. This includes different socialization experiences, such as childrearing practices. Older people today may be more religious than younger people because they were brought up in a more religious environment, not because they have become more religious with age. Other age differences may simply reflect the fact that current older persons have less education than younger cohorts. Readers might reflect on the implications of the events shaping their own cohorts for their own "old age."

Some cohorts experience events of such magnitude, and so early in their lives, that they are felt to carry an indelible generational stamp. Many older people now living grew up during the Depression of the 1930s, and it is generally believed that this permanently affected their values and life styles. It is often argued that their experience in the Depression years accounts for their preoccupation with the work ethic and material security. Glen Elder, Jr., (1974) has published one of the few empirical studies of the long-term impact of the Depression on individuals. His book, which follows a group of Oakland school children, born in 1920–21, is an excellent example of the benefits to be gained from a cohort analysis and also offers some needed warnings about the dangers of exaggerating cohort effects.

Elder begins by cautioning us against a monolithic view of the Depression years. He notes that the conditions of life varied according to age, sex, race, and place of residence, and it was not a time of great economic deprivation for at least half of the population. It was most likely to be the "worst of times" for the foreign-born, the working class, and self-employed members of the middle class. For those who were deprived, this study provides evidence of drastic alterations in patterns of living, as families adapted to hardship. Most relevant for children (the 1920–21 cohort) were changes in the division of labor and authority patterns within the family, resulting in the extension of adult responsibilities. This meant greater involvement in household affairs for girls, particularly since mothers often worked outside the home, and greater social independence and freedom from traditional parental restraints for boys, who were more likely to work. In effect, childhood was cut short.

Elder finds little support, however, for the ideas that deprivation during the Depression made these people more committed to work or more preoccupied with job security and material success. Interestingly, deprivation as a child had little impact on adult status. Among the males, deprivation seems to have spurred ambition, resulting in greater clarity of career goals and greater concentration of effort and energy to achieve those goals. In fact, Elder finds that in the middle class, those who were deprived as children were psychologically healthier as adults. The protected lives of their more privileged peers left them with reduced capacities to cope with adult problems.

A deprived childhood for women in the Depression resulted in earlier marriage and greater preference for a domestic role. These are consequences of a number of factors, including limited educational opportunities and early domestic socialization. The household was an arena of expanded responsibilities for these girls, and apparently the domestic role was sought as an emotional haven from economic hardship. The impact of deprivation on women was greater in the middle class, since domestic concerns already dominated the preoccupations of the working class.

Deprivation during the Depression seems to have made a lasting impression on individuals' perspectives on the world: greater preference for the Democratic party, greater preoccupation with domestic economic problems, and a more optimistic outlook on economic opportunities for contemporary youth. Deprivation and memories of the humiliation and shame of doing without continue to color evaluations of later life.

> Through memories and actual experiences in the 30s, hardships in the Depression made a substantial difference in the way the Oakland adults have charted their life gratification. The observed variations are consistent with the theory that Depression experiences established a frame of reference for defining life periods as relatively good or bad times. From a relative perspective, adults who remember what it was like to have very little in the 30s appear to be more appreciative of their life situation in the more affluent, secure years of the 40s and 50s. (Elder, 1974:262)

Two additional conclusions may be derived from this study. First, cohorts are themselves composed of many different subgroups defined by social class, sex, and other factors. Second, several cohorts experience the same events, but with varying effects.

It is clear that aging and cohort effects are far from simple. An example may illustrate the complexity of analyzing age differences. A number of research studies have indicated that older people today tend to be more conservative than younger people. Norval Glenn (1974) has noted that there are several possible explanations for this age difference. It may be that aspects of biological aging, such as energy decline and loss of brain tissue, result in cautiousness and resistance to change. This could be viewed as an intrinsic aging effect. Alternatively, passage through the life cycle results in the accumulation of family responsibilities, occupational mobility, and so on. This may lead to a shift away from egalitarian ideals and toward self-interest. To the extent that social age-grading creates such differences over the life cycle, this can be interpreted as a reactive aging effect. Finally, older people may be more conservative because they grew up in a more conservative society or because they have less education. This would be a cohort effect.

To further complicate matters, Glenn combines these three explanations of age differences. He suggests that as people accumulate experience, they become less susceptible to change—each new experience has a smaller "marginal" impact—and their personal characteristics stabilize after young adulthood as a natural, or intrinsic, accompaniment of aging. Whether this means that older people are more conservative or more liberal than other age groups depends on the nature of societal and cohort change. Current older people grew up in a conservative environment, followed by societal changes toward liberalism and more liberal cohorts. Though older people have followed the general trend toward liberalism, they have changed more slowly than other cohorts, and thus, appear more conservative. However, society may take a conservative trend, and the younger, more liberal cohorts of today may be followed by more conservative cohorts. Thus, in 40 years older people may be more liberal than younger people.

The existence of cohort differences points out another reason not to stereotype all "old people." We all recognize the differences between 50-year-old persons and 30-year-olds, yet we often overlook the 20-year difference between those who are 90 and those who are 70. There is tremendous variability among older people, a fact which cannot be overemphasized. Neugarten (1974) argues, for example, that there is an increasing distinction between the "young-old" (55 to 75) and the "old-old." The young-old are characterized by better health, more education, relative affluence, and greater political activism. Thus, they run counter to the negative stereotypes about aging. Neugarten suggests that the young-old have an increasing concern with the meaningful use of time and will operate as agents of change in building an "age-relevant" society. Similarly, Cain (1967) has suggested that World War I represented an historical "watershed," with the result that more recent cohorts of older persons have encountered very different educational, family, and career experiences. They are more likely to have a high school education, a longer "empty nest" period, to be native-born, and so on. Social gerontology must be sensitive to the fact that the nature of aging is partly determined by the characteristics of persons undergoing the aging process, so that aging in the future may be quite different from aging now.

Methodological Issues

Research in social gerontology requires the same decisions and encounters the same problems as other kinds of social research.[1] The researcher must be concerned with the appropriateness of different research techniques, such as interviewing, observation, and experiments: methods which have been used fruitfully in the study of aging. Measures which are used must be valid—they must accurately reflect the concepts they are intended to measure—and be reliable, so that the same results can be achieved from repeated measurements of the same phenomenon. Researchers must also be sensitive to problems of sampling, data analysis, and so on. Apart from these normal concerns, however, there are issues of particular relevance to the study of aging.

The distinctions between age differences and age changes, intrinsic and reactive aging effects, and aging and cohort effects, imply that particular care needs to be taken in the design and interpretation of research. Most gerontological research has been cross-sectional—studying one sample of people at one point in time. While the sample may include a number of age groups, cross-sectional research can only show age differences. It cannot distinguish between age differences and age changes or between aging and cohort effects. Such research is valuable, if only in a suggestive way, but there is a danger of "over-interpreting" the results.

Since the concern in much gerontological research is with the nature of age changes, a longitudinal design is an appropriate approach. Longitudinal research involves the study of samples at more than one time, as when a national sample of individuals in 1960 is compared with a similar sample in 1970. The best longitudinal approach for studying individual change is the panel study,

---

[1] For discussions of the nature of social research, see Babbie (1975) and Lin (1976).

which follows a group of individuals through time. This allows the researcher to look at the actual change shown by each individual.

If a researcher wished to study the impact of retirement on individuals, a cross-sectional design would compare workers and retirees at a single point in time. Such a study might find differences between current workers and retirees, but would not indicate whether the retirees had changed because of retirement or had always been different from this sample of workers. A panel study would gather data about the same individuals as workers and following retirement. Thus, the researcher would know whether individuals had actually changed.

A major methodological drawback of panel studies is the loss of part of the sample over time (sample "mortality"). Individuals may refuse to be interviewed again, move, or die. This can be a problem particularly in studies of older panels. For example, in one of the best studies of retirement, conducted at Cornell University (Streib and Schneider, 1972), an original group of workers was followed for a period of seven years. At the end of those seven years, only 1,969 of the original 3,793 respondents were still in the study. The danger is that the final sample is no longer representative of the original sample—dropouts may be older, in poorer health, and so forth. Thus, knowledge about the impact of retirement may be restricted to those who "survive" such panel studies.

An additional drawback of longitudinal studies is that results may be applicable only to the particular cohort which is followed over time. What is required are research designs which allow us to separate effects of cohort change, aging, and the specific social context of aging. Table 1.1 presents a design based upon suggestions by Schaie (1967), incorporating a series of cross-sectional studies over time.

The researcher can analyze such data in a number of ways. Comparisons within a data gathering period indicate cross-sectional

Table 1.1. Research design combining cross-sectional and longitudinal data gathering

Cohort Birth Date	Data gathering period			
	1950	1960	1970	1980
Cohort I: 1900	A	B	C	D
Cohort II: 1910	E	F	G	H
Cohort III: 1920	I	J	K	L
Cohort IV: 1930	M	N	O	P

age differences (comparing A-E-I-M for 1950). Change in those age differences can be studied across time (for 1950, 1960, 1970, and 1980). Age changes can be investigated for each cohort (comparing A-B-C-D for Cohort I), and the nature of these age changes can be compared across cohorts. Finally, different cohorts can be compared at the same age. For example, all cohorts can be compared at age 50 by looking at A, F, K, and P. Comparison of this data with those showing age changes within a cohort allows one to make distinctions between aging effects and cohort effects, thus accounting for cross-sectional age differences. In addition, comparisons of age changes in different cohorts yields information about intrinsic versus reactive aging effects. For example, Cohort I may become increasingly conservative while Cohort IV shows no change, indicating reactive effects. One may also find "period" effects. An example of this would be if all cohorts became more conservative in 1950 and more liberal in 1970.

Obviously, gathering the type of data represented in Table 1.1 could be exhausting, time-consuming, and costly for any single researcher. It is thus no accident that most gerontological research is cross-sectional. There is a need for the development of data archives, so that results from a variety of cross-sectional studies can be combined in this fashion. Secondary analysis of available data could serve this purpose, but studies often are not comparable because different sampling techniques and measures are used.

There have been some efforts to use archival data. As an example, Douglass and associates (1974) utilized Gallup surveys from 1940, 1950, 1960, and 1970 to study the relationship between age and political attitudes. Data were available by age for a considerable span of time, but the authors were forced to use relatively trivial questions to measure political attitudes ("What do you think is the most important problem facing our country today?"). They had to use what was available to get comparable longitudinal data. It was found that neither age, cohort, nor period had an effect on national political issues. Period had an effect for community issues, and both period and age were related to family issues. The authors concluded that "the farther removed the political issue is from the individual, the less age will have a significant effect upon his attitude toward that issue" (p. 675).

Another research issue in social gerontology is accuracy of sampling, which always is critical to good research. If the sample is not representative, the results are of questionable validity. This has been a particular problem in the study of aging, since comprehensive lists of older people are not available. Those which approach completeness, such as Social Security and Internal Revenue lists, are not available to the researcher. The telephone book omits persons without telephones, and is therefore biased against the poor and institutionalized. Organizational membership lists overrepresent those who are healthy and middle-class, while studies in institutions, such as nursing homes, overrepresent the chronically ill and senile. In addition, sampling designs too often fail to incorporate racial and ethnic subgroups in the older population, limiting much of our knowledge about aging to white, middle-class older people.

While the limitations of sampling must be kept in mind by the researcher, some research does not require perfectly representative samples. One method which achieves greater accuracy is "area" sampling, where particular types of respondents are sought.[2]

If interviewing is used, certain difficulties may arise with older respondents. The aged may be skeptical of social research, since they are likely to be wary of strangers, or may see the interviewer as a government "snoop." Hearing and vision difficulties, often coupled with mental confusion, can be particular problems with institutionalized populations. Various response biases may occur. For example, older people may have more difficulty understanding questionnaire forms and are more likely to state "no opinion" (Riley et al., 1972). Even age may be inaccurately reported. This has led to skepticism concerning claims of unusual longevity in certain cultures (Medvedev, 1974). In the interaction of an interview, respondents may attempt to "impress" the interviewer or give "correct" or "socially desirable" responses (Phillips, 1971). Older people may also be unwilling to admit loneliness, unhappiness, marginality, or self-derogation to the interviewer.

The Themes of the Book

Clearly, the study of aging is a very complex field, and the older population is characterized by great variability in ages, cohorts, personalities, health, and so on. The aged should not be studied as a separate entity, with no relationship to younger groups. Finally, social gerontology encompasses a variety of substantive areas of study—retirement, widowhood, political behavior, and so on. There is some danger that social gerontology could become a series of discrete, unrelated subject areas, lacking any sense of the integrated nature of the aging experience, its relationship to the larger society, and its overall impact on the aging individual. Maddox and Wiley (1976) have noted that:

---

[2] For an introduction to principles of sampling, see Lin (1976).

The social scientific study of aging needs but currently lacks widely shared paradigms which would provide common conceptualization of issues, standard measurements, and clearly defined agendas for the systematic testing of hypotheses derived from theory. Applied, problem-oriented studies of the societal consequences of aging predominate. (p. 4)

They also note that systematic theory development has been "strikingly absent" in gerontology.

Integrating frameworks are needed to facilitate the study of aging, while still doing justice to the complexity of the field. Two perspectives which show promise of accomplishing this will serve as themes throughout this book.

Age Stratification

The first framework recognizes the "macro" nature of aging: the fact that society and the social structure affect the nature of aging in a variety of ways. This means that all societies have an *age stratification system* (Riley, 1971; Riley et al., 1972). Because of the processes of aging and cohort succession, age groups which emerge have different characteristics and capacities. Age is also one of the criteria for determining the position of individuals in the social structure, and individuals are socialized—more or less— to accept these age-related positions. All age groups in a society can be analyzed on this basis, though the focus here will be on older age "strata."

While all societies can be characterized according to age stratification, the nature of the particular age stratification system will differ from society to society. Because of this, aging will be a different experience in different societies and in the same society at different times. By examining the age stratification system, we can understand the ways in which social structure affects the relative position and evaluation of older people. As societies change, the nature of age stratification changes, and with it the position of the aged. In American society, for example, urbanization and industrialization have been accompanied by the development of retirement as an institution, changes in family structure, and alterations of sex roles. The impact of such changes on the aging experience can be understood within a model of age stratification (see Chapter 3).

Symbolic Interactionism and Aging

The second broad perspective of this book will be a "micro" approach to aging: a recognition that the impact of aging must also be understood at the *individual* level. There are as many different aging experiences as there are aging individuals. Each person approaches old age from a unique background of experience, personality, and life style and experiences a different configuration of age-related changes. An understanding of the individual impact of aging requires an appreciation of the interpretation and meanings of the events which may accompany aging. Some persons dread retirement as an end to usefulness, others look forward to a deserved reward for a lifetime of hard work. The meaning of aging and its concomitants evolve from "symbolic interactions" between the individual and other individuals, groups, and the society.[3] Aging is a social experience, and its meanings are socially defined. But it is the individual who ultimately translates those meanings and definitions and makes sense of aging as a *personal* experience.

These two frameworks bring to mind some philosophical considerations. On the one hand, society and age structure people's lives in various ways, determining the broad parameters of the situations in which they find themselves, creating constraints, potentialities, and problems. Because of this, we can speak of patterns or trends which differentiate age groups. But it must be kept in mind that people are not totally determined by a rigid system of age stratification. They still make their own choices, based upon their own definitions of the situations they encounter. Comparison might be made with a table, which is very solid but, in fact, is composed of billions of atoms, electrons, and molecules, the position of which, physics tells us, can never be accurately determined. Out of this chaos, however, a pattern emerges at a higher level of observation. While we talk generally about "the aged," we too often ignore variations from the "usual."

Summary

There is a long history of interest in aging, as reflected in cultural themes and early scientific inquiry. The major thrust of gerontological research has come within the last 25 years, however. Gerontology has become a truly interdisciplinary field, encompassing biological, psychological, and social concerns. The primary focus of this book will be on the social aspects of aging.

Aging and the aged are not separate from the rest of the human experience, and old age is neither entirely gloomy nor completely serene. There is considerable personal continuity. Nonetheless, personal change and the social context place age-related con-

---

[3] For a more complete discussion of the symbolic interactionist perspective, see Blumer (1969).

straints on individuals which make old age a sociologically interesting period.

Age is itself a social construction. We have conceptions of distinct age periods such as "middle age" and "old age" because societies assign social positions partly on the basis of age. Societies differ in the way in which this is done, resulting in cross-cultural differences in the aging experience.

The existence of age differences may reflect a number of different phenomena: intrinsic aging effects, reactive aging effects, or cohort effects. This points to the need for more complex research designs which incorporate longitudinal as well as cross-sectional studies. There are additional methodological issues in the study of aging, including sampling and response biases.

This book has two major themes. First, all societies can be characterized by their age stratification systems, which result in age-differentiated expectations, sanctions, and rewards. Second, the meaning of aging must be sought at the individual level, as each aging person interprets the experience according to the symbolic meanings available to him or her.

References

Babbie, Earl
  1975   The Practice of Social Research. Belmont, Ca. Wadsworth.
Baltes, Paul and K. Warner Schaie (eds.)
  1973   Life-Span Developmental Psychology: Personality and
         Socialization. New York: Academic Press.
Beauvoir, Simone de
  1972   The Coming of Age. New York: Putnam's Sons.
Benet, Sula
  1974   Abkhasians: The Long-Living People of the Caucasus.
         New York: Holt, Rinehart and Winston.
Bengtson, Vern
  1973   The Social Psychology of Aging. Indianapolis: Bobbs-Merrill.
Binstock, Robert and Ethel Shanas (eds.)
  1976   Handbook of Aging and the Social Sciences. New York:
         Van Nostrand Reinhold.
Birren, James and Vivian Clayton
  1975   "History of gerontology." In Diana Woodruff and James
         Birren (eds.). Aging: Scientific Perspectives and Social
         Issues. New York: D. Van Nostrand.
Birren, James and K. Warner Schaie (eds.)
  1977   Handbook of the Psychology of Aging. New York: Van
         Nostrand Reinhold.
Blumer, Herbert
  1969   Symbolic Interactionism. Englewood Cliffs, N.J.:
         Prentice-Hall.

Brim, Orville and Stanton Wheeler
    1966   Socialization after Childhood. New York: John Wiley.
Cain, Leonard D., Jr.
    1967   "Age status and generational phenomena: The new old
           people in contemporary America." The Gerontologist 7
           (2): 83–92.
Clausen, John
    1972   "The life course of individuals." In Matilda Riley, Marilyn
           Johnson, and Anne Foner (eds.). Aging and Society.
           Volume 3: A Sociology of Age Stratification. New York:
           Russell Sage.
Datan, Nancy and Leo Ginsberg (eds.)
    1975   Life-Span Developmental Psychology: Normative Life
           Crises. New York: Academic Press.
Douglass, Elizabeth, William Cleveland, and George Maddox
    1974   "Political attitudes, age, and aging: A cohort analysis of
           archival data." Journal of Gerontology 29 (6): 666–75.
Elder, Glen, Jr.
    1974   Children of the Great Depression. Chicago: University of
           Chicago Press.
Erikson, Erik
    1950   Childhood and Society. New York: W. W. Norton.
Finch, Caleb and Leonard Hayflick (eds.)
    1977   Handbook of the Biology of Aging. New York: Van
           Nostrand Reinhold.
Fischer, David
    1977   Growing Old in America. New York: Oxford University
           Press.
Fry, Christine
    1976   "The ages of adulthood: A question of numbers." Journal
           of Gerontology 31 (2): 170–77.
Glenn, Norval
    1974   "Aging and conservatism." In Frederick Eisele (ed.).
           Political Consequences of Aging. The Annals of the
           American Academy of Political and Social Science 415
           (September): 176–86.
Gruman, G. J.
    1966   "A history of ideas about the prolongation of life: The
           evolution of prolongevity hypothesis to 1800." Philadelphia:
           American Philosophical Society.
Hall, G. Stanley
    1922   Senescence, the Second Half of Life. New York: Appleton.
Lin, Nan
    1976   Foundations of Social Research. New York: McGraw-Hill.
Maddox, George and James Wiley
    1976   "Scope, concepts and methods in the study of aging." In
           Robert Binstock and Ethel Shanas (eds.). Handbook of
           Aging and the Social Sciences. New York: Van
           Nostrand Reinhold.

Mannheim, Karl
  1952   "The problem of generations." In Karl Mannheim (ed.).
         Essays on the Sociology of Knowledge. New York: Oxford
         University Press.
Medvedev, Zhores
  1974   "Caucasus and Altay longevity: A biological or social
         problem?" The Gerontologist 14 (5): 381–87.
Mueller, Jean, Julie Moore, and James Birren
  1975   "A bibliography of doctoral dissertations on aging from
         American institutions of higher learning, 1972–1974."
         Journal of Gerontology 30 (4): 484–89.
Neugarten, Bernice
  1974   "Age groups in American society and the rise of the young-
         old." In Frederick Eisele (ed.). Political Consequences of
         Aging. The Annals of the American Academy of Political
         and Social Science 415 (September): 187–98.
Neugarten, Bernice and Nancy Datan
  1973   "Sociological perspectives on the life cycle." In Paul Baltes
         and K. Warner Schaie (eds.). Life-Span Developmental
         Psychology: Personality and Socialization. New York:
         Academic Press.
Neugarten, Bernice and Joan Moore
  1968   "The changing age-status system." In Bernice Neugarten
         (ed.). Middle Age and Aging. Chicago: University of
         Chicago Press.
Neugarten, Bernice, Joan Moore, and John Lowe
  1965   "Age norms, age constraints, and adult socialization."
         American Journal of Sociology 70 (6): 710–17.
Phillips, Derek
  1971   Knowledge from What? Chicago: Rand McNally.
Pollak, Otto
  1948   Social Adjustment in Old Age: A Research Planning
         Report. Bulletin 59. New York: Social Science Research
         Council.
Riley, Matilda
  1971   "Social gerontology and the age stratification of society."
         The Gerontologist 11 (1): 79–87.
Riley, Matilda and Anne Foner
  1968   Aging and Society. Volume 1: An Inventory of Research
         Findings. New York: Russell Sage.
Riley, Matilda, Marilyn Johnson, and Anne Foner (eds.)
  1972   Aging and Society. Volume 3: A Sociology of Age
         Stratification. New York: Russell Sage.
Rosow, Irving
  1974   Socialization to Old Age. Berkeley: University of
         California Press.
Ryder, Norman
  1965   "The cohort as a concept in the study of social change."
         American Sociological Review 30: 843–61.

Schaie, K. Warner
  1967   "Age changes and age differences." The Gerontologist
         7 (2): 128–32.
Shock, Nathan
  1976   "Current publications in gerontology and geriatrics."
         Journal of Gerontology 31 (2): 231–53.
Streib, Gordon and Clement Schneider
  1972   Retirement in American Society. Ithaca, N.Y.: Cornell
         University Press.
Walker, James and Christopher Hertzog
  1975   "Aging, brain function, and behavior." In Diana Woodruff
         and James Birren (eds.). Aging: Scientific Perspectives and
         Social Issues. New York: D. Van Nostrand.
Woodruff, Diana
  1975   "Introduction: Multidisciplinary perspectives of aging."
         In Diana Woodruff and James Birren (eds.). Aging:
         Scientific Perspectives and Social Issues. New York:
         D. Van Nostrand.

2

Characteristics of the
Older Population

~~~~~~

In assessing the sociological position and problems of any group it is important to have an understanding of who comprises that group. There are many stereotypes and claims made about the aged, many of them patently false and perhaps most of them in some way exaggerated. This chapter may confuse as much as it clarifies if its presentation of "facts and figures" is taken to mean that "the old" are a homogeneous group and that their diversity can be captured in a series of tables. With this disclaimer in mind, let us look at the *general* characteristics of older people.

Demographic Characteristics

The Population of Older People

The most striking statistical fact about the older population is the great increase during this century in the number of people over 65 in the United States. Table 2.1 indicates that the number of persons over 65 has increased from 3 million in 1900 to over 22 million in 1975. This older population has increased more rapidly than the general population, rising from 4.1 percent of the population in 1900 to over 10 percent in 1975. Projections indicate that over 30 million people will be over 65 by the year 2000 and that by that time they may comprise over 12 percent of the population. This increase is not confined to the "young-old" (60 to 75). In

26

Table. 2.1.   Population 65 and over in the United
States, 1900–2000

| | Population age 65 and over | |
| | Number (in thousands) | Percent of total population |
Year		
1900	3,099	4.1
1910	3,986	4.3
1920	4,929	4.7
1930	6,705	5.4
1940	9,031	6.8
1950	12,397	8.2
1960	16,675	9.2
1970	20,085	9.9
1975	22,400	10.5
Projection:		10.7[a]
2000	30,600	12.5[b]

[a] Assuming 2.7 births per woman.
[b] Assuming 1.7 births per woman.
Source: U.S. Bureau of the Census, 1973b, p. 2, and 1976, p. 3.

1950, persons 80 years of age and older constituted 14.1 percent
of all those over 65; by 1975, this proportion had risen to 20.2
percent.

Even if our total knowledge of aging were restricted to this
growth in the size and porportion of the older population, we
should expect some important consequences for research and social
policy. The aged generate a disproportionate demand for certain
services, including health care and financial assistance, and therefore represent an increasing "burden" on society, particularly the
younger, working population who support societal programs. The
old age "dependency ratio" (proportion of population age 65+ to
those 18 to 64) has been rising and will continue to do so (Cutler
and Harootyan, 1975), perhaps leading to conflict over scarce
resources and a decline in willingness to support special programs
such as Medicare and Social Security.

That changing age structure affects the whole society can be
seen in the effects of the post-World War II "baby boom"
cohort. When this cohort was young, schools had to be built to
accommodate them; now there are too many schools and too few
students. It has been noted that the entrance of this cohort into
old age, around the year 2010, will bring a major crunch to the
financing of Social Security and other pension plans. The impact
will also be felt in such areas as the need for more nursing-home
beds as the proportion of the "old-old" (75+) increases.

Yet this picture of the future is too simplified. While there will
be more aged in the future, they are likely to be healthier and in

better financial condition than today's aged. In addition, the rising old-age dependency ratio will be counteracted by a declining proportion of children.

Life Expectancy and the Demographic Transition

As might be expected, the growing size of the older population has been accompanied by increases in life expectancy. Life expectancy has shown a general improvement over the centuries. Cutler and Harootyan (1975) indicate that for the most part this occurred rather slowly, increasing from approximately 18 years in 1000 B.C. to 49.2 in the United States in 1900. This century has seen a marked increase in life expectancy, however, as indicated in Table 2.2. The greatest increase occurred prior to the last 30 years. Oddly, declines in *infant* mortality have contributed most to the aging of the population; Figure 2.1 indicates that life expectancy has not increased very much for those who have already reached age 65. This phenomenon, and the general "aging" of the population reflected in these statistics, are by-products of modernization and the *demographic transition* (Cowgill, 1974a). Two aspects of this transition contribute to an older population. First, the fertility (birth) rate tends to decline. Fertility sets the limit on the size of any particular birth cohort. When the fertility rate declines, already existing cohorts will be a comparatively larger part of the population. Second, public health measures (particularly in sanitation and the control of communicable diseases) result in lower mortality (death) rates. Since the greatest effect is on infant and child

Table 2.2. Average life expectancy in the United States, by race and sex: 1900–1972

	1900–02	1929–31	1949–51	1974
All:				
At birth	42.9	NA	68.1	71.9
At age 65	76.9	NA	78.8	80.6
White males:				
At birth	48.2	59.1	66.3	68.9
At age 65	76.5	76.8	77.8	78.4
White females:				
At birth	51.1	62.7	72.0	76.6
At age 65	77.2	77.8	80.0	82.6
Nonwhite males:				
At birth	32.5	57.6	58.9	62.9
At age 65	75.4	75.9	77.8	78.4
Nonwhite females:				
At birth	35.0	49.5	62.7	71.2
At age 65	76.4	77.2	79.5	81.7

Source: U.S. Bureau of the Census, p. 26.

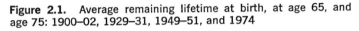

Figure 2.1. Average remaining lifetime at birth, at age 65, and age 75: 1900–02, 1929–31, 1949–51, and 1974

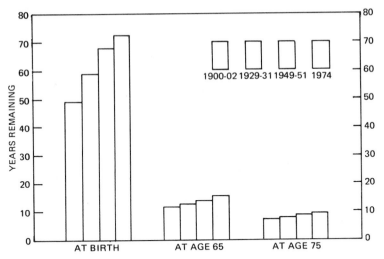

Source: U.S. Bureau of the Census, 1976, p. 27.

mortality, there will be an initial increase in younger age groups, but over time, as fertility declines, the proportion of older people rises. These trends are reflected in Table 2.2: mortality has declined during this century and fertility has declined particularly over the past 30 years.

That an aging of the population is associated with modernization can be seen from a comparison of countries with high and low percentages of those over 65 (United Nations, 1972). Modern industrialized societies tend to have higher proportions over 65: the German Democratic Republic (15.6 percent), Sweden (13.7 percent), France (13.4 percent), the USSR (11.8 percent), Canada (8.1 percent), and Japan (7.1 percent). Developing countries have much lower proportions: Mexico (3.7 percent), Syria (3.2 percent), Kenya (3.6 percent), Mali (1.6 percent), and Venezuela (2.4 percent). In some countries, life expectancy is still very low—only 37.2 years in Mali, for example (Hauser, 1976).

Table 2.2 shows that life expectancy is higher for females than for males, and for whites than for nonwhites (primarily blacks). Combining these, it is interesting that nonwhite females have a higher life expectancy than white males. The lowest life expectancy is for nonwhite males, though for those who reach 65, racial differences in life expectancy are very slight, which may reflect a "survival of the fittest" among minority groups, as well as their higher rates of infant mortality.

Sex Ratio

Since the average woman lives longer than the average man, a substantial majority of older persons are women (more than 59 percent of those over 65 in 1975). This is largely a product of changes in the past 40 years and is especially true at older levels (Figure 2.2). Currently, the average woman can expect to outlive the average man by about eight years. This difference results partly from sex differences in causes of death. Medical advances in treating infectious diseases, such as influenza and tuberculosis, have been greater than for degenerative diseases, such as cancer and heart disease, and men are more likely than women to die of degenerative diseases. Whether these mortality differences are linked to traditional sex-roles or to inherent susceptibility to certain diseases can only be speculated upon at this point. However, older women, particularly widows living alone, should be high-priority targets of social policies, given their vulnerability to low income, poor health, and crime.

Place of Residence

As with other age groups, of course, older people can be found in any number of residential settings. There are trends, however. Older people are most numerous in the largest states—nearly one-

Figure 2.2.   Sex ratios in the older ages: 1900 to 2010

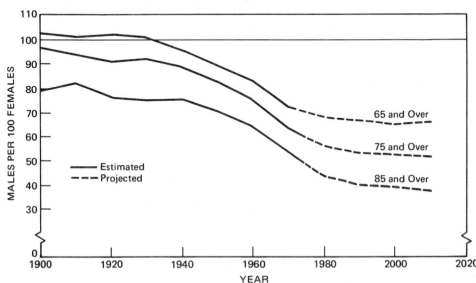

Source: U.S. Bureau of the Census, 1976, p. 12.

third of all persons over 65 reside in New York, California, Pennsylvania, and Illinois. In some states the proportions of population over 65 is very low: Alaska (2.4 percent), Hawaii (6.6 percent), and New Mexico (7.9 percent) (U.S. Bureau of the Census, 1976). Other states have relatively high proportions of older people, including Florida (16.1 percent), Arkansas (12.8 percent), and Iowa (12.7 percent).

The fact that some states are relatively "older," however, tells us very little about who those older people are, why they are there, and what the aging experience may be like for them. Younger people migrate out of some states including many midwestern states, such as Iowa, Kansas and Nebraska, as well as other states such as Maine and Arkansas. Older people migrate to other states (e.g., Florida). From 1960 to 1970, the number of persons 65 and over increased by more than 70 percent in Arizona, Florida, and Nevada. Older people who "move in" are likely to be very different from those who are "left behind," particularly since those over 65 have the lowest rate of residential mobility of any age group. Each state must develop policies to meet the needs of its own particular older population.

The United States is an urban society, and 73 percent of older people live in urban areas (Table 2.3). Older people are more likely than the general population to be concentrated in central cities and less likely to live in suburban areas. There was some increase from 1960 to 1970, however, in the proportion of older people residing in the "urban fringe" (suburbs). Older blacks are even more likely to be central-city residents: 52 percent of blacks 65 and over live in a central city.

A different picture emerges, however, when one looks at older people as a proportion of the residential population. The highest proportion of older people is found in small towns (1,000 to 2,500 inhabitants), which seem to function as farm retirement centers. The next highest proportion is found in urban areas of 2,500 to

Table 2.3. Residential distribution of the 65 and over population, 1960–1970 (percentage)

| | Urban | | | |
| | Urbanized areas | | | |
Date	Central Cities	Urban Fringe	Other Urban	Rural
1960	34.7	16.5	18.4	30.4
1970	34.1	21.2	17.6	27.1

Source: U.S. Bureau of the Census, 1973b, p. 14, and 1964, p. 149.

10,000 population, then 10,000 or more, with lowest proportions of older people in rural farm and suburban areas. There are implications for the elderly in each of these living situations. For example, rural and small-town residents may have lived there longer, and have more intact social networks, but they are likely to be more isolated from such services as health care and transportation, while the reverse is true of the aged in cities. Each segment of the older population must be taken into account in developing services for as well as theories about aging.

Housing patterns within urban areas are the result of "natural" processes of residential age segregation developing from two factors (La Gory, Ward, and Juravich, 1977). First, older people are likely to be economically disadvantaged in the competition for valuable space, and therefore more likely to be confined to areas with older, cheaper housing. La Gory and associates found that age segregation was most pronounced in larger, rapidly growing metropolitan areas in which land-use is more differentiated (including greater suburbanization) and average housing costs are higher. Second, residential age segregation results from changing needs over the life cycle (Johnston, 1971). Single and young married people are often attracted to the central city by the excitement and diversity of urban life and the accessibility to employment and city services. Families with children, however, are attracted to suburbs, which offer more living space, clean environments, better schools, and so on. In middle age and beyond there is less need for space and a tendency to move to smaller, more economical houses or apartments nearer the center of the city. Accessibility to city services, particularly public transportation, may again become important. Thus, inner zones of metropolitan areas draw the young and the old disproportionately, with few children. This assumes ability to move, of course. Low-income and minority groups may be attracted to suburban housing, but cannot move because of discrimination or inability to pay the price.

Although housing needs do change through the life cycle, older people constitute the least mobile age group in society. This can be seen in Figure 2.3. Long distance migration by relatively affluent older persons, such as to retirement communities in Florida or Arizona, has become more prevalent in the past 20 years, but still accounts for only a very small minority. Most people who retire, for example, do not move, and those who do tend to remain in the same general vicinity (Atchley, 1976). Atchley notes that older people seldom move because of climate or the desire for "retirement living." Most moves are the result of desires for better (or more economical) housing, better neighborhood, or closer proximity to family and friends. For some older

Figure 2.3. Mobility and migration rates for the population 65 years old and over and one year old and over: 1970–71

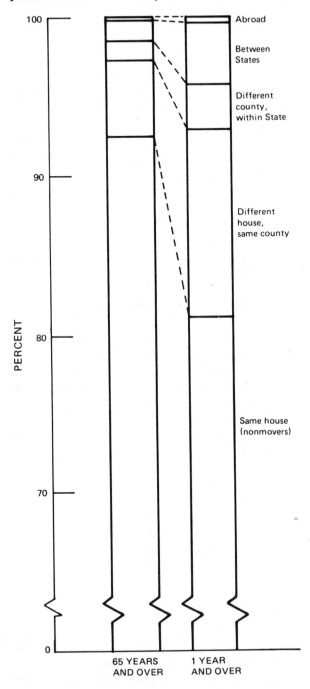

Source: U.S. Bureau of the Census, 1976, p. 20.

people, moving is a response to major life disruptions—retirement, widowhood, illness—which reduce personal independence and create dissatisfaction with current housing.

Health

Health is basic to any discussion of the aging experience, since health, particularly *self-rating* of health, is the most important determinant of satisfaction among the aged (Palmore and Luikart, 1972). Health problems constitute a very basic threat to all of us and may actually come to symbolize the aging process. In a study of heart-attack patients, Rosen and Bibring (1966) found that middle-aged males exhibited greater depression, and were more likely to be described as "hostile" or "withdrawn" by nurses, than both younger and older males. Heart attacks carry the emotional threat of helplessness and passive dependency. The authors suggested that younger men feel that they have time to bounce back, while older men have already begun to adapt to their aging. However, a heart attack forces middle-aged men to face their own aging and the possibility of decline which it represented. They have neither the luxury of time nor the benefit of previous adaptation to aging.

Before discussing "objective" indicators of health in the older population, it should be recognized that people do assess their own health, which is perhaps more important in determining satisfaction than "actual" health. Many older people do learn to accept certain pains and disabilities as inevitable or unimportant. Their self-ratings, based only in part on objective health, decline less with age than objective ratings (Riley and Foner, 1968). The definition of "good health" varies from one age group to another and changes during the life cycle. Arthritis, for example, may be viewed as normal by an older person but be intolerable for a younger person. A study conducted in the United States, Great Britain, and Denmark found that most older people say they are in good health *for their age* (Shanas et al., 1968). Unfortunately, such accommodations to expectations may constitute denial and become a barrier to seeking needed assistance.

Mortality

Death, of course, is an inevitable reality, and particularly a psychological reality for older people. While death cannot be avoided, it has been substantially postponed during this century. Since 1940 the rate of infant mortality (deaths to infants under one year of age per 1,000 live births) has declined from 54.9 to 21.4

Table 2.4. Mortality rates (deaths per 1,000 population) for selected age groups, 1900–1970

	Age						
Year	Less than 1 year	25–34	55–64	65–74	75–84	85 and over	Total
1900	162.4	8.2	27.2	56.4	123.3	260.9	17.2
1940	54.9	3.1	22.2	48.4	112.0	235.7	10.8
1970	21.4	1.6	16.6	35.8	80.0	163.4	9.5

Source: U.S. Bureau of the Census, 1975c, p. 60.

in 1970 (Table 2.4). In fact, infants died as frequently in 1900 as people over 85 do today. The mortality rate has also declined for the older population, as indicated in Table 2.4. Obviously, however, the likelihood of death increases with age. Each year, death can be expected for nearly 4 percent of those 65 to 74 and 16 percent of those 85 and over.

Lowered mortality and increased life expectancy are both caused and reflected by changes in the leading causes of death in the United States (Table 2.5), with *infectious communicable diseases* (tuberculosis, pneumonia, scarlet fever) being replaced by *chronic degenerative diseases* (cancer, cirrhosis of the liver, heart diseases) as the major causes of death. The percentage of deaths caused by heart diseases and cancer, for example, has risen from 11.7 in 1900 to 57.3 in 1975. Older people are more likely than younger people to die from these chronic illnesses, and more people are living to an age which makes them "eligible" for such diseases. Heart diseases, cancer, and cerebrovascular diseases (mainly stroke) account for over 75 percent of all deaths at ages 65 and over. It has been estimated that elimination of heart disease alone would add five years to the life expectancy of those who are 65 (Cutler and Harootyan, 1975).

Health Conditions

To simply state that older people suffer more health problems is misleading. Acute (temporary) conditions, such as injuries, pneumonia, and influenza tend to decline with age (Table 2.6). In fact, the highest rate of acute conditions occurs among children under five (as any parent could tell you). Days of restricted activity (per 100 persons per year) due to acute conditions also decline with age until 45, when restriction increases. Thus, while older people suffer fewer acute problems, those problems appear to restrict their activities more.

Table 2.5. Ten leading causes of death in the United States, 1900 and 1975: Rate (deaths per 1,000 population) and percent of all deaths

	1900		1975	
	Rate	Percent of all deaths	Rate	Percent of all deaths
1. Influenza and pneumonia	202.2	11.8		
2. Tuberculosis	194.4	11.3		
3. Gastritis and related (stomach inflammation)	142.7	8.3		
4. Heart diseases	137.4	8.0		
5. Cerebrovascular diseases	106.9	6.2		
6. Infections of the kidney	81.0	4.7		
7. Accidents	72.3	4.2		
8. Cancer and other malignant neoplasms	64.0	3.7		
9. Early infancy diseases	62.6	3.6		
10. Diphtheria	40.3	2.3		
1. Heart diseases			339.0	37.8
2. Cancer and other malignant neoplasms			174.4	19.5
3. Cerebrovascular diseases			91.8	10.2
4. Accidents			47.6	5.3
5. Influenza and pneumonia			27.0	3.0
6. Diabetes mellitus			16.8	1.9
7. Cirrhosis of the liver			15.1	1.7
8. Arteriosclerosis			13.7	1.5
9. Early infancy diseases			12.8	1.4
10. Suicide			12.6	1.4

Source: U.S. Public Health Service, 1976b, p. 3. U.S. Bureau of the Census, 1975c, p. 58.

Table 2.6. Incidence of acute conditions (per 100 persons per year) by age, 1974

	Age				
Condition	All ages	Under 6	6–16	17–44	45 and over
All acute conditions	175.7	309.0	236.7	175.1	93.6
Infectious and parasitic	19.5	47.4	30.3	16.0	8.0
Respiratory	94.4	172.6	131.3	92.5	47.5
Digestive	7.8	7.3	10.6	8.8	4.8
Injuries	30.4	33.9	38.1	33.8	19.9
All other acute conditions	23.5	47.8	26.4	24.1	13.3
Days of restricted activity	937.7	1081.2	895.9	870.9	1006.1

Source: U.S. Public Health Service, 1975, p. 8.

Chronic conditions, which are longer term or relatively permanent and can leave some lasting disability, increase significantly with age in incidence and prevalence. Indeed, approximately 80 percent of all older people have one or more chronic conditions: arthritis and rheumatism, hypertension (high blood pressure), heart conditions, atherosclerosis, cancer, blindness, and hearing defects.

These chronic conditions result in the need for greater health spending by older people. They spend more on drugs, are more likely to see a physician, and have more and longer hospital stays (Bengtson and Haber, 1975). The average person over 65 in 1975 had health-related expenses of $1,360, of which only 42 percent was covered by Medicare.

Disability

The critical question concerning chronic conditions is the extent to which these conditions handicap the aged in their daily routines, or how age affects *functional* health. Older people do have more health restrictions on their activities. Table 2.7 indicates that in 1974, 39 percent of all older people had limitations on major activities, and another 7 percent had less severe limitations. The aged also suffer more days of disability (Table 2.8). In 1974, the average person over 65 spent 52 days either restricted in activity or bedridden, compared with less than half that amount for the total population. However, *most* older persons do *not* suffer activity limitations due to health problems, an important fact to keep in mind in discussing their capabilities. The major causes of

Table 2.7. Limitation of activity due to chronic conditions, by age and sex, 1974

	Percent with no activity limitation	Percent with limitation, but not in major activity[a]	Percent with limitation in major activity[a]
Both sexes:			
All ages	85.9	3.5	10.6
Age 17–44	91.2	3.2	5.6
Age 45–64	75.9	5.2	18.9
Age 65 and over	54.1	6.6	39.3
Males:			
All ages	85.7	3.6	10.7
Age 17–44	90.8	3.7	5.5
Age 45–64	74.7	5.5	19.8
Age 65 and over	50.3	4.9	44.8
Females:			
All ages	86.0	3.5	10.5
Age 17–44	91.4	2.8	5.8
Age 45–64	77.0	4.9	18.1
Age 65 and over	56.9	7.8	35.3

[a] "Major activity" refers to ability to work, keep house, or engage in school or preschool activities.
Source: U.S. Public Health Service, 1975, p. 15.

Table 2.8. Days of disability per person, by age, 1974

	Restricted activity days	Bed-disability days
All persons	17.2	6.7
Under age 17	10.7	4.8
Age 17–24	11.2	4.6
Age 25–44	14.8	5.8
Age 45–64	23.6	8.4
Age 65 and over	38.0	14.3

Source: U.S. Public Health Service, 1975, p. 22.

limitations are arthritis and rheumatism, heart conditions, visual impairments, hypertension, and impairments of lower extremities and hips.

While institutionalization represents the most complete form of disability, stereotypes about the aged tend to exaggerate the extent to which they are institutionalized. Less than 5 percent of all persons over 65 reside in institutions, and many are there for social rather than medical reasons (see Chapter 11). This 5 percent figure is a bit misleading, however, since it refers to nursing home populations at any particular moment. There is a greater possibility that any older individual will reside in a nursing home at some time. A study of death certificates in Detroit indicated that 20 percent of all deaths to persons 65 and over occurred in nursing homes (Kastenbaum and Candy, 1973). Institutionalization does increase with age, but even for persons over 85, approximately 80 percent reside in the community at any one time. Females are more likely to be institutionalized than males, and nonwhite rates are lower in nursing and personal care homes but higher in mental institutions (Riley and Foner, 1968).

Implications of Chronic Illness

One cannot overemphasize the importance of chronic illnesses, both in shaping the aging experience and creating critical social policy needs, since chronic illnesses are an increasing part of the total illness load on society. Chronic illnesses require therapeutic approaches quite different from acute illnesses, since they must often be managed, rather than cured, and their long-term nature makes them extremely expensive.

Chronic illnesses also have a much greater impact on the individual and his or her patterns of living (Strauss, 1975). There are the psychological burdens of alternating remission and relapse, as the person is torn between hopefulness and hopelessness. The chronically ill often face prolonged regimens to control symptoms, which may be complicated, time-consuming, uncomfortable, and expensive. This may affect the person's willingness to "follow the rules," thereby affecting the course of the illness and disabilities associated with it. Persons with multiple chronic conditions face multiple and sometimes competing regimens.

> Mr. Smith has both chronic bronchitis and a stomach hernia. For the first, he is supposed to do several minutes of daily postural drainage. But this enhances the probability that he will get heartburn from his hernia. Furthermore, if he attempts to reduce the probability of his hernial heartburn by using a high pillow while sleeping, that sometimes brings on pains, ordinarily quiescent, from a pinched neck nerve. (Strauss, 1975:32)

The presence of chronic illness may require partial or complete redesigning of one's life style, partly because of the physical requirements associated with the disease. The person suffering from chronic diarrhea must reconsider such ordinary events as going to a movie or riding a bus. The following illustrates the problems faced by a person who has emphysema:

The degree of planning for an ordinary activity (shopping for groceries) becomes long and complicated. A patient lives on the second floor. He must "recoup" oxygen after walking a single block even if on flat terrain. The grocery store is uphill, so after half a block he needs to rest in order to get his breath back. If he chats with the grocer then he needs to rest for the trip back home. If he carries a bag of groceries that means still more oxygen expenditure; so, even though the route home is down-hill, he can only go 3/4 of the block before becoming winded. Then at home he has a flight of stairs with which to contend. Twelve steps is his usual oxygen supply. With the extra grocery weight he requires "getting his wind back" every six to eight steps. What normals can do in twenty minutes is stretched out to one hour or more. (Strauss, 1975:104)

Other chronic ailments—poor hearing, high blood pressure, arthritis—will have their own effects on activities and normal routines. One consequence of these limitations may be social isolation, compounded by feelings of embarrassment over visible handicaps or "distasteful" symptoms.

Public policy has not adequately addressed the growing prevalence of chronic illnesses in modern society (Strauss, 1975). The person with multiple ailments may need widely scattered sources of care, and money can become a preoccupation. The mobility needs of the chronically ill are neglected—curbstones are too high, entry doors too heavy, benches, ramps, and railings too infrequent. Although hospitals deal with large numbers of chronic problems at one stage or another, they are often poorly organized to meet the multiple needs of the chronically ill. Instead, each disease is treated in isolation. Attention is too seldom paid to the social and psychological needs of chronic patients, particularly their pain and anxiety. In general, Strauss suggests the need for a much wider range of services for those with chronic diseases, including counseling and education, redesign of physical and social environments, managerial assistance (referral and coordination, money-management), and daily-maintenance services (cooking, cleaning, transportation). Since the aged are most vulnerable to chronic health problems, they would benefit most from such services. The supports made available to aging people facing limitations on normal activities are important in shaping the aging experience.

Psychological Functioning

We tend to have an image of psychological decline in old age, whether considering perception, learning, intelligence, or some other aspect. The question of this stereotype's accuracy is complex and undoubtedly needs a book by itself, but some of the more basic trends should be noted here.

A variety of studies do indicate declines with age in sensation and perception (Riley and Foner, 1968). Vision and hearing abilities tend to decrease, and in general older people require a higher level of stimulation than younger people. For example, over half of all men 65 and over, and 30 percent of older women, suffer from some degree of hearing impairment (U.S. Public Health Service, 1971). Such impairments, combined with declines in other functions such as reaction time, can restrict activities in important ways.

The importance of sensory impairments is too easily underestimated by younger persons. Consider, for a moment, the possible effects of such impairments on life style. As taste or smell decline, there may be less interest in eating, resulting in malnutrition. Poor hearing and eyesight may be embarrassing and lead to avoidance of social interaction. Poor eyesight or a disturbed sense of balance make even such simple movements as climbing stairs or crossing streets dangerous and confusing. Some training programs for staff who work with the aged are employing simulation of these impairments—nose clips, ear plugs, parafin on fingers, goggles which make the floor appear unstable—to give them an appreciation of the world as it is experienced by their clients (Shore, 1976).

Intellectual Abilities

Probably the greatest research attention has been paid to age differences in intellectual capacity: intelligence, learning, memory, problem-solving. In general, the evidence suggests that intellectual ability does decline, but the decline may be smaller, start later, and involve fewer functions than was once thought (Botwinick, 1977). There is certainly ample evidence that older people can and do learn.

Cross-sectional studies of intelligence, using the Weschler Adult Intelligence Scale, have yielded what Botwinick (1977) terms a "classical aging pattern": a peak in intelligence in the late teens and early twenties, followed by a decline with age. Decline is greatest for psychomotor performance skills involving speed and perceptual integration, and less in verbal skills involving stored information. The greatest decline occurs after age 70. Longitudinal studies of aging and intelligence show the same pattern, though decline is less and starts later (Botwinick, 1977). These studies do indicate that people with high intelligence when they are young tend to retain it as they age, however.

What accounts for this measured decline? Part of the reason is impairment of more specific psychological functioning. Performance declines with age on certain learning tasks, particularly when time is short (Walsh, 1975; Arenberg and Robertson-Tchabo, 1977). Older people have more difficulty finding appropriate problem-solving strategies and stick more rigidly to unsuccessful strategies (Rabbitt, 1977).

Although it has become something of a cultural truism that memory fades with age, the evidence is less clear-cut. Short-term memory shows little evidence of decline, though older people may require more time to retrieve and organize information (Walsh, 1975). There does seem to be some decline for tasks requiring long-term memory, but this reflects inefficiency in entering and retrieving information rather than in the actual capacity for memory storage (Craik, 1977). Our expectation that memory declines with age may be self-fulfilling. All of us forget things throughout our lives, but generally attach no significance to it (though the consequences may be painful, indeed). When we are 65, however, the same forgetfulness becomes another sign that we are "getting old." It is a paradox that we link forgetfulness to aging, yet all of us probably know older people who can reminisce in the greatest detail about their lives (though evidence suggests an age decline in very remote memory). This simply reinforces the fact that we remember what we want to remember, and forget what we want to forget (or never cared to know).

The entire area of research on intellectual functioning is plagued with tremendous complexities. Some age differences may reflect differences in level or type of education across age cohorts. Schaie (1975) suggests that intelligence itself does not decline with age; rather, the information and skills of older people become obsolete in a changing society. It has also been suggested that declines in memory, learning or intelligence with age do not reflect a general aging effect. The "theory of terminal drop" states that "many human functions are not primarily related to chronological age as such but tend to show marked decline prior to death during a period ranging from a few weeks to a few years" (Palmore and Cleveland, 1976:76). According to this concept, the normal aged maintain stable functioning until they enter the "drop" period preceding death. Since death becomes increasingly likely with age, terminal drop will show up as a gradual decline with age in cross-sectional designs. This is an intriguing idea, but longitudinal research to test it is not conclusive.

It is also possible that although older people do not *perform* tasks which measure learning as well, their *capacity* to learn may not be impaired. For example, slower reaction times may reflect greater cautiousness and an increased willingness to sacrifice speed for accuracy. Age decrements tend to be less when time pressures are reduced. Motivation also affects performance on many of these tasks. Older people may be inappropriately and overly aroused in experimental situations, impairing their performance (Botwinick, 1973), or they may be less motivated than younger people to perform well on laboratory tasks. Perhaps older people are more difficult to "bully" into working hard on experimental tasks which are not personally meaningful. College sophomores may be more easily impressed by the chance to participate in "science" (no offense intended to sophomore readers). Finally, many of these studies indicate that older people may remember or learn less than younger people because they are unskilled at using techniques—"mediational strategies"—which organize and retrieve information more efficiently. This might be because younger people are typically better or more recently educated, rather than any innate decline in intellectual capacity with age.

There is little or no evidence of any major, general decline in mental ability with age, and there is tremendous individual variability among older people (as with any age group). Some people show sharp declines, others improve, and most show considerable stability. Even when intellectual declines do appear, however, it is not at all clear that they affect the ability of the vast majority of older people to function in their everyday lives.

These are important points to remember in developing retraining programs for older workers or adult education programs. The aged may "fail" in such programs because they lack interest or study skills, not because they cannot learn. In such cases, the fault lies as much with the program for failing to gear itself to the population being served. Older people learn best when the pace is not too fast and material or tasks are meaningful to them. They can benefit from being taught "how to learn," through strategies for organizing and mediating information. Other techniques for increasing the performance of older people include: organizing material into larger, easier to learn units, minimizing the stress associated with evaluation ("tests"), and providing sensory augmentation (presenting material both visually and orally) (Botwinick, 1973).

Finally, contrary to stereotypes of intellectual stagnation and decline in old age, creativity and personal growth can continue to the very end of life. Many of our greatest statesmen, scientists, educators, and scholars have functioned into old age: Bertrand Russell, Albert Schweitzer, Margaret Mead, and Robert Frost, to name but a few. Wayne Dennis (1966) studied productivity through the life cycle in a variety of occupations. While people in some occupations displayed the greatest productivity early in the career (mathematicians and biologists), others were most productive in their fifties and sixties (historians, philosophers, inventors, and novelists), probably requiring and benefiting from longer periods of preparation and the accumulation of experience in their work.

Psychological Disorders

In the discussion in the previous section on the normal range of psychological functioning, the relatively slight age differences which occur seem to have little effect on everyday living. As with any age group, however, older people may also suffer from more severe psychological impairment. At least some types of psychological disorder appear to increase in incidence in old age, and Pfeiffer estimates that "approximately 15 percent of the elderly population in the United States suffer from significant, substantial, or at least moderate psychopathology" (1977:652). Scattered local studies suggest that the prevalence of *psychoses* (characterized by loss of contact with reality) increases with age, but these studies have yielded no evidence of a similar increase in *neuroses* (phobias, hypochondria, hysteria, compulsive behavior), which are more common and considered less serious. The rate of hospitalization for psychiatric disorders rises with age—in 1974, 25 percent of the patients in mental hospitals (but only 2 percent of psychiatric outpatients) were over 60 (Butler and Lewis, 1977). This includes two major groups: those admitted earlier in life who grew old in the institution and those whose disorder developed late in life. Busse and Pfeiffer (1969) have suggested that there is no real increase in mental disorders with age, but *disabling* disorders do increase, resulting in greater hospitalization rates.

Psychological disorders are most prevalent among those with advanced age (75+) and in poor physical health (Pfeiffer, 1977). Rates are higher for widowed than married persons, and highest for those who are separated or divorced. There is a particularly critical need for treatment in nursing homes, where as many as three-fourths of the residents may have moderately severe or severe mental disorders. Many types of intervention have proven feasible with older people (see Eisdorfer and Stotsky, 1977), contrary to the stereotype that the elderly cannot benefit from therapy. Yet active treatment programs are quite rare in nursing homes. This is a problem we will return to in Chapter 11.

There are two basic types of psychological disorders. *Functional* disorders have no physical basis; they occur despite intact brain functioning. *Organic* disorders do have a physical basis; they occur because of impaired functioning of the brain.[1]

Functional Psychological Disorders

The most common functional disorder among older people is depression. Typical symptoms are both psychological—sadness, disinterest, pessimism, difficulty making decisions—and physical—fatigue, loss of appetite, sleeplessness. Depression is characteristically episodic and may vary considerably in severity and duration. Depression can be seen as a response to the stressful life events which may accompany aging (see Chapter 4, especially Table 4.1). Loss can become a predominant theme in the lives of older people. Adaptation to the losses they may experience—widowhood, retirement, sexual difficulties, physical illness—requires enormous amounts of physical and emotional energy. These losses can accumulate and trigger disruption or destruction of the social supports which aid in coping, and mental disorder may itself lead to increased social isolation (Lowenthal, 1964). These multiple losses can result in a number of common emotional reactions such as grief, guilt, loneliness, depression, anxiety, helplessness, rage, and eventually lead to functional mental disorders.

The second most common functional disorders for the aged are *paranoid reactions*. These are typically less serious than in younger people and may represent attempts to "make sense" of sensory deficits. Paranoid reactions are quite responsive to treatment. The third most common disorder is *hypochondriasis*, involving intensive preoccupation with bodily functioning. This increases with advancing age and is more common among women than men. *Manic reactions* are another type of functional disorder, involving elation, rapid speech, hyperactivity and periods of sadness giving way to grandiosity or belligerency.

Organic Psychological Disorders

Organic psychological disorders, or *organic brain syndromes* (OBS), account for about half the significant mental impairment of the aged, but the proportion increases with age. Organic brain syndromes may involve disturbance of a variety of functions, including memory, learning, speech, and orientation to the world, and may be associated with anxiety, depression, euphoria, delusions, and other symptoms. Approximately 10 to 20 percent of

---

[1] Much of the material in the next two sections has been drawn from Butler and Lewis (1977) and Pfeiffer (1977). For a more complete discussion, the reader is referred to these two excellent sources.

organic disorders are *reversible*, involving temporary impairment caused by such problems as congestive heart failure, diabetes, vitamin deficiencies, and alcoholism. Complete functioning can be restored in such cases, but too often there is a failure to carefully diagnose and treat reversible problems, and a tendency to see elderly patients as "only senile" (Butler, 1975).

Irreversible or *chronic* OBS results in gradual mental deterioration, caused by brain deterioration or cerebral arteriosclerosis. This is the most disabling, costly, and tragic handicap facing the aged. Wershow (1977), in a very provocative article, has argued that chronic OBS has been a taboo topic whose implications have been overlooked even by researchers. He suggests that as many as 50 percent of the residents of nursing homes suffer from some degree of chronic OBS and there has been little if any success in developing treatments. Noting the rapid increase in the old-old as a proportion of the older population, Wershow points out that chronic OBS may prove to be a critical problem in the future. For example, he estimates that by the year 2000 persons 75 and over with chronic OBS in nursing homes may account for 80 percent of the medical care expenditures for all persons 65 and over. Even if this estimate is exaggerated, it is clear that OBS deserve a high priority for research on prevention, treatment, and management.

Related Problems

Other problems of the older population are related to psychological disorders. Most notable of these are drug abuse, including alcoholism, and suicide.

Alcoholism and Drug Abuse

Butler and Lewis (1977) name alcoholism as the third leading health problem in the United States, after heart disease and cancer, and it is by no means minimal among the aging. While recorded rates of alcoholism are lower among the elderly, theirs is more likely to be a hidden condition, since most are retired and therefore less visible to the community. It has been estimated that 10 to 15 percent of the older population, and perhaps 20 percent of medical inpatients, have serious alcohol problems (Zimberg, 1974; Schuckit, 1977). Certain groups, such as elderly widowers, are particularly prone to alcoholism. There are two types of older alcoholics: lifelong alcoholics who have grown old and late-life alcoholics responding to age-related losses (Butler and Lewis, 1977).

Problems with other kinds of drugs also exist among the aged. Tranquilizers are heavily prescribed for older people and can lead to both emotional and physical dependence (Butler and Lewis, 1977). Addiction to opiates (e.g., heroin) among the aged is likely to be hidden by the family and ignored by police, but Schuckit (1977) has estimated that at least 1 percent of all opiate addicts are older people. This figure may rise in the future if the current heavier use of opiates among younger cohorts persists through the life cycle.

Suicide

Suicide rates raise particular doubts about stereotypes of the placid "golden years." Indeed, older people, who constitute only 10 percent of the population, account for 25 percent of reported suicides (Bock, 1972). Suicide rates for white females reach a peak in middle age, while those for white males continue to rise into advanced old age (Table 2.9). The age pattern is much less distinct for nonwhites. The highest rate of reported suicides occurs among white males in their eighties.

Why does this increase in suicide, at least for males, appear in many societies (Atchley, 1974)? The many stressful changes and losses experienced by the aged, such as poor health, widowhood, and retirement, may not be the whole answer. Sociological theories of suicide relate it to loss of social integration, diminishing both social supports and external restraint (Clinard, 1974). Many age-linked changes make the elderly socially marginal, disrupting ongoing social networks. Widowhood can lead to social isolation,

Table 2.9. Suicide rates in the United States, by age, sex, and race, 1970 (per 100,000 population)

Age	White males	White females	Nonwhite males	Nonwhite females
15–19	9.4	2.9	5.4	2.9
20–24	19.3	5.7	19.4	5.5
25–29	19.8	8.6	20.1	6.0
30–34	20.0	9.5	19.4	5.6
35–39	21.9	12.2	13.9	4.5
40–44	24.6	13.8	11.4	4.1
45–49	28.2	13.5	16.5	4.0
50–54	30.9	13.5	11.3	5.1
55–59	34.9	13.1	12.3	1.8
60–64	35.0	11.5	8.4	2.8
65–69	37.4	9.4	11.5	3.2
70–74	40.4	9.7	8.2	3.9
75–79	42.2	7.3	5.7	3.1
80–84	51.4	7.2	22.9	3.2
85+	45.8	5.8	12.6	6.4

Source: U.S. Public Health Service, 1974a, pp. 24–25.

and there is a well-documented relationship between widowhood and suicide (Bock, 1972). Bock also notes that low income and poor health can affect networks of social relationships. The social isolation triggered by losses associated with aging can facilitate suicide. Involvement in social networks, even formal organizations, is the best suicide preventive. Bock (1972) has found that the highest elderly suicide rate occurs in the lowest classes, who are less likely to be married, have fewer social ties in the community, and are least likely to belong to community organizations.

It is not clear why suicides continue to increase into old age for males but not for females. One possibility is that male suicides seem particularly related to work problems—retirement, unemployment, downward mobility (Maris, 1969). If this is the cause of sex differences in suicide rates, females may begin to show the male pattern as they are increasingly involved in the labor force and work becomes more central in their lives.

Social and Economic Characteristics

Education

In discussing differences between age groups, education is a critical factor. The older population has consistently had lower levels of education than the general population, and this is still true today (Table 2.10). In 1974, only one-third of those over 65 were high school graduates, compared with about two-thirds of persons between 25 and 64. This is a very important cause of cohort differences in attitudes, values, behaviors, and so on. Many characteristics of the aged, such as greater fatalism and conservatism

Table 2.10. Years of school completed (percent of population), by age and sex, 1974

	Less than high school (%)	High school (%)	College, 1–3 years (%)	College, 4 years or more (%)	Median years completed
Males:					
25–34	18.9	38.6	18.8	23.7	12.8
35–64	38.9	33.7	11.3	16.0	12.3
65+	68.8	16.4	6.2	8.6	8.7
Females:					
25–34	20.9	46.6	16.2	16.4	12.7
35–64	37.6	42.9	10.5	9.0	12.3
65+	65.4	20.9	7.8	5.9	9.0

Source: U.S. Bureau of the Census, 1975a, p. 17.

Table 2.11. Educational attainment, by age, 1957–90

Year	Percent high school graduates, 65+	Percent high school graduates, 25–64	65+ as percent of 25–64
1957–59	19.8	46.1	43.0
1969–70	28.2	60.4	46.7
1980	37.9	71.6	52.9
1990	49.4	79.7	62.0

Source: U.S. Bureau of the Census, 1973b, p. 25.

and less political activism, may really reflect these educational differences. This educational gap has been narrowing, however, and future, better-educated cohorts of older people may behave quite differently from older people today (Cain, 1967). Table 2.11 shows the trends which can be expected in the future. By 1990, it is projected that approximately half of all older people will have graduated from high school. Associated with higher education will be higher socioeconomic status, and future older people may be more involved in community roles, more politically active, more liberal, and so on.

Marital Status

The marriage relationship is an important source of both socioemotional and economic support for many people, which makes the increase in the likelihood of widowhood with age significant. This is one area, however, in which men and women experience aging very differently. Put simply, most older males are married and most older females are widowed (Table 2.12). This is true of both whites and nonwhites, though nonwhites of both sexes are more likely than whites to be widowed. Even among persons 85 years old and over, 38 percent of all males are still married, compared with only 11 percent of all females. Because of this sex difference in widowhood, older women are more likely to live alone and to be impoverished, and are more vulnerable to victimization by fraud and violent crime. It is important to remember that a woman who is widowed at age 65 can expect to live as a widow for another 10 or 15 years, and even longer in many cases.

Living Arrangements and Housing Quality

Sex differences in marital status are reflected in the living arrangements of older men and women. Older women are much

Table 2.12. Marital status of persons 65 and over, by race and sex, 1974 (percentage of population)

	Male	Female
Whites:		
Single	4.5	6.5
Married		
Spouse present	78.4	38.2
Spouse absent	1.4	1.2
Widowed	13.6	51.5
Divorced	2.1	2.6
Nonwhites:		
Single	5.2	4.7
Married		
Spouse present	59.6	25.5
Spouse absent	9.1	3.2
Widowed	22.8	64.0
Divorced	3.6	2.6

Source: U.S. Bureau of the Census, 1975b, p. 7.

Table 2.13. Living arrangements of persons 65 and over, by sex, 1975 (percentage of population)

	Male	Female
In families	79.8	56.1
Head of family	76.1	8.5
Wife	—	35.0
Other relative	3.7	12.7
Living alone	14.8	37.3
Living with unrelated individuals	1.2	1.2
In an institution	4.2	5.3

Source: U.S. Bureau of the Census, 1976, p. 48.

more likely than older men to live alone—37.3 percent to 14.8 percent (Table 2.13)—or in families with other relatives, such as their adult offspring, though the proportion of both men and women living in such families has declined, suggesting greater residential separation of the aged from their families. Whether this residential separation also implies greater social isolation from the family will be explored in Chapter 7. As Cutler and Harootyan (1975) have pointed out, there is little evidence of "communal" arrangements among the elderly as a source of companionship and pooled resources; in 1971, less than 2 percent lived with "unrelated individuals," which in fact reflects a slight decline from 1960 statistics.

We have already seen that very few older people live in institutions or any type of group setting. More than 75 percent of the aged live in detached houses (rather than duplexes or apartments), and it has been increasingly true that most older people (70 percent) live independently in homes they own, rather than rent (Carp, 1976). Home ownership and independence are deeply ingrained ideals. The psychological importance of "home" may lead some people to cling to even the most deteriorated situation.

Mrs. Salley Gruen, a 78-year-old woman holds tenaciously on to her home, which is now rat infested and dilapidated, in the inner-city slum area of Washington, D.C. Once robust and attractive, she has become thin and sallow and has to make financial choices among food on her table, prescription drugs for her ailments, and payments of her property taxes, which have been increasing in recent years. She can no longer afford repairs for her deteriorating home. She has no electricity, no heat, no water. In order to stay warm she has closed off most of the house except for one downstairs room. In the coldest days of winter she stays at the houses of her few surviving friends. Water collects in the basement. She lives by candlelight since the electricity was cut off. (Butler, 1975:104)

Although most older people own their own homes, compared with other age groups their houses tend to be smaller, older, and to have less adequate physical facilities such as heating and plumbing (Struyk, 1977). Elderly couples have better housing than those who live alone, but multi-person households headed by someone over 65 are the poorest. The greatest difference is between the urban and rural elderly. Rural older people live in poorer quality housing—for example, 15 percent lack complete plumbing (toilet, piped hot and cold water, tub or shower) and over half lack central heat—however, they have fewer neighborhood problems (street noise, crime, trash and litter). Struyk concludes that:

. . . about 17% of those residing in urban areas and around 30% of those residing in rural areas live in housing which other, more affluent segments of American society would shun. That is, they live in dwellings which are physically deficient, are plagued by problems with their mechanical subsystems (e.g., heating, plumbing), or are located in an unpleasant neighborhood environment. (Struyk, 1977:138)

Older apartment dwellers also tend to live in older buildings in older neighborhoods, in which amenities are few and safety is poor (Carp, 1976). Older people are increasingly living in mobile homes, which are easier to maintain but depreciate in value and often have fire and safety hazards (Butler, 1975).

Certain segments of the older population are particularly at risk regarding housing. The rural aged are most impoverished, suffer greater disabilities, and tend to be more isolated. Minority groups (blacks, Spanish-Americans, Asian-Americans, and others) face low income, poor health, and the worst housing, compounded by discrimination. Widows are particularly likely to live in dilapidated, isolating, and unsafe housing.

Housing is clearly a problem for many older people (though not the majority), even for those who own their own homes—it is harder to move with equity tied up in a house, they may be "trapped" in deteriorating neighborhoods, and property taxes can be a financial burden (Carp, 1976). Housing expenses consume one-third of the average older person's budget (Butler, 1975), and resources may be inadequate for necessary repairs, services, and taxes. Carp (1976) notes that while older people often say their housing is "satisfactory," this may be a response to lack of options.

Some steps have been taken to meet the housing needs of the older population. Over the years, programs supported by the Department of Housing and Urban Development have rehoused approximately 750,000 older people, including 600,000 in special housing for the elderly (Carp, 1976). But this represents only about 3 percent of the older population, and Carp estimates that for every older person in public housing there are another 40 in need of housing. Low-income public housing has been slow to develop in the United States, and urban renewal, which replaces inner-city "slums" with office buildings and luxury apartments, often simply creates greater crowding in other low-income areas. Some countries provide a greater variety of financial assistance to older people to help them remain in and maintain their own homes. In Norway, for example, older people can borrow money at favorable interest rates to modernize or recondition their homes (Carp, 1976). Programs of housing assistance and housing alternatives need to be developed on a much broader scale than at present.

Labor Force Participation

Our society, and most people in it, have come to expect retirement as a "natural" accompaniment of the aging process. But retirement as a widespread occurrence is a product of the twentieth-century United States. The proportion of older men working has declined from over two-thirds in 1900 to less than one-fourth now (Table 2.14). There are a number of reasons for this trend—

Table 2.14. Labor force participation (percent of noninstitutionalized population in labor force) by age and sex, 1900–75

	1900	1950	1960	1975
Males				
55–64	93.3	86.9	86.8	75.8
65+	68.3	45.8	33.1	21.7
Females				
55–64	14.1	27.0	37.2	41.0
65+	9.1	9.7	10.8	8.3

Source: U.S. Bureau of the Census, 1940, p. 93, and 1976, p. 51.

voluntary and compulsory retirement programs, pension systems, Social Security, changes in the occupational structure, and so forth—and the nature of retirement will be explored more fully in Chapter 6. It is important to recognize, however, that 22 percent of all males over 65 do work, so retirement is not inevitable.

Labor force participation by women has shown a very different pattern. There has been little change during this century in the proportion of women over 65 who work (approximately 8 to 10 percent), but the proportion of women between 55 and 64 who work has increased from 14.1 percent in 1900 to 41.0 percent in 1975. One way to interpret those statistics is to recognize that in 1900, only 5 percent of all women 55 to 64 experienced retirement by age 65, while in 1975, 32.7 percent, or one out of three of these women experienced retirement. Thus, as women have returned in greater numbers to the work force following childrearing (and, indeed, many never left it), their aging experience is altered by the need to adjust to retirement.

Labor force participation by older blacks is, for the most part, quite similar to that of whites, though black females of all ages have been more likely to work than white females. The gap at the older age ranges (55 and above) has narrowed considerably over the past 25 years, however, so that there are currently only slight differences.

Economic Status

There is always a danger of overlooking important differences between subgroups in the older population. Perhaps nowhere is the need for subgroup analysis greater than in the analysis of financial resources, since income varies considerably by age, sex, race, marital status, employment status, and so on. For example, persons over 80 tend to have lower incomes, different standards of living, and greater health-related financial needs than those 55 to 80. Also, in a comparison of aged households in 1973, 61 percent of those headed by persons still employed had incomes greater than $7,000, while 68 percent of those headed by an unemployed person had incomes below $7,000 (Schulz, 1976).

One major concern has been the extent to which the aged are financially handicapped, whether this means poverty or some higher but still inadequate income. Poverty is not a new problem for the aged; it was widespread in nineteenth- and early twentieth-century America (Zimmerman, 1976; Fischer, 1977). There is no question that income still declines with age. In 1974, the median annual income for families headed by someone 65 or over was only $7,298, compared with a median income of $12,836 for all families (U.S. Bureau of the Census, 1974). Unrelated individuals 65 and over also had lower median incomes than the same group in the total population: $2,956 to $4,439.

The most frequently used measure of poverty is the poverty index developed by the Social Security Administration (Schulz, 1976), which is based on the amount of money needed to purchase a "minimum adequate diet" at current prices. This amount is multiplied by three, since the average family spends approximately one-third of its income on food. The index is set at different levels for different types of families. In 1974, for example, the low-income level was $2,352 for unrelated individuals 65 and over and $2,958 for a family of two with a head 65 or over. Using this index, it appears that poverty has been declining among older people over the past 15 years (Table 2.15), though nearly one of every six older persons still lives in "official" poverty. Older people are more likely to live in poverty than persons under 65, with 15.7 percent of all older persons compared with only 8.2 percent of persons 21 to 64 years old below the low-income level in 1974. It is apparent, as well, that poverty is much greater among older blacks. In 1974, approximately 36 percent of all older blacks were living below the poverty level.

Poverty varies across subgroups of the older population, as indicated in Table 2.16. Poverty is particularly high among unrelated individuals— 31.8 percent of all older unrelated individuals and 60.5 percent of blacks were living in poverty in 1974. Single

Table 2.15. Poverty status (percent below low-income level) of the 65 and over population, by race, 1959–74

	1959	1967	1974
All persons 65+	35.2	29.5	15.7
Whites	33.1	27.7	13.8
Blacks	62.5	53.3	36.4

Source: U.S. Senate, 1974, p. 139; U.S. Bureau of the Census, 1974, p. 18.

Table 2.16. Low-income status (percent below low-income level) of persons 65 and over by family status, race, and sex, 1974

	All	Whites	Blacks
All persons 65 and over	15.7	13.8	36.4
Families with head 65 and over:			
All families	9.5	7.7	27.7
Male head	8.9	7.7	23.9
Female head	13.0	8.1	36.8
Unrelated individuals:			
All	31.8	28.9	60.5
Males	26.8	23.7	44.3
Females	33.2	30.3	68.8

Source: U.S. Bureau of the Census, 1974, p. 18.

or widowed older women who are living alone comprise over 50 percent of the aged low-income group. Also, in all the subgroups of Table 2.16, blacks have substantially higher rates of low-income status.

However, this low-income index is a rather conservative measure. How many older people are not officially "impoverished," yet live in a state of economic hardship? This is perhaps the more meaningful question in a relatively affluent, consumer-oriented society. The Bureau of Labor Statistics has developed a Retired Couples' Budget which supposedly provides a "modest but adequate" standard of living. This budget is indeed very modest. In 1971, for example, the budget included $24 a week for groceries and $139 per month for housing, including furnishings and repairs (Butler, 1975). Each year the "retired couple" was allowed 1 percent of a sofa, 7 percent of a man's coat, one house dress (but only one-fourth of a street dress), half a pair of glasses, and so on. The budget allowed $91 per year for recreation (including vacations and family visits). The assumption is made that retired couples "need" to spend less for clothing, housing, and gifts than a younger couple. There is an additional assumption of good health, and no provision is made for major medical expenses or for savings. Even with this modest budget, it has been estimated that as much as 75 percent of the older population lack an adequate income and are thus "deprived" (Bengtson and Haber, 1975).

Clearly the economic difficulties of the aged are substantial, though there are, of course, many older people who are comfortable financially. In 1974, 28 percent of older men and 8 percent of older women had annual incomes greater than $7,000. But these people are a minority, and there is no evidence that reduced income is accompanied by reduced need or desire to consume goods and services. What low income in old age often means is poor nutrition,

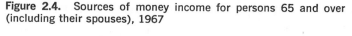

Figure 2.4. Sources of money income for persons 65 and over (including their spouses), 1967

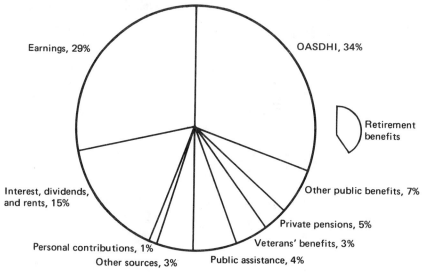

Source: Lenore Bixby, "Income of people aged 65 and older." Sound Security Bulletin (April 1970): 10.

inadequate housing, neglect of medical needs, and failure to fulfill psychological needs. Money cannot buy happiness, but how many of us would want to give up restaurants, travel, movies, and visits with family because we are old?

Unfortunately, we know relatively little about the sources of income and the financial assets of older people. The best data on sources of income are nearly a decade old (see Figure 2.4). Earnings were an important source of income, though this is obviously less true of those who are retired. Retirement benefits, particularly Social Security (Old Age, Survivors, Disability, and Health Insurance) accounted for 49 percent of all income.

Income statistics, however, do not provide an entirely accurate picture of the economic position of the aged (Schulz, 1976). For one thing, older people may receive income *in kind*, such as subsidized housing and Medicare health benefits, which soften the impact of low income. The aged may also possess assets which are not included in the income statistics: *liquid* assets, such as cash and bank deposits, which are easily converted to goods and services or money, and *nonliquid* assets, such as ownership of a house or business, which require more time to convert. However, while many older people possess such assets, they make little difference for most older people, and particularly for those who are poor. The 1968 Social Security Survey indicated that 43 percent of older couples and 61 percent of unrelated individuals had less than $1,000 in financial assets. Additionally, the homes of home-owners represented an asset of less than $10,000 for 37 percent of all couples and 44 percent of all unrelated individuals. Such assets are hardly sufficient for providing a 10- or 20-year retirement income. Although the aged also receive some tax benefits, including nontaxation of Social Security income, doubled personal exemptions, and property-tax reductions, the general picture remains of substantial economic deprivation for older people, certainly greater than the general population.

Minority Aged

It is important to keep in mind the existence of ethnic and racial subgroups in the older population. Older blacks constitute 8 percent of the aged population, and there are numerous other minority groups represented among the elderly: Mexican-Americans, Chinese, American Indians, and so on. Such older persons face a "double jeopardy" with regard to prejudice and discrimination. Until very recently, however, research on aging has largely ignored these groups. We know even less about variation within different racial and ethnic groups. After all, aged blacks are no more homogeneous than aged whites, and the fact that many blacks live in poverty should not obscure the many blacks who are relatively well off.

There is no question that minority older people are in an unfavorable position within the general aged population. As we have seen, life expectancy is lower among nonwhites, particularly among such groups as Chicanos and American Indians (Butler and Lewis, 1973; Benedict, 1971). This reflects the cumulative impact of high infant mortality, poor nutrition, and substandard living conditions. Those who survive to age 65 tend to suffer more often from chronic illnesses and disabilities (Hill, 1971; Benedict, 1971) and are less likely to receive medical care for their problems because of a variety of barriers, such as low income, scarcity of services where they live, and discrimination. It is interesting that black males over 75 tend to be in better health than their female and white counterparts, perhaps reflecting a "survival of the fittest" (Jackson, 1971).

Statistics presented in Table 2.17 reflect some important social and economic differences among white, black, and Spanish-American aged. In effect, the problems of older people are intensified by minority status. Aged blacks have less education than whites, and Spanish less than blacks. In 1970, only 8 percent of older

Table 2.17.   Comparisons of white, black, and Spanish aged, 1970

	White	Black	Spanish
Median years of education:			
Female: 65–69	9.5	7.0	6.2
70–74	8.9	6.7	5.9
75 and over	8.7	6.1	5.4
Male: 65–69	8.9	6.0	6.1
70–74	8.7	5.6	5.9
75 and over	8.4	5.1	4.9
Percent married and			
living with spouse:			
Female	34.5	26.1	30.8
Male	69.5	55.7	63.8
Percent in labor force:			
Female	9.8	13.2	7.9
Male	24.9	23.5	24.8
Median individual income:			
Female: 65–69	$2,594	$1,170	$1,270
70–74	2,305	1,098	1,248
75 and over	2,032	974	1,189
Male: 65–69	5,959	1,956	2,659
70–74	4,630	1,711	2,101
75 and over	3,621	1,503	1,735
Percent in poverty:			
Aged living in families	15.6	38.8	25.4
Aged unrelated	48.8	71.7	58.1
individuals			

Source: U.S. Bureau of the Census, 1973a (also cited in Jackson, 1974), pp. 627–29, 640–44, 679–81, 835–38, 962–65.

black males and 10 percent of females had graduated from high school. Blacks were more likely than both other groups to be widowed. Labor force participation was quite similar in the three groups, except that older black females were more likely to be working. There are substantial differences in income and poverty status, with Spanish intermediate between blacks and whites. Jackson (1974) has attributed the difference between Spanish and blacks to the greater discrimination experienced by blacks. These income differences do not simply reflect educational attainment, since the differences remain within educational categories.

One must also recognize the diversity of minorities—the special history and unique current situation of each group (Kent, 1971; Moore, 1971). Some groups, such as Chinese and Indians, face severe language barriers. Aged American Indians generally live on reservations, have an even lower level of education than most minority aged (47 percent with less than five years of schooling), and have faced a history of extreme unemployment (as high as 60 percent in some areas) (Benedict, 1971). Because of immigration patterns, most aged Chinese in the United States are unmarried males.

Variant subcultures may provide coping structures to support their aged. While the aged in some subcultures such as American Chinatowns have been almost completely isolated from the larger society, and may know nothing of the service structure "out there" (Carp and Kataoka, 1976), the institutional structures in the black community, such as the family and the church, are extremely important sources of support for older blacks (Hill, 1971; Lindsay, 1975; Davis, 1976). Studies have pointed to an apparent greater willingness of black extended families to care for their aged members. This may, however, be less from choice than the inability of older blacks to get into nursing homes (Jackson, 1973).

It is not clear whether a lifetime of experience with racial discrimination helps or hinders in coping with "ageism" (Jackson, 1971). Bengtson and associates (1977) note that older blacks and Mexican-Americans had worse functional and self-reported health than whites, considered themselves "old" at an earlier age, and evaluated aging less favorably. In this case, at least, minority status did not appear to help with life satisfaction when facing the "double jeopardy" of old age and minority-group status.

There is unquestionably a need for greater understanding of ethnic and racial differences in the older population, and of the effects of rapid change in the position of minority groups and in ethnic pride on older persons. Fortunately, there is an increasing interest in studying minority aged, though we still lack in-depth knowledge in many areas (Jackson, 1971; 1974).

Some Cautionary Notes

There is always a danger in using statistics to describe the position of any group. There are a variety of potential "social meanings" to be derived from any seemingly objective statistic. For example, though older people are more likely to live in poverty than the general population, most older people do not live in poverty.

One question which inevitably arises from the statistics reviewed here is: How well off are the aged in American society? There are two ways of answering this question. First, it is clear that older people are deprived compared to the rest of the population. In reviewing statistical trends from 1940 to 1969, Palmore and Whittington (1971) found that the relative status of the aged had declined, particularly in income. As we shall see in Chapter 3, there are sound reasons to expect that the status of older people will decline in modern industrial societies (Cowgill, 1974b).

This chapter has outlined many critical needs of older people which to a disturbing degree have not been adequately met by existing social policies. However, in a more "objective" sense, older people have probably never been better off than they are currently in American society. People are living longer, their health is better, and their average standard of living (physical shelter, food and so on) has certainly risen since preindustrial times. Even in the last 10 years the proportion of older people living in poverty has been cut nearly in half. Thus, older people are *relatively* deprived but in better *absolute* condition.

This objective standard of evaluation, however, can also be misleading. Human beings have a variety of needs beyond the simply physical. Abraham Maslow (1954) has suggested the existence of a set of "basic" needs, organized into a hierarchy, with higher level needs becoming more important as lower level needs are satisfied. His hierarchy of needs includes:

1. physiological needs (food, health)
2. safety
3. belongingness and love needs
4. esteem needs (achievement, appreciation)
5. self-actualization ("what a man can be, he must be")
6. preconditions for basic need satisfaction, which are defended because of their necessity, not as ends in themselves (freedom to speak and act)
7. desire to know and understand
8. aesthetic needs

What Maslow suggests is that once one's needs for food, good health, shelter, and so forth are satisfied, concern moves to belonging, esteem, or self-actualization. Modern societies may satisfy lower level needs but leave the aged deprived in other ways. A sufficient retirement income, for example, does not mean that one belongs, is accorded prestige and appreciation, or can continue to grow as a person. Etzioni (1968) suggests that we must question the responsiveness of social structure and societal institutions to the variety of needs felt by individuals. For older people, the question becomes whether the system of age stratification in any society makes available the kinds of roles and options which allow them to meet the needs outlined by Maslow. Without such roles, the aged will continue to be deprived in a very real sense and can experience social and psychological "starvation" in the midst of physical "comfort." This is an issue we will return to in Chapter 7.

Maslow's higher order needs may be of particular concern to older people of the future, who can be expected to be healthier, better educated, and in more favorable economic situations. Even the diversity among succeeding cohorts of the aged has been declining (Uhlenberg, 1977). Immigration has declined, so that the proportion of the elderly who are foreign-born has declined from over 30 percent in 1900 to only 10 percent in 1970. The shift from rural to urban residence is largely complete. Uhlenberg suggests that this growing stability in the nature of the older population lessens the cultural and social dislocations associated with aging. As the aged are increasingly similar to the rest of society, old age itself may be a less distinct part of the life cycle, and much of our current thinking in gerontology may require revision.

A discussion of needs and deprivations requires a balance between recognizing problems of the aged and avoiding an exaggeration of their difficulties. A recent Harris poll (National Council on the Aging, 1975) suggests that the public does exaggerate the problems experienced by older people, and this may contribute to negative stereotypes and avoidance. The general public was asked to indicate "very serious" problems experienced by "most people over 65." Table 2.18 compares these responses to the "very

Table 2.18. Personal experience versus public expectation of problems experienced by older people (percentage of population interviewed)

	Personal experience (65+)		Public expectation
	"Very serious"	"Very serious" or "Somewhat serious"	"Very serious" problems attributed to "Most people over 65"
Fear of crime	23	47	50
Poor health	21	50	51
Not enough money to live on	15	40	62
Loneliness	12	29	60
Not enough medical care	10	23	44
Not enough education	8	25	20
Not feeling needed	7	19	54
Not enough to do to keep busy	6	17	37
Not enough friends	5	16	28
Not enough job opportunities	5	12	45
Poor housing	4	11	35
Not enough clothing	3	8	16

Source: *The Myth and Reality of Aging in America,* © 1975, a study prepared for The National Council on the Aging, Inc. (NCOA), Washington, D.C. by Louis Harris and Associates, Inc., pp. 31–32. Reprinted by permission.

serious" and "somewhat serious" problems actually expressed by older persons. For example, 62 percent of the public felt that not having enough money to live on would be a very serious problem for most persons over 65, but only 15 percent of older respondents said this was actually a very serious problem for them. When one includes "somewhat serious" problems, the differences are smaller, but there does seem to be overstatement of the problems of the aged, particularly of such problems as loneliness, not feeling needed, and not having enough job opportunities. These statistics should be interpreted with some caution, of course, because older people may be unwilling to "admit" all of their feelings to an interviewer and people do have a capacity to "adjust" to even the most miserable conditions.

This chapter perhaps emphasizes the problems of aging to the relative exclusion of its joys and benefits, but there are good things about aging for many people. Take retirement as an example. Does it really sound so bad to not have to set an alarm clock when you go to bed, not have a "boss," travel and visit with family and friends? The National Council on the Aging study found that the most frequently expressed "rewards" of aging were leisure time, independence, and freedom from responsibility. Such rewards were more likely to be stressed by those with greater education and higher income, however, which indicates that one's ability to enjoy old age can be hindered by low income, poor health, or other decrements which may accompany aging.

All of this suggests that a "cost-benefit" analysis of old age is a very complex matter. There is tremendous variability from one person to another, even in what they perceive as costs or benefits. One person's boredom is another's leisure time. The results in Table 2.18, however, do suggest that a wide range of problems are experienced by at least a substantial minority of older people, and though exaggerated, there are very real difficulties and deprivations experienced by many of them, particularly among certain subgroups.

Summary

The population and proportion of older people has risen substantially in the United States during this century. Life expectancy has expanded to over 70 years for the average person. This "aging" of the population is related to declines in fertility and mortality which accompany the "demographic transition" in modern societies.

Since females tend to live longer than males, they constitute the majority of the older population. The aged are likely to reside in urban settings and are differentially distributed among the states. As a proportion of the population, the aged are most heavily concentrated in small towns and are least likely to be found in rural farm and suburban areas. Residential mobility is quite low among the elderly.

Health is a critical determinant of satisfaction among older people, and the subjective experience of health is in some ways more important than purely objective indicators. Mortality rates have declined for all age groups, and there has been a shift in the leading causes of death from infectious to degenerative diseases such as cancer and heart diseases (which are more prevalent among the aged). Older people are less likely to suffer from acute health conditions, though such illnesses may create more restrictions for them. Chronic conditions increase with age, and nearly half of all older persons have activity limitations due to chronic conditions. Approximately 4 percent of the aged reside in institutions, but this understates the proportion who enter nursing homes sometime in their lives.

Intellectual abilities tend to decline with age, but the decline is smaller, starts later, and may involve fewer functions than was once thought. Sensation and perception do decline, but results of studies of intelligence, learning, and memory are much less clearcut. Decrements may reflect cautiousness, lack of motivation, or inefficient skills, rather than declining capacity. The older population displays tremendous variability in mental capacities, and creativity and growth are not inevitably stifled by old age. Declines in functioning may reflect a "terminal drop" prior to death, rather than gradual loss caused by age per se.

Approximately one in six older persons, and perhaps 80 percent of nursing-home residents, suffer from at least moderate psychopathology. Functional disorders, lacking a physical basis, include depression, paranoid reactions, hypochondriasis, and manic reactions. Organic disorders may be either reversible or irreversible. Alcoholism and drug abuse constitute other problems in the older population. Suicide peaks in middle age for females, but continues to rise in old age for males. Suicide may be related to the social marginality experienced by some older persons.

Older people have less education, though the gap with other age groups is narrowing, and future cohorts of the aged may behave quite differently because of this. Most older males are married, while most older females are widowed. This is reflected in living arrangements—older women are much more likely to live alone. Most older people live in detached housing, though their houses tend to be older and in worse condition than those of younger persons. Housing is a particular problem for widows and rural and minority-group aged.

Retirement has come to be expected, though one-fourth of all males over 65 do work. Women have become increasingly likely to work prior to age 65, so that retirement is becoming an issue for them, as well as for men.

Though the extent of poverty among the aged has declined recently, they are more likely to have low income than younger persons, and it is still true that one in six is below the low-income level. Poverty is particularly prevalent among blacks and women who live alone. As much as 75 percent of the aged may lack a "modest but adequate" standard of living. While other sources of financial support may soften such statistics, it is nevertheless true that the aged suffer economic hardships.

Minority aged are particularly likely to be deprived in terms of low education, poor health, widowhood, and low income, as they suffer the "double jeopardy" of old age and minority status. One must recognize the differences both within and among racial and ethnic groups, however, in their special histories, unique situations, and the coping structures available to their aged.

While the aged are deprived in relation to the rest of the population, their living conditions have improved in modern societies. This may mean, however, that the aged now feel handicapped regarding other needs, both social and psychological. Additionally, we may exaggerate the problems of aging, thus contributing to negative stereotypes and avoidance.

References

Arenberg, David and Elizabeth Robertson-Tchabo
    1977   "Learning and aging." In James Birren and K. Warner
            Schaie (eds.). Handbook of the Psychology of Aging.
            New York: Van Nostrand Reinhold.
Atchley, Robert
    1976   The Sociology of Retirement. New York: Schenkman.
Benedict, Robert
    1971   "A profile of Indian aged." In Minority Aged in America.
            Occasional Papers in Gerontology No. 10, Institute of
            Gerontology, University of Michigan-Wayne State
            University.
Bengtson, Vern and David Haber
    1975   "Sociological approaches to aging." In Diana Woodruff and
            James Birren (eds.). Aging: Scientific Perspectives and
            Social Issues. New York: D. Van Nostrand.
Bengtson, Vern, Patricia Kasschau, and Pauline Ragan
    1977   "The impact of social structure on aging individuals." In
            James Birren and K. Warner Schaie (eds.). Handbook of the
            Psychology of Aging. New York: Van Nostrand Reinhold.

Bixby, Lenore
    1970   "Income of people aged 65 and older." Social Security
            Bulletin April: 10.
Bock, E. Wilbur
    1972   "Aging and suicide: The significance of marital, kinship,
            and alternative relations." Family Coordinator 21: 71–79.
Botwinick, Jack
    1973   Aging and Behavior. New York: Springer.
    1977   "Intellectual abilities." In James Birren and K. Warner
            Schaie (eds.). Handbook of the Psychology of Aging.
            New York: Van Nostrand Reinhold.
Busse, Ewald and Eric Pfeiffer (eds.)
    1969   Behavior and Adaptation in Late Life. Boston:
            Little, Brown.
Butler, Robert
    1975   Why Survive?: Being Old in America. New York:
            Harper & Row.
Butler, Robert and Myrna Lewis
    1977   Aging and Mental Health: Positive Psychosocial Approaches.
            St. Louis: C. V. Mosby.
Cain, Leonard
    1967   "Age status and generational phenomena: The new old
            people in contemporary America." The Gerontologist
            7 (2): 83–92.
Carp, Frances
    1976   "Housing and living environments of older people." In
            Robert Binstock and Ethel Shanas (eds.). Handbook of
            Aging and the Social Sciences. New York: Van Nostrand
            Reinhold.
Carp, Frances and Eunice Kataoka
    1976   "Health care problems of the elderly in San Francisco's
            Chinatown." The Gerontologist 16 (1): 30–38.
Clinard, Marshall
    1974   Sociology of Deviant Behavior. New York: Holt, Rinehart
            and Winston.
Cowgill, Donald
    1974a   "The aging of populations and societies." In Frederick
            Eisele (ed.). Political Consequences of Aging. The Annals
            of the American Academy of Political and Social Science
            415 (September): 1–18.
    1974b   "Aging and modernization: A revision of the theory." In
            Jaber Gubrium (ed.). Late Life: Communities and
            Environmental Policies. Springfield, Ill.: Charles C Thomas.
Craik, Fergus
    1977   "Age differences in human memory." In James Birren and
            K. Warner Schaie (eds.). Handbook of the Psychology of
            Aging. New York: Van Nostrand Reinhold.

Cutler, Neal and Robert Harootyan
  1975   "Demography of the aged." In Diana Woodruff and
         James Birren (eds.). Aging: Scientific Perspectives and
         Social Issues. New York: Van Nostrand.
Davis, Donald
  1976   "Growing old black." In Robert Atchley and Mildred
         Seltzer (eds.). The Sociology of Aging: Selected Readings.
         Belmont, Ca.: Wadsworth.
Dennis, Wayne
  1966   "Creative productivity between the ages of 20 and 80 years."
         Journal of Gerontology 21 (1): 1–8.
Eisdorfer, Carl and Bernard Stotsky
  1977   "Intervention, treatment, and rehabilitation of psychiatric
         disorders." In James Birren and K. Warner Schaie (eds.).
         Handbook of the Psychology of Aging. New York:
         Van Nostrand Reinhold.
Etzioni, Amitai
  1968   The Active Society. New York: The Free Press.
Fischer, David
  1977   Growing Old in America. New York: Oxford University
         Press.
Hauser, Philip
  1976   "Aging and world-wide population change." In Robert
         Binstock and Ethel Shanas (eds.). Handbook of Aging and
         the Social Sciences. New York: Van Nostrand Reinhold.
Hill, Robert
  1971   "A profile of black aged." In Minority Aged in America.
         Occasional Papers in Gerontology No. 10, Institute of
         Gerontology, University of Michigan-Wayne State
         University.
Jackson, Jacquelyne
  1971   "The blacklands of gerontology." Aging and Human
         Development 2 (3): 156–71.
  1973   "Help me somebody! I'se an old black standing in the need
         of institutionalizing!" Psychiatric Opinion 10: 6–16.
  1974   "NCBA, black aged and politics." In Frederick Eisele
         (ed.). Political Consequences of Aging. The Annals of the
         American Academy of Political and Social Science 415
         (September): 1–18.
Johnston, R. J.
  1971   Urban Residential Patterns: An Introductory Review.
         New York: Praeger.
Kastenbaum, Robert and Sandra Candy
  1973   "The 4% fallacy: A methodological and empirical critique
         of extended care facility population statistics." Aging and
         Human Development 4: 15–21.
Kent, Donald
  1971   "Changing welfare to serve minority aged." In Minority
         Aged in America. Occasional Papers in Gerontology No. 10,

Institute of Gerontology, University of Michigan-Wayne State University.

La Gory, Mark, Russell Ward, and Thomas Juravich
1977   "The age segregation process in American cities: An ecological model." Paper presented at the Annual Meeting of the American Sociological Association, Chicago, Ill.

Lindsay, Inabel
1975   "Coping capacities of the black aged." In No Longer Young: The Older Woman in America. Occasional Papers in Gerontology No. 11, Institute of Gerontology, University of Michigan-Wayne State University

Lowenthal, Marjorie
1964   "Social isolation and mental illness in old age." American Sociological Review 29: 54–70.

Maris, Ronald
1969   Social Forces in Urban Suicide. Homewood, Ill.: Dorsey.

Maslow, Abraham
1954   Motivation and Personality. New York: Harper & Row.

Moore, Joan
1971   "Situational factors affecting minority aging." The Gerontologist 11 (I–II): 88–93.

National Council on the Aging
1975   The Myth and Reality of Aging in America. Washington, D.C.

Palmore, Erdman and William Cleveland
1976   "Aging, terminal decline and terminal drop." Journal of Gerontology 31 (1): 76–81.

Palmore, Erdman and Clark Luikart
1972   "Health and social factors related to life satisfaction." Journal of Health and Social Behavior 13: 68–80.

Palmore, Erdman and Frank Whittington
1971   "Trends in the relative status of the aged." Social Forces 50 (September): 84–91.

Pfeiffer, Eric
1977   "Psychopathology and social pathology." In James Birren and K. Warner Schaie (eds.). Handbook of the Psychology of Aging. New York: Van Nostrand Reinhold.

Rabbitt, Patrick
1977   "Changes in problem solving ability in old age." In James Birren and K. Warner Schaie (eds.). Handbook of the Psychology of Aging. New York: Van Nostrand Reinhold.

Riley, Matilda and Anne Foner
1968   Aging and Society. Volume 1: An Inventory of Research Findings. New York: Russell Sage.

Rosen, Jacqueline and Grete Bibring
1966   "Psychological reactions of hospitalized male patients to a heart attack: Age and social-class differences." Psychosomatic Medicine 28 (6): 808–21.

Schaie, K. Warner
  1975 "Age changes in adult intelligence." In Diana Woodruff
         and James Birren (eds.). Aging: Scientific Perspectives and
         Social Issues. New York: D. Van Nostrand.
Schuckit, Marc
  1977 "Geriatric alcoholism and drug abuse." The Gerontologist
         17: 168–74.
Schulz, James
  1976 The Economics of Aging. Belmont, Ca.: Wadsworth.
Shanas, Ethel et al.
  1968 Old People in Three Industrial Societies. New York:
         Atherton Press.
Shore, Herbert
  1976 "Designing a training program for understanding sensory
         losses in aging." The Gerontologist 16: 157–65.
Strauss, Anselm
  1975 Chronic Illness and the Quality of Life. St. Louis:
         C.V. Mosby.
Struyk, Raymond
  1977 "The housing situation of elderly Americans." The
         Gerontologist 17: 130–39.
Uhlenberg, Peter
  1977 "Changing structure of the older population of the USA
         during the twentieth century." The Gerontologist
         17: 197–202.
United Nations
  1972 Demographic Yearbook. New York: United Nations.
United States Bureau of the Census
  1940 Comparative Occupation Statistics for the United States:
         1870–1940. Washington, D.C.: U.S. Government Printing
         Office.
  1964 United States Census of Population: 1960. Volume I,
         Characteristics of the Population. Part 1, United States
         Summary. Washington, D.C.: U.S. Government Printing
         Office.
  1973a Census of Population, 1970: Detailed Characteristics. Final
         Report PC(1)–D1, United States Summary. Washington,
         D.C.: U.S. Government Printing Office.
  1973b "Some demographic aspects of aging in the United States."
         Current Population Reports, Series P–23 No. 43.
         Washington, D.C.: U.S. Government Printing Office.
  1974 "Money income and poverty status of families and persons
         in the United States: 1974." Current Population Reports,
         Series P–60, No. 99 (Advance Report). Washington, D.C.:
         U.S. Government Printing Office.
  1975a "Population profile of the United States: 1974." Current
         Population Reports, Series P–20, No. 279. Washington,
         D.C.: U.S. Government Printing Office.

1975b "Social and economic characteristics of the older population: 1974." Current Population Reports, Series P–23, No. 57. Washington, D.C.: U.S. Government Printing Office.

1975c Historical Statistics of the United States, Colonial Times to 1970, Bicentennial Edition, Part 1. Washington, D.C.: U.S. Government Printing Office.

1976 "Demographic aspects of aging and the older population in the United States." Current Population Reports, Series P–23, No. 59. Washington, D.C.: U.S. Government Printing Office.

United States Public Health Service

1971 "Health in the later years." National Center for Health Statistics. Washington, D.C.: U.S. Government Printing Office.

1974 Vital Statistics of the United States, 1970, Volume II—Mortality, Part A. National Center for Health Statistics. Washington, D.C.: U.S. Government Printing Office.

1975 "Current estimates from the health interview survey: United States–1974." Vital and Health Statistics, Series 10, No. 100. National Center for Health Statistics. Washington, D.C.: U.S. Government Printing Office.

1976a Vital Statistics of the United States, 1972, Volume II—Mortality, Part A. National Center for Health Statistics. Washington, D.C.: U.S. Government Printing Office.

1976b "Annual Summary for the United States, 1975." Monthly Vital Statistics Report 24: 13. National Center for Health Statistics. Washington, D.C.: U.S. Government Printing Office.

United States Senate

1974 Developments in Aging: 1973 and January–March 1974. Special Committee on Aging. Washington, D.C.: U.S. Government Printing Office.

Walsh, David

1975 "Age differences in learning and memory." In Diana Woodruff and James Birren (eds.). Aging: Scientific Perspectives and Social Issues. New York: D. Van Nostrand.

Wershow, Harold

1977 "Reality orientation for gerontologists: Some thoughts about senility." The Gerontologist 17: 297–302.

Zimberg, Sheldon

1974 "The elderly alcoholic." The Gerontologist 14: 221–24.

Zimmerman, Michael

1976 "Old-age poverty in preindustrial New York City." In Beth Hess (ed.). Growing Old in America. New Brunswick, N.J.: Transaction.

3

Age Stratification: Aging in a Sociocultural Context

Aging is not the same experience in different societies or even in the same society at different times. The aged may be better or worse off, depending upon the structure of the society, the conditions of life (including the environment), attitudes toward aging, services provided to older people, family structure, and so on. One must look at the system of age grading and age stratification for a particular society to understand the position of the aged in that society. Before looking at an age stratification model in greater depth, however, it would be helpful to first have some appreciation of the position of the aged in various specific societies.

The impression is sometimes given that the aged were treated reverentially in primitive, preindustrial societies—that there existed a "golden age of aging"—and that older people are much worse off in modern societies—neglected by their families, forced into boring and meaningless retirement, and derogated by the "youth culture." But we must be wary of simplistic "before and after" statements. The reality of aging in preindustrial societies was, and is, often far from idyllic, and many of our stereotypes about the modern aged are overdrawn.

Aging in Preindustrial Societies

There are severe limitations on our knowledge of aging in pre-industrial societies. The historical study of aging, at least before

1800, derives largely from scattered literary and artistic sources and available demographic records (births, marriages, and deaths) (Laslett, 1976). Even more recent accounts of aging in preindustrial societies are often based on occasional references to the elderly in ethnological accounts by anthropologists. Nevertheless, there is ample evidence that the status of old people varied considerably among such societies. An important fact is that old age is relatively rare, except in modern industrialized societies. Very seldom was more than 1 or 2 percent of the population over 65; they constituted only 2.2 percent of India's population as late as 1948, and only 4.1 percent in the United States at the beginning of this century (Simmons, 1960). Social definitions of age may be quite different in such societies. Simmons notes, for example, that among the Bontoc Igorot of the Philippines, a woman was "getting old" at 30 and was "old" at 45. The rarity of old age may itself be a source of prestige, and such societies do not face the problems associated with the rising older population in modern societies.

A "nonsocial" variable affecting the position of the aged is the natural environment. The aged will be worse off when the climate is severe, the environment harsh, and resources inadequate. Life under such conditions becomes a daily fight for survival, and culture, religion, and sentiment are luxuries which can ill be afforded. Holmberg (1969) comments on the Bolivian Siriono tribe:

> Since status is determined largely by immediate utility to the group, the inability of the aged to compete with the younger members of the society places them somewhat in the category of excess baggage. Having outlived their usefulness they are relegated to a position of obscurity. Actually the aged are quite a burden. They eat but are unable to hunt, fish, or collect food; they sometimes hoard a young spouse, but are unable to beget children; they move at a snail's pace and hinder the mobility of the group. . . . When a person becomes too ill or infirm to follow the fortunes of the band, he is abandoned to shift for himself. (pp. 224–25)

Neglect and abandonment of the aged were apparently rather common occurrences—Simmons (1945) found it to be customary in 18 out of 39 tribes he studied. The Yakuts of Siberia, for example, expelled their aged from the family and forced them to become beggars and slaves (de Beauvoir, 1972). The killing of older people was sometimes surrounded by ritual, with their apparent consent. In some cases, this was even welcomed and demanded by the aged as their right, though one might question whether this was really their free choice. The Samoans, for example,

once buried their aged alive, and it was considered a disgrace to
the family if this was not done (Simmons, 1960). The Chukchee
tribe of Siberia engaged in ceremonial killing of the aged in front
of the entire community:

> A great feast was given in their honour, a feast in which they
> took part: the assembly ate seal-meat, drank whiskey, sang, and
> beat upon a drum. The condemned man's son or his younger
> brother slipped behind him and strangled him with a seal-bone.
> (de Beauvoir, 1972:51)

Bear in mind that the basic reason for this treatment was the
harshness of the environment and living conditions, not a barbaric
mentality.

The social rights and roles of the aged are more developed in
farming and handicraft economies, characterized by permanent
residence, stable food supply, herding and cultivation, closely
knit family relations, and the growth of magical and religious
beliefs (Simmons, 1960). These more wealthy, settled societies
enjoy a margin of security which allows them to be kinder to
those who become dependent. Indeed, it is in the adults' own
interest to look after the aged, since they may (and hope to)
reach that state themselves. Many societies, including ancient
Israel and China and the Incas of Peru, developed rules for food
sharing which involved special treatment of the old and feeble
(Goody, 1976). The position of the aged was not based solely on
charity, however. The aged assumed positions of social significance
because of abilities useful to the society and the control over
valued resources.

Also, such societies utilize the skills of older people for light
economic tasks. Simmons (1960) notes that auxiliary tasks for the
aged are less prevalent in simple collecting, hunting, and fishing
societies, but there are more opportunities for secondary economic
functions in herding, farming, and handicraft economies. For example, older people unfit for work served as scarecrows under Inca
law, and Chippewa old women winowed rice, made fish nets,
tanned hides, and supervised both the storing of fish and the
work of young girls. The aged can better preserve their economic
functions in low-productivity economies, in which any labor is of
value (Rosow, 1965; 1974). Of course, repeated demotions into
secondary menial tasks may maintain the security of the aged,
but not their status or self-esteem.

Stable farming economies may also enable the aged to attain
directive roles because of their experience or familiarity with
special skills. Simmons (1960) notes that the aged often work as

craftsmen, priests, midwives, or "beauty experts." They may also be involved in entertainment: games, songs, or storytelling.

The position of the aged is particularly related to their possession of *strategic knowledge* which is of use to the society in a number of forms (Rosow, 1974). First, the aged often use their accumulated wisdom, skill, and tact in the conduct of political, civil, and judicial affairs (Simmons, 1960). Simmons (1945) has noted that 56 out of 71 tribes which he studied had "old chiefs" (almost universally male), and older persons are frequently used as arbitrators. They may also increase their influence through secret societies and such elaborate initiation rites as the passage from youth to adulthood. Confucianism linked aging with wisdom and possession of a sense of the "golden mean" (Piovesana, 1974). The heroes of ancient China were literati and officials whose qualifications increased with age.

Age alone rarely qualifies an individual for responsibility, however. Such positions almost always go to older *males* who have demonstrated personal ability. Leadership by the aged is more likely in stable societies with advanced economies and complex social organization (Simmons, 1960). Nahemow and Adams (1974) describe a stable preindustrial society in which the aged do not enjoy authority or an advisory role, however—the Baganda tribe of Uganda. Among the Baganda, the aged have family respect and obedience, but no special position as officials or advisors. Their position is confined to the familial role of grandparent. This might be attributable to a relatively "modern" value system among the Baganda, which emphasizes individualism and a positive orientation toward achievement and change.

Older people will also be respected if they are seen as the guardians of cultural knowledge, the recollected past, and memories, thus insuring cultural continuity through time (de Beauvoir, 1972; Rosow, 1974). This gives them the strategic function of bearers and interpreters of culture—a living "storehouse" of the culture—as among the Aleuts in the northern Pacific:

> Before the advent of Russian priests, every village had one or two old men at least, who considered it their especial business to educate the children; thereupon, in the morning or the evening, when all were at home, these aged teachers would seat themselves in the center of one of the largest village courts or "oolagmuh": the young folks surrounded them, and listened attentively to what they said—sometimes failing memory would cause the old preceptors to repeat over and over again the same advice or legend in the course of a lecture. The respect of the children, however, never allowed or occasioned an interruption of such a senile oration. (Elliott, 1886:170–71)

This role is less important when traditions and knowledge are transmitted in written rather than oral form or when daily life is so hard that it prevents consideration of culture.

The aged will also be more significant when they are seen as links to the past and the supernatural in tradition-oriented societies (de Beauvoir, 1972; Simmons, 1960; Rosow, 1974). Older people often function as seers and priests, keepers of shrines, and leaders of rites. As such, they mediate between man and the unknown, relying upon subtle and esoteric methods rather than physical strength.

> The very weakness of the aged makes their blessings and curses more powerful. The ability to change the world by words alone is often seen as characteristic of those who cannot change it by other means; hence, the curse of the beggar, the gypsy, the outsider, and the weak has much greater force than that of the soldier, the chief, or the politician; it is equally so with the young and the old. (Goody, 1976:128)

Among the Polar Eskimos the aged were reputedly able to raise storms and produce calms (Simmons, 1960), and they were important in the complex Navajo culture because of their magical incantations (de Beauvoir, 1972). De Beauvoir notes that magic and religion emerge when economic life calls for more complex knowledge and the struggle against nature is less fierce, allowing for some degree of detachment.

Older persons are better off in societies which allow for the acquisition and exercise of property rights and in which property is institutionalized and guaranteed by law (Simmons, 1960; de Beauvoir, 1972; Rosow, 1965 and 1974). Property is based on right rather than strength or abilities which can decline with age. Property also gives the aged power over other age groups and, therefore, a reason to expect or demand deference. This institutionalization of property existed in Greek city-states. In agricultural societies, younger generations are dependent upon their elders for the transmission of scarce resources, such as farmland. This dependence is less in hunting societies, where individuals must rely on their own abilities rather than the accumulation of others, and in societies with open frontiers where the young can make their own fortunes ("Go west, young man!").

Related to the importance of property in settled societies is the tendency for strongly organized, relatively unchanging societies to look to the aged for support, while youth is ascendant in changing or more revolutionary societies (de Beauvoir, 1972). Respect, authority, and power were accorded to the elders of ancient

China, India, and Greece, as they upheld tradition in static, strongly hierarchical societies. This is also reflected in the gerontocratic leadership of the Roman Senate (from *senex*, aged) and the Spartan Gerusia (from *gera*, old) (Fischer, 1977).

Finally, the position of older people depends on the extent to which they are embedded in an extended family structure which provides them with positions of respect and authority as well as economic and social security (Simmons, 1960; Rosow, 1974). It was fairly common for older persons in preindustrial societies to marry younger persons and to be left in charge of the children. Older *men* often achieved power and authority from family position, as the patriarchs of Rome, China, and Japan. Deference to the aged within the family may be linked to their religious importance, as links to the past. Ancestor worship in China was centered in the family and reinforced by the teaching of filial piety in Confucianism (Piovesana, 1974).

One reason for the importance of the extended family is that it ties older people into a system of mutual dependence (Rosow, 1974). This may involve repayment for services rendered to the family earlier in life or continued opportunity to both give and receive various kinds of support. To the extent that mutual obligation within the family is weakened, older people must look elsewhere to meet their needs. As we shall see later, there has been continuing debate about the effects of modernization on family structure, and there has been a tendency to overemphasize the amount of family support received by the aged in preindustrial societies. But where a stable extended family system did exist, the aged acquired greater security.

The bases of older people's position can be condensed into four basic prestige-generating components (Press and McKool, 1972):

1. *advisory component*: the experience of older people generates expertise which is useful to others;
2. *contributory component*: older people can make valued contributions to cultural, familial, or economic activities;
3. *control component*: older people have direct control over the behavior or welfare of others because of their monopoly over necessary objects, property, ritual process, or knowledge;
4. *residual component*: older people retain prestige associated with previous statuses from which they have "retired."

Lozier (1975) has suggested that the residual component is most likely to be found in small, stable, rural communities, where the aged can "retire to the porch" and live off social credit they have accumulated in the community. The aged lack this accumulated credit in mobile, anonymous social settings, such as the city.

Respect is accorded to the aged (or taken away) on the basis of the special assets they possess. Those assets tend most often to accrue from their accumulated memory and experience, which increase their performance and judgment in certain tasks. Simmons (1960) concludes that

> . . . the basic qualities of successful aging rests, after all, upon the capacities and the opportunities of individuals to fit well into the social framework of their own times and in ways that insure prolonged but not overlong influence and security. (p. 88)

Respect accorded to the aged in general does not assure the position of any particular older person. Harlan (1964), in a study of three Indian villages, found that only a minority of older men enjoyed positions of authority, prestige, and security within the family, and the aged in general occupied precarious positions in the villages. It is also probably true, as de Beauvoir (1972) has noted, that most societies have mixed feelings about the aged—love, disgust, respect, fear. Certainly the magical and religious importance attributed to older people in many societies would suggest a mixture of respect and fear. It is still true that older people may be mocked in private but treated with public deference, or honored in words but neglected in practice.

As a final note, it appears that older men are more likely to be accorded positions of respect and authority than older women, and prestige for aged men offers no assurance for women (Simmons, 1960). Older men tend to be better off in societies characterized by a patriarchal family structure, herding or agriculture, permanent residence, constant food supply, well-regulated political system, and entrenched property rights. Older women seem to be better off under a matriarchal family structure in simpler hunting, fishing, and collection societies.

An Example: The Abkhasians

There has recently been interest in some current preindustrial societies which appear to combine extreme longevity with high status for the aged, notably groups in the Ecuadorian Valley of Vilcabamba, in the province of Hunza in Pakistan, and in Abkhazia of the Georgian Soviet Socialist Republic (Leaf, 1973). The claims of long life coming from these areas are striking. Nine persons out of 819 residents of a Vilcabamba village claimed to be over 100 years of age. Benet (1974) indicates that 2.6 percent of the Abkhasians were over 90, compared with only 0.1 percent in the

Soviet Union as a whole, and some residents claimed to be 120 or 130 years old. These ages are very difficult to verify, and there is likely to be some exaggeration (Medvedev, 1974), but longevity does appear to be substantial in these areas. Drawing from the work of Benet (1974), one can begin to outline some of the possible reasons for this in the Abkhasian culture.

The Abkhasians live in rural villages in the Caucasus Mountains of Russia. Theirs is an agricultural society, recently giving way from subsistence farming to a collective community with cash crops of tea leaves and tobacco. Though many of us would not care to live to be 120, for fear of sickness and senility, the health of the aged Abkhasians seems to be better than older people in other cultures. The physical processes of aging seem to be delayed—wrinkles and gray hair occur only in extreme age, baldness is rare, posture is erect, and the aged retain good vision, good hearing, and their own teeth. Benet notes that

> The extraordinary ability of the aged to recover from stress or illness has also been recorded on many occasions. One example is Akhutsa Kunach, one hundred fourteen years old. . . . During the previous winter, while cutting timber in the woods, he had been injured by a falling tree. Three ribs were broken. Two months later the doctors diagnosed him as fit to work, and he resumed all his former duties. He still felt responsible for his family, and directed the proper reception for his guests. (Benet, 1974: 12)

The continuation of sexual activity into old age is considered natural and healthy. Early sexual abstinence is felt to prolong sexual potency. One possible reason for this good health is the ancient and elaborate folk medicine practiced in the region. There are a number of other possible reasons for this longevity, however.

The dietary practices of the Abkhasians undoubtedly contribute to their long life. They are taught the food and medicinal value of plants at an early age. Moderation is highly valued, and fat is viewed as an illness. Cleanliness is virtually a religion and the Abkhasians never eat leftovers. Their diet consists primarily of milk and vegetables, with little meat or animal fat and few spices. The average food intake is less than 2,000 calories. Readers who have tried low-calorie diets can appreciate how little this is. This type of diet is apparently also characteristic of other long-living peoples (Leaf, 1973; Beller and Palmore, 1974). Abkhasians seldom smoke, but they do drink a lot of wine. Arteriosclerosis is virtually unknown, apparently because of the low cholesterol content of the diet.

Other possible reasons for longevity relate to the social position of the aged and the outlook on aging which it implies. The life cycle is uniform, with no sharp, stressful discontinuities among age groups. Retirement is unknown. The aged remain active up to their capacity with few feelings of uselessness. This results in a consistent, unbroken life pattern, with little need for wrenching adjustments to role transitions.

Older people among the Abkhasians assume considerable responsibility for village decision making. They are viewed as the keepers of tradition and cultural continuity, presiding over ceremonies, mediating disputes, and utilizing their knowledge of medicinal herbs. The aged also retain considerable authority in the family, remaining integrated into the extended family and community. High social status for the aged because of their wisdom and experience is characteristic of all three societies investigated by Leaf (1973).

The Abkhasian culture is also characterized by stress-avoiding mechanisms, notably a lack of competition and a stoic life style. A placid state of mind, free from worry and strain, is emphasized. This seems true of high-longevity societies, as exemplified by a Turkish proverb: "Keep your feet warm, your head cool, your heart light, and don't worry" (Beller and Palmore, 1974: 375). There is also a culturally reinforced expectation of long life and good health.

The Abkhasian culture provides a social context conducive to longevity. Much of the stress of aging in modern societies is alleviated by the continuity of the life cycle, the lack of intergenerational conflict, the high status accorded the aged, and values which stress stoicism. This, combined with dietary and other factors, makes their longevity understandable. Such conditions are by no means characteristic of all preindustrial societies, however, and even our view of the Abkhasians may be colored by our desire to fulfill the ancient hyperborean theme.

Aging and Modernization

It has been common in social gerontology to note the detrimental effects of modernization and industrialization on the relative status of the aged and describe their respect and authority in more traditional preindustrial societies. While the position of older people varied in preindustrial societies, there are processes of modernization which could be expected to undermine their status. The trend from home-based to factory production undermines the extended family. In rapidly changing modern societies, the experience of the aged becomes obsolete, they do not command new skills, tradition is less important because of future-orientation, and local group life is attenuated. These arguments imply that the prestige-generating capacities and characteristics of the aged are devalued in modern societies.

Discussions of the impact of modernization on aging have tended to be rather haphazard and integrated theoretical development has often been lacking in social gerontology. Donald Cowgill (1974a; 1974b), however, has made a laudable attempt to organize a coherent framework for understanding the effects of modernization. Cowgill's model traces the effects of what he sees as the four most salient defining aspects of modernization: (1) the application of modern health technology, (2) the application of scientific technology to the economy, (3) urbanization, and (4) mass education and the increase of literacy. The key features of the model are diagramed in Figure 3.1.

One consequence of modern health technology is the "aging" of the population, a distinctly modern phenomenon which began in western Europe as a by-product of the demographic transition. As life is prolonged, death is less effective in creating openings in the labor force. Intergenerational competition arises over jobs, and retirement emerges as a social institution for opening up the labor force to younger workers. Unfortunately for the aged, modernizing societies are also typically characterized by a work ethic and strong feelings against dependency, and they must relinquish the work role, the primary definer of their usefulness and worthiness, to take on the lower status (both financially and socially) of the retirement role. We have already seen that preindustrial societies, such as the Abkhasians, had no concept of retirement out of the major productive roles of the society.

Cowgill's model also points out that new technology creates new occupations and the young are most likely to become the occupational pioneers of developing societies. The aged remain in more traditional occupations, which are less in demand and may become obsolete. This creates additional pressure for retirement and the lowered status which may accompany it.

The third aspect of modernization is urbanization. Young people, who tend to be the most mobile members of society, are attracted to the city by the promise of exciting changes and new career opportunities. Once there, they marry and establish permanent residence, thus breaking up the extended family. This results in residential segregation of the generations and accentuation of social differences between them.

Increasing urbanization in modern and modernizing societies, accompanied by the new occupations for the young, results in social mobility. Status is inverted, with younger people occupying more prestigious positions than their parents and grandparents.

Figure 3.1. The impact of modernization on the status of the aged

Salient Aspects
of Modernization

Intervening Variables

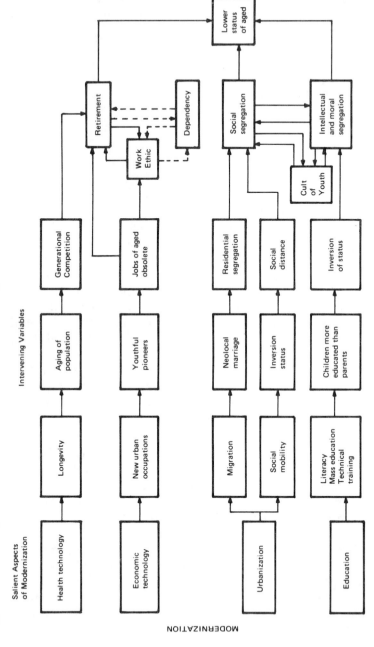

MODERNIZATION

Source: Donald Cowgill. "Aging and modernization: A revision of the theory." In Jaber Gubrium (ed.), *Late Life: Communities and Environmental Policies*, 1974, p. 141. Reprinted courtesy of Charles C Thomas, Publisher, Springfield, Illinois.

80

This serves to increase the social distance between generations. Cowgill notes that

> . . . the young move into the new, more glamorous, better-paying urban jobs, leaving behind—both physically and psychologically—the grubby, archaic, rural way of life. The young are in the stream of progress; the old are left behind. The young have improved their station; the old stand still and suffer by comparison. (Cowgill, 1974a: 13)

Finally, modernization is accompanied by a drive to promote literacy. The primary recipients of mass education efforts are the young, who thus acquire more education than their parents. Again, there is an inversion of status and, because of these educational changes, an increasing moral and intellectual difference between generations.

Cowgill suggests that this social, moral, and intellectual separation combines with other characteristics of developing countries to produce lower status for the aged. Modernizing societies have a tendency to glorify youth as the embodiment of progress and achievement, and youth is viewed as the very means for attaining that progress. The rapidity of change in such societies also means that the young are socialized for a very uncertain future. The traditions and accumulated experiences of older generations are increasingly seen as irrelevant because they no longer apply to the emerging order of things. This is perhaps the core meaning of a "generation gap."

Modernization is a process which, Cowgill suggests, results in the "transformation of a total society." The major aspects of modernization combine to place the aged in a very different position from younger generations, and the net result is lower status for the aged, as prestige-generating social structures are replaced with devaluing structures. This is a telling indictment of the view that modernization brings a more civilized culture. Certainly we do not abandon our aged on ice floes or force them to beg in the streets. But Cowgill's model suggests that the elderly are abandoned socially and psychologically, making them unnecessary, marginal, and alien to their own society. Indeed, the culture is no longer their own but belongs to the young.

This model of modernization receives at least partial support from some recent studies. Palmore and Whittington (1971) investigated the relative status of older people in the United States, focusing on four aspects of their situation: economic, social, residential, and health. They found that the status of the aged compared to the non-aged population had generally declined from

1940 to 1969 which seems to support the theory that the relative status of the aged declines in industrial societies. Palmore and Manton (1974), in a cross-cultural study of 31 countries, found the relative status of the aged lower in more modernized societies, but the most modernized societies also showed some betterment of the position of older people. Such societies may begin to create new roles for the aged, as well as provide greater social and economic security. This is supported by a recent study showing an upturn in the relative economic status of older people in the United States (Palmore, 1976).

Bengtson and associates (1975) have suggested the need to distinguish between *modernization* and *modernity*. Modernization refers to the processes of *societal* development discussed by Cowgill. Their results, from a study of six developing nations, indicate that modernization does result in more negative perceptions of aging and devaluation of the aged. Modernity, on the other hand, refers to the exposure of *individuals* to industrial technology and urban experiences which alters their attitudes and values (making them more "modern"). They found that modernity within developing societies did not lead to more negative perceptions of aging and the aged.

There are many ways in which older people are better off in modern societies than in preindustrial societies, though they may be worse off relative to others in their own society. It is important to investigate the positions occupied by older people in any society and the fit between those positions and the values and structure of that society.

The Aged in America

The impact of modernization on the status of the aged can best be examined by looking at the United States, as social historian David Fischer has done in his recent book, *Growing Old in America* (1977). This impressive work traces the position of the aged from colonial times to the present. The results suggest that while modernization has indeed accelerated the decline in status of the aged, this decline was evident even before such modern phenomena as mandatory retirement, urbanization, and mass education of the young.

Fischer's analysis begins with the Puritans of colonial times. Because of high fertility and mortality rates, old age was rare—the median age in the colonies was probably no more than 20, and fewer than 2 percent of the population was 65 and above. Old age, being so rare, was taken as a sign of the Elect, and Puritan writers made a cult of age. A large body of literature, such as the sermons of Cotton Mather, instructed people how to behave toward their elders. The respect accorded to old age was not simply a sign of affection or deference, but rather of *veneration* interwoven with religious overtones. Elders ran the churches and occupied places of honor in meetinghouses. There was no concept of retirement because of age per se; for example, clergy and schoolmasters were more likely to die in office than retire. The aged occupied positions of community leadership, and "grey champions" (to use Fischer's phrase) were particularly likely to be turned to in times of crisis.

The position of the colonial elderly was mixed. While elites were venerated, the destitute aged were often scorned and mistreated, and old age for all was often a time of physical suffering, since medical knowledge was not advanced. Fischer cites the example of Benjamin Franklin, who in his last years relied heavily on opium to relieve intense pain. When his daughter tried to console him on his deathbed with the hope of more years of life, Franklin replied, "I hope not" (Fischer, 1977: 67). Despite such suffering, the aged carried a heavy responsibility to keep active; serene, carefree retirement was denied them. As was also true of ancient Greece, literature, plays, and sermons mixed respect with feelings of resentment, conflict, satire, and rage at the senility and moral failings of the old. Fischer notes that veneration was cold, creating emotional distance and little serenity or peace.

Granting these other characteristics, the overall picture is one of great respect and authority accorded to the aged. Partly this was based on economic coercion, as control of land was retained until advanced age, guaranteeing that the elders would be surrounded by "seeking" children. Full financial independence was typically not achieved by males until age 30 or 40. But this veneration of the aged was also an instrument of conservatism in a tradition-bound society, insuring continuity, stability, and permanence. In this sense, veneration of the aged in colonial America can be likened to that of ancient China and Greece.

According to Fischer, this cult of old age was undermined in the late eighteenth and early nineteenth centuries by a number of trends. Wealth supplanted age as the basis of meetinghouse seating. Legislatures began to require retirement from office at age 60 or 70. Fashions which had previously been designed to accentuate age (such as powdered wigs) now flattered youth (the cut of men's coats, hair dyes, hairpieces). Terms which had previously indicated respect were now used to derogate (gaffer, fogy, superannuated) and new pejoratives for the aged (codger, fuddy-duddy, geezer) emerged during this period. One indication from Fischer's work that old women may have always been held in lower esteem than old men is the fact that insulting references for them have a much longer history; such terms as hag, crone, and old maid date to the fourteenth and fifteenth centuries.

Fischer attributes these changes to fundamental changes in world culture, exemplified in the American and French Revolutions, ushered in by demographic, political, economic, and ethical change. In the first place, old age was no longer so rare, due to declining fertility and mortality. In addition, the earlier closed, authoritarian societies were being broken down, supplanted by expanding ideals of equality and liberty. Growing inequality of wealth displaced other inequalities such as age, and the cultural homogeneity upon which veneration of the aged was based was lost.

What we see, then, in the period from 1770 to 1820, is not really a cult of youth which derogates the aged; rather, the ancien régime which celebrated a cult of old age was overthrown by an emerging ideal of age equality.

Fischer's study does support Cowgill's model, however, in that the modern era in American society seems to have ushered in a cult of youth, through which earlier veneration of the aged, initially supplanted by age equality, is finally replaced with derogation of the old and celebration of youth. With the institution of retirement, mass education, growing age inequality in income, and residential separation of the generations, the old came to be seen as alien and useless. The nation itself developed a youthful self-image, and its heroes and legends shifted from elders and Founding Fathers to young men, from Daniel Boone to Charles Lindbergh. Literature increasingly cast old age as pathetic and empty. As early as the nineteenth century, Henry David Thoreau stated that: "Practically, the old have no very important advice to give the young" (Fischer, 1977:115). Fischer notes that this cult of youth reached its peak in the 1960s.

There are, nonetheless, some notes of optimism concerning the place of the aged in modern America. Fischer suggests that the aged have achieved a psychic gain, despite social losses, since relations between generations are now less authoritarian and more affectionate. And the youth cult may have peaked out during the 1960s. One seldom hears anymore that "you can't trust anyone over 30," perhaps because those who espoused this view during the turbulent sixties are now themselves over 30. Rising interest in aging and the problems of the aged suggest that the future may bring more attempts to build meaningful roles for the aged in society. The cycle again seems to be moving toward an ethic of age equality.

Aging in Modern Societies

Modernization is not an entirely monolithic process. It proceeds at different rates, under different conditions, in each society. Thus, it can be expected that the similarities among modern societies in their treatment of the aged will be accompanied by some important differences, and trends in the United States are not likely to be universal. Such differences can be seen even in cross-cultural studies of Western societies. For example, mixed-age organizational memberships are more frequent in the United States, the Netherlands, France, England, and Germany than in Sweden, Denmark, and Switzerland, while clubs for older people are most developed in the Netherlands, Great Britain, and the United States, and virtually unknown in France (Havighurst, 1960). Political pressure groups of older people are more likely to be found in Sweden, Great Britain, and the Netherlands and are least evident in France, Switzerland, and the United States, though some of these trends may have changed since Havighurst's article was written. Burgess (1960b) attributes such differences to the degree of industrialization, the nature of family and organizational structure, and differences in social action on behalf of the aged. He notes, for example, that social security systems differ cross-culturally in age eligibility, sources of funding, and coverage.

Shanas and associates (1968), comparing the position of older people in the United States, Great Britain, and Denmark, suggest that the aged are more strongly integrated into industrial society than our theories indicate. This is based on findings related to general health, networks of family services, social participation, and other factors. They also note, however, that the aged are "kept at arm's length from the social structure" (p. 425) and that such societies tend formally to *accommodate* to older people rather than *integrate* them. While there were considerable similarities among the three countries, a number of differences were evident. For example, income inequality by age was less in Denmark and greater in the United States while home-help services, such as visiting nurses, were less developed in the United States. In addition, family relationships were more loosely knit in Denmark than in the United States and Great Britain.

Japan offers another example that the effects of modernization on the status of older people depends on the cultural context (Palmore, 1975a and 1975b). Japan is a modern, industrialized, urban society, yet the status of the aged has apparently remained quite high. Their integration into the family appears higher than in Western societies, since the aged are much more likely to share their children's residences and fulfill important functions within the family. They operate as caretakers, perpetuators of religious affairs, and senior advisors on family problems, and provide affectional support for grandchildren. The aged of Japan are also more likely to continue working. Although Japan spends proportionately less on social security programs than the United States, the primary reasons for continued work appear to be greater opportunities (traditions of seniority, high rates of self-employment) and a strong work ethic. There seems to be a more strongly held view that work is "normal" after age 65.

Japanese older persons also appear to be well-integrated into community life. Senior citizens clubs have multiplied rapidly since the 1950s (Maeda, 1975) and about half of Japanese over 65 belong to such groups, a much higher rate than in the United States.

The respect for the aged in Japan is reflected in the honorific language used about them, the preference given them in family matters, and both the content and language of legislation pertaining to them. For example, Respect for Elders Day has been a national holiday since 1963. Palmore argues that this respect for older people has two main roots. First, Japan is a "vertical" society which emphasizes hierarchical relationships and the deference due persons in superior positions, stressing deference and respect rather than independence and equality. Second, Japanese society stresses filial piety. Respect and obligations to parents and grandparents are learned and observed within the family, and this is connected to the importance of ancestor worship.

Japan appears to be an exception to the rule linking modernization with lower status for the aged. It may be, of course, that this cultural anachronism lingers because of the rapidity of Japanese industrialization and will fade as modernization "truly" takes hold. Only time and further research will tell.

Another example of aging within a specific modernizing society is found in Talmon's (1961) study of Israel. The Israeli collectives have solved many of the basic problems of aging by providing economic security, medical care, gradual retirement, and continued community involvement. There are still sources of strain, however. The aged occupy an ambivalent position in a future oriented, youth-centered society in which the idea of cultural continuity is still relatively new. While retirement is gradual, older persons must face continual adjustment and uneasiness about growing dependence in a society which emphasizes productivity and deemphasizes the family as a key structure. In addition, dependence on the collective is not neutral or anonymous, as it is with Social Security in the United States. Again, the meaning of modernization and its consequences depend upon the cultural context.

Distinctions between preindustrial and industrial societies also gloss over the variations within a society. The United States, for example, is comprised of ethnic and racial subcultures which have not been fully homogenized by the "melting pot" (for example, see Greer, 1974). Such enclaves present different contexts for the aging experience. This is certainly evident in the United States, with its mixture of immigrant and nonimmigrant ethnics. Japanese immigrants (*issei*) in San Francisco, who came here early in this century from a traditional, agrarian society, experience aging differently within their own cultural world (Kiefer, 1974). Similarly, the lives of the aged Chinese-Americans, many of whom have never been integrated into Western society, are conducted almost entirely within the Chinatowns (Carp and Kataoka, 1976; see Chapter 2). There are other societal subgroups which may have different responses to the aged. Wylie (1971) suggests that black Americans are more inclined to include older persons in the family structure and regard them with respect. There are apparently also some differences in the position of the aged among black, French, and non-French subcultures in Louisiana, affecting their willingness to assume the status of "old" (Harper, 1967).

Findings such as those cited in this chapter suggest the need for continuing cross-cultural comparisons to assess the differences between intrinsic and reactive aging processes. There has been an increasing interest in such studies, as indicated by a recent issue of *The Gerontologist* (1975) devoted to gerontological research in Canada, Ecuador, France, Great Britain, Japan, the Netherlands, and Sweden.

A Model of Age Stratification

The principle that the nature of the aging experience is dependent upon the characteristics of its social context is recognized in a recent attempt to develop a model of *age stratification* as a framework for organizing and understanding research on aging.[1] Every society divides people into age strata. This stratification both reflects and causes age-related differences in capacities, expected roles, and rights and privileges. We all have some awareness of social-class stratification and sex-role stratification. We know that being in the working class or upper class affects educational and occupational opportunities, political power, health, and many other things. We also know that men and women are expected to play "appropriate" roles. The recognition that age is also important in the same ways, with equally important consequences, is relatively new, however. Because the nature of the age stratification

---

[1] Much of the following discussion of age stratification is drawn from Riley, Johnson, and Foner (1972).

system differs from one society to the next, the relative position of age groups will also differ. This model can be used to study all age groups, but the focus in this book will be on its usefulness in understanding the position of the aged. The basic characteristics of the age stratification model are shown in Figure 3.2.

Models such as this are sometimes deceptively simple, since they frequently formalize what is "common sense" or "accepted knowledge." The virtue of a theoretical model, however, is that it combines these common-sense understandings of the world into a more coherent statement, thereby helping us to understand the implications of what we "know" and suggesting new directions for our thinking.

Age Strata and Age-Related Capacities

The model begins with the seemingly simple recognition that people are distributed into various age strata, just as the Grand Canyon is divided into a series of geological layers extending down from the canyon walls. These age strata are composed of different "materials." They vary in size, proportion of the population, racial composition, education, and so on (see Chapter 2).

These age strata may be defined in various ways. Chronological age is certainly one criterion, or the life cycle could be divided into developmental stages: infancy, early childhood, adolescence, young adulthood, mature adulthood, middle age, and old age. One might also define different age strata within the spheres of family or work. Depending upon how strata are defined, they may be complex or simple and the boundaries between them sharp or indistinct. Chronological age gives very clear differentiation, while the border between "mature adulthood" and "middle age" is more difficult to pin down. Conflicting age statuses may arise from varying definitions of age strata. Retirement marriages, for example, involve persons who are "old" in the work cycle yet "young" in the family cycle. The simplest division of age strata, for the purposes of this book, would be according to the developmental stages in the life cycle.

Speaking literally, these age strata arise because of *cohort flow*. As new earth forms new layers over old layers of earth in a canyon, new cohorts are born to succeed earlier cohorts. The process of aging results in individual mobility across age strata. While social-class stratification and age stratification are similar in that both order people and roles in society, one clear difference is that age mobility is universal, inevitable, and irreversible. You can not become younger or stop the flow of time.

Linked to this age stratification is the fact that there are age-

Figure 3.2. Elements in a model of age stratification

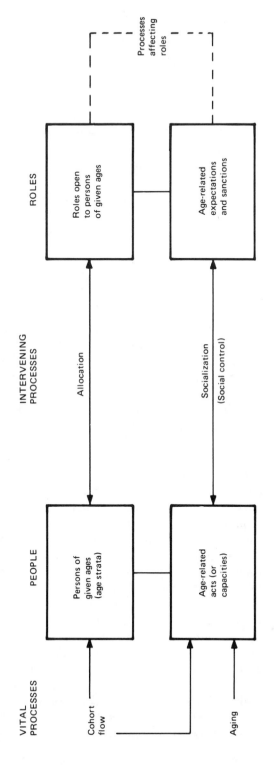

Source: Figure 1.2 from "Processes related to structural elements," in Chapter 1, "Elements in a Model of Age Stratification," in Aging and Society, Volume three: A Sociology of Age Stratification, by Matilda White Riley, Marilyn Johnson, and Anne Foner, p. 9, © 1972 by Russell Sage Foundation. Reprinted by permission.

related acts or capacities. People of different ages behave differently, have different abilities, and may be motivated by different
attitudes and values. These age differences may be attributable to
either aging effects or cohort effects, as discussed in Chapter 1.
For example, older people may have difficulty with retraining because of their poorer educational background. Additionally, if they
are more tied into the work ethic, they may be more likely than
younger people to emphasize the nonmonetary aspects of work.
Aging also creates such age differences, because of health changes
or possible psychological changes during the life cycle.

The importance of this model lies in the implications for individuals of being in an *age stratification system*, and to understand
these implications, we need to look at the rest of the model:
structural elements (roles and age-related expectations and sanctions) and processes (allocation and socialization) which link
people and roles.

Age-Grading of Roles

The model of age stratification emphasizes that age is one
criterion for determining what roles an individual will play in the
society. *Allocation* refers to "a set of mechanisms for the continual
assignment and reassignment of individuals of given ages to the
appropriate roles" (Riley, Johnson, and Foner, 1972:11). There
are a number of such allocating mechanisms, including the spread-
ing of information about roles, screening of qualifications, and
certification. It is sufficient here to simply note that one's age is
likely to determine the roles which will be played. This is true
to a greater or lesser degree in all societies.

Age operates in a number of ways as a criterion for both entering and leaving roles. Age may be a *direct* criterion. There are
formal rules which prescribe an age range for school attendance,
minimum age for entering the work force or voting, or a maximum
age for working (mandatory retirement policies). Additionally,
there are informal norms and beliefs about the kinds of roles "appropriate" for people at various ages, which reflect the values and
perceived needs of a particular society. Age norms may also be
factual regularities—the average or usual age for entering or leaving
certain roles—translated into normative standards. People may
perceive the 18-year-old college professor as "too young" or the 45-
year-old newlywed as "too old," and such norms may serve as a
barrier to behavior.

Results from a study by Neugarten and associates (1965) suggest
that there is consensus about such age expectations, as indicated
in Table 3.1. These age expectations may change as the timing of

Table 3.1. Consensus in a middle-class middle-aged sample regarding various age-related characteristics

	Age range designated as appropriate or expected	Percent who concur	
		Men (N = 50)	Women (N = 43)
Best age for a man to marry	20–25	80	90
Best age for a woman to marry	19–24	85	90
When most people should become grandparents	45–50	84	79
Best age for most people to finish school and go to work	20–22	86	82
When most men should be settled on a career	24–26	74	64
When most men hold their top jobs	45–50	71	58
When most people should be ready to retire	60–65	83	86
A young man	18–22	84	83
A middle-aged man	40–50	86	75
An old man	65–75	75	57
A young woman	18–24	89	88
A middle-aged woman	40–50	87	77
An old woman	60–75	83	87
When a man has the most responsibilities	35–50	79	75
When a man accomplishes most	40–50	82	71
The prime of life for a man	35–50	86	80
When a woman has the most responsibilities	25–40	93	91
When a woman accomplishes most	30–45	94	92
A good-looking woman	20–35	92	82

Source: Bernice Neugarten, Joan Moore, and John Lowe. "Age norms, age constraints, and adult socialization." *American Journal of Sociology* 70 (1965):712. © by The University of Chicago. Reprinted by permission.

events in the life cycle is altered. In this century there has been a "quickening" of some aspects of the family cycle and a lengthening of other periods (Neugarten and Moore, 1968). Individuals marry earlier, have children earlier, and have their last child leave the house earlier now than in 1900. Thus, they are likely to be an older couple without children in the home longer, and are also likely to be widowed for a longer time. More recently, trends toward earlier marriage and child-bearing have been reversing (Kreps and Clark, 1975). People also begin working later and end working earlier than they used to.

Age may also be an *indirect* criterion for allocating people into roles, by reflecting social, psychological, or biological characteristics. Certainly there are biological limits on the ability to enter the "mother" role. Most college professors are at least 25 by the time they acquire the necessary specialized training. The careers of professional athletes are circumscribed by age-related physical capabilities. This last example, however, involves two points which apply to all of these age criteria. First, age criteria may be more or less flexible depending upon the role. There is no flexibility in eligibility to vote, but other age criteria may be more flexible. Most professional athletes are between 20 and 40, but Joe Nuxhall pitched for the Cincinnati Reds when he was 15 and Gordie Howe continues to play hockey in his fifties. Professional athletes also provide examples of the difference in spread of ages for different roles. Most football players are "old" at 35, but professional golfers can continue to be successful into their late forties and fifties.

The existence of age norms which guide allocation into roles is universal, but the content of those norms reflects the history, structure, and values of the particular society in which they exist and can change as the characteristics and requirements of the society change. Take, as an example, the finding in Table 3.1 that "most men should be settled on a career" by age 26. This may be an anachronism from the days when people could expect to live only 40 or 50 years. Now, when the average life span is 70 or 80 years, it makes less sense to make so many crucial decisions in the first third of one's life, and we may see greater delay of such decisions in the future.

Whatever the source of age norms—tradition, negotiation, factual regularities—they are all based on assumptions about age-related capacities and limitations (Atchley, 1975). These norms are often flexible or ambiguous, however, and specific age norms may differ by social class, type of community, region, sex, or ethnicity. Thus, age norms must be "translated into reality at various social levels by particular people in particular situations" (Atchley, 1975:268). Nevertheless, age is a universal criterion for allocating roles, which creates what Atchley calls "decision demands": points in the life cycle at which individuals must choose from a field of alternative age-linked positions in the social structure. In order to understand the implications of this for the aging individual, one must understand the characteristics of the roles available to people of different ages.

There are a multitude of roles which people can play: student, spouse, worker, politician, retiree. These roles differ in a variety of ways. First, roles will emphasize different qualities. Some roles, such as the worker role, are *instrumental*—defined in terms of task-orientation or their productive content. Other *expressive* roles, such as husband or wife, have more of an emotional content. Second, roles provide different types of rewards, such as money, a sense of fulfillment, relaxation, friendships, prestige, and so on. For example, teachers may derive more prestige and fulfillment from their work, but truck drivers may be paid better. Finally, roles themselves are socially evaluated according to the values and needs of the social group, so that some roles are highly valued while others are derogated. We tend, for example, to have different feelings about the student, worker, and retiree roles.

The fact that roles are age-graded within an age stratification system and possess different characteristics creates age differences and, perhaps more importantly, structured age inequalities. *The combination of normative age expectations and social values influences the relative social positions of age strata because age stratification affects the role qualities, rewards, and identities available to people of different ages.* One can argue that older people in American society are disadvantaged because of the types of roles they occupy. Some have suggested that by retiring the aged from instrumental work roles, we cut them off from both monetary rewards and a sense of accomplishment, and force them into a negatively valued leisure role (see Miller, 1965). We will leave this argument for later discussion. The basic point, however, is that meaningful identities may or may not be available to older people, depending on the particular system of age stratification they are in.

A key element of this model is that the evaluation of a role is attached to the person or groups playing the role. Therefore, each age group will be evaluated according to the roles its members typically play and the evaluation of those roles according to the dominant values and needs of the society. Where there is a lesser amount of age-grading, as with the Abkhasians, there are fewer age differences. When societies respect the cultural knowledge and accumulated experience of the aged, and allow them to play roles which capitalize on these qualities, the aged will be respected.

When the aged are allocated into important religious or advisory roles, they will receive higher status. Modernization seems to expand the scope of age stratification, accentuating age differences. The model of age stratification (Figure 3.2) provides a framework for analyzing and understanding the cross-cultural differences based on various age-status systems discussed earlier in this chapter.

It is the age stratification of roles which both frees and limits the aged in modern societies. They are freed from many obligatory adult roles to use their time as they wish, and potentially to change and grow. Yet values, institutional structures, and norms about "age-appropriate behavior" also limit their options. Leisure pursuits, for example, are not always freely chosen, as we shall see in Chapter 7. The opportunities made available to older people will determine whether old age is a time of status or stigma, growth or stagnation, self-expression or anxiety.

Modern societies have made age a more important status variable than in the past. We have seen the emergence of "adolescence" as a distinct life period, with prolonged education, and retirement has played a major role in separating "old age" from the adult life cycle. In some respects, however, we may now be moving toward a more "age-irrelevant" society (Neugarten and Hagestad, 1976). Educational opportunities are growing for the aged. Career change is increasingly prevalent during middle age and leisure options and values are expanding throughout the life cycle. The achievement of age-irrelevance requires a loosening up of the constraints which limit the options for all age groups.

Age Norms and Socialization

There is some debate about the nature of "age-appropriate" behavior norms for older people. There do appear to be some age-related expectations in the results cited in Table 3.1, and the same study also found that older people were even more likely than younger people to subscribe to age constraints—to feel that people should "act their age" (Neugarten, Moore, and Lowe, 1965). Wood (1971) also suggests that certain age norms have emerged: a widow's grief should not be so prolonged as to make others uncomfortable or hinder adjustment, grandparents should not interfere in the socialization of children, older people should keep up their club memberships. Some researchers have suggested that specific norms may emerge in specialized settings such as retirement communities (Bultena and Wood, 1969; Messer, 1967).

Others have argued, however, that old age is really a "nonrole" characterized by normlessness, in that most norms for older people are really "middle-aged" norms—primarily related to maintaining independence, social activity, and religiosity (Bengtson, 1973; Rosow, 1974). Norms for older people tend to be quite limited and ambiguous, offering few real guidelines for behavior.

More research into the nature of age-related expectations is clearly needed. How do they arise? Norms are best viewed as emerging within specific interaction situations. The fact that there are very broad expectations about older people tells us very little about the norms encountered by particular older people within their specific social groups and situations. To what extent do age norms really constrain behavior? For example, is a 65-year-old woman really less likely to get married because it would be "age-inappropriate?" If there are age norms, how are they enforced? Norms imply sanctions—people are rewarded for following them and punished for disregarding them. More research on the operation and effects of sanctions such as social disapproval is needed. Blau (1973) suggests, for example, that various strategies are used to gain "voluntary" retirements by workers who are "too old," including overt mockery, joking, and exclusion from group rituals.

The role transitions occurring over the life course pattern our lives, creating important changes in our social and personal worlds, and age stratification means these transitions and their timing are not necessarily chosen by us, since they are shaped by various age norms and allocation processes. Thus, to understand the nature of any stage of the life cycle requires an understanding of the role transitions of that stage and the pressures and strains which accompany them. Let us take adolescence as an example. Modern societies have prolonged childhood by postponing entrance into adult family, work, and community roles. Yet these "children" feel physically, intellectually, and emotionally capable of participating in the larger community. The age stratification of roles prevents this participation, thereby contributing to such diverse youth phenomena as alienation, the generation gap, and juvenile delinquency. Gang delinquency, for example, has been seen by some as a striving for "manhood" in modern societies which provide few transitional rituals or adultlike roles for adolescents.

The intensity of the adolescent experience and the vehemence of external expression depend on a variety of factors, including the general societal attitudes toward adolescence, the duration of the adolescent period itself, and the degree to which the society tends to facilitate entrance into adulthood by virtue of institutionalized patterns, ceremonies, rites and rituals, and socially supported emotional and intellectual preparation. When a society does not make adequate preparation, formal or otherwise, for the induction of its adolescents to the adult status, equivalent forms of behavior arise spontaneously among adolescents themselves, reinforced by their own group structure, which seemingly provide the same psychological content and function as the more formalized rituals found in other societies. This the gang structure appears to do in American society, apparently satisfying deepseated needs experienced by adolescents in all cultures. (Bloch and Niederhoffer, 1958:17)

This means that the second intervening process in the age stratification model, *socialization*, is a key to an understanding of any life stage. Socialization "serves to teach individuals at each stage of the life course how to perform new roles, how to adjust to changing roles, and how to relinquish old ones" (Riley, Johnson, and Foner, 1972:11). Age stratification makes socialization a lifelong process, since people move into and out of a succession of roles as they age.

In a sense, socialization teaches people to desire what is available to them. Problems develop when individuals are not socialized for the roles they occupy, are not allocated to the roles for which they are prepared, or are prepared incorrectly for their roles. All of these situations may occur with older people. Indeed, Rosow (1974) suggests that a critical problem of aging is the lack of socialization for an "old age" role. Older people are unwilling to take on the diminished status and "uselessness" of the retirement role, and there are no institutions or situations which really help older people prepare for old age. This means that age-related capacities, attitudes, and values, reflecting both cohort and aging effects, are not adequately matched by socialization to the roles available to the aged.

Margaret Clark (1967) has argued that older people in American society face a very basic cultural discontinuity. Though certain value-orientations are stressed in adulthood—status and achievement, acquisition, competiveness, high levels of aspiration, aggressiveness, and so on—she found that virtually opposite value-orientations characterized those who had adapted well to old age—congeniality, conservation, resilience, harmoniousness, cooperation, "reasonable" aspiration. This suggests a potential imbalance between allocation and socialization. As adults, we are socialized into a set of values which cannot be achieved in old age because of the positions which older people occupy.

This should not be taken to mean that older people necessarily *ought* to be socialized to accept the roles currently open to them. Those roles may not be meaningful or rewarding, and a lack of socialization for them may constitute a pressure for needed change in the nature of age stratification. Similarly, we should not assume that no socialization occurs for old age, even if there is no "old age role."

It is undeniable that age stratification in modern societies creates the loss of formal roles for older people and that there is no "old age role" into which they can be socialized. But the consequences of these facts are not clear. Many informal roles remain for the aged which allow for considerable "role making." In other words, older people are free to make of old age what they wish, thereby personally counteracting normlessness. We need to focus on the choices made by older people from among the options available to them. These choices will be constrained by values (society's and their own), opportunities provided by social institutions (educational and others), and norms about what is "appropriate" for their age group. This applies to more specific roles associated with retirement, leisure, widowhood, bereavement, and grand-parenthood. What norms define these roles and how are these norms communicated to the elderly through socialization processes? How much agreement exists, and how much variation is there across racial and social-class subgroups? These and related questions are only now beginning to be investigated within the framework of age stratification. The model draws our attention to the many socialization experiences we all encounter throughout our lives. The relative balance between role allocation and socialization for role transitions is a key to understanding the nature of any stage of the life course.

Age is not the sole criterion for stratification, of course. Societies are also stratified according to social class, with differential access to life chances and rewards for people of different classes. Age and class stratification are intertwined to a certain extent. Neugarten and Moore (1968) point out that the timing of events in the family cycle differs according to social class, and those of higher classes tend to marry and have children later. In a sense, this means that lower- and working-class people "age" earlier than those from the middle and upper classes. Additionally, the complex of roles played will confer a greater or lesser degree of prestige upon an age group as a whole.

Societies are also stratified according to sex. To the extent that males and females play different roles throughout the life cycle, the nature of their aging experience will also differ. There is a real need to pay attention to sex differences in aging and reassess some of our assumptions along these lines.

Age stratification does not tie status strictly to age per se. Individuals of the same age may differ greatly in their social class and status, depending upon the roles they play or have played in the past. Older people who play valued roles, as in politics for example, are accorded prestige despite a general devaluation of their age group, and middle-aged persons in devalued roles may have very low status.

The age stratification model also allows for the study of social change. The position of older people, and the aging experience, will be altered by shifts in the timing of life events, roles played by the aged, or the evaluation of roles played by the aged. This is the primary implication of Cowgill's theory of the impact of modernization on the status of older people. Similarly, changes in social-class or sex-role differentiation will alter the nature of aging. Clearly the position of older people in any society is complex. The age stratification model provides an extremely useful perspective for approaching the problem in an orderly way, and we will be returning to it periodically in the chapters which follow.

Summary

The relative position of the aged in any society depends on their particular physical and social environment. Older people were not necessarily better off in preindustrial society, but are in relatively better positions in stable societies characterized by cultural development, an extended family structure, and institutionalization of property. There are four prestige-generating components: advisory, contributory, control, and residual. Age itself is very seldom the source of prestige or power. The Abkhasians present an example of a current preindustrial culture which accords considerable respect and authority to the aged and in which people appear to have extended longevity. Among the possible reasons for this longevity are diet, continuity over the life cycle, high social status for the aged, and cultural mechanisms to avoid stress.

Modernization tends to be accompanied by declining status for older people. This can be linked to the combined impact of four accompaniments of modernization: more advanced health technology, economic change, urbanization, and mass education. Declining status for the aged may have begun prior to modernization, however. Veneration of the aged in colonial America had already been replaced with an ideal of age equality by the early nineteenth century. Modernization does seem to bring in a cult of youth which derogates old age, however.

There are also ways in which the aged are better off, especially in the most advanced societies. The nature and consequences of modernization are also dependent upon their cultural context. Japan, for example, has exhibited rapid modernization, yet certain cultural features have maintained a relatively high status for their "elders."

A model of age stratification provides a coherent framework for understanding the position of older people in any society, since age is one criterion for allocating individuals into roles. This results in differential access by age to specific types of identities and rewards. If the aged are allocated into roles which are highly valued by the society, such as guardian of cultural traditions or family head, they will be accorded prestige and authority. If they are allocated into roles which are not highly valued, such as retiree, their relative position declines. Imbalance between role allocation and socialization for age-graded roles may create considerable difficulties for older people. Age stratification is also intertwined with other sources of role differentiation, such as social class and sex. Thus, characteristics of the social structure create complexities in the aging experience.

References

Atchley, Robert
  1975 "The life course, age grading, and age-linked demands for decision-making." In Nancy Datan and Leon Ginsberg (eds.). Life-Span Developmental Psychology: Normative Life Crises. New York: Academic Press.
Beauvoir, Simone de
  1972 The Coming of Age. New York: Putnam's Sons.
Beller, Suha and Erdman Palmore
  1974 "Longevity in Turkey." The Gerontologist 14 (5): 373–76.
Benet, Sula
  1974 Abkhasians: The Long-Living People of the Caucasus. New York: Holt, Rinehart and Winston.
Bengtson, Vern
  1973 The Social Psychology of Aging. Indianapolis: Bobbs-Merrill.
Bengtson, Vern, James David, David Smith, and Alex Inkeles
  1975 "Modernization, modernity, and perceptions of aging: A cross-cultural study." Journal of Gerontology 30 (6): 688–95.
Blau, Zena
  1973 Old Age in a Changing Society. New York: New Viewpoints.
Bloch, Herbert and Arthur Niederhoffer
  1958 The Gang. New York: Philosophical Library.
Bultena, Gordon and Vivian Wood
  1969 "The American retirement community: Bane or blessing?" Journal of Gerontology 24 (2): 209–17.
Burgess, Ernest
  1960b "Resume and implications." In Ernest Burgess (ed). Aging in Western Societies. Chicago: University of Chicago Press.

Carp, Frances and Eunice Kataoka
    1976   "Health care problems of the elderly of San Francisco's
            Chinatown." The Gerontologist 16 (1): 30–38.
Clark, Margaret
    1967   "The anthropology of aging: A new area for studies of
            culture and personality." The Gerontologist 7 (1): 55–64.
Cowgill, Donald
    1974a   "The aging of populations and societies." In Frederick
            Eisele (ed.). Political Consequences of Aging. The Annals
            of the American Academy of Political and Social Science
            415 (September): 1–18.
    1974b   "Aging and modernization: A revision of the theory." In
            Jaber Gubrium (ed.). Late Life: Communities and
            Environmental Policies. Springfield, Ill.: Charles C Thomas.
Elliott, H. W.
    1886   Our Arctic Province: Alaska and the Seal Islands.
            New York: Scribner's.
Fischer, David
    1977   Growing Old in America. New York: Oxford University
            Press.
The Gerontologist
    1975   "An International Issue." 15 (3).
Goody, Jack
    1976   "Aging in nonindustrial societies." In Robert Binstock and
            Ethel Shanas (eds.). Handbook of Aging and the Social
            Sciences. New York: Van Nostrand Reinhold.
Greer, Colin (ed.)
    1974   Divided Society: The Ethnic Experience in America.
            New York: Basic Books.
Harlan, William
    1964   "Social status of the aged in three Indian villages." Vita
            Humana 7: 239–52.
Harper, Dee Wood, Jr.
    1967   "Socialization for the aged status among the Negro, French,
            and non-French subcultures of Louisiana." Unpublished
            Ph.D. dissertation, Sociology, Louisiana State University
            Agricultural and Mechanical College.
Havighurst, Robert
    1960   "Life beyond family and work." In Ernest Burgess (ed).
            Aging in Western Societies. Chicago: University of Chicago
            Press.
Holmberg, A. R.
    1969   Nomads of the Long Bow. Garden City, N.Y.: Natural
            History Press.
Kiefer, Christie
    1974   "Lessons from the Issei." In Jaber Gubrium (ed.). Late
            Life: Communities and Environmental Policies.
            Springfield, Ill.: Charles C Thomas.

Kreps, Juanita and Robert Clark
1975   Sex, Age and Work: The Changing Composition of the
       Labor Force. Baltimore, Md.: Johns Hopkins University
       Press.
Laslett, Peter
1976   "Societal development and aging." In Robert Binstock
       and Ethel Shanas (eds.). Handbook of Aging and the
       Social Sciences. New York: Van Nostrand Reinhold.
Leaf, A.
1973   "Every day is a gift when you are over 100." National
       Geographic 143 (1): 93–118.
Lozier, John
1975   "Accommodating old people in society: Examples from
       Appalachia and New Orleans." In Nancy Datan and Leon
       Ginsberg (eds.). Life-Span Developmental Psychology:
       Normative Life Crises. New York: Academic Press.
Maeda, Daisaku
1975   "Growth of old people's clubs in Japan." The Gerontologist
       15 (3): 254–56.
Medvedev, Zhores
1974   "Caucasus and Altay longevity: A biological or social
       problem?" The Gerontologist 14 (5): 381–87.
Messer, Mark
1967   "The possibility of an age-concentrated environment be-
       coming a normative system." The Gerontologist 7: 247–51.
Miller, Stephen
1965   "The social dilemma of the aging leisure participant." In
       Arnold Rose and Warren Peterson (eds.). Older People and
       Their Social World. Philadelphia: F.A. Davis.
Nahemow, Nina and Bert Adams
1974   "Old age among the Baganda: Continuity and change." In
       Jaber Gubrium (ed.). Late Life: Communities and
       Environmental Policies. Springfield, Ill.: Charles C
       Thomas.
Neugarten, Bernice and Gunhild Hagestad
1976   "Age and the life course." In Robert Binstock and Ethel
       Shanas (eds.). Handbook of Aging and the Social Sciences.
       New York: Van Nostrand Reinhold.
Neugarten, Bernice and Joan Moore
1968   "The changing age-status system." In Bernice Neugarten
       (ed.). Middle Age and Aging. Chicago: University of
       Chicago Press.
Neugarten, Bernice, Joan Moore, and John Lowe
1965   "Age norms, age constraints, and adult socialization."
       American Journal of Sociology 70 (6): 710–17.
Palmore, Erdman
1975a "The status and integration of the aged in Japanese society."
       Journal of Gerontology 30 (2): 199–208.

1975b The Honorable Elders. Durham, N.C.: Duke University
       Press.
1976   "The future status of the aged." The Gerontologist
       16: 297–302.
Palmore, Erdman and Kenneth Manton
1974   "Modernization and the status of the aged: International
       comparisons." Journal of Gerontology 29 (2): 205–10.
Palmore, Erdman and Frank Whittington
1971   "Trends in the relative status of the aged." Social Forces
       50 (September): 84–91.
Piovesana, Gino
1974   "The aged in Chinese and Japanese cultures." In William
       Bier (ed.). Aging: Its Challenge to the Individual and
       to Society. New York: Fordham University Press.
Press, Irwin and Mike McKool Jr.
1972   "Social structure and status of the aged: Toward some
       valid cross-cultural generalizations." Aging and Human
       Development 3 (November): 297–306.
Riley, Matilda and Anne Foner
1968   Aging and Society. Volume 1: An Inventory of Research
       Findings. New York: Russell Sage.
Riley, Matilda, Marilyn Johnson, and Anne Foner
1972   Aging and Society. Volume 3: A Sociology of Age Stratifica-
       tion. New York: Russell Sage.
Rosow, Irving
1965   "And then we were old." Trans-Action 2:20–26.
1974   Socialization to Old Age. Berkeley: University of California
       Press.
Shanas, Ethel et al.
1968   Old People in Three Industrial Societies. New York:
       Atherton Press.
Simmons, Leo
1945   The Role of the Aged in Primitive Society. New Haven,
       Conn.: Yale University Press.
1960   "Aging in preindustrial societies." In Clark Tibbitts (ed.).
       Handbook of Social Gerontology. Chicago: University
       of Chicago Press.
Talmon, Yonina
1961   "Aging in Israel, a planned society." American Journal
       of Sociology 67 (3): 284–95.
Wood, Vivian
1971   "Age-appropriate behavior for older people." The
       Gerontologist 11 (Winter): 74–78.
Wylie, Floyd
1971   "Attitudes toward aging and the aged among black
       Americans: Some historical perspectives." Aging and
       Human Development 2 (1): 66–70.

4

The Psychological
Experience of Aging

~~~~~~~~~~~~~~~~~~~~~~~~~~~~~~~~~~~~~~~

T he "macro" approach of age stratification addresses
the impact of aging on older people as a group, given the social
context within which aging occurs, and implies that age "strata"
will themselves affect the society. However, this chapter shifts
to the "micro" approach of the individual as the unit of analysis
in considering the psychological impact of aging on the older
individual. Of course this concern cannot be divorced from the
larger social context, which defines "old age" as a social experience
and determines the accompaniments of aging and their social
meanings.

The social psychology of aging has generated considerable debate,
partly because of its implications for "successful" aging. There are
a number of research traditions, focusing on broad psychological
theories of aging, developmental stages during the life course, the
impact of stress, and so on. Yet a coherent, integrated theory of
the psychology of aging and its effects on personality and life
style is still emerging.

Social-Psychological Theories of Aging

Social gerontology has not yet produced any "grand" social
theories of aging. Current approaches are still relatively modest.
The most prominent earlier approaches are *activity theory* and
disengagement theory.

Activity Theory

Activity theory seems to have become the official "straw man" of social gerontology. Gerontologists commonly outline activity theory simply to attack it, thus rendering their own approach superior by comparison. In reality, this "theory" consists of a set of implicit assumptions and propositions with faint (or perhaps not so faint) ideological overtones.

Activity theory suggests that personal satisfaction depends on a positive self-image which is validated through continued active participation in middle-aged roles. When roles end because of age, they must be replaced to avoid feelings of decline and uselessness. Thus, sources of need satisfaction remain stable over time.

> . . . older people are the same as middle-aged people, with essentially the same psychological and social needs. In this view, the decreased social interaction that characterizes old age results from the withdrawal by society from the aging person, and the decrease in interaction proceeds against the desires of most aging men and women. The older person who ages optimally is the person who stays active and who manages to resist the shrinkage of his social world. He maintains the activities of middle age as long as possible and then finds substitutes for those activities he is forced to relinquish. (Havighurst, Neugarten, and Tobin, 1968:161)

It is true that activity tends to be positively related to satisfaction (Riley and Foner, 1968), however, the picture is more complex than that painted by activity theory. Activity can decline without affecting morale (Maddox, 1970); in fact, a more leisurely life style may be perceived by some as one of the rewards and rights of old age. A study by Lemon and associates (1972) found little support for activity theory. Their data indicated that informal friendships were related somewhat to satisfaction, but not frequency of activity in general. Havighurst and associates (1968) suggest that activity does tend to decline with age and this decline is regretted by many older people, but there is little decline in life satisfaction. Older people see this change in activity with aging as inevitable and manage to maintain a sense of self-worth and satisfaction.

Activity theory is too facile a denial of differences between "middle age" and "old age." It ignores qualitative changes accompanying retirement, declining health, or widowhood. Such age-linked events may shift both social and psychological orientations of individuals to different sources of satisfaction. Indeed, by suggesting that the aged "ought" to remain active to age "successfully" it places people who are not, or cannot remain, active in an awkward position. The "golden years" of leisure pursuits may become a cruel measure of one's own failure.

Disengagement Theory

In many ways, disengagement theory presents a view of aging opposite to that of activity theory.[1] The aging process is presented as a mutual disengaging of the individual and society. This is not very controversial, as the number of roles people play and the frequency of their interaction with others does tend to decline with age and there are some indications of a movement toward psychological disengagement. Older people tend to be more passive, more introverted, and less achievement-oriented (Riley and Foner, 1968). There may also be a greater *interiority* of personality—increased preoccupation with inner life as opposed to the outside world (Neugarten, 1969). The debate over disengagement theory concerns its discussion of the reasons for disengagement and its consequences.

According to the theory, disengagement has its ultimate basis in the probable decline with age in abilities and the universal expectation of death. The biology of aging presents the individual with an increasing inability to fulfill roles and maintain interpersonal contacts, which will be both demoralizing and alienating unless shifts occur in roles and personality toward disengagement. Older people discard task-oriented interpersonal roles in favor of more peripheral roles. There is an overall decline in love-seeking and emotional ties, with the individual focusing increasingly on himself. Disengagement may be initiated by either the individual or society, but becomes self-perpetuating.

Perhaps the two most controversial aspects of the theory are its claims that this disengagement is universal and mutually satisfying for the aging individual and society. For the individual, disengagement presumably neutralizes the potential social trauma associated with biological decline and death and frees older people from behavioral norms and expectations, allowing them to be more "eccentric." As the death of persons occupying important roles and statuses is disruptive, disengagement is also felt to be "functional" for society by gradually removing those about to die from active involvement in the social structure. Finally, the theory suggests that disengagement is universal in two respects. First, aging individuals inevitably disengage from the social world though the timing varies from individual to individual, dependng on personality and social pressures to disengage. For example, the nature

---

[1] The description of disengagement theory is taken primarily from Cumming and Henry (1961) and Cumming (1963).

of disengagement may differ for men and women because of the different roles they play. Some have suggested that the continued involvement of older people in key positions in American politics argues against the theory, however, political disengagement may simply occur later because there is less pressure to disengage. Second, it is argued that disengagement occurs in all cultures, though the particular form it takes may vary.

Disengagement theory generated immediate controversy. Some have criticized it on logical grounds. Hochschild (1975), for example, has suggested that debate and research bearing on disengagement theory have been inconclusive because of the nature of the theory itself, which provides an "escape clause." Counterevidence of engaged older persons is refuted as examples of "unsuccessful disengagers," off in their timing, or truly exceptional individuals. Additionally, there has been little agreement about how to measure disengagement. Hochschild also suggests that disengagement is seen as a unitary process, when in fact there may be several types of disengagement, such as social disengagement and psychological disengagement, and one may occur without the other. Finally, Hochschild criticizes disengagement theory for ignoring the meanings held by the individual for aging and disengagement.

There is evidence that disengagement does occur with some older people. Indeed, in the restricted sense of "relaxation" and a leisurely, less competitive life, disengagement may be viewed as one of the rewards of aging. This does not necessarily mean that disengagement is inevitable or satisfying, however. Longitudinal studies suggest that aging may have relatively little impact on activities (Palmore, 1970). Disengagement theory was originally based on the Kansas City Study of Adult Life, but other work from that study suggests that the typical pattern is actually high engagement-high satisfaction, rather than low engagement-high satisfaction (Havighurst, Neugarten, and Tobin, 1968).

Individuals may disengage socially but not psychologically, or selectively from certain areas of life, while continuing or even increasing their involvement in other activities. "Extensive social interaction may be gradually replaced by intensive local social interaction, involving fewer people. Loss of roles may heighten the subjective importance, and increase the effectiveness of those roles that remain" (Shanas et al., 1968:5). Loneliness, poor health, poverty, or self-derogation may prevent the enjoyment of a more relaxed life, making disengagement an unpleasant experience, and those who are disengaged in old age may have been so throughout their lives. Maas and Kuypers (1974), in a 40-year study of couples, found that "disengaged" older men showed some evidence of a disengaged life style as young adults.

Disengagement also may not represent personal preference but the reaction of society and the failure to provide opportunities. To illustrate, Roman and Taietz (1967) studied the engagement of "emeritus professors." This particular postretirement role allows for continuity in research, teaching, consulting, or administration. Their results indicated that one's readiness to disengage depends upon the social context since, of those still in good health, 71 percent were still engaged. This was even higher for those in research positions, which had the greatest possibilities for continued involvement. Such findings suggest that disengagement is not necessarily a natural preference of older people, but may instead be a response to the age stratification of roles and opportunities in modern societies. Disengagement may even reflect the diminished power of the aged, who withdraw from interaction exchanges because they are placed at a disadvantage and can no longer realize rewards (Dowd, 1975).

This means that disengagement is best viewed as a "reactive" aging effect rather than as intrinsic. Once this is recognized, one can explore the complexities of engagement-disengagement. We need to investigate the differnt forms which disengagement may take, variables which affect these forms and their timing, and the meaning for individuals of both engagement and disengagement (Hochschild, 1975). Distinctions must also be made between forced and freely chosen disengagement.

Opportunities for engagement exist in some societies but not others, as can be seen from the cross-cultural differences cited in Chapter 3. Opportunities for continued engagement are high among the Abkhasians and Japanese, for example, but lower in American society. Disengagement may be a consequence of modernization, which restricts the range and importance of roles available to the aged. Similarly, the individual's location in the social structure will affect the extent and timing of disengagement. Retired college professors have opportunities for continued involvement which retired college janitors lack, and they may also differ in their desire for continued involvement.

Both activity theory and disengagement theory seem to offer too simplistic a view of the aging process. They also have ideological overtones. Activity theory implies that one *ought* to remain active, while disengagement theory seems to justify withdrawal from the aged as being what they want. The evidence suggests, however, that there are a number of ways in which people can age "successfully." To understand aging and its impact, one must also under-

stand the particular aging individual and the relationship of aging
to the life cycle.

A Developmental Perspective on Aging

Disengagement theory separates aging persons from their own
pasts, while activity theory ignores the contingencies of present
old age; but to understand the individual aging experience, we
must view the aging person within the context of life-long development. Aging represents an interaction between the individual,
with previous patterns or styles of living, and constraints placed
upon the ability to follow those patterns by the processes of aging.
Throughout our lives we develop preferences, habits, and activity
patterns, and we will tend to maintain those characteristics as we
age. People are not reborn on their sixty-fifth birthday, and neither
activity nor disengagement should be assumed to be a "natural"
way to age. The aging individual makes sense of the present and
adapts to it in terms of his own past. Thus,

> . . . the individual seems to continue to make his own "impress"
> upon the wide range of social and biological changes. He con-
> tinues to exercise choice and to select from the environment in
> accordance with his long established needs. He ages according
> to a pattern that has a long history, and that maintains itself,
> with adaptation, to the end of life. (Neugarten et al., 1968:
> 176–77)

However, aging represents more than simple personal continuity.
There are many types of constraints on individuals' ability to maintain continuity. Biological decline and poor health affect capacities
and activities. Changes in roles and relationships, such as those
which accompany retirement and widowhood, will also limit continuity and require adaptation. Different societies provide varying
opportunities for older people. Social policies and institutional
arrangements, and the values which they reflect, will affect the
employment, health, and housing of the aged. Even societal
attitudes toward aging will affect the meanings attached to growing older by the individual, since it is in terms of those meanings
that the individual reacts to his increasing age and the changes
which accompany it.

A developmental view of aging suggests an adaptive interaction
between the individual and the accompaniments of aging. As such,
aging is seen as a dynamic process. One needs to take into account
personal meanings for aging, roles and relationships assumed or
lost, personality and life style, situational factors which may present stresses, and personal capacities and coping skills (Rosow,

1963). For some the outcome will be disengagement, for others engagement, and for still others something quite different from either of these. Every individual ages differently.

Personality, Life Style, and Psychological Orientation

A developmental perspective underlines the need to assess past, present, and future in attempting to understand aging as part of a life-long developmental sequence. One way in which the personal past is brought into present and future aging is through individual personality. Personality is a term we use to describe the behavioral and psychological approaches developed by individuals to meet the problems and tasks of everyday living. Over time, personality becomes a relatively stable characteristic of the self—a blueprint or recipe for living. But personality is also dynamic, continually evolving and adapting to new demands faced by the individual. This means that while personality lends continuity to old age, personality change is also possible, as aging brings new demands to be met.

Personality and life style combine to produce what might be called *patterns of aging*. Some of the more noteworthy attempts to delineate these patterns are summarized in Table 4.1. Although drawn from different sources, these typologies have certain similarities. And they all point out the individual variability of reactions to aging—variability which is not captured by either activity or disengagement theory.

The Reichard et al. (1962) and Neugarten et al. (1968) typologies are empirical descriptions of general approaches to aging and display some basic similarities. Some people ("reorganizers") substitute new activities for lost ones, corresponding rather closely to activity theory prescriptions for successful aging. Others (the "focused") become selective in their activities, withdrawing from or losing some, but maintaining and perhaps increasing others. Both of these might be subsumed under the "mature" agers described by Reichard and associates. Both the "disengaged" and "rocking-chair men" correspond to the picture painted by disengagement theory of voluntary and contented withdrawal from responsibilities and involvements. All of these patterns seem to be associated with high satisfaction and "integrated" personalities.

Other older people appear to defend themselves from the perceived threats of aging by either clinging to middle-aged patterns ("holding on") or erecting defenses against anxiety by closing in their world ("constricted"). Both of these defenses are similar to an "armored" pattern, and such individuals seem to maintain satisfaction relatively successfully.

The "succorance-seekers" maintain themselves satisfactorily so

Table 4.1. Patterns of aging

Reichard et al. (1962)	Williams and Wirths (1965)	Neugarten et al. (1968)	Maas and Kuypers (1974)
Mature	World of work	Reorganizer	Family-centered fathers
Rocking-chair men	Familism	Focused	Hobbyist fathers
Armored	Living alone	Disengaged	Remotely sociable fathers
Angry men	Couplehood	Holding on	Unwell-disengaged fathers
Self-haters	Easing through life with minimal involvement	Constricted	Husband-centered wives
	Living fully	Succorance-seeker	Uncentered mothers
		Apathetic	Visiting mothers
		Disorganized	Employed (work-centered) mothers
			Disabled-disengaged mothers
			Group-centered mothers

long as their dependency needs are met by others they can lean on. The "apathetic" pattern refers to people who had perhaps been disengaged throughout their lives for whom aging has reinforced long-standing patterns of passivity and low activity. Those who were "disorganized" showed low activity and poor psychological functioning. All three of these patterns appear to be accompanied by somewhat lower satisfaction and may correspond to the "self-haters" described by Reichard and associates.

The focus of the typology developed by Williams and Wirths (1965) differs from the others. Rather than describing reactions to aging per se, they are concerned with the main focus of an individual's style of life, which may be carried into old age. The "world of work" implies that the meaning for one's life is derived from work. It would be expected that retirement would be a particular problem for such persons. For others, life appears to revolve around the family—either the family as a whole ("familism") or the marriage relationship ("couplehood"). "Living alone" refers to inner-directed social isolates who prefer a life style of relative isolation. "Easing through life with minimal involvement" describes individuals with minimal commitment in all or most role areas: work, marriage, family. These people's activity level is rather low and they have had a long-standing pattern of disengagement from the world. Finally, "living fully" refers to people who are involved in a variety of areas, but do not focus on any one as the most important.

The typology offered by Maas and Kuypers (1974) combines elements of the other three, focusing on both patterns of aging and predominant life style. Their approach is particularly noteworthy because it is based on longitudinal data. Couples who had first been interviewed as young parents in 1930 were reinterviewed 40 years later. Despite a relatively small surviving sample (142), ten different life styles were found:

1. *family-centered fathers*, whose way of life was centered in the spouse-parent-grandparent complex of roles;
2. *hobbyist fathers*, whose home-based lives revolved around instrumental leisure activities;
3. *remotely sociable fathers*, who were active socially but corresponded to "easing through life with minimal involvement";
4. *unwell-disengaged fathers*, whose poor health had resulted in withdrawal from the world;
5. *husband-centered wives*, for whom the marriage was the center of activity;
6. *uncentered mothers*, who were not involved in work or clubs, but did much informal visiting with family and friends;

7. *visiting mothers,* who were highly involved in both informal visiting and group activities;

8. *employed (work-centered) mothers,* whose lives revolved around their work;

9. *disabled-disengaged mothers,* who showed the same basic pattern as the "unwell-disengaged fathers";

10. *group-centered mothers,* who had many recreational interests outside the family.

Maas and Kuypers were also interested in the relative stability of these life styles over the 40-year period. It is interesting that the life styles of the women depended more on their current life situation, while those of the men showed greater stability over time. For example, the "husband-centered wife" style was dependent upon a relatively advantaged social world—good health, stable residence, retired husband. The "employed mothers" exhibited considerable change over earlier life styles. In these cases, there was relief from an unsatisfactory marriage with its economic problems and entrance into a gratifying new life style of independence and new friends. Except for the "family-centered fathers," males showed considerable stability. Even the "unwell-disengaged fathers" had exhibited poor health, interpersonal conflict, and dissatisfaction earlier in life. Maas and Kuypers conclude that there is both stability and change in life style, with women apparently being affected more than men by circumstances.

Studies such as these lend themselves to three general conclusions. First, people appear to exhibit many patterns of aging, even when samples are relatively small. Thus, neither activity nor disengagement is a "typical" or "normal" reaction to growing old. Second, there also appears to be a number of ways to age "successfully," though some patterns are less successful than others. For example, "disabled-disengaged mothers" were more fearful and anxious (Maas and Kuypers, 1974) and both "apathetic" and "disorganized" patterns were associated with relatively low satisfaction (Neugarten Havighurst, and Tobin, 1968). Nonetheless, the other six patterns described by Neugarten and associates are associated with relatively high satisfaction.

As a final conclusion, all of the studies found evidence of considerable stability of personality over the life cycle, and other longitudinal studies reinforce this conclusion. Kuypers (1974) indicates that one's past affects coping and adaptation in old age and "persons are rooted in previous ways of being, perhaps prisoners to some aspects and beneficiaries of others" (p. 176). Another panel study found no significant changes on personality tests over a 25-year period (Woodruff and Birren, 1972). Such findings lead to the conclusion that:

> There is considerable evidence that, in normal men and women, there is no sharp discontinuity of personality with age, but instead an increasing consistency. Those characteristics that have been central to the personality seem to become even more clearly delineated, and those values the individual has been cherishing become even more salient (Neugarten, Havighurst, and Tobin, 1968:177)

This picture of personal stability is far from complete, however. There do appear to be age differences in psychological orientations, though these may reflect historical differences in generations, rather than age changes. Older people are generally more rigid, cautious, passive, and introverted than younger people, and they are also less achievement-oriented (Riley and Foner, 1968). There are indications that emotions such as anger and irritation are less likely to be expressed by older people (Dean, 1962) and that *covert* personality processes, which are less amenable to conscious control, may change with age (Bengtson, 1973). More *overt* characteristics, such as personality type and life satisfaction, exhibit greater stability over time.

Neugarten (1968a, 1969) has suggested that there is greater *interiority* of personality, with the increased importance of introspection in middle-age, accompanied by greater salience of "executive" personality processes—self-awareness, mastery, and competence—increased self-preoccupation and a shift in perception of the external environment:

> Forty-year-olds, for example, seem to see the environment as one that rewards boldness and risk-taking and to see themselves as possessing energy congruent with the opportunities perceived in the outer world. Sixty-year-olds, however, perceive the world as complex and dangerous, no longer to be reformed in line with one's wishes. (1968a:140)

As aging proceeds, there is less attention to the outside world and greater preoccupation with inner states.

Neugarten's concept of interiority is echoed in other approaches to the psychology of aging, such as disengagement theory, particularly subsequent revisions of the theory which placed greater emphasis on intrapsychic processes rather than societal pressures and functions (Cumming, 1963; Henry, 1965). Charlotte Buhler and her associates, following the study of individual biographies,

have argued that there are social and psychological parallels with
the biological sequence of growth, stability, and decline (Buhler,
1951; Frenkel-Brunswik, 1963). They depict the life course as a
rising curve of expansion reaching culmination during the forties,
followed by greater introspection and self-assessment, and finally
a general contraction and decline similar to disengagement.

Kuhlen (1964) has traced a similar curve of expansion and decline, linked to a basic shift in the nature of motivation. According
to Kuhlen, there is a shift in late life from growth-expansion to
anxiety and threat as the sources of motivation. Earlier in life, one's
basic motivation is toward achievement, status, self-actualization—
to gain and maintain a position as a significant person in the world.
The frustrations and limitations of old age result in constriction
as an attempt to protect those resources which remain from the
threats of aging. Thus, there is a selective disengagement away
from society-maintaining work and toward greater ego-involvement.
Kuhlen, like Neugarten, points to a shift from seeing the world
as an opportunity for growth to viewing it as complex, dangerous,
and not easily shaped to one's needs and demands.

Kuhlen's ideas receive some support from a recent study by
Lowenthal and associates (1975) of people at "four stages of life":
high school seniors, newlyweds, parents of the high school students,
and older persons nearing retirement. Among their findings was
an apparent shift in values with age. Those in the earlier stages
of the life cycle had an expansive orientation on achievement
coupled with high expectations. Middle-aged and older persons,
however, had more self-limiting orientations which stressed minimizing frustrations by coping with life's problems and not setting
one's goals too high.

All of these accounts suggest quite similar processes, whether
described as interiority, disengagement, or anxiety-produced constriction. But the sources of such changes remain unclear. Are such
shifts natural and inevitable, the reflection of the modern context
within which aging occurs, the product of a particular generation of
older persons? What is needed is a more coherent developmental
perspective on aging. The task of such an approach is to "investigate
whether or not there are orderly and irreversible changes related
to age that are significant in accounting for the differences between adults" (Neugarten, 1973:318). Further, one needs to study
the processes by which people change, the sequence and timing
of change, and the impact of individual and cohort history and
experience on developmental processes (Kimmel, 1974).

It is beyond the scope of this book to present a full developmental theory of the life cycle. Nevertheless, we can look at some
factors which frame a developmental perspective on aging. First,

each life stage may be thought of as having relatively unique developmental issues or crises which must be dealt with by the individual. Second, psychological functioning may be affected by age-linked stressful events. Finally, both of the above can be linked more generally to age-related changes in the roles and statuses occupied by individuals, thereby incorporating a developmental psychology of the life cycle within the model of age stratification.

Developmental Issues and Aging

The idea that there are specific developmental tasks which must be faced and dealt with at each stage of the life cycle is not new. Erik Erikson's theory of ego development (Table 4.2) is perhaps the most familiar of these scheme.

Erikson suggests that in middle adulthood one must develop a sense of establishing and guiding the next generation (*generativity*), thereby achieving a sense of contributing to the future. In late adulthood, the need is to develop a feeling of *ego integrity*. *Ego identity* in adolescence is the development of a self with a personal set of values. Ego integrity is the sense that one's life has been appropriate and meaningful—that the right choices were made. Erikson suggests that the failure to achieve ego integrity results in despair and a crippling fear of death.

While Erikson's approach is interesting, there is an obvious need to flesh out the details for each life stage. Let us turn to a more detailed look at the stages of interest to this book: middle age and old age.

Middle Age

Middle age might be thought of as a "confrontation between myth and reality" (Sarason, 1977:105). From youth, one's life is typically structured by early decisions concerning work and family

Table 4.2. Developmental issues over the life cycle

Stage	Developmental issue
Early infancy	Trust vs. distrust
Later infancy	Autonomy vs. shame and doubt
Early childhood	Initiative vs. guilt
Middle childhood	Industry vs. inferiority
Adolescence	Ego identity vs. role confusion
Early adulthood	Intimacy vs. ego isolation
Middle adulthood	Generativity vs. ego stagnation
Late adulthood	Ego integrity vs. despair

Adapted from Erikson (1950).

life. This structure begins to loosen in middle age, as the children leave home and the career moves toward retirement. For men, and increasingly for women, aspirations and achievements have often been expressed through work, and middle age may require adjustment of early aspirations to current realities (Brim, 1976). Workers have typically reached a plateau, beyond which further advancement is unlikely. If their achievements have not matched earlier expectations, they may have feelings of failure or desperation or a resurgence of "the dream," as mid-life reappraisal leads to one last effort to make it come true. Similar processes occur within the postparental family. Have my children turned out the way I wished them to? Are my relations with my wife (or husband) satisfactory, now that our preoccupations with the children are gone?

The middle-aged may also experience a variety of "partial deaths"—of physical attractiveness, physical strength, career opportunities (Kastenbaum, 1977). Since physical strength and attractiveness begin to decline, Peck (1956) argues that the middle-aged must come to value mental powers which withstand aging more successfully, and also that they must develop emotional flexibility:

> . . . the capacity to shift emotional investments from one person to another, and from one activity to another . . . this is the period, for most people, when their parents die, their children grow up and leave home, and their circle of friends and relatives of similar age begins to be broken by death. (Peck, 1956:45)

Middle age is also a time when one's own death becomes psychologically closer. There may be a shift in perspective from "time since birth" to "time yet to live." This contributes to reappraisal of earlier decisions and may result in intensified efforts to realize aspirations.

In their study, Lowenthal and her associates (1975) found that active reconstruction of the past peaked in middle age, revolving around past career choices and closing career options. For some this process is successful, as they work through their doubts.

> One man, for example, not only had thought about the implications of past career choices but also was attempting to work through his doubts about the proper career path: "I think about what would have happened if I had gone into another business, if I had worked strictly as an accountant or if I had gone into the real estate business with a friend of mine. I knew a great deal about real estate and he had a great deal of money. I'm

sure we would have made a successful venture. I may still do that, of course. But I keep wondering if I would have made more money at that type of work or been happier. I don't think I would have been as happy: accountants die young and real estate is dreary." (Lowenthal et al., 1975:131)

Another study found that a middle-class sample viewed middle age as the prime of life—they had a keen sense of their own competence and ability to deal with life (Neugarten, 1968b). A lower- or working-class sample, however, with a greater emphasis on physical powers (even in the work they do), might have greater difficulty resolving middle-age conflicts. Results from middle-aged respondents in the Lowenthal et al. (1975) study also suggest that middle age is not always seen as the prime of life. Many middle-aged men and women wished they were more imaginative in confronting the problems associated with rechanneling their energies into new goals and activities. A critical issue of middle age seems to concern stagnation versus growth and the development of emotional and psychological flexibility which set the stage for successful adaptation to old age. The danger lies not only in feelings of failure regarding the dreams of youth. If the middle-aged become "too set in their ways," adaptation to the new experiences and circumstances of late life will be hindered.

The "crisis of middle age" is likely to differ for men and women, since they tend to play different roles over the life cycle. In a sense, aging is confronted earlier by the woman who plays the stereotypic domestic female role. She retires from her major career—being a mother—earlier than men retire from the work role. Although this may mean that old age involves fewer wrenching transitions for women, it heightens personal change in middle age. There are some indications in the Lowenthal et al. (1975) study that this is the case. Middle-aged men tended to view themselves as industrious and in control, though some felt that they were just plodding along and something was missing. Interestingly, men were more apprehensive than women about the future, where their aging crisis lay, and one gains the impression that their concern was with laying the groundwork for a satisfying retirement life style. For middle-aged women, however, aging was a present problem, and their views of themselves and their circumstances were much less positive. Many displayed signs of desperation over the "empty nest" (when children have left the home) and limited possibilities for breaking out of the confines of the family to achieve personal growth. This indicates again that the aging experience varies, in this case according to the different roles played by men and women.

Old Age

The developmental themes of old age appear to be twofold. First, commentators on the psychology of old age often point to this as a time of "summing up." Erikson's (1950) concept of ego integrity implies that the aged need to review the appropriateness and meaningfulness of their lives, as in middle age. However, review of the past then seems to be more action-oriented, and discontent over the past may lead to behavioral change, while the "life review" occurring in old age is a more passive attempt to make sense of one's life and resolve past conflict and guilt. It may take a variety of forms—nostalgia, dreams, mirror-gazing—and may be helpful or result in more shame and regrets (Butler, 1963). There is some evidence that reminiscing promotes adaptation through a sense of self-continuity (Lewis, 1971).

The second developmental theme of old age is adjustment to new realities created by aging. One of these new realities is a changing perspective on time, which began in middle age. There is a realization that one's future is limited, as death becomes a significant possibility for the first time. Such biological and time changes may lead older people to believe that they have less ability to adjust to the world. There is some evidence, for example, that the subjective "speed" of time is greater for the aged (Wallach and Green, 1961). The feeling that time is running out may paradoxically have opposite effects, as is recognized by most students approaching a tough exam. Activity may be intensified to take advantage of what little time remains, but there may also be a feeling of impotence and inability to use what time is left, resulting in "disengagement" (e.g., going out drinking). Thus, time can become an existential dilemma.

One study of the life cycle concludes, in fact, that the use of time is the central issue of late life (Gould, 1975). Some respond to the dilemmas of time with renewed effort and energy, while time seems to slip away from many others. They report declines with age in the eventfulness of life, encountering fewer major turning points and frustrations and feeling less involved in events around them (Lowenthal et al., 1975). This study found a slower tempo of life for older respondents and more thinking about the past (though they were not less future-oriented).

Altered time is not the only new reality of old age. In many ways the aged are cut off and set adrift from familiar roles, activities, relationships, and identities because of retirement, widowhood, the death of contemporaries, or their own physical limitations. We too often forget, in stereotypes of the serene "golden years," the enormous potential for change in the later years. The person who has worked eight hours a day, five days a week, for 40 years, suddenly confronts a life without patterned work. The person who has been married for 50 years is suddenly widowed and alone. One's life-long friends die or move away, leaving one stranded in an unfamiliar social world. Such changes remind us again that while there is personal continuity through life, continuity is often challenged by the age stratification of roles and experiences.

Peck (1956) has defined three developmental issues in old age which relate to a need for a flexible self-image. First, those who can find self-worth in a variety of activities and roles will be more successful than those whose sole basis of identity is the work role. Second, old age almost inevitably brings physical problems, which Peck suggests must be transcended or people will be overcome by their bodily "insults." Finally, the new prospect of personal death must be overcome. Peck is not suggesting passive resignation or denial, but rather, the recognition of this possibility without letting it rule one's life. This would probably be easier if the other developmental issues, including ego integrity, were dealt with successfully.

These approaches to the developmental psychology of the later years clearly sensitize us to important crisis points and central issues of aging. Kimmel (1974), however, has rightly noted that for the most part these are rather general "armchair" theories which have not been rigorously tested and supported by empirical research. There are many remaining questions, the most central of which is whether these issues or adaptive tasks are universal. Aging is a very different experience in different cultures, and the ideas discussed here were developed in Western societies, in which loss is perhaps the primary accompaniment of aging. Would the same developmental tasks be found among the Abkhasians or the Japanese?

There will also be social class, sexual, or other differences in developmental issues, related to different roles and statuses and the consequent differences in the nature of aging. Neugarten's (1968b) finding of a feeling of middle-aged "mastery" among a middle-class sample might instead yield a "Death of a Salesman" feeling among other class groups. What happens to Erikson's "generativity" issue for those who do not have children? The danger is that these developmental issues are culture-bound, and therefore reactive rather than intrinsic. The threat and anxiety described by Kuhlen may be attributable to the way society structures the situations of older people.

There is also little understanding of the ways in which individuals deal with these issues. The timing and nature of age-related change will affect the aging experience of any individual. It should be remembered that aging can present the possibility of new goals and avenues of gratification as well as constriction and defensiveness. Which of these will occur depends on the meaning of change for the individual, the values attached to new opportunities, and the social supports enjoyed by the individual. If personality changes accompany aging, we need to focus on the coping processes which mediate between personality types and the environment (Neugarten, 1973). How, for example, can individuals continue to function effectively if interiority increases with age and certain cognitive functions decline? Yet most older people do seem to function effectively.

We should not lose sight of the fact that the new realities which face aging individuals offer important opportunities for positive and continuing personal growth. Certainly there are many examples of active, growing, creative life styles among the aged. A magazine recently published a series of vignettes on "ordinary" persons in their eighties who were living full, engaged, and interesting lives: an 80-year-old college student who was elected Homecoming Queen, an 89-year-old woman with an active law practice, an 86-year-old man who raises bees, an 89-year-old woman who has made three trips to the Arctic Circle and two to the Antarctic in the last five years (Jones, 1978). These people have always led intriguing lives and do not see age as a reason to disengage. There are undoubtedly many others who are "liberated" in old age from confining middle-aged roles and blossom into more complex, full-developed persons. Such older people have much to offer the young with a fascinating range of personal experiences, unique historical perspectives, and philosophies of life.

The very fact that articles such as this exist suggests, however, that these older people are exceptional. It may be, of course, that fully-lived, creative lives are exceptional among all age groups or that we consider such older people exceptional because they break our stereotypes about old age. Yet the evidence does suggest increased psychological restriction by many older people, whether we speak of disengagement, interiority, or some other term. Lowenthal and associates (1975) found that aging was accompanied by increased "blandness," with a decline in both positive and negative feelings. Older people in their study were less growth-oriented than younger people—less open, curious, and willing to experiment and change. They seemed to be seeking a relatively restricted life style and viewed the world more pessimistically, as in the following example:

One middle-aged man, acutely aware of eventual retirement, was very pessimistic and had no plans for it. His comments are typical of men and women at this stage of life: "It's just an unknown quantity. I can't see anything ahead. I suppose I could consider traveling, but that doesn't appeal to me too much now. More grandchildren? We have more than enough now. Just waiting to pass time before you die. Not knowing what to do. But age is the first thing against you in trying to do anything big or spectacular. Even if you decide on something, you may not have time to do it. I guess you have to be realistic about things. When you are young you have all of life ahead of you." (Lowenthal et al., 1975:110–11)

Rather than seeing these patterns as natural or inevitable aspects of the aging experience, we can more profitably view them as a response to the social context within which aging individuals attempt to grapple with the developmental issues of aging. Specifically, we can look at two things: the nature of stressful life events over the life cycle and the role of age stratification in shaping the options and constraints of the aging experience for individuals.

Stress and Aging

The developmental "crises" and psychological changes linked to the aging process may represent attempts to cope with stressful age-related experiences. Stress is best viewed as a subjective transaction between an individual and his situation. It results from an imbalance between the perceived demand placed upon the individual (threat) and the perceived response capability (ability to cope with the threat) (Lazarus, 1966; McGrath, 1970). The greater the perceived imbalance, the greater the stress felt by the person. Many everyday situations are somewhat threatening, and may even be exhilirating because of this (such as skiing), but they are not stressful because we can cope with them.

The situations individuals find stressful will differ. For example, most of us would find driving at 150 miles per hour more stressful than professional race drivers would. There are two possible reasons for this. The professional may see this speed as less threatening than the rest of us, or he may actually have a greater awareness of the threat (perhaps having seen friends killed in crashes), but feel that he has the experience and skills to cope with it.

There is growing evidence that stress is linked to various physical and mental illnesses (Dohrenwend and Dohrenwend, 1974; Eisdorfer and Wilkie, 1977). One could probably argue ad nauseum about which phase of life—adolescence, young adulthood, old age—is the most stressful. It is perhaps sufficient to note that old age is not necessarily a time of tranquility and relaxation. Indeed, entrance into old age can be particularly stressful because it involes the possibility of both increased threat and decreased response capability.

There are a number of types of threats or situations which can be expected to be stressful (McGrath, 1970), each of which is evident in old age. First, there is the *physical threat* of injury, pain, or death. Older people encounter increasing health problems and the prospect of personal death. The poor health or death of one's contemporaries may add greatly to a personal feeling of anxiety among the aged. *Ego threat* involves injury or pain to the psychological self. The aged are vulnerable to loses of roles defining their identity (retirement, widowhood) and their general status may be devalued. Finally, there is *interpersonal threat*—the disruption of social relationships. The poor health or death of relatives and friends may constrict the social networks of older people, as well as one's own limitations or residential mobility.

What this suggests is that certain situations or events objectively can be expected to be relatively threatening and therefore more stressful. A good illustration of the potential threat imposed by old age can be found in the Social Readjustment Rating Scale developed by Holmes and Rahe (1967). People were asked to rate life events according to their intensity and the length of time required to adapt to them, regardless of their desirability. Table 4.3 shows the resulting ranking of the disruptiveness or threat inherent in various situations. Specific rankings may, of course, differ for different social groups, as shown by Hough and associates (1976),

Table 4.3. The social readjustment rating scale

Life event	Mean value
1. Death of spouse	100
2. Divorce	73
3. Marital separation from mate	65
4. Detention in jail or other institution	63
5. Death of a close family member	63
6. Major personal injury or illness	53
7. Marriage	50
8. Being fired at work	47
9. Marital reconciliation with mate	45
10. Retirement from work	45
11. Major change in the health or behavior of a family member	44
12. Pregnancy	40
13. Sexual difficulties	39
14. Gaining a new family member (e.g., through birth, adoption, oldster moving in, etc.)	39
15. Major business readjustment (e.g., merger, reorganization, bankruptcy, etc.)	39
16. Major change in financial state (e.g., a lot worse off or a lot better off than usual)	38
17. Death of a close friend	37

Table 4.3. *(Continued)*

Life event	Mean value
18. Changing to a different line of work	36
19. Major change in the number of arguments with spouse (e.g., either a lot more or a lot less than usual regarding child-rearing, personal habits, etc.)	35
20. Taking on a mortgage greater than $10,000 (e.g., purchasing a home, business, etc.)	31
21. Foreclosure on a mortgage or loan	30
22. Major change in responsibilities at work (e.g., promotion, demotion, lateral transfer)	29
23. Son or daughter leaving home (e.g., marriage, attending college, etc.)	29
24. In-law troubles	29
25. Outstanding personal achievement	28
26. Wife beginning or ceasing work outside the home	26
27. Beginning or ceasing formal schooling	26
28. Major change in living conditions (e.g., building a new home, remodeling, deterioration of home or neighborhood)	25
29. Revision of personal habits (dress, manners, associations, etc.)	24
30. Troubles with the boss	23
31. Major change in working hours or conditions	20
32. Change in residence	20
33. Changing to a new school	20
34. Major change in usual type and/or amount of recreation	19
35. Major change in church activities (e.g., a lot more or a lot less than usual)	19
36. Major change in social activities (e.g., clubs, dancing, movies, visiting, etc.)	18
37. Taking on a mortgage or loan less than $10,000 (e.g., purchasing a car, TV, freezer, etc.)	17
38. Major change in sleeping habits (a lot more or a lot less sleep, or change in part of day when asleep)	16
39. Major change in number of family get-togethers (e.g., a lot more or a lot less than usual)	15
40. Major change in eating habits (a lot more or a lot less food intake, or very different meal hours or surroundings)	15
41. Vacation	13
42. Christmas	12
43. Minor violations of the law (e.g., traffic tickets, jaywalking, disturbing the peace, etc.)	11

Source: Thomas Holmes and Richard Rahe. "The Social Readjustment Rating Scale." *Journal of Psychosomatic Research* (1967): 213–18. Reprinted by permission.

or even different age groups. Nevertheless, it is striking that many of the most disruptive events potentially accompany aging—death of spouse, family member, or close friend, personal illness, retirement, sex difficulties, change in financial state, and so on.

Such disruptive changes may additionally be more subjectively threatening for older than for younger people, since there may be an emotional investment in familiar objects which provide a sense of continuity and security. Their loss represents a greater destruction of time and symbolic assets. For example, moving from a house in which one has lived for 40 years has a greater impact than moving from an apartment in which one has spent a much shorter time. Disruption of personal relationships, such as friendships, which have also been built up over a longer time and represent a greater commitment, by poor health or residential change becomes particularly critical.

There is evidence that such disruptive life events create problems for older people. Amster and Krauss (1974) found that a sample of older people exhibiting mental deterioration had experienced more age-linked social traumas than a matched control group. Lowenthal and Chiriboga (1973) also note that threatening events may create physical and psychological problems, though there may be complex interrelationships here with the resources available to the individual. This leads to a discussion of the response capability of the aged.

Older people may also perceive less ability to cope with disruptive life changes than younger people. They may, for example, feel that there is less time available to cope with change and replace what may have been lost, particularly with a major loss such as widowhood. Physical limitations may also hinder adaptability and lead older people to feel that they have less energy to invest in adapting to changes. Individuals with such limitations may be able to adapt to a much narrower range of situations (Lawton and Nahemow, 1973). Most of us assume that we can handle most of the events we encounter. This taken-for-granted flexibility becomes suspect, however, with the limitations of age, and a feeling of "precarious flexibility" may account for some of the cautiousness exhibited by older people (Gubrium, 1973).

Psychologically, older people may feel a lack of control over events. There is an increase with age in feelings of fatalism and passivity, which will limit coping efforts. Older persons who have internal control, who feel that they can manipulate their own world, appear to cope more adequately, to be more adaptive, and to rely less on defensive measures (Kuypers, 1972). Many of these psychological traits are related to education, which is broadly intended to provide coping skills, thus, the lower educational levels of the aged may contribute to coping difficulties.

Finally, older people's ability to cope may be reduced by the loss of social supports. Mechanic (1969) describes three components of successful personal adaptation: coping skills, motivation, and defense. These are intrapsychic resources, but they depend on the individual's group context.

> Man's ability to cope with the environment depends on the efficacy of the solutions that his culture provides . . . the ability of persons to maintain psychological comfort will depend not only on their intrapsychic resources, but also—and perhaps more importantly—on the social supports available or absent in the environment. Men depend on others for justification and admiration, and few men can survive without support from some segment of their fellows. (Mechanic, 1969:3)

The difficulty for older people is that many of the losses they face, such as retirement or widowhood, entail the weakening or loss of group ties. Thus, they must often face disruptive change without these social supports.

Apart from the experience of actual physical or mental illness, the stress of increased threat and declining coping abilities may partly account for some of the observed psychological concomitants of aging. Disengagement, rigidity, and interiority may represent attempts to conserve what remains against the perceived threats of old age. Such social and psychological constriction may well result from a refocusing of motivation toward anxiety and threat, increasingly viewing the world as complex and dangerous. These processes can become a vicious circle. Rigidity and cautiousness lead individuals to react passively and generally, rather than adapting to the peculiar characteristics of specific situations, which further hinders their ability to cope. The sense of personal incompetence and threat therefore increases, individuals become more cautious and anxious, and so on. To the extent that stress is internalized, generating self-blame, additional psychological problems may result.

> . . . the depressions of old age are primarily related to the loss of self-esteem which results from the aged individual's inability to supply his needs and drives (loss of narcissistic supplies) or to defend himself against threats to his security. (Busse, 1970:87)

However, feelings of threat and anxiety are neither inevitable nor universal among the aged, depending to a large extent on the ways society structures the aging experience. The ego threat attached to aging is determined by the position of older people in the particular system of age stratification, the nature of role changes accompanying aging, and the meanings of the roles available to the aged. Social structure and culture determine the occurrence of stress with age. The Abkhasian culture, for example, is characterized by a lack of stressful role transitions and cultural mechanisms which alleviate stress: stoicism and a lack of competitiveness. Additionally, society affects the coping resources upon which the aged may draw, including social supports and the range of services available to soften the handicapping effects of biological aging.

Aging and the Self

To understand individual responses to aging, we must look at the impact of age stratification, since age stratification defines the supports and options which will be available to the aging individual. This requires that we first understand the relationship between aging and the *social self*.

Questions of personal stability and change and of developmental tasks can be understood within the perspective of *symbolic interactionism*. Based on the work of George Herbert Mead (1934), this perspective involves the following three premises:

> The first premise is that human beings act toward things on the basis of the meanings that the things have for them. . . . The second premise is that the meaning of such things is derived from, or arises out of, the social interaction that one has with one's fellows. The third premise is that these meanings are handled in, and modified through, an interpretive process used by the person in dealing with the things he encounters. (Blumer, 1969:2)

Thus, we live in a symbolic environment in which meaning is not intrinsic to an object but is assigned to it through social interaction. We are active agents who interpret the world and act in it on the basis of our conscious perceptions of our world. Language is perhaps the best example of shared symbols developed through interaction which give meaning to the objects around us.

This perspective has important implications for the study of aging. Objects or events must be assigned social meaning to make sense. Thus, the meaning of old age, retirement, widowhood, or leisure depends on the social and cultural context in which it occurs. Similarly, if the social context in which the individual interacts changes because of aging, the self will also change.

Symbolic interactionism suggests that humans have selves because they can take the attitude of others and see themselves as an object. The meaning of the self arises from social interaction and is determined by the symbolic meanings made available to the individual. This self cannot exist apart from society, since the individual experiences himself indirectly through interaction with particular "significant others" and with the "generalized other" (society.)

Out of numerous interactions, a more or less stabilized self-conception emerges. This self is a persistent core element around which other meanings and interpretations are organized. Because the self organizes and directs behavior, individuals become consistent in their actions.

> The crucial significance of the self as a social object is that it is the only object common to all the widely varied situations in which we participate. As such, it comes to serve as the anchoring point from which we make judgments and subsequent plans of action toward the many other objects in each specific situation. . . . We may think of it as consisting of all the answers the individual might make to the question "Who am I?" (Hickman and Kuhn, 1956:43)

The self is an identity commitment evolved from a long history of interactions and shaped by validation for particular views of the self found in role-activities and symbolic interaction with others.

There are four basic variables involved in emergence of the self: (1) the individual's self-concept, (2) his perception of the responses of others toward him, (3) the actual responses of others toward him, and (4) his behavior (Kinch, 1963). Cooley's (1902) concept of the "looking-glass self" refers to a person's perception of the way others react toward him to form his self-concept. The perception of the responses of others will be based on, but not equivalent to, the actual responses of others. The self-conception, in turn, directs behavior, which will influence the reactions of others. Thus, the self evolves from a continual social process of interaction with others.

It is because of these considerations that the concept of social roles has come to occupy a place of importance in the study of aging.[2] Persons occupy various positions in the world, and role involves association of expectations with particular positions. Roles are important because they "locate" individuals in social and symbolic worlds; because we play certain roles, we have access to certain interactions, meanings, and identities. As such, roles are

---

[2] For discussions of "role theory," see Biddle and Thomas (1966) and Turner (1974).

the source of both personal stability and personal change. Continuity in one's *role set* means continuity in social, interactional, and symbolic environments; discontinuity of roles means discontinuity in these environments.

On the one hand, stability of social roles will be accompanied by stability in self-concept. Particular identities continue to be validated because the individual interacts within relatively unchanging social worlds. Indeed, Neugarten suggests that an "institutionalized self" develops:

> In a sense, the self becomes institutionalized with the passage of time. Not only do certain personality processes become stabilized and provide continuity, but the individual builds around him a network of social relationships which he comes to depend on for emotional support and responsiveness and which maintain him in subtle ways. (Neugarten, 1964:198)

This applies as well to personality, the tendency of individuals to organize their behavior consistently in different situations and over a number of years (Kimmel, 1974). It represents a "fit" between the individual and the environment, as unique adaptations to past experiences color present responses. Personality consistency evolves from the effects of memory, consistency in the situations one experiences, and habituated responses based on the accumulation of past experience (Kimmel, 1974).

The dependence of self and personality on social roles and interaction also implies the possibility of change in the self. Personality is an ongoing system which undergoes continuous change. "As the result of one's life history with its accumulating record of adaptations to both biological and social events, there is a continually changing basis within the individual for perceiving and responding to new events" (Neugarten, 1973:312). As there are changes in the social roles which individuals occupy and the social situations they encounter, there will also be changes in the nature of the interactions they have with others and with the world. This may trigger "identity transformations" (Strauss, 1962) which result in changed self-perception. External consistencies which had previously reinforced internal consistencies break up and as the self-concept changes, behavior directed by it will also change.

Aging may be accompanied by the disruption of long-term roles which had previously lent consistency to the self, due to retirement, widowhood, health limitations, and so on. Thus, there is considerable potential for personal change in response to age stratification. Role change—the relinquishing of social relationships and roles typical of adulthood and the acceptance of social relationships and roles typical of the later years—is a key to under-standing adjustment in old age (Phillips, 1957). As interactions and group memberships change, the individual internalizes new statuses, acquires new significant others and reference groups, and former statuses and significant others become less salient, and the self-concept is changed. Cavan illustrates this with retirement:

> At the point of compulsory retirement . . . the means of carry-ing out the social role disappears: the man is a lawyer without a case, a bookkeeper without books, a machinist without tools. Second, he is excluded from his group of former co-workers: as an isolated person he may be completely unable to function in his former role. Third, as a retired person, he begins to find a different evaluation of himself in the minds of others from the evaluation he had as an employed person. He no longer sees respect in the eyes of former subordinates, praise in the faces of former superiors, and approval in the manner of former co-workers. The looking glass composed of his former important groups throws back a changed image: he is done for, an old-timer, old-fashioned, on the shelf. (Cavan, 1962:527–28)

Becker (1964) suggests two other processes which link role change to personal change in adults: *situational adjustment* and *commitment*. Situational adjustment implies that individuals take on characteristics required by the situations in which they par-ticipate. We learn what is "required" of students and professors, even if such behaviors are not an integral part of our selves. Additionally, commitments which we make may constrain behavior in seemingly unrelated areas. For example, a schoolteacher might avoid X-rated movies not because of any personal moral beliefs, but because being seen there may jeopardize his or her career. As situations and roles change, these commitments and behavior patterns begin to unravel.

Personal change is more complex than this implies, however. Alteration of the "objective" social environment does not auto-matically alter self-perception, and former roles may still play a part. The retired sociologist, for example, may still define himself as a sociologist and derive esteem from that identity. Neugarten's (1969) notion of interiority implies that the self becomes less dependent on external factors for older people. The self is often more stable than one might expect. Individuals attempt to main-tain congruency among aspects of the self, interpretation of be-havior relevant to those aspects, and beliefs about how others behave toward them with respect to those aspects (Secord and Backman, 1974). They may do this by misperceiving the responses of others, avoiding incongruent interactions, downplaying certain aspects of the self, and so on. If an individual does not perceive his circumstances as changed, his self will not be altered.

On the other hand, the considerable potential for change in personal circumstances may also make personal change highly likely. Bengtson (1973) has suggested that older people may be more susceptible to social labeling because of the social reorganization they undergo. One study of older people concluded that, because of the unusual amount of personal change and status ambiguity associated with aging, "life-after-sixty shares with adolescence an intensification of the intimate and self-reflexive. At both times of life, the question, Who am I? assumes poignant relevance" (Clark and Anderson, 1967:78).

The link between role change and personal change can be related to the developmental issues discussed earlier. The usefulness of a model of age stratification again becomes apparent. Shifts into and out of roles are age-graded, with a typical sequencing of roles through the life cycle, disrupting the continuity of one's role set. Since roles are associated with qualities, rewards, expectations, and evaluations, individual's of different ages encounter different social and symbolic worlds. Because of formal events such as retirement or more informal introspection, a recognition develops that one's "me" has changed in age-related ways (Kimmel, 1974). The changes which are encountered may then result in developmental self and personality change, since roles are direct and indirect bases of attitudes, values, and behavior.

Young adulthood is a time of expansion into new roles offering more rewards and responsibilities, so it is not surprising that a critical developmental issue at this stage is personal identity and the need for a stabilized sense of self. Kimmel (1974) argues that the role changes of youth propel individuals into the external social world because of the need to master new roles and develop new personal styles to deal with them. The middle years are a time of stability and balance, with relatively less personal change, when issues seem to involve looking at the self as it has become, resulting either in feelings of mastery over the world or a sense that one has made the wrong decisions. Advancing years, at least in this society, may be accompanied by the loss of rewards, status, and long-term identities. Kimmel notes that this constriction of the social and symbolic environment is a "centripetal" force which makes internal processes more salient. The loss potentially accompanying old age and the existential dilemma created by death make both threat and ego important motivating forces.

Furthermore, the *meanings* attached to age-related transitions are important. Retirement will have a very different impact depending on whether it is seen as a reward or as an implied rejection and failure. Thus, it can be expected that the psychological issues which accompany aging will vary cross-culturally, as age transitions and the meanings of those transitions also vary.

Role Change and Socialization

There is a stereotyped notion that socialization and personality formation are confined to childhood, producing a relatively finished product. There are, however, numerous situations which may lead to socializing experiences in adulthood (Brim and Wheeler, 1966), such as demands by oneself or others for change because of dissatisfaction. Certainly the recent interest in "encounter" groups and transcendental meditation and the popularity of best sellers dealing with personal growth suggest interest in personal change. Additionally, adults move through sequences of roles and statuses during the life cycle which require meeting changing expectations. Geographic and occupational mobility require adjustment to new situations. There may be mutual socialization by couples who have just married or have just become parents. Lamaze childbirth classes and the more recent "parenting" classes represent such adult-socialization experiences.

As noted in Chapter 3, socialization teaches individuals at each stage of the life course how to perform new roles, adjust to changing roles, and relinquish old ones. Socialization is a major mechanism for integrating individuals into social groups and it adjusts their desires to what is available for those of their age.

Adult socialization is particularly relevant to *role transfer*, which combines the strain of leaving old commitments with the need to adjust to new tasks and expectations. *Anticipatory* socialization occurring before the role transition, provides continuity for a smoother transition. Many childhood activities, for example, anticipate adult roles, either inculcating broad value orientations or legitimizing particular roles. This is the essence of early sex-role socialization. Similarly, during adulthood, people are usually prepared for and looking forward to (even if with some apprehension) the new roles they will occupy—shifts from student to worker, single to married, couple to parent. On the other hand, *tenancy* socialization, occurring after entrance into the new role, does not smooth over the transition. The army draftee must be socialized into army life largely during basic training.

Thus, socialization is a life-long process of "continuous bilateral negotiation between the individual and the social system as he moves into new positions through time" (Bengtson, 1973:19), which is not always successful. Individuals may be prepared for roles they will not play, or enter roles for which they are not prepared. Irving Rosow (1974) has suggested that one of the most basic problems of older people is that they are not socialized into "old age." Throughout the life cycle, each stage has a set of norms and expectations—a distinctive pattern of activity, responsibility, authority, and privilege—but the accompanying processes of socialization break down in old age.

Properties which ease age-related transitions are no longer operative. Rites of passage, such as graduation and marriage ceremonies, ordinarily help to redefine the person, symbolize the changes being undergone, and facilitate role shifts, but such ceremonies for entrance into old age are nonexistent or vague. Retirement dinners, for example, do not adequately serve this function, and may instead "reflect the social judgment and policy of a collective that men or women beyond a certain age are not fit to work or that their services are no longer necessary" (Blau, 1973:214).

Adult role transitions typically involve an increase in responsibility and independence. Changes associated with aging, however, are more likely to represent a loss of responsibility and increased dependence. Consequently, there is little motivation to prepare for the "old age" role and much motivation to deny it. There is also little role continuity in the shifts associated with aging. The aged are left to make their own adaptations, since modern cultures do little to prepare them for the positions occupied by older people. As we shall see later, for example, preretirement programs are infrequent and typically very limited. Blau (1973) suggests that it may be more appropriate to speak of "role exit" for older people, since they do not really take on new roles. When role exits are involuntary, as with widowhood and often with retirement, there may be feelings of shame and betrayal with the implied social rejection.

There is, consequently, little motivation to enter old age, and few socializing mechanisms to assist in this age transition or norms for guidance beyond simplistic "act your age" ideas.

> . . . the norms provide almost no expectations that effectively structure an older person's activities and general pattern of life. His adjustment in this respect results essentially from his individual decisions and choices, from personal definitions of what is appropriate and desirable. . . . In this sense, an old person's life is basically "roleless," unstructured by the society, and conspicuously lacking in norms, especially for nonfamilial relationships. (Rosow, 1974:69)

One consequence of this normlessness may be uncertainty and alienation (Martin, Bengtson and Acock, 1974), although it also implies greater freedom, which may be a positive aspect of aging (Bengtson, 1973; Streib and Schneider, 1971).

Rosow also suggests that socialization to old age is confined to informal situations and the aged have not made effective use of their age peers as role models. There is a tendency to maintain involvement with old groups and to continue acknowledging previous status characteristics. Additionally, there are few or no rewards for playing the new aged role.

Riley and associates (1969) have also noted the potential failure of "societal" contributions to socialization—the lack of (1) goals and expectations, (2) facilities, resources, and support for learning, and (3) positive or negative sanctions. It is as if the older person is simply left hanging. They point out, however, that there may be individual factors which interfere with socialization of the aged. For example, motivation may decline and fatalism increase because of declining energy and physical capacities. Background experiences may also restrict further learning due to continuing commitments and long-held values. Whatever the source, however, lack of socialization (or preparation) is likely to be a major cause of psychological difficulties in the transition to old age.

Aging, Development, and Age Stratification

The individual aging experience appears to be one of personal continuity confronted by age-related changes which can potentially uproot the aging person from his or her normal and familiar worlds and identities. Identity crisis is often not a bad thing, however. It is one way in which we grow, shedding identities which no longer fit and taking on those which do, and hopefully becoming better or more complete persons in the process. Yet the literature on the developmental psychology of aging is replete with descriptions of older persons who constrict and defend rather than grow. Though many seem to find disengagement pleasant and increased interiority may in some ways represent natural aging processes, there is evidence that at least some of this disengagement results from the social context of aging.

While a lack of socialization for old age may create problems, the very vagueness of old age roles allows older people to negotiate and "make" their own roles. Perhaps more important to the psychology of aging than lack of preparation for old age roles is the actual content of those roles and options. Do the transitions of late life present aging individuals with opportunities for continued personal growth? Increasingly the answer to this question offered by commentators on the aging experience is no. In their study of stages in the life cycle, Lowenthal and associates (1975) point to the wasted potential of mature women and self-actualizing men who desire second careers but lack opportunities. Middle-aged women who seek meaningful involvement outside of the family seem especially thwarted. They suggest that psychologically "simplistic" women age more comfortably in current society than complex women, who have not acquired protective, stress-avoidant life styles.

There is growing recognition of the barriers created by modern age stratification to meaningful life experiences and options for personal change in both middle and old age. Sarason (1977) refers to the "one life–one career imperative," whereby career choices made in youth channel and "fill in" the rest of life, offering few opportunities for later change or growth. In middle age, this contributes to an early sense of aging and feelings of being trapped. In old age, one is limited to too narrow a range of options and role transitions in modern societies, which results largely in declining status and responsibility.

Despite lengthening of the expected life cycle to over 70 years, education and the major decisions about work and family careers are still confined to the first third of the life course, and major change, especially in work careers, becomes increasingly difficult with age. Sarason (1977) notes that it is far easier to change marriage partners than work careers. This situation represents a "disparity between society's rhetoric about growth and contemporary institutional realities" (Sarason, 1977:265). The age stratification system of modern societies faces the challenge of providing options for "loosening up life" (Butler, 1975) to make the later years of life more than simply playing out earlier decisions. This theme will be discussed later, particularly in relation to aging and the use of time.

Sex Differences in the Aging Experience

A developmental approach to the psychology of aging must recognize variability in the nature of aging. Age-stratification is not isolated from other mechanisms for allocating roles. One of the most important of these is the system of sexual stratification which is superimposed on the age-grading of roles and life events. Because of socialization, enticements, and barriers, men and women occupy different positions in society, and consequently their aging experiences differ. Unfortunately, our understanding in this area has been hindered by overblown stereotypes and myths about the differences between older men and women (Beeson, 1975; Payne and Whittington, 1976).

Diane Beeson has noted that "when women have been included

as subjects their experience of aging has frequently been compared to that of men and evaluated as less problematic, less traumatic, and their difficulties seen as more easily resolved" (Beeson, 1975: 52). To a large extent, this seems to be based on the assumption, exemplified in the following statement, that the life cycle is smoother for women:

> Disengagement from central life roles is basically different for women than for men, perhaps because women's roles are essentially unchanged from girlhood to death. In the course of their lives, women are asked to give up only pieces of their core socioemotional roles or to change their details. Their transitions are therefore easier. (Cumming, 1964:13)

This assumption of tranquility is questionable. Indeed, it has been suggested that if women do adjust more easily to aging, it is because they are used to ill-defined, ambiguous roles and have already experienced impermanence in the form of role loss (Kline, 1975).

Study of the aging of women has focused largely on the family role of housewife-mother, and there are some clear sources of strain in the role transitions associated with this. Lopata (1966) has noted that the housewife role begins shrinking relatively early, as children grow up and leave. Those who have invested their lives in this role may encounter considerable difficulties during the so-called "empty nest" period. Women who return to work or school may encounter feelings of inadequacy—a "reentry" syndrome (Bart, 1975). Researchers have also focused on widowhood as a particular problem for women, with its potential for isolation and financial problems which may be aggravated to the extent that women are socialized to be dependent on men (Lopata, 1973; Streib, 1975). But widowhood is often considered less traumatic than retirement because of the presumed availability of grandparenthood and other family roles (Beeson, 1975). In terms of both services and finances, less attention and support is given to widowhood, the typical major transition for older women, than to retirement, the typical major transition for older men.

Menopause is another age-linked transition for women which has received little attention. There appear to be mixed reactions to menopause. Neugarten and associates (1963) found, for example, that fewer middle-aged women than younger women saw menopause as a significant event. In fact, they quite often saw the postmenopausal period in positive terms. Menopause appears to create few problems in most societies, particularly those which attach high status to grandmother and mother-in-law roles (Bart, 1975). This suggests that, as with many of the changes associated with age, it is not the change itself which creates difficulties, but the social meaning attributed to that change.

Sex differences in aging can be linked to the more general social positions of men and women. Susan Sontag suggests that there is a "double standard of aging":

> This society offers even fewer rewards for aging to women than it does to men. Being physically attractive counts much more in a woman's life than in a man's, but beauty, identified, as it is for women, with youthfulness, does not stand up well to age. Exceptional mental powers can increase with age, but women are rarely encouraged to develop their minds. . . . "Masculinity" is identitified with competence, autonomy, self-control—qualities which the disappearance of youth does not threaten. . . . "Feminity" is identified with incompetence, helplessness, passivity, noncompetitiveness, being nice. Age does not improve these qualities. (Sontag, 1975:32–33)

Thus, aging may be more difficult for women because they are more narrowly defined. Additionally, Sontag argues that there is a "humiliating process of gradual sexual disqualification" (p. 34), which perceives women as sexually "obsolete" earlier than men. There are few, if any, female counterparts to the Cary Grants and Cesar Romeros of the male world.

There has been an assumption in the literature that retirement is rarely a problem for women because of the relative unimportance of work in their lives. The following statement exemplies this:

> Retirement is not an important problem for women because . . . working seems to make little difference to them. It is as though they add work to their lives the way they would add a club membership. (Cumming and Henry, 1961:144)

Such pronouncements seem premature, at least. Trends in labor force participation suggest an increasing importance of the work role for women, particularly older women. In fact, there are some indications that, for women who do work, adjustment to retirement may be even more difficult than for men (Streib and Schneider, 1971; Atchley, 1976). There is clearly a need for more sophisticated analysis of sex differences in the nature and impact of aging. Some of the issues in such an analysis will be indicated in later chapters.

As a final point, there is the intriguing possibility that, psychologically at least, men and women become more alike as they age and there may even be reversals in their approaches to the world. Neugarten (1968a; 1969) suggests that older men become more receptive to affiliative and nurturant needs, while older women feel less guilty about aggressive and egocentric impulses; in short, there is a "feminization" of men and a "masculinization" of women in late life. There is some empirical support for this idea. Lowenthal and associates (1975) found that men approaching retirement made fewer demands on self, were more accepting of others and the environment, and were more mellow and less ambitious and restless. Older women, on the other hand, seemed to hit their stride, becoming less dependent and more assertive. Many confronted the empty nest with a sense of relief and changing patterns of dominance. These patterns are echoed in cross-cultural studies (Gutmann, 1977). Studies of Asian, Middle Eastern, African, and Amerindian cultures display relative unanimity in the age-grading of male passivity, as old men move from active to passive styles and women move from passive to active mastery, resulting in what Gutmann calls the "matriarchy of later life." Gutmann notes that this female dominance is largely exercised informally in family settings, rather than in formal positions of power, and this often makes aged women vulnerable to charges of sorcery and witchcraft.

> The Moroccans capture the African consensus on the lethal nature of old women in this parable: each boy is born surrounded by a hundred devils and each girl is born surrounded by a hundred angels. However, with each passing year, a devil is exchanged for an angel; when a man reaches a hundred years of age, he is surrounded by angels, and the women by devils. (Gutmann, 1977:311–12)

Gutmann further suggests that aged men and women are both reverting to psychological needs which were suppressed early in life, with the taking on of family-based sex-roles. Whatever the reason, however, these findings point out that the psychology of aging is shaped by complex interactions between age stratification and other aspects of the social structure.

Successful Aging

This is not a "how to" book about aging gracefully and happily. Nevertheless, this discussion of the psychology of aging inevitably leads to the question: How does one grow old successfully? There is no shortage of conflicting prescriptions: be active, disengage; be future-oriented, review the past; conserve oneself, grow as a person. But if we have learned one thing from a developmental perspective on aging, it is that there are as many ways to age successfully as there are types of people. This challenges our own biases about what older people "ought" to be like. As one example, Lowenthal and associates (1975) found two extremely different

routes to *equally* high satisfaction in late life. Some were psychologically complex, taking a bouyant and expansive road to happiness. Others were psychologically simple, basing their satisfaction
on constriction. While this author prefers the former pattern of
aging, all persons must approach old age in a manner which is
right and consistent for themselves in order to feel satisfied.

It is not clear whether overall life satisfaction is affected much
by age. Some studies report a decline (Riley and Foner, 1968),
but others have found little change with age (Spreitzer and
Snyder, 1974). Health, particularly self-rating of health, seems to
be the most important current determinant of life satisfaction
(Palmore and Luikart, 1972), and such variables as income, family
satisfaction, and organizational activity have also been found to
be related. It is instructive that a recent four-year longitudinal
study of life satisfaction, in a sample of persons aged 46 to 70,
found no significant changes with age in level of satisfaction
"*relative to a person's own expectations*" (Palmore and Kivett,
1977:314). The best predictor of satisfaction at the end of the
study was satisfaction at the beginning. A developmental approach
to aging must always consider the personal history of the aging
individual.

It is clear that social gerontology has moved away from earlier
attempts to define "well-adjusted" or "correct" old age and to
measure successful aging against some ideal standard. It is now
more usual to let aging individuals define what satisfaction means
for themselves, in terms of their own needs, desires, interests, and
past patterns. In effect, the standard has become: if it works, it is
successful. But while this approach removes the biases of the
investigator and lends an air of value-free science to the measurement of successful aging, it is itself not entirely satisfying. Do we wish
to consider as successful aging satisfaction arrived at through defense
and denial? We all have a feeling that certain lives *should not* be
satisfying, even if they are, and if people understood the alternatives they would be dissatisfied and press for change, thereby
enriching their lives. Marxists, for example, often complain that
the working class does not understand how downtrodden and op-
pressed they are; if they did, they would develop class consciousness and seek a "new reality." This is a dilemma faced by any
movement which seeks to liberate people (workers, housewives,
old people) from the taken-for-granted realities which constrain
their lives. The very fact that these realities are taken for granted
means that people do not appreciate how dissatisfied they "ought"
to be with them.

This author does not wish to claim possession of "the answer"
to how older people ought to live their lives, but it may be pos-

sible to define successful aging in terms of what old age might look like under a different set of circumstances, in a different social context. The current system of age stratification is only one among many possible systems. The present structure of the life course may be too confining, as suggested by the concept of the "one life–one career imperative" and the need to "loosen up life," thereby robbing old age of certain potential satisfactions. The aged may well be unaware of missed options and opportunities, since the age stratification system also shapes our expectations and perceptions of the life course.

One definition of successful aging is meeting the developmental challenges presents to individuals in both a "satisfying" and an "appropriate" manner (leaving open the definition of "appropriate"). The social structure could then also be evaluated according to whether it hinders or facilitates the resolution of these challenges. A useful summary of the development issues posed by aging is provided by Clark and Anderson (1967), who outline five adaptive tasks to be accomplished in successful aging:

1. *Recognition of aging and definition of instrumental limitations:* an awareness and acceptance of the limits placed by age on one's health and energy.
2. *Redefinition of physical and social life space:* changing the boundaries of one's world to achieve an environment which can still be controlled; this may or may not require constriction (disengagement).
3. *Substitution of alternate sources of need-satisfaction:* as roles and relationships are lost, satisfaction must be found elsewhere; retirement or widowhood are critical in this respect.
4. *Reassessment of criteria for evaluation of self:* the older person must be able to find sources of self-worth which are not lost because of aging (as with retirement).
5. *Reintegration of values and life goals:* this implies that the above tasks must be accomplished and made coherent to give their "new" life meaning.

In their study, Clark and Anderson found that most older people had handled these adaptive tasks successfully. Among those who were maladapted, the most frequent problem was the failure to achieve substitute sources of need-satisfaction. This suggests that such major changes as retirement and widowhood which involve the loss of what may be central sources of need-satisfaction would have particularly severe effects on older people. Problems in achieving meaningful substitutes may stem from the prevailing nature of age stratification in modern societies. These five tasks, however, should not be taken as the only ones possible. In some ways, they seem to suggest an acceptance and adaptation to both biological and social aspects of old age as they are presented to the aging person. Again, we should not be afraid to consider alternative images of old age to those now available.

It should be clear by now that aging has exceedingly complex, and often conflicting, psychological consequences. In conclusion, the complexities of satisfying aging have been nicely stated by Raymond Kuhlen:

> Thus it would be hypothesized that the degree to which various phases of life (i.e., various age periods) offer basic gratifications or pose serious threats and thus influence adjustment will depend upon such matters as the *meaning* of life and aging to the individual, the *role* he occupies at a given age rather than his age as such, his general *"style of life"* and personality makeup (e.g., rigidity-flexibility), *situational factors* that may pose environmental stresses, and *personal factors* (e.g., capacities) which not only may be threatening in their own right but also may reduce the individual's ability to cope successfully with his environment and to achieve gratifications in usual ways and to usual degrees. (Kuhlen, 1959:892)

Summary

There have been two general social-psychological theories of aging. *Activity* theory suggests that older people should remain active and involved, thus insuring stability of need-satisfaction and a positive self-image. *Disengagement* theory argues that social and emotional withdrawal from the world by aging individuals is mutually satisfying and functional for the individual and society. Both of these approaches have some supporting evidence, but both offer an over simplified view of aging and its effects on the individual. A developmental approach is preferable, since it recognizes both stability and change. Individuals maintain previous patterns of living, but aging places constraints on the ability to maintain continuity. Each individual develops his own style of aging in light of personal history and current context.

Empirical investigations indicate a number of patterns of aging and apparently several ways to age "successfully." Individuals exhibit considerable life-style continuity, but there do appear to be psychological changes associated with aging, including a tendency toward greater interiority. There are several possible reasons for age-related psychological change.

Developmental psychology offers one set of approaches to such change. Some have characterized the life cycle as a curve of growth and decline, with growth-expansion motives being replaced by anxiety and threat. Others have focused on developmental issues unique to each life period. Middle age is characterized as a time of introspection and review, followed by a need for cognitive and emotional flexibility in adjusting to the new realities of old age. Such developmental sequences are likely to vary cross-culturally, depending on the nature of the age stratification system.

Stress may be another source of age-related psychological change. Old age may be a time of both heightened threat and declining response capability. The social context is important here, since it affects the meaning of age-linked events and the availability of resources for coping with threats. The experience of stress may be related to such psychological characteristics as disengagement and interiority.

Identity and self emerge from interactions with others, as they validate particular identities, and the self lends consistency by directing behavior. Social roles provide access to particular social and symbolic worlds. To the extent that roles change with age, the self is vulnerable to change. Thus, age stratification in concert with symbolic interactions are the ultimate sources of developmental psychological change.

This emphasis on social roles implies that socialization is an important topic throughout the life cycle. Role exit and role transfer are likely accompaniments of aging, and it has been suggested that the failure of socialization to old age is a major problem for older people. The usual mechanisms and structures which facilitate adult socialization are lacking in old age, resulting in normlessness and a "roleless role."

The nature of personal change in late life offers opportunities for positive growth, but many older people are instead characterized by psychological constriction. This may be attributable to failures of socialization and the lack of structured options in middle and old age. The age stratification system may trap people in limited and limiting roles.

There may be sex differences in the psychological impact of aging, since men and women tend to occupy different positions in society. Work in this area has been characterized by such questionable assumptions about aging for women as the experience of smoother transitions and the unimportance of retirement for them. It may be that aging is more difficult for women because of a "double standard of aging." There is also some cross-cultural evidence of a "feminization" of older men and a "masculinization" of older women, as each responds to needs suppressed earlier in life.

Finally, there have been a number of images of "successful aging." One tradition has been to set up external standards, but a preferable approach is to utilize each individual's own evaluation of aging and the life situation, recognizing the importance of personal history and individual meaning in making sense of the aging experience.

References

Amster, Leslie and Herbert Krauss
   1974   "The relationship between life crises and mental deterioration in old age." Aging and Human Development 5 (1): 51–55.
Atchley, Robert
   1976   "Selected social and psychological differences between men and women in later life." Journal of Gerontology 31 (2): 204–11.
Bart, Pauline
   1975   "Emotional and social status of the older woman." In No Longer Young: The Older Woman in America. Occasional Papers in Gerontology No. 11, Institute of Gerontology, The University of Michigan-Wayne State University.
Becker, Howard
   1964   "Personal change in adult life." Sociometry 27: 40–53.
Beeson, Diane
   1975   "Women in aging studies: A critique and suggestions." Social Problems 23 (1): 52–59.
Bengtson, Vern
   1973   The Social Psychology of Aging. Indianapolis: Bobbs-Merrill.
Biddle, Bruce and Edwin Thomas
   1966   Role Theory: Concepts and Research. New York: John Wiley.
Blau, Zena
   1973   Old Age in a Changing Society. New York: New Viewpoints.
Blumer, Herbert
   1969   Symbolic Interactionism: Perspective and Method. Englewood Cliffs, N.J.: Prentice-Hall.
Brim, Orville, Jr.
   1976   "Male mid-life crisis: A comparative analysis." In Beth Hess (ed.). Growing Old in America. New Brunswick, N.J.: Transaction.
Brim, Orville, Jr., and Stanton Wheeler
   1966   Socialization after Childhood. New York: John Wiley.
Buhler, Charlotte
   1951   "Maturation and motivation." Personality 1: 184–211.

Busse, Ewald
1970 "Psychoneurotic reactions and defense mechanisms in the aged." In Erdman Palmore (ed.). Normal Aging. Durham, N.C.: Duke University Press.

Butler, Robert
1963 "The life review: An interpretation of reminiscence in the aged." Psychiatry 26 (1): 65–76.
1975 Why Survive?: Being Old in America. New York: Harper & Row.

Cavan, Ruth
1962 "Self and role in adjustment during old age." In Arnold Rose (ed.). Human Behavior and Social Processes. Boston: Houghton Mifflin.

Clark, Margaret and Barbara Anderson
1967 Culture and Aging. Springfield, Ill.: Charles C Thomas.

Cooley, Charles Horton
1902 Human Nature and the Social Order. New York: Scribner's.

Cumming, Elaine
1963 "Further thoughts on the theory of disengagement." International Social Science Journal 15: 377–93.
1964 "New thoughts on the theory of disengagement." In Robert Kastenbaum (ed.). New Thoughts on Old Age. New York: Springer.

Cumming, Elaine and William Henry
1961 Growing Old: The Process of Disengagement. New York: Basic Books.

Dean, Lois
1962 "Aging and the decline of affect." Journal of Gerontology 17: 440–46.

Dohrenwend, Barbara and Bruce Dohrenwend (eds.)
1974 Stressful Life Events: Their Nature and Effects. New York: John Wiley.

Dowd, James
1975 "Aging as exchange: A preface to theory." Journal of Gerontology 30 (5): 584–94.

Eisdorfer, Carl and Frances Wilkie
1977 "Stress, disease, aging and behavior." In James Birren and K. Warner Schaie (eds.). Handbook of the Psychology of Aging. New York: Van Nostrand Reinhold.

Erikson, Erik
1950 Childhood and Society. New York: W. W. Norton.

Frenkel-Brunswik, Else
1963 "Adjustments and reorientation in the course of the life span." In Raymond Kuhlen (ed.). Psychological Studies of Human Development. New York: Appleton-Century-Crofts.

Gould, R.
1975 "Adult life stages: Growth toward self-tolerance." Psychology Today 8 (9): 74–78.

Gubrium, Jaber
  1973 The Myth of the Golden Years: A Socio-Environmental Theory of Aging. Springfield, Ill.: Charles C Thomas.

Gutmann, David
  1977 "The cross-cultural perspective: Notes toward a comparative psychology of aging." In James Birren and K. Warner Schaie (eds.). Handbook of the Psychology of Aging. New York: Van Nostrand Reinhold.

Havighurst, Robert, Bernice Neugarten, and Sheldon Tobin
  1968 "Disengagement and patterns of aging." In Bernice Neugarten (ed.). Middle Age and Aging. Chicago: University of Chicago Press.

Henry, William
  1965 "Engagement and disengagement: Toward a theory of adult development." In Robert Kastenbaum (ed.). Contributions to the Psychobiology of Aging. New York: Springer.

Hickman, C. Addison and Manford Kuhn
  1956 Individuals, Groups, and Economic Behavior. New York: Dryden Press.

Hochschild, Arlie
  1975 "Disengagement theory: A critique and proposal." American Sociological Review 40: 553–69.

Holmes, Thomas and Richard Rahe
  1967 "The Social Readjustment Rating Scale." Journal of Psychosomatic Research 11: 213–18.

Hough, Richard, Dianne Fairbank, and Alma Garcia
  1976 "Problems in the ratio measurement of life stress." Journal of Health and Social Behavior 17: 70–82.

Jones, Tony (ed.)
  1978 "Going strong in your 80s." Quest/78 2 (2): 113–28.

Kastenbaum, Robert
  1977 Death, Society, and Human Experience. St. Louis: C. V. Mosby.

Kinch, John
  1963 "A formalized theory of the self-concept." American Journal of Sociology 68: 481–86.

Kimmel, Douglas
  1974 Adulthood and Aging. New York: John Wiley.

Kline, Chrysee
  1975 "The socialization process of women: Implications for a theory of successful aging." The Gerontologist 15: 486–92.

Kuhlen, Raymond
  1959 "Aging and life-adjustment." In James Birren (ed.). Handbook of Aging and the Individual. Chicago: University of Chicago Press.
  1964 "Developmental changes in motivation during the adult years." In James Birren (ed.). Relations of Development and Aging. Springfield, Ill.: Charles C Thomas.

Kuypers, Joseph
 1972 "Internal-external locus of control, ego functioning, and
       personality characteristics in old age." The Gerontologist
       12 (2): 168–73.
 1974 "Ego functioning in old age: Early adult life antecedents."
       Aging and Human Development 5 (2): 157–79.
Lawton, M. Powell and Lucille Nahemow
 1973 "Ecology and the aging process." In Carl Eisdorfer and
       M. Powell Lawton (eds.). The Psychology of Adult
       Development and Aging. Washington, D.C.: American
       Psychological Association.
Lazarus, Richard
 1966 Psychological Stress and the Coping Process. New York:
       McGraw-Hill.
Lemon, Bruce, Vern Bengtson, and James Peterson
 1972 "An exploration of the activity theory of aging: Activity
       types and life satisfaction among in-movers to a retire-
       ment community." Journal of Gerontology 27 (4): 511–23.
Lewis, Charles
 1971 "Reminiscing and self-concept in old age." Journal of
       Gerontology 26 (2): 240–43.
Lopata, Helena
 1966 "The life cycle of the social role of the housewife."
       Sociology and Social Research 51: 5–22.
 1973 Widowhood in an American City. Cambridge, Mass.:
       Schenkman.
Lowenthal, Marjorie and David Chiriboga
 1973 "Social stress and adaptation: Toward a life-course perspec-
       tive." In Carl Eisdorfer and M. Powell Lawton (eds.).
       The Psychology of Adult Development and Aging.
       Washington, D.C.: American Psychological Association.
Lowenthal, Marjorie et al.
 1975 Four Stages of Life. San Francisco: Jossey-Bass.
Maas, Henry and Joseph Kuypers
 1974 From 30 to 70. San Francisco: Jossey-Bass.
Maddox, George
 1970 "Fact and artifact: Evidence bearing on disengagement
       theory." In Erdman Palmore (ed.). Normal Aging.
       Durham, N.C.: Duke University Press.
Martin, William, Vern Bengtson, and Alan Acock
 1974 "Alienation and age: A context-specific approach." Social
       Forces 53: 266–74.
McGrath, Joseph (ed.)
 1970 Social and Psychological Factors in Stress. New York:
       Holt, Rinehart and Winston.
Mead, George Herbert
 1934 Mind, Self and Society. Chicago: University of Chicago
       Press.

Mechanic, David
  1969 "Social Structure and personal adaptation: Some
        neglected dimensions." Paper presented at the Conference
        on Coping and Adaptation, Stanford Medical School,
        March 1969.
Neugarten, Bernice
  1964 Personality in Middle and Late Life. New York: Atherton
        Press.
  1968a "Adult personality: Toward a psychology of the life cycle."
        In Bernice Neugarten (ed.). Middle Age and Aging.
        Chicago: University of Chicago Press.
  1968b "The awareness of middle age." In Bernice Neugarten (ed.).
        Middle Age and Aging. Chicago: University of Chicago
        Press.
  1969 "Continuities and discontinuities of psychological issues
        into adult life." Human Development 12 (2): 121–30.
  1973 "Personality change in late life: A developmental perspec-
        tive." In Carl Eisdorfer and M. Powell Lawton (eds.). The
        Psychology of Adult Development and Aging. Washington,
        D.C.: American Psychological Association.
Neugarten, Bernice, Robert Havighurst, and Sheldon Tobin
  1968 "Personality and patterns of aging." In Bernice Neugarten
        (ed.). Middle Age and Aging. Chicago: University of
        Chicago Press.
Neugarten, Bernice, Vivian Wood, Ruth Kraines, and Barbara Loomis
  1963 "Women's attitudes toward the menopause." Vita Humana
        6: 140–51.
Palmore, Erdman
  1970 "The effects of aging on activities and attitudes." In
        Erdman Palmore (ed.). Normal Aging. Durham, N.C.:
        Duke University Press.
Palmore, Erdman and Vira Kivett
  1977 "Change in life satisfaction: A longitudinal study of persons
        aged 46–70." Journal of Gerontology 32: 311–16.
Palmore, Erdman and Clark Luikart
  1972 "Health and social factors related to life satisfaction." Journal
        of Health and Social Behavior 13: 68–80.
Payne, Barbara and Frank Whittington
  1976 "Older women: An examination of popular stereotypes
        and research evidence." Social Problems 23: 489–504.
Peck, Robert
  1956 "Psychological developments in the second half of life."
        In John Anderson (ed.). Psychological Aspects of Aging.
        Washington, D.C.: American Psychological Association.
Phillips, Bernard
  1957 "A role theory approach to adjustment in old age."
        American Sociological Review 22: 212–17.

Reichard, Suzanne, Florine Livson, and Paul Peterson
   1962   Aging and Personality. New York: John Wiley.
Riley, Matilda and Anne Foner
   1968   Aging and Society. Volume 1: An Inventory of Research
          Findings. New York: Russell Sage.
Riley, Matilda, Anne Foner, Beth Hess, and Marcia Toby
   1969   "Socialization for the middle and later years." In David
          Goslin (ed.). Handbook of Socialization Theory and Re-
          search. Chicago: Rand McNally.
Riley, Matilda, Marilyn Johnson, and Anne Foner (eds.)
   1972   Aging and Society. Volume 3: A Sociology of Age Stratifica-
          tion. New York: Russell Sage.
Roman, Paul and Philip Taietz
   1967   "Organizational structure and disengagement: The
          emeritus professor." The Gerontologist 7: 147–52.
Rosow, Irving
   1963   "Adjustment of the normal aged." In R. H. Williams,
          Clark Tibbitts, and Wilma Donahue (eds.). Processes of
          Aging II. New York: Atherton Press.
   1974   Socialization to Old Age. Berkeley: University of
          California Press.
Sarason, Seymour
   1977   Work, Aging, and Social Change. New York:
          The Free Press.
Secord, Paul and Carl Backman
   1974   Social Psychology. New York: McGraw-Hill.
Shanas, Ethel et al.
   1968   Old People in Three Industrial Societies. New York:
          Atherton Press.
Sontag, Susan
   1975   "The double standard of aging." In No Longer Young:
          The Older Woman in America. Occasional Papers in
          Gerontology No. 11, Institute of Gerontology, The
          University of Michigan-Wayne State University.
Spreitzer, Elmer and Eldon Snyder
   1974   "Correlates of life satisfaction among the aged." Journal of
          Gerontology 29 (4): 454–58.
Strauss, Anselm
   1962   "Transformations of identity." In Arnold Rose (ed.). Human
          Behavior and Social Processes. Boston: Houghton Mifflin.
Streib, Gordon
   1975   "Mechanisms for change—viewed in a sociological con-
          text." In No Longer Young: The Older Woman in
          America. Occasional papers in Gerontology No. 11, Institute
          of Gerontology, The University of Michigan-Wayne State
          University

Streib, Gordon and Clement Schneider
    1971   Retirement in American Society. Ithaca, N.Y.: Cornell
            University Press.
Turner, Jonathan
    1974   The Structure of Sociological Theory. Homewood, Ill.:
            Dorsey.
Wallach, Michael and Leonard Green
    1961   "On age and the subjective speed of time." Journal of
            Gerontology 16 (1): 71–74.
Williams, Richard and Claudine Wirths
    1965   Lives Through the Years. New York: Atherton Press.
Woodruff, Diane and James Birren
    1972   "Age changes and cohort differences in personality."
            Developmental Psychology 6 (2): 252–59.

5
Images of Aging: Personal and Social

~~~~~~~~~~~~~~~~~~~~~~~~~~~~~~~~~~~~~~~

Two important issues in a developmental perspective on the aging experience are the impact of aging on the individual's self-image and his image to others. These are critical questions because of their relevance to self-esteem and overall satisfaction with life. Under what conditions do individuals come to see themselves as old? What is the personal significance of an "old" self-concept? This latter question again brings us to a consideration of the place of the aged in any society—the relative status or stigma attributed to old age—and the psychological impact of the social context of aging, including age stratification.

Aging and the Social Self

According to the symbolic interactionist perspective we live in a symbolic world in which the meanings of objects are determined socially through interaction with others, both specific persons ("significant others") and the society or culture (the "generalized other"). The *self* is one of the objects whose meaning is socially determined, through our perception of how others see us, as we "take the role of the other." Cooley describes his concept of the "looking glass self" as follows:

> A self-idea of this sort seems to have three principal elements: the imagination of our appearance to the other person, the imagination of his judgement of that appearance, and some sort

of self-feeling, such as pride or mortification. . . . The thing
that moves us to pride or shame is not the mere mechanical
reflection of ourselves, but an imputed sentiment, the imagined
effect of this reflection upon another's mind. (Cooley, 1902:184)

Thus, as we "perform" in games, schools, and jobs, our self-judg-
ments are affected by how we imagine others see us. After all,
it is hard to view yourself as a "good golfer" when everyone snickers
during your backswing.

Social roles are important in defining the self because they give
us access to certain types of interactions (and therefore validation
of certain identities) and because we have more generalized conceptions of the meaning and evaluation of different roles. Out of
these roles and interactions, a consistent sense of the self develops
which directs behavior. Since the self is a social construct, however, it may change if the individaul's social context is altered.

The self-concept may be broadly defined as "that organization
of qualities that the individual attributes to himself" (Kinch, 1963:
381). It consists of four dimensions. The *cognitive* dimension is
the set of identity attributes the person assigns to himself (young,
middle-aged, or elderly). An individual will have many of these
cognitive identities of varying importance. The *evaluative* dimension consists of the connotative meanings attached to the cognitive identities. For example, being "elderly" may be considered
either a good or bad thing. The combination of these cognitive
and evaluative dimensions begins to determine the individual's
overall self-image. The third dimension of self-concept is *behavioral*—the individual's actions toward himself and the world
will be based on the first two dimensions. Finally, *self-esteem*, a
more global estimation of one's standing in the world (Rosenberg, 1965), is partly determined by specific cognitive-evaluative
combinations, with more central identities having a greater impact,
but is more than the sum of these parts. It is an overall assessment
of "the sort of person I am."

It might seem that self-identification as "middle-aged" or
"elderly" would simply depend on chronological age, but substantial proportions of older persons do not consider themselves
elderly. What appears meaningful from the outside may not be
meaningful for the individual. Each individual is differentially
exposed to various aspects of the social world as he occupies
specific statuses and roles and assumes group memberships. "We
come to experience and act toward ourselves, as toward all social
objects, in terms of the classifications, norms, and definitions held
by the groups of which we happen to be members" (Hickman
and Kuhn, 1956:43). As interactions and group memberships

change, the individual acquires new roles and interacts with different people and the self-concept should also change. The social self is both process and product, resulting in tension between the emerging self and the persisting, stable elements of the self. The reader has certainly experienced such changes in entering high school or college.

Aspects of the self do persist, of course. The development of the self involves integration of newly acquired meanings with existing ones, rather than mere substitution of the new for the old. Indeed, we often attempt to maintain a stable interpersonal environment in order to maintain stability of self and behavior (Secord and Backman, 1974). Even objective change in status or roles may not result in subjective changes in the self. Opposition to the perception of change comes from a sense of personal continuity. Since events must be ordered and given meaning to be comprehended, the failure to perceive change maintains stability of the self. Thus, "The awareness of constance in identity is, then, in the eye of the beholder rather than in the behavior itself" (Strauss, 1962:84). There is evidence, for example, that the perception of one's own aging is resisted because of the devalued status of the aged in American society. Nevertheless, it is clear that changes in one's personal social structure induce changes in roles, activities, and interpersonal relationships which affect self-validation. Such turning points are characterized by misalignment and the need to "try out" new and often exciting or fearful conceptions of the self.

Legitimate debate over the usefulness of the self in explaining behavior remains. In essence, it is argued that individuals behave in particular ways because they consider themselves to be "the kind of person" who behaves in those ways. But people do not generally think explicitly in those terms. Most behavior is not guided by considerations of self-identity. Do I brush my teeth because when I get up in the morning I say to myself: "I'm the sort of person who brushes his teeth in the morning"? Behavior is often constrained by prior commitments, cost-benefit calculations, and the ends it serves.

More important, some have suggested that in the course of development, our egocentric preoccupation with self-image diminishes, so that older people are less concerned with reflections on the self. The concept of interiority, discussed in Chapter 4, suggests that the self-image of the aged depends less on external factors, and preoccupation with the inner aspects of experience will result in greater consistency in the self. It is true that retired physicians, carpenters, or teachers often still think of themselves as physicians, carpenters, or teachers.

But there is also a tremendous potential for change in one's roles and circumstances with age. While the impact of these changes on self-image may be diminished in old age, it hardly seems likely that they will have no effects at all. When age-linked change accumulates—retirement, widowhood, gray hair, poor health—some consideration of self seems inevitable. This is created by the age stratification of roles and experiences. Considerations of self arise during periods of personal change or unstructured situations, which lack clear-cut recipes for action, such as adolescence and old age. Rosenberg (1965) states that there is a heightened awareness of the self during adolescence because (1) many major decisions are made during this period, (2) it is a time of unusual amounts of personal change, and (3) it is characterized by unusual status ambiguity. Similarly, aging involves an unusual amount of personal change and status ambiguity, as well as a cluster of negative stereotypes in some societies. Thus, considerations of identity, including "age identity," are important in understanding the personal experience of aging.

Subjective Age Identity

There appears to be relative agreement that people are "old" at around 60 or 65 (see Table 3.1 in Chapter 3), but substantial proportions of the over-65 population consider themselves "young" or "middle-aged" (Riley and Foner, 1968). Results from a study conducted by the author suggest that substantial numbers of persons of even advanced age continue to resist such self-labels as "elderly" or "old" (Table 5.1).[1] This is not surprising, given the general position of the aged in American society and the negative meanings attached to growing old. Asking people if they are "elderly" is not as bad as asking them if they abuse children, but it is certainly a potentially emotional question. If you doubt this,

Table 5.1. Age identification

	Age[a]		
Age Identification	60–70	71–79	80+
Young or middle-aged	64.1	39.0	26.7
Elderly or old	35.9	61.0	73.3
Number interviewed	103	159	60

[a] Age differences in age identification are statistically significant at p = .0001.

Note: Figures are percentages of population interviewed responding to the question: "Do you think of yourself as young, middle-aged, elderly, or old?"

---

[1] Data in this chapter which lacks other citation are from Ward (1974), an interview survey of 323 noninstitutionalized residents of a Midwestern city.

try an experiment with the people you know in their fifties. Refer to them as "elderly" and see their reaction. When the dust settles, be sure to explain your intent.

What is at issue here is the problematic shift in age identification from middle-aged to old. Under what conditions do people come to conceive of themselves as old and what are the consequences of this new self-concept? Certainly age itself is a factor in age identification, but age alone is insufficient to explain shifts in age identification. Age is also partly a "proxy" for events which symbolize the onset of old age. For example, the employed 80-year-old may see himself as "middle-aged," while the retired 60-year-old has developed an "old" self-concept.

Table 5.2 lists the reasons given by one sample of older people for identifying themselves as either middle-aged or old. It is obvious that activity and health are among the most important determinants of age identity. Those who are in good health (or *feel* that they are in good health) continue to see themselves as middle-aged. Older persons can frequently pinpoint a particular incident— a heart attack, breaking a hip in a fall—which made them feel "old." Health problems need not be this dramatic to cause a realization of personal aging, however. There are many nagging physical limitations which operate as daily reminders: tiring easily, having difficulty walking or driving, finding it harder to work around the house or yard.

There are two primary reasons why health is related to age identification. First, health reflects upon one's "body image," and this is closely linked symbolically to our images of "youth" and "old age." One's appearance, for example, can be an important aspect of personal identity (Stone, 1962), and aging may first enter our awareness because of wrinkles, gray hair, and the like. The occurrence of certain health problems symbolically linked to aging—deafness, arthritis, heart problems—also triggers a change in self-concept. This symbolic link between age and health also affects people's reaction to health problems. In a study of heart attack victims, Rosen and Bibring (1966) found greater depression and anxiety among 50-year-olds than in younger or older patients. They speculated that this was due to the age-symbolic nature of the illness (see Chapter 2).

The second reason for the importance of health is its effect on activity and life style. The individual is no longer able to pursue normal activities and interests, and, in this sense, a new "me" has developed. Thus, it may not be health problems per se which results in awareness of personal aging, but rather health-related inability to maintain previous patterns of living, ushering in awareness of a new developmental stage.

Table 5.2. Reasons given for personal age identification

Identification as young or middle-aged (N = 148)	Number [a]	Percentage	Identification as elderly or old (N = 172)	Number [a]	Percentage
Still active and busy	85	59.8	Particular health problem (e.g., heart attack)	49	28.5
Good physical and/or mental health	84	59.1	Retirement	38	22.1
Positive mental attitude	41	28.9	Physical slowdown (e.g., tire easily	35	20.3
Rapport with young people	20	14.1	Health restrictions	22	12.8
Youthful appearance	12	8.4	Just age (no other reason)	20	11.6
Mix with all ages	12	8.4	Change in social contacts	10	5.8
Can still handle own affairs	10	7.0	Illness or death of spouse	10	5.8
Other	10	7.0	Other	26	15.1

[a] Each respondent could give more than one response.

A number of studies have indicated that shifts in age identification are linked to changes in status or roles (Blau, 1956; Phillips,
1957). Retirement is clearly important, but it is unclear whether
widowhood has much independent effect on age identification. A
recent national survey indicated that widowhood and other family
events are more important in defining women as "old" while retirement is more important for men (National Council on the
Aging, 1975), however, these reflect existing sex-role stereotypes
and should be viewed with some caution. For women who do
work, retirement may be as age-symbolic as for men who work.
There are a number of reasons retirement should define "old
age." It is a symbol of aging, a social event which serves as a rite
of passage. There may also be an implied lack of fitness or decline,
and retirement affects other aspects of one's pattern of living:
income declines, work-related social interaction is disrupted, and
so forth. Retirement is an event whose symbolic significance is
difficult to ignore.

There are other sources of an identity as "old," such as low
socioeconomic status and institutionalization (Peters, 1971). The
results in Table 5.2 suggest that "state of mind" also defines age:
"you're only as old as you feel." Such comments were most likely
to be made by individuals who were in poor health or had retired,
so these attitudes may reflect resistance to "objective" indicators
of old age. It is interesting that, in the same study, age identification was not related to whether individuals had positive or negative attitudes about aging and "old people." It is likely that persons
identify themselves as middle-aged through continuity and habit
until retirement or poor health disrupts that continuity and
affects age identity regardless of attitudes toward growing old.

The key factor in the perception of aging and shifts in age
identification appears to be the disruption of the individual's
normal pattern of living—the extent to which aging brings change
and the intrusiveness of that change. The primary element is the
change created in activities and in the groups and individuals with
whom the person interacts. Validation of particular aspects of the
self occurs through interaction with others and the fulfillment
of roles.

Friendship networks are important in validating self-images, and
stable friendship cliques may operate as buffers against awareness
of personal aging (Blau, 1956). The sense of continuity provided
by a stable social network prevents mutual awareness of age
changes, particularly in widowhood. But associates may also be a
source of altered age definition, particularly for those who are
retired or have fewer friends. The self-image of older persons has
greater autonomy if they can resist the isolating effects of role

exit and conserve or rebuild social resources to be less vulnerable to any one set of influences (Blau, 1973).

Loss of key roles and dropping out of or being denied access to familiar groups leads to loss of external validation of prior self-images, changes in the ways others act toward the individual and loss of prior bases of prestige. The self becomes a significant issue because of this personal change, and one's own aging becomes symbolically meaningful. An old self-identity becomes the only identity validated by the individual's own experience and by others with whom he interacts. Change in one's *social* identity triggers change in *personal* identity.

Significant change must be symbolically perceived as such before changes occur in the self. For the aged, this symbolic change, which results in shifts in age identification, is *age-related deprivation*. Feelings of *relative deprivation* come from comparisons made by the individual with other persons (Hyman, 1942). Age-related deprivation has its basis in another comparison, however—comparison of one's present status with one's condition earlier in life. Persons who are "objectively" deprived (for example, socially isolated) may have been so throughout their lives, and such deprivations will not affect age identity because they are not linked symbolically to the aging process. Poor health will not lead to an "old" self-concept for persons who have always been in poor health, but change and deprivation linked to aging (occuring after about 55) may trigger shifts in age identity. Age-related deprivations may include widowhood, retirement, and declines in health, activity, social contacts, and income.

The perception of age-related deprivation is important not only for its impact on self-image and age identity; to the extent that it represents a realization of having entered a new stage of life— "old age"—it may initiate the developmental issues of old age discussed in Chapter 4. Feelings of age-related deprivation are also important determinants of overall life satisfaction, since they involve an assessment of one's situation relative to what had been normal and expected earlier.

Attitudes Toward Old People

What are the consequences of viewing oneself as "old"? This brings us to a consideration of the evaluative dimension of age identity. If negative stereotypes stigmatize old age, there may be a number of negative consequences for older people. Such stereo-types may lead to self-derogation or become self-fulfilling; stigma may be a source of isolation or disengagement; services may be shaped by negative images of "old people." Stereotyping is a common means of dealing with an unfamiliar class of objects (Brubaker and Powers, 1976). Stereotypes shape the expectations and reactions of others and, ultimately, the social field within which the individual interacts. Regardless of their truth, they have important implications for the stereotyped person.

Old Age in Literature

Even in cultures which have venerated the aged, such as ancient Greece and the Puritan colonies of America, literary treatment of old age has been ambivalent, mixing respect with resentment, conflict, satire, and ridicule (de Beauvoir, 1972; Fischer, 1977). The Puritans, for example, referred to senility and the moral failings of the elderly, as in the character of the "old miser." In twentieth-century American literature, old age is rarely a central theme, which Fischer attributes to declining status of the aged and a rising "cult of youth." He notes four major motifs in modern literary treatment of old age. The least prevalent is the young spirit conquering age, as in Ernest Hemingway's *Old Man and the Sea*. More common are themes involving the pathos of age, the emptiness of old age, and the use of old age as a revelation of the absurdity of life itself. That old age is seen as pathetic, rather than tragic, is important.

> Old age in modern American literature is not the stuff of tragedy. A truly tragic hero must have strength and dignity and purpose. But old age in twentieth-century fiction has been denied all of those qualities. When old age appears at all in a literary work, it is apt to be not tragic, but pathetic. The central theme is the weakness and dependence of age. (Fischer, 1977:124–25)

Although old age has probably always been regarded with ambivalence, there appears to be a continuing decline in the status of old age in modern literature. One study of popular magazine fiction from 1890 to 1955 concluded that there had been a "shift in the sociological prime-of-life from mature middle age (in 1890) to young adulthood (in 1955)" (Martel, 1968:56). In the more recent stories, the post-40 years were seen as anticlimactic, with a greater emphasis on competition with youth. Perhaps the most striking trend seen in Martel's study is the relative disappearance of aged characters. Studies of children's books have found similar trends (Seltzer and Atchley, 1971; Ansello and Letzler, 1975; Peterson and Karnes, 1976). Older persons are either seldom portrayed or their roles in the stories are restricted and passive. We should be careful about overemphasizing negative treatment of the aged, however. When they do appear, older characters are quite often positive. The problem is the relative invisibility of them and their real problems.

> What may be more important than the direct negative stereotyping, is the indirect picture of the older population that is shown. In an overwhelming number of cases, older people were portrayed as only shadows who moved into and out of the major flow of the story at expeditious times. . . . Problems which face real older people each day were not recognized nor struggled with in the books. Older adults led a quiet, self-sufficient life, affecting few people and being seldom affected by others. In fact, the older persons seldom really existed in the eyes of others but quietly wandered through the pages, without trouble, gratification, or suffering. (Peterson and Karnes, 1976: 230)

Aging and Television

The relative invisibility of old age in literature is echoed in network television programs. One analysis of programming from 1969 to 1971 found that older persons constituted less than 5 percent of the characters and they were more likely to be portrayed as "bad guys" (Arnoff, 1974). Another study found that the aged appeared in only 1.5 percent of all portrayals, mostly in minor roles (Northcott, 1975). While there was no particular emphasis on the problems encountered by older people, Northcott found a tendency to idealize vigor, attractiveness, and competence, and portray being "too young" or "too old" as undesirable.

It may be, however, that aging is becoming a more viable subject for television, as even situation comedies are beginning to deal with real and controversial issues (Davis, 1975). Older characters have been prominent in such recent shows as "Chico and the Man," "Sanford and Son," and "Fish." Two examples are particularly relevant. A program of a few years back—"A Touch of Grace" starring Shirley Booth—is one of the few to offer a realistic (for television) and sensitive portrayal of older persons as the major characters. Unfortunately, it was canceled. More recently, the character of Mother Dexter on "Phyllis" (since canceled) offered an extremely interesting portrayal. It "allowed" an older person (an 86-year-old woman) to be pushy, cantankerous, and her own person, without being condescending. We laughed *with* Mother Dexter, not *at* her. One episode had Mother Dexter moving into a trailer with an older man as an expression of their desire to be independent and treated as adults, not superannuated children. This was treated humorously, of course, but the humor broke the old age stereotypes rather than being directed *against* the aged. When her middle-aged son accused them of "living in sin," Mother Dexter replied: "Not yet—but we're working on it!" Tragically, Judith Lowry, the actress who portrayed Mother Dexter, died recently.

A recent Harris poll found that most television watchers feel that television presents a "fair picture" of older people, though they were more critical of portrayals in commercials, and those 65 and over were more likely to feel this way (National Council on the Aging, 1976). It is not clear what is meant by a "fair picture," however. Is the general invisibility of the aged and their problems "fair"? The portrayals of older people often tend to be humorous, as Johnny Carson's "Aunt Blabby," or idealized, as Grandma and Grandpa Walton. The Harris poll found that half of television watchers could name older persons on television who were ad-mired—the Walton grandparents, Bob Hope, and Robert Young ("Marcus Welby")—but such portrayals hardly seem typical of older people and their position in society. It is interesting to note that respondents over 65 were *less* likely than younger people to mention the Waltons and more likely to mention Lawrence Welk. Perhaps the Waltons present an idealized image of old age held by the young, which is less appropriate from the point of view of real older persons.

Aging and Humor

Humor is another type of medium for cultural communication. Palmore's (1971) analysis of humor found that 56 percent of a sample of jokes about old age were negative, while 27 percent were positive, and 17 percent neutral. Jokes about women were more negative than men and dealt with different subjects, such as age concealment and being an old maid—for example, comparing an "old maid" to "a lemon who has never been squeezed." For men, longevity, sex, retirement, and mental ability were the major topics, as with Oscar Wilde's comment that "Young men want to be faithful and are not; old men want to be faithless and cannot." It is interesting that portrayals of disengagement tended to be linked with negative jokes, while activity was seen in a more positive light.

Two more recent studies have also found humor about aging to be largely negative (Richman, 1977; Davies, 1977). Richman, for example, found that 66 percent of a sample of jokes about older people were negative or critical, while 70 percent of jokes about children were positive. The most prominent negative themes in this study involved lying about one's age, loss of attractiveness, physical or mental decline, and sexual decline. The most frequent positive themes involved sexual activity as an affirmation of life and the depiction of aging as a value in its own right.

These studies of humor hardly offer definitive statements on the position of the aged in modern societies. They are characterized by haphazard sampling of jokes, and the underlying meanings of jokes are often not clear-cut (Weber and Cameron, 1978). Nevertheless, they do add to the evidence that the images of aging are relatively negative.

Societal Attitudes About Aging

Cross-cultural studies presented in Chapter 3 indicate that the position of the aged varies according to the nature of the society and its particular age stratification system. It is rarely age itself which yields respect, however. Ethnological and historical data seem to suggest that most societies view old age as tragic, ludicrous, revolting, or some combination of these (de Beauvoir, 1972), and Cowgill's (1974) model of the effects of modernization certainly suggests that this is likely to be true of modern industrialized societies.

Numerous studies have attempted by various methods to measure attitudes toward aging and old people (McTavish, 1971; Bennett and Eckman, 1973). These studies indicate that "old age" is a meaningful concept of which somewhat distinctive and largely negative perceptions are held. Stereotypes include

> . . . views that old people are generally ill, tired, not sexually interested, mentally slower, forgetful, and less able to learn new things, grouchy, withdrawn, feeling sorry for themselves, less likely to participate in activities (except, perhaps, religion), isolated, in the least happy or fortunate time of life, unproductive, and defensive in various combinations and with varying emphases. (McTavish, 1971:97)

These images may even be resistant to cross-generational interaction. One study, for example, found that physical proximity, frequency of contact, and intimacy of contact with older persons did not break down stereotypes held by students (Drake, 1957).

Robert Butler has gone so far as to refer to *ageism*: "a deep and profound prejudice against the elderly which is found to some degree in all of us" (Butler, 1975:11). He argues that ageism makes it easier to ignore the problems of the aged and see them as different from ourselves, perhaps less than "human." This may be true generally of people whom we stigmatize:

We believe the person with a stigma is *not quite human*. On this assumption we exercise varieties of discrimination, through which we effectively, if often *unthinkingly*, reduce his life chances. (Goffman, 1963:5, emphasis added)

The disengagement of older people, for whatever reason, and their invisibility in the media encourage such feelings. Butler sees ageism reflected in a wide range of phenomena: stereotypes and myths, age discrimination, avoidance, epithets and jokes.

More important, perhaps, than individual ageism is *institutional ageism*, the extent to which institutional structures, including the age stratification system, place the aged at a disadvantage, though possibly unintentionally. Retirement is certainly not meant to create poverty, but it does so for some older people. Similarly, the ways in which educational, social, and religious institutions are structured may unintentionally deny the aged access to meaningful roles and activities (see Chapter 7).

We must again be careful, however, about exaggerating negative images of old age and old people. The danger of doing this can be seen in the results of a poll commissioned by the National Council on the Aging (1975). Responses to one set of questions concerning what people felt were the "best" and "worst" years of a person's life show that the sixties and seventies were most often considered the worst life period and least often as the best (Table 5.3). This was as true of older people as younger people. But the study also indicated that each part of the life course carried its own blend of rewards and costs, and most people could find both good and bad aspects of every age period.

Table 5.3. Attitudes in a national sample about the "best" and "worst" years of a person's life (percentage of population)

	"Best" years		"Worst" years	
	18–64	65+	18–64	65+
Teens	16	7	20	10
20s	33	17	5	7
30s	24	22	3	5
40s	13	17	3	3
50s	3	8	6	4
60s	1	6	12	14
70s	0	2	21	21
Other	1	2	6	7
Wouldn't choose any age	7	15	17	22
Not sure	2	4	7	7

Source: *The Myth and Reality of Aging in America,* © 1975, a study prepared for The National Council on the Aging, Inc. (NCOA), Washington, D.C. by Louis Harris and Associates, Inc., pp. 2, 12. Reprinted by permission.

Youth (the teens and twenties) was valued as a time of few responsibilities and pressures, allowing for more enjoyment of life, but was also seen as an unsettled age, lacking maturity or wisdom. Middle age (the forties and fifties) was valued because of financial security, children being grown and on their own, and the wisdom and experience of maturity, but its perceived costs included possible illness and a sense of going downhill. The rewards attributed to the sixties and seventies were surprisingly similar to those of youth: lack of responsibilities and pressures, and greater freedom to enjoy life. But the perceptions of old age which led people to define it as the worst period of life were illness, financial problems, inability to get around, and loneliness.

The images of old people revealed in this study were also not uniformly negative. It was generally felt that "most people over 65" are "very" "friendly and warm" and "wise from experience." On the other hand, most older people were considered only "somewhat" "good at getting things done," "bright and alert," or "open-minded and adaptable." Unfortunately, the study offers no views of persons under 65 for comparison.

We should not expect people to have monolithically views about aging. Aging is a mixed experience, as is all of the life course. The complexity of attitudes toward old people is further illustrated by a study which found that, while a representative 70-year-old was viewed unfavorably, particular older persons (presented through pictures and autobiographies) were judged more self-accepting, satisfied, adjusted, and adaptable than 25-year-olds (Weinberger and Millham, 1975). Some groups may have more positive images of the aged than others, including young people (Thorson, Whatley, and Hancock, 1974), persons with more education (Thorson, 1975), and blacks (Wylie, 1971). It is also true that not all older people hold negative stereotypes about old age and age-linked events, such as retirement (Brubaker and Powers, 1976). Finally, rejection of the aged as a group does not necessarily imply rejection of older people actually encountered. Stigmatized people frequently meet with more accepting responses than they expect, as was found in a study of homosexuals (Weinberg and Williams, 1974).

Seltzer and Atchley (1971) have suggested that social gerontologists have been overly sensitive to negative stereotypes about old age. There is some truth to this criticism, particularly in light of changing cohorts of older people. The aged in modern societies are increasingly better off regarding health, education, and income, and the public views current older people as more "independent and resourceful" than older people 10 or 20 years ago (National

Council on the Aging, 1975). In at least some segments of American society, the aged are becoming a visible and contented leisure class as our stress on productivity and the work ethic seems to be softening (Neugarten and Hagestad, 1976). Recognition of ageism has itself resulted in efforts to overcome negative stereotypes and age discrimination (Eisele, 1974).

While accuracy demands a more balanced view than the earlier stress on negative stereotypes about aging, we must also avoid an overly optimistic stance. Although relative deprivation among the aged has declined, it still exists. Chapter 2 presents ample documentation of the problems which still face many older people, often to a greater extent than the young or middle-aged. And while images of old age have also probably been improving in recent years, there is still evidence that negative stereotypes about old age and old people continue to exist. Since this is an important aspect of the aging experience, we need to understand its sources and potential consequences.

Sources of Old Age Attitudes

There are two major sources of images concerning old age and old people. The first is the social structure within which aging occurs and the nature of the age stratification system. Societies value certain qualities and roles and reward those who possess them. As noted in Chapter 3, the status of the aged is undermined by modernization because of retirement systems, perceived obsolescence of older occupations, urbanization, and mass education (Cowgill, 1974). Any stigma attached to growing old must be seen in relation to what is valued in American society and presumed lost by the aged. This society can still be characterized by an "achievement syndrome," which emphasizes activity, personal productivity, independence (self-reliance), and future time orientation (Linden, 1957). These attitudes relate directly to loss of occupation, widowhood, poor health, and other changes which may accompany aging. The older person who has lost the major roles of productivity and independence is judged to be ineffective in contributing to the goals of society, and unique roles, such as guardian of the culture or family advisor, are no longer valued or available. One available role, leisure, is seen as something for the socially immature or those no longer capable of playing "important" roles (Miller, 1965).

The second source of negative images of old age and old people is our fear of old age and the problems we associate with it: low socioeconomic status, poor health, loneliness, senility, death (Bennett and Eckman, 1973). In Chapter 2 it is suggested that such fears are often exaggerated, but this itself contributes to the problem:

> Exaggerations of the problems of old age might instill in the young a deep-seated fear of growing old. They might force the young to struggle to look and act "young," thus inhibiting maturity and preventing the young from enjoying the natural and rewarding process of aging. They may cause fears of aging that inhibit normal, rational planning for their later years. (National Council on the Aging, 1976:39)

Negative attitudes toward poor health and death are apparently good predictors of devaluation of old age (Collette-Pratt, 1976), as well as financial problems, reduced mobility, retirement, and loneliness. Many of these fears relate to the value attached to independence. Self-reliance and autonomy are deeply engrained values, and we prize our independence very highly. We are socialized to see those who are dependent as inferior, as is reflected in the stigma attached to recipients of public welfare. The importance of independence is stressed in finances, housing, personal mobility, and family relationships. These attitudes affect not only our image of the aged but also the self-image and behavior of older persons themselves. One study found that:

> Some of the aged in our sample feel that, if help can be obtained only at the expense of institutionalization, if the small sphere of respectable autonomy that constitutes the aged person's shrunken life-space can be punctured like a child's balloon— then it may be best to gamble on one's own with survival. Such people will draw their curtains to avoid critical appraisals of their helplessness; they will not get enough to eat; they will stay away from the doctor and forgo even vital drugs; they will shiver with cold; they will live in filth and squalor—but pride they will relinquish only as a last resort. (Clark and Anderson, 1967:391)

Illness is a legitimate reason for escaping obligations, however, and as such may be used by some as a "face-saving social fiction" to justify their retirement and rolelessness (Blau, 1973). It is also a mechanism for gaining attention and sympathy from family and friends. The sick role is intended to be temporary, however, and its prolonged use will alienate the older person from those around him. Additionally, there may be a tendency to allocate the aged in general into a "terminal sick role" (Lipman and Sterne, 1969), viewing old age as a period of progressive decline in both physical and mental health, with little or no possibility of recovery. This contributes to the stereotype of dependency and rapid decline from maturity to immaturity and to low status for those who care for and treat the aged.

Consequences of Old Age Stereotypes

That stereotypes about old age are important is reflected in debate over the "correct" label for older persons. The study conducted by the National Council on the Aging found considerable disagreement about such terms as "senior citizen," "elderly," and "old timer" (Table 5.4). The obvious dislike of the term "old" certainly implies some stigma attached to the aging process. Age identity is a critical issue to the extent that old age carries a stigma related to the age stratification of roles. Old age, as other types of stigma such as blindness or homosexuality, is viewed as a *master status trait*, defined by the fact that "Possession of one deviant trait may have a generalized symbolic value, so that people automatically assume that its bearer possesses other undersirable traits allegedly associated with it" (Becker, 1963:33). The master status trait is seen as the primary identifying characteristic of the individual. One is not a person who happens to be old, but an "old person," and assumed to have other attributes because of this.

Table 5.4. Terms by which people 65 and over like to be referred to (percentages)

	Like	Don't like	Doesn't matter	Not sure	Prefer
A senior citizen	50	15	34	1	33
A retired person	53	12	34	1	12
A mature American	55	13	30	2	13
An elderly person	38	30	31	1	6
A middle-aged person	37	25	34	4	3
An older American	37	28	33	2	3
A golden ager	27	36	33	4	3
An old timer	26	45	27	2	4
An aged person	19	50	30	1	1
An old man/old woman	8	67	24	1	1
None of these					3
Doesn't matter					12
Not sure					2

Source: *The Myth and Reality of Aging in America,* © 1975, a study prepared for The National Council on the Aging, Inc. (NCOA), Washington, D.C. by Louis Harris and Associates, Inc., p. 228. Reprinted by permission.

This can affect the social and psychological world of the older person in a number of ways because of the impact on the perceptions and reactions of others. Older people may be excluded from various groups and activities because of their age, making them increasingly isolated. Societal reactions toward the aged may be a cause of disengagement. Old age becomes for many a time of potential embarrassment. Older people may become aware of carrying a stigma, and be afraid to enter social situations in which they may be unable to reciprocate or perform properly and be without knowledge available to younger persons (Miller, 1965). Erving Goffman, in discussing the reaction of individuals to a "spoiled identity," notes that "shame becomes a central possibility" (Goffman, 1963:7), making stigmatized individuals hypersensitive to the reactions of others. Goffman further notes that "normals" may also be uneasy in such situations and attempt to avoid them. Persons who are crippled or blind often face this dilemma. Thus, disengagement can be viewed as a mutual withdrawal from uneasy and potentially embarrassing situations by young and old.

Stereotypes about old age may affect the behavior of older people in a variety of other ways. Older persons appear to internalize and accept the negative meanings attached to aging and view age as a reasonable criterion for evaluating behavior. We develop images of old age during our youth, which haunt us when we carry them into our own old age. To the extent that the aged are expected to be different and act differently, they will be ostracized if they step out of the "role."

> If old people show the same desires, the same feelings and the same requirements as the young, the world looks upon them with disgust; in them love and jealousy seem revolting or absurd, sexuality repulsive and violence ludicrous. (de Beauvoir, 1972:3)

Older people may accept the view of themselves as significantly different from "normal" persons—less vigorous and creative, less productive and efficient—and of old age as a time of decline in which they must forsake many normal pursuits, and act in such a way as to make the stereotypes true. The stereotype of the "sexless older years" is a case in point (Rubin, 1968). Masters and Johnson (1966) found a decline with age in male sexual performance, but attributed this primarily to social-psychological factors. Stereotypes that sexual intercourse is no longer possible and older people should not be interested in "such things" and the cultural link between youth and sexual attractiveness all contribute to the decline of sexual activity.

Sex Differences

It is not entirely clear whether men or women are hit harder by old age stereotypes. Given the nature of sex roles in modern societies, their relative dilemmas probably spring from different sources. Men have traditionally been more closely involved in the "achievement syndrome," and their major identity is the provider. Retirement ends this role and undercuts their source of prestige and power. A study by Neugarten and Gutmann (1958) asked a sample of adults to write stories about a picture containing two couples, one young and one old. This was generally viewed as a family scene, traditionally defined as the female's domain. As the respondent's age increased, the "old man" was increasingly portrayed as passive and submissive, while perception of the "old woman" moved from a subordinate to an authoritative family role, which suggests that older men lose their position of prestige and dominance.

There are also persuasive arguments, however, that aging is a more difficult experience for women. Many of our images of old woman are far from complimentary: old bag, old maid, hag, biddy (Lewis and Butler, 1972; Preston, 1975). The importance of physical attractiveness in defining the "worth" of a woman means that aging can have a particularly devastating effect (Sontag, 1975). The "double standard of aging" is particularly evident in sexual attitudes relating to older women.

> They are the neuters of our culture who have mysteriously metamorphosed from desirable young sex objects to mature, sexually "interesting" women, and finally, at about age 50, they descend in steady decline to sexual oblivion. This is the way society sees it. But this is not the way a lot of old women see it. They don't understand why older men can be considered "sexy" but never older women. They are angered that old men can attract younger women and be commended for their prowess whereas older women are seen as "depraved" or "grasping for lost youth" when they show an interest in sex at all, let alone younger men. . . . Yet in spite of their capacities, older women have limited sexual outlets. They have been trained and locked in by the culture to accept the idea that they are no longer desirable sexual partners and that only younger women have sexual perogatives. We are all familiar with the origins of this idea—namely that women are sexy as long as they are young and pretty and able to enhance a man's feelings of status and power. (Lewis and Butler, 1972:227)

Despite this rather bleak portrayal, Lewis and Butler also note that older women have a great potential for liberation because they are often free from many of the demands—childrearing and marriage—which may limit the personal expression of younger women.

The Impact of Age Identity

Regardless of which sex is hit harder by aging, both will be affected to some degree by societal reaction to aging and old people. Again, old age can be thought of as a type of stigma, which "discredits" its possessor (Goffman, 1963). Goffman has described three basic types of stigma: abominations of the body (physical deformities), blemishes of individual character (weak will or laziness), and tribal stigma (race or religion). Old age can be viewed as a combination of abominations of the body (loss of physical attractiveness, crippling chronic diseases) and blemishes of individual character (dependency, diminishing intelligence). One might even entertain the notion of old age as a tribal stigma, within the context of age stratification. Being labeled with a stigma, or labeling oneself, can critically affect self-identity and self-esteem.[2]

Individuals who are "discreditable" may, of course, attempt to deny the personal appropriateness of the label, either by denying possession of the stigmatized attribute or by "reforming." Many stigmatized attributes, such as obesity, physical disability, and old age, cannot easily be denied once the label is applied, so denial typically occurs before the fact. For example, studies indicate that the mentally retarded (Edgerton, 1967) and the blind (Strauss, 1968) may resist identification with similar others in an attempt to evade negative self-definitions. Similarly, older people may try to "pass" as young with clothing, makeup, or mannerisms. As we have seen, there is also a tendency to deny such labels as "elderly" or "old." Denial of aging may create problems, however, if it means that older people refuse to perceive problems associated with aging and are therefore unwilling to seek needed assistance.

The psychological impact of age identity for persons who come to view themselves as "elderly" or "old" because of age and age-related deprivation will depend on the meanings held by them for growing old. The psychological tension resulting from stigma can be quite profound, as illustrated by the following passage written by a homosexual:

> . . . the dominant fact in my life, towering in importance above all others, is a consciousness that I am different. . . . It is inescapable, not only this being different, but more than that, this

---

[2] For an excellent summary discussion of "labeling theory," see Schur (1971).

constant awareness of dissimilarity. . . . It is not only shame at my own debasement that demoralizes me, but a great wave of self-doubt that is infinitely more difficult to cope with. Am I genuinely as "good" as the next fellow? . . . Because I am unable to stand up before the world and acknowledge that I am what I am, because I carry around with me a fear and a shame, I find that I endanger my confidence in myself and in my way of living, and that this confidence is required for the enjoyment of life. (Cory, 1951:7, 11)

A recent study by the author suggests that attitudes toward old age and old persons have considerable effects on the self-esteem of the aged (Ward, 1977). Older respondents were presented with a series of stereotypes about "old people," resulting in a score for negative attitudes toward old people. These attitudes toward old people in general were significantly related to self-esteem, and, indeed, were the strongest predictors of self-esteem in the study, accounting for an overall decline in self-esteem with age. It is interesting that attitudes toward old people were important even for those who considered themselves "middle-aged," indicating that perhaps all persons over 60, for example, view themselves as "eligible" for the stigma they attach to being old.

The extent to which aging affects the overall self-image of individuals is still not clear. A survey mentioned earlier found that most older people considered themselves very friendly and warm, wise from experience, bright and alert, open-minded and adaptable, and good at getting things done (National Council on the Aging, 1975). The self-image of older people tended to be more favorable for whites than for blacks and for persons with higher levels of income and education. It has been argued, however, that the aged are unwilling to admit their position in modern society to others, and perhaps to themselves.

The appearance of "mellowness" in many older people is a tactic to win acceptance and support. To protest their marginality would only alienate others, and this the person without any socially useful role cannot do because he lacks the opportunities for finding alternative social resources to replace his remaining social ties . . . so the old person will pretend obliviousness to younger people's indifference and neglect in order not to jeopardize his relations with them. (Blau, 1973:154)

In summarizing findings in this area, Bennett and Eckman (1973) indicate that while results on whether self-image is positive or negative among older people are divided, there does seem to be some decline in self-image with age. They conclude that

Old people in the United States seem to hold negative views toward aging, toward the self, and toward life in general. However, it is not yet clear if this is in marked contrast to the young, the foreign aged, or to views the aged held earlier in life. (Bennett and Eckman, 1973:592)

As a final caveat, the reader must recognize that our knowledge and ideas about stereotypes of aging and their consequences (including many expressed by this author) remain highly speculative. There is a critical need to investigate the nature of old age images *as they are encountered by the aging individual*, among the people and groups with whom he or she interacts. This is an integral part of socialization for old age and must be incorporated within developmental approaches to aging and models of age stratification. As such, it is related to many other issues. How are age-related norms and expectations developed, translated, and sanctioned in the experience of aging individuals? What role models are used for successful aging? The studies we have cited about images of aging in literature and television suggest that there are relatively few positive models for older people, but perhaps they turn to other sources for guidance (see Chapter 10). To what extent is cultural imagery of aging incorporated into personal imagery, and eventually into feelings about the aging self? These are important questions which have too long been dealt with in a universalistic and speculative manner. And there is an additional need to study changing images of aging, since more recent work suggests that modern views of old age are becoming less derogatory and restrictive.

Summary

The self is a social object whose meaning is derived from interactions with others. The self-concept consists of four dimensions: cognitive, evaluative, behavioral, and self-esteem. Change will occur in these dimensions as the individual encounters and perceives change in his social world. Although self-preoccupation may decline with age, both adolescence and old age are life periods in which major personal change make considerations of the self salient.

Substantial proportions of the older population resist such labels as "elderly" and "old." Shifts in age identification occur because of age-related deprivation—perceived personal change linked symbolically to the aging process. Changes such as poor health and retirement disrupt life-style continuity and change the individual's social world, resulting in awareness of a new "me."

The aged are largely invisible in the media, and when they are portrayed it is largely in negative, passive terms. A variety of studies also indicate that largely negative stereotypes are held about "old age," though images of aging are not universally negative. The sources of such stereotypes are twofold. The status of older people is dependent on the positions they occupy in the social structure and the "achievement syndrome" of modern societies implies devaluation of the roles of the aged. An additional source of stereotypes are exaggerated fears about the problems of old age, particularly fear related to dependency.

Stereotypes about old people may be a cause of disengagement, as the aged withdraw from potentially embarrassing and discrediting social situations. They may also result in self-fulfilling prophecies, as with the stereotype of the "sexless" older years. There has been some debate about the relative impact of old age stereotypes on men and women. Men may encounter devaluation by the "achievement syndrome," while women face a double standard of aging, particularly in sexual images. Nevertheless, it is likely that both sexes encounter an old age stigma.

This stigma can have important consequences for self-identity. Older people may attempt to deny old age, but it appears that acceptance of negative stereotypes about old age results in a lowering of self-esteem. Thus, the social meanings for old age made available to the aging individual constitutes another way in which the social context affects the aging experience.

References

Ansello, E. F. and J. S. Letzler
  1975 "The depiction of the elderly in early childhood literature."
       Paper presented at the Annual Meeting of the Gerontological
       Society, Louisville, Kentucky.
Arnoff, C.
  1974 "Old age in prime time." Journal of Communication 24: 4.
Becker, Howard
  1963 Outsiders: Studies in the Sociology of Deviance. New York:
       The Free Press.
Bennett, Ruth and Judith Eckman
  1973 "Attitudes toward aging: A critical examination of recent
       literature and implications for future research." In Carl
       Eisdorfer and M. Powell Lawton (eds.). The Psychology of
       Adult Development and Aging. Washington, D.C.:
       American Psychological Association.
Blau, Zena
  1956 "Changes in status and age identification." American
       Sociological Review 21: 198–203.
  1973 Old Age in a Changing Society. New York: New
       Viewpoints.

Brubaker, Timothy and Edward Powers
  1976   "The stereotype of 'old'—A review and alternative
         approach." Journal of Gerontology 31 (4): 441–47.
Butler, Robert
  1975   Why Survive? Being Old in America. New York: Harper &
         Row.
Clark, Margaret and Barbara Anderson
  1967   Culture and Aging. Springfield, Ill.: Charles C Thomas.
Collette-Pratt, Clara
  1976   "Attitudinal predictors of devaluation of old age in a
         multigenerational sample." Journal of Gerontology 31 (2):
         193–97.
Cooley, Charles Horton
  1902   Human Nature and the Social Order. New York:
         Scribner's.
Cory, Donald
  1951   The Homosexual in America: A Subjective Approach.
         New York: Greenberg.
Cowgill, Donald
  1974   "Aging and modernization: A revision of the theory." In
         Jaber Gubrium (ed.). Late Life: Communities and
         Environmental Policies. Springfield, Ill.: Charles C Thomas.
Davies, Leland
  1977   "Attitudes toward old age and aging, as shown by humor."
         The Gerontologist 17: 220–26.
Davis, Richard
  1975   "Television communication and the elderly." In Diana
         Woodruff and James Birren (eds.). Aging: Scientific
         Perspectives and Social Issues. New York: D. Van Nostrand.
de Beauvoir, Simone
  1972   The Coming of Age. New York: Putnam's Sons.
Drake, Joseph
  1957   "Some factors influencing students' attitudes toward older
         people." Social Forces 35: 266–71.
Edgerton, Robert
  1967   The Cloak of Competence. Berkeley: University of
         California Press.
Eisele, Frederick
  1974   "Age discrimination: Definitions, victims, techniques."
         Paper presented at the Annual Meeting of the American
         Sociological Association, Montreal.
Fischer, David
  1977   Growing Old in America. New York: Oxford University
         Press.
Goffman, Erving
  1963   Stigma: Notes on the Management of Spoiled Identity.
         Englewood Cliffs, N.J.: Prentice-Hall.

Hickman, C. Addison and Manford Kuhn
   1956   Individuals, Groups, and Economic Behavior. New York:
          Dryden Press.
Hyman, Herbert
   1942   "The psychology of status." Archives of Psychology
          38: No. 269.
Kinch, John
   1963   "A formalized theory of the self-concept." American
          Journal of Sociology 68: 481–86.
Lewis, Myrna and Robert Butler
   1972   "Why is women's lib ignoring old women?" Aging and
          Human Development 3: 223–31.
Linden, Maurice
   1957   "Effects of social attitudes on the mental health of the
          aging." Geriatrics 12: 109–14.
Lipman, Aaron and Richard Sterne
   1969   "Aging in the United States: Ascription of a terminal sick
          role." Sociology and Social Research 53: 194–203.
Martel, Martin
   1968   "Age-sex roles in American magazine fiction (1890–1955)."
          In Bernice Neugarten (ed.). Middle Age and Aging.
          Chicago: University of Chicago Press.
Masters, William and Virginia Johnson
   1966   Human Sexual Response. Boston: Little, Brown.
McTavish, Donald
   1971   "Perceptions of old people: A review of research
          methodologies and findings." The Gerontologist 11 (4):
          90–101.
Miller, Stephen
   1965   "The social dilemma of the aging leisure participant." In
          Arnold Rose and Warren Peterson (eds.). Older People
          and Their Social World. Philadelphia: F. A. Davis.
National Council on the Aging
   1975   The Myth and Reality of Aging in America.
          Washington, D.C.
Neugarten, Bernice and David Gutmann
   1958   "Age-sex roles and personality in middle age: A thematic
          apperception study." Psychological Monographs 72 (17).
Neugarten, Bernice and Gunhild Hagestad
   1976   "Age and the life course." In Robert Binstock and Ethel
          Shanas (eds.). Handbook of Aging and the Social Sciences.
          New York: Van Nostrand Reinhold.
Northcott, Herbert
   1975   "Too young, too old—Age in the world of television."
          The Gerontologist 15 (2): 184–86.
Palmore, Erdman
   1971   "Attitudes toward aging as shown by humor." The
          Gerontologist 3 (3): 181–86.

Peters, George
  1971 "Self-conceptions of the aged, age identification, and aging."
        The Gerontologist 11 (4): 69–73.
Peterson, David and Elizabeth Karnes
  1976 "Older people in adolescent literature." The Gerontologist
        16: 225–31.
Phillips, Bernard
  1957 "A role theory approach to adjustment in old age."
        American Sociological Review 22: 212–17.
Preston, Caroline
  1975 "An old bag: The stereotype of the older woman." In No
        Longer Young: The Older Woman in America. Occasional
        Papers in Gerontology No. 11, Institute of Gerontology,
        The University of Michigan-Wayne State University.
Richman, Joseph
  1977 "The foolishness and wisdom of age: Attitudes toward the
        elderly as reflected in jokes." The Gerontologist 17:
        210–19.
Riley, Matilda and Anne Foner
  1968 Aging and Society. Volume 1: An Inventory of Research
        Findings. New York: Russell Sage.
Rosen, Jacqueline and Grete Bibring
  1966 "Psychological reactions of hospitalized male patients to a
        heart attack: Age and social-class differences." Psychoso-
        matic Medicine 28 (6).
Rosenberg, Morris
  1965 Society and the Adolescent Self-Image. Princeton, N.J.:
        Princeton University Press.
Rubin, Isadore
  1968 "The 'sexless older years'—A socially harmful stereotype."
        The Annals of the American Academy of Political and
        Social Sciences 376: 86–95.
Schur, Edwin
  1971 Labeling Deviant Behavior: Its Sociological Implications.
        New York: Harper & Row.
Secord, Paul and Carl Backman
  1974 Social Psychology. New York: McGraw-Hill.
Seltzer, Mildred and Robert Atchley
  1971 "The concept of old: Changing attitudes and stereotypes."
        The Gerontologist 11: 226–30.
Sontag, Susan
  1975 "The double standard of aging." In No Longer Young: The
        Older Woman in America. Occasional Papers in Gerontology
        No. 11, Institute of Gerontology, The University of
        Michigan-Wayne State University.
Stone, Gregory
  1962 "Appearance and the self." In Arnold Rose (ed.). Human
        Behavior and Social Processes. Boston: Houghton Mifflin.

Strauss, Anselm
   1962   "Transformations of identity." In Arnold Rose (ed.).
          Human Behavior and Social Processes. Boston: Houghton
          Mifflin.
Strauss, Helen
   1968   "Reference group and social comparison processes among
          the totally blind." In Herbert Hyman and Eleanor Singer
          (eds.). Readings in Reference Group Theory and Research.
          New York: The Free Press.
Thorson, James
   1975   "Attitudes toward the aged as a function of race and social
          class." The Gerontologist 15 (4): 343–44.
Thorson, James, Lynda Whatley, and Karen Hancock
   1974   "Attitudes toward the aged as a function of age and educa-
          tion." The Gerontologist 14 (4): 316–18.
Ward, Russell
   1974   "Growing old: Stigma, identity, and subculture." Ph.D.
          Dissertation, Sociology. University of Wisconsin.
   1977   "The impact of subjective age and stigma on older persons."
          Journal of Gerontology 32: 227–32.
Weber, Timothy and Paul Cameron
   1978   "Comment: Humor and aging—a response." The
          Gerontologist 18:73–76.
Weinberg, Martin and Colin Williams
   1974   Male Homosexuals: Their Problems and Adaptations.
          New York: Oxford University Press.
Weinberger, Linda and Jim Millham
   1975   "A multi-dimensional, multiple method analysis of attitudes
          toward the elderly." Journal of Gerontology 30 (3):
          343–48.
Wylie, Floyd
   1971   "Attitudes toward aging and the aged among black
          Americans: Some historical perspectives." Aging and
          Human Development 2 (1): 66–70.

6

Work and Retirement

$\sim\sim\sim\sim\sim\sim\sim\sim\sim\sim\sim\sim\sim\sim\sim$

The twin issues of work and retirement have probably been the most studied aspects of aging, and with retirement have come a number of other issues: the meaningfulness of leisure, the adequacy of retirement income, declining status related to "nonproductive" roles. Whether a particular older person, or older people in general, works or retires, is a major determinant of the aging experience. Retirement systems create new age strata, allocating the aged into new roles (and out of former roles). Retirement also creates new symbolic meanings for the aging process.

The attention given to retirement by social gerontologists is certainly warranted. Work and work-related values shape the life course in many ways, so retirement is a major transition. One cannot understand the developmental issues of old age without understanding the nature of work and retirement. Retirement is also a central component of the modern age stratification system. Many people have argued that, for better or worse, retirement defines the status of the aged in modern societies and sets off the modern aging experience from that of nonindustrial societies.

Until quite recently, retirement has been viewed as a crisis having profound social and psychological consequences in the lives of older persons. This stems from the assumption that work constitutes the central life interest at least for most men and that the work ethic requires one to work to be considered worthwhile. But the impact of retirement is often surprisingly benign, and many of our beliefs about work and retirement are facing serious challenges. Because of this, many of our traditional theories of aging are being exposed as myths which may have been true once but no longer fit current realities. Some of the issues which have been raised go to the very heart of the structure of the life course in modern societies and presage future changes in the nature of the aging experience. Before discussing retirement, however, we first need to look at the work experiences of older people.

Work and Aging

Although retirement has become the norm for persons over 65, approximately 25 percent of older males and 10 percent of older females do continue to work. They often work only part-time, however. In 1969, for example, nearly one-third of all employed males 65 and over worked 26 weeks or less during the year (U.S. Bureau of the Census, 1973). Nonetheless, work continues to be an important role for many older persons.

Certain types of people are more likely to continue working: those with high levels of education, high occupational status, and those who are still married (Riley and Foner, 1968). Occupations themselves vary in age structure. Older workers are overrepresented among such groups as managerial and sales workers, bus drivers, clergy, and welfare workers and underrepresented among skilled craftsmen, nurses, and clerks (National Council on the Aging, 1975; Smith, 1975). Such age differences reflect a matching of job demands to age-related abilities and characteristics and historical factors affecting recruitment and retirement policies. Some job-related abilities can resist age decrements better than others. Physical age declines, for example, are more likely than intellectual ones. Other considerations include the ability to make one's own decisions about work and retirement (as with the self-employed), whether the job allows some reduction in workload, the need to continue working (income and family considerations), and satisfactions derived from work.

Work Performance

One of the greatest difficulties older workers face is the stereotype of declining performance because of poor health or intellectual failings. Such stereotypes form implicit and explicit bases for age bias in hiring and compulsory retirement policies, but they have little basis in fact. While there are numerous difficulties in measuring age differences in capacity or performance, and there is a lack of longitudinal studies, the accumulated evidence suggests that older workers perform as well as, if not better than, younger workers from a number of standpoints (Riley and Foner, 1968; Meier and Kerr, 1976; Sheppard, 1976; Welford, 1977).

Older workers appear to maintain consistency and accuracy, perhaps using their experience to offset any physical decline. Studies of work involving physical effort, such as factory work, show some decline in productivity with age, but the physical strenuousness of most work has declined over the past 50 years and the physical demands of most work appear to be well within the capabilities of normal aging workers. Individual variability among older workers is considerable, and many can exceed the performance of many younger workers. Studies also indicate no decline in attendance rates; even illness absenteeism shows little increase with age. Nor is there any general rise in work-related injuries, though it has been suggested that accidents preventable by good judgment decline with age while those preventable by a rapid response may increase. A study of agricultural accidents found significant increases with age in accidents caused by falls or being hit by falling or moving objects, but declines in accidents caused by being caught in machinery and injuries inflicted by one's own tools (King, 1955). However, injured older workers tend to be disabled longer.

There are also a number of indications that older workers are more attached to their jobs than younger workers (Riley and Foner, 1968). They are less likely to switch jobs and more likely to be committed to the work they do. For example, one study found that the proportion saying they would rather do some other kind of work declined from 52 percent among workers 21 to 34 years old to 25 percent among workers 55 and older. Older workers are also more likely to report job satisfaction. It may be that younger workers are still searching for their "niche," while older workers have either found theirs or given up the hunt. These results may also reflect built-up commitments or an unwillingness to admit making the wrong decisions. Finally, older workers may simply recognize the tenuousness of their position, given the difficulties they would encounter in finding another job due to age biases in hiring practices. It should be noted that older workers have a slightly lower sense of occupational adequacy than younger workers and a lower expectation of future advancement. They may be showing a willingness to settle for what they can get.

It is enlightening that many persons continue to work, or return to work following retirement from their primary occupation. As many as one-fourth of those "retired" continue to work part-time, usually within the same broad occupational category as their full-time jobs. Such persons are more likely to have negative orientations toward retirement and have been involuntarily retired, feel economically deprived, and view work as a major source of satisfaction (Streib and Schneider, 1971; Fillenbaum and Maddox, 1974). Streib and Schneider note that these motivating factors must be accompanied by certain enabling factors, primarily good health and white-collar occupation. The latter presumably provides certain job-seeking skills and a wider range of job opportunities in which physical strength is of little relevance.

A recent Harris poll indicated that nearly one-third of those over 65 who were not working would like to work (even more among low-income groups) (National Council on the Aging, 1975). Health was a major barrier, however, and only 20 percent said they would possibly consider actually going back to work. The authors suggest that this may reflect a learned disinterest in work, perhaps attributable to societal expectations or perceived age discrimination.

Retraining and Job Redesign

While older workers seem to perform well, problems associated with aging may drive them prematurely from the labor force. The likelihood of handicaps in health and physical strength increases with age. In addition, the work role may deteriorate around the individual as he ages, with the infusion of newly trained workers and technical improvements, the creation of new occupations, or the reorganization of work roles (Riley, Johnson, and Foner, 1972). The handicap to work created by these factors is often unnecessarily high, however. Standards of health and education set by employers are sometimes too high or irrelevant to the job, needlessly disqualifying many older workers. Society, rather than aging, creates obsolescence through the lack of retraining and an unwillingness to fit jobs to people rather than people to existing jobs.

As one solution to this problem, there has been considerable interest within industrial gerontology in *functional age* (Sheppard, 1976). This entails a close look at the particular abilities and experience of any older worker, which can then be used either to match the individual to an existing job or to redesign jobs to fit his capacities. Such approaches imply a recognition that chronological age tells us little about an individual and changes which do occur with age need not be handicapping if there is a willingness to modify the work or the workplace.

An alternative approach for older workers involves retraining to compensate for job obsolescence. While some studies indicate that retraining may be more difficult for older workers, there is no doubt that it can be successful, perhaps as successful as for younger workers, and that occupational obsolescence is not inevitable or irremediable (Riley and Foner, 1968; Sheppard, 1976). Training programs for older workers must, however, be geared to their unique characteristics and capacities. Because of older workers' anxiety, lack of self-confidence, and tenuous learning skills related to low education and the length of time since their last educational experience, the techniques used for training younger people are often inappropriate. One successful approach involves such methods as treating learning as a "game," breaking learning into smaller, simpler components, using rapid feedback, and allowing for self-pacing (Belbin and Belbin, 1968; Sheppard, 1976). Tailoring approaches to the older worker may be more colstly, though, as is job redesign, and this cost is itself a barrier to the employment of older workers. Failure to use such techniques, however, means that "continued reliance on the conventional methods of teaching and training older persons may only serve to perpetuate the stereotypes about 'old dogs not being able to learn new tricks' and thus compound the problems of older workers" (Sheppard, 1976:298).

Older workers might be reluctant to seek retraining, because they are unwilling to admit their skills are obsolete or lack confidence in their ability to learn new skills (Belbin and Belbin, 1968). Retraining must acquire greater "respectability" to be successful, perhaps by building continual learning into the entire work career. As it is, the need for retraining may be viewed as stigmatizing. Despite such feelings, however, the study commissioned by the National Council on the Aging (1975) found that 37 percent of workers between 55 and 64 indicated an interest in learning new skills or participating in job training programs. Greater advantage should be taken of such feelings by directing programs to the particular needs of older workers.

Actually, workers of all ages would benefit from greater availability of retraining options. For the most part, all of our educational experience occurs early in life and is directed toward preparing us for a life-long occupation, but "mid-career crises" and the desire for a second career seem to be increasing.

> Several societal developments seem to be at the heart of this phenomenon. The first of these is the increasing rate of change in our society—technological, economic, and cultural—that modern man finds so unsettling. Related to this "future shock" is the fact that commitment to one life-long occupation is no longer as feasible as it was in the past: "Once a coal miner, always a coal miner" is no longer a valid description in an age when the mine is quite likely to close down. A second factor is quite simply that workers are living longer; a forty-year working life is a great amount of time to devote to one career. Third, the general increase in expectations and in general education

has left many workers with high aspirations in low-level jobs. For such workers a career change can be an avenue to mobility, self-actualization, and job satisfaction. (U.S. Department of Health, Education, and Welfare, 1973:123)

Growing numbers of persons are seeking greater flexibility in their options, whether through the "time-out" phenomenon in colleges or radical mid-life career changes (Sarason, 1977). Sarason cites the example of a small "New Careers" program for professionals at Columbia University which was inundated with 7,000 inquiries during its first year. Unfortunately, the search for self-realization and personal authenticity runs counter to the existing economic structure and the age stratification of both education and work. Lack of retraining opportunities, for example, are compounded by the likelihood of being unable to transfer any accumulated pension credits from one job to another.

Barriers to Employment

There are a number of reasons for the employment difficulties of older workers aside from "natural" physical declines and skill obsolescence. Despite protection afforded by seniority, unemployment is higher among males over 55 than younger age groups (Sheppard, 1976), often because of shutdowns of plants and industries or mass layoffs which cost older workers their seniority. Once unemployed, the older worker tends to remain unemployed longer and is more likely to exhaust unemployment compensation benefits. Unemployment statistics actually underestimate the problem, since many older workers who become discouraged and end their job-seeking are not included.

Part of the problem, of course, is that older job-seekers are often hampered by low education, poor health, or a lack of marketable skills. There are incentives against working, such as the Social Security ceiling on earnings, and many older persons are forced out of the labor force by mandatory retirement rules. There are also clear age biases which hinder older people in their attempts to gain employment.

One problem is the unwillingness of employers to hire older persons, stemming from negative stereotypes about their performance and skills and fear of the presumed costs (retraining, pension and insurance coverage, and so on). The Age Discrimination in Employment Act of 1967 was designed to protect workers between the ages of 40 and 65 against discrimination in hiring, termination, and compensation, and the most blatant forms of discrimination have declined with measures being taken against various firms. For example, in 1974 Standard Oil Company of California agreed to pay $2 million to 160 former employees who had been terminated because of age (Butler, 1975), and in 1975, a total of $7 million was paid to 2,400 older workers because of violations of the act (DeLury, 1976). Butler (1975) argues, however, that this legislation has not been enforced, and there has been no systematic evaluation of its impact (Sheppard, 1976). In addition, workers over 65 receive no protection. One study of aerospace employees suggests that age discrimination may indeed be quite widespread (Kasschau, 1976a). One-half of the sample said they had personally experienced age discrimination in finding, holding, or advancing in a job.

Age biases are also apparent in public and private employment agencies. Studies of employment service applicants indicate that older jobseekers receive fewer services—are less likely to receive testing or counseling or to be referred to job interviews or retraining programs—and are less likely to be placed successfully (Sheppard and Belitsky, 1966; Heidbreder and Batten, 1974). On the other hand, older persons themselves are less efficient or adaptive in their job-seeking efforts. One study found that older workers were less willing to change work methods or job-seeking techniques, to move to areas with better employment, to adjust salary expectations, or to engage in job retraining (Sobel and Wilcock, 1963). Older workers are apparently also handicapped by the fact that they use fewer job-seeking techniques and sources and contact fewer companies (Sheppard and Belitsky, 1966). Such differences may be related to lower achievement motivation and higher job interview anxiety among some older workers (Sheppard, 1976).

However, the major sources of employment difficulties for older workers are structural, not social-psychological—primarily skill obsolescence (aggravated by insufficient retraining possibilities) and age bias in job allocation processes. Middle age is often a time of assessment and reappraisal, but society places many barriers in front of the person who wishes to reorient his or her life. Given the relative inflexibility of the existing work and job structure, mid-career adjustments of any sort are extremely difficult. Additionally, there are wasted talents and skills of older persons. Robert Butler (1975) has made an eloquent plea that society take advantage of capacities which may be particularly evident in the aged because of their accumulated experience and age: teaching, counseling, historical information, preservation of dying crafts, and so on. Butler cites the following example as an illustration of the talents which may be overlooked:

Colonel Harlan Sanders, of Kentucky Fried Chicken fame, made his first million at age 73. A former gas station operator and restaurateur, Sanders was penniless when he retired at 65. With his first Social Security check for $105 he embarked on a promotion campaign for his recipe for fried chicken. Eight years later he sold the American and Canadian rights to the recipe for $4 million. "I went from rags to riches," he recalls. (Butler, 1975: 84–85)

This example, of course, is not typical of most older persons, but we need to question whether many useful talents and services are lying fallow because of the prevailing age stratification. Although new programs are being developed to utilize older persons (see Chapter 7), they are still quite limited in their coverage.

The Emergence of Retirement

Important changes have occurred during this century in the patterns of labor force participation by older men and women. There has been a steady decline in the proportion of males who work from over two-thirds of all males 65 and older in 1900 to less than one-fourth currently. However, since nearly one-half of all women between 55 and 64 now work, retirement can no longer be considered a solely male phenomenon. A number of factors have contributed to increased employment among women, including smaller family size, increased educational and job opportunities, and the desire (and need) of many families for increased income. In 1972, women comprised nearly one-third of all year-round, full-time workers. It may be that in the future these women will be more resistant to retirement as they age.

Retirement as a widespread institution is a product of twentieth-century, industrialized societies. Retirement is virtually unknown among preindustrial societies. The usual pattern is for the aged to take a second career, in which they take on different tasks (Clark, 1972). This may involve economic or family functions with less physical effort or shorter hours, or tasks for which older people are considered uniquely qualified, such as storyteller or village elder. Continued involvement in work declines substantially in modern societies, however, for a variety of reasons.

One reason for the institutionalization of retirement is the supply and demand for manpower. Demographic trends resulting in an older population structure have combined with increased worker productivity to produce heightened job competition and, by implication, heightened generational competition for jobs (Cowgill, 1974). One result of the Depression was the development of Social Security to entice older workers out of the labor force and create jobs for younger workers, and this is still given as a primary justification for mandatory retirement policies. This proves very expensive for the aged, since retirement incomes are generally quite low.

A second set of factors relates to structural transformations in the economy: (1) declines in agricultural employment and the proportion of self-employed, (2) continual upgrading and changing of the work role through education, automation, and so on, (3) increases in large, bureaucratic firms, and (4) relative increases in white-collar occupations at the expense of blue-collar occupations (Spengler, 1966; Riley, Johnson, and Foner, 1972). These changes increase retirement rates for three reasons. First, they imply an accelerated obsolescence of the knowledge and skills of older workers. Emerging occupations requiring higher education and new technical skills are taken over by the young, while older workers tend to be concentrated in slow-growth industries with fewer available jobs. Retirement need not necessarily result from work changes. Automation, by lowering physical work demands, is often well-suited for older workers, but retraining opportunities are often quite limited, even though the amount required is often minimal. In general, mechanization and automation reduce the need for the unskilled and semi-skilled occupations in which many older workers are concentrated, and a lack of job opportunities pushes workers into retirement.

Second, these transformations increase retirement because they result in less individual control over the retirement decision. Those who are in agriculture or self-employed are still more likely to continue working, but they are a smaller proportion of the work force. People increasingly work for larger, more bureaucratic organizations which develop a set of policies applicable to all employees. This involves both a "push" and a "pull" to retirement. The push is the increase in mandatory retirement policies set at specific ages. The pull is the development of pension systems which make retirement more affordable and attractive.

This brings us to the third reason for increased retirement: changes in personnel policies. Mandatory retirement provisions have risen substantially in the past 30 years, often including options for early retirement. The rapid economic growth of this century provides an economic surplus to divert into pension systems, making retirement for older people who cannot or do not wish to work economically feasible (Schulz, 1976a; Atchley, 1976a). For example, Social Security is now nearly universal in its coverage, but in 1948 only 13 percent of those over 65 were receiving payments. Similarly, private pensions cover an increasing proportion of the work force. Social Security also discourages work through the retirement test of eligibility, which exercises a strong negative influence on willingness to continue working (Schulz, 1976a).

A final possible explanation for declining labor force participation among older workers may be the declining attractiveness of work itself. We too often assume that work provides meaning and satisfaction to a worker's life when, in fact, the work may be boring or alienating. Braverman (1974) has argued that this has become increasingly true during this century. The craftsman who controls the production process from start to finish and can truly claim the product as *his* is replaced by the worker who does small, repetitive parts of some larger whole. Braverman relates this trend to monopoly capitalism, which seeks efficiency, simplicity, and routinization. This creates deadening and dead-end jobs, as illustrated by a study of automobile workers:

> Despite the claim by an automobile industry economist that "a constant upgrading of individuals is normal in the industry . . . limited only by the capacity and willingness of the individual," automobile workers cannot usually look forward to any substantial personal advancement through a series of progressively more skilled and better-paid jobs. Increasing mechanization, made profitable by the enormous volume of production, has left most automobile workers as semiskilled operatives. . . . As early as 1922, Henry Ford estimated that eighty-five per cent of the workers in his plants needed less than two weeks of training and that forty-three per cent could be working efficiently within one day. (Chinoy, 1965:19)

Braverman suggests that this "degradation of work" is characteristic of not only assembly-line workers, but office workers as well. Thus, more and more people may be willing to retire from repetitious work which involves little personal accomplishment or status.

It is probably also true that age now lends little prestige to the older worker. Accumulated experience is less important in rapidly changing modern societies, and older workers are less likely to be in a position of socializing the young to replace themselves, as was the case with craftsman-apprentice relationships. Indeed, tensions between experienced older workers and young workers with new technical skills may increase the attractiveness of retirement.

Modernization and industrialization need not lead to extremely low levels of employment among older workers. In Japan, for example, over half of all males 65 and older work, partly because so many are self-employed (Palmore, 1975). Some countries encourage work by older persons. There is no retirement test for social security benefits in Sweden (Schulz, 1976a), for example, and in 1964, the Soviet Union enacted legislation to encourage work by the elderly because of chronic labor shortages (Butler, 1975). It is nevertheless true that retirement has been established as a modern institution, to the point that most of us expect to retire and view retirement and some financial support as our right. This legitimization itself contributes to the trend toward retirement.

The Decision to Retire

People retire for many reasons, both personal (illness, desire for leisure) and institutional (compulsory retirement). Decisions about whether to retire and the preferred timing of retirement are closely linked to the meanings attached both to work and to retirement as a social role, but the concern here is the immediate reason for retirement. Regardless of attitudes or desires, what in fact propels people into retirement? The most complete information on decisions to retire comes from studies of Social Security beneficiaries. Table 6.1 indicates trends in the retirement decision from 1951 to 1963.

Voluntary Retirement

A basic distinction can be made between forced and voluntary retirement. The data in Table 6.1 indicate that approximately three of every five retirees made their own decisions. Contrary to stereotypes about compulsory retirement, there was actually an increase in voluntary retirement from 1951 to 1963. This has apparently remained quite stable, since a 1974 survey also found that 61 percent of all retirees had retired by choice (National Council on the Aging, 1975). The term "voluntary" is somewhat misleading, however. Among those who made their own decision, poor health was

Table 6.1. Reasons given for retirement by Social Security beneficiaries: 1951 and 1963 (percentages)

Reason for retirement	1951	1963
Own decision	54	61
Poor health	41	35
Preferred leisure	3	17
Other reasons	10	9
Employer's decision	46	39
Compulsory retirement age	11	21
Poor health	7	6
Laid off or job discontinued	22	8
Other reasons	7	4

Source: Erdman Palmore, "Retirement patterns among aged men: Findings of the 1963 Survey of the Aged." Social Security Bulletin 27(1964):6.

their chief reason. This is true in occupations with heavy physical demands more than in professional, managerial, and sales occupations (Riley and Foner, 1968). However, poor health has been declining as a reason for retirement as jobs have continued to be less physically demanding and the health of older people has improved (Atchley, 1976a).

In addition, retirement may be "chosen" in response to institutional or personal pressures. For example, while women (particularly married women) retire voluntarily more often than men, this may not reflect less importance attached to work but rather restricted job opportunities and the possibility that women are expected, encouraged, or even pressured to retire (Atchley, 1976a). Indeed, many older men and women may retire because of age discrimination in employment. Should this really be considered voluntary?

Voluntary retirement may be a euphemism for other reasons. Older persons may say they retired by choice to avoid the implied rejection of compulsory retirement. There may be various pressures from younger co-workers and superiors, including exclusion and mockery. As an example, Blau (1973) cites the following incident from a newspaper article:

> And in South Chicago, a young mill hand described a birthday party that had been given one 67-year-old worker. "We painted up a big sign with 'Happy Birthday' on it . . . then on the other side we drew one of those old tire company ads showing a youngster holding a candle and saying 'time to re-tire.' We all thought it was funny. But the old man didn't see the joke." (Blau, 1973:135)

White-collar workers may be more subtle, but personal coolness, failure to achieve status or salary promotions, or demotion following peak status may loosen one's work commitment and hasten retirement (Riley, Johnson, and Foner, 1972). There has been relatively little study of the impact on the retirement decision of attitudes held by co-workers, friends, and family (Atchley, 1976a), but they may be of considerable importance.

Though voluntary retirement may often result from limited job opportunities, poor health, and alienating job situations for older workers, Table 6.1 also indicates an increase in leisure as an attraction to retirement. From 1951 to 1963, there was an increase from 3 percent to 17 percent in those retiring because they prefer leisure. Thus, truly voluntarly retirement may be on the increase, perhaps linked to declining importance attached to work. Those who retire tend to be less satisfied with their jobs and less likely to see work as important in itself (Riley and Foner, 1968). Such feelings may be more advanced in the United States, since workers in Denmark and Great Britain are less likely to retire voluntarily (Shanas et al., 1968).

Early retirement is one indication of willingness to retire. Since 1962, both men and women have been able to retire at age 62 with reduced Social Security benefits. Private pension plans have also opened up possibilities for early retirement. Under a contract between the United Auto Workers and General Motors, for example, workers with 30 years of service can retire at age 56 with a monthly pension of $500 (Atchley, 1976a). Such provisions have resulted in major increases in early retirement by making it economically feasible. Even among early retirees, however, health remains important. The Social Security Retirement History Survey, begun in 1969, found that poor health was the most common reason given for early retirement and early retirement occurred disproportionately among those with poor health or long-term unemployment experience (Sheppard, 1976). A survey of early retirees in the UAW found that the primary reasons given were: adequate retirement income (47 percent), poor health (24 percent), and desire for free time (19 percent) (Pollman, 1971). The job itself was apparently of minimal importance to the decision. Economic incentives have certainly increased early retirement, but the extent to which workers choose retirement because of its attractions is still unclear.

Forced Retirement

Substantial numbers of older workers lack control over the retirement decision. Table 6.1 indicates that this may involve loss of job because of poor health, plant shutdown, and so forth, but the greatest attention has been paid to mandatory retirement policies which prevent individuals from working beyond a certain age. Between 1951 and 1963, compulsory retirement doubled in frequency, though it is probably true that many persons forced to retire in 1963 would simply have been laid off in 1951.

How many persons are actually "forced" to retire by strict age policies? Our stereotype suggests this is quite widespread, but the facts indicate otherwise. It appears that fewer than half of all workers are currently faced with even the possibility of mandatory retirement. A 1961 study found that virtually all firms without formal pension plans had flexible retirement rules (Slavick, 1966). Even among firms with pension plans, fully 60 percent had no upper age limit. Mandatory retirement policies were more prevalent among larger firms. A 1966 survey of wokers age 45 to 59 found that 46 percent faced compulsory retirement at their present place of employment (Schulz, 1976a), while a more recent study of all workers 18 and above indicated that 36 percent were faced with a fixed age (National Council on the Aging, 1975).

It is difficult to determine how many workers retire because of mandatory policies. Some workers may be "nudged" into retirement by the realization that they will have to retire in a few years anyway. Also, not all those who retire at a mandatory age are unwilling to retire. Streib and Schneider (1971), in a longitudinal study of retirement, made a useful distinction between a worker's willingness to retire and whether the decision was voluntary or administrative. By combining the two issues, it becomes clear that mandatory is not necessarily the same as unwilling. Their sample was not representative of all workers, but the distribution is illuminating. About 30 percent were "truly" voluntary—willing—retirees. A second group (about 20 percent, slightly more women than men) made their own decision, but were reluctant, probably retiring due to poor health. Some of those who were retired administratively were nonetheless willing to retire (about 20 percent), leaving approximately one-third of both men and women who were both reluctant to retire and forced to administratively. It is interesting that women were more likely to be reluctant than men (57 percent versus 49 percent), in view of the often-assumed unimportance of work for women.

Schulz and associates (1974), from a more representative sample of Social Security beneficiaries, found an even smaller proportion who had been terminated because of mandatory retirement rules. They found that:(1) 46 percent had worked in firms without mandatory policies, (2) 30 percent of the remainder retired before the fixed retirement age, (3) another 10 percent indicated they had been willing to retire anyway, (4) 4 percent were unable to work in any case, and (5) another 3 percent were able to find a new job following compulsory retirement. This left only 7 percent of all the workers whose retirement was attributable *purely* to administrative rules—who were unwilling to retire, able to work, unable to find a new job, and forced to retire by a mandatory policy. That mandatory retirement is not statistically widespread can be seen from figures for General Motors (*Time*, 1977). Although the mandatory retirement age is 68 for hourly workers and 65 for salaried employees, the average retirement age is 58; only 11 percent of salaried employees and 2 percent of blue-collar workers stay on until the mandatory age.

Control over the retirement decision varies by occupation, of course. Certainly the average physician has more control over work and retirement than the average assembly-line worker. Also, the National Council on the Aging study (1975) found that retirement was more likely to be forced for males, blacks, and persons with low income or poor education. The basic policy issue is: given the many problems already faced by older workers, need we also force them to retire simply because of age? Even if only a minority are directly affected by such policies, is not the position of all the aged altered by this type of age stratification and its implications of unfitness?

Erdman Palmore (1972) has summarized the arguments which have been made in support of compulsory retirement and indicated that each of them rests on a shaky foundation. Compulsory retirement is often justified as being simple and easy to administer and lending predictability to the retirement process. Since most people are not directly affected by fixed-age policies, however, it would seem that flexibility works reasonably well. Often the concern for predictability involves the presumed inferiority or poor health of older workers and the consequent costs to the employer of either keeping them all on or trying to "weed out" those who are unfit. Again, the problems seem greatly exagerrated. We have already seen that age alone is a very poor predictor of working ability. Techniques are being developed to assess worker capabilities, and more could be done to redesign jobs to fit older workers. It has also been argued that mandatory policies are easier on older workers—their impersonality prevents individual discrimination, saves face for the worker, and gives retirement an inevitability. It seems rather odd to justify wholesale discrimination in order to protect individuals, and it also seems that we have reached a point where "People no longer need an excuse to retire. It is an accepted part of life" (Atchley, 1976a:43). The argument that mandatory retirement does not really hurt older persons because they have adequate retirement income and can get another job if they desire also ignores the facts of the many barriers to employment for older people. Although mandatory retirement is usually linked to a pension plan, retirement income is far from adequate for many, and indeed mandatory retirement forces some people into poverty.

One of the reasons for the general institutionalization of retirement in this century is that it opens up jobs for younger workers. But are not older people as entitled as younger people to a decent income and whatever meanings are derived from work? And there are other ways to encourage older people to retire, including making retirement more attractive with activities and financial support.

It seems clear that flexible policies are preferable to mandatory retirement. Robert Butler speaks eloquently of the waste of skills and experience caused by forced retirement, citing the following example:

> Sixty-nine-year-old philosopher Paul Weiss talked animatedly about his $1 million suit against Fordham University, charging age bias. This vital and vitalizing teacher had been offered the $100,000-per-year Albert Schweitzer chair . . . but then was denied it on the basis of age. . . .
> Weiss pointed out ironically that the chair was named for the famous Dr. Schweitzer, "many of whose major achievements came after he was older than the plaintiff." Schweitzer died at 90 in 1965. ". . . America will never be of age until it knows how to make most use of its people—no matter what their color, sex or years," wrote Weiss. In the complaint the professor was described as in "excellent" physical health. "He walks eight miles every day, swims and does various calisthenics. His mental condition is also beyond question excellent." (Butler, 1975:65)

Professor Weiss lost his case, and the United States Supreme Court has repeatedly rejected challenges to the constitutionality of mandatory retirement (Quirk, 1975). A recent ruling, in 1976, involved Robert Murgia, a former lieutenant colonel in the Massachusetts State Police who was forced to retire at age 50 although he could pass required physical fitness tests. The Court upheld the law, ruling that the states have the right to set mandatory retirement ages related to the work involved.

It appears that court rulings will continue to uphold mandatory retirement policies. This does not mean, however, that there is public support for such measures. The Harris poll commissioned by the National Council on the Aging (1975) investigated this issue. Although 49 percent of the public felt that older people should retire "to give younger people more of a chance on the job," 86 percent agreed that "nobody should be forced to retire because of age if he wants to continue working and is still able to do a good job." Palmore (1972) suggests an interesting compromise, whereby workers would lose seniority rights at a certain age, no longer accumulate pension credits, and lose guaranteed continued employment, but would not be automatically retired and could continue to work up to their ability. Indeed, a law which eliminates mandatory retirement for federal employees, and moves retirement age from 65 to 70 in private industry has recently been passed.

The Consequences of Retirement

On the one hand, we have images of the "golden years" of retirement—travel, recreation, freedom. On the other hand, there are many gloomy portraits of the boredom and meaninglessness encountered by those who retire. A large body of theory suggests that retirement should constitute a severe crisis, particularly for American males. A number of observers have noted that, historically, work has been viewed as the central life task, integrating people, especially men, into the social structure by determining identity, patterns of participation, and life style (Maddox, 1966; Simpson, Back and McKinney, 1966a; Blau, 1973). A recent government report, entitled *Work in America*, asks:

> Why is a man a worker? First of all, of course, man works to sustain physical life—to provide food, clothing, and shelter. But clearly work is central to our lives for other reasons as well. According to Freud, work provides us with a sense of reality; to Elton Mayo, work is a bind to community; to Marx, its function is primarily economic. Theologians are interested in work's moral dimensions; sociologists see it as a determinant of status, and some contemporary critics say that it is simply the best way of filling up a lot of time. (U.S. Department of Health, Education, and Welfare, 1973:1)

Retirement would presumably undermine social supports and the bases of both personal and social identity, taking on major social significance as a rite of passage. In light of the general work ethic, retirement is seen as "unproductive" and not "useful."

> It is a paradox of modern times that we expect to retire when we are old whereas all our lives great emphasis is placed upon work, achievement, production, efficiency, and self-development. (Taves and Hansen, 1963:105)

The question "Who are you?" is often answered: "I'm a carpenter" or "I'm a university professor," and through co-workers, with whom one shares experiences, information, and ideas, one gains identity and prestige as well as a feeling of "belonging." There is also the personal reassurance of worth associated with a meaningful job well done. According to this symbolic interactionist perspective, when work ceases certain identities and self-feelings also cease.

Combined with the centrality attached to work is a view that retirement is an ambiguous "roleless role" (Donahue, Orbach, and Pollak, 1960; Blau, 1973; Rosow, 1974), involving few expectations about behavior and little socialization or preparation. A generally unpleasant evaluation of retirement as a useless role provides little incentive to prepare for or take the role. Thus, until meaningful social roles are created for retirement, the result will be normlessness, inactivity, depression, and disengagement.

This is certainly a gloomy portrait of retirement, and the argument seems plausible. But how accurate is this picture? The answer seems to be not very. Retirement certainly involves social and psychological trauma for some retirees, but studies of both attitudes toward and adjustment to retirement indicate that its general consequences are relatively unremarkable and in many cases quite pleasant. In fact, the major determinants of retirement satisfaction appear to be health and financial security, not the identity crises stressed by so many social gerontologists.

Attitudes Toward Retirement

Contrary to our often negative impressions, most people see retirement as "active, involved, expanding, full, and busy; as fair and good; as hopeful and meaningful; and as healthy, relaxed, mobile, able, and independent" (Atchley, 1976a:28). Most adults expect to retire by age 65, and indeed desire to do so, and only a very small minority actually seem to dread retirement. Such attitudes may reflect cohort effects, since more recent cohorts are more likely to intend to retire, have favorable attitudes toward retirement, and retire earlier. Such attitudes are important to retirement adjustment, since favorable expectations often color perceptions of events. We all know that expecting (and wanting) to like something often leads us to like it more. On the other hand, if those expectations are based upon unrealistically rosy pictures of retirement, reality may prove an even more bitter pill to swallow.

Attitudes toward retirement are not uniform, of course; they vary according to a number of individual characteristics. For example, individuals at higher levels of income, education, and occupation tend to have more favorable attitudes toward retirement. This seemingly simple relationship obscures a number of processes. Anticipated financial problems are a major determinant of negative retirement attitudes. Unskilled and semi-skilled workers have good reason to resist retirement, since it will mean poverty for many of them. Those who already have higher incomes realistically expect greater financial security in retirement. Atchley (1976a) also suggests that manual workers may perceive fewer alternatives to work, so that the job becomes the lesser of two evils. Semi-skilled and unskilled workers are likely to have developed fewer involvements outside of work, such as voluntary associations, particularly if they have not had orderly work careers (Simpson, Back, and McKinney, 1966a).

In other ways, however, social class is inversely related to willingness to retire. A survey of white males 50 and over found that 45 percent of blue-collar workers but only 24 percent of white-collar workers said they would not continue to work *if provided with an adequate income* (Sheppard, 1976). Again assuming adequate income, other studies indicate that willingness to retire is greater when work is of lower quality (less autonomy, variety, and responsibility) (Jacobsohn, 1972; Sheppard, 1972). Thus,

> . . . retirement can be viewed frequently as an escape from an undesirable, unsatisfying work role, as a negative-type decision. The fact that most studies, if not all, of "retirement adjustment" reveal a high degree of satisfaction may partly be due to this "escape" function of retirement. . . . (Sheppard, 1976:– 303)

Workers at higher educational and occupational levels find their work more interesting and are more committed to it, and are therefore less inclined to retire even though their attitudes toward retirement may be more favorable (Riley and Foner, 1968; Atchley, 1971).

The research cited above would lead one to expect that attitudes toward work and retirement are closely related. Paradoxically, this is not the case. Attitude toward work is at best a weak predictor of attitude toward retirement, even when work appears to occupy a central position in a person's life (Fillenbaum, 1971b; Goudy, Powers, and Keith, 1975; Glamser, 1976). Such attitudes do affect *whether* people retire and preferred age of retirement, but, again, this seems to be attributable to work as a plus, not retirement as a minus. Attitudes toward retirement appear to be determined more by such things as financial outlook, number of friends, social activities, and perceived preparation for the retirement role.

Various studies have also found that older workers are less accepting of retirement and are likely to prefer a later age to retire (Riley and Foner, 1968; Rose and Mogey, 1972). This may reflect a combination of aging and cohort effects. Older workers may feel that they have achieved a higher rank than they are willing to give up (Rose and Mogey, 1972), or they may be more realistic in recognizing the financial difficulties associated with retirement (Atchley, 1976a). More recent cohorts may also be more accepting of retirement than the older cohorts currently facing retirement.

Adjustment to Retirement

Although attitudes toward retirement are rather favorable, this refers only to retirement as an abstract future possibility. What happens when workers confront their own retirement? There is no question that the physical and mental health of some persons are adversely affected, as in the following extreme example:

"Mr. Winter" single-handedly ran an operation that nobody else in his company fully understood, nor in fact cared to understand. As Mr. Winter reached his 64th birthday, a bright and talented younger man was assigned as an apprentice to learn the complex set of activities so that at the end of the year, he could take over the operation and the old master could benefit from a well deserved retirement. Mr. Winter objected, claiming that he did not want to retire, but the company had rules. Not long after retirement a substantial change in Mr. Winter took place. He began to withdraw from people and to lose his zest for life. Within a year after his retirement this once lively and productive businessman was hospitalized, diagnosed as having a senile psychosis. Friends from work and even family soon stopped coming to visit as they could evoke no response. Mr. Winter was a vegetable.

About two years after the apprentice had stepped up to his new position of responsibility he suddenly died. The company found itself in a serious predicament. The function that was vacated was essential to company operations, but which no one else in the company could effectively perform. A decision was made to approach Mr. Winter and see if he could pull himself together enough to carry on the job and train somebody to take over. Four of his closest co-workers were sent to the hospital. After hours of trying, one of the men finally broke through. The idea of going back to work brought the first sparkle in Mr. Winter's eyes in 2 years. Within a few days, this "vegetable" was operating at full steam, interacting with people as he had years before. (U.S. Department of Health, Education, and Welfare, 1973:78–79)

This is by no means a general phenomenon, however. Most persons appear to remain satisfied in retirement and cope quite satisfactorily with the social and psychological changes it entails.

Generally, satisfaction is somewhat higher among the employed than those who are retired, but much of this is attributable to differences in health and income rather than the retirement role per se. A 1965 Harris poll showed that 61 percent felt retirement had fulfilled their expectations for a good life, while only a minority (33 percent) found retirement less than satisfactory (Riley and Foner, 1968). A longitudinal study which followed workers into retirement found no significant change in life satisfaction following retirement (Streib and Schneider, 1971). Although 70 percent of this sample was not fully satisfied with retirement, after four to six years of retirement only 5 percent found it worse than they had expected (and one-third found it better). Similarly, studies of a sample of retired teachers and telephone company employees have found rather quick adjustment to retirement, little effect on self-esteem and depression, and generally a low incidence of loneliness, anxiety, anomie, depression, and self-derogation (Cottrell and Atchley, 1969; Atchley, 1976b).

Retirement itself does not create widespread dissatisfaction or low self-esteem, but it may be associated with poor health, low income, widowhood, and other factors. Even feelings of usefulness are not necessarily eliminated by loss of the work role. Streib and Schneider (1971) did find a significant increase in feelings of uselessness following retirement, but only about 20 percent of their sample attributed such feelings to retirement. Loss of spouse or dependency due to illness are also likely to create feelings of uselessness. In addition, approximately three-quarters of their sample reported at least some feelings of usefulness following retirement.

There is no evidence that retirement causes poor health (Riley and Foner, 1968), though there are cases like that of "Mr. Winter." Remember that poor health is a major cause of retirement, and substantial numbers of people feel that their health improves following retirement, with the removal of the mental and physical strain of work (Streib and Schneider, 1971). This is particularly true for unskilled and semi-skilled laborers, who have been doing heavy physical work. There is also no evidence that retirement is related to mental disorders (Nadelson, 1969).

The most obvious effect of retirement is reduced income, and poverty or inadequate income is one of the greatest problems faced by the aged. Both objective and subjective financial deprivation increase following retirement, though actual income declines more than people's estimate of the adequacy of their income (Riley and Foner, 1968). The greatest financial anxiety occurs just prior to retirement and declines over time as adjustments are made (pragmatically, if regretfully).

Social participation is another area in which retirement might have an impact. Disengagement theory implies that retirement is the beginning of a more general process of social and emotional withdrawal from the world. Retirement may disrupt friendship and group ties to co-workers and work-based organizations (such as unions or chambers of commerce), but work is not necessarily a social experience, and, in any case, individuals often selectively disengage from some aspects of their life, expanding into other spheres of activity (leisure, citizenship service, and so on). The many "patterns of aging" discussed in Chapter 4 illustrated the tremendous individual variability. In their longitudinal study, Streib and Schneider (1971) found that retirement had little overall impact on other social roles. They found no change in seeing children and grandchildren, church attendance, having close friends, or taking part in associations and community activities.

But what about the retirement experience itself? What do people find satisfying and dissatisfying about being retired? Most of the research seems to be focused on sources of dissatisfaction, perhaps reflecting a cultural expectation that retirement "ought" to be dissatisfying. But retirement is unsatisfying because of difficult situations which accompany it rather than because of loss of the work role per se. It is striking that relatively few people seem to miss their jobs. The results of a national survey commissioned by the National Council on the Aging (1975) asking people over 65 who were retired or unemployed what they "missed about their jobs" (Table 6.2) suggest that it was often not the work itself which was most important, but the income, associations, and activity levels related to work. Thus, retirees may lack alternatives for the activities and social contacts (with both the public and co-workers) provided by a job. Feelings of job deprivation are most likely to occur among those who had not looked forward to retirement, had not achieved job-related ambitions, and lacked adequate income (Simpson, Back, and McKinney, 1966b).

Some people do miss a feeling of being useful and the respect of others following retirement, but it is not clear how much impact this has. In a sample of retirees in Miami, 83 percent agreed that people treat a retired man with less respect, but only 15 percent felt that they *personally* were treated with less respect (Strauss, Aldrich, and Lipman, 1976). Many of them still identified with their former occupations as "retired lawyers" or "retired doctors." This sense of continued status was strongly related to education: over one-third of those with less than a high school education felt status loss, compared with only 3 percent of the college-educated.

Table 6.2. Things retired people 65 and over missed about their jobs (percentages)

	Missed	Did not miss	Not sure	One thing missed most
The money it brings in	74	24	2	28
The people at work	73	25	2	28
The work itself	62	36	2	10
The feeling of being useful	59	38	3	11
Things happening around you	57	39	4	5
The respect of others	50	45	5	2
Having a fixed schedule every day	43	54	3	4

Source: *The Myth and Reality of Aging in America,* a study prepared for the National Council on the Aging, Inc. (NCOA), Washington, D.C. by Louis Harris and Associates, Inc., © 1975, p. 218. Reprinted by permission.

There are, however, pleasant aspects to not working as well as problems. The most frequently expressed reasons for satisfaction with retirement are: the ability to enjoy leisure pursuits (such as travel and hobbies), the freedom to do as one wishes, and a more relaxing life away from the tensions and responsibilities associated with work. The benefits of no morning alarm clock, no publication deadlines to meet, and no daily schedule to follow have occurred more than once to this author while writing this chapter.

A useful distinction can be made among retiring *back to* something (such as one's family life), retiring *from* something (such as an unsatisfying job or more general disengagement), and retiring *for* something (reengagement in different activities) (Campbell, 1971). In comparing manual and nonmanual workers, Campbell found that manual workers were more likely to be retiring back to something, less likely to be retiring for something, and equally likely to be retiring from something.

As with any aspect of the aging experience, we need to keep in mind variations in reaction to being retired. Those who retire willingly (and to a lesser extent, those who retire voluntarily) show greater satisfaction with retirement and adjust to the change more quickly (Streib and Schneider, 1971). One's occupation is also important in determining what retirement will be like. Although higher-level white-collar workers derive more intrinsic satisfactions from work, they are more satisfied with retirement than blue-collar workers, who encounter greater financial insecurity (Simpson, Back, and McKinney, 1966b; Heidbreder, 1972). Adequacy of post-retirement activity contributes to occupational differences in retirement adjustment. Retirement is more likely to cause isolation for the working class than for the middle class who typically develop broader ties outside of the work role (Simpson, Back, and McKinney, 1966a; Rosenberg, 1970). This occurs partly because semi-skilled workers are more likely to have disorderly work careers which prevent them from becoming fully integrated into their social surroundings, and new social involvements are difficult to establish following retirement. Higher-status retirees, who work with their "heads," are better able to maintain continuity than those who work with their "hands." Structured opportunities for activities similar to work also vary by occupation. A study of retired academics found considerable opportunities to continue research activities (Rowe, 1976). Many took advantage of these opportunities, particularly those with high professional visibility. Thus, the retired sociologist may have access to libraries, professional meetings, and networks of colleagues which facilitate continued involvement. Analogous opportunities are not likely to be available to retired janitors, carpenters, or clerks.

Sex differences have long been ignored as a factor in retirement adjustment, as retirement has been assumed to be primarily a male problem.

> Retirement, as this comment implies, deprives a man of the respect accorded the breadwinner in the American family and constrains him to assume a role similar to that of women. In this respect, retirement is a more demoralizing experience for men than for women. Women may choose to work, but according to cultural prescription they are not obliged to do so. Even when wives do work, it is not their occupational status, but their husband's, that determines the social status of the family. (Blau, 1973:29)

This assumption is increasingly being challenged, however. Recent studies have found that men and women attach equal importance to work and more women than men miss people at work and the feeling of doing a good job (Streib and Schneider, 1971; Atchley, 1976b). Atchley's study of retired teachers and telephone company employees found that men liked retirement more and adjusted more quickly to it, while women were "more often lonely, anxious, unstable in self-concept, highly sensitive to criticism, and highly depressed" (1976b:208). This may reflect the fact that most of our cultural models for retirement pertain to men, since women are seen as retiring back to their "real domain," the home. If retirement is ambiguous for men, what must it be like for women? As work becomes an increasingly important part of the overall pattern of life for more women, more attention will have to be paid to their problems of adjustment to retirement.

The overall impression to be gleaned from the many studies of retirement is that most people adjust favorably to it and find it a relatively satisfying experience. This conclusion deals a critical blow to gerontological approaches emphasizing the traumatic nature of the transition from work to retirement. Where did we go wrong? There are two answers to this question. First, social gerontologists have exaggerated the importance of work and work values in the lives of current cohorts, though they may have been accurate for earlier cohorts. Second, while the retirement transition may indeed be difficult and stressful, we too often overlook the capacity of people to come to grips with the most trying life events.

The Meaning of Work

The view that retirement will constitute a severe identity crisis stems from the assumption that work is a central life interest which defines one's "mission in life" and one's personal identity.

But this assumption is questionable. The ancient Hebrews and Greeks, for example, saw work only as a painful necessity which brutalized the mind (Parker and Smith, 1976). It was only later that work came to be viewed as a "calling." During the Renaissance, creative work was viewed as a joy in itself, and the "Protestant work ethic" of Martin Luther and John Calvin portrayed work as the path to salvation. Such work ethics no longer seem so widespread, however, and there is growing evidence of alienation and job dissatisfaction at virtually all occupational levels.

In the first place, work means different things to different people. Work may be variously seen as a source of: (1) income, (2) something to do to pass the time, (3) self-respect and recognition from others, (4) friendship and collegial relationships, or (5) meaningful life experience through one's purpose in life, creativity and self-expression, novel experiences, or service to others (Friedmann and Havighurst, 1954). To say, then, that work may be missed in retirement says nothing about which of these aspects will be missed.

In addition to various meanings for work, there are many sources of satisfaction and dissatisfaction in any particular job. Attachment to and satisfaction with work depends on such things as: relations with co-workers, financial rewards, convenience and "creature comforts," opportunities for career advancement, the provision of adequate resources to do a good job, and whether the work is interesting and meaningful (Kalleberg, 1977). *Work in America*, the report of a Special Task Force of the Department of Health, Education, and Welfare (1973), concludes that "interesting work" is the most important aspect of a job, and the most oppressive aspects are constant supervision, lack of variety, isolation from others, and meaningless tasks. A recent study found such intrinsic aspects of work as autonomy, participating in decision making, and being able to work on a "whole" job the most important determinants of job satisfaction (Kalleberg, 1977). Willingness to continue working and reluctance to retire are more pronounced among those who emphasize the noneconomic, intrinsic qualities of their work (Friedmann and Havighurst, 1954).

While most workers develop bonds of attachment to some elements of their work, the extent to which work is a central life interest varies by occupation and organizational setting (Dubin, Hedley, and Taveggia, 1976). Studies indicate that the working class is less likely to see their jobs as intrinsically interesting or meaningful (Friedmann and Havighurst, 1954; Morse and Weiss, 1955). In addition, job satisfaction declines when work involves considerable routine and low levels of skills (Dubin, Hedley, and Taveggia, 1976), characteristics which are more prevalent in blue-collar than white-collar jobs.

Retirement might be easier for blue-collar workers, as indicated in a study which asked workers in various occupations: "What type of work would you try to get into if you could start all over again?" The percentage who would voluntarily choose the same work over again is indicated in Table 6.3. Clearly, the average blue-collar worker is less attached to his work than the average white-collar worker, but even more impressive is the fact that while occupations such as lawyer and professor appear to be satisfying, only 43 percent of the *white*-collar workers would choose the same job, despite the fact that such jobs presumably offer more intrinsic satisfactions.

A number of recent works have argued that both blue- and white-collar jobs are becoming less intrinsically meaningful, and more alienating and confining (U.S. Department of Health, Education, and Welfare, 1973; Braverman, 1974; Sarason, 1977). *Work in America* suggests that declining intrinsic satisfactions from work partly account for increasing absenteeism, sabotage, worker turnover, wildcat strikes, and similar problems for industry. For one thing, there is less opportunity to be one's own boss, as the workforce has come to be dominated by large corporations and the government which attempt to maximize control and predictability at the expense of worker independence. The goal of efficiency has often made tasks simplified, fragmented, compartmentalized, and under continuous supervision, which results in worker alienation.

Table 6.3. Percentages in occupational groups who would choose similar work again

Professional and lower white-collar occupations	%	Working-class occupations	%
Urban university professors	93	Skilled printers	52
		Paper workers	42
Mathematicians	91	Skilled autoworkers	41
Physicists	89	Skilled steelworkers	41
Biologists	89	Textile workers	31
Chemists	86	*Blue-collar workers, cross section*	24
Firm lawyers	85		
Lawyers	83	Unskilled steelworkers	21
Journalists (Washington correspondents)	82	Unskilled autoworkers	16
Church university professors	77		
Solo lawyers	75		
White-collar workers, cross section	43		

Source: Reprinted from *Work in America,* by the U.S. Department of Health, Education and Welfare, 1973, p. 16, by permission of the MIT Press, Cambridge, Massachusetts.

Alienation exists when workers are unable to control their immediate work processes, to develop a sense of purpose and function which connects their jobs to the over-all organization of
production, to belong to integrated industrial communities, and
when they fail to become involved in the activity of work as a
mode of personal self-expression. (Blauner, 1964:15)

At the same time, new cohorts of workers are less authoritarian,
better educated, and apparently more concerned with meaningful
work which provides an opportunity for personal growth.

Attention is usually focused on blue-collar work in studies of
such alienation, and this report does point to the "blues" of those
who feel that their careers are blocked and manual labor is deni-
grated. An auto-worker explains:

"If you were in a plant you'd see—everybody thinks that General
Motors workers have it easy, but it's not that easy. Some jobs
you go home after eight hours and you're tired, your back is sore
and you're sweatin'. All the jobs ain't that easy. We make good
money; yeah, the money is real good out there, but that ain't all
of it—cause there's really a lot of bad jobs out there." (U.S.
Department of Health, Education, and Welfare, 1973:37)

Dissatisfaction with the meaning of work is not restricted to manual
labor, however. Low-level white-collar jobs held by college graduates in factory-like offices, such newly created occupations as
medical technicians and computer keypunch operators, and middle-
level managers all often lack autonomy and participation in decision making and overall goals. A former corporation executive comments that:

"You felt like a small cog. Working there was dehumanizing
and the struggle to get to the top didn't seem worth it. They
made no effort to encourage your participation. The decisions
were made in those rooms with closed doors. . . . The serious
error they made with me was not giving me a glimpse of the big
picture from time to time, so I could go back to my little detail,
understanding how it related to the whole." (U.S. Department
of Health, Education, and Welfare, 1973:48)

Sarason (1977) has suggested that even highly educated professionals, such as physicians, lawyers, and university professors, are
finding increasing dissatisfaction from work. Physicians, for example, confront growing independence of new health professionals,
heavy paper-work and regulations, large bureaucratic settings for

medical practice, and a decline in the attribution of Godlike qualities to them by patients. Many professionals lose their autonomy, becoming mere functionaries in bureaucratic organizations. As such trends continue at all occupational levels, work will decreasingly be *the* organizing center in life.

This means that we must be careful about predicting retirement troubles. Even 20 years ago a study found that work was not the central life interest for three out of four industrial workers (Dubin, 1956), and Atchley's (1971) more recent study indicated that only a small minority of retired teachers and telephone company employees carried a high degree of work orientation into retirement. It may be that individuals do find retirement discouraging and meaningless, but this is apparently true of work as well and perhaps reflects a more general malaise in modern society.

We need to reassess the importance of retirement to the age stratification system and to the status of the aged in modern societies. While retirement continues to be an important and often difficult transition, its consequences are by no means monolithically negative. In many cases retirement frees older persons for more meaningful activity patterns which may provide more opportunities for personal growth. Dubin (1976) suggests that changing meanings of work may result in a shift in definition of a "good citizen" from being productive to being a socially relevant consumer, which would mean that retirement will no longer imply a highly devalued status for older people. This may be one reason for the upturn in status for the aged in advanced modern societies noted in Chapter 3.

Retirement as a Process

Although the general consequences of retirement seem relatively benign, the retirement experience is not necessarily simple or unimportant or adjustment to it easy. Retirement is a *process* which affects one's life in many ways (Atchley, 1976a), and it is also both an event and a role. Unfortunately, we know very little about the complexity of the retirement transition as it is experienced by individuals.

Retirement as an event is a rite of passage from the world of work. Rites of passage, such as baptisms, weddings, or graduations, are designed to publicly redefine an individual by symbolizing status change, thereby facilitating role transition (Rosow, 1974). The retirement event, however, is very informal and seldom an adequate rite of passage (Rosow, 1974; Atchley, 1976a). Atchley points out, for example, that ceremonies such as retirement dinners tend to focus on past achievements and expressions of gratitude rather than attractions in store, as do weddings and graduation ceremonies. This is no doubt a reflection of the uncertain status of retirement as a role, but the nature of retirement ceremonies is highly variable.

> The social position of the individual who is retiring probably influences the likelihood that a retirement ceremony will take place and what it will consist of. For example, retiring professors who are well known in their fields are often given an impressive send-off with speeches, academic papers, and perhaps even a book of tributes to the work of the Great Man. These ceremonies can take as much as two or three days and draw colleagues and friends from a great distance. For the lesser-known professors and administrators, a faculty tea will usually do, and it is not uncommon to see several people being dispatched at one of these affairs. Finally, Old Charlie in the maintenance department is made the subject of a special coffee break, at which all of his co-workers look at their shoes while the boss tries to remember exactly what it was that Charlie did around there for all those years. (Atchley, 1976a:55)

Very little is known about the nature of other aspects of the retirement event—what the last day of work is like or the symbolization and impact of retirement gifts (Atchley, 1976a).

Retirement can also be thought of as a role, presumably involving various norms and expectations, rights and duties. There is considerable debate about whether old age and retirement are normless or roleless (see Chapter 3), but some argue that there are certain expectations about the retired—they should manage without assistance (not become dependent), live within their incomes—as well as certain rights involving economic support, freedom of time, and so on (Atchley, 1976a). We need a better understanding of the expectations which really do face retirees as they interact with friends, family, or former co-workers and the impact that this aspect of the retirement role might have.

In viewing reactions to retirement, bear in mind that it is not simply a question of being retired or not being retired. There are a variety of retirement phases through which individuals may "travel" (Figure 6.1):

1. *Preretirement:* As retirement approaches, workers develop expectations and fantasies about what it will be like. Relatively few formally prepare for retirement, but realistic expectations can make the transition smoother, while unrealistic fantasies can create difficulties. Workers may adopt a "short-timer's attitude" toward the job as they prepare to leave it (Atchley, 1976a).

Figure 6.1.   The phases of retirement

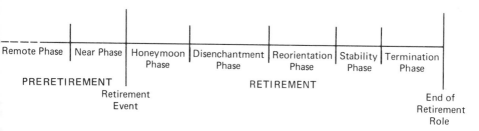

2. *Honeymoon:* A euphoric period may follow retirement, in which

> people try to "do all of the things I never had time for before." The honeymoon period tends to be a busy time, filled with hunting, fishing, card-playing, sewing, seeing the grandchildren (or greatgrandchildren) and traveling, all at the same time. A typical person in this phase says: "What do I do with my time? Why, I've never been so busy!" The person in the honeymoon period of retirement is often like a child in a room full of new toys. He flits from this to that, trying to experience everything at once. (Atchley, 1976a:68)

Some individuals never experience this because they cannot afford it or because they have very negative attitudes toward retirement and the leisure role. The honeymoon period may be quite short or last a considerable time.

3. *Disenchantment:* If the individual fails to develop a satisfying, stable routine, disenchantment may set in—activities are limited by low income or poor health, he cannot adjust to freedom from work, or he is inadequately prepared for the realities of retirement. Retirement, after all, is more than just a long vacation; it may last 20 years or more, and feelings of emptiness and boredom can occur.

4. *Reorientation:* In this period, the individual "takes stock," assesses the realistic choices available, and tries to develop a satisfying routine. He may receive help in this from family, friends, and community groups (such as senior citizen clubs).

5. *Stability:* In this phase, individuals achieve the capacity to deal routinely with retirement living and the changes which accom-

pany it. They are aware of abilities and limits and can live self-sufficiently. However, Atchley is careful to point out that "Many people pass into this phase directly from the honeymoon phase; others reach it only after a painful reassessment of personal goals; others never reach it" (1976a:70).

6. *Termination:* People may reach a stage where retirement per se is no longer a relevant concern. Some return to work, but termination is more likely the result of illness and disability. Thus, the person moves from the retirement role to the role of "dependent."

These retirement phases constitute an ideal type. For example, some may never experience disenchantment, others may experience little else. However, these phases do indicate the variety of experiences retirement may entail for any individual. Such phases probably characterize all major role transitions; certainly similar phases can be identified for marriage. More research needs to be done on the factors which affect people's experience of any of these phases and the timing of progress through them. There have been many studies of retirement, but there is still much to be learned about the process of retirement *as it is experienced by the individual.*

It is often assumed that retirement creates a void requiring substitutes for the satisfactions derived from work, as illustrated in the following statement:

> In summary, it appears fairly clear that most do not want more work as such, but meaningful substitutes for work—activities that are interesting, challenging, and enduring enough so that the person can find himself in them without assuming a lot of responsibility or enduring undue stress. Most elderly people want to keep thinking, to do useful things, and to stay active, the achievement of which requires reasonably complex tasks or activities that stimulate and reward for long periods of time—not just occasional entertainment. (Taves and Hansen, 1963:116)

But how often does work "stimulate and reward for long periods of time"? The fact that money and health are the most important determinants of retirement satisfaction raises doubts about this type of "substitution theory." It is more appropriate to view retirement adjustment as an ongoing accommodation to changes in the scheduling of activities and personal contacts, which may affect one's entire pattern of behavior—leisure, level of living, physical functioning, and self-concept (Shanas, 1972).

Relevant to this concept of accommodation, Marvin Sussman (1972) has proposed an analytical model which focuses on options available to the retiree and the extent to which those options are limited by both societal and individual attributes. This is a very promising approach. There are many optional new "careers" available to retirees—another work career, leisure, education, dependency—however, they may be limited by society and the nature of age stratification.

Sussman's approach reminds us that retirement is not really "roleless"; rather the choices themselves are not clearly prescribed. It is perhaps like buying a new car. We lack total freedom, since our range of choices is shaped by the auto manufacturers, but we do confront many options—rack-and-pinion steering, radial tires, stratified-charge engines, and so on. These things sound very nice, but those of us who are not mechanics often feel that we are groping in the dark in choosing one over another. So it is with the retiree, who is unfamiliar with the new options presented by retirement.

Sussman argues that the retiree needs to retain his options in the face of various constraints and that there is a need to systematically study the factors which affect the availability and choice of options. The very fact that people retire within a particular social context is important. For example, the services society provides and values relating to both work and retirement affect options. Numerous preretirement factors, both situational-structural (cause of retirement, social class, marital status) and individual (life style, personality, values), determine one's perception of retirement options and their likely outcomes. When viewed in this light, retirement can be seen as an extremely complex transition, which often requires hard work, wrenching reassessment of one's life, and considerable time to move through the phases of retirement.

Retirement Income

In modern societies, which both pressure and encourage older workers to retire, retirement support becomes a major social issue. Low income is a major problem for the aged—nearly one in five has income below the poverty level and as many as three-fourths may lack an "adequate" income (see Chapter 2)—and we have seen that financial security is a major determinant of retirement satisfaction.

The family has often been expected to assume a major responsibility in supporting the aged. This may even have accounted for greater fertility in earlier times when social security meant having children who would someday support you. In 1800, for example, the average couple needed four children to be 95 percent certain that a male would survive until the parents' old age (May and Heer, 1968). A recent national survey found that only 11 percent of adults between 18 and 64 felt that children should support their parents during retirement, however, so family expectatons have apparently declined (National Council on the Aging, 1975).

Retired people can also support themselves through accumulated savings. We do still expect people to make some financial arrangements, but many people do not or cannot do so adequately. Thus, group pensions have become commonplace in modern societies, as a type of insurance, which spread out the risk and uncertainty associated with retirement through collective arrangements.

Social Security

Compulsory old age insurance has a long history, dating back to 1889 in Germany, 1906 in Austria, 1908 in Great Britain, and 1913 in Sweden (Fischer, 1977). By 1973, at least 105 countries had some type of old age/invalidity/survivors program (Schulz, 1976b). The United States was a latecomer to the provision of such insurance, however. Early in this century, Teddy Roosevelt called the lack of old age insurance an "outrage" on the conscience of the American people (Fischer, 1977). There was great resistance to the idea of compulsory old age pensions, because of the fear that it would destroy the spirit of individual enterprise and lead to socialism. During the 1920s and 1930s, however, there was rising support for a social security program because of growing recognition of poverty among the aged and the impact of the Depression. Political movements, such as the Ham and Eggs Movement and the Townsend Movement, began to pressure for change, and in the early 1930s received support from the American Federation of Labor and both the Democratic and Republican parties. Despite counterpressure from Chambers of Commerce and Associations of Manufacturers, most states had at least rudimentary old age insurance programs by 1933 (Fischer, 1977).

With the Social Security Act of 1935, the United States became the last major industrial country to establish a public retirement pension. This legislation, originally intended to create jobs for younger workers, was only secondarily motivated by humanitarian concern for the aged. The program was weak and ineffectual in comparison with other Western nations, but it has been strengthened considerably since 1935, expanding to include such programs as survivor's benefits, disability insurance, and the Medicare health program for the elderly—OASDHI (old age, survivors, disability, and health insurance). The number of persons covered by the program has also expanded. In 1948 only 13 percent of all persons 65 and over were receiving Social Security payments (Riley and Foner, 1968); this has risen to about 90 percent of all older people (Atchley, 1976a), excluding only federal employees and some state and local government employees with other pension coverage, low-income farm and domestic workers, and low-income self-employed persons (Schulz, 1976a). The recent major changes in the system were incorporated in the 1972 Social Security Amendments which increased benefit levels, set up automatic cost-of-living increases (tied to the Consumer Price Index), increased payroll taxes, and established *Supplemental Security Income* (SSI) to replace aid to the indigent aged, blind, and disabled. SSI establishes an income "floor" below which no aged person should fall.

The old-age pension embodied in Social Security has achieved legitimacy, therefore policy-makers are reluctant to make changes for fear of raising questions about the entire system. The national poll conducted for the National Council on the Aging (1975) found that 81 percent of the public felt that "the government should help support older people with the taxes collected from all Americans," 76 percent felt older people should be provided with enough to live on "comfortably," and 97 percent agreed that there should be cost-of-living increases for Social Security. This strong public support has been accompanied by expansion of the financial importance of the system, making it the largest income maintenance program in this country: in 1973, $42 billion was paid out to 25 million recipients (Hollister, 1974). Without Social Security, poverty would be substantially greater among the aged; it is the major source of income for nearly 60 percent of those over 65 (National Council on the Aging, 1975). In 1966, 60 percent of all recipients would have been below the poverty line without this assistance, and 90 percent of these were lifted from poverty by their income from Social Security (Hollister, 1974).

Certain basic principles have been built into Social Security legislation. Great pains have been taken to avoid a "welfare" stigma (with apparent success), so there is no means test. Participation is compulsory for workers in designated groups because

. . . those who do not insure [for retirement] will have to be supported anyway—perhaps at lower levels and in humiliating and respect-destroying ways—when they are in the nonproductive phase of life, but . . . will escape the burden of paying premiums when they are in the productive phase. In fairness to those who insure voluntarily, and in order to maintain the self-respect of those who would not otherwise insure, insurance should be compulsory. (Boulding, 1958:239)

Social Security combines both equity and adequacy, by relating benefits to prior earnings and establishing both minimum and maximum benefit levels.

It is by no means true that you are paid simply on the basis of what you have contributed to the system.

> The first American social security benefit ever paid was $22 a month and was received by Miss Ida Fuller, a retired law firm secretary, in early 1940. . . . . Miss Fuller (who died in 1975) lived to be over a hundred, paid into the program less than $100, and over the years received more than $20,000 in social security benefits. (Schulz, 1976a:88)

While this is an extreme example, Social Security redistributes income in two ways: first, from the young to the old as taxes paid by current workers subsidize the retired; second, to workers who had lower lifetime earnings through weighted benefits and minimum levels. Altogether, about two-thirds of the benefits of the average Social Security beneficiary are "unearned" (not based on past contributions). This proportion will decline, however, since new and future retirees have been paying into the system for a longer time.

While financial adequacy is one aspect of the benefit structure, the level of adequacy is rather low, since the intent has not been to provide comfortable incomes through Social Security alone. The minimum benefit (rising to $121 per month in 1979), which more than 10 percent of all recipients receive, is below the poverty level. In 1972 the average annual Social Security pension was $3,270 for married couples, $2,124 for single men, and $1,682 for single women, clearly an inadequate income by most standards (Atchley, 1976a). A final aspect of Social Security legislation is the "retirement test," reducing benefits for persons between 65 and 72 who earn more than a specified level.

The pension system provided by Social Security includes the following elements:

1. Benefits are financed by payroll taxes paid by both employers and employees on income up to a certain level. In 1978 this tax was 12.1 percent (6.05 percent withheld from employees) on the first $17,700 of income, which will increase to 12.26 percent (6.13 percent from employees) on the first $22,900 in 1979.

2. Once persons under 72 receive outside income above a certain level (4,000 in 1978), benefits are reduced by one dollar for each additional two dollars earned. The level of this retirement test increases automatically with increases in the Consumer Price Index.

3. Benefits are paid to persons who have worked for a minimum period of time on a covered job. In addition to the minimum benefit, there is a maximum benefit limited by the ceiling placed on earnings on which the worker had made contributions. At the end of 1978, for example, the maximum monthly benefit was $456.80.

4. Early retirement benefits, which are actuarially reduced, may be received beginning at age 62. Workers who delay receiving benefits after age 65 have an additional 1 percent added to their benefits for each year they do not receive Social Security from 65 to 72.

5. Dependents and survivors of beneficiaries are also entitled to benefits. Wives and children receive a dependent benefit of 50 percent of the worker's basic benefit. Widows 65 and over (60 and over if disabled) receive the full benefits to which the worker was entitled. Various other dependents and survivors are eligible for benefits under certain conditions. About 40 percent of Social Security pensions are now paid to survivors and disabled workers and their dependents (Schulz, 1976a).

A number of questions have been raised in recent years about the Social Security system.[1] One issue is the equity of coverage for certain groups, notably females and blacks. Women are disadvantaged in a variety of ways (Cohen, 1975; Sommers, 1975). Benefits which are calculated by averaging earnings, tend to be lower for women because they are more likely to have erratic or marginal work careers with low earnings. Housekeeping yields no credit as work, leaving a housewife dependent on her husband's benefits. Women who are divorced before ten years of marriage are not entitled to any of their husbands' benefits. Widows with survivor's benefits tend to be better off—only 11 percent of these draw the minimum benefit, compared with 28 percent of retired women workers (Atchley, 1976a).

Blacks (and other minority groups) are similarly disadvantaged by lower lifetime earnings. For all categories of pension recipients, blacks receive about $20 per month less, and blacks account for

---

[1] For a more complete discussion of the issues surrounding Social Security, see Boskin (1977).

approximately one-fourth of the men and one-fifth of the women receiving minimum benefits (Atchley, 1976a). Jacquelyne Jackson (1974) has suggested that Social Security should take into account the fact that blacks have lower life expectancy by increasing benefits or lowering minimum eligibility ages for blacks.

Major debates have also surrounded financing and eligibility aspects of Social Security. The retirement test, for example, discourages older people working, and thereby supporting themselves, through what amounts to a 50 percent tax on earnings above a certain level. This retirement test is no longer needed to open up jobs for younger workers, and its elimination might relieve some of the public burden for supporting retirees. Another criticized aspect of Social Secuity is that although husbands and wives are separately taxed if both work, only the higher benefit is actually received.

In addition to these apparent inequities, the payroll tax is a regressive tax. Since only the first $17,700 (in 1978) of income is taxed, those with higher incomes pay a lower proportion of their overall income. For example, a janitor earning $10,000 a year pays 5.85 percent of that to Social Security, but an executive earning $50,000 a year pays only about 1.8 percent of his total income. Thus, payroll contributions are a relatively heavier burden for lower-income workers, though such workers can expect to receive proportionately higher benefits when they retire. It is also likely that the employer's share of Social Security taxes is in fact partly borne by employees, in lower wages or reduced fringe benefits such as private pensions. What Social Security amounts to is support of current retirees by current workers, with workers making less contributing a higher proportion. As realization of this fact grows among workers, Social Security financing may become a political issue involving conflict between young and old.

Financing questions also relate to the adequacy of Social Security benefits. Current levels clearly fail to provide truly adequate standards of living, in both an absolute and a relative sense. Schulz (1976a) has estimated that, in order to maintain the same living standard in retirement as existed just prior to retirement, retirement pensions should replace approximately 60 to 65 percent of gross income for a middle-income worker. While some European countries have replacement rates as high as 70 percent, median Social Security pension replacement rates in the United States ranged from 29 to 47 percent in 1974; workers with earnings above the maximum received only 25 percent replacement of preretirement average earnings (Schulz, 1976a). These replacement levels require substantial lowering of the standard of living of the average retiree.

While these issues are important, the most basic question about Social Security concerns the solvency of the system itself. As with all pension systems, Social Security has a *trust fund* to support payment of benefits. This trust fund was accumulated during the early years of Social Security, when more revenue was taken in from taxes than was paid out in benefits. By 1976, however, Social Security was paying out $4.3 billion more than it was taking in, and by projection the trust fund, reduced to $34.3 billion in 1976, will be exhausted by the mid-1980s (Boskin, 1977). This growing deficit is a consequence of many things: a falling birth rate resulting in an "older" population, earlier retirement, a longer average time between retirement and death, and inflation. The fiscal crisis of Social Security will become particularly acute between 2010 and 2020, when the postwar baby-boom cohort reaches retirement age.

Does this mean that Social Security will go bankrupt, depriving millions of older Americans of the pensions they have planned on? This is not a realistic possibility, since the ultimate guarantor of the solvency of Social Security is the taxing power of the federal government, but some hard decisions about its future will have to be made. There are many possibilities for relieving the financial crunch: increasing payroll taxes (the tax rate or the maximum taxable wage), financing benefits through general tax revenues, reducing benefits or taxing them, increasing the retirement age, placing more reliance on private pensions (Schulz, 1976a; Boskin, 1977). Proposals involving almost all these alternatives are currently being debated in Congress, and each will encounter resistance. Payroll taxes are already considered too burdensome by many workers, and increasing them might stretch our willingness to support the aged beyond the breaking point. By 1981, Social Security taxes on employees and employers will rise to 13.3 percent on the first $29,700 of income. Anything which reduces benefits will be adamantly opposed by retirees and their supporters. There is great reluctance to finance all or part of Social Security through general tax revenues for fear it will come to be viewed as "just another welfare program," thereby jeopardizing the strong political support and public legitimacy which it currently enjoys.

These suggested reforms all assume that Social Security will at best operate at current levels, but other suggestions would increase benefits, thereby exacerbating the financial problems of the system. If Social Security is to provide an adequate retirement life, benefits will obviously have to increase to higher levels of income replacement. Although benefits are now adjusted for inflation, some have suggested that they should also be adjusted for economic growth to give the aged their fair share of more prosperous standards of living in the society as a whole.

Social Security is an essential program which must and will continue. Not only are the aged a disproportionately low-income group, but their ability to improve their own financial situation is quite restricted. Personal savings are a difficult, risky, and uncertain method of providing for one's retirement, and private pensions are still inadequate. Barriers to older persons' working further contribute to the need for Social Security. Rather than tinkering with this or that aspect of the Social Security system, we need to decide just what we wish to accomplish through it. For example, Social Security has involved two somewhat contradictory goals: to provide forced insurance based on past earnings and to insure, through income redistribution, adequate support from society for all the aged (Hollister, 1974). Are these goals better pursued through separate programs, or would their separation jeopardize support for both? There is a need to carefully consider goals in supporting retirees, how those goals are best achieved and financed, and how a Social Security system fits within the overall social programs and policies for the aged, and indeed how programs for the aged relate to other policies directed at the well-being of the population.

Job-Related Pensions

While Social Security provides nearly universal coverage and constitutes the most important source of income for retirees, many older persons receive pensions specifically linked to their jobs. Such pensions were slow to develop in the United States (Fischer, 1977). The first private pension plan was established in 1875 by the American Express Company and was followed by railroad pension plans. Industrial corporations were slower to act, and it was not until the period from 1900 to 1915 that such corporations as U.S. Steel, Standard Oil, DuPont, and Westinghouse instituted pensions for their employees. However, these plans protected only a small minority of long-term, loyal employees, were viewed as a favor rather than a right, and were small and easily lost.

Public employees were even worse off.

The United States government treated its animals better than its human work force. Four-legged federal workers retired on full rations, much to the fury of many employees. John W. Perry, a postal worker, was astonished to read in his union newspaper that an artillery horse named Rodney was retired from active duty with full support to the end of his days. "For the purpose of drawing a pension," Perry wrote, "it would have been better had I been born a horse than a human being. I have been a 'wheel horse' for the Government for the past fifty years and can not get a pension." (Fischer, 1977:167)[2]

Few police, firemen, or teachers were covered. The first pension coverage for federal civilian employees was provided by the Civil Service Retirement Act of 1920.

Prior to the enactment of Social Security, only 3 to 4 million workers were covered by private pensions. There has been tremendous recent growth in such coverage, however, for a variety of reasons, including continued industrialization of the economy, periodic wage freezes encouraging growth in fringe benefits, tax inducements (for example, the Revenue Act of 1942 made employer pension contributions tax deductible), a Supreme Court decision in 1949 that pensions were a proper issue for collective bargaining, recognition by unions of the need to supplement Social Security, and the development of multi-employer pension plans (Schulz, 1976a). Unions began to negotiate for pension plans during the 1940s, beginning with the mineworkers, steelworkers, and autoworkers (Greenough and King, 1976). The assets of pension funds more than doubled from 1961 to 1971 to a total of $240 billion, and such funds owned 10 percent of the shares on the New York Stock Exchange (Butler, 1975). By 1972 an estimated 44 percent of wage and salary workers in private industries were covered by private pensions (Kolodrubetz, 1974).

Still, only a minority of all workers are covered by such pensions. They are more prevalent in larger firms with higher wages and higher rates of unionization, particularly in communications and public utilities, mining, and manufacturing (Kasschau, 1976b; Schulz, 1976b). Older workers, women, blacks, and low paid workers in small, nonunion plants are least likely to be covered by private pension plans. Table 6.4 indicates the variations in private pension coverage.

Job-related pensions have generally been designed as supplements to Social Security coverage, resulting in low average benefits. In 1973, about 6 million persons received a total of $11.2 billion in private pension benefits, or an average of less than $2,000 per beneficiary (Schulz, 1976a). An additional 3.7 million persons received $15 billion from the civil service retirement pension program. Even in the federal system most received less than $300 per month as of 1971 (Butler, 1975). The National Council on the Aging survey (1975) found that job-related pensions were the largest source of income for very few: company pensions (5 percent), government pensions (3 percent), railroad pensions (3 per-

---

[2] Quoted in Epstein (1922).

Table 6.4.   Private pension coverage, April 1972

Wage and salary workers in private industry	Percentage
All full-time and part-time employees	43.7
Full-time employees only	47
Men	52
Women	36
Whites	48
Nonwhites	39
Full-time employees, by industry	
Communications and public utilities	82
Mining	72
Manufacturing	
Durable goods	63
Nondurable goods	57
Finance, insurance, and real estate	52
Transportation	45
Trade	
Wholesale	48
Retail	31
Construction	34
Services	29
Full-time employees, by earnings	
Men earning less than $5,000	26
Women earning less than $5,000	31
Men earning $5,000–9,999	58
Women earning $5,000–9,999	58

Source: Walter Kolodrubetz, "Employee-benefit plans, 1972," Social Security Bulletin 37(1974): 15–21; and Walter Kolodrubetz and Donald Landay, "Coverage and vesting of full-time employees under private retirement plans," Social Security Bulletin 35(1973): 20–36 (cited in Schulz, 1976b).

cent), and teacher's pensions (2 percent). While such pension coverage has increased, and benefit levels should improve as the plans mature, the rate of growth in coverage has slowed, and expansion to areas not yet covered may be difficult (Atchley, 1976a). In addition, Kasschau (1976b) points out that unions are often dominated by younger workers, rendering retirees and their needs relatively invisible.

James Schulz (1976a) provides a good overview of private pension characteristics. Most covered workers (80 percent) are in noncontributory plans (financed solely by the employer), since only employer contributions are tax free. Multi-employer plans cover only one-third of the workers but are more prevalent in certain industries (mining, construction, trade, transportation, and service). Most plans provide benefits by either: (1) a uniform amount to all eligible retirees (minimum age and/or years of service requirements), (2) relating benefits to years of service, or (3) relating benefits to both prior earnings and length of service. Survivor's benefits have been a problem, since most plans reduce benefits to those who elect to protect their spouses. While there have been recent increases, a sample survey in 1971 found that only 12 percent of private plans provided automatic survivor's benefits (Hodgens, 1973). Most private plans have early retirement options.

There have been some real problems connected with private pensions. The lack of auditing, for example, has resulted in financial irregularities. More important, however, is the often tragic loss of pension rights which may be experienced by older workers. When Studebaker went out of business, for example, workers under 65 lost all the money they had paid into the company's pension fund. Pensions have been lost by workers laid off only a year or two before retirement age, or with other irregularities in their work careers, as in the following case:

> Mr. X began employment for a Midwest meat-packing company in 1927, at one of the employer's two plants in the same city. During World War II, he was sent to work in the other plant in the city because of the need to fulfill government contracts. He remained there until 1965 when the plant closed. The employer would not permit him to transfer back to the former plant as a regular employee, but only as a casual and intermittent laborer at the former plant. When the plant was closed, Mr. X was paid a total of $231.55 for his accrued pension benefits, despite 38 years of continuous employment with the same employer. Since he was reemployed in his old plant as a casual laborer, he was not eligible for any pension benefits after 1965.

> In 1970, he was dismissed because he was overage at 65. He did not receive any pension benefits. In sum, this employee was dismissed at age 66 after 43 years of continuous employment with the same employer and with no benefits to him except $231.55, paid to him in 1965. Had he been permitted to carry his pension benefits and credits from both plants with the same employer, which were located a few streets apart, Mr. X would have been eligible for a pension. (Cummings, 1974:81–82)

Three major problems have been associated with private pensions. First, such pensions have not been insured against the company or its pension fund going bankrupt. Second, vesting provisions have typically been inadequate. If a person is vested, he or she can leave the company before retirement age and still be guaranteed benefits. For example, a person could work for Firm A for 10 years, move to firm B until retirement at age 65, and then receive pensions from both firms based on years of service. In the past, workers were required to remain until retirement or work for a long time (20 or 30 years) before any benefits were vested. The third problem is a lack of *portability*, that is, pension contributions and rights with one organization are not transferrable to another. Take the case of a worker who spends 20 years with one company and 20 years with another. Assuming full vesting of benefits with both companies, the combination of two 20-year-service pensions would amount to less than one 40-year-service pension with portability of the 20 years of service in the first company to pension rights in the second company.

The Employee Retirement Income Security Act of 1974 was a response to such problems and included some very commendable provisions (Skolnick, 1974; Schulz, 1976b). For example, all private pension plans must vest benefits according to one of three alternatives:

1. 25 percent of pension benefits would be vested after 5 years with the company, increasing to 100 percent after 15 years of service.
2. Full vesting (100 percent) after 10 years of service.
3. 50 percent vesting when age and years of service total 45 years, followed in 5 years by 100 percent vesting (but all employees must be 50 percent vested after 10 years and fully vested after 15 years of service).

Thus, all covered workers would be guaranteed a full pension upon retirement (however that is determined by the company) after 10 or 15 years with the company, regardless of whether they stayed until retirement. The legislation also strengthens standards for financing and administering pension plans and has new requirements for disclosure to participants and the Social Security Administration. The Pension Benefit Guarantee Corporation offers insurance (up to $750 per month) to workers whose pension plan collapses because of insufficient funds. Finally, workers without pension coverage may establish their own tax-exempt *individual retirement account* (IRA).

While this legislation is certainly a positive step, there are important gaps or omissions (Butler, 1975; Schulz, 1976a). Pension plans are still voluntary, leaving over half the private work force uncovered, and nothing is said about the adequacy of benefits. State and local government plans are not covered by the law. Portability remains low, and this continues to hinder worker mobility and career change. Adequate portability might be an incentive to older workers to retrain for other careers rather than hang on to deadend jobs. Survivor's benefits, still usually not available, are quite low. Thus, much remains to be done in providing adequate and equitable retirement benefits.

Pension Policy[3]

Some retired persons do receive adequate incomes. In fact, some (20 percent of all retired couples in 1967) receive two pensions, both Social Security and a job-related pension (Atchley, 1976a). Approximately 43 percent of retired federal employees are "double-dippers," drawing both civil service and Social Security retirement benefits by taking a minimal second job covered by Social Security (Campbell, 1977), a practice which has drawn much criticism. Such persons are relatively well off, but they tend to be concentrated in well-paying industries and occupations. There are many more retirees for whom retirement benefits and other income sources are far from adequate.

One as yet unanswered policy question is: What is the best mixture of public and private pensions? Most industrialized countries rely either on public pensions or some mixture with strong regulation of the private sector. We have already seen some of the criticisms of Social Security. Private pensions do have certain advantages, notably their flexibility to the needs and desires of different worker groups and the investment of pension funds in the national economy (Schulz, 1976a), but numerous problems are associated with them: it is difficult to cover all workers, they are usually not inflation-proof, administrative costs are relatively high, and portability is difficult to achieve (Schulz, 1976b). Social Security has the advantages of low costs—administrative expenses were only 1.5 percent of contributions in 1974 (Schulz, 1976a)— nearly universal coverage, combined with cost-of-living adjustments; guarantee of the financial integrity by the taxing power of the government allowing benefits to be provided without the large reserves needed to cover private pensions.

It is likely that the United States will continue to have a mixture of public and private pension systems in the foreseeable future. Private pensions will become more prevalent, but by no means universal, and Social Security benefits may improve, but probably not to "comfortable" levels. Robert Butler (1975) has suggested what seems to be an ideal pension system: universal coverage with immediate 100 percent vesting and portability, full insurance, with full survivor's benefits, and two escalators (tied to the cost of

---

[3] For a more complete discussion of pension policy issues, see Greenough and King (1976).

living and the overall economic productivity of the country) to conform to current standards of living. Unfortunately, the acceptance of such a plan, if it occurs at all, is a long time in the future.

Preparation for Retirement

Retirement generally represents a considerable change in patterns of living for most people (for better or worse), though generally, older people appear to adjust reasonably well to its ambiguity. Streib and Schneider (1971) suggest three reasons for this: (1) the "roleless" role actually has multiple role possibilities from which to choose, (2) ambiguity may itself be protective by reducing demands on the aged and making them more free, and (3) there is always the possibility for "reliving" past roles (reminiscing) or achieving vicarious gratification (through children or grandchildren). Thus,

> A clearly-defined role facilitates activity and gives a sense of security to a person involved in a network of impersonal universalistically-oriented judgements and evaluations. This may not be the kind of world in which many older people live. In the later years of life, the *important* persons in one's life—friends and relatives—know who the older person is and, therefore, he moves in a world that is familiar to him, and with which he is familiar. He may not need a sharply-defined extra-familial "role" to give him an identity or to facilitate his own activity in his everyday world. We suggest, therefore, that so far as the older person himself is concerned, his willingness to leave the work force and perhaps his satisfaction with other aspects of life are not dependent upon whether he has a clearly defined alternative role or not. (Schneider, 1964:56)

However, any role transition is facilitated by "anticipatory socialization," through which people learn what to expect as well as what to desire from a new role (Rosow, 1974), and lack of preparation or unrealistic expectations will certainly have an impact on the retirement experience. There are many aspects of retirement which can benefit from planning—financial, health, social, marital. Prospective retirees need to develop a greater understanding of the options available to them, as well as competence in selecting options and handling interactions with the many bureaucracies which affect retirement. A substantial minority of workers find retirement difficult, and others approach it with fear or resistance which, though it may later prove excessive, makes the transition more difficult.

The Prevalence of Preparation

Most people do little definite planning for retirement. The National Council on the Aging study (1975) compared what people 65 and over said were "very important" steps which ought to be taken to prepare for one's later years with those steps they had actually taken (Table 6.5). Some steps, particularly those involving health and income, had generally been taken, but this may not have occurred *before* retirement. Some things, such as building up savings, have to be started rather early in life. The study did find that 35 percent had not prepared a will, 65 percent had not sought information from older people, and 92 percent had not participated in formal preparation programs. Older blacks and those with low incomes were least likely to have prepared.

When asked what they would have done differently to prepare for old age, people were most likely to indicate a need for more savings and investments (26 percent) and more or better education (14 percent) (National Council on the Aging, 1975). Finances

Table 6.5. Public 65 and over who consider steps "very important" compared with those who have already taken steps

	Percentage who consider step "Very important"	Percentage who have already taken step
Make sure you'll have medical care available	88	88
Build up your savings	85	73
Learn about pensions and Social Security benefits	85	87
Prepare a will	79	65
Buy your own home	75	74
Develop hobbies and other leisure-time activities	61	62
Decide whether you want to move or continue to live where you are	53	72
Talk to older people about what it's like to grow old	27	35
Plan new part-time or full-time jobs	26	16
Enroll in retirement counseling or preparation programs	19	8
Move in with children or other relatives	7	9

Source: *The Myth and Reality of Aging in America,* a study prepared for The National Council on the Aging, Inc. (NCOA), Washington, D.C. by Louis Harris and Associates, Inc., © 1975, p. 120. Reprinted by permission.

should certainly be a focus for any planning effort. One study of a large manufacturing corporation found that most workers expected financial difficulties in retirement and were willing to save (Morrison, 1976). Few of them were able to save very much, however, and most had unrealistic expectations about postretirement earnings. There was a general lack of good information on which to base financial planning. The fact that education was mentioned second in the NCOA study suggests that the use of time and possession of skills and interests which withstand aging are important concerns.

There appear to be social class differences in retirement preparation (Simpson, Back, and McKinney, 1966c; Atchley, 1976a). Upper-status workers, who are more reluctant to retire, see little need for formal preparation, since they are used to manipulating their world. Semi-skilled workers may be more fatalistic and in any case have less access to formal programs, but there is evidence that they are interested in preretirement programs (Fillenbaum, 1971a). Exposure to retirement information is greatest among middle-status workers, who tend to be favorably disposed to retirement and work in organizations with preretirement programs.

Those who do some planning for retirement tend to have more favorable orientations, though which causes which is unclear, and they also appear to have higher morale and fewer feelings of job deprivation following retirement (Riley and Foner, 1968; Simpson, Back, and McKinney, 1966c), and formal preretirement programs have demonstrated some utility in easing the transition from work to retirement.

Preretirement Counseling

Preretirement counseling is a relatively new phenomenon which is still not very widespread. A 1963 survey of 1,600 plants, each with at least 50 employees, found that only 12 percent had preretirement counseling programs (Shultz, 1963). They are somewhat more widespread now, but are largely confined to larger companies and government agencies. There are three basic models: informational lectures, group discussions, and more interpersonal "T-group" approaches (Pyron and Manion, 1973). Most programs are limited rather than comprehensive, involving little more than information about retirement options and Social Security and pension benefits. Most are geared for literate, middle-income workers, which may limit their usefulness (Atchley, 1976a). This is unfortunate, since Simpson and associates (1966c) found that exposure to information about retirement was particularly likely to encourage planning among semi-skilled workers.

Obviously there are many things on which such programs could focus. "Hard" information, particularly regarding finances and health, should always be a priority. Financial programs such as Social Security and job-related pensions, as well as health and social services for older people, can be very confusing. Ideally, however, such programs should also help ease the social and psychological transition from work to retirement and foster flexibility, since retirement is a varied and changing experience. Preretirement programs, especially those involving group discussions, offer an excellent opportunity to explore the individual's attitudes toward both work and retirement and to help people deal more effectively with situations encountered following retirement. Peers in one's retiring cohort, and those who have retired earlier, can offer helpful suggestions and serve as role models and a particularly important source of anticipatory socialization.

There is evidence that preretirement counseling can be effective (Pyron and Manion, 1973; Atchley, 1976a). Presumably adjustment to retirement is enhanced by better preparation and more realistic expectations, resulting in higher postretirement involvement, lower job deprivation, better self-rated health, and greater satisfaction with retirement income. Interestingly, such effects may occur regardless of whether participants thought the program was useful (Green et al., 1969). Postretirement counseling can compensate somewhat for a lack of preretirement counseling, but the latter seems to be more effective (Pyron and Manion, 1973).

While preretirement programs seem to be helpful, little is known about the relative usefulness of different types. A study by Glamser and DeJong (1975) exemplifies the type of research needed. They randomly assigned older workers at six glass manufacturing plants into three groups:

1. A control group with no preretirement counseling.
2. An individual briefing program, involving booklets and an individual meeting with the personnel manager.
3. A group discussion program of eight sessions on the meanings of work and retirement, Social Security and Medicare, financial planning, health, leisure, family and friends, and living arrangements.

Participants in the group discussion program gained significantly more information about Social Security, Medicare, income, and health. Surprisingly, individual briefing was no more effective in teaching this information than no program at all. Compared with

Table 6.6. Selected retirement preparation activities undertaken, by type of preretirement program (percentage)

Activity	Group discussion	Individual briefing	Control group
Have figured out retirement income	63	55	35
Talked over retirement plans with spouse	90	35	55
Have made a will	63	35	30
Have reviewed insurance policies	52	22	30
Try to eat a well-balanced diet	79	65	50
Have arranged for health insurance	42	30	20
Have worked out ways to cut expenses	79	35	20
Have checked house for safety hazards	58	40	30
Have done some reading about retirement	79	70	35
Saving a little more money lately	79	52	50

Source: Francis Glamser and Gordon DeJong. 1975. "The efficiency of preretirement preparation programs for industrial workers." *Journal of Gerontology* 30:599. Reprinted by permission.

the control group, neither preretirement program resulted in changes in morale or attitudes toward retirement or the company. All of these attitudes were relatively positive to begin with, however, which suggests that results might be different when worker attitudes are more negative. Workers in the group discussion program were more likely to feel prepared, and data in Table 6.6 indicate that they were more likely to plan and prepare for retirement (for example, make a will and talk over plans with spouse). Individual briefing was only slightly better than the control group in fostering such preparations.

Preretirement programs need more interpersonal approaches dealing with the social and psychological implications of being retired. The traditional "learning model" of most classrooms is often inappropriate, since resistance, fear, and unrealistic fantasies distort the message. Group interaction approaches can be used to develop self-diagnostic skills, communication and interpersonal skills, independent attitudes, and skills in planning and problem-solving (Pyron and Manion, 1973).

This approach is taken in a group discussion program developed at the University of Michigan (Hunter, 1973). Designed to create an atmosphere permitting the expression of concerns, fears, expectations, and interests, the program provides both information and an interchange of ideas and experiences relevant to common problems and fears. It attempts to stimulate people to think and make decisions on their own, since any formal program is necessarily limited, and deals with such issues as work and retirement, income and money management, physical and mental health, family and friends, living arrangements, legal questions, use of free time, and utilization of community resources. A wide variety of program materials are used, including a retirement readiness checklist, essays and short stories, and thematic films and photographs.

Some orientation to retirement should begin very early in life, when attitudes and expectations are first being formed, and formal programs concerned with financial planning and the creative use of leisure time could begin at age 45. The transition into retirement could also be made more gradual, through shorter work weeks or longer vacations as workers near retirement.

This implies that preparation for, and adjustment to, retirement is the result of lifelong patterns, and how to use time meaningfully cannot be taught suddenly. Such capabilities must be carefully cultivated, but our age stratification system has created a sudden transition into retirement and made available relatively few options.

Summary

Many older people continue to work, even after retiring from their primary occupation. The ability and desire to do so depends on occupation, family situation, health, and other considerations. In most respects, older workers are as capable as younger workers and seem to be more committed to their work (for various reasons). Nevertheless, the potential for physical decline and job obsolescence create difficulties for older workers, and little has been done in this society to facilitate career changes at any age. High unemployment among older workers is partly due to their relatively low education, poor health, and inefficient job-seeking techniques, but it is also caused by age discrimination in hiring and employment services.

Retirement is a product of modern, industrialized societies. Structural transformations in the economy create skill obsolescence among older workers, remove individuals from the retirement decision, and result in new personnel policies which both "push" and "pull" toward retirement. It may also be that work is less meaningful than in the past, particularly when age no longer lends prestige to the older worker, creating less attachment to work and greater willingness to retire.

Most workers retire "voluntarily," though usually because of poor health, and often because jobs are not available or they are pressured into it. The attraction of leisure has grown, however. While compulsory retirement has increased, relatively few able workers are forced to retire against their will. It is questionable whether mandatory policies are ever justified, but the constitutionality of such policies has continually been upheld. There is little public support for mandatory retirement, however, and flexible alternatives could be encouraged more than they are.

It has been suggested that retirement is a major crisis for both social and personal identity, but most adults expect and desire to retire. Such attitudes are affected by occupational status and age. In addition, most retirees appear to adjust to retirement, with health and income being the primary determinants of retirement satisfaction. Relatively few people miss their jobs, and if they do it is often because of a lack of alternative activities and associations. Retirement does offer rewards—leisure pursuits, independence, relaxation from responsibilities. Blue-collar workers have more problems adjusting to retirement, because of financial problems and greater social disruption. The assumption that retirement is a male problem is unfounded, and women may actually have more difficulty adjusting to retirement than men.

One reason for the relatively unremarkable consequences of retirement is the fact that work is not necessarily a central life interest. There is growing evidence that both blue-collar and white-collar work is becoming less meaningful and satisfying. Thus, we must be careful in assessing the "loss" felt at retirement.

Retirement is a complex process. As a particular event it is seldom an effective rite of passage for easing role transition, and little is known about its overall nature. Additionally, relatively little is known about the expectations and rights associated with retirement as a role, though some have suggested that its ambiguity can create problems for retirees. Individuals may face a variety of retirement phases—preretirement, honeymoon, disenchantment, reorientation, stability, and termination—which vary by individual, further emphasizing the complexity of the retirement process. Retirement adjustment is a matter of overall accommodation to changes in one's patterns of living.

Retirement income is a major concern, since families and individuals often cannot or do not provide adequate finances. The Social Security Act of 1935 has been expanded to include about 90 percent of the aged. This program has strong public support and it has become the largest income maintenance program in the United States. Social Security is a contributory insurance program which also redistributes income. Questions have been raised about the equity of coverage for women and blacks. Other issues are the retirement test, the regressive nature of the payroll tax, and the adequacy of support levels. While numerous reform proposals have been made, there is a reluctance to institute change for fear of jeopardizing support for the program.

Coverage from private pensions has grown considerably in recent years, though they still involve only a minority of all workers and average benefits are rather low. The Employee Retirement Income Security Act of 1974 was enacted as a response to financial irregularities and problems of vesting and portability. This legislation outlines vesting requirements, strengthens requirements for managing pension plans, and provides pension insurance. Many problems remain with private pensions, however, though some mixture of public and private pensions is likely to continue in the foreseeable future.

While the ambiguity of the retirement role may be overstated, preparation for any role change is advisable. Most people do little planning for retirement, however. Financial expectations seem to be a particular problem. Exposure to retirement information is greatest among middle-status workers. In general, preretirement counseling is relatively new and not widespread and is likely to be limited in scope, despite the need for social and psychological preparation as well as the provision of information on health and finances. Retirement preparation should be thought of as a lifelong process, and there are indications that preretirement counseling can produce a more positive retirement experience. Group approaches emphasizing social and psychological aspects of retirement appear to be most effective.

References

Atchley, Robert
  1971 "Retirement and work orientation." The Gerontologist
    11: 29–32.
  1976a The Sociology of Retirement. New York: Schenkman.
  1976b "Selected social and psychological differences between men
    and women in later life." Journal of Gerontology 31:
    204–11.
Belbin, Eunice and R. M. Belbin
  1968 "New careers in middle age." In Bernice Neugarten (ed.).
    Middle Age and Aging. Chicago: University of Chicago
    Press.
Blau, Zena Smith
  1973 Old Age in a Changing Society. New York: New
    Viewpoints.

Blauner, Robert
1964 Alienation and Freedom. Chicago: University of Chicago Press.

Boskin, Michael (ed.)
1977 The Crisis in Social Security: Problems and Prospects. San Francisco: Institute for Contemporary Studies.

Boulding, Kenneth
1958 Principles of Economic Policy. Englewood Cliffs, N.J.: Prentice-Hall.

Braverman, Harry
1974 Labor and Monopoly Capital: The Degradation of Work in the Twentieth Century. New York: Monthly Review Press.

Butler, Robert
1975 Why Survive?: Being Old in America. New York: Harper & Row.

Campbell, M. P.
1971 "Retirement and disengagement." Human Relations 24: 255–78.

Campbell, Rita
1977 "The problems of fairness." In Michael Boskin (ed.). The Crisis in Social Security: Problems and Prospects. San Francisco: Institute for Contemporary Studies.

Chinoy, Ely
1965 Automobile Workers and the American Dream. Boston: Beacon Press.

Clark, Margaret
1972 "An anthropological view of retirement." In Frances Carp (ed.). Retirement. New York: Behavioral Publications.

Cohen, Wilbur
1975 "Social Security: Next steps." In No Longer Young: The Older Woman in America. Occasional Papers in Gerontology No. 11, Institute of Gerontology, University of Michigan-Wayne State University.

Cottrell, Fred and Robert Atchley
1969 Retired Women: A Preliminary Report. Oxford, Ohio: Scripps Foundation.

Cowgill, Donald
1974 "Aging and modernization: A revision of the theory." In Jaber Gubrium (ed.). Late Life: Communities and Environmental Policies. Springfield, Ill.: Charles C Thomas.

Cummings, Frank
1974 "Reforming private pensions." In Frederick Eisele (ed.). Political Consequences of Aging. The Annals of the American Academy of Political and Social Science 415 (September): 80–94.

DeLury, Bernard
1976 "The Age Discrimination in Employment Act: Background

and highlights of recent cases." Industrial Gerontology 3 (1): 37–40.

Donahue, Wilma, Harold Orbach, and Otto Pollak
1960 "Retirement: The emerging social pattern." In Clark Tibbitts (ed.). Handbook of Social Gerontology: Societal Aspects of Aging. Chicago: University of Chicago Press.

Dubin, Robert
1956 "Industrial workers' worlds." Social Problems 3: 131–42.
1976 "Work in modern society." In Robert Dubin (ed.). Handbook of Work, Organization, and Society. Chicago: Rand McNally.

Dubin, Robert, R. Alan Hedley, and Thomas Taveggia
1976 "Attachment to work." In Robert Dubin (ed.). Handbook of Work, Organization, and Society. Chicago: Rand McNally.

Epstein, Abraham
1922 Facing Old Age: A Study of Old Age Dependency in the United States and Old Age Pensions. New York: Alfred A. Knopf.

Fillenbaum, Gerda
1971a "Retirement planning programs—at what age, and for whom?" The Gerontologist 11: 33–36.
1971b "On the relation between attitude to work and attitude to retirement." Journal of Gerontology 26: 244–48.

Fillenbaum, Gerda and George Maddox
1974 "Work after retirement: An investigation into some psychologically relevant variables." The Gerontologist 14: 418–24.

Fischer, David
1977 Growing Old in America. New York: Oxford University Press.

Friedmann, Eugene and Robert Havighurst
1954 The Meaning of Work and Retirement. Chicago: University of Chicago Press.

Glamser, Francis
1976 "Determinants of a positive attitude toward retirement." Journal of Gerontology 31: 104–07.

Glamser, Francis and Gordon DeJong
1975 "The efficacy of preretirement preparation programs for industrial workers." Journal of Gerontology 30: 595–600.

Goudy, Willis, Edward Powers, and Patricia Keith
1975 "Work and retirement: A test of attitudinal relationships." Journal of Gerontology 30: 193–98.

Green, Mark, et al.
1969 Pre-retirement Counseling, Retirement Adjustment and the Older Employee. Eugene: University of Oregon Graduate School of Management.

Greenough, William and Francis King
1976 Pension Plans and Public Policy. New York: Columbia University Press.

Heidbreder, Elizabeth
1972 "Factors in retirement adjustment: White-collar/blue-collar experience." Industrial Gerontology 12: 69–79.

Heidbreder, Elizabeth and M. D. Batten
1974 ESARS II—A Comparative View of Services to Age Groups. Facts and Trends No. 4. Washington, D.C.: National Council on the Aging.

Hodgens, Evan
1973 "Survivors' pensions: An emerging employee benefit." Monthly Labor Review 96 (July): 31–34.

Hollister, Robinson
1974 "Social mythology and reform: Income maintenance for the aged." In Frederick Eisele (ed.). Political Consequences of Aging. The Annals of the American Academy of Political and Social Science 415 (September): 19–40.

Hunter, Woodrow
1973 "Preretirement education programs." In Rosamonde Boyd and Charles Oakes (eds.). Foundations of Practical Gerontology. Columbia: University of South Carolina Press.

Jackson, Jacquelyne
1974 "NCBA, black aged and politics." In Frederick Eisele (ed.). Political Consequences of Aging. The Annals of the American Academy of Political and Social Science 415 (September): 139–59.

Jacobsohn, Dan
1972 "Willingness to retire in relation to job strain and type of work." Industrial Gerontology 13: 65–74.

Kasschau, Patricia
1976a "Perceived age discrimination in a sample of aerospace employees." The Gerontologist 16: 166–73.
1976b "Retirement and the social system." Industrial Gerontology 3:11–24.

Kalleberg, Arne
1977 "Work values and job rewards: A theory of job satisfaction." American Sociological Review 42: 124–43.

King, H. F.
1955 "An age-analysis of some agricultural accidents." Occupational Psychology 29: 245–53.

Kolodrubetz, Walter
1974 "Employee-benefit plans, 1972." Social Security Bulletin 37: 15–21.

Kolodrubetz, Walter and Donald Landay
1973 "Coverage and vesting of full-time employees under private retirement plans." Social Security Bulletin 35: 20–36.

Maddox, George
1966 "Retirement as a social event in the United States." In

John McKinney and Frank deVyver (eds.). Aging and
Social Policy. New York: Appleton-Century-Crofts.
May, David and David Heer
1968 "Son survivorship and family size in India: A computer
simulation." Population Studies 22 (2): 199–210.
Meier, Elizabeth and Elizabeth Kerr
1976 "Capabilities of middle-aged and older workers: A survey
of the literature." Industrial Gerontology 3: 147–56.
Morrison, Malcolm
1976 "Planning for income adequacy in retirement: The
expectations of current workers." The Gerontologist
16: 538–43.
Morse, Nancy and Robert Weiss
1955 "The function and meaning of work and the job."
American Sociological Review 20: 191–98.
Nadelson, Theodore
1969 "A survey of the literature on the adjustment of the aged
to retirement." Journal of Geriatric Psychiatry
3: 3–20.
National Council on the Aging
1975 The Myth and Reality of Aging in America.
Washington, D.C.
Palmore, Erdman
1964 "Retirement patterns among aged men: Findings of the
1963 Survey of the Aged." Social Security Bulletin 27:
3–10.
1972 "Compulsory versus flexible retirement: Issues and facts."
The Gerontologist 12: 343–48.
1975 "The status and integration of the aged in Japanese
society." Journal of Gerontology 30: 199–208.
Parker, Stanley and Michael Smith
1976 "Work and leisure." In Robert Dubin (ed.). Handbook
of Work, Organization, and Society. Chicago:
Rand McNally.
Pollman, A. William
1971 "Early retirement: A comparison of poor health to other
retirement factors." Journal of Gerontology 26: 41–45.
Pyron, H. Charles and U. Vincent Manion
1973 "Preretirement counseling." In John Cull and Richard
Hardy (eds.). The Neglected Older American. Springfield,
Ill.: Charles C Thomas.
Quirk, Daniel
1975 "Public policy note: The Supreme Court and mandatory
retirement." Industrial Gerontology 2: 301–03.
Riley, Matilda and Anne Foner
1968 Aging and Society. Volume 1: An Inventory of Research
Findings. New York: Russell Sage.
Riley, Matilda, Marilyn Johnson, and Anne Foner

1972   Aging and Society. Volume 3: A Sociology of Age
        Stratification. New York: Russell Sage.
Rose, Charles and John Mogey
1972   "Aging and preference for later retirement." Aging and
        Human Development 3: 45–62.
Rosenberg, George
1970   The Worker Grows Old. San Francisco: Jossey-Bass.
Rosow, Irving
1974   Socialization to Old Age. Berkeley: University of
        California Press.
Rowe, Alan
1976   "Retired academics and research activity." Journal of
        Gerontology 31: 456–61.
Sarason, Seymour
1977   Work, Aging, and Social Change. New York: The Free
        Press.
Schneider, Clement
1964   "Adjustment of employed women to retirement." Un-
        published doctoral dissertation, Cornell University, Ithaca,
        New York.
Schulz, James
1976a   The Economics of Aging. Belmont, Calif.: Wadsworth.
1976b   "Income distribution and the aging." In Robert Binstock
        and Ethel Shanas (eds.). Handbook of Aging and the
        Social Sciences. New York: Van Nostrand Reinhold.
Schulz, James et al.
1974   Providing Adequate Retirement Income—Pension Reform
        in the United States and Abroad. Hanover, N.H.: New
        England Press for Brandeis University Press.
Shanas, Ethel
1972   "Adjustment to retirement: Substitution or accommoda-
        tion?" In Frances Carp (ed.). Retirement. New York:
        Behavioral Publications.
Shanas, Ethel et al.
1968   Old People in Three Industrial Societies. New York:
        Atherton Press.
Sheppard, Harold
1972   Where Have All the Robots Gone?—Worker Dissatisfac-
        tion in the 1970's. New York: The Free Press.
1976   "Work and retirement." In Robert Binstock and Ethel
        Shanas (eds.). Handbook of Aging and the Social Sciences.
        New York: Van Nostrand Reinhold.
Sheppard, Harold and A. Harvey Belitsky
1966   The Job Hunt. Baltimore: Johns Hopkins Press.
Shultz, Edwin
1963   A study of Programs of Preparation for Retirement in
        Industry. Ithaca, N.Y.: New York State School of Industrial
        and Labor Relations.

Simpson, Ida, Kurt Back, and John McKinney
1966a "Attributes of work, involvement in society, and self-evaluation in retirement." In Ida Simpson and John McKinney (eds.). Social Aspects of Aging. Durham, N.C.: Duke University Press.
1966b "Orientations toward work and retirement, and self-evaluation in retirement." In Ida Simpson and John McKinney (eds.). Social Aspects of Aging. Durham, N.C.: Duke University Press.
1966c "Exposure to information on, preparation for, and self-evaluation in retirement." In Ida Simpson and John McKinney (eds.). Social Aspects of Aging. Durham, N.C.: Duke University Press.
Skolnick, Alfred
1974 "Pension reform legislation of 1974." Social Security Bulletin 37: 35–42.
Slavick, Fred
1966 Compulsory and Flexible Retirement in the American Economy. Ithaca, N.Y.: Cornell University Press.
Smith, John
1975 "Occupations classified by their age structure." Industrial Gerontology 2: 209–21.
Sobel, Irvin and Richard Wilcock
1963 "Job placement services for older workers in the United States." International Labor Review 88: 129–56.
Sommers, Tish
1975 "Social Security: A woman's viewpoint." Industrial Gerontology 2: 266–79.
Spengler, Joseph
1966 "Some economic and related determinants affecting the older worker's occupational role." In Ida Simpson and John McKinney (eds.). Social Aspects of Aging. Durham, N.C.: Duke University Press.
Strauss, Harold, Bruce Aldrich, and Aaron Lipman
1976 "Retirement and perceived status loss." In Jaber Gubrium (ed.). Time, Roles, and Self in Old Age. New York: Human Sciences Press.
Streib, Gordon and Clement Schneider
1971 Retirement in American Society. Ithaca, N.Y.: Cornell University Press.
Sussman, Marvin
1972 "An analytic model for the sociological study of retirement." In Frances Carp (ed.). Retirement. New York: Behavioral Publications.
Taves, Marvin and Gary Hansen
1963 "Seventeen hundred elderly citizens." In Arnold Rose (ed.). Aging in Minnesota. Minneapolis: University of Minnesota Press.

Time
   1977   "Now, the revolt of the old." October 10: 18–33.
U.S. Bureau of the Census
   1973   "Employment status and work experiences." Census of
           Population: 1970. Subject Report PC(2)–6A. Washington,
           D.C.: U.S. Government Printing Office.
U.S. Department of Health, Education, and Welfare
   1973   Work in America. Cambridge, Mass.: MIT Press.
Welford, A. T.
   1977   "Motor performance." In James Birren and K. Warner
           Schaie (eds.). Handbook of the Psychology of Aging.
           New York: Van Nostrand Reinhold.

7

The Use of Time: Opportunities and Constraints

~~~~~~

Economic growth has made it possible for modern societies to support retired older persons (though often quite modestly). As a result, the use of time has become an important issue for the older population in particular. This century has witnessed steady growth in the amount of "free" time available to the average person, with shorter work weeks, longer paid vacations, labor-saving household devices, and the like. Some of these trends are illustrated in Figure 7.1. As time, money, and facilities have become more broadly available, "leisure elites" have given way to mass participation, but it is the retired who are truly our new "leisure class," since the free time of even young people is limited by education and work requirements (Kreps, 1976). How this extra time is used will have important consequences for our overall enjoyment of life, now and in the future.

Aging presents critical challenges to the use of time. Older people may be cast adrift from familiar worlds and identities—by retirement, widowhood, declining health, residential change, and so on. How people use their time to accommodate to these disruptions of their normal styles of living will determine the nature of their aging experience. Release from normal, expected, or obligatory activity patterns may open new outlets for creativity, experimentation, self-expression, and personal growth, but we have already seen that the psychological consequences of old age are often constriction, disengagement, defensiveness, and passivity. The reasons for

Figure 7.1. Hours of work and hours of free time per week 1900–1960

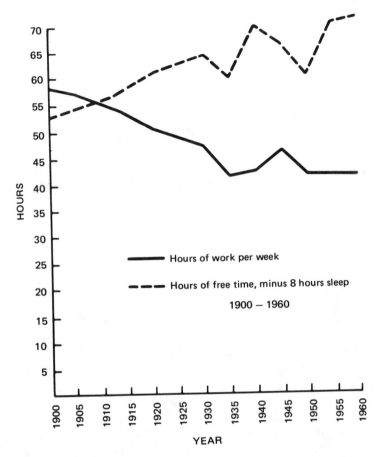

Source: Max Kaplan, *Leisure: Theory and Policy,* © 1975 by John Wiley and Sons, Inc., p. 368. Reprinted by permission.

this involve limitations in options for using time, as well as barriers and constraints in using those options.

The factors affecting the use of time correspond to some of the major themes and topics of this book. Aging frees time for new uses, but at the same time may create barriers of poor health or low income. Such psychological accompaniments of old age as new time perspectives focused on "time left to live" will affect perceptions about available options and their feasibility. Aging persons are also prisoners of their own pasts in at least two respects. First, each of us enters old age with particular personalities and styles of living through which we assess the appropriateness for ourselves of alternative roles and activities. Second, our membership in a specific cohort shapes our use of time through shared socialization and historical experiences. While current cohorts of older people have relatively low levels of education, have been brought up on the work ethic, may have experienced greater religious socialization in childhood, and so on, the activity patterns of succeeding cohorts can be expected to change.

One of the most important factors affecting the use of time by older persons is the social context within which choices are made. Options are restricted by the prevailing age stratification system in modern societies. In the broadest sense, this means that the choice between activity or disengagement is determined by the society, so that restricted role opportunities account for the social and psychological withdrawal of many older people. Age stratification also channels activities through the relative availability of leisure pursuits, voluntary associations, service roles, and the like in more subtle ways, however. Thus, the roles and activities of older people are a product of the complex interaction of personal history and preference, cohort differences, age-related opportunities and constraints, and the patterns facilitated or constrained by age stratification.

The critical issues we need to address regarding the use of time by older people are:

1. What factors determine the activity patterns of the aged?
2. What are the meanings of these activities and the satisfactions derived from them?
3. How do the uses of time affect the individual aging experience? What contributions do they make to the psychological and developmental issues confronting the aged?
4. What changes are needed or likely in the activity options available to older people?

Leisure

"Leisure" is a term which is both recognizable and difficult to define. Clearly we view leisure as "nonwork," but not all such activity is truly leisure. There may be complex relationships between work and nonwork activities (Kelly, 1972). Some things are done as preparation for, or recuperation from, work, while others are engaged in as compensation for work (travel as an escape from factory work) or because it is "expected" of us (the businessman who belongs to Rotary). Still other pursuits are more freely chosen but still related to work (reading by college professors or the business golf game). *Unconditional leisure* refers to activities which are not escapes or work-related, but are engaged in as ends in themselves (Kelly, 1972). Thus, leisure partly implies activity with a minimum of obligation. It is *expressive* activity, engaged in for its intrinsic satisfactions (Gordon, Gaitz, and Scott, 1976). Leisure is also expected to be pleasant, though it may at times make us unhappy (when we lose a game or fail to master a musical instrument).

These meanings of leisure can be seen in the following definitions:

> Leisure is an activity—apart from the obligations of work, family, and society—to which the individual turns at will, for either relaxation, diversion, or broadening his experiences and his spontaneous social participation, the free exercise of his creative capacities. (Dumazedier, 1967:16–17)

> Leisure . . . consists of relatively self-determined activity-experience that falls into one's economically free-time roles, that is seen as leisure by participants, that is psychologically pleasant in anticipation and recollection, that potentially covers the whole range of commitment and intensity, that contains characteristic norms and constraints, and that provides opportunities for recreation, personal growth, and service to others. (Kaplan, 1975:26)

These definitions point out some critical aspects of leisure. Although leisure is considered pleasant and relatively nonobligatory, it is not simply amusement or idleness—potentially it can be as intense and meaningful as any activity (including work). Work is not the only source of creativity, sociability, or self-respect, and many people may be turning elsewhere for meaningful self-expression. Thus, the study of leisure is important to an understanding of the meanings and satisfactions of life itself, particularly for the retired.

These definitions also indicate that leisure may have many functions. Such pursuits as meditation, hobbies, and spectator sports can provide relaxation, diversion, entertainment, or escape. Other activities provide opportunities for personal growth and development (cultural events, travel, artistic pursuits, education). Another form of leisure described by Kaplan is service to others, though we do not often think of volunteer roles as leisure. Finally, *sensual transcendence*, activities which provide an intense "peak-experience" such as highly competitive sports and sexual activity, may be an objective of some leisure activity (Gordon, Gaitz, and Scott, 1976). What relationships do these options for meaning and satisfaction in leisure have to the aging experience?

Leisure and the Life Cycle

It would not be surprising to find that the use of time varies by age, if only because age is related to income, education, and other social characteristics. The quality of leisure time is also different for older people—the time available to them for leisure is greater and less fragmented (Kaplan, 1975). Leisure patterns are also related to age in that they may contribute to achievement of the developmental issues and tasks facing persons at different stages in the life cycle, and in any case will be shaped by the needs and preoccupations of each stage.

The relationship of leisure to developmental tasks can be seen in many ways. The play and games of childhood provide rehearsal for adult roles ("playing house"), opportunities to learn cooperation with others (think of the cooperation needed for a successful neighborhood football game), and reinforcement of personal competence and self-enterprise. Throughout life leisure is shaped by the preoccupations and needs of each life stage (Berlyne, 1969; Rapoport and Rapoport, 1975). Adolescents, for example, are concerned with developing personal identity, so their leisure pursuits involve exploration of the environment and sampling of new experiences. Young adults, on the other hand, leave age-graded groups to identify with more general social institutions. Interests may focus more narrowly on occupation and family, rather than developing broader interests which can be sustained into middle age and retirement. During the 30s and 40s, when one's life becomes structured by work and family, leisure patterns often become very home- and family-centered. People often transfer habits from other contexts into their free time—work in another form, family activities, work-related citizenship roles—rather than developing new or creative patterns in the use of time. This may create problems in late middle age, leaving people unprepared for the new opportunities for expansion and enjoyment created by the empty nest and the winding down of the work career. This is illustrated by the following comment from a middle-aged housewife:

> You lose something of yourself by getting too involved in a house and children. The more you do, the more you want to do. My husband says I sound like I'm searching for something—well, there's so much to do, and you can waste it doing nothing. (Rapoport and Rapoport, 1975:257)

Leisure in middle age may help reorient people to new interests as they move toward retirement, but this may be difficult to achieve without an earlier base of activities to build on.

One of the critical "tasks" faced by older persons is adjustment to the new realities brought by aging. With retirement, for example, we have seen that accommodation to disrupted familiar patterns involves choosing among optional new "careers" in the use of time. Thus, a major function of leisure in old age is the search for new sources of personal meaning and social integration to replace earlier sources which have been lost. We need to look at the patterns older people use to achieve this goal, and their relative success.

Patterns of Leisure in Old Age

The most obvious point to make is that older people have more potential nonwork time available to them. This time is not necessarily "free," however. Leisure is an element of life-style and as such is related to and constrained by social class, education, age, sex, and many other social characteristics (Zablocki and Kanter, 1976). Income certainly affects options in the use of time, and education is also related to tastes, values, curiosity, and so forth. The development of mass culture may limit true freedom of leisure selection to the latest fads (Kaplan, 1975). Even one's residential location can affect leisure patterns. Urban living provides access to "strange" styles of behavior unavailable to the rural resident, as well as a wider variety of cultural and recreational opportunities, though the complexity of the city can be confusing or even dangerous to the potential user of time (Kaplan, 1975).

Older people face additional limitations on their use of free time. Even the most avid golfer may have to forsake the sport because of severe arthritis or low income. Because of physical limitations on mobility, older people may feel that restaurants, libraries, parks, theaters, recreation centers, and sports events are not "convenient" to get to (National Council on the Aging, 1975). The age stratification system also affects activity patterns by structuring the availability of educational opportunities, service roles, voluntary associations, and so on.

Because of age-related limitations, the level of activity tends to decline with age, though not drastically until the seventies and eighties (Riley and Foner, 1968; Gordon, Gaitz, and Scott, 1976). Older people engage in many of the same activities as younger people, but there are age differences in the overall patterns of activity. And while the aged engage in a wide variety of pursuits to fill their leisure time, some older people (especially the very old and those with low income or education) find that they have very little to do.

We have very little data indicating whether activity *patterns* change over the life cycle, since almost all of the research has used cross-sectional designs. As with most characteristics, the major picture which emerges shows considerable continuity in both amount and type of activity, but age differences do exist. In general, older people have fewer activities and a narrower range, and their pursuits tend to be less intense and physically demanding (Gordon, Gaitz, and Scott, 1976). Age differences are much smaller or nonexistent for home-centered activities which are more sedentary, such as spectator sports, television, and socializing. Gordon and associates found that age differences were greatest for more "hedonistic" pursuits involving "sensual transcendence." Differences in activity patterns obviously reflect certain effects of aging. But there are undoubtedly also cohort differences in leisure preferences, related to early socialization experiences, educational levels, and historical fads. Younger cohorts may view leisure in general as more meaningful and be receptive to a wider variety of specific pursuits. More work on the nature of leisure throughout the life cycle is clearly needed. We know virtually nothing about the perceived appropriateness of different uses of time for different age groups and the ways in which this aspect of age stratification shapes leisure patterns. This partly reflects the fact that, at least until recently, leisure has been considered an unimportant or "frivolous" topic in sociology.

Studies indicate that older people are most likely to engage in socializing with friends, watching television, reading, gardening or raising plants, and sitting and thinking (see Beyer and Woods, 1963; Pfeiffer and Davis, 1971; National Council on the Aging, 1975). Only relatively small minorities have hobbies, participate in sports, do volunteer work, or participate in clubs or other groups. These are very broad statements, however, and a closer look at some of these activities is in order.

Socializing, particularly in the context of the home, is clearly a favored activity, which suggests that there is little disengagement from family and friends. Older people are also heavy users of the mass media, especially television, though they watch television only slightly more than younger people (an average of about three hours a day). Television can be an important source of companionship and contact with the larger world, particularly for persons with limited mobility. Since older people are more likely than younger people to select programs with serous content (particularly informational programs) and to seek out *local* news programs, television appears to be more than just a way to pass the time—it can perhaps partly compensate for a shrinking social world by providing electronic contact with the larger community. Older people also appear to prefer "personal," nonfiction programs ("wholesome" variety shows, "oldtime" music, quiz programs) which are not as intense as detective shows or love stories (Meyersohn, 1961; Tennant, 1965; Davis, 1975).

Older people are more likely to read newspapers but less likely to use other media, such as books, magazines, and movies. Attendance at cultural events such as plays and concerts is also lower among older people. The major barriers expressed by the elderly are poor health and transportation difficulties, and they also have less access to information about such events (Harris et al., 1975). Participation could be enhanced by careful scheduling with older people in mind and utilizing various clubs as funnels for information (Johnson and Prieve, 1975).

There are relatively few age differences in involvement in handiwork, crafts, and similar hobbies, though outdoor activities, with the exception of gardening, tend to be lower among the aged. The most common outdoor pursuits for older people are driving for pleasure, picnics, sightseeing, walking, and fishing (for men). Travel is an important activity for many older people, but it is limited by income (Carp, 1972; Friedsam and Martin, 1973).

Older people are not all alike, of course, so one would expect variations in activity according to such characteristics as sex, education, and ethnicity. Older men are more likely to participate in sports, fishing, travel, and gardening, while women more frequently favor "cultural production" (handiwork and crafts), television watching, socializing, and reading (Pfeiffer and Davis, 1971; Gordon, Gaitz, and Scott, 1976; Payne and Whittington, 1976). Men do appear to become more home-centered in their activities as they age, however (Zborowski, 1962).

Socioeconomic status is another important determinant of overall life style, including leisure pursuits. Numerous studies indicate that the activities of lower status persons are more likely to include television watching, family socializing, hunting, fishing, and hobbies, often in same-sex groups, while higher status people are more likely to prefer clubs and organizations, cultural events, travel, and parties (Havighurst, 1973; Gordon, Gaitz, and Scott, 1976). These patterns are partly due to income differences, but they also reflect more basic differences in life style. The life styles of the middle class appear to be more community-oriented, while those of the working and lower classes are more home-centered (Havighurst and Feigenbaum, 1959). Unfortunately, we know virtually nothing about racial and ethnic differences in leisure pursuits among the elderly.

This catalogue of activities engaged in by the elderly tells us only what they *do*, not what *satisfactions* are derived from leisure patterns or what *functions* they serve, nor what they are *capable* of doing with a wider range of options. More important than the "what" of leisure is the "so what?" We need to consider the meanings of leisure patterns and their consequences for the aging experience.

The Functions of Leisure

We all have leisure pursuits we consider trivial and others we feel are as important as anything we do. For some of us, home repairs are just a chore; for others, they represent a creative outlet and a source of self-worth.

Characteristics of free-time activities vary widely. For example, they vary according to whether they involve: (1) autonomy (or are other-directed), (2) creativity, (3) enjoyment (or are simply time-killers), (4) opportunities to develop talents, (5) instrumental ("productive") as opposed to expressive (emotional) outlets, (6) physical energy, (7) complementary or competitive relationships to work, (8) gregariousness, (9) service (as opposed to personal pleasure), (10) status or prestige, (11) relaxation from anxiety, and (12) ego-integration (as opposed to not fitting one's overall life style) (Havighurst, 1961). Havighurst found that middle-class older persons were more likely than lower-class persons to engage in activities involving creativity, personal enjoyment, development of talent, and social prestige. High personal adjustment was associated with activities characterized by autonomy, creativity, enjoyment, talent, instrumentality, physical energy, gregariousness, service to others, status, and ego-integration (compared with their opposites). Such findings suggest that not all leisure pursuits are equally meaningful and satisfying. One study of an all-male sample, for example, found that social or physical activities had the most positive effects on satisfaction, even controlling for health, income, and other determinants (Peppers, 1976).

If inherent differences among leisure pursuits are so important, we need to know how specific activities are viewed by participants, but unfortunately, there is little information to go on. An early study by Donald and Havighurst (1959) does shed some light on this matter. They asked respondents in Kansas City to indicate their reasons for engaging in various activities, and those most frequently expressed were: just for the pleasure of it (68 percent), welcome change from work (48 percent), new experience (42 percent), contact with friends (28 percent), chance to achieve something (23 percent), and makes the time pass (23 percent). Different activities served different typical functions. For example, fishing resulted in pleasure and a welcome change from work, but not new experiences, achievement, or creativity. Handicrafts yielded feelings of achievement and creativity, but were not typically a source of new experiences or contact with friends.

At least some older people derive creative or artistic satisfaction from a wide variety of leisure-time activities, including reading, gardening, sewing, carpentry, listening to music, and watching television (Harris et al., 1975). A study of older participants at a legalized gambling (poker) club in Gardena, California (Stone and Kalish, 1973) provides another example of the variability of functions of leisure. Their average respondent made two or three visits to the club per week, with an average of six hours per visit, and despite expenses of about $30 (travel and table costs) and little expectation of winning, they were enthusiastic about participating. Stone and Kalish offer some reasons for this. Gambling offers both social life and at least a chance of winning, and one attraction may be that these clubs were *not* designed for "senior citizens." At a deeper level, older people lose many of their decision-making options and the excitement of facing personal success or failure (as they might on a job), which gambling changes by offering a real payoff and the opportunity to pit one's own skill and luck against others regardless of age (gambling is an age leveler). It also offers the possibility for social, emotional, and psychological engagement in an interesting activity, the opposite of disengagement.

The author does not wish to suggest that gambling is "the answer" for all older people. Many organizations, such as senior centers and nursing homes, attempt to develop activity programs for the aged, however (though activities are more likely to be successful when initiated by participants), and we must pay attention to participants' perceptions of activities. Lakin and Dray (1958) cite the example of a "hobby shop" set up in a nursing home. While this provided an outlet in self-expression for some residents, even most of those who participated derogated the activities as "foolishness." A "sheltered workshop," through which people were paid for their work, proved to be a better source of positive self-images. While it may be unfortunate that being paid is what makes an activity meaningful, such perceptions must be carefully taken in account. This particular study offers an illustration of how values held by a particular cohort—in this case, seeming attachment to a relatively narrow work ethic—constrains the choice of activity options and determines whether particular uses of time are worthwhile for them.

Consequences of a Leisure Career

A most important consideration is the impact of choosing a leisure "career" in old age, since leisure is widely regarded as an important facet of late life. One of the reasons that retirement is often considered a difficult and even traumatizing role transition is the presumed meaninglessness of leisure pursuits, resulting in feelings of boredom or personal worthlessness. Stephen Miller (1965) has been the most eloquent spokesman for this point of view, referring to the "social dilemma" of the leisure participant. Miller argues that the leisure role has not achieved legitimacy as a replacement for work or as a source of identity and self-respect: it "only supports the position of the old as non-meaningful, non-functional or, at best, superannuated." There is an embarrassing stigma attached to leisure which Miller suggests results in social withdrawal (disengagement) by the aged.

Miller's argument that work is a primary source of identity and commitment focuses primarily on the retired. In a broader sense, problems associated with leisure have also been attributed to all members of modern societies. Kaplan (1975) has suggested that the rapid emergence of a "middle-class leisure class" has not been accompanied by changes in the work ethic and that managers and proprietors may be most alienated from leisure and least capable of true play. In general, the argument has been that the values associated with the work ethic inhibit our ability to take full advantage of free time—to open ourselves up to new experiences or simply enjoy the passage of time (see, for example, Martin, 1969; Mendel, 1971). The capacity to use our inner resources is suppressed and scorned, and leisure is equated with idleness and laziness. The following passage exemplifies this argument:

> We still have a work-oriented ethic that is essentially anti-pleasure, anti-creativity, anti-joy, anti-leisure, and anti-laughter. If this ethic is left unaltered and continues as a vehicle for socializing our children, we will ensure that the next generation will face the new world of leisure with guilt and boredom, and without creativity or freedom. We will lay the groundwork for alienation, depression, impaired self-esteem, and misery while the next generation endures a leisurely existence. (Mendel, 1971:1690)

Pfeiffer and Davis (1971) found that over half derived greater satisfaction from work than from leisure, while only about one in six derived greater satisfaction from leisure. They also found that dissatisfaction with leisure is apparently related to sex-linked transitions from "work" roles. Women were most dissatisfied from age 46 to 55, when family roles are being altered. Men, on the other hand, were least satisfied with leisure time from 66 to 71, the usual time for adjusting to retirement. Thus, transitions from work to leisure are neither easy nor automatic for many, and some encounter boredom and identity crises.

Such arguments have important implications for all of us as available nonwork time continues to expand in the future. But how much truth is there to this assessment? We have already seen that retirement is often not the crisis we assume it to be, and there is evidence that the same is true of the use of leisure time.

Arguments about leisure problems partly assume an overarching importance for the work role, but work is often not that important for individuals and its intrinsic satisfactions may be declining. Similarly, attachment to work does not necessarily lead to poor retirement adjustment. People derive self-conceptions from many roles and identities, and work-related identities often continue in retirement (Atchley, 1971). Even highly work-oriented people have been able to take up a satisfying leisure role. Thus,

> Each person generally has several roles that he stakes his identity on. Work may be at or near the top, but not necessarily so. There simply is not the kind of homogeneous consensus on the value of work that would keep it at the top for everyone. In fact, the many systems of competing values in a complex society insure that there will be a wide variety of self-values. Thus, the probability that retirement will lead to a complete identity breakdown is slight, and there may be just as many people who rely on leisure pursuits for self-respect as there are who rely on work, particularly among those with unsatisfying jobs. (Atchley, 1971:17)

The weight of the evidence suggests that leisure pursuits are neither traumatizing nor demoralizing for most older people. The rather unremarkable effects of retirement cited in Chapter 6 certainly support this conclusion, as do findings from the Scripps Foundation studies of retirement (Atchley, 1971; 1977). Embarrassment and identity loss associated with retirement are minimized by continuity in other activities—family, friends, church, and so on—creating retirement cohorts which may legitimize leisure. Generally, reluctance toward the leisure role is negligible when income is secure. The expansion of leisure time is not viewed negatively, and desired leisure pursuits are often a cause of retirement.

That most people adapt relatively satisfactorily to the transition from work to leisure does not necessarily mean that they are fully utilizing their capacities for self-expression, personal growth, or community involvement in a wide range of activity options, however. Many people may be responding to retirement by choosing a leisure "occupation" which resembles work. Residents of retirement settings, for example, often come to view some of their activities as their "work," though they receive no pay (see Chapter 9). White-collar workers seem best able to transfer their styles of work to retirement, since their jobs yield the types of interpersonal skills useful in retirement (Simpson, Back, and McKinney, 1966).

The leisure pattern of other older people seems little more than the playing out of remaining middle-aged activities. One gets little sense from the literature that many older people use their increased free time to experiment with new sources and forms of self-expression, but this is less a result of what older people are capable of than of limited opportunities for cultivating more open approaches to the use of time earlier in life and the unavailability of wider options in old age.

Voluntary Associations

Group activities offer a variety of satisfactions for persons of any age, but membership in voluntary associations can offer important benefits for older people particularly. Such groups may be a source of social integration to fill the vacuum created by role losses such as retirement or widowhood. Pluralist political theories suggest that voluntary organizations promote democratic processes by distributing power more broadly, creating satisfaction with democratic procedures, and providing a mechanism for social change (Smith and Freedman, 1972). Finally, any type of group participation offers opportunities for self-expression and personal involvement.

The fact that older people are less likely to belong to voluntary associations than younger people has been taken as evidence of disengagement. More recent evidence suggests, however, that such age differences primarily reflect the lower average socioeconomic status of the aged (Cutler, 1977). Cutler's longitudinal studies indicate considerable stability in the general level of associational participation by older people, at least in their sixties. There is considerable *individual* change. Some people increase their participation in response to declining work and family responsibilities. Others report a decline with age because of poor health, transportation problems, residential change, or the loss of group-related roles (such as retirees who are no longer active in unions). But the overall picture is one of continued engagement, with relatively widespread membership and participation in voluntary associations.

Age patterns of participation vary across types of associations. Data in Table 7.1 show these patterns for a representative sample of persons 18 and older in the United States (Cutler, 1976a). Older people (65+) are most likely to belong to church-affiliated groups, fraternal groups (e.g., lodges), labor unions, and veterans' groups. There is a steady increase with age in membership in fraternal and church-related organizations, which Cutler suggests is due to generational differences in the types of groups which appeal to people. The functions performed by lodges and fraternal groups, for example, are now available elsewhere (Smith and Freedman, 1972). Greater membership in sports groups among the

Table 7.1. Percentage belonging to 16 types of voluntary associations, by age

Type of Association	Age						
	18–24	25–34	35–44	45–54	55–64	65–74	75+
Fraternal groups	3	9	14	15	15	17	23
Church-affiliated groups	27	34	46	45	48	48	52
Sports groups	26	23	23	19	12	8	5
Labor unions	13	16	17	21	22	11	7
Professional or academic societies	12	15	17	13	10	9	5
School service groups	8	22	31	18	8	5	1
Youth groups	13	11	19	10	5	4	1
Veterans' groups	2	4	9	14	13	8	11
Service clubs	4	8	11	13	9	8	8
Literary, art, discussion, or study groups	7	13	8	9	9	8	7
Farm organizations	3	3	4	6	6	4	4
Political clubs	2	5	6	4	4	4	7
Hobby or garden clubs	8	12	10	7	10	9	9
School fraternities or sororities	5	6	4	5	3	4	3
Nationality groups	3	3	3	4	2	3	3
Other groups	7	11	10	9	7	12	11

Source: Adapted from Stephen Cutler, "Age profiles of membership in sixteen types of voluntary associations." Journal of Gerontology 31 (1976): 464. Reprinted by permission.

young is only partly due to the poorer health of older people (Cutler, 1976a). Membership in some groups reaches a peak in middle age and declines thereafter: labor unions, professional or academic societies, school service groups, youth groups, veterans' groups, service clubs (e.g., Rotary), and literary, art, discussion, or study groups. Many of these memberships are related to work and family roles relinquished by older people. Thus, age stratification of roles affects patterns of group association. However, many groups exhibit no significant age differences: farm organizations, political clubs, hobby or garden clubs, school fraternities or sororities, and nationality groups (ethnic clubs).

Membership in voluntary associations is not evenly distributed among the older population. Older women are more likely than older men to belong to religious, volunteer, and cultural organizations, while older men are more likely to belong to unions, service clubs, and fraternal organizations (Cutler, 1976a; Payne and Whittington, 1976), and men display a greater decline in overall group participation with age than do women. Blacks of all ages have higher rates of participation in voluntary associations than whites, perhaps as a compensation for racial discrimination (Clemente, Rexroad, and Hirsch, 1975). Clemente and associates found that older blacks are particularly likely to belong to church-related groups and social or recreational clubs, while older whites are more likely to belong to ethnic organizations and senior citizen clubs. And group participation among the elderly is greater for those with better health, higher income, and greater education (Riley and Foner, 1968).

Participation in voluntary associations serves many functions and results in a variety of satisfactions, however, there has been little investigation of the perceptions of participants about their involvement. A study by the author suggests some ways in which the functions of group activities may differ (Ward, 1977). Group participants were asked to indicate three reasons they enjoyed the group activities in which they engaged (Table 7.2). Not surprisingly, socializing was the most frequent response. Other frequently mentioned reasons included opportunities for new experience, activities which are pleasurable in themselves, and helping society and others. Older people probably do receive status and popularity from group associations, but are unwilling to admit such "egotistical" reasons.

Surprisingly, there is no evidence that membership in such groups contributes much to the psychological well-being of older people. Although many studies indicate that older people who participate in voluntary associations have higher morale (Riley and Foner, 1968), such persons also have better health, higher income,

Table 7.2.   Reasons for enjoying group participation

Reason	Percentage[a]
It brings me into contact with friends.	73
It gives me new experience; I feel I learn something from it.	36
I like it just for the pleasure of doing it.	35
It makes the time pass.	34
I like it because I like to do things that will be of benefit to society.	30
I get to help other people.	23
It gives me a chance to achieve something.	19
It is a welcome change from my work.	12
I feel I can respect myself for doing these things.	11
It gives me more standing with other people.	8
I feel that I am being creative.	6
It makes me popular among other people.	6
It helps me financially.	2
Other	2

[a] Respondents were asked to indicate 3 reasons.
Source: Russell Ward, "The quality of group activities." Paper presented at the Annual Scientific Meeting of the Gerontological Society, San Francisco, 1977.

and more education. When such individual characteristics are controlled, group membership is apparently unrelated to overall life satisfaction (Bull and Aucoin, 1975; Cutler, 1976b). Cutler did find a small effect of church-affiliated groups on satisfaction, but he noted that this could be due to various factors: a general effect of religiosity, intensity of involvement, or greater age homogeneity of such groups.

There are a number of possible reasons for the relative unimportance of group involvement. First, older people who belong to voluntary associations have typically been "joiners" throughout their lives; relatively few take them up in old age as compensation for other social losses (Lowenthal and Robinson, 1976). This suggests that we are prisoners of past activity patterns and there may be few new or attractive associational options available to older people. Many voluntary associations are linked to the roles and activities of young adulthood and middle age; relatively few are geared to the interests and needs of older people.

The lack of a relationship between voluntary association participation and overall morale may also reflect a general lack of "meaty" roles or personally meaningful involvement for all but a small leadership group within most associations. This may be particularly true of the aged who may be shunted aside by younger group members. For many, participation may yield little more than social interaction. In the study cited earlier (Ward, 1977), the third most frequent first reason for group participation was "it makes the time pass," which is hardly a glowing affirmation of the significance of their involvement. If voluntary associations offer little more than "lukewarm" social integration, they fail to serve as creative, self-expressive accommodations to new needs in the use of time.

Some types of group involvements seem to be more beneficial than others. Persons with higher morale are more likely to stress such reasons for group involvement as new experiences, achieving something, being creative, and being helpful to others, and active participation through discussions, planning, and leadership involvement resulted in more novel experience and greater feelings of achievement and creativity (Ward, 1977). This was also related to higher levels of satisfaction. Participants in more social or recreational activities (such as card-playing) tended to stress simply the pleasure involved and passing the time. These findings suggest that group participation by the elderly will be experienced as more "meaningful" and satisfying when it provides opportunities for active, intense involvement.

Age-Homogeneous Groups

The voluntary associations we have been discussing may include older people, but they are not organized by or for them. To the extent that the activity needs of older people are not adequately addressed in such groups or memberships are lost through moving or role change accompanying aging, groups which are more age-homogeneous should be encouraged.

There are both costs and rewards involved in participating in more homogeneous "old age" groups (Havighurst, 1949). One risks the possible stigma of associating with "old folks" and loses a sense of involvement in the larger community, but such groups can address the specific interests of older people and provide opportunities for prestige and leadership which may be limited in younger groups. These groups are likely to be most successful when they are run by older people, rather than for them and when they allow for active participation—speakers, discussions, lobbying on their own behalf, and so on. As such, they can offer a more meaningful use of time (see Rose, 1960).

The increasing size of the older population and growing awareness of their shared problems and interests heighten the likelihood that groups specifically designed for older people will be increasingly prevalent. This appears to have occurred in Japan, where "old people's clubs" have rapidly multiplied since the 1950s to include nearly half the older population in over 90,000 clubs throughout the country (Maeda, 1975). The emphases of these clubs, in order of importance, have been recreation, making crafts for money, learning (discussions, lectures, outings), health-related activities, and volunteer community service. In the United States, where senior citizen groups are usually sponsored by social service, recreation, and adult education agencies, a similarly wide range of programs may be found, from purely social activities to social action and the provision of services (Hacker, 1973). There are also various nationally organized associations for older persons, such as the American Association of Retired Persons/National Retired Teachers Association (AARP/NRTA), which has nearly 5 million members (Butler, 1975). But participation in such organizations is much lower in the United States than in Japan. A recent national survey found that only 18 percent of those over 65 (and 8 percent of those between 55 and 64) had attended a "senior citizen center" during the prior year (National Council on the Aging, 1975), and probably no more than 5 percent of the older population participates in such organizations on a regular basis (Riley and Foner, 1968).

Level of participation in old age voluntary associations are relatively low partly because people are busy with other involvements, not interested in the activities which are offered, in poor health, or simply do not wish to associate with "old people." But there is also untapped interest in such groups. The National Council on the Aging study (1975) found that 19 percent of those over 55 (39 percent among blacks) would like to attend, but were too busy, lacked convenient facilities, had inadequate transportation, or were in poor health. Fully 50 percent of the entire older sample did not have a senior center which they felt was "convenient" to go to; such centers were least accessible for blacks and in rural and Southern areas.

Participation is also limited by the fact that senior citizen clubs tend to draw members from a narrow local area and include primarily higher-status older people who have had a "joining" life style (Riley and Foner, 1968; Trela, 1976). National organizations, such as the American Association of Retired Persons, are particularly likely to have an upper-middle-class membership. Lack of participation by the poor and disadvantaged limits the use of such organizations as a type of social agency (Taietz, 1976). For those who do participate, however, old age associations offer the potential for self-expressive uses of time which are more directly related to the aging experience. Unfortunately, we know virtually nothing about the consequences of this participation for older persons.

Education and Aging

Education is one use of time from which older people might clearly profit. It can be an interesting activity in itself or open doors to a variety of other activities and interests. Unfortunately, education has not been an important activity for older people and society has done relatively little to encourage their participation, which has contributed to the distance between age groups and the difficulties accompanying the transitions from middle age to old age.

Modern societies have segregated education, work, and leisure into different parts of the life cycle, with important consequences for the age stratification system as a whole (Parelius, 1975). The tendency to think of education as something for the young creates more separated age strata in modern societies, such as "adolescence." Since education is highly age-graded, new knowledge and socialization experiences produce social distance between generations. With education a major determinant of occupational placement, older people are at a disadvantage in occupational advancement or entering new occupations.

A more continuous integration of educational, work, and leisure opportunities would offer many potential benefits. There is a tendency for life in modern societies to become too programmed and rigid (Butler, 1975; Sarason, 1977). Education focuses too narrowly on preparation for careers which may become obsolete, rather than preparing young people to meet the opportunities and challenges of their whole life span. More flexible career counseling, as well as courses related to entrepreneurial skills, leisure-time preparation and usage, and aging and retirement may be needed (Department of Health, Education and Welfare, 1973; Peterson, 1975). Preparation (in the broadest sense) for retirement should be combined with educational opportunities throughout the life cycle as it is likely to be too late when one is 60. Older workers may face obsolescence or boredom because of a lack of opportunities for continual education and retraining. One proposal has been to institute paid sabbaticals (a "self-renewal program") for all workers to remove obstacles to mid-career change (Department of Health, Education and Welfare, 1973). Educational opportunities for older people should include more than work-related options, however; indeed, adult education has perhaps been oriented too much to work skills. One can also derive more intrinsic satisfactions from education, and educational experiences could be oriented toward the meaningful use of time and general preparation for retirement and postretirement.

While such proposals seem quite simple, their effects could be quite far-reaching. Lifelong education has a tremendous potential for creating change in society, particularly in the blurring of age distinctions (Parelius, 1975). Adolescents would participate more widely in the "adult world," perhaps through apprenticeship programs, and would experience less pressure to make so many important decisions early in life. As opportunities are opened for greater flexibility, there may be more identity crises during adulthood (which Butler (1975) suggests would help to "loosen up life"). This might make new opportunities available particularly for women. There might even be more marital disruptions due to a greater likelihood of personal change during the adult years (Parelius, 1975). Finally, the "generation gap" between the young and middle-aged or older people would be narrowed, and continuous educational opportunities would provide new meaningful roles and activities in the later years.

There has been some movement toward opening up education for older people. Approximately 40 percent of American colleges and universities offer nondegree adult education (Butler, 1975) and there is a growing trend toward tuition-free courses for the elderly. As college enrollments have been declining, there has been increasing recognition by educational institutions of the need to recruit new types of students, including the aged.

Progress has been very limited, however. While we have probably all read stories about 90-year-old high school or college graduates, both educational participation and the desire to learn more decline with age (Riley and Fover, 1968). A recent survey found that only 2 percent of all persons over 65 are enrolled in some type of course (National Council on the Aging, 1975). This partly reflects the low educational background of current older cohorts, and educational involvement in old age should rise in the future, as older cohorts have higher levels of education. But despite recent growth, programs directed at the aged are still quite limited. Both formally and informally, our educational institutions remain "youth ghettos," with both social and psychological barriers for older persons. The major reasons given by older people for not participating in educational courses are: lack of interest (45 percent), being "too old" (27 percent), poor health (22 percent), and not having enough time (13 percent) (National Council on the Aging, 1975). The first two reasons indicate that our youthful orientation to education may discourage participation by the elderly, who come to view education as "inappropriate" for their age group.

There are additional barriers to involvement in education, including vision and hearing problems and lack of transportation. Educational opportunities for older people must be carefully planned. Scheduling and location are critical, since home responsibilities often make it difficult for older students to follow strict schedules, and physical restrictions, transportation problems, and fear of crime at night can limit mobility. Grading may often be inappropriate, given the different goals of older students and the likelihood (particularly for older men) that tests will be viewed as threatening to one's self-image (Goodrow, 1975). Involvement by older persons may also be resisted by younger students. One study of age-integrated classes at a university (Auerbach and Levenson, 1977) found increasingly negative attitudes by young students toward older students who were viewed as unfair competition, since they could focus on just one course, and as "cluttering up" the classroom with irrelevant personal anecdotes. Students tended to segregate themselves from those of different ages.

Such problems do not mean that we should abandon efforts to achieve wider involvement by the aged in existing educational institutions, but they do suggest that we must be flexible and experiment with other forms and media of education. Television, for example, offers a particularly relevant tool for life-long education (Davis, 1975). Older people view television as a dependable, trusted medium of communication, and will therefore be more likely to accept information related to retirement preparation, health counseling, or the range of benefits and services available to them. Indeed, television offers largely untapped opportunities for influencing the entire population about aging and being old. Simply relying on existing patterns of educational opportunities will only perpetuate its age stratification and fail to offer the aging creative new options for the use of time.

Religion and Aging

We do not generally think of religion as a "use of time," but religious activities have long been considered important for the aged. Fear of death, for example, is often assumed to be a mainspring of religious commitment (Stark, 1968); as death presumably grows psychologically near in old age, people may turn to religion for personal solace. Since religious affiliation represents the most widespread group involvement among older people, it may also represent their most important source of social integration. Religion is a very complex phenomenon, however. There are many religions and many denominations within them. There are also many dimensions of religiosity, including emotional experience, beliefs (e.g., belief in an afterlife), ritual practices, and personal knowledge and information (Moberg, 1965). Although most people identify themselves with some type of religion, this tells us very little about the nature and significance of their religious experience.

While religious involvement may become more important with age, it may also decline. Disengagement theory would suggest a decline in religious participation, though perhaps not in the more personal aspects of religion. Religious activities may peak in early and middle adulthood because church membership is "expected" of persons in certain roles or the presence of children encourages attendance as a model for socialization (Bahr, 1970). Thus, the relationship of religion to age is not likely to be a simple one, nor are its consequences for the aging experience likely to be clear-cut.

Church attendance apparently reaches a peak in middle and old age, with a small drop in frequency after age 80 (primarily due to poor health) (Riley and Foner, 1968; National Council on the Aging, 1975). The latter study found, however, that even among those over 80, 68 percent had attended a church or synagogue within the past year.

The leadership of established religious organizations tends to be heavily concentrated among older people (Lehman, 1953). Older people are also more likely to read the Bible and participate in personal devotional observances, such as praying at home (Riley and Foner, 1968). Thus, ritualistic practices outside the home tend to decline slightly in old age, primarily due to poor health, low income, or transportation difficulties, but these are at least partly compensated for by activities inside the home, such as reading the Bible or following religious broadcasts on the television or radio (Moberg, 1965).

Older people are more likely to express a belief in God and an afterlife, and in general subscribe to more conservative religious beliefs than younger people (Moberg, 1965; Riley and Foner, 1968). Such beliefs are apparently quite stable. In a longitudinal study of older people lasting 17 years, Blazer and Palmore (1976) found gradual declines in religious *activity* but considerable stability in religious *attitudes*.

There are important variations in religiosity within the older population, related to education, income, and residential stability. Catholics are most likely to continue attending church; Protestants are intermediate, and Jews are least likely to continue attending (Riley and Foner, 1968). Older women are more likely than older men to participate in religious activities and to feel that religion is an important part of their lives, but their involvement also shows a greater decline with age than for men (Payne and Whittington, 1976). Church participation also appears to be greater for older blacks (Kent, 1971).

There is little evidence in these studies that people turn to religion as they age, though those who had been slightly religious may become more so. A study by Wingrove and Alston (1971) found that all cohorts displayed declines in church attendance after 1965. If this reflects a general secularization of American society, one would expect religion to be less important for older people in the future. A more recent study by Wuthnow (1976) indicates that such predictions are risky, however. He notes that most evidence shows a religious revival during the 1950s, followed by declining religious commitment since the early 1960s. Using evidence from Gallup polls over this period, he shows that this declining religious participation is greatest among youth, resulting in much larger age differences than in the past (Figure 7.2). He attributes this to youthful involvement in the "counterculture," which has sought alternatives to established religions (Marxism, mysticism, and other philosophies). Thus, each cohort develops its own patterns of religious involvement as a consequence of its unique history. We may, in fact, be witnessing a new religious revival, as evidenced by the success of such groups as Campus Crusade for Christ.

The consequences of religious involvement by older people are not clear. While many find religion to be more helpful than earlier in their lives, nearly equal numbers find it *less* comforting and satisfying, and the aged generally derive greater satisfaction from family and friends (Riley and Foner, 1968). On the other hand, older people are more likely than younger people to consider religion "very important" in their lives (National Council on the Aging, 1975). A longitudinal study found positive associations between both religious activities and religious attitudes and happiness, usefulness, and adjustment in old age, and the strength of these associations increased over time (Blazer and Palmore, 1976). Other studies have found that holding conservative religious beliefs is associated with greater serenity and less fear of death (Moberg, 1965) and that the mentally ill often seek emotional support from religion (Clark and Anderson, 1967). But it is not clear from this research whether religiosity *itself* is beneficial, since religious participation is related to other types of group involvement. Satisfaction, serenity, or acceptance of death may result not from faith, but from participation in social networks and reference groups which offer support and security.

The meaningfulness of religious participation in the lives of older people is restricted by a number of factors. As is true of all the activities we have looked at, religiosity in old age is related to religiosity earlier in life. In addition, church programs directed specifically at the elderly are still relatively infrequent; while churches accept participation by older people, few actively solicit their involvement (Atchley, 1977). The emphasis placed on youth by many churches may lead to disengagement by older members

Figure 7.2. Weekly church attendance by age, 1954–1971

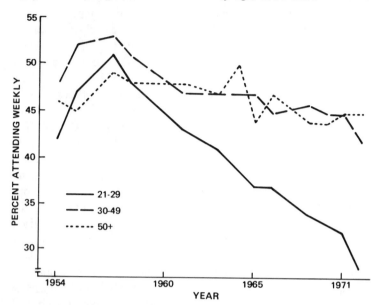

Source: Robert Wuthnow, "Recent patterns of secularization: A problem of generations?" *American Sociological Review* 41 (1976): 857. Reprinted by permission.

or to generational conflicts within the congregation. This is not meant to deny the important role played by some churches in developing and providing services for the aged. Social groups for the elderly are often sponsored by churches and synagogues and retirement housing, hospitals, and nursing homes are often run by religious institutions. Other services, such as Meals-on-Wheels, benefit from the cooperation of local churches. But the social and psychological importance of religion in the everyday lives of most older people remains unclear. Certainly much more study of the impact of religion in old age, as well as the effects of older participants on religious institutions, could be undertaken.

The Volunteer Role

Time spent in service to others is time well spent, regardless of one's age. Few other activities can rival volunteer work as a source of "good feelings" about oneself. For older people, the volunteer role is a potential source of meaningful activity and status which can counteract the marginality and demoralization of old age. Some have viewed service as a way of loosening up rigid age and sex role-grading to allow for greater creativity and self-discovery throughout the life cycle (for example, see Blau, 1973, and Butler, 1975). As we are becoming increasingly service-oriented, there are many "public tasks" which offer far more than just "make-work." Blau has even suggested a redefinition of citizenship to include obligatory public service, yielding benefits to both participants and society.

> The young need an opportunity to perform useful, socially relevant roles so as to establish a sense of efficacy; older people need productive roles for the same reason. The answer to both groups' needs, it seems to me, lies in the creation of new obligatory social roles in the public sector. Massive problems confront American society. Despite its enormous wealth, despite modest attempts to deal with our national problems in the areas of poverty, health care, and education, the ills of our society persist and proliferate. Much significant, essential work lies waiting while there are millions of young and old people eager to be useful. These human resources, now wasted, can and must be mobilized and organized to perform the work. (Blau, 1973:204)

In other words, we and the aged will both benefit from seeing the aged as *providers* of services, not just recipients.

Some service roles are already available to the elderly. The federal government, for example, sponsors a variety of work programs to provide supplementary income to low-income older people, such as:

1. *Foster Grandparents*, which recruits and trains older people to provide personalized care to institutionalized children.
2. *Green Thumb* (sponsored by the National Farmers Union), which provides part-time employment for conservation and community improvement in rural areas.
3. *Senior Opportunities for Services Programs* (SOS), in which older workers provide services to older people in nutrition, outreach programs, referral, and so on.
4. *Senior Aides* (National Council of Senior Citizens), *Senior Community Service Aides* (National Council on the Aging), and *Senior Community Aides* (NRTA/AARP), through which older people are employed in homemaker services, home repair, nutritional programs, and the like.

These are relatively small programs, however, and by no means adequate substitutes for full-scale employment efforts. Other government programs, some not restricted to older people, provide additional volunteer opportunities for the aged. The Peace Corps and Volunteers in Service to America (VISTA) though often considered youth-oriented opportunities, have included older volunteers. Lillian Carter, the mother of President Carter, was a Peace Corps volunteer in India while in her seventies. Other volunteer programs are specifically for older persons, including:

1. *Retired Senior Volunteer Program* (RSVP), which places volunteers in libraries, hospitals, schools, and many other settings, reimbursing them for travel and meal expenses.
2. *Service Corps of Retired Executives* (SCORE), through which retirees help small businesses with their management problems, again getting reimbursement for expenses.

The elderly have proven to be effective in such service roles provided they are given adequate training, careful placement, and meaningful tasks. None of us enjoys trivial tasks or work which is frustrated by inadequate preparation. The elderly have shown a willingness to engage in such activities, even when pay is low or nonexistent, but we must be wary of exploiting them simply because their income is very low or they desire more meaningful community involvement. The programs described here have been successful in this regard and have proven beneficial for both older participants and the recipients of the services they offer.

The Foster Grandparents program is an excellent example of how service roles for older people can be mutually beneficial. A small-scale evaluation of one program suggested the existence of a special compatability of emotional needs between the older volunteers and institutionalized children (Saltz, 1971). They seemed to develop real "family" feelings, despite the relatively temporary nature of the relationship. The "grandparents" performed well, even when their health was poor. They displayed good job stability and attendance, had a beneficial impact on the children, and received favorable ratings from supervisors, and the volunteer experience was conducive to better health, vigor, and life satisfaction for them. They expressed satisfaction over having regular and purposive activity and the opportunity to be useful and appreciated.

Although volunteerism declines with age, approximately one in five persons 65 and over engage in some type of volunteer activity, and another 10 percent would like to do so (National Council on the Aging, 1975). This means that there is an available pool of nearly 7 million older volunteers. The most frequent activities of older people involve health and mental health (hospitals and clinics), transportation (driving the handicapped), civic affairs (voter registration and lobbying), psychological and social support services (telephone reassurance for shut-ins), giveaway programs (thrift shops and emergency food), and family, youth, and children-oriented services (foster children and day care). The major barriers to such participation, as for almost all types of activity, were poor health and lack of transportation. While poor health is perhaps difficult to deal with, service agencies could clearly increase their recruitment of older volunteers by providing transportation.

Volunteer participation is greater among older whites and those who are employed or have higher income (National Council on the Aging, 1975). A study by Monk and Cryns (1974) found that the volunteer role most attracted those who were younger, owned their own homes, were better educated, had a broader range of social interests, were interested in organized senior citizen activities, and believed that they could make a valuable contribution. Other research indicates that volunteers are most likely to be female and widowed (Payne and Whittington, 1976). Men seem to view volunteer work as a substitute for the instrumental work role, whereas women view it as an expressive role ("doing good"). Payne and Whittington suggest, however, that women may increasingly be finding the values and status associated with work in the service role.

The service role offers both meaningful activity for many older people and benefits to society. The elderly have not been effectively trapped as a resource, however. We need greater understanding of what makes different volunteer activities attractive and successful. There is also a need to develop ways of encouraging older people to participate, particularly those who have been relatively uninvolved. The results of the Monk and Cryns (1974) study suggest that we should encourage the feeling that their skills and contributions are valuable. This is hampered by societal stereotypes about the work deficiencies of the aged, but expanded service roles may help counteract many of the stigmatizing myths of old age.

Social Change and the Use of Time

Old age and retirement, rather than being roleless, offer many possible roles, options, and careers. The difficulty is that there are little preparation and few guidelines for making choices, and while the options are numerous, their depth and quality are less certain. One wonders how socially and psychologically "meaty" these roles are for older people.

Many factors constrain the use of time. The middle-aged uncreative user of time is likely to remain the same in old age. The most important constraints, however, relate to how time and its uses are structured for us by the social structure and the age stratification system.

The structured use of time has changed over the course of industrialization and modernization (Miller, 1965; Dumazedier, 1967; Hochschild, 1975; Kaplan, 1975). Preindustrial societies did not separate work and leisure into distinct worlds, and older people were encouraged and expected to work and rewarded for doing so. Thus, the use of time was less of a "problem." Industrial societies, however, have separated work from leisure, while still attaching great importance and status to productive work. The use of time is an issue particularly for older people, who leave the world of work, yet are still judged by the standards of that world.

We are now entering what some have referred to as the post-industrial society, however, which may reunite work and leisure, while leisure itself may be on the verge of being a dominant value. Kaplan (1975) cites the following trends as contributing to a new convergence of work and leisure:

1. growing criticism of technology combined with a new humanistic ethos
2. extension of marketing expertise to leisure goods and services, thereby promoting the value of leisure
3. fragmentation of jobs which lessens their intrinsic meaningfulness
4. growth of transportation and communication, increasing options in leisure selection
5. democratization of economically free time

Others point to a shift in cultural values toward self-actualization, self-expression, interdependence, and "capacity for joy" (Emery and Trist, 1973), which would "dis-inhibit" our free choice of options in the use of time.

This certainly paints a favorable future for leisure careers. Whether future cohorts of older people (or of all ages) actually achieve this Nirvana remains to be seen, however. The young may not be as guilt-free about leisure as they seem. One wonders, for example, how much of the interest in Transcendental Meditation arises from an unwillingness to say: "I'm just sitting here thinking." More important, post-industrial values about the use of time must be expressed and realized within the structure of society, and here the age stratification system comes into play.

Our society has done relatively little to promote creative or self-expressive uses of time throughout the life cycle. The separation of leisure from the rest of life impairs "the application of imagination to ordinary life" (Rapoport and Rapoport, 1975:348) and prevents us from enriching all aspects of our lives through more creative uses of time. In addition, little is done to promote resourcefulness in using time. Education is geared toward vocational pursuits, rather than "socialization for life," and leisure interests are subsidiary to work and family careers. Entering old age without sustainable leisure patterns, older people are unprepared to explore new options in using time.

Available activities may be shallow and unfulfilling, because they are set up for older people or allow them few truly meaningful roles. Older people shy away from education because they are "too old" or from service roles because they question their own usefulness in a society which expects them to retire from "productive" roles, and few roles are available to them.

The author does not wish to overstate the case. Older people are relatively satisfied in their leisure pursuits, but in relation to what? That people can accommodate to reality does not justify that reality. In all respects, a satisfying old age is best built upon a satisfying youth and middle age. But we must also experiment with new options for older people, inventing and upgrading social roles for them. The freedom of time given to the aged by modern societies presents a challenge to use that time in mutually beneficial ways.

There is room for optimism. Future cohorts of older people will have more education and money and better health, making them more capable and resourceful, as well as more demanding of meaningful involvement in community life. They may be more concerned with the "higher-order" needs discussed at the end of Chapter 2: esteem, self-actualization, the desire to know and understand, and aesthetic needs. There already seems to be growing interest in opening up such involvement, evidenced in the recent "revolt" against compulsory retirement. While this is a favorable trend, it is also somewhat beside the point, since most older people do not need or desire to keep working but need expanded nonwork options. Much more exploration of new options in the use of time and the factors which facilitate and encourage participation by older people needs to be done. There is also a critical need to investigate the meanings and consequences for older people of the activities they pursue. The ways in which older people choose, and are constrained to choose, uses of time are major determinants of the aging experience.

Summary

The use of time is an important issue for the aged in modern societies. Many options are available, but choice is constrained by the accompaniments of aging, past activity patterns, cohort experiences, and age stratification of opportunities.

Leisure activity is generally considered expressive, pleasant, and relatively nonobligatory. It is not simply amusement or escape, but rather covers a wide range of intensity and functions. Patterns of leisure are likely to vary over the life cycle in response to the developmental needs of each period. Although interests tend to narrow during adulthood, leisure in old age may focus more broadly on the search for new personally engaging involvements and social integration.

Although older people have more nonwork time, their freedom is often limited by poor health, low income, transportation difficulties, and so on. Their most frequent activities are socializing, television, and reading. Age differences are evident in such things as media preferences and attendance at cultural events. Although most of the data are cross-sectional, intense, physically demanding activities appear to decline with age, while more sedentary home-centered pursuits remain stable. Leisure patterns vary by sex and social class.

Leisure pursuits vary widely in meaning, and individual variability in these meanings must be kept in mind, particularly when designing activity programs for the elderly.

It has been argued that leisure is considered degrading in industrial societies because of the importance attached to the work role. This argument overstates the importance of work. While most people appear to derive greater satisfaction from work than leisure, most adjust satisfactorily to a leisure "career," particularly when income is adequate and work styles can be transferred to leisure.

Voluntary associations offer a potentially important source of interesting activities, social integration, and social action on behalf of the elderly. There are a variety of barriers to their participation, however, including poor health, inadequate transportation, residential mobility, and role loss. Age differences in membership patterns reflect such constraints, as well as cohort differences and the age-grading of social roles. Older people are most likely to belong to church-affiliated groups, fraternal groups, labor unions, and veterans' organizations. Formal associations vary by social class, sex, and race, and those who belong are likely to have been "joiners" throughout their lives.

There is little evidence that participation in voluntary associations *itself* contributes to morale. As with all uses of time, older people derive many meanings from group participation. Morale is higher for those who stress new experience, achievement, creativity, and service to others. These meanings are more likely to be derived from active than from passive participation.

Although age-homogeneous groups can specifically address the desires and needs of older people, relatively few participate in "senior citizen" clubs. Again, there are many barriers limiting their involvement. Members tend to be "joiners," and there is little evidence that the poor and disadvantaged are drawn to such groups.

The age-grading of education has contributed to the social gaps between age strata and hindered the opportunity for mid-life career change and general preparation for retirement and old age. If education, work, and leisure were integrated throughout the life cycle, life would be less rigidly programmed, with potentially far-reaching consequences for society. While educational opportunities are opening up for them, very few older people are involved in educational pursuits. Greater care is needed in developing programs appropriate to their capacities and needs.

The link between religion and aging remains unclear. Religious activities outside the home tend to decline, but inside activities show some increase with age. Older people are more likely to express a variety of religious beliefs and to consider religion an important part of their lives, but there is no clear evidence that religion *itself* contributes to the psychological well-being of the aged. Of course, the activities of religious institutions are often beneficial to the elderly. Predictions about the future religiosity of older people are risky, due to the mixture of general secularization and unique cohort experiences.

The volunteer role has been pointed to as a source of meaningful activities for the aged. A number of work and volunteer programs are available, and participation by older people has proven highly successful. There are barriers to their involvement, however, and we know relatively little about what makes various service roles attractive.

The relationship between work and leisure has been altered in the transition to an industrial society. The post-industrial society may again achieve a convergence of work and play, supported by values stressing self-expression. Realization of greater freedom in the use of time will require alterations in the age stratification of structured time, however.

References

Atchley, Robert
    1971   "Retirement and leisure participation: Continuity or crisis?" The Gerontologist 11: 13–17.

1977   The Social Forces in Later Life. Belmont, Calif.:
        Wadsworth.
Auerbach, Doris and Richard Levenson, Jr.
1977   "Second impressions: Attitude change in college students
        toward the elderly." The Gerontologist 17: 362–66.
Bahr, Howard
1970   "Aging and religious disaffiliation." Social Forces 46: 60–71.
Beyer, Glenn and Margaret Woods
1963   "Living and activity patterns of the aged." Research
        Report No. 6. Ithaca, N.Y.: Center for Housing and
        Environmental Studies, Cornell University.
Berlyne, D. E.
1969   "Laughter, humor, and play." In Gardner Lindzey and
        Elliott Aronson (eds.). Handbook of Social Psychology.
        Reading, Mass.: Addison-Wesley.
Blau, Zena
1973   Old Age in a Changing Society. New York: New
        Viewpoints.
Blazer, Dan and Erdman Palmore
1976   "Religion and aging in a longitudinal panel." The
        Gerontologist 16: 82–85.
Bull, C. Neil and Jackie Aucoin
1975   "Voluntary association participation and life satisfaction."
        Journal of Gerontology 30: 73–76.
Butler, Robert
1975   Why Survive?: Being Old in America. New York: Harper
        & Row.
Carp, Frances
1972   "Retired people as automobile passengers." The
        Gerontologist 12: 66–72.
Clark, Margaret and Barbara Anderson
1967   Culture and Aging. Springfield, Ill.: Charles C Thomas.
Clemente, Frank, Patricia Rexroad, and Carl Hirsch
1975   "The participation of the black aged in voluntary associa-
        tions." Journal of Gerontology 30: 469–72.
Cutler, Stephen
1976a   "Age profiles of membership in sixteen types of voluntary
        associations." Journal of Gerontology 31: 462–70.
1976b   "Membership in different types of voluntary associations
        and psychological well-being." The Gerontologist 16:
        335–39.
1977   "Aging and voluntary association participation." Journal of
        Gerontology 32: 470–79.
Davis, Richard
1975   "Television communication and the elderly." In Diana
        Woodruff and James Birren (eds.). Aging: Scientific
        Perspectives and Social Issues. New York: D. Van Nostrand.
Donald, Marjorie and Robert Havighurst
1959   "The meanings of leisure." Social Forces 37: 355–60.

Dumazedier, Joffre
1967   Toward a Society of Leisure. New York: The Free Press.
Emery, F. and E. Trist
1973   Towards a Social Ecology. London: Plenum.
Friedsam, H. and C. Martin
1973   "Travel by older people as a use of leisure." The
        Gerontologist 13: 204–07.
Goodrow, Bruce
1975   "Limiting factors in reducing participation in older adult
        learning opportunities." The Gerontologist 15: 418–22.
Gordon, Chad, Charles Gaitz, and Judith Scott
1976   "Leisure and lives: Personal expressivity across the life
        span." In Robert Binstock and Ethel Shanas (eds.).
        Handbook of Aging and the Social Sciences. New York:
        Van Nostrand Reinhold.
Hacker, Abbe
1973   "Senior centers for the older citizens." In John Cull and
        Richard Hardy (eds.). The Neglected Older American.
        Springfield, Ill.: Charles C Thomas.
Harris, Lou et al.
1975   Americans and the Arts: A Survey of Public Opinion.
        New York: Associated Councils of the Arts.
Havighurst, Robert
1949   "Old age—an American problem." Journal of Gerontology
        4: 298–304.
1961   "The nature and values of meaningful free-time activity."
        In Robert Kleemeier (ed.). Aging and Leisure. New York:
        Oxford University Press.
1973   "Social roles, work, leisure, and education." In Carl
        Eisdorfer and M. Powell Lawton (eds.). The Psychology
        of Adult Development and Aging. Washington, D.C.:
        American Psychological Association.
Havighurst, Robert and Kenneth Feigenbaum
1959   "Leisure and life style." American Journal of Sociology
        64: 396–404.
Hochschild, Arlie
1975   "Disengagement theory: A critique and proposal." American
        Sociological Review 40: 553–69.
Johnson, Alton and E. Arthur Prieve
1975   "Older Americans, arts administrators and audience
        participation." Paper presented at the 28th Annual
        Scientific Meeting of the Gerontological Society,
        Louisville, Ky.
Kaplan, Max
1975   Leisure: Theory and Policy. New York: John Wiley.
Kelly, John
1972   "Work and leisure: A simplified paradigm." Journal of
        Leisure Research 4: 50–62.

Kent, Donald
  1971 "The Negro aged." The Gerontologist 11 (1, Part 2):
        48–51.
Kreps, Juanita
  1976 "The economy and the aged." In Robert Binstock and
        Ethel Shanas (eds.). Handbook of Aging and the Social
        Sciences. New York: Van Nostrand Reinhold.
Lakin, Martin and Melvin Dray
  1958 "Psychological aspects of activity for the aged." American
        Journal of Occupational Therapy 12: 172–75.
Lehman, Harvey
  1953 Age and Achievement. Princeton, N.J.: Princeton
        University Press.
Lowenthal, Marjorie and Betsy Robinson
  1976 "Social networks and isolation." In Robert Binstock and
        Ethel Shanas (eds.). Handbook of Aging and the Social
        Sciences. New York: Van Nostrand Reinhold.
Maeda, Daisaku
  1975 "Growth of old people's clubs in Japan." The Gerontologist
        15: 254–56.
Martin, Alexander
  1969 "Idle hands and giddy minds: Our psychological and
        emotional unpreparedness for free time." American
        Journal of Psychoanalysis 29: 147–56.
Mendel, Werner
  1971 "Leisure: A problem for preventive psychiatry." American
        Journal of Psychiatry 127: 1688–91.
Meyersohn, R.
  1961 "An examination of commercial entertainment." In Robert
        Kleemeier (ed.). Aging and Leisure. New York: Oxford
        University Press.
Miller, Stephen
  1965 "The social dilemma of the aging leisure participant." In
        Arnold Rose and Warren Peterson (eds.). Older People
        and Their Social Worlds. Philadelphia. F. A. Davis.
Moberg, David
  1965 "Religiosity in old age." The Gerontologist 5: 78–87.
Monk, Abraham and Arthur Cryns
  1974 "Predictors of voluntaristic intent among the aged: An
        area study." The Gerontologist 14: 425–29.
National Council on the Aging
  1975 The Myth and Reality of Aging in America.
        Washington, D.C.
Noll, P.
  1973 "Site selection criteria for housing for the elderly." Paper
        presented at the 26th Annual Scientific Meeting of the
        Gerontological Society, Miami, Fla.

Parelius, Ann
  1975 "Lifelong education and age stratification." American
       Behavioral Scientist 19: 206–23.
Payne, Barbara and Frank Whittington
  1976 "Older women: An examination of popular stereotypes and
       research evidence." Social Problems 23: 488–504.
Peppers, Larry
  1976 "Patterns of leisure and adjustment to retirement." The
       Gerontologist 16: 441–46.
Peterson, David
  1975 "Life-span education and gerontology." The Gerontologist
       15: 436–41.
Pfeiffer, Eric and Glenn Davis
  1971 "The use of leisure time in middle life." The Gerontologist
       11: 187–95.
Rapoport, Rhona and Robert Rapoport
  1975 Leisure in the Family Life Cycle. London: Routledge
       and Kegan Paul.
Riley, Matilda and Anne Foner
  1968 Aging and Society. Volume 1: An Inventory of Research
       Findings. New York: Russell Sage.
Rose, Arnold
  1960 "The impact of aging on voluntary associations." In Clark
       Tibbitts (ed.). Handbook of Social Gerontology: Societal
       Aspects of Aging. Chicago: University of Chicago Press.
Saltz, Rosalyn
  1971 "Aging persons as child-care workers in a Foster-Grandparent
       program: Psychosocial effects and work performance." Aging
       and Human Development 2: 314–40.
Sarason, Seymour
  1977 Work, Aging and Social Change. New York:
       The Free Press.
Simpson, Ida, Kurt Back, and John McKinney
  1966 "Continuity of work and retirement activities, and self-
       evaluation." In Ida Simpson and John McKinney (eds.).
       Social Aspects of Aging. Durham, N.C.: Duke University
       Press.
Smith, Constance and A. Freedman
  1972 Voluntary Associations. Cambridge, Mass.: Harvard
       University Press.
Stark, Rodney
  1968 "Age and faith: A changing outlook or an old process?"
       Sociological Analysis 29: 1–10.
Stone, Ken and Richard Kalish
  1973 "Of poker, roles, and aging: Description, discussion, and
       data." Aging and Human Development 4: 1–13.
Taietz, Philip
  1976 "Two conceptual models of the senior center." Journal
       of Gerontology 31: 219–22.

Tennant, F.
   1965   "A descriptive estimate of the adequacy of network tele-
          vision service to older viewers." Unpublished Master's
          Thesis. University of Southern California.
Trela, James
   1976   "Social class and association membership: An analysis of
          age-graded and non-age-graded voluntary participation."
          Journal of Gerontology 31: 198–203.
U.S. Department of Health, Education, and Welfare
   1973   Work in America. Cambirdge, Mass.: MIT Press.
Ward, Russell
   1977   "The quality of group activities." Paper presented at the
          Annual Scientific Meeting of the Gerontological Society,
          San Francisco.
Wingrove, C. Ray and Jon Alston
   1971   "Age, aging, and church attendance." The Gerontologist
          11: 356–58.
Wuthnow, Robert
   1976   "Recent patterns of secularization: A problem of
          generations?" American Sociological Review 41: 850–67.
Zablocki, Benjamin and Rosabeth Kanter
   1976   "The differentiation of life styles." Annual Review of
          Sociology. Volume 2. Palo Alto, Calif.: Annual Reviews,
          Inc.
Zborowski, Mark
   1962   "Aging and recreation." Journal of Gerontology 17: 302–09.

8

The Family Life of Older People

W hile the nature of family relationships has changed in many ways because of modernization and industrialization, the family is still a major source of *primary* relationships, providing long-lasting, intimate, emotional ties with others. The marriage relationship is generally viewed as the keystone to the satisfaction of emotional needs, but interactions with other kin—offspring, parents, aunts, uncles, and so on—also offer a broad range of gratifications, from the purely social or emotional to financial support and other services. Thus, the extent to which older people are embedded in a system of family relationships has a great potential impact on the aging experience. The 80-year-old widow with no living children and few contacts with relatives is in a very different position from the 65-year-old wife who lives near, and interacts daily with, her children and grandchildren.

Family relationships affect the aging experience in many ways. Family-based roles are an important part of the age stratification system, and they shift in response to larger social changes. We saw in Chapter 3 that involvement of the aged in networks of kin often results in greater status and economic security, but industrialization, urbanization, and the democratization of family interaction in modern societies may have altered the nature of family ties. With expanded longevity such roles as widow and grandparent have become more prevalent. Cohorts may also attach different values to family relationships. The Depression, for ex-

271

ample, may have instilled an image of the family as an emotional and social haven in the minds of some segments of present older people (Elder, 1974). The meanings, functions, and consequences of various family roles in the lives of older persons need to be considered.

In truth, we all belong to several "families," each resulting in a different complex of roles. The *family of orientation* is the one into which we are born, in the roles of daughter, son, sister, and brother. The *family of procreation* is the one in which our own reproductive behavior occurs (at least according to society's expectations), making us a husband, wife, father, mother, grandparent, or widow. From these basic families we also "inherit" an *extended family* of aunts, uncles, cousins, and in-laws. Kinship relations obviously offer broad possibilities for support or companionship in themselves or as compensation for other ties we have never made (because of singlehood) or have lost (because of widowhood). The effects and effectiveness of this broad network for the aged will be explored in this chapter, however, first we will look at the marriage relationship in old age and the consequences of its loss through widowhood.

The Aging Couple

Despite all of the talk about a "sexual revolution," marriage remains a typical experience for adults (some experiencing it more often than others). Very few older people (about 8 percent) have never been married. Because the spouse role implies intimacy and sharing, it may assume considerable importance in fulfilling social and emotional needs, particularly in old age when other roles and associations may be lost through retirement, poor health, and other age-related changes. This is one reason for the possibility of important sex differences in the nature of aging, since most older men are married while most older women are widowed.

While marriage is an important source of many gratifications, we should not assume that single older people are thereby "sentenced" to loneliness and unhappiness. In one of the few studies of single elderly, Gubrium (1975) found that single respondents were more socially isolated but *not* more lonely than married persons. These people had developed a "single" life style, preferring more solitary pursuits and greater independence. For them, being single was "just another way of life"—they saw no stigma associated with it and could not understand why people would expect them to be lonely. Gubrium also points out one "benefit" of being single—you do not experience the disruptive and isolating effects of the death of a spouse.

Nevertheless, most of us do marry, and the increased longevity of modern society means that we will have more time together as a couple, including more time after the children have left and after retirement. Most people are still middle-aged by the time their children "move on," leaving them another 20, 30, or more years of living together. It is important to remember that marriage is not a static experience; the family has its own "life cycle," involving a sequence of realignments in family structure and family relationships. Hill (1965) has provided an idealized sequence of stages representing this cycle:

1. *Establishment:* newly married, childless
2. *New Parents:* oldest child under three
3. *Preschool Family:* oldest child between three and six
4. *School-Age Family:* oldest child between six and 12
5. *Family with Adolescent:* oldest child between 13 and 19
6. *Family with Young Adult:* oldest child 20 until first child leaves home
7. *Family as Launching Center:* from departure of first to departure of last child
8. *Post-Parental Family:* after children have left home until retirement
9. *Aging Family:* after retirement

Even a cursory consideration of these stages suggests differences in the marriage relationship. Becoming parents inevitably imposes some constraints on the freedom of a married couple and also affects residential choice, as space needs and other considerations are affected. Hill suggests that early stages are future oriented, while later stages bring an easing in the pressure on resources.

The quality of the marriage relationship may itself vary among these stages in the life cycle, as is illustrated in a study of couples at different stages conducted by Rollins and Feldman (1970). They found that: (1) the percent indicating that the marriage was "going well all the time" declined to a low when children were of school age, then rose to its highest point during retirement, (2) the percent who considered their present stage "very satisfying" declined to a low point during the launching stage, then rapidly recovered to a high point in retirement, and (3) the percent reporting positive companionship experiences was highest at the beginning, declined until the preschool age, and remained stable thereafter. To understand the sources of such variations, let us turn to the stages most relevant to this book: the post-parental family and the aging (or retirement) family.

The Post-Parental Couple

The "empty nest" following the departure of children involves a major shift in the middle-aged family. As with most major role changes which accompany aging, this period brings both problems and benefits.

The empty nest period appears to be more problematic for women than for men. Deutscher (1964), for example, found that wives were more likely than their husbands to see this phase as *either* better or worse than previous phases. Similarly, Lowenthal and associates (1975) found the empty nest to be more salient for, and more negatively viewed by women. Because of the sexual stratification of roles which encourages and restricts women, especially in current middle-aged and older cohorts, to take on primarily family roles, loss of the "motherhood role" may trigger a crisis of purposelessness which can result in depression (Bart 1971). This may be aggravated by the husband experiencing at the same time peak success and authority in his work (Thurnher, 1976).

The usual prescription for this "empty nest syndrome" is to substitute new roles (hobby, school, work), but this may be quite difficult, especially for working- and lower-class women. Inability to fill this gap may be combined with other difficulties, including menopause or other physical changes and a feeling of failure in one's work career or in childraising, as when one's hopes and ambitions for children are not realized.

"Things hurt you a little deeper when you get older. (Q.: What kinds of things?) Oh, if you have real trouble, it hurts you worse. If your children have traits—(Q.: What do you mean by traits?) Maybe you've been religious and gone to church and sent the kids to Sunday School regularly and, you know, put yourself out. Well, sometimes it ends up that the kids won't go near a church. They just say, 'I had all the church I need.' And education— well, you can't help but feel that they are foolish there. You have to know their personality. You can't make them over; you have to find out the hard way . . . (pause). . . . He had a voice like Nelson Eddy. Just beautiful. I tried to encourage him, but it didn't do any good. He would never do anything with it." (Deutscher, 1964: 57)

A more general marital "disenchantment" may also occur at this stage, resulting in less marital satisfaction, loss of intimacy (confiding and kissing), and less sharing of activities (Pineo, 1961). Despite "efficient" selection of a spouse, unforeseen changes in situation, personality, or behavior or different roles and experiences as adults can lead people who are very similar during their youth to drift apart. The marital relationship often becomes subordinate during the childrearing years (Blood and Wolfe, 1960), which may also lead spouses to grow apart. This mid-life crisis in marriage is reflected in rising rates of middle-aged divorce, since people no longer have to stay together "for the sake of the children" and divorce has lost some of its stigma.

However, the evidence suggests that this disenchantment is not a widespread phenomenon. Most studies indicate that marital satisfaction is as high or higher among older couples as it is among childrearing couples, and older couples typically report fewer problems and feelings of inadequacy (Riley and Foner, 1968; Rollins and Feldman, 1970; Rollins and Cannon, 1974). As with findings showing rising work satisfaction, such cross-sectional data should be viewed with caution, since those who are most dissatisfied have gotten a divorce and there may simply be a tendency to justify any situation which has lasted for 20 or 30 years to avoid appearing foolish. And although disenchantment is apparently not wide-spread, most people do not view this as the "best" time of marriage (Treas, 1975).

Nevertheless, the empty nest does offer rewarding possibilities to older couples. Many view this as a time of new freedom: freedom from financial responsibilities, freedom of movement, freedom from housework, freedom to be oneself. The following comment illustrates such feelings:

> "There's not as much physical labor. There's not as much cooking and there's not as much mending and, well, I remarked not long ago that for the first time since I can remember my evenings are free. And we had to be very economical to get the three children through college. We're over the hurdle now; we've completed it. Last fall was the first time in 27 years that I haven't gotten a child ready to go to school. That was very relaxing." (Deutscher, 1964: 55)

Lowenthal and associates (1975) found that most married people looked forward to the empty nest, and many experienced improved marital relationships based on greater closeness and companionship, increased mutual dependence, and the possibility for more undivided attention to each other.

Other studies indicate that post-parental couples may exhibit fewer sex-role boundaries and place greater emphasis on expressive aspects of the relationship (sharing and caring for each other), rather than on the spouse is a "good housekeeper" or "good provider" (Clark and Anderson, 1967; Thurnher, 1976).

The Retirement Couple

The second major change in the later years of the family cycle occurs with retirement. Most research in this area has focused on the strains associated with a male retiree entering the wife's role sphere—the household. This domain has typically defined the wife's self-image, in which case the retiring husband may be seen as an "intruder" who is suddenly under foot all the time, and even threatens to encroach on her sphere of influence.

Most retirement couples seem relatively satisfied with the marital relationship, and expressed satisfaction may even reach its peak at this stage (Riley and Foner, 1968; Rollins and Feldman, 1970; Dressler, 1973). Researchers disagree, however, on the most effective role adjustments for achieving this satisfaction. Ballweg (1967) suggests that sex-role task differentiation continues, with husbands assuming responsibility for a select group of "masculine" household tasks (repairs, bill-paying), which may involve physical strength or mechanical skills, while wives retain more "feminine" tasks (laundry, dusting). A similar division of labor has been found among older black couples (Jackson, 1972). Lipman (1962), however, argues that these instrumental role conceptions are difficult for males who lose the "provider" role to maintain, even if they take on the kinds of "quasi-instrumental" tasks described by Ballweg, and more problems will result if husbands and wives continue to adhere to purely instrumental role definitions. Townsend (1957), in his studies of English families, found that couples often did retain their earlier sex-role divisions, but this frequently meant that the wife was jealous of her daily routine and the husband did little, resulting in friction and frustration over the disruptions attending retirement and feelings of uselessness for husbands. Lipman suggests that feelings of usefulness will be greater for both spouses who emphasize expressive qualities (affection, companionship, and understanding) through sharing and cooperation. However, there may be sex differences here. Stinnett and associates (1972) found that men were most dissatisfied with lack of respect from their wives, while wives tended to be dissatisfied with poor communication. Nonetheless, it does appear that love, companionship, and the ability to express true feelings are the most rewarding aspects of older marriages, and poor communication may create more problems for older than for younger couples (Thompson and Chen, 1966).

This sharing and cooperation does not always occur. In a study of three generations, Hill (1965) found that the "grandparent" generation was least likely to have an egalitarian marriage, and most likely to follow conventional lives of role specialization (Table 8.1). However, the greatest incidence of "double unconvention-

Table 8.1. Percentage distribution of families by generation on role specialization and role conventionality

	Married child	Parent	Grand-parent
Role Specialization			
High specialization, both spouses *always* do certain household tasks	57	65	78
Medium specialization, spouses usually but not always do the same specified tasks	37	29	14
Low specialization, great shifting about in who does tasks	6	6	8
Role Conventionality			
Both conventional in doing sex-typed tasks, and/or wife conventional with husband only crossing the line	17	21	42
Husband conventional, wife crossing line, and/or both crossing line	70	62	32
Combinations of unconventionality: both crossing line and systematic role reversals	13	17	26
Number of Families	107	100	98

Source: Reuben Hill, "Decision making and the family life cycle," in *Social Structure and the Family: Generational Relations,* by Ethel Shanas and Gordon Streib, © 1965, p. 128. Reprinted by permission of Prentice-Hall, Inc., Englewood Cliffs, New Jersey.

ality" was among these older couples, and other studies (e.g., Dressler, 1973) also report greater sharing of household tasks following retirement. While this sharing appears to be associated with greater marital satisfaction, social class differences have been found. Sharing is welcomed by wives and seen as desirable by both spouses in the middle and upper strata (Kerckhoff, 1966a), probably reflecting a greater general acceptance of egalitarianism in such marriages. In working-class marriages, which tend to be more authoritarian and less companionate, however, activities and tasks are more likely to be segregated by sex. Wives expect more exclusive control over household affairs and husbands are less involved prior to retirement, therefore both view increased involvement by the husband as undesirable, resulting in greater irritation for the wife and guilt for the husband (Kerckhoff, 1966a; Heyman and Jeffers, 1968).

One additional issue addressed by researchers is the relative power of husbands and wives in retirement marriages. Jackson (1972) found some support among older black couples for Smith's (1965) theory that husbands will have greater power in the marital dyad because of the relative scarcity of older males. Others have suggested, however, that the husband's power declines when he loses the "leverage" provided by the "breadwinner" role. Blood and Wolfe (1960) found that the decision-making power of husbands declined with age, particularly after retirement, and Hill (1965) found a greater incidence of "wife-centered" families among retirement couples. Another study by Neugarten and Gutmann (1958) indicated that older respondents were more likely than younger respondents to see "old women" as the central figure in pictures dealing with family situations, with "old men" taking a more passive and peripheral role. Loss of authority for retired males may stem not only from their retirement, but also from continued employment by wives and the higher occupational status often enjoyed by adult offspring.

Both theories may have some truth. Adams (1975) has suggested, for example, that retired husbands might continue to control major decisions concerning finances or residence, while wives run the socio-emotional aspects of the marriage. This interpretation is supported by the cross-cultural studies (cited in Chapter 4) showing that older women exercise greater authority, but it is largely informal. There may also be social-class differences in the relative power of retired husbands. Hochschild (1976) has suggested that the husband's power in working-class marriages may derive simply from being the male, which allows them to retire to the home without losing a sense of efficacy. In the middle-class family, where power may derive from occupational status, realignments occur following retirement.

The research resulting from these marital studies is not entirely satisfactory. Many of the conclusions drawn about realignments are too broad and vague to yield a sense of the processes involved for both spouses in adjusting to the transitions of retirement and the empty nest. How do husbands and wives adjust their expectations concerning appropriate roles in retirement, where do those expectations come from, and through what processes is their relative power altered? Additionally, the studies have been hindered by stereotyped conceptions of sex roles in which the husband retires into the wife's domain. What realignments are required when the wife, or both spouses, retire? Assuming greater sex-role flexibility in the future, what will be the nature of retirement marriages? Such questions remain to be addressed.

Sexuality in Old Age

While sexual interest and activity are by no means confined to the marriage relationship, marriage has been the usual focus for sexuality, particularly for older cohorts. There is no physiological reason for most older people not to have an active and satisfying sex life. Unfortunately, our cultural norms and stereotypes often imply that sex is neither possible nor necessary in old age (Rubin, 1968; Lobsenz, 1974). Our youth-oriented culture reserves images of sexual interest and attractiveness for young people, and as children, we often have difficulty imagining our parents making love. The aged may be tragically cut off from legitimate feelings and gratifications by such stereotypes, shutting off normal sexual feelings because of shame, embarrassment, or fear of ridicule or censure.

> I was told of a recently remarried 78-year-old man whose daughter greets him every morning with a derisive "How did it go last night?" A Florida psychiatrist reported two instances where children tried to commit their parents to a mental institution because they had moved in with friends of the opposite sex. It's not just coincidence that we never refer to even the most profligate youth as a "dirty young man," but are quick to label any older person who shows some interest in sex as a "dirty old man." (One California septuagenarian struck back with a bumper sticker on his sports car: "I'm not a dirty old man, I'm a sexy senior citizen.") (Lobsenz, 1974)

Lobsenz also states that institutions for the aged are particularly likely to be "desexualized," even keeping spouses apart. The following is but one example of the problems which may be encountered:

> A vigorous woman of 71 recently complained to the director of a convalescent home because there was neither the opportunity nor the facility for her to have a sexual relationship with her husband, who was a patient there. "He entered the home to be cared for during his recovery from a serious eye operation," the woman said. "I can't take care of him properly at home. But there is nothing else wrong with him, no reason why we cannot make love. Yet when I come to visit him we must meet only in 'public' areas. Even if we could be alone in his room, there's only a narrow hospital bed there. When I suggested to the home's director that he put at least a three-quarter bed in my husband's room, the man looked at me as if I were some sort of sexual monster." (Lobsenz, 1974)

Such feelings may be particularly difficult for older women, given the sexual double standard which reserves sexual initiative for men and the ability of older men to project a "Cary Grant" image.

There is a tendency for sexual interest and activity to decline with age, partly because of a greater likelihood of physiological problems, but studies clearly show a continuing sexual capacity for most, and stable or even increasing activity is not unusual (Masters and Johnson, 1966; Pfeiffer, Verwoerdt, and Davis, 1972). The research conducted by Pfeiffer and associates at Duke University is a good example. Their study included 261 male (98 percent were married) and 241 female (71 percent were married) volunteers who were relatively healthy. The data, reported in Tables 8.2 and 8.3, do show declines with age for both sexes in current sexual interest and frequency of sexual intercourse, and there is also a widening gap with age between interest and activity. Nevertheless, sexuality is far from nonexistent, particularly for males: only 10 percent of the men 66 to 71 reported no sexual interest and 24 percent no sexual intercourse. It was a different story for women between 66 and 71: 50 percent reported no sexual interest and 73 percent no intercourse. Partly this reflects the fact that men report higher rates of sexual activity at all ages. But Pfeiffer and associates did find that sexuality continued to play an important role for the majority of both sexes.

Sex differences in such studies appear to indicate that in marriage it is the man who determines whether sexual activity will continue or cease. The most frequent reasons given by men for stopping were inability to perform, poor health, and loss of interest (Pfeiffer, Verwoerdt, and Davis, 1972). Masters and Johnson (1966) report that the most important reasons for declining sexual performance in older males are sociopsychological, particularly a "fear of failure." While women may experience painful coitus due to steroid

Table 8.2. Current level of sexual interest for a group of older subjects, by age and sex

| | Number | Level of sexual interest (percentage) | | | |
		None	Mild	Moderate	Strong
Men					
46–50	43	0	9	63	28
51–55	41	0	19	71	10
56–60	61	5	26	57	12
61–65	54	11	37	48	4
66–71	62	10	32	48	10
Total	261	6	26	56	12
Women					
46–50	43	7	23	61	9
51–55	41	20	24	51	5
56–60	48	31	25	44	0
61–65	43	51	37	12	0
66–71	54	50	26	22	2
Total	229	33	27	37	3

Source: Eric Pfeiffer, Adriaan Verwoerdt, and Glenn Davis, 1972, "Sexual behavior in middle life," *American Journal of Psychiatry* 128 (10): 1264. Reprinted by permission.

Table 8.3. Current frequency of sexual intercourse for a group of older subjects, by age and sex

		Frequency of sexual intercourse (percentage)				
	Number	None	Once a month	Once a week	2–3 times a week	More than 3 times a week
Men						
46–50	43	0	5	62	26	7
51–55	41	5	29	49	17	0
56–60	61	7	38	44	11	0
61–65	54	20	43	30	7	0
66–71	62	24	48	26	2	0
Total	261	12	34	41	12	1
Women						
46–50	43	14	26	39	21	0
51–55	41	20	41	32	5	2
56–60	48	42	27	25	4	2
61–65	44	61	29	5	5	0
66–71	55	73	16	11	0	0
Total	231	44	27	22	6	1

Source: Eric Pfeiffer, Adriaan Verwoerdt, and Glenn Davis, 1972, "Sexual behavior in middle life," *American Journal of Psychiatry* 128 (10): 1264. Reprinted by permission.

starvation, which can be dealt with through hormone therapy (Masters and Johnson, 1966), their most frequent reasons for ceasing sexual activity were the death, illness, or inability of spouse (Pfeiffer, Verwoerdt, and Davis, 1972). The sexual activity of older women is more completely determined by marital status and age than for men (Pfeiffer and Davis, 1972), whose declining sexuality is largely a function of their own biological and psychological problems and fears. Such feelings may create severe problems for older couples and lead a wife to feel rejected if she does not understand her husband's fear of impotency. For older women, the greatest problem is the unavailability of socially sanctioned, capable partners, because of the sex ratio among the aged and social disapproval of sexuality in single or widowed older women.

There are also other variables affecting sexuality among the aged. Sexual activity is greater among those with higher socioeconomic status or good health (Pfeiffer and Davis, 1972). More important, continued sexual activity and enjoyment depend on previous sexual behavior and experience, with much less decline among those who were sexually active in their middle years (Masters and Johnson, 1966; Pfeiffer and Davis, 1972). It appears that the Abkhasians are misguided in thinking that early abstinence prolongs sexual capacity (Benet, 1974).

Widowhood

We are social beings, which implies that our ability to validate personal identities and achieve a wide variety of other gratifications is determined by the nature of our social relationships. For many of us, marriage is a central social relationship because of both its intrinsic importance and the links it provides to other social activities and social networks. The sense of "desolation" experienced with widowhood is caused by the severe changes in everyday life and other associated social roles it entails. The new widow can no longer play the role of confidant, lover, housekeeper, or "member of a couple," and these changes may have far-reaching effects on one's style of living.

Many types of gratification accrue from our associations with others. Schutz (1966) has proposed three basic interpersonal needs for which we seek to establish and maintain satisfying social relationships:

1. *Inclusion:* the need to be recognized and to belong, to share experiences and ideas, to feel that the self is significant and worthwhile
2. *Affection:* the need for intimate emotional attachments, to feel that the self is lovable, the need for both nurturance and support
3. *Control:* the need for public esteem in order to feel that the self is competent and responsible

All three of these needs can be met in the marriage relationship. Certainly companionship and affection are major reasons for marrying, and interaction with one's husband or wife ideally engenders trust, emotional understanding, and ready access. Control needs can also find an outlet. For one thing, marriage involves a dyad in which one partner may exercise power over another. In a less "Machiavellian" sense, one can acquire feelings of competence and mutual respect from satisfactory role performance and mutual decision making.

There is also a tendency to specialize our relationships—spouse, friend, colleague—to fulfill different needs, and a variety of relationships is needed to fill them all (Weiss, 1969). When a specialized relationship is lost, it may be difficult to transfer our needs elsewhere.

Generally there is so much resistance to change of definition of a relationship that if a person loses the relationship that provided a particular function—as through the death of a spouse—he will be able only temporarily to alter his remaining relationships to fill the gap. Among members of Parents Without Partners, for example, we found a good deal of bitterness that stemmed from the failure of their friends to respond to their new relational needs. (Weiss, 1969:38)

Marriage may assume even more critical importance for older people. Because of commitments and emotional investments, some relationships come to be viewed as unique, fragile, irreplaceable, and nontransferable (McCall and Simmons, 1966). This is likely to occur with older marriages. In addition, older people lose other roles and relationships when children leave home and with retirement, and limited physical mobility may restrict the range of relationships providing fulfillment of their interpersonal needs. Widowhood is therefore a potentially critical aspect of the aging experience.

The Cultural Context of Widowhood

As with all aspects of the aging experience, the consequences of widowhood depend on its cultural context, particularly in the extent to which being widowed disrupts one's wider social network and roles. The degree of disruption can be thought of as a continuum (Lopata, 1973a), with the *suttee* cultural tradition, involving self-immolation on the husband's funeral pyre, as the most "disruptive" and the tradition of *widow inheritance*, in which the lost husband is soon replaced with another man from the same group, as the least disruptive. Other cultures, such as traditional India, have an intermediate *status role* of widow, resulting in isolation reinforced by special clothing or physical characteristics. The tradition of widows wearing black or a veil for a period of time would fulfill this function. A variety of roles may be assigned to widows (Lopata, 1973a). They may be expected to continue the role of wife by tending the grave or remarrying. Societies in which a high "bride price" is paid may require widows to continue working for the husband's family, who invested so much in her.

Most societies incorporate widows into the extended family in some fashion, though status may be lost (Lopata, 1973a). Lopata suggests that roles for widows are most restricted in patriarchal societies which institutionalize extensive rights of men over women. Modern societies exercise less control over widows because of the declining importance of the extended family, strong rights of property inheritance for widows, increased independence for women, and greater choice of both marital partners and other social relationships; but this often means that widows are also more likely to be isolated in modern societies. The lack of expectations and institutionalized structures for widows creates both greater freedom and the possibility that many widows will be set adrift psychologically and socially.

The Personal Consequences of Widowhood

As one might expect, widowhood often has negative consequences for older people. For example, those who are widowed report greater anticipation of death (Riley and Foner, 1968), though this may only be true of the recently widowed (within ten years) (Kutner, 1956). They also display higher rates of mortality and suicide (though suicide is even greater among those who are divorced) (Riley and Foner, 1968). While many people do give some thought to the possibility of widowhood, and the death of others may precipitate a type of "rehearsal," there is the clear potential for severe disruption of self-identity. After all, the roles associated with being a spouse are no longer available, and one's spouse is lost as a source of interpersonal need fulfillment.

We must be careful, however, about overstating the impact of widowhood. Former identities can be preserved through memory or children, just as status derived from work often continues in retirement, nor is "wife" a central role for all women. Lopata's (1973a) study of widows, age 50 and over, in Chicago indicated that lower-class and black women, compared with more highly educated and white widows, tended to downgrade the wife role. Middle-class marriages are generally more couple-companionate. The hardships of lower-class life may result in anger directed at the husband, and such marriages tend to involve less communication and greater segregation of activity by sex. Lopata found that black and lower-class women had less satisfying relationships with their husbands. It is also true that the lower morale experienced by widows may partly come from things which *accompany* widowhood (such as financial problems or poor health), rather than widowhood *itself* (Morgan, 1976).

Widowhood may also have its positive aspects. Relief may be the predominant feeling for those with unhappy marital histories.

One of the NORC interviewers was so struck by the vehemence of a widow's feelings that she explained in the margin: "This woman went on about how little she thinks of men. Let me tell you, she hates them!" This respondent had tried marriage twice and was miserable both times. "There is nothing good I can say about it. I would go to bed unhappy and cursing while my husband was alive. After he died, I could say my prayers and go to sleep in peace. Women in those days married a man and stuck it out, going about their routine of washing, ironing and cooking regardless of how miserable they were. But the Lord did me a favor and removed my husband, so I would live out the rest of my days in peace." (Lopata, 1973a:83)

Another type of relief may follow the end of a long, lingering illness. In addition, many widows mention the independence and release from duties which accompany widowhood, as illustrated by the following comment: "You don't have to cook if you don't want to: your time is your own; you can come and go as you want; you don't have to be home if your husband isn't there" (Lopata, 1973a:75–76). In fact, half the widows in Lopata's sample reported that they "like living alone."

None of this denies the very real problems experienced by many widows. There is, for example, the "grief work" associated with loss of a spouse. Partly because of the lack of a socially institutionalized period of grief, Lopata (1973a) found that 20 percent of her sample was still going through the bereavement process, though nearly one-half had ended their grief within a year of widowhood. In his study of 22 recent widows, Parkes (1969) found considerable "separation anxiety," similar to that experienced by young children at the loss of a parent. This feeling was expressed in attempts to recover the lost object through hyperactivity, continual "searching," preoccupation with memories, a recurring sense of the person's presence, and calling out for the lost person.

"Husband sanctification" appears to be typical early in widowhood. In her studies Lopata (1973a; 1976) found that husbands were idealized as "extremely good, honest, kind, friendly and warm," particularly by older widows, whites, higher-educated persons, and widows who attached greater importance to the "wife" role. Lopata suggests that husband sanctification serves to boost status and morale and to facilitate successful "grief work" by eliminating feelings of resentment or jealousy.

Obviously there are many other problems which may be associated with widowhood. We have already seen that aged widows comprise a large percentage of the older poverty population, and taking on unfamiliar roles—such as financial manager for many women and housekeeper for many men—always requires adjustments. Many of the widows in Lopata's (1973a) study were quite ignorant of financial matters, since traditional role specialization within the family had not prepared them. In fact, economic advice was especially likely to be a source of strain with family and friends. Many felt acutely vulnerable to bad financial advice or being cheated, and approximately one-half felt that "people take advantage of you when they know you are a widow." The most important consequences of widowhood, however, were its effects on social networks and potential isolation and loneliness.

The Social Consequences of Widowhood

Widowhood inevitably results in at least short-term social disruption and the need to fulfill many tasks during an often grief-stricken time. As we shall see in greater detail later, one's family (adult offspring as well as the extended family) can be an important source of emotional, social, and financial support. The adult children of older widows may replace the husband as objects of attention and care, perform tasks previously done by their father, or serve as an outlet for close interpersonal ties (Lopata, 1973a). Lopata's results indicate that these functions are more likely to be performed by unmarried children. Widows were also emotionally closer to their daughters, while sons were most helpful dealing with funeral arrangements and financial matters. It is interesting that there was considerable unwillingness on the part of the widows in Lopata's study to undertake too many obligations toward their adult children, and one-third felt that children do make unwarranted demands. For example, babysitting was often seen as an imposition. It appears that many widows have a keen sense of vulnerability to exploitation (financial, social, or otherwise), and are not "desperate" for just any kind of social contact.

While children and other relatives can be important sources of support, widowed persons are increasingly likely to live alone. The proportion of the widowed who live alone has increased from less than 20 percent in 1940 to 50 percent in 1970 (Chevan and Korson, 1972). The widows in Lopata's (1973a) study preferred "intimacy at a distance." Having been accustomed to running their own homes, they did not wish to become dependent subordinates in someone else's house. This was a particular concern with married children, where moving in might involve considerable role reversal, status loss, and competition. In addition, these widows did not wish to impinge on the right of their children to lead their own lives, free from outside "meddling." The likelihood of living with relatives does increase after age 80 (due to physical and financial problems), however, and is greater among nonwhites, females, lower socioeconomic groups, and those with children (Chevan and Korson, 1972). Perhaps as a reflection of differences in cultural expectations, the widowed are less likely to live alone if they are foreign-born, live in a rural area, or come from a traditional Catholic background.

Although family contacts are generally available to those who are widowed, and this availability itself lends a sense of security, there is little evidence of major new involvement in family affairs. Lopata (1973a) found, for example, that while nearly one-third of her widows felt their sibling relationships were more important following widowhood, fewer than 15 percent saw a sibling as often as once a month. Another study of the elderly widowed in Missouri towns found no change in family involvement by widows, while the involvement of widowers rose in the first five years, but then fell to even less than when they were married (Pihlblad and Adams, 1972). It also appears that older black widows are no more likely than whites to have close ties with their extended families (Lopata, 1973b; Arling, 1976). Contact with in-laws, in fact, is quite likely to be broken by widowhood (Lopata, 1973; Rosenberg and Anspach, 1973).

Other social networks beyond the family are likely to be disrupted by widowhood. In Lopata's (1973a) study, 38 percent reported declining intensity of social life while only 12 percent reported an increase. Friendship interaction was particularly low during the first year of widowhood. This disruption of social networks is quite unfortunate. Apart from providing the usual gratifications of friendships, friends can help recent widows by keeping them occupied, offering sympathy and understanding, helping with bereavement, and so on. In fact, at least one study suggests that contact with friends is a more important determinant of satisfaction than contact with family (Pihlblad and Adams, 1972). Social interaction does not decline for everyone, however. Those who tend to experience little change are those who were immersed in family contacts, home-based housewives, highly isolated during marriage, or social activists while married (Lopata, 1973a).

Why would widowhood disrupt social networks? One reason is that accompaniments of widowhood, such as poor health or poverty, have isolating effects. But it is also true that widowhood itself creates problems. Many social activities—visiting, attendance at public places—are engaged in as a couple with other couples. Widowhood threatens one's continuation in this "society of couples" (Blau, 1961, 1973; Lopata, 1973a). The recent widow may feel like a "third wheel" or be viewed by wives as a potential rival. Interests and needs may change and the widow may feel dependent for transportation. The lack of a male escort in a "couple-companionate world" may engender a feeling of alienation because of status loss.

"I feel that. Well, how can I put it in words? Second class citizen, that's true, you do feel that way. Well, I think just the fact that you don't have an escort when you go places—I think that this is very pronounced and very evident if you go out to dinner. I

don't like to go out to dinner alone, so consequently you try to
get on the phone and call somebody else up and see if they're in
the mood to go. This sets you apart, you see a couple of women
. . . I can remember down in Miami, I hate Miami for that
reason. When I was not a widow yet, you'd see groups of beauti-
fully gowned, elegant looking elderly women, you knew they were
all widows. Immediately they were an isolated segment of society
in my mind at that time, and I'm sure when we go into a
restaurant, maybe two or three or four of us, I'm sure that other
people look at us the same way." (Lopata, 1973a:191)

Lopata found that while few widows limited their contacts solely
to other widows and most retained at least some of their former
friends, most had experienced some strains in their friendships.
Involvement in the larger community, through neighbors or voluntary associations, may offer some compensation, but Lopata indicates that neighboring is largely sporadic as few are used to such
visiting as a major source of social contacts, and few clubs actively
encourage membership by widows. Widows attempting to establish
new roles, relationships, and activities may also experience a "reentry syndrome," characterized by feelings of inadequacy and low
self-confidence (Bart, 1975), particularly recent widows attempting
to enter the world of education or work after a lifetime of being a
housewife.

The disruptive effects of widowhood depend upon one's position
in the social structure regarding both age and sex peers and social
class. Blau (1961, 1973) suggests that the prevalence of widowhood among one's age-sex peers is extremely important. For example, women over 65 may become involved in a "society of
widows" because widowhood is actually the norm for them
(Cumming and Henry, 1961), but younger widows may experience
a greater decline in social position. Morgan (1976) found that
widows had lower morale than married women, but older widows
catch up with (and may even surpass) the morale of the married.
Widowhood is also less prevalent among males, and may therefore be more socially disruptive, since it places them in an "unusual" position. Pihlblad and Adams (1972), for example, found
a greater disruption of friendships for widowers than for widows.
As with women, being placed in an odd social category by widowhood would decline with age.

There are also important, though in some ways contradictory,
social-class differences in the disruptiveness of widowhood. The
greater sharing of activities and friendships in middle-class marriages, which are more couple-companionate (Lopata, 1973a),
would suggest greater problems for middle-class widows. But this
is apparently more than counteracted by the greater social oppor-

tunities and social skills possessed by better-educated middle-class women. While they have been more involved in the marital relationship, they have also developed a wider network of interpersonal relationships and a greater variety of social activities (Lopata, 1973c), and their greater education gives them more self-confidence and better skills in building social relations. The social contacts of lower- and working-class women are more likely to be minimal and sporadic, yielding a smaller reservoir of social opportunities (Blau, 1973).

Loneliness

The social disruption which often accompanies widowhood implies that feelings of loneliness may be a particular problem. In Lopata's (1973a) sample of widows, 48 percent said that loneliness was their greatest problem. Loneliness is not the same as aloneness, however. A useful distinction can be made between *isolation* and *desolation* (Townsend, 1957). Isolation means few social contacts, but some prefer this and others get used to it over a period of time. Desolation refers to a sudden decrease in interpersonal contact below accustomed levels. The desolated person may in fact have more contacts than the isolate, but experiences *subjective* deprivation resulting in loneliness. Thus, loneliness is "caused not by being alone but by being without some definite needed relationship or set of relationships" (Weiss, 1973:17).

There are two types of isolation which may result in feelings of loneliness (Weiss, 1973).[1] *Emotional isolation* is the lack of a truly intimate tie. It involves separation anxiety and utter aloneness which cannot be alleviated by just any alternative social relationship. This is likely to accompany widowhood because of the intimacy and sense of uniqueness attached to the marital relationship, which make it very difficult to transfer the needs satisfied through marriage to other relationships. The widowed are also likely to experience *social isolation*—lack of a network of involvements with peers—which engenders feelings of boredom, aimlessness, and marginality. Social isolation is more easily dealt with than emotional isolation, since a wider variety of social relationships are satisfactory.

There may be age differences in emotional and social isolation (because of the availability of a "society of widows" as age increases), but there is no reason to expect that emotional isolation, and attendant grief or separation anxiety, will lessen with age. Longer spouse relationships may be seen as more irreplaceable,

---

[1] Weiss refers to these as types of isolation, but their meanings are closer to our concept of desolation.

and the loss (through death, poor health, or mobility) of other long-term intimates may have heightened the importance of the marital interaction.

Lopata (1969; 1973a) found that there are many types of loneliness which may be experienced by widows. One can be lonely for an individual as a *person*, or miss having someone around, someone to share experiences with, or someone to care for and love. The loss of a companion is expressed by the following:

> I don't think anyone who hasn't experienced it can understand the void that is left after losing a companion for so many years— all the happy little things that come up and you think, 'Oh, I must share that'—and there isn't anyone there to share it with. . . ." (Lopata, 1969:251)

A younger divorcee expresses the emptiness from lacking someone or something around which to organize oneself:

> "How can I explain it? Your house is so noisy all day long, phones, people, kids, all kinds of action going on and come eight o'clock everybody's in bed, and there's this dead silence. Like the whole world has just come to an end. All of a sudden you get this feeling that you're completely alone, that there is no one else in the world. You look out the windows, you walk back and forth from room to room, you watch television, and you're dead." (Weiss, 1973:136)

Lopata (1973a) notes that widows are especially likely to feel lonely at dinnertime. Not only must they eat alone, but the entire rhythm of the housewife role is disrupted when there is no "object" for one's tasks. Widows may also feel lonely because they miss being the object of someone else's activities and love. Finally, there is the loneliness felt for life style or set of activities engaged in as a couple.

There are a variety of ways to combat loneliness, of course. The usual prescription is to "keep busy," which may involve a self-conscious scheduling of activities, as engaged in by one widow:

> "I find that the lonesome part of the day is at dusk. I don't have my mail delivered and I usually go out and get my mail or do some shopping at this time—just to get away from the house then. People say they call me up at 6:00 and 'you're not home.'— I tell them it may be a good time for most people but it isn't a good time to get me because then I feel too lonesome. I just get out. I have a car so I drive around a little. I generally eat dinner late at night. . . . I have a little TV in the kitchen too so I can

eat out there. I think it's kind of lonely to eat alone—that's why I watch TV or read the papers." (Lopata, 1969:256)

Many widows seek new roles and relationships, through activities with family, friends, or voluntary associations, but success in this depends on the prevalence of widows among one's age-sex peers and the prior development of social interests and skills.

Sex Differences

Most of this discussion has drawn on studies of female widows. But assumptions that widowhood is a "female problem" do not appear to be warranted.

Bell (1971) has suggested that widowhood is more difficult for women because of traditional sex-role socialization and expectations, which make the marital role a more important part of the self for women. Their lesser social aggressiveness is combined with less opportunity and encouragement to remarry, and widows typically face a bleaker financial future and possess fewer skills for financial management. Atchley (1975), for example, found that widowers had greater social participation than widows because of the economic supports they possessed. Lopata (1971) has referred to widows as a disadvantaged minority group. They are often victimized, restricted by poverty, and socially handicapped by the emphasis on couples. Lopata suggests that because women live in a male-dominated society and have been socialized into restricted roles, they face severe difficulties in developing broader social engagement following widowhood.

It may well be that widows are placed at a disadvantage by existing patterns of sex-role differentiation, but the same can be said of men. Some observers, such as Berardo (1968; 1970) and Blau (1961), suggest that men have more difficulty adjusting to widowhood than women and encounter greater social isolation because of it. Table 8.4 presents data from a study by the author (Ward,

Table 8.4. Loneliness by marital status and sex for ever-married older respondents (60 and over)

Loneliness	Female[a] (percentage)		Male[b] (percentage)	
	Married	Widowed	Married	Widowed
Never or hardly ever	60.8	46.4	80.5	40.0
Sometimes or often	39.2	53.6	19.5	60.0
Number of respondents	51	110	87	45

[a] Differences for females not significant at p = .05.
[b] Differences for males significant at p = .0001.

1974) which suggest that widowhood is more likely to result in increased loneliness for men than for women. There are several possible reasons for such findings. First, widowhood is more unusual for men, so a "society of widowers" is more difficult to achieve. Second, just as the wife may be relatively unprepared for certain tasks (financial management), the husband may be unprepared for the daily tasks of running a household (cooking, cleaning, and so on). Third, widowhood may more often constitute a double blow for men, who are more likely to have already experienced the social disruptions of retirement. Finally, men may experience greater difficulty satisfying emotional needs outside of marriage, since their friendships tend to be less expressive and close than those of women, and they retain fewer close family ties. Townsend (1957), for example, found stronger bonds between mothers and children, based on greater past involvement and the special tie between mothers and daughters. A common consequence of widowhood for men was less interaction with children. Because of sex-role socialization, men are more dependent on the intimacy and expressive freedom found within the marital relationship.

Both of these views are partly valid. In some ways widowhood is more difficult for women, in other ways for men. What these findings suggest is that restricted roles and the failure to develop multidimensional social relationships will make any kind of role loss more traumatic. In any case, widowhood is clearly a difficult experience for most. Lopata (1973a) has drawn certain conclusions from her study of widows in Chicago. First, widows need help with "grief work," since society largely leaves the individual to his or her own resources (see Chapter 12). A second pressing problem is companionship. Lopata observed an almost paranoic anxiety concerning social relationships. The larger community may be of assistance through widow-to-widow programs or adequate scheduling and transportation for social activities. Finally, Lopata suggests that what the widowed need is not a lot of advice, but rather confidence-building experiences which would encourage them to rebuild their patterns of living for themselves.

Remarriage

One course of action following widowhood is remarriage, though this is not a widespread phenomenon. Many older people view remarriage as inappropriate, and there are additional barriers created by opposition from children and loss of Social Security benefits (Treas, 1975). Nevertheless, in 1970 there were approximately 60,000 marriages involving older people, almost all of

which were remarriages (Treas and Van Hilst, 1976). The likelihood of remarriage is quite high for those widowed in their thirties
or forties, but declines rapidly with age. Men tend to remarry
sooner and at all ages are substantially more likely than women to
remarry following widowhood (Cleveland and Gianturco, 1976;
Treas and Van Hilst, 1976), possibly because of their greater
emotional dependence on marriage, but also there are simply more
available older women than men. McKain (1972) found a high
rate of success in a sample of 100 older newlyweds. He argues that
success is more likely when the couple have known each other
well for a long time, friends and relatives approve, income is
sufficient, adjustment to aging has been satisfactory, and they do
not move into a house from an earlier marriage.

One might speculate on the likelihood of future experimentation by the aged with alternative life styles such as cohabitation or
group marriage. Adams (1975) suggests that there might be a
"reverse socialization," whereby elders learn from the examples of
youth. To date, however, there is little evidence of such experimentation, though the 1970 Census indicated that at least 18,000
couples 65 and over were unmarried and living together (Lobsenz,
1974).

Aging and the Extended Family

Our discussion to this point has treated only one part of the
family life of the aged—the marriage relationship. Obviously the
family is a much broader social context which can affect the aging
experience in many ways. As a source of social and emotional outlets, and a variety of personal services, an older person's family can
have tremendous benefits. On the other hand, the family can be
a source of conflict and strain. For example, the aged are very
reluctant to become dependent on their children because of the
implications of role reversal and value conflict. In order to understand the impact of family ties on older people we first must understand their position in the larger family structure.

Modernization and the Family

The *classical extended family* of preindustrial societies has been
described as a patriarchal organization of parents, unmarried children, married sons and their families, and occasionally brothers
and their families, who lived together under the authority of the
extended family (Sjoberg, 1956). Extended kin relationships were
primary factors in determining occupational and political success.

Beginning in the 1940s, articles appeared announcing the "death" of the extended family and its replacement by a more autonomous, even isolated *nuclear family* (parents and children) (e.g., Parsons and Bales, 1955; Parsons, 1959; Goode, 1963). This was attributed to the related processes of industrialization and urbanization. The new occupational system engendered by industrialization reduced family "inheritance" of occupation and required greater mobility, thereby dispersing the family. New institutions emerged to take over functions formerly played by the extended family: economic production, education, financial support, health care. The more impersonal and segmented urban milieu fostered greater nonfamily involvement and smaller residences reduced the ability of families to live together. Finally, values stressing freedom of movement and democratic relationships were antithetical to the authority of the extended family.

This is a *structural-functionalist* argument that family structure is a reflection of family functions. As modernization reduced the functions of the family, its structure could be expected to change. The presumed remaining functions of the family—socialization of children and stabilization of adult personalities through the marital relationship—could best be performed in an autonomous nuclear family. Thus, major obligations and solidarity are focused on the nuclear family, while extended kin are at most peripheral. This tendency should be most advanced in the urban middle class. If this shift from extended to nuclear family is real, the aged will be cut off from family supports they may have enjoyed in the past. But how much truth is there to this argument?

It should first be noted that, despite our nostalgic images of families such as "The Waltons," the classic extended family has never been widespread. In the Plymouth colonies, for example, the nuclear family was typical (Demos, 1970). Those who did survive to old age, however, were likely to live in a three-generational family, because of both values and norms and housing shortages. Older persons in the past also often controlled family property, but young people now are less dependent on family property, and values tend to support residential separation.

Nevertheless, recent evidence from empirical studies suggests that the demise of the extended family has been greatly exaggerated (Adams, 1970; Troll, 1971). Interaction among kin remains quite frequent, with reciprocal provision of services, and people still consider their kinship ties important, even in the absence of residential proximity. It does not appear that urban life necessarily results in family deterioration or the replacement of kin ties by friends, neighbors, or voluntary associations. In his study of Greensboro, North Carolina, Adams (1968) found that 45 percent of the middle class and 60 percent of the working class had at least one set of parents living in the same city and that interaction between parents and offspring was quite regular.

What seems to have evolved is not an isolated nuclear family, but rather a *modified extended family*. The extended family has become more geographically dispersed, has lost its occupational importance, and no longer exercises rigid authority. Kin relations have become more open and voluntaristic. But family ties remain important in fulfilling social and emotional needs and providing a wide range of services. Even young people agree that people *should* maintain contact with families (Hill, 1970), and an ideology of "taking care of one's own" persists among younger cohorts, though they allow other social institutions to take major responsibility (Sussman, 1976).

Why has the extended family continued to play important roles in modern society? A combination of affection, general obligation, and long-term reciprocal commitments results in a "positive concern" for the well-being and activities of kin (Adams, 1967), because of which family ties tend to be more persistent than friendships, more narrowly based on sociability and similarity. How many of our friendships from college survive for 10 or 20 years? When we do develop "positive concern" about friends, we often say the person is "like a sister" or "like a father." This mutual interest keeps family ties alive over the years and across the distances which separate people. These family ties are sustained through ceremonies and holidays—weddings, funerals, christenings, Christmas.

Modernization has not entirely stripped the extended family of its functions. For example, the first source of aid during illness or disasters is more likely to be the family than formal community agencies, which are still not a preferred source of help (Quarantelli, 1960; Hill, 1970). Family assistance is not considered welfare, but stems instead from a long history of reciprocity. Mobility need not reduce family ties, since a dispersed family can aid individuals who move (Litwak, 1960). Litwak and Szelenyi (1969) suggest that the extended family has survived because modern communication and a monetary economy allow the family to communicate and exchange services without face-to-face interaction. Neighbors can be of immediate assistance because of their proximity. Friends provide a reference group and consensus-based sociability. The virtue of the family is the long-term commitments and reciprocity which are built up. In addition, the extended family offers a network of interpersonal relationships to compensate for or replace ties which are missing or lost, for those who are single or widowed, for example. Thus, the aged can at least *potentially* be enmeshed in a complex family network of affectional ties and reciprocal assistance.

Family Involvement of Older People

One aspect of family involvement is living arrangements. Most older people prefer not to live with their children or other relatives. Shanas and associates (1968) found that only 8 percent of a national sample of older people said they preferred to live with children or other relatives, while 83 percent preferred their own home. Even when ill or disabled, most older people opposed moving in with relatives (Riley and Foner, 1968). In recent decades the aged have increasingly lived in their own households (and more often with spouse) rather than with relatives, but a substantial minority still share a household with others. Shanas and associates (1968) found this to be true for 35 percent of the elderly in the United States, 45 percent in Great Britain, and 27 percent in Denmark. Those who live with their children are likely to be older, widowed or unmarried, in worse health, and have lower income. Thus, the family remains an important alternative for those who need it.

Probably a more important aspect of family involvement is the extent of actual interaction with kin. Nearly 80 percent of all older people have living children, and in their reviews of the literature, both Adams (1970) and Troll (1971) conclude that there is considerable interaction between older parents and their children. For one thing, they are likely to live in close proximity to their children. Table 8.5 presents data on residential proximity for a study

Table 8.5. The proximity of the nearest child to people aged 65 and over in Great Britain, the United States, and Denmark

	People with living children		
Proximity of the nearest child	Britain (%)	U.S. (%)	Denmark (%)
Same household	41.9	27.6	20.1
10 minute's journey or less	23.5	33.1	32.0
11 to 30 minute's journey	15.9	15.7	23.0
31 minute's to 1 hour	7.6	7.2	12.4
Over 1 hour but less than 1 day	9.1	11.2	11.2
1-day journey or more	1.9	5.2	1.3
N =	1911	2012	2009

Source: Jan Stehouwer, "Relations between generations and the three-generation household in Denmark," in *Social Structure and the Family: Generational Relations,* by Ethel Shanas and Gordon Streib, © 1965, p. 147. Reprinted by permission of Prentice-Hall, Inc., Englewood Cliffs, New Jersey.

conducted in the United States, Great Britain, and Denmark (Stehouwer, 1965). In the United States, over three-quarters of those with living children live within 30 minutes of at least one child, and this proximity was utilized. Again for the United States, 65 percent of those with living children had seen a child within the past day and another 19 percent within the past week. Contacts are often maintained with other family members, as well. Between one-third and one-half of all older people see a sibling every week or two (Shanas et al., 1968; National Council on the Aging, 1976). At the very least, it appears that most older people are not isolated from their children and other kin, and even those who do not live near their children compensate by telephoning and writing letters.

What needs does the family meet for the aged? For one, there is the companionship and affection embodied in the "primary" nature of family ties, which make the extended family important in its own right and also as a wide-ranging network for compensation and replacement of interpersonal relationships. The aged are susceptible to social loss because of retirement, widowhood, illness or death of peers, and limited personal mobility. Relations with neighbors are typically restrained anyway, and older people may find it hard to make new friends because of poor health or low income (which restrict both going out and entertaining). An English study found that the percentage who had been visited by a friend or neighbor during the previous week declined from 74 percent among respondents aged 50 to 59 to only 53 percent among those 70 and over (Willmott and Young, 1960). The large number of relationships available in the extended family can compensate for such losses. Shanas and associates (1968) found that older people without living children were nearly twice as likely to. feel lonely, and those who are widowed are more likely to see their children and live with single children.

The family may also compensate for relationships never established. Willmott and Young (1960) found that 43 percent of single older people had been a sibling in the past 24 hours, compared with only 6 percent of those who had been married. Similarly, those with no children or who do not see them as often maintain more frequent contact with siblings.

It is apparent that extended family ties are important to the aged, and aged family members may also play a key role in maintaining extended kin ties. Contacts with siblings, and particularly with more distant kin such as aunts, uncles, or cousins, may occur through intermediaries like older parents. If so, the death of this older intermediary may loosen or break up the extended family network.

In addition to the fulfillment of interpersonal needs, the extended family can provide more tangible help and services: help during illness, financial aid, child care, advice, gifts, and so on. Such mutual assistance is a widespread pattern in both middle- and working-class families (Sussman and Burchinal, 1962; Shanas et al., 1968; Bild and Havighurst, 1976). For example, Shanas and associates found that approximately two-thirds of their respondents in the United States received help from children and a considerable minority relied on relatives as the sole source of assistance for everyday personal and household tasks. Assistance does not only flow to the aged; throughout the life cycle there are mutual and reciprocal patterns of aid. Networks of aid can become quite complex, as illustrated in the following case:

> Mrs. Rilk, an infirm widow in her early sixties, lived alone. A married daughter living nearby regularly did her cleaning and gave her meals on Sundays. Her shopping was done by a 13-year-old grandson. "He comes every morning before school." As for washing, another grandson "calls in when he's on his milk round on Sunday and collects it. My daughter gets it done on a Monday and Charlie (the grandson) brings it back." Her grandchildren chopped firewood for her, exercised her dog and took her to the cinema or to the bus-stop. Her daughter collected the pension. But Mrs. Rilk prepared a meal for her daughter and grandchildren six days of the week, often entertained her relatives in the evenings and once or twice a week she took a meal to an old lady in the same block of flats. (Townsend, 1957:45)

Over half of all older persons also assist their children (Sussman and Burchinal, 1962; Shanas et al., 1968). This is more likely to occur in middle-cass families and is, of course, determined by the physical and financial capabilities of the older person.

This pattern of mutual aid can be illustrated by a study of three-generation families (Hill, 1965). Table 8.6 indicates the types of assistance both given and received by each generation. No generation is entirely a "giver" or "receiver," but giving is generally highest for parents and lowest for grandparents, though differentials are least in the economic sphere. Not surprisingly, married children received the greatest assistance with child care, while the grandparent generation was most likely to require help for illness and household management. Note, however, that 32 percent of the grandparents also provided illness assistance to younger generations, such as the grandmother who becomes a "live-in nurse" for a sick grandchild. So the aged are not simply reduced to "cashing in" the obligations accrued from their parental assistance.

Though the extended family can offer tremendous benefits to its

Table 8.6. Comparison of help received and help given by generation for chief problem areas (percentages)

	Type of crisis									
	Economic		Emotional gratification		Household management		Child care		Illness	
	Gave	Rec'd	Gave	Rec'd	Gave	Rec'd	Gave	Rec'd	Gave	Rec'd
Grandparents	26	34	23	42	21	52	16	0	32	61
Parents	41	17	47	37	47	23	50	23	21	21
Married children	34	49	31	21	33	25	34	78	47	18

Source: Reuben Hill, "Decision making and the family life cycle," in *Social Structure and the Family: Generational Relations*, by Ethel Shanas and Gordon Streib, © 1965, p. 125. Reprinted by permission of Prentice-Hall, Inc., Englewood Cliffs, New Jersey.

aged members, a few words of caution are in order. In one sense, the extended family is even more prevalent in modern societies than in preindustrial societies. The three- and four-generation family is no longer rare. Shanas and associates (1968) found that 44 percent of their older sample were members of a three-generation family, and another 32 percent of four-generation families. Thus, older persons may find themselves at the pinnacle of a vast network of literally hundreds of kin relationships. But there is great diversity in family structure, and many widowed or single older people find themselves completely isolated from social contacts. The extremes are illustrated by the following case histories:

> Mr. Fortune, aged seventy-six, lived alone in a two-room council flat . . . Mr. Fortune had been a cripple from birth and he was partly deaf. He was unmarried and his five siblings were dead. An older widowed sister-in-law lived about a mile away with an unmarried son and daughter. These three and two married nieces living in another borough were seen from once a month to a few times a year. . . . He spoke to one or two of the neighbors outside his flat but he had no regular contact with any of them. He had one regular friend, living a few blocks away, who came over to see him on a Sunday about once a month. (Townsend, 1957:171)

> A married woman of sixty-four lived with her husband, a single son, and a granddaughter. She had a part-time occupation as an office cleaner. Three married daughters lived nearby and she saw them and four of their children every day. She saw two of their husbands nearly every day and one once a week, her eldest son and his wife only once or twice a week. The surviving members of the husband's family were not seen, but two of the wife's nieces called every fortnight. She had a widowed friend living alone whom she visited once a fortnight but she took pride in not having any regular association with a neighbor. She went to the cinema once or twice a month. (Townsend, 1957:168)

Townsend (1957) suggests that isolates such as "Mr. Fortune" are likely to be unmarried or childless, infirm, retired, and with few surviving relatives.

Kerckhoff (1965) suggests that while we express norms which support a modified extended family, actual *behavior* is less likely to display this mutual support. Kinship relations have lost much of their obligatory nature and become more permissive and voluntary. Thus, not all kin are truly "available." Distance divides children into intimates, week-enders, and holiday companions, and other family members are characterized as either "intimate" or "recognized" (seen only on ritual or holiday occasions) (Townsend,

1957). A study of working-class kinship in Philadelphia found that if the only proximate kin are *distant* relatives (aunts, uncles, grand-parents), contacts are likely to be only sporadic (Rosenberg and Anspach, 1973). Thus, the available extended family may be effectively limited to children and their spouses and siblings. Rosenberg and Anspach also found that the aged often experience an atrophy in their kin pool, as relatives die or widowhood severs contact with in-laws, and they often have difficulty extending family relationships to compensate for losses. They conclude that neither the isolated nuclear family nor extended family integration gives a truly accurate portrayal of the familial position of the aged.

The research on family involvement of the aged has largely focused on the frequency of family contacts, leading one to wonder about their quality and meaning. Irving Rosow (1965) points out that these studies do not necessarily indicate *emotional* closeness or warmth. Emergency aid is not the same as stable, continual interaction, and involvements may be largely ritualistic, as with holiday family gatherings. Blau (1973) has speculated that the "intimacy at a distance" seemingly preferred by older people may be a pseudo-intimacy which reflects an unwillingness to admit their marginal status in the family. Older people value indepen-dence for their children and themselves, but there is also some ambivalence. They do not wish to impose or be dependent, but neither do they wish to be neglected or ignored: "They shouldn't *have* to visit me or take care of me, but it would be nice if they did."

Variations in Family Structure

The position of the aged in the family is affected by a number of factors, the most noteworthy being social class, sex, and racial and ethnic membership. Numerous studies indicate that the work-ing class has a stronger kin orientation, living closer and interacting more regularly with family, than does the middle class (see Adams, 1970; Troll, 1971). For example, studies of working-class areas around London suggest that most of the basic rights, obligations, and needs of individuals are expressed and satisfied within a three-generation extended family characterized by close residential proximity, daily interaction, and such reciprocal services as shop-ping, cleaning, and illness care (Townsend, 1957; Willmott and Young, 1960). Middle-class families partly compensate for greater geographic dispersion with the use of transportation and com-munication facilities, however, and are also involved in inter-family help networks (Sussman and Burchinal, 1962; Shanas et al., 1968). While the working-class family appears more important throughout the life cycle, the family's salience may increase for the middle-class aged. Willmott and Young (1960) investigated the frequency with which parents of respondents lived in the same dwelling or within five minutes. Differences were large for parents under 65—40 percent of the working class but only 16 percent of the middle class lived this close to their parents—but were much smaller when parents were 65 and over—53 percent in the working class and 47 percent in the middle class.

One can perhaps speak of three types of family structures, varying by social class. The *patriarchal extended family* has survived in the upper classes because elite status is still tied to the patrilineal line of descent (the Rockefellers or the Kennedys). The *maternal extended family* is more characteristic of the working class. It involves close daily interaction and reciprocal aid among localized family members, revolving around mother-daughter-granddaughter ties. The *modified extended family* is most characteristic of the urban and suburban middle class. The family is more dispersed because of residential and occupational mobility, and the marital relationship assumes greater importance. Although contact is less stable and continuous, the extended family is still bound together by affectional ties and reciprocal aid, particularly financial assistance.

These structures reflect differences in family values. Kerckhoff (1966b), in one study in North Carolina, has found three conceptions that older people have of family norms:

1. The extended family cluster: parents live near children with considerable mutual aid and affection (expressed in 20 percent of the families)
2. The modified extended family cluster: mutual aid and affection, but no necessity for nearness (60 percent of the families)
3. The nucleated family cluster: expected to neither live near children nor engage in mutual assistance (20 percent of the families).

The modified extended family was clearly the modal category for this sample. Extended family values were most likely to be expressed by the rural working class with large families, while nuclear family values came largely from urban, well-educated, and mobile white-collar respondents with small families. Kerckhoff points out that these older people are likely to be pleasantly surprised by the extent to which mutual affection and aid continues in modern societies, while those holding extended family values may well be disappointed.

Another source of variation is the critical role played by women

in modern kinship. Women tend to be closer to their kin, to consider them more important, to interact more with family, and to
be more active in kinship activities and obligations than men, who
focus more exclusively on the marital relationship (Adams, 1970;
Troll, 1971). This has a number of consequences for older people.
Older people are more likely to have contact with daughters than
sons and to live with the daughters' family, and older women are
more likely to interact with and receive assistance from their
children (Riley and Foner, 1968; Shanas et al., 1968). Such differences help to account for the greater social and emotional difficulties encountered by widowed men. In his study of older workers,
for example, Rosenberg (1970) found that solitary males were
most restricted in their family involvement.

Finally, racial and ethnic subcultures affect family structure.
The black family is sometimes portrayed as a "pathological" structure weakened by the effects of slavery and poverty. Billingsley
(1968) found, however, that research often fails to recognize
variations in structure among black families as adaptations to both
historical and contemporary social and economic conditions. Extended family ties can provide mutual support—material, social,
and emotional—to assist survival in an environment hostile to a
disadvantaged minority (Adams, 1970; Hays and Mindel, 1973).
A number of studies provide evidence of considerable interaction
and mutual aid within black extended families (Feagin, 1968;
Hays and Mindel, 1973; Sussman, 1976). Wylie (1971) suggests
that blacks have greater acceptance of the extended family and
are more likely to include the aged in family affairs, partly as a
reflection of the importance of elders in African culture and the
perceived role of grandparents as the repository of folk wisdom.
Older blacks may also serve as symbols of unity within the family
(Sussman, 1976).

The Grandparent Role

A final family role available to older people is that of grandparent. Actually, this is becoming a middle-aged role, since it is
increasingly common to have grandchildren in one's forties and
fifties, and with widespread emergence of four-generation families,
approximately 40 percent of the aged are great-grandparents.
Grandparenting is a potentially important source of gratification
and responsibility since it is one of the few new roles open to
older people. We have already seen that the aged are involved in
fairly regular interaction within the modified extended family,
and grandparents can be an important source of assistance during
family emergencies. Most of the research on grandparenthood,

however, indicates that the role has limited significance for most older people and is often primarily symbolic and ritualistic with little meaningful involvement of grandparents in the lives of their grandchildren (Kahana and Kahana, 1971; Wood and Robertson, 1976).

Views of Grandparents

The most extensive study of the grandparent role was conducted by Neugarten and Weinstein (1964), through interviews conducted with 140 grandparents in Chicago. Although most grandparents expressed comfort and pleasure in the role, nearly one-third mentioned some type of discomfort derived primarily from seeing the grandparent self-image as alien ("I'm too young to be a grandmother!"), conflict with parents over childrearing, or indifference (and occasional guilt because of it) to responsibilities for grandchildren.

The most prevalent meaning of the role was as "a source of *biological renewal* ('It's through my grandchildren that I feel young again') and/or *biological continuity* with the future ('It's through these children that I see my life going on into the future' or 'It's carrying on the family line')" (Neugarten and Weinstein, 1964:202). Although this was more likely to be expressed by grandmothers, the sample was biased toward the daughters' children. The next largest group felt remote from their grandchildren, expressing considerable psychological distance. Third in significance was emotional self-fulfillment through a new emotional role. Very few of these grandparents functioned as resource persons or achieved vicarious fulfillment. The overall pattern of these results suggests little authority over or involvement in the lives of grandchildren. Another study found that the grandparent role was limited to occasional babysitting, outings to the zoo or movies, and similar short-lived interactions (Wood and Robertson, 1976). Fewer than half reported ever telling grandchildren about family history and customs or teaching special skills (such as cooking or fishing).

Reported "styles" of grandparenting also reflect a relative lack of involvement. The most frequent style was a *formal* one, reflecting a "proper" role which clearly separated parental and grandparental functions. While minor services and indulgences were allowed, care was taken not to "interfere" in childrearing. Two other roles were prevalent: *fun-seeking*, emphasizing informality, playfulness, and mutual satisfaction, and *distant figure*, largely confined to ritualized family gatherings. The *parent surrogate* was confined to grandmothers and very few functioned as a *reservoir of family wisdom.*

Variations in the grandparent role partly reflect the position of older people in the larger culture. Where the aged retain economic power, grandparents tend to have more authoritarian and formal relations with grandchildren (Apple, 1954). When they are removed from positions of authority in the family (as in modern societies), their relationships tend to be warmer and more egalitarian or indulgent. It also appears that maternal grandmothers and paternal grandfathers show the greatest closeness and warmth toward grandchildren (Kahana and Kahana, 1971). Apparently grandchildren are seen as more similar to one's own children through the father-son and mother-daughter relationships. We have also seen that family ties revolve around grandmother-daughter-granddaughter relationships. Because of the relative stability of the housewife role, grandmothers may have more relevant skills to offer granddaughters than grandfathers have for grandsons. Institutionalized older people have less interaction with grandchildren and the grandparent role has little significance for them (Kahana and Kahana, 1971). Their relationships with grandchildren tend to be extremely formalistic, perhaps reflecting the depersonalizing effects of institutional living. There are also indications that the grandparent role is more enjoyable and significant when interaction with grandchildren is frequent, involves trust and mutual respect, and is relatively free of interference from the parent generation (Kahana and Kahana, 1971; Lopata, 1973a).

Jackson (1971), in a study of 68 black grandparents, found patterns similar to those indicated for whites. Interaction with grandchildren was relatively infrequent and grandparents did not play central roles within the black family. Interaction was more frequent for grandmothers and for those who were younger or lived alone. While the majority expressed strong affectional closeness, and they did provide a variety of supports, Jackson concluded that there was no support for the stereotyped view of black families as "powerful matriarchies" ruled by "black grannies."

Views of Grandchildren

There are few studies of grandparenting from the point of view of the grandchild, but two stand out. Kahana (1970), in a study of young children, links grandparenting to the changing needs of the developing grandchild. For children four or five years old, the grandparent is valued for his or her indulgent qualities—as someone who is "nice" and allowed to "spoil" the child. By age eight or nine, the grandparent's active, fun-sharing role is stressed.

But by the age of 11 or 12, there is a greater distance as the child grows away from the "doting grandparent." There is no indication here that the grandparent plays an authoritative role or a continuing significant part in the child's ongoing life.

Robertson (1976) studied 86 adult grandchildren (age 18 to 24), who had quite favorable attitudes toward their grandparents. For example, they did not view them as too old-fashioned or likely to spoil children. They tended to view them as friends, rather than "elders." Grandparents are sometimes notably lenient toward their grandchildren, engaging in a "privileged disrespect" between alternate generations (Townsend, 1957). The grandchildren in Robertson's study felt a responsibility to visit grandparents, provide emotional support, and give tangible help when needed. There were indications, however, that the grandparent role was not considered very significant. Grandchildren had few explicit behavioral expectations beyond gift-giving and being the bearers of family history. Grandparents were not chosen as companions, advisors, liaisons with parents, role models, or financial supporters. The ideal grandparent was, first, "one who loves and enjoys grandchildren, visits with them, shows an interest in them," and secondarily as one "who helps grandchildren out when they can, when asked or needed." The most important characteristics were being loving, helpful, understanding, a friend, and among the least important were their roles as mediators, companions, and teachers.

These findings suggest that although being a grandparent is often enjoyable and satisfying, the role is unlikely to be significant or meaningful. Infrequent or sporadic social involvement is hardly a role to build one's identity around or to fill voids created by retirement and widowhood. Grandparents and grandchildren can have close emotional ties, but the role of grandparent is one of diffuse nurturance or formal distance. While grandchildren may use their grandparents as role models when they eventually enter their own old age, this is of little significance to the grandparents themselves. Grandparents have become "nice people" to whom we are tied by bonds of affection, but they have little impact on our lives.

Aging and the Family: Some Conclusions

Although the literature on the family is voluminous, there are critical gaps in our understanding. We know little about the processes of marital adjustment to retirement. Sex and age variations in the consequences of widowhood remain highly speculative. The nature and quality of family interaction, including grandparenting, need much more investigation. All of these questions require a greater emphasis on the point of view of individuals encountering and attempting to adapt to their own aging.

Despite these questions, we can draw some conclusions about the family life of older people. The extended family continues to be a viable institution for assisting with *acute* problems facing the aged—illness, financial help, support during bereavement. Every effort should be made to support the family's role in this regard, whether through financial assistance, counseling, home delivery of services, or some other mechanism. But the extended family now seems poorly suited to meeting the *chronic* material, social, and emotional needs of the aged. A societal response is essential for problems of income, health care, housing, and transportation, which are too costly to be met by the family for more than a small minority of older persons.

The effectiveness of the family as a helping institution may further decline in the future (Treas, 1977). Because of declining fertility rates, aging parents will have fewer descendants to call upon for assistance. There are also increasing numbers of "old-old" (75+) persons, whose offspring are themselves elderly and less able to provide help. We have noted that women have been the mainstays of family networks, but Treas suggests that this involvement may be affected by the changing social roles (and interests, obligations, and constraints) of modern women.

Finally, one does not get a sense that family interaction provides many outlets for prestige, self-esteem, self-actualization, or meaningful uses of time. The family appears to have limited importance in the everyday lives of older people. Meaningful roles and activities must be sought elsewhere, perhaps in the kinds of participations discussed in Chapter 7. Another possibility is growing involvement with age peers, in the larger community or in retirement settings, which is the topic of the next chapter.

Summary

The family is a major source of primary social and emotional relationships. The marital relationship is particularly important because of the intimacy and sharing it implies, though we should not assume that single older people are necessarily lonely or unhappy. In moving through the life cycle of the family, middle and old age bring two major transitions: the "empty nest" and retirement. The empty nest creates the potential for identity crises and disenchantment in the post-parental marital relationship, but it also carries the possibility of greater freedom and independence and a renewal of couplehood. Retirement is a second transition requiring realignment of family roles. While husbands and wives may divide household tasks into "masculine" and "feminine," the key to retirement adjustment appears to be an emphasis on expressive qualities—companionship, sharing, and affection—in the middle-class more than in the working class. It is not clear whether retirement affects the balance of power in older marriages, and if so in what direction.

Although most older people are physiologically capable of active and satisfying sex lives, cultural stereotypes about "the sexless older years" may lead the aged to shut off normal sexual needs and gratifications. Sexual interest and activity tend to decline with age, but sexuality is far from nonexistent, particularly for males. The sexual performance of older males is often affected by socio-psychological factors, while older women are dependent on the availability of legitimized, capable partners. Sexual activity is also related to health, socioeconomic status, and previous sexual behavior.

The marriage relationship is important to older people because it is a focus for the fulfillment of all three interpersonal needs (inclusion, affection, and control) and because of a sense of uniqueness and irreplaceability attached to it. It is therefore not surprising that the widowed are less able to fill interpersonal needs, have higher rates of mortality and suicide, and are more likely to worry and be depressed. Although widowhood is not devastating for everyone, it can result in disrupted identity, poverty, and social and emotional isolation. One of the greatest problems is loneliness, though widows may experience various types of loneliness. The social disruptiveness of widowhood depends on one's social and cultural context. Unlike earlier societies, the modern role of widow is quite unstructured. Also, widowhood is more disruptive if it is unusual among one's age-sex peers. For example, elderly widows may benefit from the availability of a "society of widows." Men appear to experience greater emotional and social disruption following widowhood, though they may be better off financially than widowed women. Men also have greater opportunities for remarriage.

While some have suggested that modernization disrupts the extended family, a modified extended family has apparently survived even in the middle class to provide both tangible services and social and emotional support to older people. Older people prefer not to live with children, though poor health, low income, or widowhood may lead them to do so. But the aged tend to live near their children and to interact regularly with them, and many also interact with other relatives, such as siblings. The extended family provides a wide-ranging network of potential sources of interpersonal need fulfillment. There is also considerable evidence of intergenerational exchange of services within the family. The extent to which older people are embedded in extended family relationships varies by social class, sex, and race. While the extended family does retain importance for the aged in modern societies, more study is needed of the quality of these relationships.

The grandparent role does not appear to be a highly significant one for most older people. The primary styles are formal, fun-seeking, or distant; few play authoritative or involved parts in the lives of their grandchildren. Grandparenting styles may be linked to the changing needs of the developing grandchild. Though attitudes of adult grandchildren are largely favorable, with feelings of both responsibility and affection, expectations are few and grandparents are not seen as companions, advisors, or role models. Even their role as bearer of family tradition has been sharply reduced.

References

Adams, Bert
1967 "Interaction theory and the social network." Sociometry 30: 64–78.
1968 Kinship in an Urban Setting. Chicago: Markham.
1970 "Isolation, function, and beyond: American kinship in the 1960's." Journal of Marriage and the Family 32: 575–97.
1975 The Family: A Sociological Interpretation. Chicago: Rand McNally.
Apple, D.
1954 "Grandparents and grandchildren: A sociological and psychological study of their relationship." Unpublished doctoral dissertation. Radcliffe College.
Arling, Greg
1976 "Resistance to isolation among elderly widows." Aging and Human Development 7: 67–86.
Atchley, Robert
1975 "Dimensions of widowhood in later life." The Gerontologist 15: 176–78.
Ballweg, John
1967 "Resolution of conjugal role adjustment after retirement." Journal of Marriage and the Family 299: 277–81.
Bart, Pauline
1971 "Depression in middle-aged women." In Vivian Gornick and Barbara Moran (eds.). Women in Sexist Society. New York: New American Library.
1975 "Emotional and social status of the older woman." In No Longer Young: The Older Woman in America. Occasional Papers in Gerontology No. 11. University of Michigan-Wayne State University Institute of Gerontology.

Bell, Robert
1971   Marriage and Family Interaction. Homewood, Ill.: Dorsey.
Benet, Sula
1974   Abkhasians: The Long-Living People of the Caucasus.
        New York: Holt, Rinehart and Winston.
Berardo, Felix
1968   "Widowhood status in the U.S.: Perspectives on a neglected
        aspect of the family life cycle." Family Coordinator 17:
        191–203.
1970   "Survivorship and social isolation: The case of the aged
        widower." Family Coordinator 19: 11–15.
Bild, Bernice and Robert Havighurst
1976   "Senior citizens in great cities: The case of Chicago." The
        Gerontologist 16 (1–Part II).
Billingsley, Andrew
1968   Black Families in White America. Englewood Cliffs, N.J.:
        Prentice-Hall.
Blau, Zena
1961   "Structural constraints on friendship in old age." American
        Sociological Review 26: 429–39.
1973   Old Age in a Changing Society. New York: New Viewpoints.
Blood, Robert and Donald Wolfe
1960   Husbands and Wives. New York: The Free Press.
Chevan, Albert and J. Henry Korson
1972   "The widowed who live alone: An examination of social
        and demographic factors." Social Forces 51: 45–53.
Clark, Margaret and Barbara Anderson
1967   Culture and Aging. Springfield, Ill.: Charles C Thomas.
Cleveland, William and Daniel Gianturco
1976   "Remarriage probability after widowhood: A retrospective
        method." Journal of Gerontology 31: 99–103.
Cumming, Elaine and William Henry
1961   Growing Old: The Process of Disengagement. New York:
        Basic Books.
Demos, John
1970   A Little Commonwealth: Family Life in Plymouth Colony.
        New York: Oxford University Press.
Deutscher, Irwin
1964   "The quality of postparental life." Journal of Marriage and
        the Family 26: 52–59.
Dressler, D.
1973   "Life adjustment of retired couples." Aging and Human
        Development 4: 335–49.
Elder, Glen, Jr.
1974   Children of the Great Depression. Chicago: University of
        Chicago Press.
Feagin, Joe
1968   "The kinship ties of Negro urbanites." Social Science
        Quarterly 49: 660–65.

Goode, William
  1963   World Revolution and Family Patterns. Glencoe, Ill.:
         The Free Press.
Gubrium, Jaber
  1975   "Being single in old age." Aging and Human Development
         6: 29–41.
Hays, William and Charles Mindel
  1973   "Extended kinship relations in black and white families."
         Journal of Marriage and the Family 35: 51–57.
Heyman, Dorothy and Frances Jeffers
  1968   "Wives and retirement: A pilot study." Journal of
         Gerontology 23: 488–96.
Hill, Reuben
  1965   "Decision making and the family life cycle." In Ethel
         Shanas and Gordon Streib (eds.). Social Structure and the
         Family: Generational Relations. Englewood Cliffs, N.J.:
         Prentice-Hall.
  1970   Family Development in Three Generations. Cambridge,
         Mass.: Schenkman.
Hochschild, Arlie
  1976   "Disengagement theory: A logical, empirical, and phenom-
         enological critique." In Jaber Gubrium (ed.) Time,
         Roles, and Self in Old Age. New York: Human Sciences
         Press.
Jackson, Jacquelyne
  1971   "Aged blacks: A potpourri towards the reduction of racial
         inequalities." Phylon 32: 260–80.
  1972   "Marital life among aging blacks." Family Coordinator
         21: 21–27.
Kahana, Eva
  1970   "Grandparenthood from the perspective of the developing
         grandchild." Developmental Psychology 3: 98–105.
Kahana, Eva and Boaz Kahana
  1971   "Theoretical and research perspectives on grandparenthood."
         Aging and Human Development 2: 261–68.
Kerckhoff, Alan
  1965   "Nuclear and extended family relationships: A normative
         and behavioral analysis." In Ethel Shanas and Gordon
         Streib (eds.). Social Structure and the Family: Generational
         Relations. Englewood Cliffs, N.J.: Prentice-Hall.
  1966a "Family patterns and morale in retirement." In Ida Simpson
         and John McKinney (eds.). Social Aspects of Aging.
         Durham, N.C.: Duke University Press.
  1966b "Norm-value clusters and the strain toward consistency
         among older married couples." In Ida Simpson and John
         McKinney (eds.). Social Aspects of Aging. Durham, N.C.:
         Duke University Press.

Kutner, Bernard
  1956   Five Hundred over Sixty: A Community Survey of Aging.
         New York: Russell Sage Foundation.
Lipman, Aaron
  1962   "Role conceptions of couples in retirement." In Clark
         Tibbits and Wilma Donahue (eds.). Social and Psycho-
         logical Aspects of Aging. New York: Columbia University
         Press.
Litwak, Eugene
  1960   "Geographical mobility and extended family cohesion."
         American Sociological Review 25: 385–94.
Litwak, Eugene and Ivan Szelenyi
  1969   "Primary group structures and their functions: Kin, neigh-
         bors, and friends." American Sociological Review 34: 465–81.
Lobsenz, Norman
  1974   "Sex and the senior citizen." New York Times Magazine,
         20 January.
Lopata, Helena
  1969   "Loneliness: Forms and components." Social Problems 17:
         248–61.
  1971   "Widows as a minority group." The Gerontologist 11:
         67–77.
  1973a Widowhood in an American City. Cambridge, Mass.:
         Schenkman.
  1973b "Social relations of black and white women in a Northern
         metropolis." American Journal of Sociology 78: 1003–100.
  1973c "The effects of schooling on social contacts of urban
         women." American Journal of Sociology 79: 604–19.
  1976   "Widowhood and husband sanctification." Paper presented
         at Annual Meeting of American Sociological Association,
         New York.
Lowenthal, Marjorie et al.
  1975   Four Stages of Life. San Francisco: Jossey-Bass.
Masters, William and Virginia Johnson
  1966   Human Sexual Response. Boston: Little, Brown.
McCall, George and J. L. Simmons
  1966   Identities and Interactions. New York: The Free Press.
McKain, Walter
  1972   "A new look at older marriages." Family Coordinator 21:
         61–69.
Morgan, Leslie
  1976   "A re-examination of widowhood and morale." Journal of
         Gerontology 31: 687–95.
National Council on the Aging
  1976   The Myth and Reality of Aging in America.
         Washington, D.C.
Neugarten, Bernice and David Gutmann
  1958   "Age-sex roles and personality in middle age: A thematic

apperception study." Psychological Monographs 72:
No. 470.

Neugarten, Bernice and Karol Weinstein
1964 "The changing American grandparent." Journal of Marriage
and the Family 26: 199–204.

Parkes, C. Murray
1969 "Separation anxiety: An aspect of the search for a lost
object." In M.H. Lader (ed.). Studies in Anxiety. Ashford,
England: Headley Brothers.

Parsons, Talcott
1959 "The social structure of the family." In Ruth Anshen (ed.).
The Family: Its Function and Destiny. New York:
Harper & Row.

Parsons, Talcott and Robert Bales
1955 Family Socialization and Interaction Process. Glencoe, Ill.:
The Free Press.

Pfeiffer, Eric and Glenn Davis
1972 "Determinants of sexual behavior in middle and old age."
Journal of the American Geriatrics Society 20: 151–58.

Pfeiffer, Eric, Adriaan Verwoerdt, and Glenn Davis
1972 "Sexual behavior in middle life." American Journal of
Psychiatry 128: 1262–67.

Pihlblad, C. T. and David Adams
1972 "Widowhood, social participation and life satisfaction."
Aging and Human Development 3: 323–30.

Pineo, Peter
1961 "Disenchantment in the later years of marriage." Marriage
and Family Living 23: 3–11.

Quarantelli, Enrico
1960 "A note on the protective function of the family in disasters."
Marriage and Family Living 22: 263–64.

Riley, Matilda and Anne Foner
1968 Aging and Society. Volume 1: An Inventory of Research
Findings. New York: Russell Sage.

Robertson, Joan
1976 "Significance of grandparents: Perceptions of young adult
grandchildren." The Gerontologist 16: 137–40.

Rollins, Boyd and Kenneth Cannon
1974 "Marital satisfaction over the family life cycle: A re-evalua-
tion." Journal of Marriage and the Family 36: 271–82.

Rollins, Boyd and Harold Feldman
1970 "Marital satisfaction over the family life cycle." Journal
of Marriage and The Family 32: 20–28.

Rosenberg, George
1970 The Worker Grows Old. San Francisco: Jossey-Bass.

Rosenberg, George and Donald Anspach
1973 Working Class Kinship. Lexington, Mass.: Lexington
Books.

Rosow, Irving
1965 "Intergenerational relationships: Problems and proposals."
In Ethel Shanas and Gordon Streib (eds.). Social Structure
and the Family: Generational Relations. Englewood Cliffs,
N.J.: Prentice-Hall.
Rubin, Isadore
1968 "The 'sexless older years'—a socially harmful stereotype."
Annals of the American Academy of Political and Social
Science 376: 86–95.
Schutz, William
1966 The Interpersonal Underworld. Palo Alto, Calif.: Science
and Behavior Books.
Shanas, Ethel et al.
1968 Old People in Three Industrial Societies. New York:
Atherton Press.
Sjoberg, Gideon
1956 "Familial organization in the pre-industrial city." Marriage
and Family Living 18: 30–36.
Smith, Harold
1965 "Family interaction patterns of the aged." In Arnold Rose
and Warren Peterson (eds.). Older People and Their Social
World. Philadelphia: F. A. Davis.
Stehouwer, Jan
1965 "Relations between generations and the three-generation
household in Denmark." In Ethel Shanas and Gordon
Streib (eds.). Social Structure and the Family: Generational
Relations. Englewood Cliffs, N.J.: Prentice-Hall.
Stinnett, N., Linda Carter, and J. E. Montgomery
1972 "Older persons' perceptions of their marriages." Journal of
Marriage and the Family 34: 665–70.
Sussman, Marvin
1976 "The family life of old people." In Robert Binstock and
Ethel Shanas (eds.). Handbook of Aging and the Social
Sciences. New York: Van Nostrand Reinhold.
Sussman, Marvin and Lee Burchinal
1962 "Kin family network: Unheralded structure in current
conceptualizations of family functioning." Marriage and
Family Living 24: 231–40.
Thompson, P. and R. Chen
1966 "Experiences with older psychiatric patients and spouses
together in a residential treatment setting." Bulletin of the
Menninger Clinic 30: 23–31.
Thurnher, Majda
1976 "Midlife marriage: Sex differences in evaluation and per-
spectives." Aging and Human Development 7: 129–35.
Townsend, Peter
1957 The Family Life of Old People. London: Routledge and
Kegan Paul.

Treas, Judith
    1975   "Aging and the family." In Diana Woodruff and James
            Birren (eds.). Aging: Scientific Perspectives and Social
            Issues. New York: D. Van Nostrand.
    1977   "Family support systems for the aged: Some social and
            demographic considerations." The Gerontologist 17: 486–91.
Treas, Judith and Anke Van Hilst
    1976   "Marriage and remarriage rates among older Americans."
            The Gerontologist 16: 132–36.
Troll, Lillian
    1971   "The family of later life: A decade review." Journal of
            Marriage and the Family 33: 263–90.
Ward, Russell
    1974   "Growing old: Stigma, identity, and sub-culture." Unpub-
            lished Doctoral Dissertation. University of Wisconsin.
Weiss, Robert
    1969   "The fund of sociability." Trans-Action 6: 36–43.
    1973   Loneliness: The Experience of Emotional and Social Isola-
            tion. Cambridge, Mass.: MIT Press.
Willmott, Peter and Michael Young
    1960   Family and Class in a London Suburb. London: Routledge
            and Kegan Paul.
Wood, Vivian and Joan Robertson
    1976   "The significance of grandparenthood." In Jaber Gubrium
            (ed.). Time, Roles, and Self in Old Age. New York:
            Human Sciences Press.
Wylie, Floyd
    1971   "Attitudes toward aging and the aged among black Amer-
            icans: Some historical perspectives." Aging and Human
            Development 2: 66–70.

9

Older People
in the Community

W̲e have been speaking of the aged as if they were
displaced persons whose social ties are limited to work-related or
family contacts. But older people are also residents of communities,
living in neighborhoods and making friends. Too often we think of
the elderly as not really part of their communities, as being helpless, dependent, and disengaged. Smith and Turk (1966) have
pointed out, however, that this stereotype fails to recognize that:
(1) older people are often important in keeping families together,
(2) they often occupy positions of power in the community, (3)
many prefer integration into the larger community to special age-
homogeneous residences, and (4) they are likely to be the longest
and most stable residents of a community. Thus, older people are
important members of their communities, and their position in
the community may be quite important to them. As occupational
and marital roles are lost in old age, the local neighborhood and
surrounding community often assumes greater importance in the
fulfillment of their personal needs.

Aging and Friendship

Age is related in many ways to the formation, duration, and disruption of friendships. For one thing, friendships are typically
formed by people of similar ages, partly because of the age-grading
of roles which results in relatively age-homogeneous settings for
people to meet and become friends: the college populated by

316

youth, the suburb in which young families reside, the workplace of middle-aged persons, and so on. But age is also a measure of the type of *homophily*, or similarity, upon which friendships are based (Hess, 1972). There are two reasons that age yields similarity of experiences, interests, and activities. First, people of the same age come from the same birth cohort, with common historical events and socializing experiences. Second, people of the same age are likely to share the same stage in the life course—college, marriage, retirement. The shared interests and needs arising from this are the bases for friendships.

Hess (1972) suggests that age as a source of homophily, overriding other status attributes, is most important when roles are least differentiated. In middle age, people play a variety of roles which are likely to cut across age boundaries, but in youth and old age roles are more restricted and age-linked.

It should also be remembered that older people are likely to have longer lasting friendships, and "old friends" may indeed be the best friends. Not only do they share age-based similarities, but their own relationship has a long history. As with work and marriage, increasing commitment is attached to friendships which persist, and such friendships can acquire the quality of "positive concern" more usually reserved for family relationships. These long-lasting friendships can be a tremendous source of social and emotional support during transitions associated with aging, but their loss (through death, illness, or residential move) can also be especially devastating. Just as widowhood may be especially difficult for the aged, so also may be the loss of even one long-time friend.

This implies that age is also related to disrupted friendships. This is partly due to restrictions brought by illness, moving, and the death of friends. Age-related disruption of social networks is also caused by the age stratification of roles, however, and the fact that friendships are often *fused* to roles (Hess, 1972), that is, we make friends through the roles we play. Parents of young children meet other parents of young children because they join the PTA or their children play together. We make friends with co-workers. These friendships would not have been made except for the playing of certain roles, and older people, who are particularly likely to lose certain roles (through retirement, widowhood, and so on), are also vulnerable to losing the friendships associated with those roles. Loss of a role does not automatically sever friendships acquired through it, but friendships are highly voluntary and therefore quite fragile. They carry a connotation of "peership"—equality and similarity of status—which must be continually reaffirmed. A study by Lowenthal and associates (1975) found that similarity was the most important quality attributed to one's friends by people of varying ages. Role loss or role change removes this similarity, and if other bases of similarity are not present, the friendship will be lost.

Of course, the loss of one role often means taking on another, such as "retiree" or "widow." Such roles may themselves be fused to friendships, as with the "society of widows" discussed in Chapter 8. But these roles do not usually open up opportunities for interaction, the way work or marriage might. The role transitions of old age are largely role "exits" (Blau, 1973), involving a net loss of social opportunities. These role exits will be particularly disruptive of social participation when they set the aging individual apart from his or her age-sex-social class peers, differentiating their interests and experiences from those of peers and reducing the mutuality upon which friendships are based (Blau, 1961; 1973). Thus, the early retiree or the young widow often finds that role loss is particularly isolating. The aged of today are further handicapped by limited social resources: education, income, social class. Since they possess fewer social "badges" which elicit respect, interaction with the aged will be less attractive to others (Smith, 1966). This is perhaps an overly callous view of friendship formation. The point, however, is that there is a narrowing range and scope of social opportunities for many older people, partly as a consequence of the age stratification of roles.

Interaction with Friends and Neighbors

Interaction with friends and neighbors obviously does occur, and is often substantial. A recent national survey found that 60 percent of a sample of persons 65 and over had seen a "close friend" in the last day or so, and an additional 31 percent within the last week or two (National Council on the Aging, 1976). Thus, the aged as a group are not isolated from these social contacts (though many aged individuals are). This contact appears to be less prevalent than with kin, however. Shanas (1962) found that older people were twice as likely to see children during a week as they were to visit neighbors. Also, most older people report that they have fewer friends than in the past, although declines in friendship participation are not likely to be pronounced until the mid-seventies and eighties (Riley and Foner, 1968). In general, older people play fewer roles, have less interaction, and experience a smaller variety of social contacts. Their "social life space" displays constriction in number, intensity, and variety (Williams and Loeb, 1968).

The older population is not homogeneous in social participation, of course. Not surprisingly, healthier older people have more friends and see them more often (Riley and Foner, 1968). Socioeconomic status (income, occupation, education) appears to be more important than age in determining social participation (Foskett, 1955; Taietz and Larson, 1956). Persons with higher status have more friends. One reason for lower social participation by the aged may be their low status, particularly concerning education. This suggests that future cohorts of older people will exhibit more active social participation, since their levels of education and occupational status will be higher. There appear to be few sex differences in the quantity of the social participation, but as we shall see, the quality of friendships may differ for men and women.

A critical aspect of social participation is the social context within which the older individual resides—"normal" city neighborhoods, retirement villages, nursing homes, and so on. If the older person is not surrounded by similar others (peers) to become friends with, in an environment which encourages friendship formation, isolation will result. One study found that nearly half of a sample of persons 65 and over drew most of their friends from their own neighborhood (Riley and Foner, 1968). This appears to be particularly true of the working class, for which the immediate neighborhood constitutes the available social world (Whyte, 1943; Gans, 1962; Rosenberg, 1970). In Rosenberg's study of a working-class sample, three-quarters of all those who had seen friends in the previous week said that *all* their friends lived on the same block. Thus, working-class older people may be particularly vulnerable to the need to live immediately among people who can be their friends (peers) to avoid social isolation.

Sadly, many people may have lost the capacity to "neighbor." Lack of a sense of neighborhood is a frequent complaint of apartment dwellers. Lopata (1973) found that most of the widows in her study were quite restricted in the use of urban resources, perhaps because of a declining importance of "community" in modern, urbanized society. These widows were not accustomed to using neighbors as a source of social contacts. Interaction was largely sporadic, and "dropping over" was not a frequent occurrence. It may be that true neighboring is largely restricted to middle-class neighborhoods of young couples with children, stable working-class neighborhoods, and, for older people, age-segregated settings.

Having neighborhood friends is related to length of residence in an area (Riley and Foner, 1968). While social contacts are not completely disrupted by moves, mobility can have isolating effects. Older people in large cities are also less likely to know people in their neighborhoods than those in smaller communities and rural areas. This may partly reflect the length of residence or that older

residents are "left behind" in a changing neighborhood, leaving
them surrounded by people of a different social class or racial
group.

The Functions of Friendship

The reader does not need to be told that friendships fulfill many
social needs. Not surprisingly, social isolation is related to loneliness, feelings of futility and frustration, negative self-image, and
a felt lack of love and affection among older people (Riley and
Foner, 1968). In a four-year longitudinal study, Graney (1975)
found that declining social participation was generally accompanied
by a decline in overall happiness. There is no automatic association
between amount of social contact and well-being, however. The
distinction made in Chapter 7 between *isolation* and *desolation*
is pertinent here. Also, we need to distinguish between voluntary
and involuntary social withdrawal (Lowenthal and Robinson,
1976). Declining social participation may be less important than
whether it was chosen or forced upon the individual.

There is reason to believe that the importance of friendships
increases with role loss. Blau (1973) suggests that the superficial-
ity of many friendships is not important so long as we continue
to perform major institutional roles but that an active social life
can counteract the demoralizing effects of role loss by providing
alternatives to occupational and marital roles. Table 9.1 presents
data from Blau's study in Elmira, New York, during the mid-
1950s. These results suggest that informal social contacts may
affect morale primarily for those who lack institutional roles—who
are retired, widowed, or single—and have little impact for the aged
who are employed or married.

Table 9.1. Incidence of low morale by extent of social participation, by employment status and marital status

| | Extent of participation | | | |
	Low[a]	High[a]	Difference	N
Employment status:				
Employed	25	14	11	164
Retired	69	27	42[b]	91
Housewives	52	34	18[b]	103
Marital status:				
Married	33	20	13	209
Widowed	61	31	30[b]	160
Single	65	24	41[b]	50

[a] Numbers refer to percent with low morale.
[b] Statistically significant at p = .05.
Source: Zena Smith Blau, *Old Age in a Changing Society*, New
York: New Viewpoints, 1973, p. 64. © 1973 by Zena Smith Blau.
Reprinted by permission.

The *quantity* of friendship interaction may also be less important than its *quality*. Lowenthal and Haven (1968) found that the presence of even one *intimate* friend serves as a buffer against age-linked social losses. Older people with this kind of confidant were able to experience declining social activity with considerably less depression. The stability inherent in intimate friendships or friendship networks lends a sense of continuity to the self. Lowenthal and Haven found that such confidants were more prevalent among women, married persons, and those of higher socioeconomic status. The sex difference is particularly important, since it implies different qualities of friendship for older men and women. In Chapter 8 we spoke of an "expressive hardship" for men which might make widowhood more difficult for them than for women. Lowenthal and Haven found that wives were the most likely confidants for men, while women were more likely than men to turn to children, other relatives, and friends. Women had greater flexibility in their intimate relationships, making them less dependent on the marriage relationship. Another study found that men are more likely to stress similarity in friendships while women place greater emphasis on reciprocity (support, understanding) (Lowenthal et al., 1975). To perhaps oversimplify, men seem to have "buddies," while women have "confidants" who can buffer social loss.

In addition to fulfilling social and emotional needs, friends and neighbors can offer various assistance, though they are utilized less than extended kin. They help out in emergencies, such as with illness care or more ordinary services like shopping, primarily for those who live alone or have no nearby kin (Riley and Foner, 1968). In winter, for example, when many older people find it difficult to get out by themselves, friends may provide rides to and from grocery stores or doctor's offices. Financial assistance from friends is quite rare, however (Riley and Foner, 1968). Such aid is apparently considered appropriate only within the family. Regular contact with friends also provides an outlet to the outside world and at least an indirect check on the well-being of older persons. As with the extended family network, this assistance is usually reciprocal, though not necessarily so.

A final function of friendship is that of socialization. Throughout our lives, as an integral part of the age stratification system, peers make many contributions to the socialization processes: emotional support during role transitions, provision of information about new and future roles, mutual opportunities for role rehearsal (Hess, 1972). Childhood play groups, for example, prepare children in many ways, both general and specific, for the adult roles they will play in the future, with such seemingly simple things as "playing house," learning to abide by the rules of a game, and being able to cooperate in group efforts. Age peers can also be particularly helpful in preparing older persons for old age and assisting their adaptation to new situations and identities. Among the potential functions of age peer groups are the provision of emotional support, new group memberships and roles to replace those which are lost, norms and expectations to counteract the "normlessness" of old age, insulation from stigma, and real role models.

The Age Mix of Housing for the Aged

A question which arises is whether older people are "better off" in age-integrated settings, surrounded by a "normal" age mixture, or in age-segregated settings such as retirement communities or apartments for the aged. This question will not have a simple answer, since the "best" living arrangement varies among individuals, but it would be useful to explore the relative advantages and disadvantages of the two types of housing arrangements. Age-segregated settings, be they retirement village or nursing homes, are sometimes seen as "dumping grounds" for the aged who are not wanted by their children or society. This impression is unfair and overlooks a variety of benefits to be gained from age concentration.

Resistance to age-segregated settings lies in the very fact that only older people live there, as indicated in the following comments from a community sample of older people:

"People in those places get to be chronic complainers and its just because they are just with their own age groups and have no outside interests. . . . I don't think it's neighborly. I like to be with all ages and with children."
"Most older people are fussy and crabby and they would complain if you had younger people with children visiting you."
"As far as I am concerned they are places you go to die. All you see is old age—very depressing. It is not conducive to an optimistic way of life. I like to look at the bright side of life."
" . . . Old people need the association of younger people. It helps keep them young. You can't live in the past, you have to live in the future."
"Friends of mine that live in them tell me that they miss children and it seems like they are always going to funerals. You can't help wondering if yours will be the next one."
"I try to keep from old people. It's repugnant to me. With young people I am lively and cheerful and forget my stroke."
(Sherman, 1971:131)

These respondents also disliked the loss of privacy, regimentation, and dependency implied by congregate living. They may simply not yet feel a need for the specialized services available in such housing. Those who have moved to old-age housing stress ease of maintenance and provision of services as their primary reasons (Sherman, 1971; Mangum, 1973; Heintz, 1976). They have found their homes too large and property taxes too high, and are seeking smaller, low-cost housing which still has certain amenities (particularly maintenance). Because of changes in physical strength and health, residents of old-age housing are also concerned that their health and personal needs can be cared for.

A second set of reasons stressed by movers to age-segregated settings is a desire for a better living environment. Climate is certainly one attraction of southern and western communities. Winter can be an especially difficult season for the aged. Residents are also attracted to the sociability and recreational facilities of retirement communities. Hoyt (1954) found these to be particularly important qualities of life in a retirement trailer park. People also move because they dislike their present neighborhoods. Heintz (1976) and Sherman (1971) found considerable antipathy to city life among the residents of retirement communities, including: bad neighbors (perhaps invasion of the neighborhood by "undesirables"), pollution, congestion, crime, too many children. These people were looking for a more relaxed, pleasant, and secure environment.

Interestingly, Sherman (1971), in her study of six different types of old-age housing, found that only one-third of respondents expressed a desire to be with members of their own age group as an important factor in their decision to move. While they were highly appreciative of the presence of friends, the decision to move into old-age housing was based primarily on a desire for various services and convenience.

There are many types of age-segregated housing. The choice among them is likely to be based on any number of site-specific characteristics, such as cost, climate, nearness to family, and security (Sherman, 1971). There is also no reason to believe that all types of age-segregated settings are similar in their nature or consequences. We will look more closely at three settings: old-age apartments, communes, and retirement communities.

Old Age Apartments

While retirement communities in Florida or Arizona have received much attention, the aged are more likely to live together within "old age" housing developments in age-integrated communities. The most impressive early work on such settings was done by Irving Rosow (1961; 1967). Rosow recognized that normal, or age-integrated, living arrangements could be successful, but only when certain conditions were met: (1) long-term residence in an area, (2) a relatively stable neighborhood which is socially homogeneous (in such things as class, race, or ethnicity), and (3) intact local primary groups (family and friends). While these conditions are met for some, there are many older people who lack this social environment, such as the widow living in a fringe area of rapidly changing social composition, surrounded by people too different to be true friends. Rosow also argues that the stigma of aging and role losses experienced by the elderly results in a marginality best counteracted by age segregation. Age peers, because of their mutual interests and problems, offer the possibility of continued social involvement. Thus, the aged can achieve social integration within a segregated setting, rather than being isolated in integrated settings.

Rosow (1967) tested his ideas in a study of apartment buildings in Cleveland, where he found that older people had more local friends and greater interaction with neighbors when there was a more dense concentration of age peers and, in any case, tended to choose friends from older residents. Put simply, older people had more friends (higher social integration) when surrounded by other older people. This local dependence was more pronounced for women, the working class, and those who were widowed. A study of six California retirement settings also found that residents reported more new friends and greater visiting with neighbors than matched controls living in integrated settings (Sherman, 1975a; 1975b). However, all older people do not benefit from age concentration. Rosow found that the morale of "isolates" declined as age density increased, since they did not wish to associate with neighbors.

These studies also found networks of mutual assistance among the residents of age-concentrated housing, though there were limits to the utility of this support. Rosow found that the family was still the most important source of aid, and it did not appear that neighbors compensated for lack of family ties or could eliminate emotional dependence on children. Thus, there are limits to the benefits which may be achieved by age segregation. Sherman also points out that not all of the sites she studied exhibited greater mutual assistance than the matched controls. Mutual dependency was greatest when the setting was isolated from the larger community and the residents were older, unmarried, and less mobile.

Illustrations of the type of social community which can arise in age-segregated settings are provided by two in-depth case studies of old-age apartment complexes: Merrill Court in San Francisco (Hochschild, 1973), and Les Floralies in France (Ross, 1977). In both cases there were already bases for the development of a sense of community among the residents. They were socially homogeneous to begin with: rural-born, working-class widows in Merrill Court, retired construction workers and their spouses in Les Floralies. Along with cohort similarities and shared problems of old age, this contributed to the feeling of being "all in the same boat." Residents were also faced with a "hostile" outside world which devalued and neglected the aged. Rather than seeing themselves as dependent because they lived in retirement housing, they viewed mutual assistance from age peers as making continued independence (from family and from society) possible. The importance of this background of shared experiences and problems is heightened by feelings that there is no place else to go. In the words of one Les Floralies resident: "After all, we are here for the rest of our lives" (Ross, 1977:85).

These background factors in these two residences set the stage for the emergence of social communities, which was further facilitated by events and processes occurring within the residences. Community-wide interaction was centered at the Recreation Room in Merrill Court, and at the communal noon meal at Les Floralies. Parties and elections (and resident decision making) were also focal points for community life. While interaction was initially fostered by formal activities and roles, it soon spread to informal networks and loyalties on the living floors. Patterns of mutual assistance emerged, including exchange of goods and services (knitting, recipes, repairs) and help during illness. The residents of Merrill Court developed a systematic way of checking up on each other's well-being.

> Neighboring is also a way to detect sickness or death. As Ernestine related, "This morning I looked to see if Judson's curtains were open. That's how we do on this floor, when we get up we open our curtains just a bit, so others walking by outside know that everything's all right. And if the curtains aren't drawn by mid-morning, we knock to see." (Hochschild, 1973: 53)

There are a number of indications of a true community in these residences. Residents had a keen sense of territory. Les Floralies residents, for example, defended an image of a residence, rather than a nursing home, and felt that "sick people should stay in their place" (Ross, 1977:89). A consensus emerged about "our way" of doing things which counteracted the usual ambiguity and normlessness of old age. Some activities were defined as "work"—making things for charity, playing in a five-piece band at nursing homes, working on the residents' committee—while others were "pure fun"—card parties, potluck dinners. Obligations were built up, such as the "Secret Pal" system at Merrill Court, whereby residents were anonymously paired to give $2 gifts on birthdays. Hochschild describes this as an "emotional insurance policy" to distribute a feeling of being remembered.

There was social pressure at Merrill Court to keep active and involved in the life of the community.

> Downstairs and in the privacy of their apartments, the residents expressed definite opinions about Daisy. As one put it, "Daisy doesn't want to be down gadding about with us. She likes being upstairs, just sittin'. What's the use of living if you're not up to somethin'?" Daisy was gently chastised for not coming down to the potluck dinners on Fridays. She claimed that she was on a salt-free diet, but, as the others brought out, there was salt-free food downstairs. When she still declined, they brought some up to her, for which they were mildly thanked. The group knew the details of Daisy's physical ailments, as they did those of almost everyone in the building, and they made assessments about how much of her inactivity was due to physical decline and how much was not. The consensus was that she could be more sociable if she wanted. (Hochschild, 1973: 34)

Gossip was used as a means of social control and a way to relay information. This may seem oppressive, but all groups are oppressive in getting members to live up to the group's expectations. Les Floralies lacked this pressure to "be active," but residents there had their own norms; conflict was disapproved, extreme flirtation was frowned upon, protection of individual privacy was stressed. Violation of norms was met with various sanctions, including "social quarantine" (e.g., no one would sit with the person at lunch).

A further indication of the true "groupness" of the setting was the emergence of an *internal* system of social status. Status was not determined by characteristics brought in by the residents, such as education or occupation, at least partly because there was such homogeneity. At Les Floralies, status was based on "work" roles in the residence and position within the two primary political factions (Communist and non-Communist) which served as bases for interaction patterns and loyalties. Despite a norm against conflict, there was a considerable interpersonal gulf between these factions. Ross suggests that the very existence of political conflict shows that community life was important to residents. Status at Merrill Court had a different basis: the distribution of "luck" within a "poor dear" hierarchy.

Those in politics and recreation referred to the passive card players and newspaper readers as "poor dears." Old people with
passive life styles in good health referred to those in poor health
as "poor dears" and those in poor health but living in independent housing referred to those in nursing homes as "poor
dears." Within the nursing home there was a distinction between
those who were ambulatory and those who were not. Among
those who were not ambulatory there was a distinction between
those who could enjoy food and those who could not. Almost
everyone, it seemed, had a "poor dear." (Hochschild, 1973:
60–61)

Thus, members of a marginal, relatively disadvantaged group which
is often lumped together by society were able to define their situation positively.

Because of reciprocity and similarity residents were much freer
around each other. They could improvise new roles, act "silly,"
reminisce, joke about old age, or discuss death—things they would
do only in the presence of age peers. For example, they would
rarely discuss death with kin or young people, but needed to express their feelings somewhere. They also had access to role models
of both successful and unsuccessful aging.

These peer relationships could not provide everything, however.
Relationships with children constituted an emotional tie which
peers could never be, and residents turned to kin in real emergencies. Hochschild notes that:

In a deep sense and over the long run, the two kinds of relationships did not really compete; one could not replace the other
even in the "time filling" sense. To the widows, children are a
socio-emotional insurance policy that peers can never be. Kin ties
run deeper and have a longer history than peer ties. When a
grandmother is in deep trouble, she turns to blood ties first.
When a widow needs a lot of money, she turns to kin; when she
needs "something to tide her over till payday," she turns to a
neighbor. When there was an accident or death in the building,
peers were the first to find out, but kin were the first to be
called. (Hochschild, 1973: 96)

Neither residence was isolated from the larger community, and
there was considerable contact with relatives and friends outside.
Residents were also hesitant to incur too much obligation or more
intimacy than was desired. Hochschild notes, for example, that they
were more willing to invite someone in for a cup of coffee than for
a meal, since a meal has deeper social implications. Nevertheless,

the tit-for-tat quality of these peer relationships seem to offer benefits unattainable in more age-integrated housing arrangements.

Communes for the Aged

Streib and Streib (1975) have suggested that communes may provide an alternative supportive living environment particularly suited to the economic, health, and social needs of older people. Some communal living arrangements do exist for the aged. The Share-A-Home Association, in Winter Park, Florida, involves a dozen older persons living as a communal family (James, 1972; Sussman, 1976), who actually won a court ruling that they were living as a family, and therefore not violating local zoning restrictions. These people jointly own a 27-room mansion, share expenses according to ability to pay, and hire a staff to run the house. Wax (1976) has described another experiment in communal living— the Weinfeld Group Living Residence in Evanston, Illinois. For $500 a month, partly supported by the Council for Jewish Elderly, a dozen older women (average age 82) share a residence and have apparently developed close, family-like relationships.

While such communal living arrangements may increase, Streib and Streib (1975) suggest that they are not likely to become widespread. Since communes are still viewed as deviant, communards must cope with hostility from the outside. Although this may be more true of youthful communes, it does indicate the need for considerable dedication in keeping communal feelings going. The high turnover likely among the aged, due to poor health and death, further limits the continuity and cohesiveness of communal ties. Finally, communal arrangements are probably not attractive to the majority of older people, who lack strong identification with age peers, are attached to the value of private property, and generally prefer independent living. Nevertheless, it appears that communal arrangements are quite successful for some older persons.

Retirement Communities

With the possible exception of institutions for the aged, such as nursing homes, retirement communities represent the most age-segregated type of environment for older people. They are primarily a post-World War II phenomenon, apparently originating in Florida (Mangum, 1973). The earliest communities were run by nonprofit fraternal, church, and union groups to provide low-cost housing for their retired members, but private builders have become increasingly involved in planned communities. Such places have emerged to meet the need for smaller, cheaper, easily maintained housing, and to facilitate leisure life styles for retirees.

There is tremendous variation among retirement communities. For one thing, they are no longer confined to sunbelt states like Florida and Arizona. Heintz (1976) has published a study of five retirement communities in the area between Philadelphia and New York City. Most retirement communities have age eligibility requirements (usually around 50 or 55) and have planned services, housing design, land use, shared recreational facilities, and so on. They are usually relatively small, containing from 1,500 to 7,000 housing units (Heintz, 1976). Communities vary in the range of services and facilities offered to residents—hospital, buses, golf courses, and so on—the types of housing design—single-family dwellings, apartments, trailer parks—and therefore also in their costs. In her study, Heintz found that the initial purchase price for a home varied from $16,407 to $30,996 among five communities, with a range from $9.82 to $77.80 for monthly maintenance. In 1973, annual costs to live in an average retirement community were $6,000 for single persons and $8,000 for couples (Butler, 1975), making it beyond the means of most older people.

Various studies have found high morale among residents of retirement communities, in some cases higher than the aged in integrated settings (Hoyt, 1954; Messer, 1967; Bultena and Wood, 1969; Heintz, 1976). Bultena and Wood, for example, compared residents of four planned communities in Arizona with a group from the midwestern states these residents had left. They suggest three reasons for the higher morale in the retirement communities. First, the migrant retirees represented an elite in socioeconomic and health status. Second, such communities offer a pool of age peers as potential friends, yielding the benefits found in Rosow's research. Finally, retirement communities facilitate a leisure life style (Bultena and Wood, 1970). Those who had moved to these communities were apparently already more oriented to leisure pursuits, and such settings provide facilities, including a wider range of specialized activities, as well as a social environment and peer reference group supportive of leisure. Thus, they are insulated from any stigma attached to leisure careers by the larger society. Bultena and Wood found that only about 10 percent of the residents of these communities were not regularly involved in recreational activities. Messer (1967) also suggests that residents of age-segregated settings can become less active ("disengage") without feeling guilty. Thus, interaction among age peers in an age-homogeneous setting encourages the development of their own values and norms, making them less dependent on the invidious judgments of society.

Residence in a retirement community does not necessarily imply isolation from family or the larger society. Heintz (1976) found that nearly half of the residents she studied participated in activities outside the retirement community, and Bultena and Wood (1969) found that migration to retirement communities did not precipitate separation or isolation from children. Nearly one-fifth of the residents still had a child living within 20 miles. The presence of children does affect the decision to move; compared with non-movers, residents of retirement communities had smaller families, were more likely to be childless, and were less likely to have had a child living in their community before the move. It is also true that one reason for moving to retirement communities is to avoid becoming dependent on children.

An additional issue concerning retirement communities is their impact on nearby or surrounding communities. There may be concern that a retirement community means a smaller tax base, greater service needs (particularly medical), and possible political dominance by conservative older voters, affecting such local issues as school budgets, but Heintz (1976), in a study of five Eastern retirement communities, found these fears were groundless. Actually, all five generated a substantial revenue surplus for their respective municipalities. The property taxes they paid outweighed their use of local services—for example, they supported schools which they did not use. Although residents used more health services than the nonaged population, this was not a fiscal burden on local communities since their use was largely supported by third parties (primarily Medicare). There was no evidence that residence in retirement communities resulted in mobilization of an "old age" political bloc. Extensive analysis indicated that their voting turn-out was apparently not a significant factor in the approval or rejection of proposed school budgets.

While the picture painted so far has been quite positive, the reader should not be left with the impression that retirement communities are necessarily the best of all possible worlds. Although most published studies indicate considerable satisfaction by residents, they may miss such things as certain services (stores, restaurants), old friends and neighbors, and former houses. A study by Jacobs (1974) of a retirement community he calls "Fun City" offers ample evidence that such settings are not always what they seem. Although this was a planned community, with many recreational facilities and social clubs, only about 500 of the 6,000 residents participated in planned activities. An estimated 25 percent virtually never left their homes. The following illustrates a typical day in the passive way of life led by most residents:

> Mr. N.: Well, for me a typical day is—I get up at six a.m. in the morning generally, get the newspaper. I look at the financial

statement and see what my stocks have done. I generally fix
my own breakfast because my wife has, can eat different than
I do. So I have my own breakfast—maybe some cornflakes
with soy milk in it—milk made out of soybeans that they sell
in the health food store. And uh, then at eight a.m. my wife
gets up. The dog sleeps with her all night. And uh, she feeds
the dog. Then the dog wants me to go out and sit on the
patio—get the sun and watch the birds and stuff in our back-
yard and we have quite a few rabbits back in there. And I
finish my paper there. And then she sits and she looks at me.
She'll bark a little bit. And uh, then she'll go to my wife, stand
by my wife and bark at her. She wants me to go back to bed.
So I have to go back to bed with her. So about eight-thirty
a.m. I go back to bed again with my dog for about an hour.
And then I get up and I read. And then I walk up around
here and I go over to oh, the Mayfair [supermarket] and sit
there and talk to people. We go over to the bank. They have
a stockroom over there. For people that own stock. We discuss stocks and events of the day. And then I come home and
maybe have lunch if I want to or not—it doesn't make any
difference. *In fact, down here it doesn't make any difference
when you eat or when you sleep. Because you're not going any
place. You're not doing anything. And uh, if I'm up all night
reading and sleep all day, what's the difference.* But then, I'll
sit around and read and maybe a neighbor will come over or
I'll go over to a neighbor's and sit down and talk about something. And lots of times, we go over to a neighbor's and we
play cards 'til about five p.m. and then we come home and
have our dinner. And the evening is . . . we are generally
glued to the television until bedtime comes. And that's our
day.
Dr. J.: Is that more or less what your friends and neighbors do?
Mr. N.: Some of them do. Some of them don't do that much.
(Jacobs, 1974: 31)[1] [Emphasis added.]

Jacobs describes the community as an unnatural setting which
fostered a "blasé attitude" and social isolation. Fun City was
isolated from other communities and was not itself a true community—it lacked its own fire, police, major medical facilities,
public transportation, and adequate shopping. Despite being
socially homogeneous to an extreme, residents tended to withdraw from all but casual and innocuous interactions to avoid giving
or taking offense. Most of the residents had moved to Fun City
from a large metropolitan area and experienced considerable "cul-

---

[1] From *Fun City: An Ethnographic Study of a Retirement Community* by
Jerry Jacobs, Copyright (c) 1974 by Holt, Rinehart and Winston. Reprinted
by permission of Holt, Rinehart and Winston.

ture shock." All in all, Jacobs presents a rather dismal picture of what one resident called a "false paradise."

Age Segregation: Pros and Cons

Jacobs' study points out that age segregation can have negative consequences, but there are more general arguments which may be made against it. The most important is that integration—whether age, racial, religious, or any other—presumably promotes tolerance through a broadening exposure to people different from oneself. As the restriction of education to youth creates "youth ghettos" and cross-generational feelings of suspicion and fear (Lofland 1968), lack of contact with the elderly may exacerbate negative stereotypes and fears concerning aging. In addition, the young themselves are deprived of the experience of their elders and of role models for the aging process. Perhaps housing integration could foster meaningful intergenerational contacts.

Unfortunately, housing heterogeneity appears to be a limited source of increased contact and tolerance. Studies of interracial contact indicate that tolerance can result only with positive experience and cooperative interaction (Katz, 1970). Likewise, less favorable attitudes toward the aged result if contacts are negative, as in hospitals or nursing homes, which may only confirm negative stereotypes (Rosencranz and McNevin, 1969). In order to be effective, age-heterogeneity in housing must be balanced by the similarity in interests and attitudes which leads to true friendships. Simply locating people near each other does not guarantee meaningful association—familiarity can breed contempt instead of tolerance.

Jacobs (1975) reports on a study of "High Heaven," a high-rise retirement complex located on a university campus. It was hoped that shared facilities and activities—dining room, snack bar, films, volunteer programs—would foster interaction between residents and students. Indeed, the older residents liked to be around students, missed them when they were on vacation, and wanted to be involved, despite differences in their backgrounds. Unfortunately, Jacobs concludes:

> As things now stand there is little direct interaction between the residents of High Heaven and the university students. In fact, many students are literally unaware that retired persons live in High Heaven or that there is or ever was any affiliation between the residents and students. Most students are neutral to the presence of a limited number of residents in the student dining hall and some are puzzled; others are openly hostile. This is not to say that students do not from time to time help residents with

their trays or show them other courtesies; they do, but the overall picture is one of indifference and clanishness, both on the
part of students and residents. Each group stays very much to
itself even when in the other's presence. (Jacobs, 1975: 24)

Differences between the groups were too great, and even when
interaction developed, it might be more along the lines of volun-
teer-to-dependent than young friend-to-old friend.

It might also be argued that age integration would benefit not
only society and young people by encouraging a more favorable
view of old age, but also a "stigmatized" group like the elderly by
lessening their isolation from mainstream society. Alienation can
result from age segregation when the older person is cut off from
outside family and friends and contacts within the complex fail to
develop (Larson, 1974).

On the whole, though, age-segregated housing appears to offer
some real potential benefits to older people: accessible peers for
friendships, more similar others for comparison, a new normative
reference group, and mutual assistance, which promote social
integration and new bases of identity. Age-segregated settings can
also promote leisure activities and offer more tangible benefits.
Specialized housing may be more economical and can incorporate
design features such as grab-rails and low cupboards. Centralized
services—personal maintenance, housekeeping, meal preparation,
medical care—can be delivered more efficiently in group housing.
But these residences are *not* nursing homes, objectively or in the
minds of residents, and these services do not mean that residents
are dependent. The combination of a supportive peer group and
personal and health services provides an environment which
facilitates continued independence.

Perhaps the clearest evidence that age-segregated residences can
be beneficial for the aged comes from a national survey of older
residents of public housing (Teaff, Lawton, Nahemow, and Carlson, 1978), which found that greater age segregation was associated
with greater morale, housing satisfaction, activity, and neighborhood mobility. This was attributed to increased feelings of personal security and the emergence of age-specific activity patterns
and norms. The authors further estimate that 1,250,000 older
people would prefer living with age peers—four times the number
currently residing in housing for the elderly.

Separation and segregation are negatively viewed by many
because they imply discrimination. Ross (1977) also suggests that
age segregation makes us feel guilty about the status of the aged
and their rejection by society. But it is not unusual for people to
seek out those who are similar and familiar, both for greater

sociability and for greater feelings of security. Patterns of urban residential segregation, for example, may be partly a response to the pace of life and cultural diversity of cities, which can create a stressful feeling of "stimulus overload" (Milgram, 1970).

Age-segregated housing is not a panacea for the problems experienced by older people, however. For one thing, many older people (perhaps most) prefer contact with diverse age groups, including children, and do not desire association with "those old folks." Only about 10 percent of American older people live in age-segregated settings (Ross, 1977). Winiecke (1973) found that interest in public housing for the aged among low-income persons was highest for renters who lacked strong social or family ties and had transportation problems, and we have seen that receptivity to such housing is related to declining physical strength and health. Rosow's (1967) study suggests that age segregation has little effect for persons who desire isolation or are oriented toward broader community involvement. Another suggestion has been that older people with limited "activity resources" (health, income, social supports) will have higher morale in age-segregated settings where activity expectations are geared to older age groups (Gubrium, 1973). This may be true, but only up to a point. Hochschild (1973) has argued that the community of Merrill Court might not have developed in a nursing home, where residents are less able to engage in the independent interactions out of which friendships evolve.

Jacobs' (1974) study of Fun City also indicates that the structure of an age-segregated community affects its success. Fun City was both too isolated and not a true community. Houses were laid out on a grid, like so many suburban tracts, providing no easy or common space for interaction. Merrill Court, on the other hand, had apartments opening onto a common area which facilitated interaction.

The variation among age-segregated settings is illustrated by Sherman's (1971, 1972, 1974, 1975c) comparisons of residents of six such settings—a retirement hotel, a rental village, an apartment tower, a purchase village, a cooperative village, and a life-care facility—with a matched group of community residents. Satisfaction with the retirement housing was approximately the same as the neighborhood satisfaction of the community sample. The greatest differences occurred *among the age-segregated sites*, with more urban (less isolated) sites seeming to work better. Dissatisfactions were site-specific, relating to meals, management, and proximity to community facilities. Residents of one site were particularly concerned about the lack of a hospital and sufficient doctors, which led them to worry more about their health, adversely affecting their overall morale. The primary reason for moving to group settings seems to be a desire for various services, therefore when such services are inadequate (as in "Fun City"), independent coping is not supported and satisfaction declines. This is exacerbated when residents are also isolated from the facilities of the larger community.

Sherman's research also indicates that old-age housing does not always facilitate leisure activity (this was also true of "Fun City"). Such activity was enhanced in only three of the six settings she studied because of differences in site facilities, access to the larger community, and self-selection for leisure life styles. There was also only a moderate relationship between activity and morale, which Sherman suggests is a consequence of restricted meaningfulness of available activities, continuity of life style, and variation in styles of aging.

Thus, the impact of age-segregated housing may be limited. Nevertheless, age-segregated housing arrangements have a clear promise for at least some older people under favorable conditions. The lack of structure to old-age roles in modern societies provides freedom to "make" roles, but age stratification may set older people adrift socially and psychologically from familiar realities. However, the lack of "macro" structure to old age may be compensated for by "micro" structures which provide norms, role models, interpersonal support, and socialization experiences. It is this micro structure which is represented by the emergence of community in some age-segregated settings.

The Impact of Housing

Because of the tremendous heterogeneity in the older population, no one type of housing can be said to be the best. However, housing has a potentially decisive impact on the life style and well-being of older people. By housing, we mean the total "context for living" in which the older individual is embedded (Carp, 1976a), which includes a number of relevant dimensions: physical characteristics, the interpersonal and social environment, characteristics of the surrounding neighborhood, availability and convenience of services (Lawton and Nahemow, 1973).

All of us are affected in many ways by where we live. Do we have pleasant neighbors? Is our housing in good physical condition? Do we feel safe on the streets? The answers to such questions affect feelings of happiness and security, and this may be especially true for the aged. Lawton and Nahemow (1973) note that aging often results in reduced cognitive and physical competence, which leads to retrenchment and a preference for simplicity, resulting in an *environmental docility* among many older people. This means that a greater proportion of behavior is due to *environmental* characteristics than to *personal* characteristics. Thus, older people may be affected more than younger people by their immediate environment and be more passive in manipulating their surroundings to their own advantage.

An excellent example of the effects housing can have is provided by a series of studies conducted by Carp (1965; 1967; 1975b; 1976b; 1977) in Victoria Plaza, a public housing development for the elderly located in San Antonio, Texas. This complex included eight stories of apartments, with a county Senior Center on the ground floor. Interviews were conducted with applicants for housing who were then living in physically substandard housing or were socially isolated or in stressful situations (such as friction within a family). Those who eventually moved into the complex were compared with nonmovers in followup interviews conducted 12 to 15 months after the move. While nonmovers exhibited little change, movers showed dramatic improvement in a wide variety of areas, including happiness, number of activities, number of friends, self-rated health, and optimism about the future. Residents expressed fewer problems generally, not just concerning housing, and overall evaluation of their lives improved. Social relationships formed quickly, including some romances and even one marriage within the first year. Residents felt the security of physical safety and having a nice place to live out the remainder of their lives. The effects were not simply short-lived "honeymoon reactions"—they were reflected in another followup after eight years. Residents of Victoria Plaza even had better health and a lower mortality rate than nonmovers.

Carp is careful to point out that Victoria Plaza is not perfect. For example, residents were quite independent and capable of caring for themselves. And some problems were expressed, such as lack of privacy and inconvenience of certain special design features: refrigerators placed high to avoid stooping were difficult to defrost; clothes rods placed low to avoid reaching tended to droop. Overall, however, the results suggest the favorable impact which improved housing can have. Carp notes that this indicates that dissatisfactions expressed by the elderly are often quite realistic and can be alleviated by dealing with their causes.

It is clear that housing for the aged can benefit enromously from proper planning, which should involve older people themselves, to maximize flexibility and choice. Hartman and associates (1976) used slides to illustrate housing options and small group discussions to determine the preferences of potential users. They found this type of "user needs survey" yielded quite satisfactory results. As examples of the kinds of preferences which may be expressed (and not realized by planners), they found that:

1. modern-looking buildings were preferred because they seemed cleaner and more prestigious
2. most wanted commercial use on the ground floor, if it did not bring in undesirable "outsiders"
3. concern for street safety resulted in a desire for quick, secure entryways
4. an aesthetically pleasing landscaped courtyard was overwhelmingly rejected as a "lovely place for a mugger to hide"
5. most (and particularly men) wanted a lobby as a "hanging out" place.

These older people were very conscious of "territory," their own dignity, and personal safety.

The City as a Living Environment

Since most older people live in cities, increasing attention has been paid to both their advantages and disadvantages for the aged. Even such living situations for the elderly as "single room occupancy" hotels (Stephens, 1975) and skid row (Rooney, 1976) have attracted research interest. Most older urbanites live in more favorable surroundings, of course, but Clark (1971) refers to "geriatric ghettos" of impoverished, isolated inner-city elderly who have been left behind by the flight to the suburbs.

One thing to recall is the limited mobility of many older persons. Their activities are neighborhood-based, and often neighborhood-bound, with a maximum radius of perhaps only ten city blocks (Cantor, 1975). Cities may offer benefits to such persons, by providing a more accessible concentration of local services essential to the daily needs of the aged—grocery stores, drug stores, churches, banks—than the "sprawling" suburbs (Carp, 1975a; Cantor, 1975). Also, public transportation is more readily available in cities than in suburban and rural areas for nonlocal services, and the relative density of age peers within cities may provide greater possibilities for social interaction. Carp's (1975a) study of San Antonio found that areas closer to the center of the city presented a more "viable" environment for older people—they experienced less "lost time," got out into the community more often, and had better social networks.

Some aspects of urban life, however, constitute obstacles to mobility—crime and fear for personal safety, inconvenient bus stops and routes, stairs. Many seemingly insignificant barriers may combine to severely restrict movement.

> And the structure of downtown cities denies that the old and the feeble may wish to move among us; denies that we can be old in any decent public form while still in the world. The speed of traffic light changes prohibits easy walking for one who is slow; the height of the sidewalk above the street-level makes hopping up and down an effort. There is the absence of enough public toilets, the lack of benches in shopping centers, and housing developments and apartment houses that provide few facilities for the uninstitutionalized old. (Rakoff, 1973: 154)

The physically handicapped of all ages are denied full use of the environment, since urban design is based on the "mobility, size, strength, and capabilities of the average-sized, healthy, thirty-year old male" (Bednar, 1977:1–2). There are many barriers—poor drainage, unsafe storm drains, irregular surfaces (bricks, cobblestones), long flights of stairs—which are invisible to the nonhandicapped, but limit the freedom of many older people, and "tell" them, through daily reminders, that they are less competent (Steinfeld, Duncan, and Cardell, 1977).

Other urban problems include lower quality housing, deteriorating neighborhoods, crowding and noise and high costs of living (Cantor, 1975; Carp, 1975a).Cantor notes that the aged are often fearful of those who are different: different ethnic and racial groups, different life styles, and so on. Thus, the cultural diversity of cities, which many find attractive, may prove to be unpleasant for some older persons. In addition, while some city services are readily accessible, others are widely scattered and fragmented, particularly medical care. The complexity, fragmentation, and depersonalization of urban health services often proves confusing and virtually impenetrable to many older persons (Cantor and Mayer, 1976). Public transportation is not well-suited to going here for one doctor, there for another, and somewhere else to a hospital. Some elderly people just give up, with tragic results.

The benefits of city living may be lost by the weakening of the traditional neighborhood "community" and the fact that older people are often unaware of the services available to them (Lopata, 1975). Lopata found that under-users of urban resources were more likely to be women, rural-born or second-generation urbanites with little formal education, and nonmembers of voluntary organizations. Elderly immigrants may be particularly disadvantaged, though they may receive support within ethnic communities.

Clearly city living offers both advantages and disadvantages. The balance between the two depends on the desires and capability of each older individual and the nature of the community in which he or she lives. The neighborhood must be analyzed as an "environmental support system," whether assessing existing housing or planning new housing for the elderly (Regnier, 1975). Regnier notes that there are "critical distances" beyond which most older people will not travel for a particular service—one block for a bus stop, one to three blocks for a bank, four to ten blocks for a supermarket, and so on. These distances are often subjective, being affected by such things as hills, fear of crime, or climate. Distance barriers are more likely to be overcome for very significant purposes (medical care, seeing children), and less likely to be overcome when combined with economic barriers (barber/beauty shops, restaurants) (Lawton, 1977). These barriers imply two needs in planning a livable neighborhood environment for older people (Regnier, 1975). First, there is a minimal core group of services which should be located within walking distance: bus stop, grocery store, drug store, bank, post office, church. Second, there should be accessible (and inexpensive) transportation to reach other services, such as: medical care, clubs, parks, libraries, luncheonettes, dry cleaners.

Crimes Against the Elderly

Considerable attention has recently been given in the media to crimes against the elderly. Wide coverage was given to one particular incident which occurred in November of 1976.

> Hans Kabel, 78, and his wife Emma, 76, lived in an apartment in the South Bronx. In good health, with $23,000 in the bank, they seemed to be quite well off. But both had been victimized by crime. Hans Kabel had been mugged and his head bashed against a staircase. A year later, a man had broken into their apartment and stolen $100. Emma Kabel was beaten and tortured by another robber, who stole $200. Not long afterward, Hans and Emma Kabel were found dead in their apartment in an apparent double suicide.

Older people are particularly vulnerable to many types of crime. Their low, fixed income, isolation and loneliness, and desperation over illness make them susceptible to quackery and fraud (to be discussed in Chapter 11). The fact that they are often concentrated in high-crime inner-city areas, and may be sickly or weak, makes them vulnerable to purse-snatchings, muggings, and break-ins.

> The couple inched painfully from Fordham Road into a wasteland of The Bronx. Clinging to each other for support, the old

man and woman mounted a curb and struggled for a moment while she regained her balance. Then, slowly, they went on. Watching them shuffle into the shadows of late afternoon, Detective Donald Gaffney sighed heavily and said, "There goes prime meat." (*Time*, 1976: 21)

Young criminals refer to attacks on older people as "crib jobs," since it is as easy as taking candy from a baby (*Time*, 1976). They may wait for Social Security checks to be left in mailboxes, or linger outside banks and stores to snatch purses or follow the person to force their way in.

Actually, fewer crimes are committed against older people than against other age groups, regardless of whether one looks at official crime statistics ("crimes known to the police") or victimization surveys in the community. This is illustrated by the data in Table 9.2, drawn from the National Crime Survey conducted in 1973, in which persons were asked about crimes committed against them (whether or not they had reported them to the police). Such crimes as assault, robbery, and rape are concentrated among the young, while some 'types of personal larceny (purse snatchings, picked pockets) are more evenly distributed by age (Antunes, Cook, Cook, and Skogan, 1977). The typical crime against the elderly involves less violence and is more likely to occur in or near their homes.

Such statistics are perhaps less important than the *fear* of crime felt by older people, which limits their autonomy and security. This fear has a "chilling effect" on life style. Older people become afraid to go out, even for food, much less for such "luxuries" as church or social clubs. Traveling by bus becomes a major expedition into dangerous territory. When they do go out, they may be afraid to come back, for fear that someone has broken in. These fears are not unrealistic for those older persons who are already in poor health or quite frail—simply being knocked down can mean a long convalescence with a broken hip, or even death. In the words of a *Time* magazine article, older people can become "prisoners of fear."

In an attempt to assess the prevalence of such fearfulness, national surveys conducted by the National Opinion Research Center have asked people of all ages whether there is "any area right around here—that is, within a mile—where you would be afraid to walk alone at night" (Lebowitz, 1975; Clemente and Kleiman, 1976). Older people were only slightly more fearful than the rest of the population (51 percent of those over 65 were fearful; 41 percent of those under 65). But certain groups of the elderly were especially vulnerable to such fears, notably older women (though

Table 9.2. Reported crime victimization by age (rates per 1,000 population)

	Age 12 and over			Age 65 and over		
	Total	Male	Female	Total	Male	Female
ALL PERSONS:						
Total selected crimes	64.0	75.2	53.9	15.1	18.4	12.8
Rape	0.5	—	1.0	a	—	a
Robbery						
with injury	1.2	1.6	0.8	1.0	a	1.1
without injury	2.3	3.6	1.2	1.5	2.1	1.1
Assault						
aggravated	5.1	7.7	2.8	0.8	a	0.9
simple	8.1	10.3	6.1	1.1	1.6	a
Personal larceny	46.7	52.0	42.0	10.6	13.2	8.8
HOUSEHOLDS (BY AGE OF HEAD):						
Total selected crimes	103.9			55.3		
Burglary	44.0			28.5		
Household larceny	51.4			24.8		
Motor vehicle theft	8.5			2.0		

a Base too small for rate to be statistically reliable.
Data are from the 1972 National Crime Survey.
Source: U.S. Bureau of the Census, 1975.

sex differences were less than for younger age groups), blacks, and those living alone or with lower income. Size of the community was particularly important, as indicated in Table 9.3. Age differences were virtually nonexistent in rural areas and small cities, but older residents of larger cities were quite likely to be fearful for their personal safety. Thus, low-income residents of inner-city areas, especially women and blacks, will feel least secure because of the fear of crime. And there is likely to be some basis in fact for such fears. A study of one public housing development in Boston found that the assault rate against older residents was 783 percent higher than the national average, and burglaries and break-ins were 590 percent higher (Loether, 1975). Small wonder that some older people are distrustful prisoners in their own homes.

There are a number of possible approaches to dealing with this crime problem. Programs in California, for example, have taken an informational approach, telling older people about security measures (locks, property identification), teaching them about confidence games and consumer fraud, and encouraging older women not to carry purses (Younger, 1976). A bimonthly information bulletin, "Senior Crime Preventer's Bulletin," was mailed out to older people. Other programs include increased surveillance and escort services (e.g., for going to the bank), and increased penalties for crimes against the elderly have been suggested, but the constitutionality and effectiveness of such an approach are questionable. Teaching self-defense techniques to older persons is also highly questionable, since attempts at self-defense by victims often only provoke violence, increasing the likelihood of their injury (Hindelang, 1976).

There is some evidence that age-segregated housing arrangements may affect criminal victimization and fear of crime. Sherman and associates (1976) compared age-integrated, age-segregated, and mixed (an age-segregated high-rise in the midst of low-rise housing for younger families) housing projects. Older residents of age-integrated housing were more likely to have been victims of crime. The greatest differences were in *feelings* of safety, however—residents of some type of segregated arrangement (including mixed) felt substantially more secure. The authors suggest that this was not due to objectively greater security arrangements (such as patrolling); rather, informal groups developed to provide natural surveillance, such as questioning strangers about their purposes. For example, interviewers in the study were much more likely to be questioned about their presence in the age-segregated buildings. In this sense, such housing increases the existence of "defensible space" (Newman, 1972) for elderly residents by fostering a sense of social territory.

Table 9.3. Percentage fearful[a] by age and place of residence

Age	Place of residence[b]									
	Rural		Small city		Suburb		Medium city		Large city	
	%	N	%	N	%	N	%	N	%	N
Under 40	24	135	38	168	31	97	44	88	53	184
40–59	23	108	37	110	42	94	48	79	60	106
60 and over	19	101	39	66	50	34	63	35	71	78

[a] Respondents who said "yes" to the question: "Is there any area right around here—that is, within a mile—where you would be afraid to walk alone at night?"

[b] Rural: in open country, on a farm, or in a small town under 2,500; Small city: 2,500 to 50,000; Suburb: suburb near a large city; Medium city: 50,000 to 250,000; Large city: over 250,000.

Data are from a national survey conducted in 1973 by the National Opinion Research Center.
Source: Barry Lebowitz, "Age and fearfulness," *Journal of Gerontology* 30 (1975):699. Reprinted by permission.

Whether various policies directed at reducing crime against the aged are really effective is perhaps less important than their effects on *feelings* of safety. Fear of crime contributes to a general perception of the world as complex and dangerous. It may be that such fear will decline because of cohort succession. Future older people will less frequently come from rural backgrounds, be immigrants, or have low educational and occupational status, and will therefore be less likely to possess the psychological characteristics—external locus of control, passivity, fatalism—which contribute to a fearful perception of the world.

Summary

Age and friendships are linked in many ways. Similarities related to age—shared life-cycle and historical experiences—lead people to select most of their friends from age peers, particularly the elderly. Old friendships can also take on enduring qualities, similar to family ties. However, age also brings the disruption of friendships because of role loss, poor health, or residential moves. Role losses such as retirement and widowhood are particularly disruptive when they set the aging individual apart from his or her peers.

Most older people interact quite frequently with friends and neighbors, though less than with kin. But most report declining social interaction. This is much less true of those with good health and higher socioeconomic status. The aged, especially those in the working class, are dependent on their local residential settings for the provision of peers to interact with. Unfortunately, many older people may have lost the ability to "neighbor." Stable residents are more likely to have local friends.

Friendships fulfill many social and emotional needs, and involvement in social networks is especially critical for those who have experienced role loss. But quality of interaction may be more important than quantity, with even one confidant acting as a buffer against age-related losses. Such confidants were more prevalent for women, married persons, and those with higher socioeconomic status. Friends and neighbors are also sources of more tangible assistance, but they are used less than the family. Finally, age peers can make contributions to socialization for old age.

Age-segregated settings—apartments, communal living, and retirement communities—offer potential benefits to the aged, including greater sociability, mutual assistance, group norms, and a positive reference group. There is considerable variation in types of retirement communities. Residents are drawn to them by their economy and the desire for a better living environment (climate, recreational facilities, security). They tend to have higher morale, partly due to self-selection, but also because of the availability of age peers and norms supporting leisure. Retirement communities apparently do not have detrimental financial or political effects on surrounding areas.

Age segregation can also have negative consequences. It may increase intergenerational intolerance and distrust, increasing the marginality of the aged. Housing is a limited source of such tolerance, however, and age integration may only heighten social isolation for some older people. Poorly planned retirement communities may create many problems, and many older people reject the idea of specialized housing. For those who are receptive, however, and may have limited "activity resources," age-segregated settings appear to be beneficial.

The nature of neighborhood and housing arrangements may be particularly critical for older people, given their greater likelihood of "environmental docility." Studies indicate that improved housing for the aged can have a tremendous impact on life style and well-being, and older people can make valuable contributions to the planning of their living environments.

City living presents both advantages and disadvantages for older people. Urban neighborhoods often have greater accessibility to a variety of local services, complemented by the availability of public transportation. Social integration may also be enhanced by the greater availability of age peers. Other aspects of cities create problems, however—poor housing, deteriorating neighborhoods, street crime. Health services are particularly likely to be fragmented and confusing to the elderly. In addition, older persons may fail to take advantage of those urban resources which do exist. The assessment of neighborhoods must take into account the presence or absence of a core group of local services and accessibility to more scattered services and facilities.

Crime is one negative aspect of city living for the aged. Although fewer crimes are committed against the elderly than other age groups, fear of crime can severely restrict life style. Such fears are most prevalent among older people living in cities, and among older women, blacks, and those with low income.

References

Antunes, George, Fay Cook, Thomas Cook, and Wesley Skogan
  1977   "Patterns of personal crime against the elderly: Findings
         from a national survey." The Gerontologist 17: 321–27.
Bednar, Michael (ed.)
  1977   Barrier-Free Environments. Stroudsberg, Pa.: Dowden,
         Hutchinson and Ross.

Blau, Zena
    1961   "Structural constraints on friendship in old age." American
            Sociological Review 26: 429–39.
    1973   Old Age in a Changing Society. New York: New Viewpoints.
Bultena, Gordon and Vivian Wood
    1969   "The American retirement community: Bane or blessing?"
            Journal of Gerontology 24: 209–17.
    1970   "Leisure orientation and recreational activities of retirement
            community residents." Journal of Leisure Research 2:
            3–15.
Butler, Robert
    1975   Why Survive?: Being Old in America. New York:
            Harper & Row.
Cantor, Marjorie
    1975   "Life space and the social support system of the inner city
            elderly of New York." The Gerontologist 15: 23–26.
Cantor, Marjorie and Mary Mayer
    1976   "Health and the inner city elderly." The Gerontologist
            16: 17–24.
Carp, Frances
    1965   "Effects of improved housing on the lives of older people."
            In U.S. Department of Health, Education, and Welfare.
            Patterns of Living and Housing of Middle-Aged and Older
            People. Washington, D.C.: U.S. Government Printing
            Office.
    1967   "The impact of environment on old people." The
            Gerontologist 7: 106–08.
    1975a   "Life-style and location within the city." The Gerontologist
            15: 27–34.
    1975b   "Impact of improved housing on morale and life satisfac-
            tion." The Gerontologist 15: 511–15.
    1976a   "Housing and living environments of older people." In
            Robert Binstock and Ethel Shanas (eds.). Handbook of
            Aging and the Social Sciences. New York: Van Nostrand
            Reinhold.
    1976b   "User evaluation of housing for the elderly." The Gerontol-
            ogist 16: 102–11.
    1977   "Impact of improved living environment on health and life
            expectancy." The Gerontologist 17: 242–49.
Clark, Margaret
    1971   "Patterns of aging among the elderly poor of the inner city."
            The Gerontologist 11 (1, P. II): 58–66.
Clemente, Frank and Michael Kleiman
    1976   "Fear of crime among the aged." The Gerontologist 16:
            207–10.
Foskett, John
    1955   "Social structure and social participation." American
            Sociological Review 20: 431–38.

Gans, Herbert
1962 Urban Villagers. New York: The Free Press.
Graney, Marshall
1975 "Happiness and social participation in aging." Journal of Gerontology 30: 701–06.
Gubrium, Jaber
1973 The Myth of the Golden Years: A Socio-Environmental Theory of Aging. Springfield, Ill.: Charles C Thomas.
Hartman, Chester, Jerry Horovitz, and Robert Herman
1976 "Designing with the elderly: A user needs survey for housing low-income senior citizens." The Gerontologist 16: 303–11.
Heintz, Katherine
1976 Retirement Communities: For Adults Only. New Brunswick, N.J.: Center for Urban Policy Research, Rutgers-The State University of New Jersey.
Hess, Beth
1972 "Friendship." In Matilda Riley, Marilyn Johnson, and Anne Foner (eds.). Aging and Society. Volume 3: A Sociology of Age Stratification. New York: Russell Sage.
Hindelang, Michael
1976 Criminal Victimization in Eight American Cities. Cambridge, Mass.: Ballinger.
Hochschild, Arlie
1973 The Unexpected Community. Englewood Cliffs, N.J.: Prentice- Hall.
Hoyt, G. C.
1954 "The life of the retired in a trailer park." American Journal of Sociology 59: 361–70.
Jacobs, Jerry
1974 Fun City: An Ethnographic Study of a Retirement Community. New York: Holt, Rinehart and Winston.
1975 Older Persons and Retirement Communities: Case Studies in Social Gerontology. Springfield, Ill.: Charles C Thomas.
James, M.
1972 "A commune for old folks." Life (May 12): 53–57.
Katz, Irving
1970 "Experimental studies of Negro-white relations." In Leonard Berkowitz (ed.). Advances in Experimental Social Psychology. Volume 5. New York: Academic Press.
Larson, Calvin
1974 "Alienation and public housing for the elderly." Aging and Human Development 5: 217–30.
Lawton, M. Powell
1977 "The impact of environment on aging and behavior." In James Birren and K. Warner Schaie (eds.). Handbook of the Psychology of Aging. New York: Van Nostrand Reinhold.
Lawton, M. Powell and Lucille Nahemow
1973 "Ecology and the aging process." In Carl Eisdorfer and

M. Powell Lawton (eds.). The Psychology of Adult Development and Aging. Washington, D.C.: American Psychological Association.

Lebowitz, Barry
1975   "Age and fearfulness: Personal and situational factors."
       Journal of Gerontology 30: 696–700.

Loether, Herman
1975   Problems of Aging. Encino, Calif.: Dickenson.

Lofland, John
1968   "The youth ghetto." Journal of Higher Education 39:
       121–43.

Lopata, Helena
1973   Widowhood in an American City. Cambridge, Mass.:
       Schenkman.
1975   "Support systems of elderly urbanites: Chicago of the
       1970's." The Gerontologist 15: 35–41.

Lowenthal, Marjorie and Clayton Haven
1968   "Interaction and adaptation: Intimacy as a critical variable."
       American Sociological Review 33: 20–31.

Lowenthal, Marjorie and Betsy Robinson
1976   "Social networks and isolation." In Robert Binstock and
       Ethel Shanas (eds.). Handbook of Aging and the Social
       Sciences. New York: Van Nostrand Reinhold.

Lowenthal, Marjorie, et al.
1975   Four Stages of Life. San Francisco: Jossey-Bass.

Mangum, Wiley
1973   "Retirement villages." In Rosamonde Boyd and Charles
       Oakes (eds.). Foundations of Practical Gerontology.
       Columbia: University of South Carolina Press.

Messer, Mark
1967   "The possibility of an age-concentrated environment becoming a normative system." The Gerontologist 7: 247–50.

Milgram, Stanley
1970   "The experience of living in cities." Science 167: 1461–68.

National Council on the Aging
1976   The Myth and Reality of Aging in America.
       Washington, D.C.

Newman, Oscar
1972   Defensible Space. New York: MacMillan.

Rakoff, Vivian
1973   "Psychiatric aspects of death in America." In Arien Mack
       (ed.). Death in American Experience. New York:
       Schocken Books.

Regnier, Victor
1975   "Neighborhood planning for the urban elderly." In Diana
       Woodruff and James Birren (eds.). Aging: Scientific
       Perspectives and Social Issues. New York: D. Van
       Nostrand.

Riley, Matilda and Anne Foner
 1968   Aging and Society. Volume 1: An Inventory of Research
        Findings. New York: Russell Sage Foundation.
Rooney, James
 1976   "Friendship and disaffiliation among the skid row popula-
        tion." Journal of Geronotology 31: 82–88.
Rosenberg, George
 1970   The Worker Grows Old. San Francisco: Jossey-Bass.
Rosencranz, H. and T. McNevin
 1969   "A factor analysis of attitudes toward the aged." The
        Gerontologist 9: 55–59.
Rosow, Irving
 1961   "Retirement housing and social integration." The
        Gerontologist 1: 85–91.
 1967   Social Integration of the Aged. New York: The Free Press.
Ross, Jennie-Keith
 1977   Old People, New Lives. Chicago: University of Chicago
        Press.
Shanas, Ethel
 1962   The Health of Older People: A Social Survey. Cambridge,
        Mass.: Harvard University Press.
Sherman, Edmund, Evelyn Newman, and Anne Nelson
 1976   "Patterns of age integration in public housing and the inci-
        dence and fears of crime among elderly tenants." In Jack
        Goldsmith and Sharon Goldsmith (eds.). Crime and the
        Elderly: Challenge and Response. Lexington, Mass.:
        Lexington Books.
Sherman, Susan
 1971   "The choice of retirement housing among the well-elderly."
        Aging and Human Development 2: 118–38.
 1972   "Satisfaction with retirement housing: Attitudes, recom-
        mendations and moves." Aging and Human Development
        3: 339–66.
 1974   "Leisure activities in retirement housing." Journal of
        Gerontology 29: 325–35.
 1975a "Patterns of contacts for residents of age-segregated and age-
        integrated housing." Journal of Gerontology 30: 103–07.
 1975b "Mutual assistance and support in retirement housing."
        Journal of Gerontology 30: 479–83.
 1975c "Provision of on-site services in retirement housing." Aging
        and Human Development 6: 229–47.
Smith, Joel
 1966   "The narrowing social world of the aged." In Ida Simpson
        and John McKinney (eds.). Social Aspects of Aging.
        Durham, N.C.: Duke University Press.
Smith, Joel and Herman Turk
 1966   "Considerations bearing on a study of the role of the aged
        in community integration." In Ida Simpson and John

McKinney (eds.). Social Aspects of Aging. Durham, N.C.: Duke University Press.

Steinfeld, Edward, James Duncan, and Paul Cardell
1977   "Toward a responsive environment: The psychosocial effects of inaccessibility." In Michael Bednar (ed.). Barrier-Free Environments. Stroudsberg, Pa.: Dowden, Hutchinson and Ross.

Stephens, Joyce
1975   "Society of the alone: Freedom, privacy, and ultilitarianism as dominant norms in the SRO." Journal of Gerontology 30: 230–35.

Streib, Gordon and Ruth Streib
1975   "Communes and the aging: Utopian dream and gerontological reality." American Behavioral Scientist 19: 176–89.

Sussman, Marvin
1976   "The family life of old people." In Robert Binstock and Ethel Shanas (eds.). Handbook of Aging and the Social Sciences. New York: Van Nostrand Reinhold.

Taietz, Philip and Olaf Larson
1956   "Social participation and old age." Rural Sociology 21: 229–38.

Teaff, Joseph, M. Powell Lawton, Lucille Nahemow, and Diane Carlson
1978   "Impact of age integration on the well-being of elderly tenants in public housing." Journal of Gerontology 33: 126–33.

Time
1976   "The elderly: Prisoners of fear." November 29: 21–22.

U.S. Bureau of the Census
1975   "Social and economic characteristics of the older population." Current Population Reports. Series P-23, No. 57. Washington, D.C.: U.S. Government Printing Office.

Wax, Judith
1976   "It's like your own home here." New York Times Magazine. November 21: 38+.

Whyte, William
1943   Street Corner Society. Chicago: University of Chicago Press.

Williams, Richard and Martin Loeb
1968   "The adult's social life space and successful aging: Some suggestions for a conceptual framework." In Bernice Neugarten (ed.). Middle Age and Aging. Chicago: University of Chicago Press.

Winiecke, Linda
1973   "The appeal of age segregated housing to the elderly poor." Aging and Human Development 4: 293–306.

Younger, Evelle
1976   "The California experience in crime prevention programs with senior citizens." In Jack Goldsmith and Sharon Goldsmith (eds.). Crime and the Elderly: Challenge and Response. Lexington, Mass.: Lexington Books.

10

The Politics of Age

~~~~~~

The "politics of age" has attracted increasing attention in American society over the past 20 years, focusing largely on the politics of youth, with the rise of various "youth movements," campus activism surrounding such social issues as the Vietnam War, and the so-called "generation gap." These issues themselves are important in understanding the nature of aging and its effects throughout the life cycle. Do they represent true social change and the emergence of cohorts with a new political consciousness and set of values or simply an eternal rebelliousness of youth which dissipates in middle age?

There are also important questions related to the "politics of old age." Old age itself is increasingly being defined in legal terms, through Social Security regulations, mandatory retirement policies, and other legislation directed at specific age groups (Cain, 1974). The possibility of age inequality and discrimination is becoming an important legal issue. The position of the aged in American society raises the questions of whether they will develop activist political movements on their own behalf, and whether such movements imply increasing conflict among age groups in society.

We sometimes forget the extent of conflict among age groups. Even the socialization of children can be viewed in terms of the relative ability of parents and children to "get their own way" by exercising power through rewards and punishments (Collins, 1975). Any system which structures opportunities and rewards carries within it the seeds of conflict. So it is with age stratification. We have seen that the aged in modern societies suffer disproportionately from a number of material disadvantages and they often face limited options in the meaningful use of time and some stigma attached to being old. We can expect that these problems would be reflected in a lack of political power and of resources by which to gain more power. But they could also lead to greater political activism by the aged on their own behalf, as they attempt to improve their material and social standing.

Age Stratification and Age Conflict

The model of age stratification suggests that some age conflict is inevitable. Since social positions are age-based, age becomes a basis for "structured social inequality" (Foner, 1974). In the political sphere, for example, there is likely to be age inequality in access to political power. The age stratification of roles and access to rewards and resources helps explain age differences in alienation and the existence of a generation gap. In Chapter 3, we spoke of the potential imbalance between the roles into which older (or younger) people are allocated and the degree of socialization for those roles. This imbalance may create a pressure for change in patterns of age stratification, providing the basis for a social movement among the aged. Although age conflict is always possible, however, there are factors which reduce age conflict by forging ties across age strata and reducing age-group solidarity (Foner, 1972; 1974). These factors warrant our attention because of their implications for future age conflict.

First, multiple group affiliations tend to reduce conflict in complex societies. Age-heterogeneous groups, such as the family or work groups, may reduce age conflict for a number of reasons. They foster common goals and interests—a sense of common fate— which override age differences. They also forge emotional ties and feelings of loyalty and responsibility across age boundaries, and people of different ages can socialize each other. There is considerable evidence of cross-generational value transmission within families. This works in both directions, with children often affecting the attitudes and values of their parents, as well as vice versa. Foner suggests that a lack of age-heterogeneous affiliations may partly account for the "rebelliousness" of college students.

A second factor reducing age conflict is the inevitability of aging ("age mobility"). Younger people may anticipate their future age status and older people can empathize with youth because they have been there themselves (though we often forget what it was like). This softens the perception of severe age differences.

Foner suggests that these conflict-reducing mechanisms are most effective with *material* issues concerning the distribution of economic resources. Such class-based issues tend to cut across age lines. *Ideal* issues, involving ethics and values, are much broader questions which may call forth generational differences. They tend to have an urgency and emotionality which limits compromise, and may also reflect on the status or power of specific age groups, particularly if they are rebuffed in their efforts.

The analysis of age conflict has tended to focus on youth versus middle age. Using Foner's ideas, however, we can begin to question whether age conflict regarding old age might not increase in the future. First, what is the evidence on age-heterogeneous affiliation? Cowgill's (1974) model of modernization suggests that physical and social separation of the aged occurs in modern societies, and, as indicated earlier, there is age-segregation in urban settings and the continuing solidarity of the extended family is questionable. As cross-age contacts diminish, the potential for age conflict increases. It is also possible that "material" issues are becoming more age-based as young and old people are increasingly in competition over support from general revenues. This is reflected in conflict over school budgets and the cost of Social Security. Social Security has implications for conflict over the old-age "dependency ratio," with current workers subsidizing older nonworkers (a "dependent" population) and the ratio of non-workers to workers rising, and along with it the tax burden for supporting Social Security. As this burden increases so may unwillingness to provide a sufficient subsidy. In discussing the possibility of a "backlash" against the elderly, Ragan (1976) quotes from an editorial appearing in the *Los Angeles Times*:

> The significant, semihidden story in the new federal budget is that America's public resources are increasingly being mortgaged for the use of a single group within our country: the elderly. . . . This is a ticklish subject to write about. No one wants to be accused of being niggardly toward his elders, and it is a matter of pride, not regret that in recent years this country has moved decisively to alleviate a long and shameful history of neglect. . . . But it is also a fact that the decision to meet those needs has been taken without a general awareness . . . of the tradeoffs involved. . . . As a result, there is a serious danger of a backlash against this belated policy of generosity toward the elderly, when today's wage earners begin to understand what has happened—and who is paying for it. . . . Clearly, this trend

cannot continue for long without causing a bitter political struggle between the generations. (Broder, 1973)

Additionally, the aged may increasingly come into conflict with other minorities over health and welfare resources.

This suggests that there is at least the potential for future conflict surrounding the problems of old age. The form which this might take depends partly on solidarity and activism within the older population. To more fully understand the future of age politics, however, we must first understand past and present political action and the effects of both aging and cohort change as they relate to the age stratification of political activity and political conflict.

Age and Political Participation

Political participation refers to a number of distinct types of involvement such as voting, interest in politics, formation of opinions, political leadership, party affiliation. Each of these appears to be related to age, but trends are by no means consistent. However, there is little evidence of any general disengagement by older people from the political arena, therefore the potential for activism on their own behalf does exist.

Voting

Studies of voting behavior have consistently shown the same age pattern: low voter participation among the youngest age groups (21 to 24), a steady increase to a peak in the forties and fifties, and a decline in participation in the sixties and seventies (Riley and Foner, 1968). It is interesting to note, however, that those over 75 still vote more frequently than the 21 to 24 age group. Table 10.1 reflects this pattern for reported voting in the presidential elections of 1964, 1968, and 1972. There are a number of possible reasons for the relatively low voter turnout among the

Table 10.1. Reported voting in Presidential elections, in percentages, by age

| | Presidential election | | |
	1972	1968	1964
Total (21+)	64.3	67.9	69.4
21–24	50.7	51.1	51.3
25–44	62.7	66.6	69.0
45–64	70.8	74.9	75.9
65+	63.5	65.8	66.3

Source: U.S. Bureau of the Census, 1973, p. 3.

young: lower partisanship (party identification), difficulties in registering for the first time, high rates of mobility, lack of full integration into the community (young people are still establishing their social positions), and less commitment to a society which has been structured for them by others (Foner, 1972). Part of the decline in voting by the aged is certainly attributable to health and transportation problems, which account for declines in many types of activities. Disengagement among some older people may also account for some of the decline, since there is evidence that political activity by the aged depends on their objective and subjective involvement in the total life of the community (Turk, Smith, and Myers, 1966).

Factors other than age also affect voting patterns, of course. Education appears to be the most important of these. For all age groups and both sexes, those with higher levels of education are significantly more likely to vote (Table 10.2) and age has the greatest impact among the least educated, since the best-educated appear to vote at all ages. Thus, the decline with age in voting may weaken as future cohorts of the aged are better-educated.

Sex differences in voting are slight through most of the life cycle, but older women show a greater decline with age than older men. The reasons for this are not entirely clear, though Foner (1972) has offered some suggestions. Older women are likely to be widowed and may have formerly voted with their husbands; they

Table 10.2. Percent voting in November 1964, by sex, age, and education

| | Years of education | | | | | | |
| | Elementary | | High school | | College | | |
	0–7 years	8 years	1–3 years	4 years	1–3 years	4 years or more	Total
Males							
21–24	14	30	34	56	70	80	53
25–44	43	58	65	76	82	87	71
45–64	63	79	81	88	88	93	79
65+	66	79	80	88	91	88	74
Total 21+	58	73	69	80	82	88	73
Females							
21–24	22	21	33	55	69	78	52
25–44	34	52	58	76	85	87	68
45–64	52	69	75	84	87	92	74
65+	46	63	72	76	82	93	61
Total 21+	45	63	63	76	83	89	68

Source: U.S. Bureau of the Census, 1965:16–19.

are more likely to be in poor health; and women of this particular cohort may not be used to voting, since many were socialized prior to women's suffrage.

Political Interest and Commitment

Voting is only one form of political participation and a weak one at that. Evidence suggests that, in a variety of additional ways, older people retain an interest in political affairs. Glenn (1969) found that when the effects of education were controlled, older people were slightly more likely to hold political opinions than younger people. Compared with people in their twenties, persons over 50 and 60 are more likely to follow public affairs through newspaper reading and television viewing, and they are also more likely to keep up with political information such as the names of their senators (Riley and Foner, 1968). Thus, there is no support for a view of the older voter as disinterested, disengaged, or mis-informed, at least to any greater extent than the general electorate.

These are largely sedentary activities, but membership in political associations is also maintained, though only a small minority of the population belongs to such groups (Riley and Foner, 1968). Additionally, older people are more attached to a particular party than younger people, apparently because of a sense of commitment built up over time (Campbell, 1971). Campbell also indicates that though political activism, measured by such behaviors as party work and attendance at political meetings, is greatest in the thirties and forties and declines thereafter, older people still retain a greater level of activism than the young. In general, the aged are actively engaged in moderate forms of political participation and are under-represented only in more intensive forms (Hudson and Binstock, 1976).

Political Leadership

Since the status of the aged seems to fall in modern societies, one might expect to find few older persons occupying positions of political leadership. On the contrary, however, "older people appear to be better represented than younger people among the elite who play strategic roles in the body politic" (Riley and Foner, 1968: 475). Modern political leaders in the United States—senators, representatives, Supreme Court justices, presidents, and cabinet members—are older than their counterparts from the 1700s and 1800s (Lehman, 1953; Fischer, 1977). Even at the local community level, middle-aged and older people are overrepresented in such roles as community decision maker, museum leader, and trustee of an educational institution (Riley and Foner, 1968). We seem to be a society which celebrates youth, but is controlled by the middle-aged and elderly.

How is it that so many individual older persons achieve status and power, despite the devalued status of the aged as a group? First, such positions typically require demonstrated excellence of achievement in other roles. To the extent that the structure of professions delays such achievement until at least middle age, the pool from which leaders are drawn will exclude the young. Supreme Court justices, for example, must work their way up various judicial and political ladders to achieve an attention-attracting prominence. Second, tenure is still an important correlate of political power. The concept of retirement without functional incapacities has been slow to reach the political arena. Political "bosses," like former Mayor Richard Daley of Chicago, can retain power as long as they can exercise it, and power becomes stronger over the years. Finally, trends toward "gerontocratic" leadership are more pronounced in stable, entrenched groups. Young elites emerge during periods of revolutionary change, such as the early history of the Nazi movement in Germany and Communism in China (Hudson and Binstock, 1976).

One word of caution is in order. The fact that many political leaders are older does not necessarily mean that older people and their interests are being well represented. There is no evidence that such politicians vote on the basis of their age.

Age and Political Attitudes

There has been a tendency to stereotype the aged as conservative and rigidly opposed to change, leading some to suggest that the "graying of America" will cause cultural stagnation. Such views are unwarranted because of the complexity of the effects of both aging and cohort change on political attitudes. The aged of today are conservative in some ways, liberal in others, and the aged of tomorrow may well be a different breed of political cat.

Party Affiliation

One measure of political attitudes is party affiliation: Democrats are presumably more liberal, Republicans more conservative. Older voters are more likely than younger voters to identify themselves as Republicans, with approximately equal numbers of Republicans and Democrats among the aged (Riley and Foner, 1968). This should not be taken as evidence of a general trend with age toward conservatism, however, as people do not appear to shift from Democrat to Republican as they age (Cutler, 1969), and younger voters can be expected to retain their current affiliations as they age.

Recent cohort phenomena suggest some changes in the patterns of partisan loyalties (Abramson, 1975). The relationship between social class and party affiliation (working-class Democrats, middle-class Republicans), forged during the Depression, has been weakening in recent presidential elections, and there has been a rising proportion of voters who express no party affiliation. Both of these trends are most notable in cohorts which have entered the electorate since World War II, and the evidence suggests that they will continue over the life course of these cohorts. Since this opens up the possibility of new coalitions based on factors other than party loyalty or social class, it removes one barrier to coalitions based on age. As these cohorts enter old age, they may be more willing to vote according to age interests rather than class interests or party affiliation.

Conservatism

In general ideological terms, older people appear to be more conservative than younger people. For example, they are more resistant to change and less tolerant of nonconformity (Riley and Foner, 1968). On specific issues, older people have been found to be less supportive of school busing to achieve racial balance, legalization of marijuana, women's rights, and federal involvement in protecting civil rights (Cutler and Schmidhauser, 1975).

The general finding that conservatism is greater among the elderly must be tempered by other considerations, however. Certainly all older people are not more conservative than all younger people, nor are they monolithically conservative. While the young are apparently more receptive to change in general, older people can be more liberal on policies which would benefit them as a group, such as governmental programs directed at medical care (Bengtson and Cutler, 1976). Young cohorts in some societies may in fact be more conservative than older cohorts. The right-wing Nazi party in Germany received its major support from youth and the youngest cohorts in Cuba tend to be less supportive of Fidel Castro's leftist revolution (Foner, 1974). Even a general conservatism may lead to positions which are considered liberal. The conservative isolationism on foreign policy which characterizes older people resulted in a more "dovish" stand on the Vietnam War than even the young (Campbell, 1971).

It should be apparent that the relationship between age and conservatism is complex. Foner has suggested two hypotheses:

Hypothesis 1: On specific issues, each cohort tends to change as it ages in line with the general trend in the society.

> Hypothesis 2: On the *general* question of conservative versus liberal allegiance, each cohort tends to change as it ages toward a more conservative position. (Foner, 1972:133–34)

Thus, all age groups may show similar trends (*either* more conservative or more liberal) on issues like abortion or crime, so that people can become more liberal as they age. But general support for the existing system, and a generalized resistance to change, may increase with age.

Why might this general conservatism increase with age? Glenn (1974) notes that there are a number of meanings for conservatism: resistance to change, holding "old" attitudes, upholding the status quo or authority, unwillingness to take risks. Age might be related to such dimensions for a variety of reasons. The impact of biological aging and social stresses may lead to rigidity and a fear of change. Also, one's position in the social structure (related to age stratification) affects political attitudes. As individuals assume family responsibilities and reach higher socioeconomic levels, they may oppose liberal feelings of humanitarianism and egalitarianism in their own self-interest, though this does not explain the conservatism of older people who lose family responsibilities and often experience downward mobility. Glenn also suggests that attitudes may begin to stabilize as adult life "settles down," and new experiences have less effect as people accumulate them. Thus, attitudes developed in middle age are more stable because they are based on a greater range of experiences, and the searching and experimentation of youth are left behind. Increases in conservatism may reflect a "developmental stake"—the fear that "if youth rejects the society I have built, my own life is meaningless" (Bengtson and Kuypers, 1971). Finally, perhaps it should be recognized that conservatives like Barry Goldwater might argue that increasing conservatism reflects a more accurate view of the world!

Age differences in conservatism arise from a combination of aging and cohort effects (Glenn, 1974). Glenn cites evidence that American society as a whole has become more liberal over the past 50 years. Older people have shown the same trend, but to a lesser degree. This makes them more conservative than other age groups, even though they have moved in a liberal direction. If the society were to move in a conservative direction, the same processes would make the aged appear more liberal by comparison.

Alienation

Interest in alienation has a long history in sociology, and there has been considerable debate about its meaning and measurement

(Seeman, 1975). The most widely held conceptualization recognizes six dimensions to feelings of alienation: powerlessness, meaninglessness, normlessness, cultural estrangement, self-estrangement, and social isolation (Seeman, 1972). Many of our stereotypes about youth imply a sense of alienation. Their "newness" on the social scene, the fact that their values are still being formed, youthful identity crises, and the apparent rebelliousness reflected in youth "movements" imply the possibility of heightened alienation from society or from the self.

One can also see the possibility of heightened alienation among older people. To the extent that the aged are disengaged or become socially isolated, they may experience a sense of cultural estrangement. If Rosow (1974) is correct about the failure of socialization to old age, feelings of normlessness or meaninglessness will also arise. This, combined with changing bases of identity and a possible "identity crisis" in old age, may create self-estrangement.

As with other age differences, relationships between age and alienation can be attributed to either aging or cohort effects. There may be life-cycle changes in alienation, linked to the age stratification of roles and resources. Martin and associates (1974) suggest that the middle-aged are the "command" generation. They control many of the resources of the social system and participate most fully in that system. Both older and younger people may have heightened feelings of alienation, but the psychological consequences may differ. Youthful alienation may result in attempts to forge a new political ideology, while alienation among older people simply yields a sense of stagnation and despair.

Two recent studies indicate the complexity of the relationship between age and alienation. Cutler and Bengtson (1974) were concerned with political alienation—a sense of powerlessness and an inability to identify with the political system (estrangement). The question was whether alienation displayed aging effects, cohort effects, or period effects (all age groups are affected in the same way by historical periods). They used the following measures of political alienation from election surveys in 1952, 1960, and 1968 (thus allowing them to use the type of cohort analysis illustrated in Chapter 1):

1. "I don't think public officials care much what people like me think."
2. "People like me don't have any say about what the government does."
3. "Sometimes politics and government seem so complicated that a person like me can't really understand what's going on."

Cutler and Bengtson found that older cohorts expressed greater political alienation, but not when educational differences were taken into account. All cohorts showed essentially the same trends: a decline in alienation from 1952 to 1960, followed by an increase in 1968 to higher levels than in 1952. On question 2 ("people like me have no say"), for example, 31 percent agreed in 1952, 27 percent in 1960, and 41 percent in 1968. The evidence suggests a period effect, whereby all age groups are affected similarly by historical events. They conclude that "There is no evidence of a process of aging which produces, or is in other ways related to, political alienation among adults during the period studied" (Cutler and Bengtson, 1974:174).

Martin and associates (1974) looked at more diverse dimensions of alienation: powerlessness, meaninglessness, normlessness, isolation, and self-estrangement. They expected alienation to vary with participation in the social structure, being lowest in middle age, highest in youth, and intermediate in old age. This expectation was largely confirmed, but the patterns of alienation were complex. The aged exhibited their greatest alienation in feelings of powerlessness and meaninglessness, even more so than the young, yet they were the lowest of the three age groups in social isolation and self-estrangement. This suggests that disengagement and identity crises may be less widespread than some have suggested. Older people were most alienated from political life, and less alienated from family life.

Perhaps the clearest implication of these studies of conservatism and alienation is that the relationship between age and political attitudes is highly complex, reflecting the interaction of aging, cohort, and period effects. They also reflect the age stratification of roles. Young and old people may be more alienated because their roles are marginal, with little meaningful involvement in the social and political life of the community. Finally, it should be remembered that age is not the only factor affecting political attitudes and beliefs. Social class, race, ethnicity, and sex are but a few of the factors which may interact with age to affect political attitudes. While there are no simple age patterns, one important conclusion is justified: "*old age is not a period of political quiescence*" (Bengtson and Cutler, 1976:153).

Generations and Politics

If we are to understand future political behavior by older people, we must understand the extent to which political phenomena are rooted in cohort backgrounds. One way to do this is to look at what has been called "the generation gap."

During the 1960s, there was much discussion of the nature and extent of a gap in values and attitudes between young people and their parents. Some argued that youth was antithetical to parental values, while others suggested this was simply a reflection of normal rebelliousness which would fade in mature adulthood. This debate is important because of its implications for social change as well as for the future of the aging experience and age-based politics.

While issues of generational discontinuity can be traced back to the nineteenth century in sociology, the generation gap became a major social and political issue in the late 1960s. People apparently do perceive the existence of a gap. Bengtson (1971), in a study of three-generation families, found that all three generations felt there was such a gap in society, though they also felt there was a lesser gap *within their own family*. The grandparent generation was least likely to perceive a gap in the family, while grandchildren were most likely to perceive one.

That there are age differences in beliefs, attitudes, and values is already apparent from our discussion of age and politics. A review by Bengtson and Lovejoy (1973) suggests evidence of age differences in specific dimensions of values, such as politics and religion. Often such differences can be attributed to social change, as new cohorts experience a different social world from their predecessors. For example, there appears to be a trend toward less authoritarianism and hopelessness and greater independence in rural areas as the work ethic erodes and there is greater participation in the metropolitan environment (Youmans, 1973).

Studies have also found differences on specific issues within families. For example, Hill (1970) found that younger generations took a less "traditional" approach to parenthood, emphasizing personal development and growth rather than obedience and respect. Nevertheless, Hill's study found considerable value consistency across generations, and others have found a similar consistency on attitudes toward drugs, politics, business, and so on (Thomas, 1974). Even student activists exhibit familial similarity in values and opinions, in that they may simply be carrying their parents' values to their logical conclusion (Bengtson, Furlong, and Laufer, 1974).

The youth "counterculture" may display similarity in attitudes while being different in more basic value orientation—it may be more present-oriented, more concerned with "being" than "doing," more interested in harmony with nature than mastery over it (Thomas, 1974). Bengtson and Lovejoy (1973) investigated differences within three-generation families on two value dimensions: *materialism-humanism* and *individual-institutional* orientation. They reasoned that value orientations might vary by social class, age, or sex because of their dependence on location in the social structure. They found considerable homogeneity across these subgroups, however, indicating the pervasiveness of cultural values and the impact of cross-generational transmission through socialization. While there were no age differences on materialism-humanism values, they did find that younger people were more likely to emphasize individualistic values, which was a cohort difference rather than simply a reflection of maturational processes.

It appears that the generation gap is somewhere between "great" and "illusory" (Bengtson, 1970). Apart from these objective dimensions, however, are the *perceptions* held by each generation of other generations. In a study of students and their parents, Bengtson and Kuypers (1971) found that both saw some generational conflict. Parents tended to minimize this conflict as involving only personal habits and traits, however, while students saw friction in more basic issues of values, morality, politics, and life goals. Bengtson and Kuypers argue that these tendencies are related to *fear of loss* and a *developmental stake*. Each generation is afraid of losing something because of the other's behavior. Youth fear powerlessness and meaninglessness if their generation is not made distinctive from the parent generation. The desire to build their own world and establish their own identity, not simply carry out their parents', makes a perception of conflict essential. Parents, on the other hand, have a "stake" in having youth accept their values and priorities. If the world they have constructed is rejected by the young, their efforts have been meaningless. This approach suggests that perception of a generation gap reflects one's developmental stage in the life cycle.

It appears from these studies that age differences in values and attitudes, and perceptions of those differences, do exist, though their importance may have been exaggerated. There are two major interpretations of such age differences (Bengtson, Furlong, and Laufer, 1974; Braungart, 1974). One approach attributes generation gaps to "maturational" processes—the sequence of biological, psychological, and social events in the life cycle. Intergenerational conflict results from the weak integration between age groups and society (Parsons, 1963; Eisenstadt, 1965). Since the middle-aged hold the major positions of responsibility, they are most attached to the status quo. In complex societies, other age groups (notably the young) become less integrated. Adolescence has become prolonged, so that young people feel ready to assume adult positions before they are permitted to, resulting in skepticism and detachment and encouraging rebellion to take their "rightful place" in society (Braungart, 1974). Thus, the generation gap is a natural conflict attributable to personality development and age-based social positions, which all cohorts undergo as they attempt to adapt to and prepare for adult roles.

An alternative approach attributes age differences in values and attitudes to "cohort-historical" processes, reflecting a true gap between generations which will persist. A "generational consciousness" may arise as successive cohorts experience unique historical events and socialization experiences (Mannheim, 1952). Mannheim argues that not all cohorts become generations, in the sense that they differ distinctively from other cohorts. New cohorts can take unique perspectives on the world because of their "fresh contact" with the social system—they can perceive the social structure in new ways because they lack previous experience with it. Additionally, social change means that new cohorts encounter a different social world and different social institutions from those encountered by their parents. Thus, cohort flow results in a "stratification of experience." When social change is sufficiently great, a truly new generation emerges. This cohort-as-generation is one factor which accounts for social change (Ryder, 1965).

If age differences reflect only maturation over the life cycle, there is little reason to expect change in the nature of "youth," "middle age," or "old age." But if age differences reflect generational differences, the door is opened for many changes in the future. More work is clearly needed on the question of generational differences. If our youthful activists of the past decade remain activist, for example, the politics of old age may be very different in 30 or 40 years. How much cohort homogeneity will be transferred into old age? This relates to potential change in the nature and meaning of political involvement in old age and leads us to a discussion of the past, present, and future of old-age activism.

The Senior Movement: Past, Present, and Future

Our impressions of political movements tend to focus on youth, but there has actually been a long history of groups pushing for more favorable treatment of the elderly. Partly as a result of this activism, the needs of the aged currently enjoy considerable visibility, and although many problems still confront older people, programs directed at them have continued to grow during a time of inflation and increasing fiscal conservatism. What does the future hold for the "senior movement"? If the aged grow increasingly activist in pushing for better material conditions and more meaningful involvement in modern society, will they encounter growing resistance from other groups, heightening the conflict among age groups or between the elderly and other disadvantaged

Figure 10.1. Normal pattern for the "natural history" of a social movement

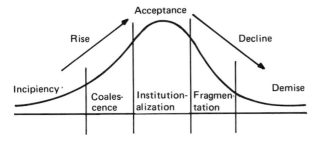

Source: Armond Mauss, *Social Problems as Social Movements,* Philadelphia: J. B. Lippincott, 1975, p. 66.

groups over scarce resources? To answer such questions, we must understand the history and present status of old-age political activism and the processes through which social movements either progress or die away.

Mauss (1975) has described five stages in the "natural history" of social movements (Figure 10.1). Any particular social movement may vary from this ideal progression, depending on the response it receives from society, but this offers a very useful framework for looking at the past, present, and possible futures of the senior movement (Figure 10.2).[1]

Incipiency is the first stage of any social movement. This is a period of unorganized, uncoordinated efforts by a "concerned public" (the aged and their supporters) seeking an identity based on their perception of a threat to their interests. The basis of activism by the aged lies in the processes of modernization discussed in Chapter 3, which set them apart from society and create the kinds of shared problems and frustrations—inadequate pensions, poor housing, expensive medical care, devalued status—which can generate mass action. This incipiency stage lasted roughly from 1920 to 1950, as the few organizations which emerged were relatively short-lived and ineffectual.

The origins of the "senior movement" can be traced to a few individuals and groups campaigning for old-age pensions during the 1920s. Although these groups attracted relatively few adherents, pension experts such as Abraham Epstein did have some influence on Franklin Roosevelt and policy groups which were shaping Social Security legislation. The Townsend Movement was the largest mass organization. Emerging in California during the 1930s, Dr. Francis Townsend eventually attracted over a million

---

[1] Material on the history of the senior movement is drawn from Henry Pratt's recent book, *The Gray Lobby* (1976).

Figure 10.2. A selective history of the senior movement

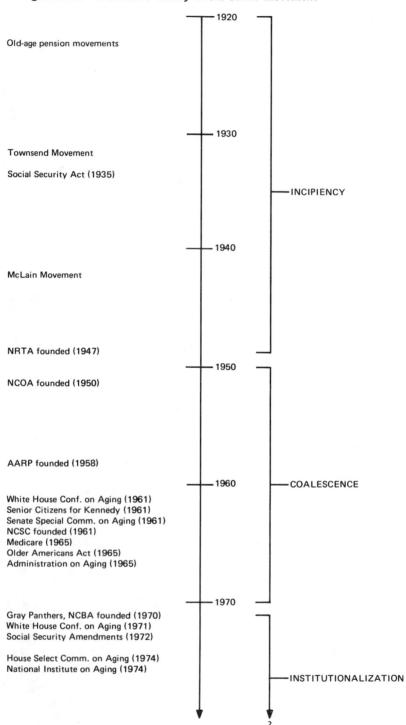

Old-age pension movements

Townsend Movement

Social Security Act (1935)

McLain Movement

NRTA founded (1947)

NCOA founded (1950)

AARP founded (1958)

White House Conf. on Aging (1961)
Senior Citizens for Kennedy (1961)
Senate Special Comm. on Aging (1961)
NCSC founded (1961)
Medicare (1965)
Older Americans Act (1965)
Administration on Aging (1965)

Gray Panthers, NCBA founded (1970)
White House Conf. on Aging (1971)
Social Security Amendments (1972)

House Select Comm. on Aging (1974)
National Institute on Aging (1974)

1920

1930

INCIPIENCY

1940

1950

1960 — COALESCENCE

1970

INSTITUTIONALIZATION

?

followers for his plan to provide a pension of $200 per month to those over 60 who would retire (Holtzman, 1963). More than just a pension plan, this was designed to end the Depression by opening jobs and giving buying power to masses of older people. The movement came too late to really influence Social Security policies, however, and eventually died out.

These early groups influenced the climate of public opinion, but had no genuine direct political access or mass support. Rivalry among the groups prevented collaboration, and their appeals ran counter to the values of thrift, self-reliance, and free enterprise preached by opponents. The early activity surrounding Social Security lapsed into what Pratt calls "the dismal years" of the 1940s. The only major old-age movement during these years was George McLain's "Citizens Committee for Old Age Pensions," which was supported by hundreds of thousands of older people in California and did contribute to rising state expenditures on behalf of the aged. The national scene was quiet, however, despite obvious needs for reform in Social Security.

The second stage of social movements is *coalescence*, as formal and informal organizations emerge and begin to form common alliances, possibly in response to disappointment over the failure of society to adequately address their needs. Pratt (1976) notes that the aged have come to expect economic security and adequate health care, and their "revolution of rising expectations" has made them increasingly restive over the pace of progress. Coalescence of the senior movement encompassed roughly the period from 1950 to 1970, culminating in the White House Conference on Aging of 1971.

Pratt attributes the true birth of the senior movement to trends in the 1950s. Efforts by public agencies to reach the aged and the growth of senior centers, combined with a growing sense of injustice, contributed to increased political consciousness among older people. Organized labor became interested in the needs of retirees, eventually helping in the push for Medicare. New leaders also emerged, such as Ethel Percy Andrus of the National Retired Teachers Association/American Association of Retired Persons (NRTA/AARP) and Charles Odell of the United Auto Workers retiree organization. Two events were particularly critical, however, to increasing the political access and effectiveness of old-age organizations: the involvement of older people in Kennedy's presidential campaign and the White House Conference on Aging of 1971.

The traditional association between older voters and the Republican party, partly due to Democrats being associated with inflation and high taxes, began to decline during the 1950s, and the Democratic party begin to pay more attention to older voters. Although "Senior Citizens for Kennedy" did not convert many older voters, it did persuade party leaders to court older voters to a greater degree. State and local conferences related to the White House Conference on Aging of 1961 also enlarged the base of popular support for old-age issues. During the 1960s, legislation such as Medicare and the Older Americans Act, and the establishment of the federal Administration on Aging (AOA) and the Senate Special Committee on Aging, served as additional focal points for old-age activism.

It is the White House Conference on Aging of 1971, however, which Pratt cites as the most critical watershed for old-age political influence. After initial resentment by such groups as AARP and the National Council of Senior Citizens (NCSC) at being ignored in conference planning, steps were taken to involve national organizations in the conference, and they eventually came to play a major role. Thus, the conference provided a forum for involvement and cooperation by old-age associations and forced them to clarify and relate their own goals to the broad needs of the elderly. The conferences also heightened the level of old-age awareness among government officials and increased the awareness among older people of the existence and potential benefits of national old-age organizations. Both of these results strengthened the political leverage available to the aged.

Pratt argues that the White House Conference was more than just a "noble experiment" with few consequences. Recommendations were made in many areas—income, employment, health care, housing, nutrition, and so on. While much obviously remains to be done, many of the recommendations have been embodied in subsequent legislation, and old-age associations have achieved greater political visibility and access. For example, AARP has developed both formal and informal channels to Congress and the AOA, and legislative lobbying has become an ongoing feature of this organization, involving full-time staff members. Pratt cites evidence that the NCSC was instrumental in formulating and passing the 1972 Social Security Amendments, involving costly and inflationary measures benefitting the aged.

The senior movement now appears to be in the stage of *institutionalization*, characterized by society-wide organization and coordination, a large base of members and resources, regular political involvement, and growing respectability. Some old-age associations are now quite large. The NRTA/AARP now has over 9 million members, and offers a wide range of services to its members, including insurance, travel, prescription drugs, and lobbying. The

NCSC now has over 3 million members in some 3,000 affiliated senior citizen clubs.

Other groups are smaller, but nonetheless have considerable visibility. The National Council on the Aging (NCOA), established in 1950, is largely a group of subject-matter specialists for planning and consultation. The Gray Panthers, founded in 1970 by Margaret Kuhn, a retired church worker, is a very activist group (Butler, 1975). Disdaining senior citizen clubs as "playpens for the old," Kuhn hoped to "radicalize" the elderly through a coalition of all ages to attack ageism in society. The following exerpt from their 1972 "Rationale for Social Change" indicates the thrust of the group:

> We constitute one of the nation's largest reservoirs of human experience, skill and wisdom, but our resources are grossly wasted and disregarded because of our society's bias against old people. . . . This society tends to think of the aging process as a disease, if not a disaster. . . . Agism, defined as discrimination against persons and groups solely on the basis on chronological age, oppresses both the young and the old, depriving both groups of power and status and the right to control their own lives and destinies. . . . Many of us over 65 are no longer willing to accept this powerless state. We are becoming radicalized and militant about the injustice and inhumanity around us. The revolution of retirees has only begun.

As a final example, the National Caucus on the Black Aged (NCBA) emerged in 1970 to insure greater representation of the needs of elderly blacks at the 1971 White House Conference (Jackson, 1974). It was composed of professionals in the field of aging who were concerned that the Conference "would dilute the critical and special needs of the black and other minority aged, thereby weakening the effects of the total attack on the problems of the elderly of the nation" (Jackson, 1972:22). The NCBA did result in greater black participation at the White House Conference and special sessions concerning the black aged, and it has continued to hold annual conferences, establishing in 1973 the federally funded National Center on Black Aged for research and training.

These old-age organizations have become an established part of the political scene, with access to policy makers. Pratt concludes that:

> . . . senior-citizen leaders have managed to achieve increasing levels of generalized acceptance in Washington. This has come about because their constituents have a well-documented basis

for making claims on society and because the leaders have learned to present their case in a manner appealing to politicians. Congressmen and senators need specialized, technical information as a basis for legislation—senior groups stand ready to provide it; lawmakers want reassurance that by responding positively to the elderly other articulate groups will not charge that their needs have been ignored—senior-group leaders can help them weigh the political costs and rationalize a positive posture; politicians want to be reelected—old age associations, though not able to deliver votes or participate directly in campaigns, do have access to a large home-district reading audience, and a favorable personal reference in one of their house organs presumably can make a decided impression on an election-conscious lawmaker. (Pratt, 1976:198)

These groups are more effective than earlier old-age associations for a number of reasons.

One important factor is greater public and official receptivity to the needs of the aged than in the 1930s and 1940s. Pratt (1976) suggests that the aged have become an "unrivaled minority"—no one wants to be "against" old people. In a sense, the problems of old age have become "fashionable." Nearly 80 percent of the adult population agree that "there is a real need for people to join together to work toward improving the conditions and social status of people over 65," and 37 percent say they would "certainly" or "probably" join such a group (National Council on the Aging, 1975). Talk about actually joining a movement should be viewed with some skepticism, but this does reflect receptive attitude. Official receptivity is symbolized by the establishment of the federal Administration on Aging and the National Institute on Aging.

Old-age associations have also been more effective in taking advantage of this receptivity and access because they are stronger, more viable organizations (Pratt, 1976). For one thing, they have become bureaucratized, therefore less dependent for survival on a charismatic leader (as with the Townsend Movement) and they are less subject to internal divisiveness. This bureaucratization, combined with expanded membership and greater financial resources, makes them more effective in political lobbying. These groups have also been more effective at manipulating symbols to appeal to the public and attract committed members, as can be seen in the growing support of the concept of "institutional ageism," analogous to institutional racism and sexism.

What will be the future of the senior movement? This brings us to the final two stages in Figure 10.1: fragmentation and demise. Ironically, the success of a movement in attaining official adoption of its goals may mean the death of the movement itself. Improvement, even if it is only a surface or symbolic success, leads to a bleeding off of mass support, as people feel that "something is being done" and move on to other concerns. This may lead to rivalry and conflict among the remaining segments of the movement, as in the recent history of the civil rights and feminist movements. The demise of the movement may eventually occur either because it succeeds or because it loses support. In some respects, these have both been the fate of the New Left and the anti-war movement.

That success can dampen the zeal for reform can be seen in the death of groups pushing for pension reform following the passage of Social Security (Pratt, 1976). But this fragmentation and demise is not likely to happen in the near future to current old-age associations. For one thing, the senior movement is not likely to achieve total success in improving the position of older people in modern society. These groups have focused primarily on adjustments to existing programs ("tinkering"), and the very nature of "interest group politics" limits their ability to achieve more fundamental changes in the institutions affecting the lives of the aged (Binstock, 1974). Additional constraints are presented by the complexity of congressional politics and the unwieldly nature of the federal bureaucracy (Pratt, 1976). In other words, access by no means guarantees success. Also, the status of the aged as an "unrivaled minority" may well change in the future, as workers complain about Social Security taxes or other disadvantaged groups complain about "special treatment" of the old.

But even partial success can lessen the mass support for a movement. The relative material status of the aged has been improving, though very slowly in many areas. To retain broad commitment, old-age associations will have to continue to broaden their goals. Institutional ageism might be a profitable theme. In Chapter 7 we noted the impediments created by age stratification to meaningful options in the use of time and community involvement. These structural barriers could become the focus of old-age activism, and are perhaps already reflected in the "revolt" against compulsory retirement.

In the final analysis, however, it is support *by the aged* of old-age politics which will determine the future vitality of the senior movement. Their widespread participation depends upon emerging feelings of *aging group consciousness*, defined as:

> . . . elderly persons who become aware, not merely that they are old, but that they are subject to certain deprivations because they are old, and they react to these deprivations with resentment and with some positive effort to overcome the deprivation.

Further, they are aware that most, or all, older persons are subject to these deprivations, and they feel a positive sense of
identification with other elderly persons for this reason. For
them, the elderly are a group, and not merely a category. (Rose,
1965b:19)

This consciousness contributes to feelings of belonging to a *subculture of the aging*. There is evidence that older people who identify themselves as "old"' are more liberal, particularly on issues
affecting the aged, such as government intervention in inflation
and medical care (Bengtson and Cutler, 1976).

Does this kind of age consciousness exist? Arnold Rose (1965a;
1965b) has argued that a subculture is already developing among
older people in American society, which he attributes to such
recent trends as the growing number and proportion of older persons in the population, better health and education among the
aged, the emergence of "retirement communities," and the emergence of unifying grievances such as the cost of health care. Others
have argued, however, that the aged do not constitute a true
"minority group" partly because they lack widespread feelings of
group identity and readiness to organize on their own behalf
(Streib, 1965; Rosow, 1974). Such feelings depend on more than
just age.

There are understandable barriers to the feelings of group
solidarity represented by aging group consciousness, not the least of
which is resistance to the perception of personal aging because of
the stigma attached to old age. "But old people are also mirrors
for one another, mirrors in which they do not care to see themselves—the marks of old age they behold vex them" (de Beauvoir,
1972:472). The aged are also not accustomed to thinking in terms
of age identification. Other bases of differentiation have been
salient throughout their lives—race, sex, ethnicity, religion, social
class. The older college-educated, middle-class white may feel he
has little in common with the older lower class black. Feelings of
age solidarity are further minimized by contacts with other segments of society through the family or the mass media and the use
of them as reference groups. These "bonds of pluralism" limit
feelings of alienation from the larger society (Seeman, 1975).
Poor health and transportation problems accompanying old age
may also prevent older people from associating with one another.

There are conditions which might foster aging group consciousness, however. What is required is a perception of similarity
with age peers based on past experiences and current common fate.
Proximity, in the form of some type of age-segregated situation,
would allow older people to develop a sense of the situation of age

peers and of their similarities in interests, needs, and attitudes. Hochschild's (1973) study of Merrill Court shows the development of this sense of community in an age-segregated setting (Chapter 9). Membership in such age-segregated residential settings is still not widespread, however, and the development of solidarity typically requires homogeneity on factors other than age. This type of age concentration can result in aging group consciousness, but not as a widespread phenomenon throughout the older population.

Membership in old-age associations may also foster aging group consciousness. One study found that participation in age-graded groups fostered greater activist self-interest based on age—greater desire for political change, more receptivity to appeals for organized political activity, and an increased willingness to engage in activist political behavior (Trela, 1972). Groups like the NCSC and AARP can provide an opportunity for older people to more clearly define their interests and the political problems which confront them collectively, but membership in such groups still accounts for only a small minority of the older population.

As with class consciousness (Laumann and Senter, 1976), aging group consciousness implies certain perceptions by the individual. There must be a recognition by the older person that his life chances depend on the group, rather than just personal resources. This implies an awareness of the age stratification system and the extent to which one's own relative position is determined by it. Thus, the aging group conscious would attribute problems to the age-based system rather than to personal failure. There is little evidence of such feelings among the aged, and stigma combined with cross-generational associations will probably limit its emergence. There is also little evidence that the aged view the age stratification structure as undesirable or changeable, perceptions which Laumann and Senter suggest are related to group consciousness. Indeed, there is evidence that older people attribute greater legitimacy to norms of age-appropriateness than younger people.

Rosow (1974) has argued that the stigma attached to old age will continue to be a barrier to group identification and that, while there seems to be growing concern about the problems of the aged, the age stratification of modern societies will still dictate low status and restricted roles for them. He further argues that the aged will still be substantially disadvantaged, giving them little effective social leverage or political power. Binstock (1974) is also skeptical about the possibility of "senior power," arguing that the aged will continue to be too heterogeneous to form an effective political bloc.

The picture is not all one-sided, however. The aged are not

quiet when it comes to voting, political interest, and the like, and they can be quite "liberal" about programs which would directly benefit them (Aren't we all?). The growing size of the older population, rising interest in gerontology, the visibility of old-age associations, and the ability of some older groups to coalesce despite their internal cleavages all indicate the possibility of continued or growing political activism by the aged. More important, the sources and facilitators of political activism still exist and may increase in the future.

Social movements arise from feelings of alienation, relative deprivation, and status inconsistency. Status inconsistency is the feeling that one's status in one area is out of line with one's status in another area, providing conflicting expectations, instability of the self, and a perception that rewards do not correspond with one's aspirations (Trela, 1976). Combined with feelings of deprivation compared to other groups or to one's expectations, this can create a preference for change in the political order, in the form of either political liberalism or extremism. Feelings of status inconsistency and relative deprivation may occur in older people, particularly those who move from higher middle-aged status to a lower status in old age (loss of authority, financial problems). The Townsend Movement was a response to status loss caused by the Depression and consisted largely of professionals, businessmen, and skilled workers who had been driven into the ranks of the deprived aged (Trela, 1976). We have also seen that the aged often experience heightened alienation, particularly political powerlessness, which can lead to political activism. Members of one old age movement, the McLain Movement, tended to feel dissatisfied and distrustful (Pinner, Jacobs, and Selznick, 1959).

Paradoxically, these feelings of status inconsistency and alienation may rise as we alleviate some of the most dire economic and medical problems of older people. Betterment of individual status may heighten feelings that the position of older people *as a group* is unjust. Thus, institutional ageism may be more pronounced for older people who are better off individually, but still treated as "just another old person." The "young-old" in particular can be expected to push for more meaningful involvement in community life (Neugarten, 1974).

It must be recognized, however, that status inconsistency and alienation present only a *potential* for political mobilization which may not be realized. Most older people do not see the political system as unresponsive or illegitimate, despite increases in alienation with age. Their relative satisfaction with political affairs, combined with well-established norms of self-reliance and a reluctance to burden other generations, limits the development of political activism. Additionally, downward mobility experienced by the aged does not necessarily result in generalized alienation or distrust. Tissue (1970) found that older recipients of public assistance from middle-class backgrounds were dissatisfied with their own situations, but had not lost faith in the fairness of the larger social order. Thus, rather than political activism, status inconsistency and relative deprivation may result in stress-related psychological problems or social withdrawal (disengagement) (Trela, 1976).

Studies of student activism suggest that alienation in itself is also not enough to create political activism but that high perceived powerlessness in relation to the *system* must be combined with a low sense of *personal* powerlessness (Seeman, 1975). Older people tend to be more fatalistic than young people, however, and if aging results in lower self-esteem, this may also lessen feelings of personal efficacy (Ragan and Dowd, 1974). Other potential psychological accompaniments of aging, such as disengagement, conservatism, and interiority, would also limit activism, and the lack of political efficacy is compounded by low income and poor health. In addition, minority-group elderly, such as Mexican-Americans (Torres-Gil and Becerra, 1977), have encountered a long history of intimidating barriers to political participation.

But, since many of these psychological traits represent cohort differences rather than the effects of aging, feelings of political efficacy should be higher among older people in the future. Future older people will be better equipped for effective political involvement, because of higher levels of education, and more accepting of protest politics (Table 10.3). If such attitudes reflect a political "generation," they will be carried throughout the life cycle, and there is some indication that this may occur. A followup of former

Table 10.3. Percent approving "non-conventional" political participation, by age

Percent approving of	Age	
	18–35	60+
Protest politics	26.4	10.2
Civil disobedience	22.0	9.3
Sit-ins	10.8	3.2

Data are from the University of Michigan Center for Political Studies 1972 national presidential election survey.
Source: Neal Cutler and John Schmidhauser, "Age and political behavior," in Diana Woodruff and James Birren (eds.), *Aging: Scientific Perspectives and Social Issues*, New York: D. Van Nostrand Company, 1975, p. 402. Reprinted by permission.

civil rights activists found that they had neither "matured out" of their activism nor "dropped out" because of disillusionment (Fendrich, 1974). They were concentrated in knowledge and human service industries and in change-oriented voluntary associations, and they were still committed to radical political and economic change.

Ragan and Dowd (1974) point to other developments which might enhance future political activism by the aged. Increased involvement in age-graded voluntary associations and lobbying groups such as AARP may increase feelings of political efficacy to combine with subjective dissatisfaction and political distrust. Area Agencies on Aging are supposed to encourage political participation by older people in the development of services. Increased attention by the media to the problems of older people also contributes to an ideological basis for political movements.

So there is a *potential* for aging group consciousness and political activism. The very fact that societies are age-stratified is an objective basis for age consciousness, since the relative position and status of the aged are structurally determined. Since older people already constitute about 15 percent of eligible voters and tend to vote regularly, they are a potential "swing" vote in close elections. It is true that "there is no evidence to indicate that aging-based interest appeals can swing a bloc of older persons' votes from one party or candidate to another" (Binstock, 1974:202–203). But objective reality may be less important than the perceptions of political leaders. One indication of the perceived importance of older voters is the appearance of the National Council of Senior Citizens on the "enemies list" of the Nixon administration.

There is no reason to believe that "senior power" can ever occupy a position of overriding political importance, that older voters will polarize around a few issues, or even that the aged can achieve the status of organized labor or organized business. The interests and needs of older people will continue to be seen as one set of problems among many others. But there is also no reason to expect that old-age activism will fragment and die out in the foreseeable future. National old-age associations are now well-established on the political scene, and are both visible and accessible. Support from older masses may well increase among future cohorts, and people will continue to participate in old-age social movements for a variety of reasons: their friends belong, they agree with the group's purposes, they see the movement as a way to achieve their own goals, they can utilize their political expertise, or they simply have time on their hands (Ragan and Dowd, 1974). The aged will represent an important force in pressing for political and social change. Whether they will be effective in pursuing their goals and interests depends on many things, including receptivity from the larger society and competition with other groups making claims, and predictions are fraught with uncertainty.

The Consequences of Aging Group Consciousness

One obvious potential consequence of aging group consciousness, and political activism based on it, is improvement of the position of older people in society. Even if this does not happen, however, there are benefits to be derived from age consciousness and involvement in what might be considered a subculture of the aging. Part of our self-image comes from the groups we identify with.

> The groups to which a person belongs serve as primary determiners of his self-esteem. To a considerable extent, personal feelings of worth depend on social evaluations of the groups with which a person is identified. Self-hatred and feelings of worthlessness tend to arise from membership in underprivileged or outcast groups. (Cartwright, 1950:440)

Given the devalued status of old age in modern societies, it is not surprising that the aged might resist identifying with other older people, in the same way that the mentally retarded (Edgerton, 1967) and the blind (Strauss, 1968) often resist identification with similar stigmatized others. Yet we have seen in earlier discussions (notably Chapters 4 and 5) some of the identity problems which may arise in old age, which association with age peers may help to handle.

A subculture, such as the subculture of the aging, represents the development of a separate cultural system, a mutual sharing of perceived norms which may partially accept, deny, or construct opposites to the norms of a larger culture (Wolfgang and Ferracuti, 1967). It develops as a response to situations or problems shared by interacting persons. In this sense, subcultures may be defined as "a set of acquired patterns of conduct, a way of life that provides its participants with adaptive techniques to deal with a set of recurring problems" (Sarbin, 1970:31).

Stigmatization and isolation of the aged, as a reflection of their devalued status in the modern stratification system, creates shared problems of adjustment. It is the perception of these shared problems which we have called aging group consciousness. In this sense, a subculture of the aging is conceptually similar to various "deviant" subcultures, such as delinquent gangs (Cohen, 1955) and the homosexual subculture (Hooker, 1966), which are attempts by stigmatized individuals to adjust to shared problems caused by "conventional" society's reaction to their activities or attributes.

Such deviant subcultures fulfill three primary functions for their members, and a subculture for older people might serve similar functions.

First, deviant subcultures allow individuals to pursue deviant activities with less interference, by providing "facilitating" places, hardware, and skills (Lofland, 1969). While the aged are not usually thought of as "deviant" in this sense, we have seen in Chapter 9 that age-segregated settings may allow the aged to "let their hair down" more freely or to pursue a leisure career without guilt.

Reactions to deviants often result in their exclusion from normal roles and activities, perhaps because they are considered "tainted" or "unpleasant" in other ways (Becker, 1963; Goffman, 1963). Therefore, a second function of deviant subcultures is to reduce the marginality and isolation felt by those who are excluded from conventional groups. This will be important for the aged to the extent that society disengages *from* them.

The third function of deviant subcultures is perhaps most important, since it relates to self-concept. Reference groups and subcultures act as mediators of culture, affecting our attitudes (including self-attitudes) through the evaluative information they provide about such cognitive categories as "homosexual," "blind person," or "old person" (Woelfel and Haller, 1971). Meanings available for stigmatized identities in the conventional culture are largely negative and can result in self-derogation. This is true for the aged, whose self-esteem may be lowered if they accept negative stereotypes about old age. A subculture of the aging might provide a more positive definition of "old person" and meaningful roles within which self-worth can be validated.

Old age can be a difficult turning point in personal identity because of the stigma attached to it and the disruptive changes in roles and relationships which may accompany it. This is compounded by the breakdown of socializing processes (Rosow, 1974), particularly the lack of reference groups which could provide new self-conceptions and roles. According to Cavan (1962), satisfying adjustment in old age requires culturally approved positive values for old age, acceptance and respect of those values by society and the specific groups to which the aging individual belongs, and new roles for the expression of the new self-image. This could be provided by the age peer group in a subculture of the aging. While Rosow (1974) points out that the peer group might simply allow collective denial of aging, it can also be a major socializing influence, because of the basic functions which peer groups can provide: group support, new memberships to replace those which have been lost, new roles and role models, a *positive* reference group, insulation from stigma, and new self-images. As an example, role models like Albert Schweitzer, Bob Hope, or Grandpa Walton are too exceptional to be useful to the average older person, but one's peers can provide *real*, personal role models of successful aging.

A study by the author attempted to measure aging group consciousness and its consequences for self-esteem (Ward, 1977). Responses to several questions were combined to indicate the degree of aging group consciousness felt by the individual. Among those who considered themselves "elderly," aging group consciousness was related to significantly higher self-esteem, but not for those who considered themselves "middle-aged." This was apparently a reflection of reference group or comparison processes. Persons who lack aging group consciousness still view the middle-aged as their reference group, and this group is likely to be better off in health, income, and other aspects. When people compare themselves with others who are better off, feelings of relative deprivation and self-derogation are likely to result (Parker and Kleiner, 1968). With aging group consciousness, one's relative standing in a more similar comparison group appears more advantageous and self-esteem can be maintained.

Summary

Age stratification creates the potential for age conflict by making age a basis for structured social inequality. This conflict may be reduced by age-heterogeneous group ties and the inevitability of "age mobility," and will be more pronounced for "ideal" than for "material" issues. Modern societies may heighten generational separation and create age-based material issues, however, which could exacerbate age conflict.

Old age is not a time of political quiescence. The aged continue to vote, are interested in politics, and often are part of the political leadership. The political attitudes of older people do not fit simplistic stereotypes of conservatism. They are more likely to be Republicans, but this may be a cohort phenomenon. The aged are generally more conservative than younger people, but they can be liberal on policies which would benefit them and have followed recent trends toward liberalism in the larger society (though at a slower rate). There are a number of reasons conservatism might increase with age—role change, accumulation of experience, developmental stake—but such age differences may also reflect cohort effects. There are reasons to expect heightened feelings of alienation among both the young and the old. The aged appear to feel greater powerlessness and meaninglessness, but less social isolation and self-estrangement, and more alienation politically than in the family. Age trends in both conservatism and alienation are far from clear-cut, however.

Much has been made of the "generation gap" in modern societies. This could reflect either the generational consciousness of new cohorts or the natural rebelliousness of developing youth. While such a gap is perceived by most people, it does not appear to be an extensive one, at least within families.

The senior movement has gone through a long history of incipiency and coalescence, culminating in the White House Conference on Aging of 1971. Since then, old-age associations have enjoyed a good deal of political visibility and access, and have been effective in shaping some of the policies directed at the aged. The future of old-age activism depends on many things: official adoption of their goals, resistance from other groups, and their breadth of appeal. Political consciousness within the older population has an uncertain future. Barriers such as the perceived stigma of old age, the diversity within the older population, continuing contracts with other segments of society, and limited mobility will continue to exist, and alienation and status inconsistency do not inevitably result in political activism. But future cohorts of older people are likely to have greater feelings of political efficacy, because of their greater education and history of activism. Thus, the aged represent a potentially important political force.

To the extent that it represents a subculture of the aging, aging group consciousness may yield psychological benefits for the aged. Age peers represent an important reference group, providing role models, social supports, and more favorable images of aging. Thus, other older persons represent a positive factor in shaping self-esteem.

References

Abramson, Paul
    1975   Generational Change in American Politics. Lexington, Mass.:
            Lexington Books.
Becker, Howard
    1963   Outsiders: Studies in the Sociology of Deviance. New
            York: The Free Press.
Bengtson, Vern
    1970   "The generation gap: A review and typology of social-
            psychological perspectives." Youth and Society 2: 7–32.
    1971   "Inter-age perceptions and the generation gap." The
            Gerontologist 11: 85–89.

Bengtson, Vern and Neal Cutler
   1976   "Generations and intergenerational relations: Perspectives
           on age groups and social change." In Ethel Shanas and
           Robert Binstock (eds.). Handbook of Aging and the Social
           Sciences. New York: Van Nostrand Reinhold.
Bengtson, Vern, Michael Furlong, and Robert Laufer
   1974   "Time, aging, and the continuity of social structure: Themes
           and issues in generational analyses." Journal of Social
           Issues 30: 1–30.
Bengtson, Vern and Joseph Kuypers
   1971   "Generational difference and the developmental stake."
           Aging and Human Development 2: 249–60.
Bengtson, Vern and Mary Lovejoy
   1973   "Values, personality, and social structure: An intergenera-
           tional analysis." American Behavioral Scientist 16: 880–912.
Binstock, Robert
   1974   "Aging and the future of American politics." In Frederick
           Eisele (ed.). Political Consequences of Aging. Annals of
           the American Academy of Political and Social Science
           415: 199–212.
Braungart, Richard
   1974   "The sociology of generations and student politics: A
           comparison of the functionalist and generational unit
           models." Journal of Social Issues 30: 31–54.
Broder, David
   1973   "The old: Benefits put a dangerous drain on U.S. funds."
           Los Angeles Times, February 1.
Butler, Robert
   1975   Why Survive?: Being Old in America. New York:
           Harper & Row.
Cain, Leonard
   1974   "Political factors in the emerging legal status of the elderly."
           In Frederick Eisele (ed.). Political Consequences of Aging.
           Annals of the American Academy of Political and Social
           Science 415: 70–79.
   1975   "The young and the old: Coalition or conflict ahead?"
           American Behavioral Scientist 19: 166–175.
Campbell, Angus
   1971   "Politics through the life cycle." The Gerontologist 11:
           112–17.
Cartwright, Dorwin
   1950   "Emotional dimensions of group life." In Martin Reymart
           (ed.). Feelings and Emotions. New York: McGraw-Hill.
Cavan, Ruth
   1962   "Self and role in adjustment during old age." In Arnold
           Rose (ed.). Human Behavior and Social Processes. Boston:
           Houghton Mifflin.

Cohen, Albert
1955 Delinquent Boys: The Culture of the Gang. Glencoe,
Ill.: The Free Press.
Collins, Randall
1975 Conflict Sociology. New York: Academic Press.
Cowgill, Donald
1974 "Aging and modernization: A revision of the theory." In
Jaber Gubrium (ed.). Late Life: Communities and Environmental Policies. Springfield, Ill.: Charles C Thomas.
Cutler, Neal
1969 "Generation, maturation, and party affiliation: A cohort
analysis." Public Opinion Quarterly 33: 583–88.
Cutler, Neal and Vern Bengtson
1974 "Age and political alienation: Maturation, generation, and
period effects." In Frederick Eisele (ed.). Political Consequences of Aging. Annals of the American Academy of
Political and Social Science 415: 160–75.
Cutler, Neal and John Schmidhauser
1975 "Age and political behavior." In Diana Woodruff and
James Birren (eds.). Aging: Scientific Perspectives and Social
Issues. New York: D. Van Nostrand.
de Beauvoir, Simone
1972 The Coming of Age. New York: Putnam's Sons.
Edgerton, Robert
1967 The Cloak of Competence. Berkeley: University of
California Press.
Eisenstadt, S. N.
1965 From Generation to Generation. Glencoe, Ill.: The Free
Press.
Fendrich, James
1974 "Activists ten years later: A test of generational unit
continuity." Journal of Social Issues 30: 95–118.
Fischer, David
1977 Growing Old in America. New York: Oxford University
Press.
Foner, Anne
1972 "The polity." In Matilda Riley, Marilyn Johnson, and Anne
Foner (eds.). Aging and Society. Volume 3: A Sociology
of Age Stratification. New York: Russell Sage.
1974 "Age stratification and age conflict in political life."
American Sociological Review 39: 187–96.
Glenn, Norval
1969 "Aging, disengagement, and opinionation." Public Opinion
Quarterly 33: 17–33.
1974 "Aging and conservatism." In Frederick Eisele (ed.). Annals
of the American Academy of Political and Social Science
415: 176–86.
Goffman, Erving
1963 Stigma: Notes on the Management of Spoiled Identity.
Englewood Cliffs, N.J.: Prentice-Hall.

Hill, Reuben
   1970   Family Development in Three Generations. Cambridge,
          Mass.: Schenkman.
Hochschild, Arlie
   1973   The Unexpected Community. Englewood Cliffs, N.J.:
          Prentice-Hall.
Holtzman, Abraham
   1963   The Townsend Movement: A Political Study. New York:
          Basic Books.
Hooken, Evelyn
   1966   "The homosexual community." In James Palmer and
          Michael Goldstein (eds.). Perspectives in Psycho-Pathology.
          New York: Oxford University Press.
Hudson, Robert and Robert Binstock
   1976   "Political systems and aging." In Robert Binstock and
          Ethel Shanas (eds.). Handbook of Aging and the Social
          Sciences. New York: Van Nostrand Reinhold.
Jackson, Hobart
   1972   "The White House Conference on Aging and black aged."
          In Jacquelyne Jackson (ed.). Proceedings of Research
          Conference on Minority Group Aged in the South. Durham,
          N.C.: Duke University Center for the Study of Aging.
Jackson, Jacquelyne
   1974   "NCBA, black aged and politics." In Frederick Eisele
          (ed.). Political Consequences of Aging. Annals of the
          American Academy of Political and Social Science 415:
          138–59.
Laumann, Edward and Richard Senter
   1976   "Subjective social distance, occupational stratification,
          and forms of status and class consciousness: A cross-national
          replication and extension." American Journal of Sociology
          81: 1304–38.
Lehman, H. C.
   1953   Age and Achievement. Princeton, N.J.: Princeton University
          Press.
Lofland, John
   1969   Deviance and Identity. Englewood Cliffs, N.J.:
          Prentice-Hall.
Mannheim, Karl
   1952   "The problem of generations." In Karl Mannheim (ed.).
          Essays on the Sociology of Knowledge. New York: Oxford
          University Press.
Martin, William, Vern Bengtson, and Alan Acock
   1974   "Alienation and age: A context-specific approach." Social
          Forces 53: 266–74.
Mauss, Armand
   1975   Social Problems as Social Movements. Philadelphia:
          J. B. Lippincott.

National Council on the Aging
   1975   The Myth and Reality of Aging in America. Washington,
           D.C.
Neugarten, Bernice
   1974   "Age groups in American society and the rise of the young-
           old." In Frederick Eisele (ed.). Political Consequences of
           Aging. Annals of the American Academy of Political and
           Social Science 415: 187–98.
Parker, Seymour and Robert Kleiner
   1968   "Reference group behavior and mental disorder." In
           Herbert Hyman and Eleanor Singer (eds.). Readings in
           Reference Group Theory and Research. New York:
           The Free Press.
Parsons, Talcott
   1963   "Youth in the context of American society." In Erik
           Erikson (ed.). Youth: Change and Challenge. New York:
           Basic Books.
Pinner, Frank, Paul Jacobs, and Philip Selznick
   1959   Old Age and Political Behavior. Berkeley: University
           of California Press.
Pratt, Henry
   1976   The Gray Lobby. Chicago: University of Chicago Press.
Ragan, Pauline
   1976   "Another look at the politicizing of old age: Can we expect
           a backlash effect?" Paper presented at the Annual Meeting
           of the Society for the Study of Social Problems, New York.
Ragan, Pauline and James Dowd
   1974   "The emerging political consciousness of the aged: A
           generational interpretation." Journal of Social Issues 30:
           137–58.
Riley, Matilda and Anne Foner
   1968   Aging and Society. Volume 1: An Inventory of Research
           Findings. New York: Russell Sage.
Rose, Arnold
   1965a "The subculture of aging: A framework for research in
           social gerontology." In Arnold Rose and Warren Peterson
           (eds.). Older People and Their Social World. Philadelphia:
           F. A. Davis.
   1965b "Group consciousness among the aging." In Arnold Rose
           and Warren Peterson (eds.). Older People and Their Social
           World. Philadelphia: F. A. Davis.
Rosow, Irving
   1974   Socialization to Old Age. Berkeley: University of California
           Press.
Ryder, Norman
   1965   "The cohort as a concept in the study of social change."
           American Sociological Review 30: 843–61.
Sarbin, Theodore
   1970   "The culture of poverty, social identity, and cognitive out-

comes." In Vernon Allen (ed.). Psychological Factors in Poverty. Chicago: Markham.

Seeman, Melvin
1972   "Alienation and engagement." In A. Campbell and P. Converse (eds.). The Human Meaning of Social Change. New York: Russell Sage.
1975   "Alienation studies." Annual Review of Sociology. Volume 1. Palo Alto, Calif.: Annual Reviews.

Strauss, Helen
1968   "Reference group and social comparison processes among the totally blind." In Herbert Hyman and Eleanor Singer (eds.). Readings in Reference Group Theory and Research. New York: The Free Press.

Streib, Gordon
1965   "Are the aged a minority group?" In Alvin Gouldner and S. M. Miller (eds.). Applied Sociology. Glencoe, Ill.: The Free Press.

Thomas, L. Eugene
1974   "Generational discontinuity in beliefs: An exploration of the generation gap." Journal of Social Issues 30: 1–22.

Tissue, Thomas
1970   "Downward mobility in old age." Social Problems 18: 67–77.

Torres-Gil, Fernando, and Rosina Becerra
1977   "The political behavior of the Mexican-American elderly." The Gerontologist 17: 392–99.

Trela, James
1972   "Age structure of voluntary associations and political self-interest among the aged." Sociological Quarterly 13: 244–52.
1976   "Status inconsistency and political action in old age." In Jaber Gubrium (ed.). Time, Roles, and Self in Old Age. New York: Human Sciences Press.

Turk, Herman, Joel Smith, and Howard Myers
1966   "Understanding local political behavior: The role of the older citizen." In Ida Simpson and John McKinney (eds.). Social Aspects of Aging. Durham, N.C.: Duke University Press.

U.S. Bureau of the Census
1965   "Voter participation in the national election, November, 1964." Current Population Reports. Series P-20, No. 143. Washington, D.C.: U.S. Government Printing Office.
1973   "Voting and registration in the election of November 1972." Current Population Reports. Series P-20, No. 253. Washington, D.C.: U.S. Government Printing Office.

Ward, Russell
1977   "Aging group consciousness: Implications in an older sample." Sociology and Social Research 61: 496–519.

Woelfel, Joseph and Archibald Haller
1971   "Significant others, the self-reflexive act and the attitude

formation process." American Sociological Review 36: 74–87.

Wolfgang, Marvin and Franco Ferracuti
1967 The Subculture of Violence. London: Tavistock.

Youmans, E. Grant
1973 "Age stratification and value orientations." Aging and Human Development 4: 53–65.

11

Services for Older People

~~~~~~~~~~~~~~~~~~~~~~~~~~~~~~~~~~~~

Throughout this book we have tried to strike a balance between recognizing the problems experienced by the aging and avoiding a stereotyped exaggeration of those problems. This chapter will necessarily focus more heavily on the former, discussing service needs, delivery, and utilization, however, many older people have no need, or minimal need, for these kinds of services. In addition, some older people are "over-serviced," that is, institutionalized because of a lack of sufficient alternatives which could support them in the community. With this note of caution, this chapter will cover two broad areas of concern. First, what institutional services are required by the aged, how are they organized, and what are the effects of institutionalization on the older individual? Second, what community-based services are available (or should be available), and what factors affect their development, delivery, and use?

The most basic theme of this book has been that the nature of aging is shaped by its social context, a critical part of which is the network of services made available to the aging individual. A distinction must be made between *problems* and *handicaps*. For example, being confined to a wheelchair is certainly a problem, but the extent to which it is a handicap depends on people's willingness to hire such persons, the presence of architectural barriers such as stairs (instead of ramps), and other aspects of the "environment." By providing or failing to provide support, societal services affect the extent to which aging handicaps the individual and lowers the quality of his life.

Older people's needs for services also relate to many of the issues discussed in earlier chapters. The longevity characteristic of modern societies means that a greater part of the resources must be allocated to support an older population. This increase in the old-age dependency ratio may then become a political issue. The perceived needs of the elderly also affect their relative status by shaping stereotypes and fears attached to aging. It is probably true, for example, that most younger people exaggerate the need for nursing homes, and this colors their overall image of the aged.

Institutionalization of the Aged

The likelihood of living in an institutional setting increases with age, as indicated in Table 11.1. Only a relatively small minority of the aged are institutionalized, however—less than 5 percent of those over 65, and less than 10 percent of those over 75. Such statistics are somewhat misleading, since approximately one of every five older persons will *at some time in his life* reside in an institution (Palmore, 1976). But the fact remains that it is unusual, even rare, for an older person to be in an institution such as a nursing home. At all ages, women are more likely than men to be institutionalized. Whites are more likely to reside in nursing and personal care homes, while nonwhites are more likely to be in mental hospitals, which may simply reflect a greater difficulty for nonwhites in finding nursing homes which will accept them.

The proportion residing in old age institutions varies by state, reflecting differences in the characteristics of the older population (Manard, Kart, and van Gils, 1975). "Retirement states," which attract more able and mobile elderly, have lower proportions—for example, 1.8 percent in Arizona, and 2.0 percent in Florida. States in which the aged are less mobile have higher rates—for example, 7.5 percent in South Dakota, and 7.2 percent in Minnesota. The institutionalized population is an older one (median age is about 81), and 85 percent of those who enter nursing homes die there

Table 11.1.   Rate of institutionalization per 1,000 in nursing and personal care homes, by age, sex, and race: 1969

	Total	Male	Female	White	Nonwhite
All ages 20+	6.5	4.2	8.5	6.9	2.7
20–64	0.9	0.9	0.9	0.9	0.8
65–74	11.6	9.9	12.9	11.7	9.6
75–84	51.7	36.0	62.3	54.1	22.9
85+	203.2	130.8	247.6	221.9	52.4

Source: U.S. Public Health Service, 1974:7.

(Butler, 1975). The average stay is only about one year, and one-third of those who enter die within the first year (Butler, 1975).

There are many types of institutions which may house the aged, including chronic disease hospitals (e.g., tuberculosis hospitals) and mental hospitals. Institutions for the aged date back at least to the Gerontochia established by the Christian church in the third and fourth centuries, but the more typical pattern was to house them in "poor houses" or "work houses," along with the sick, mentally ill, destitute, and criminal. Because of this, institutionalization of the aged came to be viewed as the penalty for "improvident or dissolute life" (Townsend, 1964:15). Such attitudes linger on, contributing to a stigma attached to nursing-home residence.

In recent years, the aged have increasingly been housed in specifically old-age institutions: nursing homes, rest homes, and homes for the aged. From 1960 to 1970, the number of older persons residing in old-age institutions increased by 105 percent (Manard, Kart, and van Gils, 1975). This reflects a number of trends: an increase in the older population, changes in family living arrangements, and changes in federal financing programs (particularly Medicare and Medicaid). It also reflects an increased willingness by nursing homes to accept a greater variety of patients. A 1968 survey of old-age institutions found that, as a "general rule," 52.6 percent would accept mentally retarded patients, 48.7 percent would accept psychiatric transfers, and 24.3 percent would accept mentally ill patients (Manard, Kart, and van Gils, 1975).

The share of the institutionalized older population residing in mental hospitals declined from 24 percent to 10 percent between 1940 and 1970. To a great extent this is a result of the revolution in psychiatric care accompanying the use of tranquilizing drugs, which has produced a general deemphasis of hospitalization for mental disorders. This was supposed to bring more humane and accessible treatment to the mentally impaired, while maintaining their community ties, but for the aged it has often meant substitution of a nursing home for a mental hospital, since there are few community services available to "senile" older people (Frankfather, 1977). It has been estimated that since 1967 there have been more mentally ill elderly in nursing homes than in all other types of psychiatric facilities (Shanas and Maddox, 1976). There has been little study of the effects of this transfer, and Butler (1975) has argued that it may be ill-advised in many cases. As we shall see in a later section, relocation itself carries many hazards. In addition, the needs of the aged with mental disorders are ignored and neglected because the facilities and staff of nursing homes may be ill-equipped to meet them.

Processes Leading to Institutionalization

One obvious reason for entering a nursing home is the presence of physical problems such as chronic heart failure or strokes which make living in the community impossible. But many nursing-home residents could benefit from supportive services in the community and are forced into institutions because of the lack of such alternatives. There are also many older people whose physical or psychological problems are equal to or worse than those of institutional residents, but who are nevertheless able to remain in the community. In his discussion of mental hospitals, Erving Goffman (1961) has suggested that mental patients suffer from "contingencies" as much as from mental illness. Persons may enter or leave mental hospitals not because they are necessarily "sicker" than those on the outside or are cured, but because of their social class, marital status, family ties, and other nonmedical factors.[1] Similar processes operate with the elderly. Older persons who enter institutions are more likely to have no or few children, be single or widowed, and be living alone or with nonrelatives prior to entry (Riley and Foner, 1968; Manard, Kart, and van Gils, 1975; Palmore, 1976).

What these findings suggest is the necessity of a balance between need for support and available networks *in the community* which can provide support. As losses occur, the aged try a variety of alternatives, including living with family, and typically display high residential mobility prior to entrance into a nursing home. Thus, the institution is often a last resort after other avenues have been exhausted or when they are not available. Premature admission to an institution results from a lack of social or financial supports in the community. In effect, socioeconomic needs are met with a health care "solution."

The stereotype that older people are in nursing homes because they have been rejected or forgotten by their families has little basis in fact (Shanas and Maddox, 1976). Many lack such support because they have never married, have no children, or have few children nearby. In some cases, living with family may create severe friction, as in the following example from an English study.

> Mrs. Mooney, a widow of 82 renowned for her belligerent language, formerly lived with her married daughter and family. "My daughter's husband said to me, 'You're nowt but an old nag,' and I goes up to him and I says, 'If I'm an old nag, it's thee has made me one, with coming to look after thy wife and looking after thy children. You were fain to run to me when thy

---

[1] For a discussion of social factors in mental hospitalization, see Spitzer and Denzin (1968).

wife were ready to be confined. Put that in your pipe and smoke it.' He said, 'It's time you went,' and I gave him such a one across his chops, and I says 'Take that.' I thought there'd be nowt left of me if I stopped with that lot. My daughter said she'd found a nice place for me." Mrs. Mooney is very infirm, is anaemic and incontinent, and can scarcely walk. She had been living in a small house not only with her married daughter and son-in-law but with an unmarried daughter and five grandchildren. The case file reports that her daughter was ill with a "nervous complaint." (Townsend, 1965: 184)

This hardly sounds like an ideal living situation! In other cases, the family support system may break down because the family can no longer manage the burdens involved. Loss of a supportive relationship may trigger entry into a nursing home:

In many personal accounts the sudden loss of a supporting relative was plainly critical. A wife died or went into a hospital. A son was killed in an accident. A daughter emigrated to Canada with her husband and family. A widowed sister became more infirm and moved to live with her married children. A niece was no longer able to live with her aunt because she took a residential nursing appointment. The death or the sudden illness of close relatives were the most common events precipitating admission. (Townsend, 1965: 176)

Those who are supported in the community may reach a stage where there is no alternative to institutionalization. On the other hand, those who are most isolated may not come to the attention of social welfare agencies until their problems are too advanced for community services. Thus, while some families clearly do reject or forget their aged members, a deterioration in the balance between need and available community supports appears to be the primary precipitant to institutionalization.

The "Political Economy" of Nursing Homes

The past 15 years have seen a virtual explosion in the availability of nursing homes; for example, the number of nursing-home beds tripled from 1960 to 1970 (Manard, Kart, and van Gils, 1975). By 1974, there were 23,000 nursing homes in the United States, housing over 1 million older persons (Butler and Lewis, 1977). The reason for the rise of nursing home industry is simple: profits were made possible by federal financing of nursing-home care, particularly with the enactment of the Medicare and Medicaid programs in 1965. *Medicare* provides national health insurance for the elderly through the Social Security program and finances up to 100 days in a "skilled nursing facility" for posthospitalization care. Medicaid, which is financed jointly by federal and state governments, provides medical insurance for the indigent (of all ages), including unlimited nursing-home benefits for those who qualify (eligibility rules vary by state). By 1974, nearly 60 percent of the $7.5 billion income of the nursing-home industry came from Medicare and Medicaid alone (Butler and Lewis, 1977). This financing has increased the number of nursing homes run for profit. By 1974, 75 percent of all nursing homes were proprietary (private commercial ownership), as opposed to nonprofit homes run by the government or various voluntary groups (such as churches). This period has even seen the emergence of nursing-home chains.

Government financing in nursing-home care is essential, given the often low income of older persons and the often catastrophic expenses related to such care. The average monthly charge for nursing-home care in 1974 was $479, and 71 percent charged over $500 (U.S. Public Health Service, 1975). In a study of a sample of Massachusetts nursing homes conducted in 1973, the monthly charge for private residents ranged from $660 to $1,650, with a median of $840 (Manard, Kart, and van Gils, 1975); for publicly assisted residents, average monthly costs ranged from $434 to $741, with a median of $613. The involvement of the government has been a mixed blessing, however.

There are various types of nursing homes, related to level of care provided and certification under Medicare and Medicaid. Extended care facilities (ECF), certified for Medicare, provide extensive professional nursing and supportive staffs. Skilled nursing facilities (SNF), originally certified only for Medicaid but now also for Medicare, provide less extensive services. Intermediate care facilities (ICF), certified for Medicaid, provide an even less extensive range of services (such as personal hygiene, administration of medication) as a cheaper alternative, though they must have at least one licensed practical nurse (LPN), or an "equivalent," on full-time duty during the day shift. Other nursing homes may be called "personal care homes," "foster care homes," and the like. Of the nursing homes in existence in 1974, 26.8 percent were certified for both Medicare and Medicaid, 50.3 percent only for Medicaid (as either SNF or ICF), and the remaining 22.9 percent for neither (U.S. Public Health Service, 1975). Those which are certified tend to be larger, cost more, and have higher staff-to-patient ratios.

Nursing Home Exposés

This section is not meant to imply that all nursing homes, or perhaps even most, are "bad" places. Institutions can have a beneficial impact, and many useful studies and programs have emerged from nursing homes. Nevertheless, there is sufficient evidence from various exposés of the nursing-home industry to indicate the existence of a number of "horror stories" connected with nursing-home care. Townsend's (1964) review of institutional care in Great Britain was one of the first of these, citing many gross inequities and shortcomings among residential facilities for the aged. Later studies in the United States echoed these problems (in particular, see Townsend, 1971; Butler, 1975; Mendelson, 1975). Some of the practices found in nursing homes represent abuse of the public, through fraud and corruption. More serious and tragic, however, are the frauds and abuses perpetrated on residents of nursing homes.

Many of these abuses stem from the structure of financial arrangements surrounding nursing homes. Two mechanisms have been used to finance nursing-home care (Mendelson and Hapgood, 1974). With the *flat-rate* method, until recently used by some states for Medicaid, nursing homes receive a set fee per patient per day. Profits could be increased by cutting the cost of services, thereby catching the patient in the middle of a financial squeeze. Mendelson (1975) cites the example of a nursing home in Chicago which fed patients on an average of 78 cents per day. Corners can also be cut in hiring staff, failing to meet building requirements, and the like. Fortunately, as of 1977 both Medicaid and Medicare are based on *cost-plus* financing, whereby nursing homes are reimbursed for their actual costs, plus a "reasonable" profit. This removes one incentive for patient abuse, but opens the doors for the reporting of inflated costs and charging for services never rendered. Studies have reported "kickback" arrangements between nursing homes and pharmacists or laboratories to increase profits from such "ancillary" services.

> Sometimes the kickback is paid in cash, other times in more unusual ways: buying a car for the nursing home operator or paying his way on his vacation. One pharmacy paid two nursing homes $4,400 a year supposedly to maintain "drug supply rooms": the rooms turned out to be broom closets. The presence of those closets permitted the homes to obtain a higher rate from Medicare on the grounds that they were offering an extra service. To speed their profitable transactions, one nursing home has a direct phone line to its favored pharmacy. (Mendelson, 1975: 178)

Medicaid patients (or, rather, the government) may be charged more for services than other patients, or be charged for services they have not received. Mendelson (1975) cites the case of 11 dentists who collected $1 million in one year from Medicaid. Mendelson and others have also reported the occurrence of "gang visits" to nursing homes by physicians who "cruise" quickly through the home and charge each patient for an individual visit.

> The GAO, in its Ohio investigation, found not a few examples of such gang visits. One doctor billed the government for 71 patient visits in a single day and 56 on another; he charged the taxpayers for a total of 960 patient visits in one three-month period. Another doctor billed for 487 visits to patients in a six-teen-day period, including 90 on one day and 86 on another. A podiatrist put in for 750 visits, including 32 on one Sunday. All these doctors were also handling their usual load of non-Medicaid patients. (Mendelson, 1975: 44)

Some of the abuses described in these studies involve manipulation of ownership or mortgages, to artificially increase apparent nursing-home costs, in order to hide high profits (Mendelson and Hapgood, 1974). One such technique is "pyramiding," where heavy mortgages are taken out on nursing homes to finance other business enterprises. These manipulations allow nursing-home owners to get the most revenue and pay the least taxes, all the while complaining that they cannot make a profit.

The most serious abuses, however, are those which directly affect quality of care and the safety of residents. Nursing homes are often deficient in many ways: poor hygiene, malnutrition, inadequate records, lack of preventive and emergency care (Butler, 1975). In 1974, at least 60 percent of all nursing homes failed to meet at least some federal standards (U.S. Senate, 1974), and the Senate Special Committee on Aging has noted that even these regulations are often inadequate. For example, regulations for intermediate care facilities require no licensed nursing personnel for two of three shifts during the day, allow almost anyone to qualify as a nutritionist or food manager, and are extremely vague about such things as toilet and bathing facilities.

One problem which has captured periodic public attention is nursing-home fires. From 1961 to 1971, 267 residents died in multiple-death nursing-home fires in the United States (Butler, 1975), and an unknown number in single-death fires. In January of 1970, 32 patients died in a fire at a Marietta, Ohio nursing home.

> Harmar House was a classic example of the breakdown in standard enforcement. From 1967 to 1969, the home was listed as deficient in "specifications of alarm signals, frequency of fire drills, and assignment of personnel responsibility in a crisis." In

April, 1969, the county health department nurse surveying the facility reported that the deficiencies had been removed; apparently they had not been. At the time of the fire, Harmar House had had no fire drill in ten months, although Medicare standards require a drill at least three times a year. Employees testified that they had no idea what their duties were in case of an emergency. The aid who rescued the patient in room 104 had been working at the home for several months but had never been told that one of the first principles of confining fire is to close the door of the room where the fire starts. The four-minute delay in notifying the fire department was due in part to her mistaken belief that the room sensor automatically signaled the fire department. (Townsend, 1971: 63–64)

Despite tragedies such as this, as recently as 1974 59 percent of all "skilled nursing facilities" had "serious fire safety violations" (U.S. Senate, 1974); yet all of these homes were still licensed and certified by the federal government.

Other abuses exist, such as carelessness in the prescription and administration of drugs and possible overdrugging for "ease of maintenance." A retired nursing-home administrator comments:

A layman doesn't know what to look for in a nursing home. He walks in and sees a patient is nice and quiet and he thinks this guy is happy. And the nurse tells him: "This is John. John is one of our best patients. He sits here and watches television."

But you just take a look at John's pupils, and you'll see what condition John is in. John is so full of thorazine that it's coming out his ears. Thorazine—that's a tranquilizer they use. It's a brown pill. It looks like an M&M candy.

The nursing home where I worked kept at least 90 percent of the patients on thorazine all the time. They do it for the money. If they can keep John a vegetable, then they don't have to bother with him. They never have to spend anything to rehabilitate him. (Townsend, 1971: 114)

Staffing presents continual problems. Geriatric medicine has traditionally had a low status, the combined result of ageism, stereotypes that the elderly are "untreatable," feelings that resources should go to younger patients, and the often demoralized and depressed state of nursing-home patients. Thus, there has been a chronic shortage of physicians, nurses, therapists, and other professional staff. Regulations regarding who can administer a nursing home are sometimes quite minimal. Aides, who in many ways have the most demanding jobs and the most extensive and intimate contact with residents, are paid very low wages and typically given little or no training. This, combined with the often depressing nature of the work in some nursing homes, results in an annual turnover among aides of about 75 percent (Townsend, 1971). The situation may in some cases lead to patient abuse, as suggested in letters written to Congressman David Pryor of Arkansas:

> It was a prank for revenge for one shift to load the patients with laxatives so the next shift would have to work cleaning up. One of the patients was so weak she was almost dead from laxatives and fleet enemas.

> Several times I found people lying on the floors and when I reported this to the nurses at the nursing station I was told that they would take care of that patient when they got around to it. I found that this was very common along with other things such as the nurses on the evening and night shifts turning off the call system so they do not have to be bothered since many of the nurses and aides sleep on the evening and night shifts. (Townsend, 1971: 102)

Stannard (1973) cites the case of a confused nursing-home resident who was left unattended in a bath; he was later found sitting in a tub of scalding water, and eventually died from the burns. Stannard suggests that patient abuse can occur with relative impunity because aide-patient interaction is largely invisible and hostility and suspicion separate aides and other staff (particularly nurses), which limits control. Abuse often represents discipline of "troublesome" patients who wander or are incontinent.

If problems like these can occur in nursing homes, for which many regulations have been enacted, it may be that abuses are even more widespread in other settings which receive less scrutiny. Roberts (1974) reports on a survey of boarding homes, which are essentially unregulated and receive the most impoverished elderly. While approximately half of the homes are rated good to excellent, the rest were little better than "human warehouses." For example, 38 of the 81 homes had "emergency" or "major" structural violations of building codes. Although medical problems were prevalent among residents, many of the homes lacked individualized care, dietary programs, or trained medical personnel.

Factors Affecting Quality of Care

There is obviously wide variation in the quality of care provided by nursing homes, and abuses are far from universal. Quality of care is difficult to define, however. On the one hand, it refers to the availability of treatment resources—professional staff, records and facilities, therapeutic programs, and so on. While the "best" nursing home for any particular older person depends upon the level of care he or she requires, one can make certain general statements about correlates of "objective" treatment resources. Nursing homes which are certified for Medicare, conform to licensing standards, and are accredited (by such organizations as the Joint Committee on Hospital Accreditation) tend to offer more treatment resources (Kosberg and Tobin, 1972; Kosberg, 1973; Levey et al., 1973; Kart and Manard, 1976). These studies indicate few differences depending on ownership; beliefs that nonprofit homes provide better care than proprietary homes do not seem warranted regarding objective resources. Larger nursing homes which are more expensive and have more professional staff have more treatment resources.

This suggests that, as in so many other ways, the poor are disadvantaged in nursing-home care. Blacks and persons supported by public aid reside in poorer quality nursing homes, while homes located in higher-income, suburban areas have more treatment resources (Kosberg and Tobin, 1972; Kosberg, 1973). Kosberg also found that poor residents are more likely to receive only custodial care from staff. Part of the problem is that regulations often are not, and cannot be, enforced because there are a limited number of nursing homes willing to take Medicaid patients.

Quality of care also involves the social and psychological milieu of the nursing home, however, which can have a tremendous impact on resident well-being. Unfortunately, few studies have investigated social and psychological quality of care. Smaller nursing homes appear to be more "homelike," with greater sociability (Kart and Manard, 1976). As is so often true in medical settings, greater size brings better technical care, but at the cost of a more impersonal, bureaucratic environment. Kart and Manard also suggest that voluntary nonprofit homes have better staff attitudes and social milieu, with public homes the worst and proprietary homes intermediate.

How can the quality of nursing homes be improved? Regulation of the industry does seem to help, since certification and licensing produce higher quality care. Particular attention should be given to institutions housing low-income older people, whose care can be quite invisible to the public. It also appears that nursing homes should be large enough (and expensive enough) to support a full range of treatment resources, while not becoming so large that they are impersonal bureaucracies. Some have suggested that nursing homes should be run by the public (the government), but there is no indication that private, profit-making nursing homes have lower quality care in general. Certainly the government has displayed no particular expertise in running high quality institutional programs.

Average quality no doubt has improved. Levey and associates (1973), for example, found an increase in the quality of Massachusetts nursing homes between 1965 and 1969. There is certainly room for additional improvement, however. A myriad of regulations for nursing homes exist but have not been effectively enforced for a variety of reasons. Agencies which inspect nursing homes are typically understaffed. In 1972, for example, there were only two nurses and two sanitarians available to inspect 144 nursing homes in a five-county area of Wisconsin. Even when problems are uncovered, there may be no alternative—a substandard home is better than none at all. Medicaid patients in particular are often shunted to the worst institutions, which are in effect subsidized by public money. There is also the problem of corruption, or of abdication of responsibility to fiscal intermediates, which are themselves controlled by the health industry. In addition, regulation of nursing homes is so fragmented that no single agency has clear authority.

A number of suggestions for increasing the accountability of nursing homes have been offered: tying reimbursement to quality of care rather than quantity (Kosberg, 1974), "shopper's guides" to facilitate choice (and competition) (Anderson, 1974), publication of agency ratings (Townsend, 1971), and so on. One study found that better care was given to those who received visitors from the community (family, friends, personal physicians), implying the existence of someone in the community who might hold the nursing home accountable (Gottesman and Bourestom, 1974).

Families are often not very thorough or sophisticated in placing their aged members in nursing homes. According to one study, 51 percent of a sample of families had not even visited the nursing home before placement (York and Calsyn, 1977). The major reasons for selecting a nursing home were availability of a bed and location—hardly the best indicators of quality. Such factors as quality of staff, physical care, activity programs, and cleanliness were much less influential in family decisions.

Perhaps the essential problem is the failure of the public to pay sufficient attention to the nursing-home industry and the treatment received by the elderly. Kart and Manard conclude that *"lack of continued effective public pressure is the most basic reason for the failure of nursing home regulation"* (1976: 255).

The Impact of Institutionalization

We referred in Chapter 8 to the concept of *environmental docility*—as physical and intellectual competence declines, behavior is increasingly shaped by the environment, and the individual becomes less able to shape the environment to meet his or her needs. Residents of nursing homes are likely to have experienced reduced competence, therefore the nature of the nursing home as a living environment is critically important. The institutional world can have a tremendous impact on residents, for better or worse.

Relocation Studies

Institutionalization can literally be a life-or-death issue. Aldritch and Mendkoff (1963) studied an elderly sample which had to be relocated after the closing of an institution. When they compared mortality rates following the move with expected rates (based on the previous ten years at the institution), it was apparent that the likelihood of death increased for all ages (Table 11.2). This rise in mortality occurred primarily within the first three months. The following case is an example:

Miss E. W., aged 85, had been in the Home for twenty-four years following a back injury. She walked with a cane and had been an active and alert participant, requiring no nursing supervision. She was anxious about the Home's closing, expressed fear of any change in her situation, and became depressed and withdrawn. After arranging her belongings and taking care of her personal affairs, she withdrew further and lost all interest in the daily activities of the Home. She frequently spoke of death and

Table 11.2. Comparison of calculated anticipated death rates and actual death rates during first year following relocation

Age of patients	Anticipated[a] mortality (%)	Actual mortality (%)	N
Under 70	13	20	59
70–79	19	33	45
80–89	28	45	56
90+	28	30	20
All 70 and older	23	38	121
All ages	19	32	180

[a] Based on records for 10 years prior to relocation.
Source: C. Knight Aldritch and Ethel Mendkoff, "Relocation of the aged and disabled," *Journal of the American Geriatrics Society* 11 (1963):187. Reprinted by permission.

stated that she had no reason to live. While efforts were being made for transfer, she died, apparently of arteriosclerosis. (Aldritch and Mendkoff, 1963: 190)

A number of other studies have also found that relocation, from home to institution or from one institution to another, can result in physical, psychological, and social deterioration, and even death (Liebowitz, 1974; Lieberman, 1974; Schulz and Brenner, 1977). In some ways, those most in need of relocation, because they require more supportive services, are most vulnerable to such tragic consequences. It appears, however, that the stress of relocation can be at least partly alleviated in two ways (Lieberman, 1974; Schulz and Brenner, 1977). Increasing predictability, achieved by involving patients in decisions, trial visits, and making the new environment as similar as possible to the old one, lessens the need for wrenching adjustments. And, the impact of relocation is less when residents can exercise greater control—when the move is voluntary or the new environment encourages autonomy, interaction, and integration in the outside community. Liebowitz (1974) has suggested that the greatest negative impact occurs when residents are moved into cold, dehumanizing environments which foster dependency. Relocation to an *improved* environment can have a decidedly *beneficial* result (see Chapter 9).

The Consequences of Being Institutionalized

A number of studies indicate that institutionalized older people share certain negative characteristics, including low morale, negative self-image, preoccupation with the past, feelings of personal insignificance, intellectual ineffectiveness, docility and withdrawal, anxiety and fear of death (Riley and Foner, 1968; Tobin and Lieberman, 1976). Many have taken this as an indication that nursing homes create more problems than they cure, which may be the case in many instances, but there are three alternative explanations which may also contribute to this "institutional syndrome" (Tobin and Lieberman, 1976). First, selection biases are involved in who enters institutions. The physical illnesses of those who enter nursing homes may account for their psychological states, or there may be a "dependent personality" which responds in a particular way to institutional life. Second, there may be "preadmission effects," linked to feelings of separation or rejection and negative attitudes toward entering an institution. Finally, relocation research suggests that environmental discontinuity may account for the impact of institutionalization. These explanations indicate a complex variety of reactions to the stress imposed by the losses which create dependency and a need for institutional services, loss of familiar supports, entrance into a strange environment, and labeling effects of being in a nursing home.

Certainly there are many aspects of the preadmission period which might have detrimental effects on older people. The aged have largely negative views of institutions (even more than the general population), preferring to live in their own homes or with relatives (Riley and Foner, 1968). There are many negative symbols attached to nursing homes: the lingering image from earlier times of the "poorhouse," a sacrifice of highly valued independence, an underlining of the losses associated with aging and the nearness of death, feelings of being "cast aside" by family and society. In addition, there may be little preparation (anticipatory socialization) for entrance into the nursing home, heightening feelings of confusion and personal distress. These reactions to institutions may lead those who enter to dwell on the past or withdraw socially and psychologically from an unpleasant reality.

There are also good reasons to expect that the institutional environment itself will have an impact on residents. Robert Scott, in a thought-provoking study, argues that agencies for the blind often make the blind more dependent—more "blind"—than they need to be.

> The disability of blindness is a learned social role. The various attitudes and patterns of behavior that characterize people who are blind are not inherent in their condition but, rather, are acquired through ordinary processes of social learning. Thus, there is nothing inherent in the condition of blindness that requires a person to be docile, dependent, melancholy, or helpless; nor is there anything about it that should lead him to become independent or assertive. Blind men are made, and by the same processes of socialization that have made us all. (Scott, 1969: 14)

Erving Goffman (1961) used the term *total institution* to refer to places (such as mental hospitals, prisons, army barracks, or monasteries) which are cut off from the surrounding world and impose regimented schedules on "inmates," presumably to achieve some overall goal—treatment, rehabilitation, conversion. Goffman is concerned with the effects of such institutions on residents, particularly in creating social and psychological disabilities, such as "curtailment of self." Inmates lose control of many seemingly trivial things which define their individuality in institutional uniforms, furniture, haircuts, and so on, and they lose their autonomy and spontaneity in regimentation of eating, sleeping, play, and work from "above." A gulf of suspicion, hostility, and derogation separates staff and residents, limiting meaningful interaction.

There is a loss of privacy, or "the right of the individual to decide what information about himself should be communicated to others and under what conditions" (Pastalan, 1970: 89), further limiting personal autonomy and opportunities for emotional release and self-evaluation. In all of these ways "total institutions disrupt or defile precisely those actions that in civil society have the role of attesting to the actor and those in his presence that he has some command over his world" (Goffman, 1961: 43).

The concern is that residents may eventually lose the capacity to be an individual—to act in a self-directed, autonomous fashion—as decisions are constantly made for them. Being labeled and treated as incompetent, particularly for the institutionalized aged who are already confused and dependent, may result in what Zusman (1966) calls the social breakdown syndrome. The individual becomes increasingly oriented to the world of the institution and isolated from the outside world, thereby losing the capacity to exist independent of the institution.

One can assess degrees of "totality" in an institution. A "shopping list" or sorts can be used to determine the totality of any nursing home (Bennett and Nahemow, 1965; Kiyak, Kahana, and Lev, 1975). Some criteria relate to life inside the home: sequential scheduling of activities, few provisions for personal property, involuntary recruitment, dormitory-style living, formalized rules and sanctions, little resident involvement in governance; others relate to access to the outside world: availability of private phones, proximity and ease of travel to the community, allowances for leaving during the day or for a weekend, scheduled activities outside the institution. A "total" nursing home is one which provides a custodial, protected environment for its residents, severing ties to the community. It is oriented toward an orderly routine, rewarding residents who perform the "proper" role of dependency and passivity. This may involve an aspect of "infantilism," where first names or a patronizing "dear" are always used for residents. Residents are stereotypically perceived as having little capacity for autonomy or personal growth.

Scattered studies do suggest that as totality and length of residence within such nursing homes increase, there is a decline in morale and increased depersonalization, or deteriorated self-concept, independent of actual health (e.g., Dick and Friedsam, 1963; Coe, 1965; Lawton and Nahemow, 1973). In fact, the impact seems to be greatest for those who are in better health or have remaining ties in the community (such as children or other family ties), suggesting a type of relative deprivation. Larger nursing homes appear particularly likely to isolate residents from the community and from interactions with other residents and staff, engendering an incapacity for self-initiated activity (Curry and Ratliff, 1973; Lowenthal and Robinson, 1976).

Nursing-home residents may encounter the loss of autonomy and privacy which contribute to social breakdown, as illustrated in the following example from Townsend's study in Great Britain:

> The staff took the attitude that the old people had surrendered any claims to privacy. The residents were washed and dressed and conveniently arranged in chairs and beds—almost as if they were made ready for a daily inspection. An attendant was always present in the bathroom, irrespective of old people's capacity to bathe themselves. The lavatories could not be locked and there were large spaces at the top and bottom of the doors. The matron swung open one door and unfortunately revealed a blind old women installed on the w.c. She made no apology. In a dormitory she turned back the sheets covering one woman to show a deformed leg—again without apology or explanation. (Townsend, 1964:5)

They may also encounter loss of the aspects of self associated with personal possessions. Institutional coldness, combined with hospital-like smells and routine, implies a loss of "home" and the little details associated with it.

> "It isn't home here. I woulda' liked to have stayed with the children. We had a cat and I miss that cat quite a bit. I miss my little radio and the window I had where you could see the dog in the yard next door. Sometimes I really miss that nice little carpet I had next to my bed. I was used to that." (Gubrium, 1975: 87)

These problems are compounded by the disruption of social interaction. Those who enter nursing homes have already experienced disruption of daily habits and routines. Loss of access to old friends combines with difficulty adjusting to new ones. Social and psychological withdrawal may substitute for the lack of physical privacy (Lawton, 1970). In addition, residents are restricted in doing things for each other—cooking, caring during illness, and so on.

> The residents of Weldon Manor are actively discouraged from helping one another, as I saw for myself during the two days I was there. One of the women said, "We are not supposed to help. It does seem short-sighted to a good few of us here. I think it's made me rather unkind." Another added to this, "I'm not supposed to lift a finger for anybody and I'm not even allowed to wash up. I'd like to. . . . We're not always good-

tempered with each other. It's a lonely life, you know, with
nothing to do and plenty of time to do it in." (Townsend,
1964:82)

While these restrictions are no doubt motivated by concern for
both the safety and well-being of the residents and the liability
of the institution, they nevertheless prevent the development of
reciprocal relationships on which friendships can be built.

Gottesman and Bourestom (1974) conducted an observational
study of 1,144 residents in 169 Detroit nursing homes. They found
that 56 percent of the residents' time during the day was spent
doing *nothing*; only 17 percent of the time were they observed in
contact with any other person; and only 7.5 percent of the time
were they in contact with nonstaff. The residents typically developed few close friends within the institution, and other studies
indicate that staff maintain considerable social distance from residents, turning the nursing station into a "staff refuge" (Watson
and Maxwell, 1977).

This does not mean that nursing homes do not develop their
own social systems. For example, Gubrium's (1975) in-depth
study of "Murray Manor" did find a complex social environment.
Friendship was important to residents, and cliques developed along
lines similar to the "poor dear" hierarchy discussed in Chapter 9.
There was a keen sense of territoriality concerning room assign-
ments, seating in the dining room, and the use of lounges, as is
illustrated by the following:

> Dorothy Porath, whose room is in the south wing, has been
> known to watch television in the north lounge and fall asleep on
> the couch, "letting it run until late at night." She's been told
> by several women with rooms near the lounge to "go to the
> other end, Dorothy, where you belong." Don Staats, who also
> resides in the south wing and who is considered to have a "dirty
> mouth," often sits in the north lounge with a friend who has a
> room near it. Whenever these women run into him there they
> scoff at his presence and snidely tell him that he has his "own
> place down at the other end." They add, "Why do you want to
> bother everyone down here?" Don typically spits back, "Go to
> hell, you goddamn bags!" (Gubrium, 1975: 27)

But social relationships were not encouraged by staff, and were
even hindered by staff orientations. Gubrium notes, for example,
that while administrative ("top") staff gave lip service to social
and emotional needs as part of "total care," since they really only
checked on physical care, this is what floor staff concentrated on.
Their concern was with meeting routine schedules, and residents

were considered unrealistic or irrational when their demands could not be met within the normal routine. Although dignity and respectful care were important to residents, such concerns, as well as the social relationships among residents, were largely ignored in staff decisions.

> Rarely does top staff seek social explanations for clientele behavior. It believes that people do things because of their personal desires or "quirks." Although top staff often casually recounts the interaction between persons that led to the particular actions of a patient or resident, such interaction is not given serious attention as an official explanation of behavior. The official causes of clientele behavior lie within the persons themselves, not in the contingencies of their everyday lives in or out of the Manor.

> The idea that patient and resident behavior is basically a product of individual acts, past and present, influences top staff's administrative decisions about clientele care. The nursing care memos or care plans sent to the floors typically direct floor staff to deal with individuals, not with cliques, socially emergent situations, small social movements, or social ties. (Gubrium, 1975: 46)

A study by Frankfather (1977) also found that staff in one nursing home viewed conversation among residents as silly and meaningless and in some cases disruptive.

These studies imply that nursing homes, at least partly because of their characteristics as total institutions, create demoralized, depersonalized, passive, and withdrawn residents. They do not "nurse," but rather foster dependency and an incapacity to function in the community. These studies are suggestive, however, rather than conclusive, because of the difficulties in separating the effects of the institution from the other explanations for the characteristics of institutional populations (selection biases, preadmission effects, and the impact of relocation).

Tobin and Lieberman (1976) have conducted one of the few studies which attempts to assess the relative importance of these effects. They interviewed 100 persons on a waiting list for admission to three nursing homes, and reinterviewed those who entered (85 persons) both two months and one year following admission. Two groups were used for comparison: a sample of community residents and a sample of relatively healthy persons who had lived in these homes for one to three years. From the initial interviews, it was apparent that "most of the psychological qualities attributed to the adverse effects of entering and living in an institution were already present in people on the waiting list" (p. 77) (emphasis added). Persons on the waiting list were more like the institutional sample than the community sample, and in some ways were worse than those already in the institution. Tobin and Lieberman suggest that the most significant transition may be from community to waiting list, rather than waiting list to institution. This is a time of accumulating losses, dependency, and deterioration in social networks, colored by feelings of separation and abandonment.

Problems of adjusting to the institution were most acute during the first few months, as people felt resentment toward family, left behind prized possessions, experienced a sometimes overwhelming sense of institutionalization (e.g., group bathrooms, large dining halls), and had low status in the resident social system. Nevertheless preadmission characteristics generally persisted. Contrary to Goffman's picture of the total institution, there was considerable stability in self-concept. New residents did feel less capable of caring for themselves, but this may be an inevitable consequence of institutional reminders of frailty and physical decline.

> Before admission, Mrs. A. said that she had difficulty walking up and down stairs. While this difficulty persisted, she had no need to climb stairs in the home. After admission to the home, she claimed difficulty in getting out of doors "because of my eyes," and in washing and bathing. Before admission she did not complain of difficulties in these two areas. Apparently, living in the home had made her conscious of these difficulties. The home's medical milieu probably created an expectation of managing with difficulty. To some extent, this effect of life in a home for the aged is unavoidable, because caretakers in the home wish to protect older persons such as Mrs. A., who might stumble in an unfamiliar outdoor area as a result of poor eyesight. Thus, one can understand why anxiety over falling and a fearful self-consciousness absent in the past became manifest in Mrs. A.'s behavior after she moved into the home. Washing and bathing oneself is made a more difficult task in the home because the tubs are designed for bathing the most deteriorated residents. Fixtures such as swinging metal seats used to ease the weak into the tub make it easier, if not necessary, for the ablest of people to ask for help in washing and bathing. Residents such as Mrs. A. are thus continually made aware, in a very personal sense, of actual or potential deficits in their capacity for the caring of themselves. (Tobin and Lieberman, 1976: 160)

In their followup conducted one year after admission, Tobin and Lieberman found that, among those who had not died or shown extreme deterioration, there was no evidence of psychological deterioration. Indeed, as residents began to establish their own slot in the world of the home, they became more satisfied and less anxious. They conclude that "the status of the 'old-timer' appears to be largely a function of his status just before admission"

(p. 198). Postadmission reactions were largely a function of the "culture shock" involved in moving from a familiar community setting to an unfamiliar institutional setting.

Tobin and Lieberman's research raises important doubts about the impact of institutions, but it does not disprove the deleterious effects on residents of nursing homes, as institutions. Their samples were small, with limited comparability and representativeness, and the three nursing homes studied were apparently of high quality and relatively "nontotal." There is a great need for comparative research among different types of nursing homes. This study does caution us, however, that the creation of passive, withdrawn, dependent institutional populations is not an inevitable effect of nursing homes. Nursing homes should strive to have beneficial impacts on the social and psychological functioning of residents; at the very least, they should be structured to prevent further decline among persons who have already experienced deterioration of psychological and social skills.

Social Reconstruction in Nursing Homes

There is ample evidence that nursing homes can benefit residents. It is clear, for example, that older people can make effective use of the entire range of mental-health services (Butler and Lewis, 1977). In an 11-year study of over 1,000 patients discharged from one skilled nursing home, Kaplan and Ford (1975) found that 61 percent were discharged to independent living in their own households. They attribute this to the effective use of a multidisciplinary team: physicians, nurses, physical therapists, occupational therapists, speech therapists, social workers. The reader needs only to glance through issues of *The Gerontologist* to find many favorable evaluations of a variety of "milieu therapies," with such names as "reality orientation," "independence training," and "interpersonal skill training." The provision of "therapy" does not automatically imply therapeutic consequences, of course. Gubrium (1975) relates the following "theater of the absurd" involving "reality orientation":

AIDE: [Pointing to the weather on the RO board, which reads "raining."] What's the weather like today, Emma?
Emma turns her head slightly and quickly looks out the window.
EMMA: Well, it looks like the sun is shining kinda bright.
The sun happens to be shining at the moment.
AIDE: Are you sure? It says it's raining. Doesn't it? [Finger still pointing to board.]
EMMA: Well, it doesn't look like it from here.

AIDE: What does it say here, Emma? [Directing Emma's attention to the board.]
EMMA: It says it's raining.
AIDE: [Warmly] That's correct. Very Good. (Gubrium, 1975:
192)

Despite the existence of such incidents, nursing homes are capable
of "nursing."

What approaches need to be taken? For one thing, Tobin and
Lieberman (1976) point out that there are four distinct phases
connected with institutionalization: (1) predecision (leading to the
need for institutional services), (2) anticipatory (being on the
"waiting list"), (3) initial adjustment to the institution, and (4)
longer term adaptation. Their study suggests that phases 2 and 3
may be most critical. Support can be provided through realistic
familiarization with the new environment and humanization of
the institution, perhaps providing objects from the resident's
former world as anchors.

Since interaction is critical to self-concept and adaptation, efforts
should be directed at facilitating social involvement. Social integration is enhanced when the nursing home constitutes a self-
contained community giving the residents a sense of permanency
(Bennett and Nahemow, 1965). Social interaction is also heightened by physical arrangements which facilitate interaction while
protecting personal privacy. Cluff and Campbell (1975), for example, found that interaction in nursing homes was greater when
the environment was personalized and there was a central sitting
room, allowing easy access to others and free movement without
infringing on others' space.

Seemingly simple changes in the environment can have quite
large effects. This is illustrated by a study conducted by Robert
Sommer (1969) on a ward for older women in a state mental
hospital. Although this ward had recently won an award for
physical improvements—new furniture, tiles, air conditioning, and
so on—interaction among residents was minimal. Sommer noted
that furniture had been positioned for ease of maintenance, along
walls and facing outward around pillars, in completely inadequate
orientations for conversation. Yet patients did not move the chairs
to converse; they accepted the routine (environmental docility).
Sommer tried an "experiment," in which the chairs were grouped
around tables decorated with artificial flowers and magazines.
Despite resistance from both staff (whose routine was upset by the
"clutter") and residents (whose routine and territoriality were
also upset), there was a substantial increase over a period of two
weeks in both brief and sustained interactions.

Figure 11.1. The social reconstruction syndrome

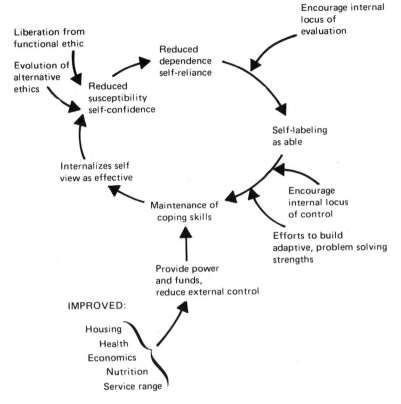

Source: Joseph Kuypers and Vern Bengtson, "Social breakdown and competence," *Human Development* 16 (1973):197. Reprinted by permission of S. Karger AG, Basel, Switzerland.

Of primary importance in institutions is the development of an environment which fosters and facilitates feelings of competence among residents. Kuypers and Bengtson (1973) refer to the *social reconstruction syndrome,* diagramed in Figure 11.1. This model was developed for older people in the community and is most appropriate for noninstitutional settings, but it does suggest some important considerations for institutional care. Recognizing the susceptibility of the aged to social labeling, three types of inputs are suggested to bolster coping abilities and a sense of efficacy. First, the aged need to be liberated from the "functionalist ethic," which stigmatizes them for not playing "productive" roles. Second, there is a need for services which enhance adaptive capacities and a lessening of debilitating environmental conditions. Too often, living environments set up barriers which penalize the elderly, continually calling into question their competence and attacking self-esteem.

> . . . those who choose furniture utilized in settings for older persons tend to ignore the penalties imposed by chairs or sofas too low or too soft or without arms on those who by virtue of arthritis or restricted mobility or stiffness or other deficits find it enormously difficult to get in and out of such chairs. The same criteria can readily be applied to other aspects of the environment which presume to serve the aged: poorly designed beds; storage space so low or so high as to be virtually inaccessible to the elderly; tables of unsuitable height or dimensions; visual and other orienting cues virtually indistinguishable or nonexistent; windows, elevators, water faucets, and heat controls almost impossible to manipulate by stiff fingers or aged joints; wheelchairs which are unstable or allow discomforting and even unsafe slumping by the elderly occupant; heavy doors and "blind" entry and exit portals; eating and cooking utensils and stoves, medicine cabinets, storage bottles and stairs which often range from the inconvenient and unsuitable for the aged to the unsafe and positively dangerous. (Schwartz, 1975: 290)

The third input to social reconstruction—encouraging internal locus of control—is most important for the social environment within institutions. The implication is that aged residents are too often protected, rather than encouraged to have self-determination and responsibility. Bennett and Nahemow (1965) have noted that nursing homes and mental hospitals often have virtually no social adjustment criteria; nothing is expected, so nothing is rewarded. Without the opportunity to succeed (or fail) on their own, residents become dependent, apathetic, and withdrawn. In an experimental study, using control groups, Langer and Rodin (1976) found that when decision making, personal responsibility, and freedom were encouraged among nursing-home residents, they were happier and received more favorable nurses' ratings on alertness, general improvement, sociability, and activity.

Nursing-home environments need to be richer, more complex, and more challenging to residents, while keeping in mind their existing limitations. As pointed out by Lawton and Nahemow (1973), institutions should strive for a match between residents' competence (both cognitive and physical) and environmental demands. When environmental challenge is too low, people experience either deprivation or complacency; when it is to high, they experience overload. Lawton and Nahemow suggest the need for "minimal goals" rehabilitation, where environmental demands are slightly above the person's accustomed level of performance. This encourages increased feelings of competence and personal power, without putting people out on a limb. There are many ways to encourage initiative and responsibility within nursing homes, from room decoration to resident governance. And the evidence suggests that increased assertiveness is correlated with benefitting from therapeutic programs (Tobin and Lieberman, 1976).

Community-Based Services for the Aged

Although institutions can have beneficial effects, it seems generally preferable to keep the aged in the community whenever possible. Some type of institution will always be necessary, but there have been many complaints that some residents of nursing homes are there needlessly. The proportion is difficult to determine, but it may be substantial. A 1971 study of Massachusetts nursing-home residents, conducted by Brandeis University's Levinson Gerontological Policy Institute, concluded that while 37 percent needed full-time skilled nursing care, 26 percent needed only minimally supervised "living," 23 percent required only periodic home visits by nurses, and 14 percent needed nothing (U.S. Senate, 1971). In other words, 63 percent were "overinstitutionalized." As indicated in Figure 11.2, only 41.6 percent of all nursing-home residents in 1969 required intensive nursing care (intravenous injection, oxygen therapy), full bed bath, or less intensive nursing care (application of sterile bandages or dressings); the remainder required only routine nursing care (special diet, help with dressing), or no care. In addition, only 37 percent of nursing-home residents were confined to either bed or wheelchair (U.S. Public Health Service, 1974). Thus, many institutionalized older people might remain in the community were sufficient services available, and others are handicapped by the lack of a full range of services, though they manage to remain in the community.

The older population would clearly benefit from a wider range of community-based services. Apart from the potentially negative effects of institutionalization, "home" is an important idea for all of us, and particularly for the elderly. Home is part of their identity, lends a sense of familiarity, and helps the aged maintain personal autonomy and control. Congregate living of any type is often seen as a loss of personal liberty and dignity.

Types of Community Services

There are no set answers to the provision of services to older people in the community. Each individual's own living situation must be assessed for its match to his or her competence. Many things are involved: functional health, psychological well-being,

Figure 11.2. Percent distribution of residents in nursing and personal care homes by level of patient care, according to age

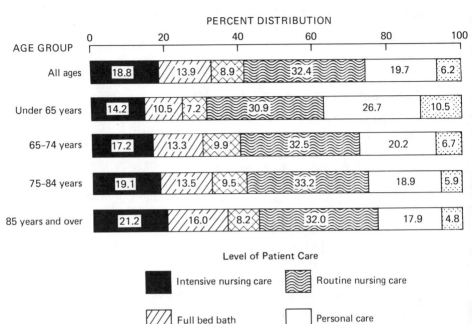

Source: U.S. Public Health Service, 1974:20.

potential support from family and friends, and so on. Butler and Lewis (1977) note that many skills are required for independent community living—orientation to time, place, and person, cooking and feeding oneself, bathing, dressing, grooming, toileting, continence, transferring from bed to chair, standing and walking, climbing stairs, fire and accident security, shopping, money management, ability to follow instructions (medication), ability to seek assistance when needed, social participation. Community services should be designed to further and protect the dignity, independence, and integration of the individual. The concept of "social reconstruction" is important in this regard (see Figure 11.1). Keeping in mind this complexity in the types of community services which may be required, there appear to be four basic types of necessary community-based services: (1) preventive services, (2) treatment services, (3) protective and support services, and (4) linkage services.[2]

---

[2] For more complete discussion and references concerning these services, see Beattie (1976) and Ward (1977).

Preventive Services. Some programs are needed to prevent the occurrence of difficulties which lead to a need for costlier services. These include encouraging the aged to use preventive medical and dental services. Counseling programs offered through community mental health agencies can also be effective. Even social clubs and activities can be viewed as preventive services. An important element of prevention concerns the architectural barriers and dangers in the environments of older people, given declines with age in strength and coordination, vision and hearing, and speed of response. Each year accidents account for approximately 30,000 deaths (26 percent of all accidental deaths in the population) and 800,000 disabling injuries among older people, with falls constituting the greatest danger (Butler and Lewis, 1977). Attention should be paid to such things as the visibility of steps, nonskid floors, and handrails. Sometimes a change in environment can be disorienting and dangerous, as indicated in the following case:

A 73-year-old carpenter moved to Florida after living in his home for thirty-six years. He was accustomed to turning to the left from his bedroom door to enter the bathroom. Suffering from nocturia, he had to get up several times a night. In his new home a stairway was to the left. Several nights after moving, he fell down the stairs and fractured his hip. (Butler and Lewis, 1977: 225)

The aged also face dangers outside their homes. For example, older people account for approximately 25 percent of all pedestrian traffic fatalities (Carp, 1976), which implies a need to consider traffic volume, the safety of crosswalks, and the brightness of lights in areas they frequent.

Treatment Services. The second type of service involves delivery of treatment while older people still live in the community. Outreach programs are needed to screen and diagnose health problems. As alternatives to institutionalization, access to outpatient programs or "day hospitals" is needed for older people to receive the benefits of hospital or nursing-home care while living in the community. Other programs extend health care into the home, through visiting nurses or physician assistants. A 1968 survey indicated that nearly 1.5 million older people were receiving some type of home health care: 80 percent receiving "personal" care (bathing, meals) and 25 percent receiving "medical" care (injections, changing bandages) (Shanas and Maddox, 1976).

Protective and Support Services. Other programs are not strictly treatment-oriented, but are designed to support relatively independent community living. These include legal services, friendly visitor and telephone reassurance programs, consumer education, housekeeping and personal maintenance, meals, home repair, and fiscal management. By the mid-1970s, nearly 2,000 agencies, employing 20,000 homemakers, were providing home-help services (Beattie, 1976). Federal funding of meal services, either to the home ("Meals on Wheels") or through congregate dining, was begun in 1973. By 1974, nearly 180,000 older people were being served by such programs, with another 117,000 on waiting lists (Beattie, 1976). The term "protective services" usually refers to programs for mentally-impaired persons which "oversee" their needs; for example:

A mildly confused elderly woman developed paranoid ideas about the gas company, which resulted in her not paying her bills for several months. She was threatened with having the gas turned off, which would leave her without heat in mid-winter. Had she been without help, her gas probably would have been turned off; after a while police and medical help would have been called for, and her eventual transfer (probably in a very deteriorated condition) to an inpatient psychiatric ward would have been necessary. With protective services, the crisis with the gas company was averted. A casework aide, under the supervision of a social worker, was able to gain the woman's confidence enough to convince her to pay the gas bill. Since she had no money for an immediate payment, protective services made a partial payment of the bill and arranged with the gas company for the woman to pay the rest later. Continuing contact with the protective service worker enabled the women to continue living in her own home. A homemaker was also provided for a few hours a week. All these helpers used psychiatric consultants to help them react appropriately to the client's psychiatric condition. (Butler and Lewis, 1977: 231)

Such programs lessen the need for institutionalization in marginal cases. Services should also be directed at maintaining and strengthening the role of natural support systems in the community, such as the family.

Linkage Services. The final type of service involves efforts to link older people to the services they need, or to link one service to another. Referral and placement are crucial components of any program—one must find out who needs a particular service, and those who need services must know about them and be able to reach them. Thus, efforts to provide information to would-be clients, or to those who can refer would-be clients (such as personal physicians), are important. Organizations such as Area Agencies on Aging can operate as information clearinghouses and encourage coordination of care. Transportation is also a critical type of linkage service. One increasingly common approach to linkage services is using "senior centers" as a hub for a wide variety of medical and social services.

Referral and placement should not be considered subsidiary to "real" treatment programs. Inadequate assistance can often be traced to inappropriate placement. Nursing homes and hospitals, for example, may too seldom consider individual needs for service referrals and have little real followup or aftercare (Townsend, 1964; Frankfather, 1977). Mentally impaired older people face particular problems. Frankfather (1977), in a study of one community, found that the "confused elderly" were bounced around from one agency to another. Because their "senility" was considered irreversible, handling them was considered a waste of resources. Defined as inappropriate cases ("dump jobs"), the confused elderly were quickly referred elsewhere, in a perpetual cycling through the service system.

> Old people are just moved around like so much rotten fruit. (administrator, Thompson Nursing Home Corporation)
> It's just like dropping a hot potato. Maybe someone will stop and pick it up. (psychiatric nurse, emergency room, PH)
> They ship them out of here as if they were a side of beef. (social worker 1, CH) (Frankfather, 1977:156)

Placement was more often based on negotiation over institutional needs than on consideration of patient needs. For example, nursing homes would accept a few "bad" patients (e.g., incontinent) from hospitals, expecting to get some "good" ones later.

This sort of nonplacement for nonservice benefits no one. A particular linkage need is for oversight of a specific individual's service needs. Many older people have multiple problems—physical, mental, economic, social—which must be dealt with through many programs and service providers. Too often there is no coherence to the provision of these services—the left hand rarely knows what the right is doing.

In addition to the kinds of services discussed here, a variety of alternative living arrangements offering a continuum from independent community living to dependent institutional care is needed. Many older people can live in their own homes with supportive services, including household repairs, to prevent disruptive relocation. Others could benefit from various group-living arrangements, which may include special architectural features and certain minimum services. Such a group home was established by the Philadelphia Geriatric Center in 1965 (Bronson, 1972). For $40 a month, residents lived in their own rooms, sharing a bathroom, living room, dining room, and kitchen, with building maintenance, limited social services, and weekly housekeeping provided. Foster homes are another stage prior to institutionalization. Finally, geriatric institutions themselves sometimes specialize in convalescent as opposed to chronic care.

Estimating Need and Cost

One reason for the recent increased interest in community services is the belief that they are less costly than institutional approaches. This is true only up to a point. One must consider many types of costs connected with maintaining the aged in the community: housing, nutrition, personal care, volunteer expenses and so on. When the intent is to support family-based care, one must also assess social and psychological costs to the family. This is illustrated by a study of the relative values of hospital and home treatment for schizophrenic patients (Pasamanick, Scarpitti, and Dinitz, 1967). Although home care and hospital care were equally effective in rehabilitating patients, and home care was much less expensive, the first six months of home care were quite costly to the family in worry, disruption of work and social activities, physical and psychological strain, and conflicting responsibilities. If the family is seen as an important caring institution, which it often is with older people, it must be given support.

The financial benefits of community or institutional care for the elderly depend on their impairment level and the quality of care being provided (Pollak, 1976). When impairment is low, home care is more economical than nursing home care. Beyond a certain level of impairment, however, it becomes more costly to support community living because too many costly services are required. What this level of impairment is depends on the quality of care provided in the alternative settings. When fewer home services are provided, home care will be "economical" for a longer time; but the "costs" are then transferred to the older person.

We must be wary of viewing community services as always "the answer" to unnecessary or inadequate nursing-home care. Too often, such personnel as visiting homemakers are poorly trained and poorly paid. In at least one state, welfare recipients are required (forced) to work in such roles. This hardly seems the best way to insure competent or dedicated service providers. The growing tendency for states to contract with private agencies for the provision of community services to the aged also opens the door to abuses similar to those found in the nursing-home industry. Indeed, there is already growing evidence in New York State of mismanagement, fraud, and poor care from such services. Foster care, involving placement of older persons in small, home-like settings, while it often provides worthwhile assistance (Sherman and Newman, 1977), sometimes merely means the worst aspects of nursing-home care without the formal safeguards applied to institutions.

There are still very few good indicators of the extent of need for services in any community. Thus, planners are often uncertain about how many visiting nurses, group homes, or congregate meals are needed. However, there are some beginning attempts, such as using available census data to estimate the need for new group housing in a community (Heumann, 1976). But there is a great need for better information concerning all aspects of service development and delivery.

Factors Affecting Delivery and Use of Services

It has been pointed out for many years that certain community or institutional services would be helpful to older people, yet services for the aged are still woefully inadequate in many respects. Services which are "ideally" needed may never be "really" implemented, and even when services are developed there is no guarantee that older people can, or will, use them. There are three types of factors which affect the delivery and use of services: (1) predisposing factors, (2) enabling factors, and (3) illness level factors (Andersen and Newman, 1973; Ward, 1977).

Predisposing Factors

Predisposing factors are characteristics which affect the likelihood that individuals will need services and seek assistance. Increased age is itself associated with greater need for a variety of services. Within the older population, there are also certain subgroups—such as, widows and minority-group aged—with greater service needs. Thus, when communities assess the likely demand for future medical and social services, with an eye toward rational planning, they should begin by looking at the demographics: the future proportions of "old-old" (75+) persons, widowed people, low-income aged, and so on. Current "retirement states," such as Florida and Arizona, will have to give some thought to the aging of their retirement populations over the next 20 years, as this affects the dependency ratio and the demand for services.

Other predisposing characteristics affect service use through their association with values, attitudes, beliefs, and behavior patterns. For example, low education is related to less use of preventive services, and blacks are also less likely to use preventive services (Ward, 1977). Such facts must be kept in mind when targeting services for particular subgroups of the aged.

Willingness to use services is often affected by attitudes and beliefs. Older people tend to be fatalistic and have less "scientific" health orientations than younger people and are more likely to consider health problems unavoidable and medical treatment unsuitable for their afflictions (Riley and Foner, 1968; Phillips, 1970).

Independence is an important value for older people, and they may be unwilling to use certain services—food stamps, homemakers, Meals on Wheels—because of the dependency they symbolize. This is aggravated by a potential "welfare" stigma attached to special programs for the elderly. One study of attitudes toward 13 social programs (such as Aid to Families with Dependent Children and Unemployment Compensation) found that Social Security was the least stigmatized (Williamson, 1974). But other programs for the aged may not fare as well; for example, Williamson found that public housing was a relatively stigmatized program. And the extent to which "old age" itself bears a stigma is a potential barrier to the provision of important social and medical services, since people will deny aging and its associated problems.

Enabling Factors

Assuming that people are willing to use a service, they must also have access to it. This access is affected by a number of enabling factors: (1) the service must exist, (2) delivery of the service must be structured in such a way that people actually receive assistance, (3) people must know that the service exists, (4) the service must be accessible to people, and (5) the service must be affordable. The failure of any one of these means that even the most brilliantly conceived program will fail.

The federal government has played a major "enabling" role (discussed in a later section) through its policies and programs directed at the aged. The structure of services and related financial arrangements represent only one set of enabling factors, however. Information and transportation are also important enabling variables. Unfortunately, those at whom services are most clearly aimed (with poor health, low income, over 75) are often least knowledgeable about what services are available. A study of older people in Boston found that only 46 percent knew about the existence (much less the name or location) of home nursing services, and only 14 percent were aware of homemaker services (Fowler, 1970). This lack of knowledge may lead people to be unaware of even their need for services. Personal physicians can be an effective referral source, but many older people, particularly recent movers and those with low income, do not have a regular physician. We knew very little about the sources of information and referral used by the aged. They probably depend on the community setting.

Taietz (1975) indicates, for example, that direct knowledge and word-of-mouth are effective in rural areas, but the aged must rely on mass communication in more complex urban areas.

Transportation difficulties are most likely to affect social and recreational activities, but they also affect access to, and convenience of, virtually all services (Golant, 1976). Older people at all income levels are less likely to own an automobile and more likely to depend on public transportation or friends, particularly older women. Even public transportation presents many problems for the aged. Their transportation needs often run against established "home-to-work" mass transit patterns, resulting in time-consuming and inconvenient schedules and transfers (Kaye, 1973). Such things as high steps, fast-moving doors, and exposed stops create additional problems. Consider using the New York City subway system with the physical limitations (not to mention fear of crime) of many older people, and even a 50¢ bus fare can be a financial burden for the low-income older person. Public transportation has become increasingly important with the decline of the neighborhood as a center for services and the rise of large suburban shopping centers.

A number of programs which attempt to alleviate these transportation problems have been developed (Golant, 1976). Reduced-fare programs have consistently resulted in increased use of mass transit, particularly during off-peak periods. West Virginia has experimented with "transportation stamps" for low-income and handicapped older people. Some newer systems, such as San Francisco's Bay Area Rapid Transit (BART), have incorporated special design features, including wider doors and extended handrails. So-called "demand responsive" services, such as dial-a-ride or special bus routes, have proven reasonably efficient, especially when computerized. But transportation continues to be a critical need for many older people, particularly for those who live in rural and suburban areas where public transportation is least developed and special programs are usually very costly.

Illness Level Factors

Even though people may be predisposed to use a service and have access to that service, they may fail to use it. Studies in the sociology of health show that many social and psychological factors affect decisions to seek help (Mechanic, 1962). The tendency of people to deny aging may translate into a reluctance to admit age-related difficulties, whether medical, psychological, or social. The aged may also shift their frame of reference for evaluating need from *objective* to *subjective* indicators, which change less with age (Riley and Foner, 1968). This reflects people's ability to "settle for" what they have, yet it constitutes a potential barrier to the provision of services which are objectively needed.

It is also true that the *evaluation* of need by service providers, or by those who might refer older people to services, is a vital link in the processes by which services are delivered. There is evidence of at least some age biases among the various helping professions, which historically have dealt with the needs of younger people for acute problems (Beattie, 1976). There has long been a serious shortage of staff for services directed at the aged; for example, there are only about 10 percent of the number of homemaker-home health aides needed (Butler, 1975). Butler (1976) also notes that medical schools have paid scant attention to geriatric medicine— few students are exposed to the problems of older patients (through courses or clinical experience, as in nursing homes) and few faculty have geriatric expertise. The older patient is practically invisible in both curricula and textbooks. Many physicians have been unwilling, for a variety of reasons, to accept Medicare and Medicaid patients. Schofield (1974) has referred to the YAVIS syndrome among psychotherapists—the tendency to prefer young, attractive, verbal, intelligent, and successful (well-paying) clients. One study of psychiatrists found that less than 2 percent of their time was spent with older clients.

The lack of receptivity to dependent or impaired older persons extends beyond service providers to include the larger community. Frankfather (1977), for example, found senior citizen centers to be closed societies of middle-class women who were intolerant of deviance and forced "outsiders" to withdraw from involvement. Nursing-home residents in particular were stereotyped as "mumblers and droolers," and made to feel unwelcome at the center. This lack of tolerance and general support for the impaired elderly is a significant barrier to their maintenance in the community. Those who do manage to remain in the community may become the sort of wandering "street characters" found in any community.

. . . Coughin' Annie (chef, Main Street Luncheonette). . . . the Cryer—She spends all day feeding pigeons and crying (chef, luncheonette). . . . the Picker—The old guy comes in here every day. He spends about an hour going through the barrels. If he finds anything of obvious value, he returns it to us. I guess he's just looking for something to do, and it's safer and warmer in here than out on the street (clerk, post office). . . . the Night Watchman—He walks the streets all night. About two A.M. he's at the fire station getting coffee, then at four he's over at the post office, and by six the luncheonette is open so he goes there (policeman 1). (Frankfather, 1977:28)

Even when the aged reach treatment, they may still encounter age bias. Aged patients are often stereotyped as bothersome and complaining, and treated with avoidance, paternalism, and infantilism (Butler, 1975). The complaints may be written off as "just old age," and most older persons are not as forthright as the following gentleman in challenging such assertions:

> Mr. Morris was one of the volunteers for study at the National Institute of Health at the age of 92. He lived to be 102 years old. Near the end of his life he was having pain in his left leg and went to see his doctor. The doctor declared, "Sam, for Pete's sake, what do you expect at 102?" Sam retorted, "Look, my right leg is also 102 but it doesn't hurt a bit. Now explain that!" (Butler, 1975: 182)

The stereotyped reaction that the aged cannot benefit from therapy and services should go to more "hopeful" (youthful) clients persists. Thus, the aged may not be referred to needed services or are sent too late in the course of their problem for services to be effective. This problem of the "reluctant therapist" appears to be most pronounced with psychiatric services (Kastenbaum, 1964; Ginsburg and Goldstein, 1974), but it also affects the use of medical and social services.

"Senility" presents a particular problem, as indicated in Frankfather's (1977) study of service providers in one community. He found that "senile" had become a catchall phrase for dependent or deviant behavior by confused older persons. Such persons were then labeled as irreversible and therefore hopeless; worse yet, perhaps, these cases were not even "interesting." Almost universally, professionals (physicians, social workers, psychiatrists) considered handling mentally impaired older people to be "dirty work" which wasted their skills. Their prejudice is indicated in the following statement by a medical resident:

> We say there are two ways to identify these old people, with the "O" sign and the "Q" sign. If they lay there with their mouths open, that's the "O" sign. If their tongue hangs out because they've had a stroke, that's the "Q" sign. (Frankfather, 1977: 132)

These older people are powerless to challenge the diagnostic stereotypes of professionals. As a result, the label "senile" can be used to remove "troublesome" older people from the community, while offering little hope for real treatment.

The labels "senile dementia" and "organic brain" syndrome are the only diagnostic categories that define the deviant as totally beyond rehabilitation. Only for such elderly is an assumption of therapeutic failure incorporated into the agents' perspective. Senility is like no other deviant label, and its unique quality serves an explicit social function: the diagnosis legitimizes, with the authority invested in the scientist, the exclusion and removal of old people who constitute a social problem. The empirical pattern is clear: those labeled senile presumably cannot be rehabilitated and therefore need only be maintained, generally in nursing homes. While society hopes that confused elderly are not ill-treated under maintenance strategies, it demands that they are efficiently and economically removed. If they are "senile," it does not matter where they go. (Frankfather, 1977:190)

The nature of service organizations may constitute yet another barrier to the utilization of services (McKinlay, 1972). Older clients may be discouraged or antagonized by the impersonality of bureaucratic agencies—long waits, inattention to their psychological or social needs, failure to understand what is expected of them. The cautiousness and fatalism felt by many older people may lead them to withdraw rather than actively challenge and pursue what they need. It is too easy to blame older clients for inability to communicate their needs or follow instructions, when providers are at least equally to blame for communication breakdowns (McKinlay, 1975). Organizations themselves develop a "culture" which may be supportive, neutral, or antagonistic to the culture of client groups, such as the aged (Berkanovic and Reeder, 1974). Unfortunately, we know very little about the nature of the actual interactions which take place between older clients and service providers.

The Government and Services for the Aged

For most of human history support of the aged has been a private concern, shouldered by the family, religious groups, and other voluntary and charitable sources. The late nineteenth century represented a major turning point, however, as problems of the aged became a public concern (Hudson and Binstock, 1976). Because of the dislocations created by industrialization, and ideological changes concerning the role of government, industrial societies began to undertake major social programs as part of the birth of the modern welfare state. Germany led the way during the 1880s, enacting a series of health, accident, and old age/invalidity programs, followed over the next 25 years by emerging policies in such countries as Demark, New Zealand, Great Britain, and Sweden. As noted earlier, the United States was a comparative latecomer, enacting the Social Security Act in 1935.

The need for a range of core social services is generally recognized in industrial societies (Brocklehurst, 1975; Kamerman, 1976; Beattie, 1976). Some form of income maintenance is virtually universal, and most industrialized countries supplement this with comprehensive health insurance and services. Beyond these similarities, however, there are important variations in the emphases of national programs. Some countries (e.g., Canada and Yugoslavia) are still expanding their long-term care facilities. Swedish policy, on the other hand, is directed at supporting family care. The greatest emphasis on home medical care appears to occur in Great Britain and the Soviet Union. Approximately 20 countries have developed home-help services (both personal and health care). These are most advanced in such countries as Sweden, Norway, and Great Britain, and least developed in the United States, France, Japan, and Italy.

The locus of responsibility for services to the aged also varies cross-culturally. In socialist societies, the government plays an overriding role. The United States, on the other hand, has less government coordination and delivery of services. In Great Britain, 90 percent of all long-term care facilities are publicly run, compared with only 23 percent in the United States. The tendency in the United States has been for the government to financially back services delivered by private agencies. This is particularly evident with home-help services and the nursing-home industry.

Great Britain has been a leader in the development of community services for the elderly, and was the first country with a comprehensive national aging policy (Kamerman, 1976). For example, meals-on-wheels programs originated in England, under the auspices of the Women's Royal Volunteer Service. The Health Services and Public Health Act of 1968 transferred and centralized services for the elderly as the responsibility of local authorities.

The United States still lags behind other countries in such areas of service for the aged as home-help. The earliest programs were only designed to supplement efforts of families and charities. As recently as 1962, 35 states in this country still had "responsible relatives" laws, requiring children and other relatives to support the aged (Rheinstein, 1965). The following paragraph is drawn from one such law:

Every person who shall be in need and unable to earn a livelihood in consequence of any unavoidable cause shall, except as herein otherwise provided, be supported by his spouse or person

holding himself out to be his spouse, father, mother, a person in
loco parentis to a child, children, brothers, or sisters if they or
either of them be of sufficient ability. (Rheinstein, 1965: 247)

Laws governing inheritance are also partly designed to encourage
care of aged relatives. The Depression of the 1930s, however, made
clear the inadequacy of charity, local relief, and family support,
and the widespread deprivation could no longer be attributed
simply to moral failure or laziness. It became clear that poverty
was a product of the social structure, and the federal government
has since become increasingly involved in social welfare programs.

Certain characteristics of government social welfare programs can
be traced to the Elizabethan Poor Law of the seventeenth century
(Komisar, 1974). Even then, a distinction was made between the
"deserving" poor (the blind, the old, children) and the "unde-
serving" poor (able-bodied employables). Public welfare has historically been partly based on the principle of *less eligibility*—
those on relief should be no better off than the lowest-paid independent laborer—to discourage going on relief. Unfortunately,
those who are unable to work, such as the disabled and the very
old, are caught up in the same system. This attitude is still reflected
in the often minimal support and services provided by such programs as Supplemental Security Income (SSI) and Medicaid.

The United States has not been entirely miserly toward its older
citizens. On the contrary, programs and services for the aged have
acquired strong legitimacy and grown enormously over the years.
By 1973, cash and service programs for older people amounted to
$58.5 billion (Viscusi and Zeckhauser, 1977). The federal Admin-
istration on Aging, begun as a symbolic gesture with a budget of
only $10 million, now oversees programs with a $400 million
budget. The establishment in 1974 of a National Institute on
Aging catches us up with the Soviet Union, which had already
established a national institute of gerontology, in Kiev. Indeed,
the aged receive about one-fourth of governmental special assistance outlays (for selected subgroups of the population) (Gold,
Kutza, and Marmor, 1977).

The proliferation of programs for the aged stems from many
sources. Governmental involvement is essential because of the
inability of normal market mechanisms to meet the needs of the
aged, given their disproportionately low incomes and difficulties
improving their financial position, and the often catastrophic
expenses associated with aging (particularly chronic health care).
Such programs are also justified as rewards for past contributions
of the aged to society. In addition, the perceived voting power

of the elderly has played some role. Finally, the aged benefit from one fact which other disadvantaged groups lack: while whites do not expect to become blacks, and men do not expect to become women, young people expect (and hope) to grow older. Thus, support of older people by the young will hopefully benefit them in the future.

The federal government has played six roles in the provision of services: (1) insuring adequacy of income (Social Security), (2) provision of noncash benefits (Medicare and low-income housing), (3) protection of the rights of the aged, (4) financing of research and training, (5) financial support to public and private organizations at the state and local level, and (6) orchestration and coordination of the first five goals (Gold, 1974). These roles are embodied in a number of different types of programs (Gold, Kutza, and Marmor, 1977). Some are specifically for the elderly (age-entitlement programs)—Social Security, Medicare, Supplemental Security Income—other programs affect them indirectly. Those based on financial need (need-entitlement programs) often benefit the aged disproportionately because of their low income. For example, about 40 percent of all Medicaid benefits go to the aged, and older people also benefit from various housing subsidies and food stamps, Many tax provisions also aid older persons. In 1974, nearly three-quarters of the tax privileges granted to special categories of taxpayers went to older people. Such provisions as an additional personal exemption on federal income tax and nontaxation of Social Security income added $5.6 billion to their incomes in that year. Finally, the aged may be affected by even more generalized programs, such as biomedical research.

We have also seen throughout this book, however, that such programs are too often inadequate, leaving important needs unmet. Many of the programs, including Social Security, SSI, and Medicare, emerged in a crisis atmosphere, rather than from rational consideration of long-term needs and consequences (Kerschner and Hirschfield, 1975). Caught in the middle of competing interests and a system of fragmented power, such programs are compromised in both adoption and implementation to secure support and neutralize opposition (Binstock and Levin, 1976). The fragmented nature of "interest group liberalism" inevitably limits the effectiveness of social intervention through compromise, resistance to real innovation by existing organizations, and the ability of service providers to neutralize regulatory machinery. This has been the history of Medicare and Medicaid, and accounts for many of the abuses within the nursing-home industry. Binstock and Levin also note that politicians are often most interested in passing legislation that yields tangible, quantifiable short-term results, which are not necessarily the most effective over the long haul.

There are many issues concerning the "best" structure of delivery systems to meet the needs of the aged (Ward, 1977), but two seem particularly important. First, should programs be directed specifically at the aged, or should they be subsumed within more general approaches? We have seen (in Chapter 10) that the political power of the aged is limited, and their needs may conflict with those of other powerful groups. Recognizing this problem, Robert Atchley has concluded that the aged are better off in coalitions with other groups:

> Everything we have discovered thus far indicates that if success is the measure of good, then low priority in a large coalition is the only hope older people have. Their needs must be incorporated into general programs to enjoy any real possibility of success. For example, combining the transportation needs of older people with those of the poor could result in gains for both. This type of combination is the essence of political coalitions. Many political scientists are convinced that since Social Security and Medicare have both been enacted, there will never again be an issue relating primarily to older people that will mobilize the support of the young. Accordingly, the only hope that older people seeking government action on their problems have is to attach their requirements to broader proposals. Over the past several years, the track record of lobbyists using this strategy has been encouraging. (Atchley, 1977: 256)

It may become increasingly difficult in the future to justify special programs for the aged, although they suffer disproportionately. It can be argued that people should be helped because they are *in need*, not because they are *old* and in need (Neugarten and Havighurst, 1977). Unfortunately, such general programs often result in fragmented responsibility for services to the aged, and their needs may be lost in the shuffle.

The problem of fragmentation was addressed in the 1973 Comprehensive Services Amendments to the Older Americans Act, which created Area Agencies on Aging to determine and meet unmet needs of older people in local areas through monitoring of existing programs, advocacy of new ones, and planning and coordination. This is a promising attempt to lend rationality to the delivery of services, thereby increasing access ("enabling") for those in need. By 1975, there were 475 Area Agencies, covering 70 percent of the older population (Beattie, 1976). Some have suggested, however, that their impact may be minimal (Estes, 1974;

Hudson, 1974). Organizational realities—lack of real authority, domination by existing organizations, ambiguity of tasks—may result in "goal displacement." Hudson, for example, suggests that Area Agencies will be least effective in mobilizing new services and redirecting existing ones, since these tasks bring them into conflict with the domains of existing service organizations. They may settle on linking and coordinating existing services as the path of least resistance—a task which is spelled out in greater detail and involves less conflict.

The Levison Gerontological Policy Institute at Brandeis University has proposed the establishment of Personal Care Service Systems at the community level (Beattie, 1976). These would offer a range of services (home-finding, foster care, home-helps, meal preparation, transportation), and would arrange and finance other services provided by other agencies. This, or some other approach, would help meet the pressing need for better service coordination and continuity of care, designing service programs which are appropriate to each older individual's specific needs.

A second delivery issue concerns the type of program which is most effective in meeting needs. Broadly, two strategies have been employed: (1) direct provision of income, so that the aged can buy necessary goods and services, and (2) provision of "income-in-kind" (housing, food stamps, medical care). Both approaches have advantages and disadvantages (Williamson, 1975). Income strategies, such as Social Security and SSI, are simple and have low administrative costs, but they assume that the market is capable of meeting the needs of older people if they have money. Strategies which directly provide goods and services can meet immediate needs and are a corrective for faulty markets or poor consumer choice, but disadvantages include high administrative costs, local inequities due to eligibility rules and quality control, the stigma which is often attached to such programs as food stamps, restricted freedom of choice, and the inferiority of services which can result from having a "guaranteed" market. These disadvantages are quite evident with Medicaid—enormous amounts of red tape, public subsidization of inferior nursing homes, the unwillingness of many physicians to accept Medicaid patients, local differences in eligibility, and so on. Thus, Medicaid subsidizes poor care for the elderly poor, supporting class bias in medical services. Yet direct income strategies may result in no health care at all.

Medicare

The Medicare program is a good example of both the potentials and the limitations of a social policy aimed at increasing access to needed services. Health care is a big business in the United States;

in 1976, a total of $139.3 billion was spent on health care, or an average of $638 per person (Gibson and Mueller, 1977). And those over 65 account for a disproportionate amount of these expenses; in 1975, nearly 30 percent of all health care spending was by older people (Mueller and Gibson, 1976). Inflation in health costs have been rampant; per capita health expenses for the aged tripled from 1966 to 1975, rising from $445 to $1,360. Given their disproportionately low income, it is clear that the aged need assistance if they are to get the health care they require.

Enacted in 1965, Medicare was designed to eliminate at least some of the financial barriers to health care for the older population. It has two parts. Hospital insurance (Part A), financed through the Social Security payroll tax, covers 90 days of inpatient hospital care, 100 days of post-hospital care in a "skilled nursing facility," and up to 100 home health visits connected with the hospitalization for persons eligible for Social Security and certain other groups (nearly 23 million people are currently enrolled). There is some cost-sharing; for example, in 1976, those eligible had to pay the first $104 of the hospital bill and an additional $26 for each day over 60. Supplemental medical insurance (Part B) covers physician services, home health services not linked to prior hospitalization, and various other medical services, such as laboratory fees and ambulance service. This is a voluntary program, though about 98 percent of those covered under Part A also have Part B (Gornick, 1976). Part B is jointly financed from general tax revenues and premiums paid by enrollees (currently $7.20 per month).

Although the most basic goal of Medicare was to increase access to health services, it was also hoped that Medicare would encourage greater coordination and comprehensiveness of health care for the aged and facilitate more diversity (preventive care, home-health services, extended care). How well have these goals been met? Medicare has certainly been beneficial. In 1975, Medicare covered 42 percent of the total health expenses of older people (other public money covered another 24 percent), compared with only 30 percent of expenses covered by public money in 1966 (Mueller and Gibson, 1976). In 1976, Medicare reimbursements totaled $17.8 billion (Gibson and Mueller, 1977). The initial impact of Medicare was increased short-stay hospitalization, partly because payment for nursing-home care was linked to this (Shanas and Maddox, 1976), but the greatest increase has occurred in hospital outpatient services (Gornick, 1976). The use of skilled nursing facilities increased to a peak in 1969, but has declined since then.

Medicare financing has increased access to health care, but there are critical gaps in the coverage. While Medicare and other public money cover most of the costs of hospital care, nursing-home care, and physicians' services, substantial per capita costs remain in these categories, as well as for such things as dentists' services, drugs, eyeglasses, and hearing aids which are not covered by Medicare (Table 11.3). Private health insurance fills in only some of the gaps; over 50 percent of the aged have private insurance which covers hospital and physician costs, but only a small minority have coverage for things excluded under Medicare, and approximately 30 percent pay all of the cost-sharing amounts required under Medicare (Gornick, 1976) (Figure 11.3). Costs connected with Medicare have been steadily rising; from 1966 to 1976, the hospital deductible under Part A rose from $40 to $104, and the monthly premium for Part B increased from $3 to $7.20. This, combined with the tremendous inflation of health costs, has meant that the direct out-of-pocket health expenses of the average older person have actually increased since the enactment of Medicare, from $237 (53 percent of all expenses) in 1966 to $390 (29 percent of all expenses) in 1975 (Gornick, 1976).

The uniform financing mechanisms of Medicare have also failed to guarantee equal access to medical care for all older people. Those who are most disadvantaged are older people who are poor, black, or reside in the South (Davis, 1975). For example, the average older white receives 40 percent more Medicare benefits than the average older black, and nearly double the benefits for skilled nursing facilities. Davis notes that such disparities are a consequence of a number of factors. Cost-sharing provisions (deductible and coinsurance) bear most heavily on the poor, acting as a deterrent to their use of services. Discrimination and the unequal distribution of medical facilities limits access for certain groups, particularly minority groups and those in the South. Reimbursement policies, based on "customary fees," in effect reward most highly physicians in high-income areas, and may lead to charging excessive fees for Medicare patients.

A further disappointment of Medicare has been its minimal impact on the organization and delivery of health services. It was hoped that Medicare would encourage greater coordination of care and an increased emphasis on preventive and home health care, but this has not occurred. In 1971, for example, $900 was spent on hospital coverage by Medicare for every dollar spent on home-health services (Brocklehurst, 1975). A longitudinal study of the impact of Medicare in five midwestern communities found that: (1) physicians were not making more home visits or nursing-home calls, (2) there was no decline in the use of traditional nursing homes, (3) care for the elderly was not better coordinated,

Table 11.3. Per capita expenses for health services and type of coverage, by age: 1975

	Age 19–64			Age 65+		
	Total	Private (%)	Public (%)	Total	Private (%)	Public (%)
Total health expenses	$471.88	70.0	30.0	$1360.16	34.4	65.6
Hospital care	229.82	59.1	40.9	602.89	10.2	89.8
Physician services	99.91	80.9	19.1	217.66	40.9	59.1
Dentist services	44.51	96.0	4.0	24.17	93.0	7.0
Other professional services	9.84	83.0	17.0	19.74	49.8	50.2
Drugs and drug sundries	48.96	92.6	7.4	117.68	87.0	13.0
Eyeglasses and appliances	11.63	94.2	5.8	22.65	98.5	1.5
Nursing-home care	9.25	7.9	92.1	342.47	46.6	53.4
Other health services	17.98	31.2	68.8	12.89	8.2	91.8

Source: Marjorie Mueller and Robert Gibson, "Age differences in health care spending, fiscal year 1975." *Social Security Bulletin* 39:6 (1976):20.

Figure 11.3. Per capita personal health care expenditures for the aged, by source of funds: 1966–1975

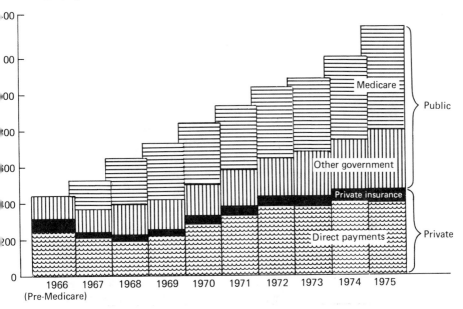

Source: Marian Gornick, "Ten years of Medicare: Impact on the covered population," *Social Security Bulletin* 39:7.

and (4) sharp initial increases in home care programs during the late sixties had been followed by a decline thereafter (Coe, Brehm, and Peterson, 1974). Other than increased institutional staffs to process Medicare information, expansion of traditional acute-care capacities, and some increase in skilled nursing facilities, the authors conclude that "Medicare has not appreciably altered the organization of health care services in our study communities" (p. 260).

Older people are better off with Medicare than without, but the substantial gaps and inequities which still exist have led some to suggest its replacement with a more general national health insurance program. Health care for the aged continues to be fragmented, with little emphasis on preventive or home care. Medicare is geared primarily to acute illness episodes requiring hospitalization, rather than to the prevalent chronic conditions of older people which create a need for long-term, often prohibitively expensive, community-based or institutional services.

Exploitation of the Aged

Many of the problems we have discussed in this chapter constitute a type of victimization of the aged. The losses associated with aging and the failure to meet their needs elsewhere also make older people vulnerable to a variety of frauds and confidence games. Butler (1975) refers to the "loneliness industry"—travel cruises, dating services, dancing studios—which prey on feelings of isolation. Older people seeking a retirement home may succumb to high-pressure real estate schemes.

> Many dream lots in Hawaii are on the slopes of active volcanoes, those in Florida are sometimes under water, and those in the southwest are often in the midst of desert wastelands. In some locations it is necessary to bring water in by truck. Distances are often misrepresented. Facilities said to be minutes away are often hours away. (Loether, 1975: 117)

Other fraudulent activities involve fees to publish books or songs, and preneed burial services.

> One of many examples of what the purchase of a "funeral" and/ or "funeral" merchandise can needlessly cost is the Julesburg, Colo., contract calling for the advance purchase of two caskets, two vaults, and a gravestone for $1,650. In 10 years if this money were placed in a savings account at the rate of interest paid in Julesburg (componded semiannually) it would earn $810.44. Therefore, if the merchandise was not needed for 10 years—it would cost not $1,650 but $2,460.44. And, no matter when death occurred, whatever the cost for the merchandise might be, no services are included. Someone would have to be called to care for the body and provide the facilities, equipment, and personnel for the funeral services. (U.S. Senate, 1964: 19)

Elderly women living alone are vulnerable to the "bank examiner" swindle. They receive a call from a "bank examiner," asking them to withdraw a large sum of money in order to trap a bank employee suspected of embezzlement. After handing over the money, receiving a receipt and a promise of a bonus for her assistance, the widow waits in vain for the return of her money (often her life savings). Variations on this theme involve impersonations of police or Social Security agents. The movie, "Paper Moon," portrayed Ryan O'Neal as an engaging confidence man who preyed on recent widows by checking the obituaries, then arriving at the door with a Bible which had been "ordered" by the husband before his death.

The most tragic types of fraud involve health quackery, which takes advantage of the painful and progressive nature of such chronic conditions as cancer and arthritis. Fraud involving vitamins and fake "health foods"—bottled seawater, "ozone generators," miracle cures—account for an estimated 500 million dollars a year (Loether, 1975). Loether describes rejuvenation schemes involving such things as turtle oil, vitamin lotions, and hormone creams. Arthritis, which can be a particularly painful disease, seems to especially lend itself to quackery. A startling figure is Butler's (1975) estimate that $25 is spent on fraudulent arthritis "treatments" for every $1 spent on arthritis research. These treatments have included lying on top of uranium ore, special milk, and alfalfa tea (Loether, 1975).

Older people are vulnerable to fraud for a number of reasons: social isolation, feelings of hopelessness and desperation concerning chronic illness, a desire for the "golden years" of retirement living, low levels of education, low and fixed incomes which make them susceptible to get-rich-quick schemes, and the mental confusion which may accompany age-related problems. There is a clear need for better consumer education and protection directed at the older population. Younger (1976) has described some approaches which have been taken in California. Programs have focused on teaching older people about the types of bunco and confidence games they may encounter. The aged are told to avoid impulse buying and to consult with authorities about door-to-door salespeople. They are also trained in the provisions of consumer protection laws.

Summary

Certain service needs increase with age. The extent to which age-related problems become handicaps depends on the network of services available to the aging individual. Approximately 5 percent of the older population resides in institutions, though there may be a 20 percent chance that any individual will be institutionalized at some time. The aged are increasingly placed in old-age institutions such as nursing homes, rather than in chronic disease hospitals or mental hospitals. The processes leading to institutionalization are best viewed as a deteriorating balance between need and available support, with the institution being a last resort when other alternatives have failed.

There has been tremendous growth in the nursing-home industry, particularly since the passage of Medicare and Medicaid. Most nursing homes are run for profit and can be classified according to the level of care provided. Regulation of nursing homes has been lax, and many abuses still exist—kickbacks, gang visits, failure to meet fire safety standards, inadequate staffing, overdrugging. Better quality care is apparently available in larger, more expensive homes which are certified and conform to licensing standards, while smaller homes are more likely to foster sociability. The poor in particular are consigned to the worst institutions. Poor quality care is a consequence of understaffed regulatory agencies, fragmented responsibility, lack of alternatives, and insufficient public pressure for reform.

The impact of institutionalization is an important issue. Relocation can literally be lethal when it involves considerable environmental discontinuity. Institutionalized older people share many negative social and psychological traits, arising from various sources: the type of people who enter institutions, reaction to the losses which create a need for institutional services, the stigma attached to nursing homes, and the impact of the nursing home as a total institution. "Social breakdown" is neither a necessary nor an inevitable consequence of nursing-home residence, however. There is ample evidence that "social reconstruction" can be fostered in institutional settings. It is important to encourage social integration and coping skills, while providing support during the critical premove and institutional adjustment periods. Competence and environmental demands should be carefully matched.

The aged can benefit from a wide range of community services, but they are sometimes forced into institutions because of the lack of alternatives. Needed programs include preventive services, treatment services, protective and support services, and linkage services. A continuum of living arrangements between full independence and institutionalization would also be beneficial. Estimating the need for, and relative cost of, community services is at present a very difficult task, however.

Three factors affect the delivery and use of services. Predisposing factors, including demographic characteristics and service-related attitudes, affect the likelihood of older people seeking assistance. Enabling factors, including income, knowledge, and transportation, affect access to services. Illness level factors, such as denial of age-related problems and age biases among helping professionals, affect the likelihood that older people will actually come in contact with services.

Organized social programs for the aged first emerged with the birth of the modern welfare state in the 1880s. There continue to be important cross-national differences in these programs, with Great Britain apparently offering the most comprehensive national aging policy. The federal government has played an increasingly prominent role in the United States. Programs are often less effective than they might be, however, because of compromise, fragmented responsibility, and the air of crisis in which many programs are enacted.

The Medicare program exemplifies the potentials and limitations of social policy. Although it has increased access to needed health services, many gaps and inequities remain, and Medicare has had little impact on the ways in which services are organized and delivered.

Because of age-related losses, isolation, and the desperation associated with long-term problems, older people may be vulnerable to a variety of frauds, including high-pressure real estate schemes or financial swindles. Most tragic are those frauds involving miracle cures, particularly for cancer and arthritis.

References

Aldritch, C. Knight and Ethel Mendkoff
   1963   "Relocation of the aged and disabled: A mortality study."
          Journal of the American Geriatrics Society 11: 185–94.
Andersen, Ronald and John Newman
   1973   "Societal and individual determinants of medical care
          utilization in the United States." Milbank Memorial Fund
          Quarterly 51: 95–124.
Anderson, Nancy
   1974   "Approaches to improving the quality of long-term care for
          older persons." The Gerontologist 14: 519–24.
Atchley, Robert
   1977   The Social Forces in Later Life. Belmont, Calif.:
          Wadsworth.
Beattie, Walter
   1976   "Aging and the social services." In Robert Binstock and
          Ethel Shanas (eds.) Handbook of Aging and the Social
          Sciences. New York: Van Nostrand Reinhold.
Bennett, Ruth and Lucille Nahemow
   1965   "Institutional totality and criteria of social adjustment in
          residences for the aged." Journal of Social Issues 21: 44–76.
Berkanovic, Emil and Leo Reeder
   1974   "Can money buy the appropriate use of services?: Some
          notes on the meaning of utilization." Journal of Health and
          Social Behavior 15: 93–99.
Binstock, Robert and Martin Levin
   1976   "The political dilemmas of intervention policies." In Robert
          Binstock and Ethel Shanas (eds.). Handbook of Aging and
          the Social Sciences. New York: Van Nostrand Reinhold.
Brocklehurst, J. C. (ed.)
   1975   Geriatric Care in Advanced Societies. Baltimore: University
          Park Press.
Bronson, Edith
   1972   "An experiment in intermediate housing facilities for the
          elderly." The Gerontologist 12: 22–26.

Butler, Robert
    1975   Why Survive?: Being Old in America. New York:
           Harper & Row.
    1976   "Medicine and aging: An assessment of opportunities and
           neglect." Testimony before the U.S. Senate Special
           Committee on Aging.
Butler, Robert and Myrna Lewis
    1977   Aging and Mental Health. St. Louis: C. V. Mosby.
Carp, Frances
    1976   "Urban life style and life-cycle factors." In M. Powell
           Lawton, Robert Newcomer, and Thomas Byerts (eds.).
           Community Planning for an Aging Society:
           Designing Services and Facilities. Stroudsberg, Pa.:
           Dowden, Hutchinson and Ross.
Cluff, Pamela and William Campbell
    1975   "The social corridor: An environmental and behavioral
           evaluation." The Gerontologist 15: 516–23.
Coe, Rodney
    1965   "Self-conception and institutionalization." In Arnold Ross
           and Warren Peterson (eds.). Older People and Their Social
           World. Philadelphia: F. A. Davis.
Coe, Rodney, Henry Brehm, and Warren Peterson
    1974   "Impact of Medicare on the organization of community
           health resources." Milbank Memorial Fund Quarterly
           52: 231–64.
Curry, Timothy and Bascom Ratliff
    1973   "The effects of nursing home size on resident isolation and
           life satisfaction." The Gerontologist 13: 295–98.
Davis, Karen
    1975   "Equal treatment and unequal benefits: The Medicare
           program." Milbank Memorial Fund Quarterly 53:
           449–88.
Dick, Harry and Hiram Friedsam
    1963   "Adjustment of residents of two homes for the aged."
           Social Problems 11: 282–90.
Estes, C. L.
    1974   "Community planning for the elderly: A study of goal
           displacement." Journal of Gerontology 29: 684–91.
Fowler, Floyd
    1970   "Knowledge, need, and use of services among the aged."
           In Carter Osterbind (ed.). Health Care Services for the
           Aged. Gainesville: University of Florida Press.
Frankfather, Dwight
    1977   The Aged in the Community. New York: Praeger.
Gibson, Robert and Marjorie Mueller
    1977   "National health expenditures, fiscal year 1976." Social
           Security Bulletin 40 (4): 3–22.

Ginsburg, Arlene and Steven Goldstein
1974 "Age bias in referral for psychological consultation." Journal of Gerontology 29: 410–15.

Goffman, Erving
1961 Asylums. Garden City, N.Y.: Anchor Books.

Golant, Stephen
1976 "Intraurban transportation needs and problems of the elderly." In M. Powell Lawton, Robert Newcomer, and Thomas Byerts (eds.). Community Planning for an Aging Society: Designing Services and Facilities. Stroudsberg, Pa.: Dowden, Hutchinson and Ross.

Gold, Byron
1974 "The role of the federal government in the provision of social services to older persons." In Frederick Eisele (ed.). Political Consequences of Aging. Annals of the American Academy of Political and Social Science 415: 55–69.

Gold, Byron, Elizabeth Kutza, and Theodore Marmor
1977 "United States social policy on old age: Present patterns and predictions." In Bernice Neugarten and Robert Havighurst (eds.). Social Policy, Social Ethics, and the Aging Society. Washington, D.C.: U.S. Government Printing Office.

Gornick, Marian
1976 "Ten years of Medicare: Impact on the covered population." Social Security Bulletin 39 (7): 3–21.

Gottesman, Leonard and Norman Bourestom
1974 "Why nursing homes do what they do." The Gerontologist 14: 501–06.

Gubrium, Jaber
1975 Living and Dying at Murray Manor. New York: St. Martin's.

Heumann, Leonard
1976 "Estimating the local need for elderly congregate housing." The Gerontologist 16: 397–403.

Hudson, Robert
1974 "Rational planning and organizational imperatives: Prospects for area planning in aging." In Frederick Eisele (ed.). Political Consequences of Aging. Annals of the American Academy of Political and Social Science 415: 41–54.

Hudson, Robert and Robert Binstock
1976 "Political systems and aging." In Robert Binstock and Ethel Shanas (eds.). Handbook of Aging and the Social Sciences. New York: Van Nostrand Reinhold.

Kamerman, Sheila
1976 "Community services for the aged: The view from eight countries." The Gerontologist 16: 529–37.

Kaplan, Jerome and Caroline Ford
1975 "Rehabilitation for the elderly: An eleven-year assessment." The Gerontologist 15: 393–97.

Kart, Cary and Barbara Manard
    1976   "Quality of care in old age institutions." The Gerontologist
            16: 250–56.
Kastenbaum, Robert
    1964   New Thoughts on Old Age. New York: Springer.
Kaye, Ira
    1973   "Transportation problems of the older American." In John
            Cull and Richard Hardy (eds.). The Neglected Older
            American: Social and Rehabilitation Services.
            Springfield, Ill.: Charles C Thomas.
Kerschner, Paul and Ira Hirschfield
    1975   "Public policy and aging: Analytic approaches." In Diana
            Woodruff and James Birren (eds.). Aging: Scientific
            Perspectives and Social Issues. New York: D. Van Nostrand.
Kiyak, Asuman, Eva Kahana, and Nira Lev
    1975   "The role of informal norms in determining institutional
            totality in residences for the aged." Paper presented at the
            Annual Meeting of the Gerontological Society, Louisville, Ky.
Komisar, Lucy
    1974   Down and Out in the USA: A History of Social Welfare.
            New York: New Viewpoints.
Kosberg, Jordan
    1973   "Differences in proprietary institutions caring for affluent
            and nonaffluent elderly." The Gerontologist 13: 299–304.
    1974   "Making institutions accountable: Research and policy
            issues." The Gerontologist 14: 510–15.
Kosberg, Jordan and Sheldon Tobin
    1972   "Variability among nursing homes." The Gerontologist
            12: 214–19.
Kuypers, Joseph and Vern Bengtson
    1973   "Social breakdown and competence: A model of normal
            aging." Human Development 16: 181–201.
Langer, Ellen and Judith Rodin
    1976   "The effects of choice and enhanced personal responsibility
            for the aged: A field experiment in an institutional setting."
            Journal of Personality and Social Psychology 34: 191–98.
Lawton, M. Powell
    1970   "Ecology and aging." In Leon Pastalan and Daniel Carson
            (eds.). Spatial Behavior of Older People. Ann Arbor:
            University of Michigan-Wayne State University Institute of
            Gerontology.
Lawton, M. Powell and Lucille Nahemow
    1973   "Ecology and the aging process." In Carl Eisdorfer and
            M. Powell Lawton (eds.). The Psychology of Adult
            Development and Aging. Washington, D.C.:
            American Psychological Association.
Levey, Samuel et al.
    1973   "An appraisal of nursing home care." Journal of Gerontology
            28: 222–28.

Lieberman, Morton
  1974   "Relocation research and social policy." The Gerontologist
         14: 494–500.
Liebowitz, Bernard
  1974   "Background and planning process." The Gerontologist
         14: 293–95.
Loether, Herman
  1975   Problems of Aging. Encino, Calif.: Dickenson.
Lowenthal, Marjorie and Betsy Robinson
  1976   "Social networks and isolation." In Robert Binstock and
         Ethel Shanas (eds.). Handbook of Aging and the Social
         Sciences. New York: Van Nostrand Reinhold.
Manard, Barbara, Cary Kart, and Dirk van Gils
  1975   Old Age Institutions. Lexington, Mass.: Lexington Books.
McKinlay, John
  1972   "Some approaches and problems in the study of the use of
         services—an overview." Journal of Health and Social
         Behavior 13: 115–52.
  1975   "Who is really ignorant—physician or patient?" Journal of
         Health and Social Behavior 16: 3–11.
Mechanic, David
  1962   "The concept of illness behavior." Journal of Chronic
         Diseases 15: 189–94.
Mendelson, Mary
  1975   Tender Loving Greed. New York: Vintage Books.
Mendelson, Mary and David Hapgood
  1974   "The political economy of nursing homes." In Frederick
         Eisele (ed.). Political Consequences of Aging. Annals of the
         American Academy of Political and Social Science
         415: 95–105.
Mueller, Marjorie and Robert Gibson
  1976   "Age differences in health care spending, fiscal year 1975."
         Social Security Bulletin 39 (6): 18–31.
Neugarten, Bernice and Robert Havighurst (eds.)
  1977   Social Policy, Social Ethics, and the Aging Society.
         Washington, D.C.: U.S. Government Printing
         Office.
Palmore, Erdman
  1976   "Total chance of institutionalization among the aged."
         The Gerontologist 16: 504–07.
Pasamanick, Benjamin, Frank Scarpitti, and Simon Dinitz
  1967   Schizophrenics in the Community: An Experimental Study
         in the Prevention of Hospitalization. New York: Appleton-
         Century-Crofts.
Pastalan, Leon
  1970   "Privacy as an expression of human territoriality." In Leon
         Pastalan and Daniel Carson (eds.). Spatial Behavior of
         Older People. Ann Arbor: University of Michigan-Wayne
         State University Institute of Gerontology.

Phillips, Derek
   1970   "Age and the utilization of medical aid in a small town."
           In Carter Osterbind (ed.). Health Care Services for the
           Aged. Gainesville: University of Florida Press.
Pollak, William
   1976   "Costs of alternative care settings for the elderly." In
           M. Powell Lawton, Robert Newcomer and Thomas Byerts
           (eds.). Community Planning for an Aging Society:
           Designing Services and Facilities. Stroudsberg, Pa.:
           Dowden, Hutchinson and Ross.
Rheinstein, Max
   1965   "Motivation of intergenerational behavior by norms of law."
           In Ethel Shanas and Gordon Streib (eds.). Social Structure
           and the Family: Generational Relations. Englewood Cliffs,
           N.J.: Prentice-Hall.
Riley, Matilda and Anne Foner
   1968   Aging and Society. Volume 1: An Inventory of Research
           Findings. New York: Russell Sage Foundation.
Roberts, Pearl
   1974   "Human warehouses: A boarding home study." American
           Journal of Public Health 64: 269–76.
Schofield, William
   1974   Psychotherapy: Purchase of Friendship. Englewood Cliffs,
           N.J.: Prentice-Hall.
Schulz, Richard and Gail Brenner
   1977   "Relocation of the aged: A review and theoretical analysis."
           Journal of Gerontology 32: 323–33.
Schwartz, Arthur
   1975   "Planning micro-environments for the aged." In Diana
           Woodruff and James Birren (eds.). Aging: Scientific
           Perspectives and Social Issues. New York: D. Van
           Nostrand.
Scott, Robert
   1969   The Making of Blind Men. New York: Russell Sage
           Foundation.
Shanas, Ethel and George Maddox
   1976   "Aging, health, and the organization of health resources."
           In Robert Binstock and Ethel Shanas (eds.). Handbook of
           Aging and the Social Sciences. New York: Van Nostrand
           Reinhold.
Sherman, Susan and Evelyn Newman
   1977   "Foster-family care for the elderly in New York State."
           The Gerontologist 17: 513–19.
Sommer, Robert
   1969   Personal Space. Englewood Cliffs, N.J.: Prentice-Hall.
Spitzer, Stephan and Norman Denzin (eds.)
   1968   The Mental Patient: Studies in the Sociology of Deviance.
           New York: McGraw-Hill.

Stannard, Charles
  1973 "Old folks and dirty work: The social conditions for patient abuse in a nursing home." Social Problems 20: 329–42.
Taietz, Philip
  1975 "Community complexity and knowledge of facilities." Journal of Gerontology 30: 357–62.
Tobin, Sheldon and Morton Lieberman
  1976 Last Home for the Aged. San Francisco: Jossey-Bass.
Townsend, Claire
  1971 Old Age: The Last Segregation. New York: Bantam Books.
Townsend, Peter
  1964 The Last Refuge. London: Routledge and Kegan Paul.
  1965 "The effects of family structure on the likelihood of admission to an institution in old age." In Ethel Shanas and Gordon Streib (eds.). Social Structure and the Family: Generational Relations. Englewood Cliffs, N.J.: Prentice-Hall.
U.S. Public Health Service
  1974 "Measures of chronic illness among residents of nursing and personal care homes. U.S., June-August 1969." Vital and Health Statistics, Series 12, No. 24. National Center for Health Statistics. Washington, D.C.: U.S. Government Printing Office.
  1975 "Selected operating and financial characteristics of nursing homes. U.S.: 1973–74 National Nursing Home Survey." Vital and Health Statistics, Series 13, No. 22. National Center for Health Statistics. Washington, D.C.: U.S. Government Printing Office.
U.S. Senate
  1964 Preneed Burial Service. Special Committee on Aging. Washington, D.C.: U.S. Government Printing Office.
  1971 Alternatives to Nursing Home Care: A Proposal. Special Committee on Aging. Washington, D.C.: U.S. Government Printing Office.
  1974 Development in Aging: 1973 and January-March 1974. Special Committee on Aging. Washington, D.C.: U.S. Government Printing Office.
Viscusi, W. Kip and Richard Zeckhauser
  1977 "The role of social security in income maintenance." In Michael Boskin (ed.). The Crisis in Social Security: Problems and Prospects. San Francisco: Institute for Contemporary Studies.
Ward, Russell
  1977 "Services for older people: An integrated framework for research." Journal of Health and Social Behavior 18: 61–70.
Watson, Wilbur and Robert Maxwell
  1977 Human Aging and Dying: A Study in Socio-Cultural Gerontology. New York: St. Martin's.

Williamson, John
    1974   "The stigma of public dependency: A comparison of
             alternative forms of public aid to the poor." Social
             Problems 22: 213–28.
    1975   Strategies Against Poverty in America. New York:
             Schenkman.
York, Jonathan and Robert Calsyn
    1977   "Family involvement in nursing homes." The Gerontologist
             17: 500–05.
Younger, Evelle
    1976   "The California experience in crime prevention programs
             with senior citizens." In Jack Goldsmith and Sharon
             Goldsmith (eds.). Crime and the Elderly: Challenge and
             Response. Lexington, Mass.: Lexington Books.
Zusman, Joseph
    1966   "Some explanations of the changing appearance of psychotic
             patients: Antecedents of the social breakdown syndrome
             concept." Milbank Memorial Fund Quarterly 64: 363–94.

12

Death and Dying

~~~~~~~~~~~~~~~~~~~~~~~~~~~~~~~~~~~~

By both coincidence and design, death and dying are the subjects of the final substantive chapter of this book. Discussion of these issues in connection with social gerontology is appropriate from a number of points of view. Death is, after all, the inevitable final act in the aging experience. We need to understand how the aged confront their own finitude and how the social context affects this confrontation. In modern societies, death has also been increasingly confined to the end of the "natural" life span; simply put, it is increasingly the old who die. This link between old age and death may thus contribute to our fears and stereotypes about aging and old age, and attempts to deny our own finitude through "distancing" behaviors may also lead us to withdraw from the aged, who mirror our mortality. This link also gives special relevance for the aged to many current public issues surrounding dying and death, such as euthanasia, medical definitions of death, and debates over "appropriate death."

The fact that death becomes a more salient experience in old age may affect the aging experience in many ways. As the deaths of friends and family occur with greater frequency, older people may experience what Kastenbaum and Aisenberg (1976) call "bereavement overload." Psychological correlates of old age, such as rigidity, cautiousness, or fatalism, may be linked to the perception of impending death. We saw in Chapter 2 that psychological and intellectual age differences may reflect a "terminal drop" just prior to death rather than general effects of aging per se. Disengagement theory, still one of the most influential approaches to aging, attributes basic social, psychological, and emotional changes to individual and societal preparation for death.

A discussion of death is also relevant to the study of aging because it is relevant to the human condition in general. Many human activities and institutions are shaped by inevitable mortality. Some have even suggested that death is a primary motivating force—that one can interpret human existence in terms of anticipation of death. Ernest Becker, in *The Denial of Death*, argues that:

> . . . the idea of death, the fear of it, haunts the human animal like nothing else; it is a mainspring of human activity—activity designed largely to avoid the fatality of death, to overcome it by denying in some way that it is the final destiny for man. (Becker, 1973:ix)

But before considering individual responses to death, let us look at the societal aspects of death.

Death and Social Structure

Society structures the nature of death. Since it is a universal and recurring event, which in many ways threatens to disrupt the social order, all cultures develop values, beliefs, and practices concerning death (Volkhart and Michael, 1957; Blauner, 1966). These cultural practices shape individual orientations and reactions to death, both one's own and the deaths of others. It is also true that death affects the social structure, and thereby the lives of the living.

While the inevitability of death has not been altered, other aspects of death have changed over the centuries, particularly as a consequence of the "mortality revolution" which has accompanied modernization (Goldscheider, 1971). In preindustrial societies, death rates were very high (and life expectancy low) and fluctuated widely with time and location in response to the largely uncontrolled effects of climate, epidemics, war, and famine. Compared with today, death was particularly high in the early years of the life course. For example: (1) life expectancy in Europe between the thirteenth and the seventeenth centuries ranged between 20 and 40 years, (2) even among the British aristocracy of the sixteenth and seventeenth centuries, approximately 20 percent of all infants failed to survive, (3) during the fourteenth century, an estimated one-fourth to one-third of the entire population of Europe died of plague, and (4) 44 percent of the population of Marseilles, France, died during an epidemic in 1720–22 (Goldscheider, 1971).

Exposure to death in these "high-mortality" societies was considerable for all members of society, and there seemed to be little control over the "mysterious" forces of nature. The nature of death may account for some of the structural aspects of these societies (Goldscheider, 1971; Kastenbaum and Aisenberg, 1976).

First, there was an emphasis on the extended family, as a more permanent and less precarious structure than the small, autonomous nuclear family, made possible only by extending life and reducing infant deaths. One mechanism for reducing the disruptiveness of death is to reduce the "importance" of those who die. Thus, in high-mortality societies there are reduced emotional attachments within the nuclear family, and infants especially are unlikely to be viewed as real "people." Because of high rates of infant mortality, high fertility will be encouraged. Romantic love may be downplayed in favor of arranged marriages; there is little time to dawdle through time-consuming, haphazard searches for "true love."

Very low life expectancy means little time or energy to go beyond subsistence or to plan for the future. Thus, while moderinzation usually causes lower mortality, mortality reduction is also required to allow time for the career planning, specialized training, and future-orientation which facilitate social and economic development. The prospect of an early death stands in the way of progress.

With the regular presence of uncontrolled death, there is a press for religious and magical explanations and the development of more elaborate rituals and procedures to manage the disruptiveness of death, which is more likely to occur to those in the "prime of life" who are still vital to society's business. Blauner (1966) suggests that ghosts are reifications of these people who die with "unfinished business," and elaborate rituals evolve to appease the dead. In the Middle Ages in Europe, with no technological defenses against death and religious imagery of eternal torture and damnation, a preoccupation with death developed, perhaps as a way of controlling fear, which was reflected in art, children's "death games" ("ashes, ashes, all fall down"), dancing manias, and witchcraft.

By the nineteenth century in Europe, however, the mortality revolution was lowering mortality rates and reducing the wide fluctuations (except for those due to warfare). This was a consequence of medical advances, improved sanitation and public health measures, and a general rise in living standards. Although Europe and the United States led the way in these advances, developing countries have shown very swift recent changes, as seen in some examples cited by Goldscheider. From 1921 to 1951, Jamaica showed reductions in mortality which required 130 years in Sweden. Infant mortality in Singapore declined from 168 to 28 per 1,000 births between 1930 and 1960. In Mauritius, deaths due to malaria declined from 3,534 in 1945, to only 3 in 1955. These changes have altered some of the realities of death, as we have already seen in Chapter 2. Death has increasingly become the "province" of the old, which affects the entire society.

The location of death has also changed in modern societies. Two or three generations ago, most people died at home, surrounded by family and friends in a familiar environment. Now perhaps two-thirds of all deaths occur in institutions, primarily general hospitals (Lerner, 1970). The proportion of all deaths which occurred in nursing homes also doubled from 1962 to 1972, and approximately one-fifth of the deaths to persons 55 and over now occur in nursing homes (Ingram and Barry, 1977). The fact that people are increasingly likely to die within an institutional environment, with its potential for depersonalization, partly accounts for recent concern over "appropriate death" and the "right to die."

Thus, the nature of death is very different in modern societies. In someways, we are insulated from the perception of death (Blauner, 1966; Kastenbaum and Aisenberg, 1976). The aged, who are most likely to die, are already socially disengaged and therefore less "important" to society, and the young can maintain a social and psychological distance from death, which is not a "real" prospect for them. Dying and death are segregated from our worlds through bureaucratization—special dying institutions (hospitals, nursing homes) and death specialists (the mortuary industry). Children especially are unlikely to be exposed to death. We have also achieved a type of technological mastery over death, enormously reducing the capriciousness of death and the possibility of "premature" death.

Since death is not as real or as uncontrollable, and the dead are seen as less powerful, there is less social disruption and therefore less need for elaborate traditions and rituals. Blauner (1966) suggests, for example, that stress on ghosts and extrahuman forces has declined because it is largely the aged who die. Religious institutions must change from an "other world" to a "this world" orientation (Goldscheider, 1971). Funerals are criticized as irrelevant and exploitative, and, at the very least, are less important to the group as a whole.

The social substructure of the funeral is weakened when those who die tend to be irrelevant for the ongoing social life of the community and when the disruptive potentials of death are already controlled by compartmentalization into isolated spheres where bureaucratic routinization is the rule. Thus participation and interest in funerals are restricted to family members and friends rather than involving the larger community, unless an important leader has died. Since only individuals and families are affected, adaptation and bereavement have become their private responsibility, and there is little need for a transition period to permit society as a whole to adjust to the fact of a single death. (Blauner, 1966:386)

Although death may be less disruptive for the society, it may have become more so for the individual. Elisabeth Kübler-Ross (1969) argues that as death has been removed from family and home into lonely, dehumanized institutional environments, dying has become a more difficult experience, for both those who die and their survivors. Secularization of society means that the hereafter no longer offers a reward for suffering, making it seem purposeless. The deritualization of death means that individuals are left on their own to handle bereavement and grief. The lack of structured expectations about grieving—"When have I grieved long enough?"—may prolong it and leave unmet needs which create hostility and guilt (Volkhart and Michael, 1957; Blauner, 1966). This brings us to a consideration of societal attitudes and values concerning death, and of the problems faced by those who are dying, those who care for the dying, and those who are bereaved.

Attitudes Toward Death

Attitudes toward death are extremely complex and changeable, shifting with situation, mood, and cultural surroundings, and they vary by age, sex, education, religiosity, and so on. Death-related attitudes are also very difficult to study, because of their sensitive emotional quality. Until recently, there was relatively little work in this area, and the vast majority of studies have been conducted with highly specialized populations: college students, medical staff, terminal patients, and so on. The validity of responses to questions about death is also difficult to ascertain. Suppose someone tells you that he has little fear of death, and seldom thinks about his own death. On the surface, this might seem to indicate "acceptance" of death, but this very acceptance may instead be a type of denial.

Despite these problems, however, there do seem to be some consistencies in attitudes toward death, stemming from the impact of the social and cultural context on our images, values, beliefs, and feelings. The larger culture is one source of our views of "death as a thought," to use Kastenbaum and Aisenberg's (1976) phrase. For example, although Western societies tend to see life and death as separate entities, other cultures take different approaches (Knutson, 1970). Greek literature abounds with visits of the living to the land of the dead, and vice versa. Buddhism views life as a continuous existence through which the soul migrates in different forms. Even Western thought has run the gamut from death as a mere natural, organic fact, to death as the distinguishing feature of human existence (Marcuse, 1959). In this section, we shall explore three questions: (1) What does death mean for the individual and society? (2) Is there denial or acceptance of death in modern societies? and (3) How do reactions to death change over the life cycle?

The Meanings of Death

Death has two kinds of meaning for us. First, there are various interpretations of what it means to "be dead" (Kastenbaum, 1977a). Death may be seen as enfeebled life, a view often held by young children, but also by some ancient religions. For the Hebrews during Old Testament times, the dead dwelt in Sheol, as shadows of their former selves. Kastenbaum also notes that some tribal societies viewed death simply as a transition to more "life as usual." Death may be a time of sleeplike waiting for a Day of Judgment. Other philosophies stress perpetual development, with death as a removal to a higher spiritual plane, or a type of recycling or rebirth, in the Mandala—the "great wheel of life." Finally, there are more "rational" interpretations of death as a biological endpoint or as simply the absence of life.

Death can also be seen as having an "ultimate" meaning or purpose (Kastenbaum, 1977a). Death is the "great leveler," providing a sense of revenge for the poor and the downtrodden. Death may also be seen as the "great validator" of our worth and status. This is evident in such things as wishing to "die with my boots on" and the use of the funeral as a show of status. Death alters our relationships with others. It obviously entails separation, but also unites friend and foe, brings us into company with God or reunion with those who died earlier. Finally, death may be seen as either the "ultimate problem"—the worst enemy of society and the individual, something which defies understanding—or the "ultimate solution"—genocide and suicide.

One way to explore the meanings of death is to look at the ways in which it is pictured and personified as harpies, skeletons, and the like. Kastenbaum and his associates have investigated personifications of death held by various types of people by asking: "If death were a person, what sort of a person would Death be?" (Kastenbaum and Aisenberg, 1976). Four images seemed to predominate. The *Macabre* image presents death as a repulsive, overpowering, typically very old person, as in the following quote from a male undergraduate:

> Physically, Death is a walking death. He is a male, about 89 years old, and is very bent over. His hair is scraggly, his face is wrinkled, almost not recognizable as human flesh.

> His eyes are sunken, his teeth are rotting (the ones left). As noted above, he is bent, if not a hunchback, and can hardly move. His hands and other appendages are also in terrible shape. Personality-wise, he's grouchy, cranky, sullen, sarcastic, cynical, mean, evil, disgusting, obnoxious, and nauseating—most of the time—only, very, very seldom does his good side show through. (Kastenbaum and Aisenberg, 1976:128)

The *Gentle Comforter* offers a very different view of death as a strong and tender middle-aged person. A young nurse comments:

> Psychologically, Death would be very comfortable and comforting. He would bring the meaning of life, the quiet whisper would allow one to know what life is about. The entire reason each one is living will become clear when Death comes. He will be kind, tender, and gentle. He will come to envelop and take me with a quietness. (Kastenbaum and Aisenberg, 1976:130)

The third personification of death is the *Gay Deceiver*, who entices and cons people into death:

> Death is either a man and/or a woman. This death person is young to middle-aged and very good looking. The man is about 35 or 40 with dark hair, graying at the sides. The woman is tall, beautiful with dark hair and about 30. Neither is repulsive in any way. Both have very subtle and interesting personalities. They're suave, charming, but deceitful, cruel, and cold. While death may be cruel, however, it's a pleasant cruelty at times. . . . You like them and they lead you on. (Kastenbaum and Aisenberg, 1976: 134)

The final image is the *Automaton*—death as an objective, unfeeling instrument, lacking human qualities.

> He would never speak. He would be void of all emotions. He would exist under a superhuman type of energy. He would move slowly as if remorsefully, but he would not be so in the slightest. He

would never tire, nor would he ever become energetic. He would just go about his business in a matter-of-fact way. (Kastenbaum and Aisenberg, 1976: 132)

Images of a death-person reflect our interpretations of and attitudes toward death. The Macabre picture is perhaps a legacy of the Middle Ages, when death was omnipresent and often horrible. Kastenbaum and Aisenberg suggest that the Automaton represents a reaction to modern science and technology, where death has become sterile and meaningless.

The Automation is the funeral service that alienates both the deceased and the survivor through its routine, remote generalizations. He is the medical technology that relates to the dying man through his orifices while casting a calculating eye upon organs worth the detaching. He is the professional indoctrination that dulls our nerve endings so that human feeling gains neither entry nor exit while we remain captive within our roles. He is our scrap heap orientation toward the aged which leads a person to feel "as good as dead" while still on this side of the grave. He is the casual brutality of our cities. He is the war machine. (Kastenbaum and Aisenberg, 1976:366–67)

There is some evidence in their work of a relatively accepting view of death, however. In a multiple-choice version of the study, death was most frequently pictured as male, late middle-aged or elderly, and "gentle, well-meaning."

Denial or Acceptance?

One continuing argument has revolved around whether our attitudes and behaviors concerning death constitute acceptance or denial (Dumont and Foss, 1972). Denial implies that we refuse to truly believe or recognize death as a personal possibility. Acceptance, on the other hand, means personal awareness of our own finitude, planning for death, and perhaps even approving of it.

One can find various types of evidence for the denial of death. At the very least, death symbols are emotion-laden, and some have argued that death has become the great "taboo" of modern societies, perhaps replacing sex as the "new pornography" (Gorer, 1965). Dumont and Foss (1972) point to funeral customs which mask the reality of death—cosmetic embalming, cushioned caskets —and the many euphemisms which soften death—pass away, cross over the bar, kick the bucket. There may also be the feeling that they will die, not me, or that if I don't go to the doctor, my symptoms can't be serious, a type of magical immortality (Kastenbaum, 1977a).

Humans have many strategies for circumventing the finality of death, thereby achieving a "symbolic immortality" which transcends physical death (Toynbee et al., 1968; Lifton, 1977). This may occur biologically, by living through our descendants, or it may involve a merging or oneness with nature. We achieve immortality through our works or fame that lives on. This book may give the author some small sense of immortality. The famous among us are often concerned about their "place in history," and write memoirs to assure it. The immortality of the soul, perhaps dwelling in an afterlife, also denies the finality of death.

Why should we fear or deny death? It is, after all, as natural as life itself, and some would argue that denial of death is morbid and a sign of psychological maladjustment. Others suggest, however, that fear of death and denial are natural responses to the dilemma of knowing that "people" die, yet being unable to really comprehend our own death or nonexistence (Becker, 1973; Hinton, 1972). We gain comfort by denying the death of ourselves and our loved ones, except as very distant possibilities. The inability to comprehend and face death may be greater in modern societies than in the past, since death is more removed from our experience. Lifton and Olson (1974) suggest that the nuclear age, with its unimaginably destructive weapons, creates the ultimate threat of meaninglessness and total destruction of the entire human race. This is a reality we cannot accept in any meaningful sense.

Many specific fears are linked to fear of death (Hinton, 1972; Kastenbaum and Aisenberg, 1976). There is ample evidence that the dying and the dead are "repulsive" to us; they remind us of our own mortality and we may fear the power that the dead hold over the living (as ghosts, for example). Many funeral rituals, particularly in earlier times, are designed to appease the dead. The uncertainty of death is unsettling, and fear of dying may be greater than fear of death. There is a common desire to die relatively quickly (once dying begins), with little suffering, and with honor or dignity. Fear of death may be linked to fear of other things—separation, punishment, chaos—and some have suggested that all fears are ultimately tied to fear of death.

Diggory and Rothman (1961) investigated the relative importance for an adult sample of seven "values" destroyed by death. These values (or reasons for fearing death), in decreasing order of importance, were:

1. My death would cause grief to my relatives and friends.
2. All my plans and projects would come to an end.
3. The process of dying might be painful.

4. I could no longer have any experiences.
5. I would no longer be able to care for my dependents.
6. I am afraid of what might happen to me if there is a life after death.
7. I am afraid of what might happen to my body after death.

The ranking of these values varies according to the sample used. Schneidman (1971), using a sample which was primarily young, female, single, and of high socioeconomic status, found that the loss of experiences was most important, followed by the pain of dying and concern for dependents, with the cessation of plans and grief to others falling in importance. Kalish and Reynolds (1976), with a somewhat older sample of lower socioeconomic status, found that grief to others was most important, followed by concern for dependents and the pain of dying. Thus, there is no universality to the values threatened by death.

There are indications that women are more concerned with the grief of others, effects on the body, and the pain of dying, while men are more disturbed by the ending of plans and projects (Diggory and Rothman, 1961; Kastenbaum, 1977a). Married persons are more concerned than the unmarried about inability to care for dependents (Diggory and Rothman, 1961). Many of these differences reflect the fact that social roles (and their age stratification) influence the goals which are important to us—personal experience for the young, care of dependents for older, married persons, and so on—thereby determining the values threatened by death (Kastenbaum and Aisenberg, 1976).

Kalish and Reynolds (1976) investigated age differences in these fears or concerns. They found that the middle-aged (40 to 59) were most likely to stress the grief to others and the end of their plans and prospects. Older respondents (60+) were more likely to be concerned with what would happen to their bodies (perhaps reflecting greater body preoccupation in old age), but were less concerned with grief to others, inability to care for dependents, and the ending of experiences.

While fear of death is multidimensional, and probably natural, it might be argued that the best way to cope with this fear is to meet it head on. Hinton (1972) notes that many philosophers have argued for total acceptance of the reality of death. American society in particular tends toward rationality, and with medical advances, death is increasingly viewed as the natural completion of the life cycle in old age. Death may also be perceived as acceptable because it represents release from misery and suffering, a reunion with loved ones, or as one's own possession (Kastenbaum and Aisenberg, 1976). This last idea implies that control over one's own death may be very important to people. A 93-year-old man, while discussing the prospect of his death, stated that: "It's mine. . . . Don't belong to nobody else" (Kastenbaum and Aisenberg, 1976:103).

Surveys indicate that when asked directly, relatively few adults consider fear of death important compared with other concerns, and their attitudes about death primarily reflect acceptance (Kastenbaum and Aisenberg, 1976; Kalish, 1976). Riley's (1970) survey of a national sample offers good examples of this. His findings included the following:

1. 89 percent agreed that death can "sometimes be a blessing," 82 percent agreed that it is "tragic only for the survivors," while only 53 percent felt that death "always comes too soon," and 14 percent said that "to die is to suffer."
2. Approximately one-third of the respondents "often" thought about death; such thoughts were often triggered by illness, the death of others, and accidents or "near misses."
3. 80 percent felt that it was better to make plans concerning death than to ignore or deny it.
4. Many had made preparations regarding death: 70 percent had bought life insurance, 50 percent had talked about death with others, 25 percent had made funeral arrangements and drawn up a will.

Kalish and Reynolds (1976) also found that most of their respondents in Los Angeles appeared unafraid of death, seldom thought about their own death, and would accept it peacefully. They also found that, although death may be less intrusive in modern societies, their respondents were not isolated from death experiences. Within the previous two years, over 80 percent knew someone who had died, two-thirds had gone to a funeral, and over one-third had visited or talked with a dying person.

There is evidence, then, that we both deny and accept the reality of death. Such conflicting attitudes may be inevitable, given what Weisman (1972) terms the "primary paradox" surrounding death: while we can recognize the universality of death, we cannot imagine or comprehend our own death. Other factors contribute to rational, intellectual acceptance of death, coupled with emotional, psychological denial (Dumont and Foss, 1972). Kalish and Reynolds (1976) found that their younger respondents "expected" not to die until they were 75. While the decline of religious and ritualistic practices surrounding death may indicate greater acceptance, loss of these reassuring supports may also create greater apprehensiveness. Finally, our death-related experiences are never totally positive or negative, leaving a complex mixture of feelings and emotions. Kalish and Reynolds conclude from their study that "The overall impression is one of a practical and reasonable approach to the handling of death with perhaps a dash of avoidance when personal-emotional aspects are touched upon" (Kalish and Reynolds, 1976:49).

Fear and denial of death vary among individuals, of course. Persons with less education tend to think more about death, make fewer plans, and feel more threatened by death (to say, for example, that death always comes too soon or that to die is to suffer) (Riley, 1970). Interestingly, courses on death seem to have little effect on fear of it, though they seem to make discussion less taboo and may facilitate the development of personal philosophies concerning death (Bell, 1975; Leviton, 1977). Religiosity has complex relationships to death attitudes. Those who are most religious tend to display lower death anxiety, but this may also be true of those who are most confirmed in their lack of religious beliefs (Kalish, 1976). Age is also related in various ways to attitudes surrounding death.

Death and the Life Cycle

It is reasonable to expect that changes in conceptions of death and attitudes toward death will occur over the life cycle, at least partly in response to developmental processes. This can be seen in Maria Nagy's (1948) classic study describing these stages in the child's developing conception of death:

1. Ages 3 to 5: death is viewed as reduced life, and as temporary, with predominant themes of departure and separation.
2. Ages 5 to 9: children recognize the finality of death, but personify a Death-man as an outside agent who might still be eluded.
3. Ages 9 and above: death is recognized as personal, universal, and inevitable.

Death is an abstract concept whose "full" meaning requires an appreciation of other concepts, such as object and self constancy and a sense of futurity (Kastenbaum and Aisenberg, 1976). A sense of one's future may not be fully comprehended until adolescence, and death may not be a "real" possibility even for college-age young people who live in the present.

One must be careful, however, about exaggerating the inability of even very young children to develop perceptions and feelings about death. Children are exposed to many types of death—the death of flowers, pets, or family members, death images on television—and adults can often recall very early encounters with death, some of which may contribute to later emotional and behavioral problems (Kastenbaum and Aisenberg, 1976). Children often display considerable curiosity about death, and experiment with "being" and "nonbeing" ("peek-a-boo," "all gone").

Children's conceptions of death depend on many things—developmental level, inquisitiveness, types of experiences with death, communication and support from others (Kastenbaum, 1977a; 1977b). Kastenbaum notes that the sociocultural context affects death experience, so one could expect different conceptions of death from children in the Middle Ages or during wartime (as in Vietnam or Northern Ireland). Adult ambiguities, evasions, or myths about death may only confuse children. The best policy seems to be not to treat discussions with children of death as taboo, but rather to be open, direct, and accurate, and to use the many childhood encounters with death to recognize natural feelings and questions, creating an open environment for the expression of feelings (Kastenbaum, 1977b; Bluebond-Langner, 1977).

Young adults appear to take a stance toward death which sets them apart from other age groups. Kalish and Reynolds (1976) suggest that younger persons may be more introspective, enabling them to conceptualize better their own "nonexistence." It is also true that they are only beginning to develop the emotional ties with others which make their grief and the inability to care for dependents more important in later adulthood. Other results from Kalish and Reynolds' study indicate that while the young are more open about death in some ways (they are more likely to advocate that a dying person should be told that he or she is dying), they are also more fearful of death, and would fight against their own death more actively. This anxiety is partly alleviated by seeing death as only a distant possibility.

Middle age is another stage of the life cycle which affects our relationship to death (Kastenbaum, 1977b). This may be the time when we encounter our first personally relevant or disturbing death, such as the death of our parents. Kastenbaum notes that we develop a "pecking order of death"—we expect certain people to die before we do. When parents die, this brings one's own death psychologically closer. Middle age is also a time when death is less uncommon among peers, and the middle-aged may experience "partial deaths"—of attractiveness, physical strength, career opportunities. Kalish and Reynolds (1976) found that their middle-aged respondents expressed the most anxiety about the interview itself, perhaps because of some realization that youthful postponement of the possibility of death can be maintained for only a short time more.

A sense of impending death has long been considered important in the psychology of old age. Presumed consequences include social and emotional disengagement, the need for a sense of ego integrity, and the tendency to engage in a life review. This awareness of finitude is not simply a function of chronological age; it is affected by such things as parents' age at death, number of living siblings, health, and the deaths of friends (particularly age peers) (Marshall, 1975a). Obviously, death is a realistic concern for the aged and may be related to fear of abandonment or of dying in an "inappropriate" way.

Older people are more likely than younger people to think about death and talk about it with others (Kalish, 1976), and generally display more acceptance than fear of death. For example, older people are more likely than younger people to agree that "death is sometimes a blessing" and to make plans regarding death (Riley and Foner, 1968). Kalish and Reynolds (1976) found that older respondents (60+) thought more about death, had made more preparations (funeral arrangements, writing a will), were less afraid of death, felt better able to face dying, and would accept death more peacefully than younger and middle-aged persons. They suggest a number of reasons for this apparent greater acceptance of death. As death becomes a more imminent reality, the aged may engage in some anticipatory socialization for dying (perhaps with the help of age peers). Having reached their "expected age," they may also feel that they are living on borrowed time, making death seem less unfair. Kalish and Reynolds found, for example, that the death of an elderly person was almost universally considered the least tragic type of death. Finally, problems associated with aging and processes of disengagement may diminish the value of life. This disengagement (for whatever reason) helps account for the decreased importance for older people of grief to others and inability to care for dependents. Fear of death, while low, is greater among older people who have less education, live alone, have greater feelings of rejection and depression, and have less belief in an afterlife (Jeffers, Nichols, and Eisdorfer, 1961; Riley and Foner, 1968).

Kalish and Reynolds (1976) have found that older people appear to react differently from younger people to the possibility of their own death (Table 12.1). There was a decline with age in the likelihood of altering life style or attempting to complete projects and an increase in a more contemplative approach to impending death. Interestingly, older respondents were also more likely to consider sudden death more tragic than slow death. Apparently

Table 12.1. Responses (percentage) of 434 respondents to the question: "If you were told that you had a terminal disease and six months to live, how would you want to spend your time until you died?"

Use of time	Age		
	20–39	40–59	60+
Marked change in life style, self-related (travel, sex, experiences, etc.)	24	15	9
Inner-life centered (read, contemplate, pray)	14	14	37
Focus concern on others, be with loved ones	29	25	12
Attempt to complete projects, tie up loose ends	11	10	3
No change in life style	17	29	31
Other	5	6	8

Source: Richard Kalish and David Reynolds, *Death and Ethnicity: A Psychocultural Study,* p. 68, © 1976 by The Ethel Percy Andrus Gerontology Center, University of Southern California. Reprinted by permission.

they wanted more time to see loved ones one last time, bring their affairs together, and reminisce.

Other older people can be an invaluable source of support against death and dying. Studies of age-segregated settings indicate that they facilitate discussion of death, allowing the aged to come to grips with their own feelings and achieve an acceptance of death which does not require denial (Hochschild, 1973; Marshall, 1975b). Age peers serve as role models of how to "face up" to death, how to react appropriately to the death of others, and how to die in a "good," or dignified, way. This is not a morbid preoccupation with death. Marshall, in his study of one retirement village, found that death was managed in a low-key manner: funerals were held elsewhere, grief was restrained, obituaries were discreet. But through interaction with other older people, discussing feelings which could not be discussed as easily with family or younger people, they were able to view death as an "appropriate" completion of the life cycle. An 88-year-old woman comments that "it's time people shuffled off by 90." An 81-year-old widow remarks:

"Heavens! I've lived my life. I'd be delighted to have it end. The sooner the better. I nearly went with a heart attack. It would have been more convenient to go when my daughter was in _____ rather than in _____. I feel I've lived my life, and I don't want to be a care to anybody. That's why I'm glad to be here [in Glen Brae]. No, I don't want to mourn when I go. I've had a good life. It's time." (Marshall, 1975b:1127)

Table 12.2. Attitudes toward death in a retirement village and in a national sample of adults

Would you agree or disagree with the following statements?	Percent agreeing		
	Glen Brae[a]	61+[b]	18+[b]
Death is sometimes a blessing.	98	91	89
Death is not tragic for the person, only for the survivors.	91	85	82
Death always comes too soon.	12	51	53
Total N	79	249	1,428

[a] Retirement village.
[b] National sample (Riley, 1970).
Source: Victor Marshall, "Socialization for impending death in a retirement village," *American Journal of Sociology* 80:1127. © 1975 by The University of Chicago Press. Reprinted by permission.

Table 12.2 compares some attitudes toward death among the residents of this retirement village with those from Riley's (1970) national sample. The results do indicate greater acceptance of death, as "sometimes a blessing," "tragic only for the survivors," and not "always coming too soon."

While these findings are interesting and informative, they are based on only scattered studies which include age as a factor in death-related attitudes. This is an area which needs much more investigating, particularly in explaining why such age trends occur. Are these differences truly consequences of age, or do they reflect cohort phenomena instead? Current cohorts of older people are more religious and have less education, for example, and these variables themselves seem to have important effects on attitudes about death. Until recently, death and dying have been neglected topics in social gerontology. A recent survey of books on aging found that little attention was given to death and dying: nearly two-thirds gave less than 1 percent of their space to this subject (Wass and Scott, 1977). This neglect is unfortunate, and overlooks the relevance of thanatology (the study of death) to the aging experience. Hopefully, more attention, research, and discussion will be generated in the future.

Reactions to the Dying

To this point, we have discussed attitudes toward death as an "abstract" possibility. What happens when death is a "real" possibility? How are the dying reacted to by others, and how do they themselves react to the process of dying?

There are many indications of a social and psychological withdrawal from the dying by those around them. Families may use pretense to stave off the reality of dying, or visit less frequently. Hospital staff find ways to avoid contact with death.

Nurses can also find ways to delegate the death watch, usually to someone who is not quite aware of the task he is being asked to perform (another use of "role switching"). If the dying patient is in a room with an alert patient, the nurse may leave the room with a "pressing work" excuse, asking the alert patient to call her immediately if he notices a change in the other patient. Nurses will also ask an ever-present family member, or perhaps a chaplain, to sit with the patient. If no one is available, a patient may be left to die alone, between periodic checks, though nurses find this outcome most disturbing unless he is already comatose. (Glaser and Strauss, 1966:247)

One study found that nurses responded more slowly to bedside calls from terminal patients (Bowers et al., 1964). There are many reasons for this "distancing" from the dying: the implied failure associated with death, particularly for health professionals, our own fears and insecurities concerning death, and feelings of inadequacy about how to respond ("What do I say?") (Kastenbaum and Aisenberg, 1976).

Death, in modern societies, is increasingly likely to be a frequent occurrence in nursing homes and on some wards of general hospitals. David Sudnow (1967), in a study of a county hospital, notes that it was a mark of sophistication for staff that they could no longer count the number of deaths they had witnessed, except for unusual types of death. To lessen the social and emotional disruptiveness of death, such institutions "bureaucratize" it by isolating death from other aspects of the setting and developing predictable, routinized procedures for managing it.

One way to manage death is to contain and isolate it from the "normal" social world. In *Passing On*, Sudnow (1967) describes some of the strategies designed to isolate death in one county hospital. Dying patients are typically moved to private rooms, or curtains are drawn around their beds. When patients die, their bodies may be removed under pretense of going for an x-ray, and they are never moved during visiting hours. Similar processes seem to go on in nursing homes: closing doors, pulling curtains, removing bodies during meal times, handling the dead as if they were still alive (Gubrium, 1975). In Sudnow's study, the hospital morgue was located in an inaccessible part of the basement, and the morgue attendant made every effort to avoid others when carrying out his duties. For example, he would carry a logbook and keep looking downward to avoid interactions while going to get a body or transporting one. Because of his association with death, the morgue attendant was also something of a social outcast.

Another way of managing death is through predictability, which allows staff to handle death through "routine" procedures, coordinate their treatment of the individual, and avoid disruptive "scenes" which arise from unexpected death. This implies that the determination that someone is *dying* is as much a socially created prediction as a medical fact.

> "Dying" becomes an important, noticeable "process" insofar as it serves to provide others, as well as the patient, with a way to orient to the future, to organize activities around the expectability of death, to "prepare for it." The notion of "dying" appears to be a distinctly social one, for its central relevance is provided for by the fact that it establishes a way of attending a person. In the hospital, as elsewhere, what the notion of "dying" does, as a predictive characterization, is place a frame of interpretation around a person. (Sudnow, 1967:68–69)

Glaser and Strauss (1968) refer to staff conceptions of a *dying trajectory*—the expected shape and duration of the dying process for the patient—which affects their attitudes toward, and treatment of, the individual. There are four types of death expectations, based on its certainty and time remaining (Glaser and Strauss, 1968):

1. death is certain and will occur at a known time
2. death is certain, but the time is unknown
3. death is uncertain, but there is a known time when certainty will be established (e.g., following a series of tests)
4. death is uncertain, and it is not known when this uncertainty will be resolved.

Staff members experience greater stress and disorganization when these expectations are not clearly communicated, or when death occurs unexpectedly, too slowly, or too quickly. It is better for staff when death occurs "on schedule," permitting normal procedures for handling it. All of this relates to an attempt to rationalize death.

The primary responsibility for announcing and coordinating the dying trajectory lies with the physician. Predictions are based on many things other than the illness. The timetable of the "dying career" in a nursing home, for example, may be based on social activity, mobility, functional control (continence), and mental capacity (Gustafson, 1972). In another study, Marshall (1976) found that the perceived dying trajectory in a nursing home was related to successive residential transitions from a private or dormitory room to the infirmary, and finally to "dying rooms."

One important implication of the dying trajectory is that it affects the attitudes and behaviors of others toward the dying person. With expected, lingering dying, for example, active diagnosis and treatment may be suspended, and dramatic rescue scenes in the final hours are unlikely. The focus of treatment shifts from cure to comfort and attempts to relieve suffering. A more unfortunate possibility is that *social* death will precede *biological* death, involving withdrawal and treating the person as if he or she were already dead.

> *Social death* must be defined situationally. In particular, it is a situation in which there is absence of those behaviors we would expect to be directed toward a living person, and the presence of behaviors we would expect when dealing with a deceased or nonexistent person. Social death is read by observing how others treat and fail to treat the person with whom we are concerned. The individual himself may be animated enough and potentially responsive. As a matter of fact, the individual may be desperately seeking recognition, attention, interaction. The concept of social death recognizes that a significant aspect of being a person is being a person in the eyes of others. In other words, this concept calls attention to the basic status of being a person in society. We may appreciate more keenly how contingent and even precarious being a person in society can be when we are alert to the possibility of a living human being treated as though dead or nonexistent. (Kastenbaum, 1977a:31)

Sudnow offers a number of illustrations of social death, including the following:

> A nurse on duty with a woman who she explained was "dying," was observed to spend some two or three minutes trying to close the woman's eyelids. This involved slowly but somewhat forcefully pushing the two lids together to get them to adhere in a closed position. After several unsuccessful moments she managed to get them to stay shut and said, with a sigh of accomplishment, "Now they're right." When questioned about what she had been doing, she reported that a patient's eyelids are always closed after death, so that the body will resemble a sleeping person. After death, however, she reported, it was more difficult to accomplish a complete lid closure, especially after the body muscles have begun to tighten; the eyelids become less pliable, more resistant, and have a tendency to move apart; she always tried, she reported, to close them before death; while the eyes are still elastic they are more easily manipulated. (Sudnow, 1967:74)

While this example of social death is rather bizarre, the more tragic instances involve patients who are still conscious of their world and recognize the declining frequency of visits, the tendency of staff to discuss their "case" as if they were not present, and similar withdrawal from the individual as a social being. Nursing-home residents may engage in a frantic struggle against this dying time-table, as in the hoarding of greeting cards to signify that one is still socially alive (Gustafson, 1972).

All of these reactions to death represent institutional responses to the implied failure of death and the lingering potential for guilt (Mauksch, 1975). Dying threatens the normal routinization of emergencies in hospitals. But reactions to the dying are more than just institutional responses; they are also attempts by individual staff members to deal with their own feelings.

Although health professionals such as nurses and physicians may encounter death frequently, particularly within certain specialties, they are largely left on their own in handling the dying and be-reaved. They carry their own fears and insecurities into medical situations. It has been suggested that physicians are even more fearful of death than the average person, and that becoming a physician may represent an attempt to master those fears (Schulz and Aderman, 1976).

Fear of death, and attempts to avoid contact with it, may be further reinforced by the nature of medical education. It appears that far fewer than half of all medical students even now are exposed to courses on death and dying (Liston, 1973), but they do learn certain stances regarding death (Kastenbaum and Aisenberg, 1976; Coombs and Powers, 1976). Early contact with cadavers and autopsies desensitizes them to death stimuli, teaching a detached "scientific" approach to death. They are taught to maintain a "detached concern" for patients, emphasizing objectivity and lack of emotional involvement. The physician is idealized as the bulwark against death; stress placed on saving lives makes death a sign of failure, ineptitude, and lack of mastery. Helping people die in a dignified or accepting way runs counter to this perception of the healing role.

These aspects of medical education make death and dying very stressful for the physicians. Various strategies, which may be mal-adaptive to the interactional needs of the dying patient, are used to deal with this stress. Physicians may avoid the dying; when cure is impossible, the task of comforting is left to other staff. Patients and their families may be dealt with impersonally, as "cases" ("the kidney in 307"), rather than as whole persons with social, psychological, and emotional needs. Failure to keep this emotional distance may make death very disturbing, as illustrated in the fol-lowing statement by a staff member on an intensive care unit:

We found Richard to be a very interesting, intelligent, and likeable person. He had worked in a hospital previously and therefore understood much of what was happening to him and what his prognosis was. His attitude was one of kindness, concern, and warmth, all which was easy to return. He had a wife and family that were very concerned about him and were equally considerate and kind to the staff. Because of these qualities in Richard and his family, it became very easy to become involved in them. Richard became not just a patient but also a person. His care was made more emotionally difficult by the fact that, unlike most patients, everything he asked for was preceded and followed by "please" and "thank you." He sincerely appreciated everything that we did for him. We found it difficult to care for him because we knew he was going to die. We tried to be cheerful to him, despite the fact that most of us felt quite depressed concerning him and his condition. Many of us who took care of him often wished he would stop being so nice, so considerate, and be the opposite—almost as though it would be easier for us to adjust to his death if we could be angry at him. Even now, many years after his death, we find ourselves remembering him and the emotional difficulties encountered in his care. (Swanson and Swanson, 1977:248)

In some ways, nurses may have greater difficulty handling death and dying than physicians, since they have the most intimate daily contact with dying patients, particularly in emergency and intensive care settings, where there is a constant state of readiness and tension (Benoliel, 1977). Nurses are often the first to discover death and bear the major emotional burden of lengthy terminal care, which lacks the tangible satisfaction of "nursing" someone back to health. This intimate contact with death is compounded by the "responsibility vacuum" created by their subordinate status to the physician; for example, it is not their decision when or whether to tell a patient of his or her status, or to inform the family of a death (Kastenbaum and Aisenberg, 1976). As with physicians, there is little educational preparation for handling death. Studies cited by Kastenbaum and Aisenberg indicate that nurses tend to cling to a model of efficient, impersonal care, in which they should avoid making mistakes or "giving in" and letting their feelings show. When a sample of nurses was asked how they would react to a patient saying, "I think I'm going to die soon" or "I wish I could just end it all," the most likely response was to "turn off" the patient, by changing the subject, engaging in denial, or taking a fatalistic approach. Only 18 percent said that they would be willing to discuss the patient's feelings. Yet such discussions are often very important and beneficial for the dying.

Reactions of the Dying

One increasing concern is that modern societies create a "crisis in dying." As people increasingly die in unfamiliar, depersonalized institutions, an acceptable, dignified, or appropriate death becomes more difficult to achieve. Weisman (1972) notes that common misconceptions about the terminally ill—they do not want to know what the future holds, reconciliation and preparation for death are impossible to achieve, only the suicidal or psychotic are willing to die—become rationalizations for withdrawal or ignoring their human needs. The dying process is usually relatively short (75 to 80 percent of the mortally ill die within three months of their last hospital admission) and only a minority experience unrelieved pain (Hinton, 1972). Even among terminal geriatric patients, most are able to communicate and are conscious of their surroundings up to the very end (Weisman and Kastenbaum, 1968). Yet institutional staff too often pay little attention to the psychological well-being and needs of the dying.

Awareness of Dying

How aware are the terminally ill of their condition, and how much should they be told? Glaser and Strauss (1966) have found four types of *awareness contexts:* (1) *closed awareness*, where the patient is unaware of his condition, (2) *suspected awareness*, in which the patient is suspicious but not sure, (3) *mutual pretense*, where patient and staff both know but deny knowledge to each other, and (4) *open awareness*, when patient and staff acknowledge the "reality" of the situation. It appears that most terminally ill patients have at least some awareness of their condition, since they receive many clues: direct and overheard statements, bodily symptoms, changes in the behavior of others or in treatment routines, changes in physical location (Kalish, 1970; Hinton, 1972). Even terminally ill children are usually aware that they are dying, despite efforts by staff and parents to shield them, and may experience feelings of isolation or anger concerning the overprotectiveness of others (Binger et al., 1969; Waechter, 1971). This awareness, however, is often what Weisman (1972) calls *middle knowledge*, between open acknowledgment and total denial. The terminally ill may fluctuate between open and closed awareness, in response to changes in the course of the illness or equivocation by others. Weisman also notes that they may display an awareness of the diagnosis, but not of its implications.

In mutual pretense, denial is typically shared by avoiding dangerous topics (death itself, future plans) and maintaining little fictions (Glaser and Strauss, 1966). Family and staff are unlikely to initiate discussions of death, often because they feel this is best for the patient, and the patient picks up these signals. To protect their feelings and avoid jeopardizing what few social relationships remain, the patient "plays along." While this lends a certain amount of privacy and minimizes embarrassment, mutual pretense creates very strained, "unreal" interactions and prevents the patient from expressing feelings and concerns within close personal relationships. There may be a severe sense of isolation, as shown in the following statement by a cancer patient:

> I began to realize I desperately needed to talk to someone. But there was no one. The nurses at the hospital were friendly but cautious about answering my questions. The doctors were efficient but very busy. I couldn't talk to my wife because I didn't want to upset her. I tried to talk to some of my friends, but I saw it was bothering them. Some told me not to worry because everything was going to be all right. The doctors certainly knew more about my prognosis than they indicated, so I knew they were just trying to evade the issue. Some of my other friends were affected emotionally by what had happened to me, and they didn't make very good listeners. They were concerned but couldn't bear to discuss anything with me. (Kelly, 1977:185–86)

There may eventually be a break to open awareness, when suffering and the need to talk make the pretense too difficult to maintain, but the convenient fictions are not always easy to break through. Pretense may also be engaged in with some people, but not with others.

Since most terminally-ill people sense their predicament anyway, the ability to talk about it usually brings a feeling of relief. At the very least, they should be granted real opportunities to express their feelings. While this is somewhat less true for older people, most persons prefer to be told of their condition, though they also need to retain some hope and reassurance (Kalish, 1976). The dying may give off many cues, both verbal and nonverbal, of their willingness to engage in "open awareness." It does appear that doctors are increasingly likely to inform terminal patients of their condition. One study of physicians from ten specialties found that only 22 percent would refuse to inform such patients, and 53 percent felt a duty to give these patients extra time (Rea, Greenspoon, and Spilka, 1975). This was more true of younger physicians and those who more frequently encounter the dying, such as oncologists. Pediatricians and cardiologists were less likely to fully share their diagnoses.

Reactions to Dying

In many ways the terminally ill show few emotional differences from the seriously ill, or even the healthy (Kalish, 1976). They are, however, more likely to exhibit anxiety (Hinton, 1972; Kastenbaum and Aisenberg, 1976). There are, after all, many naturally fearful aspects to dying: physical distress, strange tests and treatments, loneliness and separation, loss of control and personal identity, and so on. Fears are attached both to dying and to death. Nevertheless, the dying do not appear to be overwhelmed by fear. Lieberman (1965) found little fearfulness or preoccupation with death among a sample of terminal geriatric patients. Kalish (1969), in a study of persons who had been "reprieved" from a "close call" with death (automobile accidents, near-drownings), found that only 23 percent had been fearful or in panic; the most frequent first reaction had been concern for family and other survivors. Various reports of "out-of-body" experiences by those who "died" and were brought to life by medical rescue often stress peacefulness and serenity and occasional anger over being saved.

While anxiety may be linked to dying, depression seems to be a more frequent response (Hinton, 1972). This includes depression about one's own loss of health and control, and reactions to impending death. It also involves concern for others—their grief, and the extent to which the dying patient is a burden to them.

Some persons react more favorably to the dying process than others. Hinton (1975) found better adjustment to terminal illness among those who had coped well with problems throughout their lives and viewed their lives as more satisfying or fulfilling. These personal differences may actually affect longevity. In a study of cancer patients, Weisman and Worden (1975) found greater than expected longevity among those who were assertive and had established cooperative, mutually responsive relationships with others. Because of their positively expressed assertiveness, they received more attention and better care. On the other hand, those who were apathetic, had death wishes, or had a long-standing pattern of mutually destructive relationships survived a shorter time. They possessed traits which created alienation, both in their personal lives and in encounters with staff.

In her groundbreaking work with the terminally ill, Elisabeth Kübler-Ross (1969) suggests that the dying may experience five stages in their reactions to impending death:

1. *Denial.* According to Kübler-Ross, nearly all patients initially react with denial, which is a healthy buffer. Unfortunately, this may continue if others are not open to dealing with the person's

fears and concerns. She notes that most patients were eventually willing to talk about dying, but have little opportunity to do so.

2. *Anger.* The second stage involves a "why me?" reaction, and anger may be displaced on family or staff. The following statement by a leukemia patient reflects the mixture of anger and guilt which may be felt by dying patients over the behavior of others and loss of personal control.

> Often when Art and the children came, I was too drained and sick to do much talking. I felt guilty about Art having to drive back and forth, handle the children, our home, and his business as well. So, at times, I would urge him to remain at home. At other times, when I was feeling more energized, I would become resentful that he couldn't spend more time with me. I was angry, too, that no one was around to give him the support I felt he needed.
>
> The bulk of my anger became displaced on my hospital environment, particularly those aspects that threatened my own sense of control. These aspects included having to endure endless waiting in the x-ray department when I was racked with chills and fever; experiencing the traumatic loss of my hair that became symbolic for all my potential losses; seeing my body waste away and having no appetite to combat it; vomiting perpetually and continually; feeling trapped in a bleak, grey room that overlooked the barren rooftops of the city. (Jaffe and Jaffe, 1977:200–01)

Such feelings need to be respected and understood, but they often lead instead to withdrawal and avoidance.

3. *Bargaining.* In the third stage, the patient may bargain, often with God, to live long enough to reach some deadline, or to postpone death as a "prize" for good behavior. This may reflect a partially successful "will to live." One study found a reduction in deaths during the month prior to a birthday and an increase following birthdays (Phillips and Feldman, 1973); and John Adams and Thomas Jefferson both died on the Fourth of July, a date of obvious significance to them.

4. *Depression.* The fourth stage represents a natural grief over the final separation of death—grief for oneself and also for those who will be left behind. As with anger, others must "open the door" for the expression of such feelings.

5. *Acceptance.* The final stage, acceptance, is achieved only if the dying person is able, or allowed, to express and deal with earlier feelings, such as anger and depression. This is not a happy stage, but is rather almost void of feelings. There is a sense that one's tasks have been accomplished, the struggle is over. It is, in

the words of one patient, "the final rest before the long journey" (Kübler-Ross, 1969:113).

Kübler-Ross suggests that those around the dying person should not force the stages, but should be open to the individual moving through the stages as he or she is ready to do so. Withdrawal and denial only make a final acceptance more difficult to achieve. Kübler-Ross also notes that some feelings of hope usually persist through all stages, and conveyed hopelessness by others makes the dying process extremely difficult.

The work of Kübler-Ross indicates the importance of allowing the dying to express their feelings, however uncomfortable this may be for us. It is not easy for the family to encounter anger and depression, but such feelings may be necessary for the dying person. However, her scheme is best thought of as an inventory of possible moods or orientations. There is no evidence that the dying experience a universal or invariant sequence of stages (Schulz and Aderman, 1974; Kastenbaum, 1977a). The person may shift back and forth between denial and acceptance, or follow apparent acceptance with more anger or depression. There is a danger that these five stages could become a self-fulfilling prophecy, as patients are forced to follow the expectations. Weisman and Kastenbaum (1968) note from their studies of the terminally ill that, although acceptance of death seemed to be the most frequent response, there were other reactions: apathy, apprehension, anticipation.

> Acceptance refers to patients who spoke about death in a dispassionate and realistic way; apathy describes patients who seemed indifferent to almost any event, including death; apprehension refers to patients who openly voiced fear and alarm about death; and anticipation applies to patients who showed acceptance plus an explicit wish for death. (Weisman and Kastenbaum, 1968:22)

There is no "typical" way to die. The dying process is shaped by an individual's own personality and life style, the specific illness, and, finally, by the context within which it occurs. In questioning the universality of Kübler-Ross's stages, Charmaz (1976) points out that emotional reactions by the dying may be created by the environment—patient denial as a response to staff denial, or anger as a fitting response to staff attitudes and behavior. The openness stressed by Kübler-Ross is an important aspect of this environment and leads to a discussion of caring for the dying.

Caring for the Dying

It is obviously difficult to present any "manual" for caring for the dying. Many of the responses to the dying person which we have discussed—dying trajectories, limiting the obtrusiveness of death—are best seen as natural responses by individuals and organizations to exceptionally difficult social and emotional situations. And in some cases they represent commendable sensitivity, as in the unobtrusive removal of dead bodies from nursing homes. But organizational and staff responses to death and dying can also create a wall of denial and social distance around dying patients, meeting organizational needs at the expense of the needs of the dying.

The goal of those who care for the dying should be to help them achieve an "appropriate death."

> The concept of an appropriate death is based upon the view that dying can be a positive act, not just a calamity that overtakes a person. In appropriate death, the patient is helped to resolve conflict within the limits of his personality and in accordance with the aspirations of his ego ideal. Admittedly, an appropriate death is usually only partially attained, but it is a feasible goal to work toward. An appropriate death is, essentially, one that the patient might have chosen for himself, had he a choice. Conversely, whatever is done to impoverish, demean, or reduce a patient's autonomy and self-esteem will necessarily be a defeat for those who look after him. (Weisman and Kastenbaum, 1968: 43)

Achieving a death which is appropriate to the individual requires a number of things (Weisman and Kastenbaum, 1968; Weisman, 1972; Kalish, 1976; Kastenbaum, 1977a). Relief from physical suffering should be a high priority of treatment. The individual's preferences and life style should be respected, and opportunities to exercise control and responsibility provided. Weisman (1972) notes that sickness eats away at control over our own lives, attacking the person's viability as a competent, responsible actor. Those who care for the dying must support their decision-making options, paying attention to privacy and individuality. This must be balanced with a sense of security and protection. Issues discussed in Chapter 11—the "prosthetic environment," the "social reconstruction syndrome"—should not be discarded simply because someone is dying. Hope for the dying does not depend solely on survival or absolute control, but rather on what Weisman (1972) calls "significant survival": "the belief that we do something worth doing, and that others think so too" (p. 21).

Achieving an appropriate death also requires an open awareness context, combined with warm and intimate personal relationships which provide encouragement and reassurance. Patients, family, and staff all need opportunities to vent their feelings. Sometimes this means nothing more than good listening. There is also a need for privacy and personal leave-taking, which require respect for the dignity of the individual and more relaxed visiting rules.

An open context does not mean that dying persons should be "forced" to be open about their feelings. There is tremendous individual variability in reactions and preferences concerning dying, and we should be wary about any list of rules. There is a danger, for example, in misinterpreting Kübler-Ross's stages of dying to mean that everyone "ought" to follow a fixed sequence or they are dying "unsuccessfully." And not everyone appreciates total openness. Kalish and Reynolds (1976) found that older persons were less likely to feel that dying persons should be informed of their condition, apparently because they placed a greater value on the privacy of such feelings.

All of this suggests that the dying need not suffer, physically, emotionally, or socially, nor inevitably deteriorate. Unfortunately, these conditions are too seldom met in hospital environments. Dying is a total experience, involving the total person, which runs counter to the hospital's fragmented emphasis on "the disease" (Mauksch, 1975), and expression of anger or depression violates the "culture" of the hospital. The dying face a "death valley" atmosphere of isolation, little communication, and hushed tones (Weisman and Kastenbaum, 1968). They experience perhaps the most "total" of institutions, with constricting rules and regulations which yield no autonomy. Weisman and Kastenbaum cite a case where such an environment had clearly negative effects:

> For unspecified administrative reasons, the patient was transferred to another ward where she was essentially unknown. Patients in the new ward were more deteriorated than she, but the head nurse presented the greatest difficulty. She was an elderly woman who called her charges "little girls," and, by assuming a patronizing attitude, fostered extreme dependency. The patient objected when the head nurse first called her by a diminutive version of her given name and demanded that she be called by her proper title. The nurse then sarcastically chided her for wanting to be the "Queen Bee!"

> Three weeks later, a consultant found the patient in a state of delirium. She muttered servile pleas to go back to her original ward, reached out desperately to grab his hand and kiss it. By this time she had deteriorated so much that return to the former ward was no longer possible, and before other arrangements could be made, she died. (Weisman and Kastenbaum, 1968:15)

Problems in caring for the dying may be especially acute in nursing homes, where death is prevalent. In 1972, for example, the average nursing home experienced nearly two deaths every month (Ingram and Barry, 1977). Nursing-home personnel are too seldom prepared for care of the dying, and the frequency of death may be one reason for the high turnover among workers in nursing homes.

There are alternatives to the hospital or nursing home in caring for the terminally ill. St. Christopher's Hospice, opened in 1967 in Great Britain by Cicely Saunders, is literally geared toward providing "hospitality" to the dying.

> Those who welcome each patient to St. Christopher's do so with the conviction that he or she is an important person and that hospitality to a stranger is a prime necessity. Those concerned take care to know the name of newcomers before they arrive, and a senior nurse joins the stewards at the ambulance to welcome them personally. The patient is lifted directly into a warm bed, and his family travels in the lift with him to the ward. It is impossible to overemphasize what such a welcome means to a mortally sick person who has so often felt alien and rejected. He has been the "failure" who cannot get better in the acute ward, feeling obscurely that it is his own fault, or he has suffered long pain at home which has led to despair of ever finding peace. (Saunders, 1977:163)

This emphasis on a personal touch, rather than technology, is found throughout the program of the hospice. Communication and family involvement are stressed. Control of chronic pain is a primary goal; drugs are given regularly according to need, rather than being rationed out according to an implied stoicism. A domiciliary service supports terminal patients in their homes and provides continuity between home and the hospice. This approach seems to be effective. Saunders (1977) notes that 8 to 10 percent of those who enter St. Christopher's return home, and some have achieved unexpected remissions of up to five years. In a comparison with matched patients who were dying in more traditional settings, residents of St. Christopher's had greater mobility, rated their pain as less severe, and were less likely to view the staff as "busy" (Saunders, 1977). In addition, 78 percent felt that "the hospital is like a family," compared with only 11 percent of the comparison group.

Such settings are useful if an appropriate or acceptable death is to be achieved. There have been some recent attempts to transplant the hospice approach to the United States (e.g., in New Haven), but openness in care of the dying is still unusual. Dempsey (1975) has estimated that only about 1 percent of the

7,000 private hospitals in the United States have active counseling programs for dying patients.

Bereavement

Death is never truly an isolated, individual event. There are always survivors who themselves have social, psychological, and emotional needs related to the death experience. Survivors need not have an intimate relationship to the deceased to have severe reactions. Disaster victims often display feelings of guilt ("Why did I live?") or depression. For example, Lifton (1967) found feelings of profound guilt and a "psychic numbing" which made the resumption of meaningful activity nearly impossible among the survivors of the atomic bomb dropped on Hiroshima. The response to death may even be death, as evidenced in the increased death rate six months following widowhood (Parkes, 1973). Since these deaths are mostly attributable to heart diseases, Parkes suggests that we can perhaps literally speak of death from a "broken heart." Thus, just as the dying need supportive assistance in handling death, so also do the survivors of death need help in managing their "grief work." Kübler-Ross (1969) suggests, for example, that her "stages" of dying also apply to the dying patient's family.

A few definitions are in order before we proceed. *Bereavement* refers to both the status of being deprived—one occupies a new social role—and the process of reacting to this loss; *grief* is the response made to this bereavement; and *mourning* signifies culturally patterned expectations about the expression of grief. Although the nature of grief seems to have certain universal qualities, the definition of who is bereaved varies among cultures, as does the content of the prescribed mourning role.

> In cross-cultural terms, the specific content of the role varies widely: weeping; personal preparation of the corpse for burial, gashing one's own body with knives or sharp sticks, protracted seclusion; fasting, wreaking vengeance on those responsible for the death, special religious obligations of prayer or sacrifice, sharp and humiliating alterations in dress and appearance, and so on. (Volkhart and Michael, 1957:297)

How do people respond to the death of others? Lindemann (1944) argues that acute grief constitutes a definite syndrome.

> The picture shown by persons in acute grief is remarkably uniform. Common to all is the following syndrome: sensations of somatic distress occurring in waves lasting from twenty minutes to an hour at a time, a feeling of tightness in the throat, choking

with shortness of breath, need for sighing, and an empty feeling in the abdomen, lack of muscular power, and an intense subjective distress described as tension or mental pain. (Lindemann, 1944:142)

Grief symptoms may occur immediately or be delayed or distorted, but they must be resolved through satisfactory "grief work," which emancipates the bereaved from the deceased and allows readjustment to the "new" world and new relationships without the deceased. Both over- and underreactions to grief may result in certain "pathologies," including suicidal impulses and a lasting loss of social interactions (Lindemann, 1944).

Bereavement and grief encompass complex processes. Common reactions include: shock and disbelief, psychological numbness, depression, loneliness, fatigue, loss of appetite, sleeplessness, and anxiety about one's ability to reorganize and carry on (Lindemann, 1944; Parkes, 1970; Hinton, 1972; Glick, Weiss, and Parkes, 1974; Kalish, 1976). There may be self-questioning and guilt—"Could I have done more?"—which may be linked to anger and resentment, as in the following:

The mother of a fatally injured eight-year-old boy could not allow herself to go into his hospital room. Eventually she confessed to a sympathetic nurse that she desperately wanted to see the dying youngster, but she could not stand by his bedside without the overwhelming urge to "beat the hell out of him." She had told her son repeatedly to keep away from the farm machinery. He had disobeyed her orders and had been fatally injured in the moving mechanism. How could he do this to himself and to her? (Easson, 1977:161)

Restlessness may combine with an inability to initiate activity; routines related to the deceased have now lost their significance, and new patterns have not emerged as replacements.

In a longitudinal study of widows and widowers under 45, Glick and associates (1974) found that although grief and its associated reactions were most severe during the first few weeks, the impact of bereavement persisted and recurred throughout the first year. After the first year, most felt in control of their lives; grief had faded, though feelings of loneliness continued. Even this was not universally true, however; at the end of the year, 28 percent of the widows still agreed that they "would not care if I died tomorrow."

Glick and associates also found that support during bereavement comes from many sources—the immediate atmosphere of warmth and concern constituted "society at its best." Contrary to some of our earlier observations of reactions by hospitals to dying patients, hospitals were often seen by these widows and widowers as quite supportive, as in the following case:

> As far as the doctor was concerned, and the nurses, they were just fantastic. Even the ward helper, the floor scrubbers even. I mean I was just like a member of the family in there. At 3:30 every afternoon I went down to the kitchen and made a pot of tea and we [she and her husband] both had a cup of tea. And I just had my dinner in there if I stayed. They just served me off the tray. Any time I went down to talk to the doctors, they were more than helpful to me, and any time that Bill asked for anything they gave it to him immediately. So that is the one thing I know, that he had the best of care, the very best. (Glick, Weiss, and Parkes, 1974: 80–81)

Kin were particularly helpful. Women generally assisted in household tasks, and brothers-in-law were often especially supportive of widows.

Reactions to loss often intensified following the funeral, however, when the "prescribed" mourning period was over, others returned to their own lives, and the bereaved were left to face their "new life" on their own. There was often uncertainty about the type and length of "appropriate" mourning, and some were defensive about returning to normality This bereavement period was managed by strenuous efforts to "carry on," particularly controlling feelings around others to avoid losing their respect. Gradually during the first year of bereavement, there occurred an acknowledgment of reality and a reconstruction of patterns of living, though there were still intermingled periods of grief and despair. By the end of the year, most had acquired a sense of competence in managing their new lives, as reflected in the following statement:

> I never thought I could take what I have had to take. I thought I would fall apart. But I fought my way back. So maybe I'm stronger than I ever realized. I always leaned on Phil. I always felt that I leaned on him. But now I've got to stand on my own two feet. I just never thought I could do it, but I have. I found out I was a bit stronger than I thought I was. (Glick, Weiss, and Parkes, 1974: 215)

A key finding of the study was that adjustment to bereavement was much less successful when death was sudden or unexpected. Expected death did not reduce subsequent grief, but there was better eventual adjustment, apparently because of emotional and psychological preparation for the changes to come. Sudden death seems to constitute a shock which overwhelms coping capacities, and the reality of death is much more difficult to accept. This is one reason death of the aged is less disruptive; in a sense, their death is always expected, even when sudden.

The benefits of "anticipatory grief" should not be overstated, however. Interaction during a terminal period is very intense—an emotional pressure cooker. This may be a particular problem for women, who typically bear the most responsibility in caring for the dying (Kalish, 1977). As a reflection of the strains involved in "waiting" for death to occur, a recent study of aged widows and widowers found that adjustment to widowhood was less satisfactory when there had been an extended period of anticipatory grief (Gerber et al., 1975).

Mourning involves cultural assumptions about bereavement behavior, which are intended to assist individuals in their "grief work." But it has been argued that this assistance has broken down in modern societies and bereavement has been deritualized, leaving the survivors on their own to handle grief privately (Volkhart and Michael, 1957; Hinton, 1972; Kastenbaum, 1977a). Continued grief is seen as deviant, and there are few socially appropriate channels for the expression of natural grief reactions. The bereaved are therefore likely to view their feelings as "abnormal" and be unable to resolve feelings of guilt, anger, or depression. This may be exacerbated by other types of roles; for example, men seem to have more difficulty expressing grief (Glick, Weiss, and Parkes, 1974; Kalish and Reynolds, 1976). There are other barriers to expression of grief. Kalish and Reynolds found that emotional expression is considered appropriate in private but not in public, and older people are less willing to express their grief through tears, perhaps as a way of protecting themselves from bereavement overload.

Much of this concern about bereavement problems has focused on the modern funeral. As the social disruptiveness of death declines, the funeral becomes less important to the community (Blauner, 1966), but also less functional for the bereaved.

The Death System and the Funeral

Although there has been a certain deritualization of death in modern societies, all cultures still develop values, beliefs, and practices related to death. This cultural system, which Kastenbaum (1977a) has called the *death system*, has many components: people (funeral directors, florists, life insurance agents), places (funeral homes, hospitals, historic battlefields), times (Memorial Day, Good Friday), objects (tombstones, skull and crossbones), and symbols (black armbands, funereal music). The death system serves many functions, including prediction and prevention of death, care of the dying, disposal of the dead, and lending meanings to death. The greatest focus, however, has been on the sociological and psychological functions of the death system in helping both society and the individual to deal with the problems created by death. These functions are felt to be exemplified in the funeral.

Typical arrangements following death currently involve embalming, a "wake" (viewing of the body) which allows people to pay their respects, some type of funeral service (usually religious), and a brief committal service at the cemetery (Pine, 1975; Raether and Slater, 1977). Alternatives exist, but they are seldom used: cremation occurs in about 5 percent of all deaths, donation of bodies to medicine is still very infrequent, and memorial societies (no viewing of the body, cremation, and memorial services) have only approximately 500,000 members (Dempsey, 1975). Although funeral rituals have a very long history, such widespread modern practices as cosmetic embalming and viewing of the body emerged during the Civil War (Raether and Slater, 1977).

The funeral and related rituals such as the wake and burial ceremonies are necessary for disposing of the dead. It is also felt, however, that the funeral fulfills important functions for the living, both the immediately bereaved and the larger social group (Mandelbaum, 1959; Pine et al., 1976). In this sense, "a funeral ceremony is personal in its focus and is societal in its consequences" (Mandelbaum, 1959:189). All cultures have developed such rituals and ceremonies, though their form varies considerably.

One function of the funeral is to serve as a "rite of passage" for the deceased, an appropriate and fitting conclusion to the person's life. Eulogies and respectful gatherings pay tribute to the deceased, emphasizing their worth and helping us put their lives and significance for us into perspective.

Funerals and related ceremonies also provide important functions for the bereaved, by serving as a focal point for expressing grief, accepting the reality of death, and accomplishing the transition back into the normal social world. Prescribed mourning behavior provides a legitimized outlet for grief in a situation in which the support of others is made available. Tasks and rituals bring home the reality of death. Funeral directors often claim that this is facilitated by viewing the body after cosmetic embalming, though there is no real evidence to support this contention. These rituals also help the bereaved determine when they have grieved "enough."

Finally, funerals are important for the social group as a whole by providing an opportunity to display solidarity and reaffirm the values of the group. The funeral demonstrates family cohesion and shows that the social order goes on, despite the disruptiveness of individual death. Funerals also remind those present of their own finitude, and perhaps underline the meaning of death in that culture.

The modern funeral has been challenged as being irrelevant to the needs of the bereaved—as a hollow, artificial ceremony, which encourages irrational responses and serves largely to enrich the $2-billion-a-year funeral industry and its allies (roughly two-thirds of the revenue of florists comes from funerals [Mitford, 1963]). The best-known critic of the funeral industry has been Jessica Mitford, in *The American Way of Death*.

If the Dismal Traders (as an eighteenth-century English writer calls them) have traditionally been cast in a comic role in literature, a universally recognized symbol of humor from Shakespeare to Dickens to Evelyn Waugh, they have successfully turned the tables in recent years to perpetrate a huge, macabre and expensive practical joke on the American public. It is not consciously conceived of as a joke, of course; on the contrary, it is hedged with admirably contrived rationalizations.

Gradually, almost imperceptibly, over the years the funeral men have constructed their own grotesque cloud-cuckoo-land where the trappings of Gracious Living are transformed, as in a nightmare, into the trappings of Gracious Dying. The same familiar Madison Avenue language, with its peculiar adjectival range designed to anesthetize sales resistance to all sorts of products, has seeped into the funeral industry in a new and bizarre guise. The emphasis is on the same desirable qualities that we have all been schooled to look for in our daily search for excellence: comfort, durability, beauty, craftsmanship. The attuned ear will recognize too the convincing quasi-scientific language, so reassuring even if unintelligible. (Mitford, 1963:15–16)

Mitford criticizes the elaborate, profit-seeking nature of funerals. A 1974 survey in Washington, D.C., found that average funeral expenses were $1,886, not including grave plot (Dempsey, 1975). This may be an understatement, as indicated in the sample expenses for a "simple" funeral in 1972 shown in Table 12.3. Mitford argues that there is no evidence to support a public hygiene function for embalming or the view that the "final memory picture" provided by cosmetic embalming helps the bereaved. Indeed, most of the widows in the Glick and associates study (1974) found viewing of the body repugnant. Mitford notes that funeral customs in England are much less ostentatious: embalming is infrequent, and morticians are viewed as craftsmen, not professionals.

The evidence on the utility of funerals is not clear-cut, however.

Table 12.3. Sample expenses of funeral and burial services in 1972 for what undertakers describe as "simple" arrangements

FUNERAL	
Professional services	$ 578.00
Casket (metal; tailored cream-colored interior)	1,154.00
Vault	360.00
Dress	42.50
Slippers	4.95
Limousine	40.00
Obituaries (two papers)	33.60
Death certificates (4) @ $1 each	4.00
Sales taxes	48.00
	$2,265.05
AT THE CEMETERY	
Lot itself	$ 300.00
Open and close ($30 more on Saturday)	170.00
Headstone (actually a flat stone)	210.00
Pallbearers (6) @ $10 each	60.00
Limousine	40.00
	$780.00
TOTAL	$3,045.05

Source: Table 6, p. 382, from *Why Survive? Being Old in America* by Robert N. Butler, M.D. Copyright © 1975 by Robert N. Butler, M.D. Reprinted by permission of Harper & Row, Publishers, Inc.

Fulton (1965; 1976) notes that most people approve of traditional funerals and that such funerals may result in fewer adjustment problems. He also suggests that recent "national" funerals—John and Robert Kennedy, Martin Luther King—have fulfilled important social functions. Glick and associates (1974) found that above all widows wanted the funeral ceremony to be fitting and proper and were not concerned about the cost. They were aware of who had attended, and attendance *itself* was seen as a tribute, as well as offering support and reaffirmation.

> He had a very large funeral and of course when you're young you have not only your own friends, but your family and your family's friends, and he had thought a great deal of many of the people who came. It was very dignified and very simple. It was the way he lived, in a very dignified and simple manner. This meant a lot to me, that so many people would pay him such a great tribute. It was a tremendous funeral procession and the church was packed. I think he would have been kind of proud to have known this. (Glick, Weiss, and Parkes, 1974:116)

Nearly all expressed gratitude to funeral directors for their comfort and support and for their professionalism, while clergy interestingly, were seen as providing little personal solace or counsel.

There may be religious differences in the importance of the funeral. In a study of recently bereaved, Khleif (1976) found that

Catholics saw funerals as being "for the deceased," while Protestants stressed their functions "for the living." Khleif also found that older people were less upset by funeral plans and more pleased with cosmetic restoration.

The funeral will undoubtedly continue as a response to death, and some type of group ritual appears to be beneficial. Greater authenticity is sometimes achieved by adapting arrangements to the life style of the deceased, as in the following example.

> But on one particular occasion about three years ago residents blinked at a strange procession indeed. The familiar gray hearse was followed by a single limousine and twenty-five motorcycles. Even at its funeral pace, the cortege was unusually noisy; to many spectators, it was an unseemly way to pay one's respects to the dead. The helmeted riders—some with their girlfriends perched on the pillions—were wearing blue jeans and leather jackets.
>
> Three days before, a member of their motorcycle club had been killed in an accident. At first the funeral director had resisted the idea of letting the young people ride to the cemetery on cycles; it just wasn't done. But the club leader convinced him, and the boy's family, too, that the deceased would have wanted it that way. The members were paying their respects out of deep feeling, rather than convention. For in a sense, they were his true family. (Dempsey, 1975:167–68)

But it also seems clear that many of the trappings of modern funerals, including cosmetic restoration of the body, are unnecessary. Kastenbaum and Aisenberg (1976) suggest that funerals should be less expensive and take more sensible physical approaches, focusing instead on the psychological and social needs of the survivors. They also point out, however, that the problems of funerals are often simply reflections of a general lack of clear cultural norms to meet the needs of the bereaved.

Grief Specialists

How well do those whose task it is to counsel and comfort the bereaved fulfill their function? Two actors in the death system carry this primary responsibility: funeral directors and clergy.

Funeral directing as a modern occupation began at the end of the nineteenth century, and the role has changed in response to the secularization of death (Pine, 1976). Funeral directors have come to emphasize their status as *professionals*, based on underlying theory and knowledge, ethics, and service to others (Pine, 1975). In recent years, they have particularly advanced a view of themselves as professionals who "serve the living" as "grief specialists," which is shown in the following statement by a funeral industry spokesman:

> Firstly, we are true *professionals*. Licensees in most states are required to invest at least five years beyond high school in academic preparation for examination and licensure. The body of knowledge and demand for more knowledge of the dying, death and bereavement process is expanding day by day.
>
> Our professional counseling is an important help for the bereaved. We bring order out of family chaos. We help families in bereavement to make proper decisions at a time when these decisions are most vital. We assist people in grief and in the process we help mend lives. We give the early aid in the bereavement and grief process and assist people as they take their first steps back into a meaningful life, adjusted to their loss and successful in their grief. These are the goals of our professional practice. (Hausman, 1976:171)

Others are skeptical of such claims to professional status. In their studies of funeral directors and mortuary students, Kastenbaum and Goldsmith found little intellectual interest or output, and their attitudes concerning death were not especially deep or mature. When death-related issues were raised in a classroom of mortuary students:

> Instantly the room was filled with cigarettes that looked like so many emergency flares burning for help; the young men and women began to twitch as though their chairs had just been electrified, and there was a scattering of giggles and obscene remarks. This was by far the strongest reaction either of the researchers had ever encountered when introducing the topic of death in a classroom situation—and the students were tomorrow's funeral directors! (Kastenbaum and Aisenberg, 1976:169)

One-third of the funeral directors in the United States have only a high-school education or less (Pine, 1975). Pine also notes that in terms of specialized training, 12 percent have no training, 62 percent have one year or less, and only 26 percent have college-level training in "mortuary science."

The funeral director is in a difficult position, faced with conflicting demands as businessmen, coordinators, and counselors (Fulton, 1965; Pine, 1975). They must mitigate the reality of death, while at the same time calling attention to the special services they provide, and they may be the scapegoat for our guilt and anxiety concerning death. As with the morgue attendant in Sudnow's (1967) study, funeral directors are "tainted" by their proximity to death. Pine (1975) notes that much of their work involves impression management, to create an orderly and appropriate setting; they must be professionally impersonal but sympathetic, solemn but not depressing.

The most ancient and traditional "grief specialists" have been the clergy. Kastenbaum and Aisenberg (1976) suggest that clergy can be helpful precisely because they serve no medical or technological function, but that they are most useful when they simply offer comfort rather than theological lectures. Clergy, of course, have their own difficulties dealing with death, including the expectations of others that they will "naturally" know how to handle death and dying. Too often this leads to defensive styles: ritualized religiosity, a businesslike manner, denial of death (Bowers et al., 1964; Wood, 1976). Wood (1975), in a study of 31 ministers, found that some took a "humanist" approach, attempting to open up the bereaved to their feelings, while others were more "traditionist," emphasizing the religious and spiritual aspects of death.

To some extent, funeral directors and other counseling professionals are in competition with the clergy, threatening them with a loss of function and status.

> Today clergymen see the new-found prestige enjoyed by doctors, lawyers, and other professional men in the community and are aware, as well, of the material rewards that these professions offer. Relative to these professions many clergymen sense a loss of status, for in a manner of speaking, these other professions have moved ahead more rapidly than the clergy. But in addition, clergymen discover that the cabinet maker who assisted him yesterday in the conduct of a funeral, today not only offers to take complete charge of the funeral, but also is prepared to hold the service in his own "chapel." To many clergymen this is not only galling personally, but is also contrary to the tenets of their faith. (Fulton, 1961:323)

This appears to be less true of Catholic priests, since the Catholic church has been more insistent on keeping the funeral service within the church, with a clearly religious focus (Fulton, 1961). But the counseling role of the clergy may be on the decline. Kalish and Reynolds (1976) found that younger people were much less likely than those over 60 to turn to religion or the clergy for comfort during bereavement.

Issues in Death and Dying

We have noted many times that the changing nature of death in modern societies has altered the ways we deal with it, in some cases creating problems for the dying and bereaved. Complex philosophical, social, and legal issues have also resulted, to a great extent from advances in medical technology which blur the distinction between life and death and create a mechanized atmosphere which threatens "death with dignity." These issues are not unique to aging but have a special relevance for the aged.

The Definition of Death

For a small but growing number of cases involving irreversible coma with brain damage, advances in medical technology have made the traditional signs of death—absence of heartbeat, pulse, and respiration—inadequate, because of the ability to sustain such functions artificially. Decisions about when death has "occurred" are particularly urgent in cases involving organ transplants, since the organ itself (kidney, heart) must still be "alive" for the transplant to be successful. But concern that the pronouncement of death be correct has a much longer history than this. During the nineteenth century, there was considerable concern about premature burial linked to a state of trance or suspended animation ("catalepsy") (Kastenbaum and Aisenberg, 1976); an eighteenth-century physician wrote of 52 alleged cases of premature burial, and 72 cases of mistaken certifications of death (Mant, 1968), and Dempsey (1975) has described coffins sold during the nineteenth century equipped with a chain to ring a bell at the surface in case of premature burial.

The definition of death is of obvious importance to patients and medical staff, but it also has far-reaching legal implications involving such things as burial, inheritance, and homicide. This is illustrated in the following case:

> In Arkansas, a man and his wife were killed in a car crash. What mattered in this case was the order of death, which had to be established for inheritance purposes. Although witnesses agreed that the husband had died almost instantly, two of them testified that the wife exhibited signs of life for a short time— she had moved, gasped for breath and moaned. Despite this, the husband's heirs went to court, contending that technical advances in medicine had outmoded the coroner's definition of death. A proper definition, they argued, would not be based on the cessation of breathing and heartbeat, but on medicine's inability to resuscitate. Both the lower and an appeals court, however, disagreed, and the wife's heirs inherited the estate. (Dempsey, 1975:23)

In another case, a gunshot victim was placed on a respirator, two days later pronounced to have suffered "brain death," and then his heart was removed for transplantation (Meyers, 1975). The assailant's attorney argued that, since the heart was still "alive" when it was removed, his client could not be charged with murder. The court held, however, that death had indeed resulted from the gunshot wound and not from removal of the heart. The law has generally treated death as a medical question of fact rather than a statutory definition of criteria.

The most widely accepted alternative to traditional criteria of death is that of *brain death*. The criteria for brain death, as defined by the Ad Hoc Committee of the Harvard Medical School to Examine the Definition of Brain Death (1968), are:

1. unreceptivity and unresponsivity to externally applied stimuli and inner need (i.e., even painful stimuli yield no groan or change in respiration)
2. no spontaneous muscular movement or spontaneous breathing when removed from the respirator (under certain conditions, patients may be removed from a respirator for up to three minutes without damage, in order to test this criterion)
3. no elicitable brain reflexes (e.g., no dilation of the pupil in response to bright light)
4. a flat electroencephalogram (EEG), with repeat testing, after 24 hours.

These criteria are to be used in combination. When they are met, the patient is declared dead and disconnected from the respirator. Experience with these criteria indicates that they are reasonable and valid measures of death (Institute of Society, Ethics and the Life Sciences, 1972). An increasing number of states have enacted brain death criteria into law, including Kansas, California, Georgia, Maryland, Michigan, New Mexico, and Virginia (Devins and Diamond, 1977).

Veatch (1972) has rightly pointed out, however, that the concept of brain death is not strictly a medical opinion, but rather a social and ethical judgment about the nature of life. It represents a consideration of what makes living things alive—a beating heart or a functioning brain? The emphasis in brain death is on the quality of life and the distinction between a human *organism* and a *human* organism. This has led some to speak of "neocortical death," arguing that meaningful human existence resides in the "higher" brain functions, which are not always adequately measured by an EEG.

The Right to Die

The concern over the quality and meaningfulness of human life is reflected in debates over abortion, genetic engineering, and compulsory sterilization (Ostheimer and Ostheimer, 1976). More relevant to this discussion is debate over the "right to die" and the right of others to help people die through euthanasia, sometimes called "mercy killing." Recent interest in this issue has focused on the case of Karen Quinlan, who was hospitalized in April of 1975 with a diagnosis of drug-induced coma (Kastenbaum, 1977a). Suffering from severe and irreversible brain damage, she has never regained consciousness, and her breathing was maintained by a respirator. When physicians refused to remove her from the respirator, Karen Quinlan's parents asked the courts to name them legal guardians, so that she could be allowed to die. The New Jersey Supreme Court ruled in their favor, stating that the respirator could be turned off if physicians agreed that there was no chance of her regaining consciousness. Fourteen months after lapsing into a coma, Karen Quinlan was removed from the respirator. At the time of this writing, 13 months later, Karen Quinlan is still alive in a nursing home and still in a coma.

This case illustrates some of the exceedingly complex medical, legal, social, and ethical issues surrounding the question of euthanasia. Under what conditions should people be "allowed" or "helped" to die, and who should make the decision? Note that Karen Quinlan did not meet the criteria for brain death—she still breathes without a respirator, and the EEG continues to show very weak tracings. Kastenbaum (1977a) also notes that "death with dignity" is an empty phrase in this case; the special poignancy arises from the suffering of those around Karen Quinlan. But her case is not unique; what is unique is that the decisions have surfaced to public attention.

Debate over euthanasia has a long history. In the first century A.D., the Roman philosopher Seneca stated:

> If I can choose between a death of torture and one that is simple and easy, why should I not select the latter?—Why should I endure the agonies of disease—when I can emancipate myself from all my torture?—I will not depart by death from disease as long as it may be healed and leaves my mind unimpaired—but if I know that I will suffer forever, I will depart, not through fear of pain itself, but because it prevents all for which I live. (Russell, 1975:54)

Some form of euthanasia has been advocated by such persons as Sir Thomas More, Francis Bacon, and Benjamin Franklin, and condemned by such others as St. Augustine and St. Thomas Aquinas (Mannes, 1973; Russell, 1975). Something of a social movement has arisen around euthanasia since the 1930s, when the Voluntary Euthanasia Legalization Society was formed in England, followed by the Euthanasia Society of America. The Euthanasia Education Council was founded in 1972, and now has 30,000 members (Heffernan and Maynard, 1977). But attempts to legalize euthanasia have been defeated in Great Britain (in 1936, 1950, and 1969) and New York State (in 1947) and have languished in the legislative committees of a number of states over the past decade.

Euthanasia involves two issues: an appeal to mercy for the dying and the *right* of the dying to die (Bok, 1975). These issues revolve around three distinctly different types of patients: the terminally ill who are conscious, the irreversibly comatose (such as Karen Quinlan), and brain-damaged or severely debilitated patients with good chances for survival but at a low level of existence (severely deformed new-borns, senile aged) (Crane, 1975).

Different meanings and types of patients make euthanasia a very tangled issue. In an attempt to bring some order to the discussion, Fletcher (1968) has defined four types of *elective death*. The first is *voluntary and direct*, where death is chosen and carried out by the patient, in effect, a form of suicide. Patients do have a right to refuse treatment, and suicide is not illegal. Helping someone commit suicide *is* illegal, however, so family and staff may incur legal liabilities in such cases. Physicians may administer pain-relieving drugs which have the additional effect of hastening death, since causing death is not the primary motive in such cases, but it is not legally clear whether physicians have a duty to prevent suicide, given the nature of the doctor-patient relationship (Cantor, 1975; Meyers, 1975).

The second form of elective death is *voluntary and indirect*, where the patient, though no longer conscious, has granted discretion to others to cease "heroic" or "extraordinary" treatment. This type is embodied in the "Living Will," an example of which is shown in Figure 12.1. California recently passed a "right to die" law, allowing physicians to disconnect life-support equipment when the patient has signed a Living Will. It must be signed at least 72 hours before the act, witnessed by two unrelated persons who are not included in the estate, and renewed every five years.

A third elective death is *indirect and involuntary*, where treatment is ceased and the patient is "allowed" to die, sometimes called *passive* or *negative* euthanasia. Such actions have a very uncertain legal status. Meyers (1975) and Cantor (1975) note that the special nature of the doctor-patient relationship probably imposes a duty to continue "ordinary" treatment, but that there are no clear legal or medical standards about what constitutes "extra-ordinary" treatment, or whether treatment must be continued in "hopeless" cases. The concept of brain death only partly alleviates these problems, and physicians may potentially be liable to prose-

Figure 12.1. Sample of a "Living Will"

TO MY FAMILY, MY PHYSICIAN, MY CLERGYMAN, MY ATTORNEY:

If the time comes when I can no longer take part in decisions for my own future, let this statement stand as testament of my wishes:

If there is no reasonable expectation of my recovery from physical or mental disability, I, _____ , request that I be allowed to die and not be kept alive by artificial means or heroic measures. Death is as much a reality as birth, growth, maturity and old age—it is the one certainty. I do not fear death as much as I fear the indignity of deterioration, dependence, and hopeless pain. I ask that drugs be mercifully administered to me for terminal suffering even if they hasten the moment of death.

This request is made after careful consideration. Although this document is not legally binding, you who care for me will, I hope, feel morally bound to follow its mandates. I recognize that it places a heavy burden of responsibility upon you, and it is with the intention of sharing that responsibility and of mitigating any feelings of guilt that this statement is made.

The above form is based on "A Living Will," developed by the Euthanasia Educational Council, 250 West 57th Street, New York, New York 10019.

cution for murder or manslaughter, though such cases are almost never prosecuted.

The final type of elective death is *direct and involuntary*, where an affirmative action, such as a lethal injection, is taken to end life although the patient is not capable of giving consent. This *active* or *positive* euthanasia is closest to the idea of "mercy killing." Uruguay is the only country which does not punish such homicides, when they occur at the victim's request and are motivated by compassion (Fletcher, 1973). In other countries, including the United States, life is given a preeminent value, and neither good motives nor consent are legal defenses (Meyer, 1975; Cantor, 1975). However, few cases are prosecuted and juries are often unwilling to convict.

Many arguments have been made both for and against the concept and practice of euthanasia.[1] Proponents emphasize compassion for the suffering of the dying and a concern for human dignity

---

[1] For more complete discussions of thought and debate regarding euthanasia, see Behnke and Bok (1975) and Russell (1975).

and choice in achieving a "good death." They argue that life is not an *absolute* good, but its quality and meaningfulness should be considered.

> An increasing number of vital functions can be maintained by mechanical respirators, artificial kidneys, cardiac stimulators and other ingenious devices. No one will doubt their importance when used for an acutely ill patient, who may thereby survive a crisis and return to reasonable health. Nevertheless, the use of such mechanical aids to prolong a very limited form of life in an incurably ill person remains debatable. If such measures can be continued to bring some useful, enjoyable life, most would wish to use them. If they can only maintain a truncated semblance of life, as in a permanently unconscious being, there is little justification. They can easily cause distress to the living— the fully living. (Hinton, 1972:141)

Treatment in such cases really prolongs dying, not living, and remote chances for recovery are not felt to justify prolonged suffering. Proponents of euthanasia typically point out that most religious teachings do not require maintenance of life as a supreme obligation. Pope Pius XII, for example, stated in 1957 that termination of extraordinary measures in certain circumstances and relief of pain with drugs which also hasten death were acceptible. It is also argued that physicians are not obligated to continue heroic measures in hopeless cases. Fletcher (1968), for example, refers to the "vitalistic error," which places biological life above all other considerations.

These arguments may have particular poignance for the aged. Having reached the end of a "natural" life span, many older people may find the dying process, with its attendant possibilities of pain, dwindling personal competence, and isolation, more fearful than death itself. The following comments of an 88-year-old psychologist, who has himself researched the aging experience, are illustrative:

> At the age of 88, crippled by rheumatism, plagued by insomnia, of failing vision, must I wait out a "natural" death—perhaps becoming mindless, incontinent, locked in a back ward of a nursing "home"? Do I have any rights as to the time and nature of my dying? . . . In antiquity, the old wishing to die might so petition the authorities who, if they approved, would arrange an occasion like a banquet (Russell, 1975) where these oldsters would gather, drink a lethal potion, and die honored by their fellows. Perhaps again! Old couples like the Van Dusens longing to go together, old friends wishing so to go, the many, many lonely old and the many in stresses of dying—what indeed a

mercy if wise and humane laws might give such their wish! (Pressey, 1977:296)

Opponents of euthanasia have focused on a number of issues. One argument is that medical diagnosis and prognosis are not infallible and in some "hopeless" cases the patients have survived to lead meaningful lives. The possibility of new medical discoveries is also held out, and there is the additional fear that euthanasia will be based not on the best interests of the *patient*, but on such considerations as the emotional or financial burden for others, the need for organs to transplant, or the "social worth" of the patient. In *Passing On*, Sudnow (1967) cites cases of a child and an elderly person who entered the emergency room with virtually identical symptoms; the elderly person was almost immediately pronounced dead, while the child received strenuous and prolonged treatment from a large team of professionals. Even when consciously made, there is some question about whether patient requests for euthanasia are truly voluntary or a product of temporary pain and depression, lack of full awareness about their condition, or concern about being a burden to others.

Probably the most basic objection raised to euthanasia is that it cheapens life and may be too tempting a solution for those considered too burdensome or unproductive by society; that it will dull our sensitivities to the helpless and "defective." In other words, where will we draw the line on who is "worth" saving? Reiser (1975) cites the example of Nazi Germany:

> In 1939, after Hitler came to power, all state institutions submitted reports on patients who were ill and were unable to work the previous five years to a central bureau, which selected patients for euthanasia. An organization devoted to determining appropriate children for euthanasia also existed, having the title: Realms Committee for Scientific Approach to Severe Illness Due to Heredity and Constitution. The hundreds of thousands of people killed through these organizations included mentally ill, epileptics, the aged sick, and sufferers from neurological diseases such as infantile paralysis and brain tumors. (Reiser, 1975: 43–44)

Concern is raised that euthanasia, or even the concept of a "natural death," may lead us to prematurely reject the will to live of the "useless" elderly and become tantamount to a form of "gerontocide" (Kastenbaum and Aisenberg, 1976).

Decisions concerning euthanasia have largely been confined to physicians, with relatively little visibility. The traditional stress on "saving lives" as an absolute medical ethic seems to allow little room for positive definitions of death, but this view conflicts with the other task of the physician—to alleviate suffering. Indeed, despite its uncertain legal status, passive euthanasia appears to be a widely accepted part of medical practice. Williams (1973b) found that 87 percent of a sample of physicians approved of passive euthanasia in principle, and 81 percent had practiced it. Duff and Campbell (1973) documented 43 deaths from 1970 to 1972 in the special-care nursery of Yale-New Haven Hospital, all involving rejection of further treatment when there was a hopeless prognosis for "meaningful life," as with multiple deformities. They noted that this is accepted medical practice, though it receives little publicity.

Crane (1975), in a study of attitudes among a national sample of physicians, found ample evidence that nonmedical, social criteria—notably, expected quality of life—are used in determining how actively to treat patients.

> Evidence from the present study suggests that physicians respond to the chronically ill or terminally ill patient not simply in terms of physiological definitions of illness but also in terms of the extent to which he is capable of interacting with others. The treatable patient is one who can interact or who has the potential to interact in a meaningful way with others in his environment. (Crane, 1975:61)

The emphasis was on social *capacity*, rather than social *value*, and the priority for active treatment was: (1) salvageable with physical damage, (2) salvageable with mental damage and unsalvageable with physical damage, and (3) unsalvageble with mental damage. Physicians were highly critical of "unnecessary" resuscitations, and a study of hospital records showed that patients with brain damage were less likely to be resuscitated. Under various conditions, decisions about treatment were affected by such other nonmedical criteria as patient attitudes, financial burdens, and age. For example, hospital records indicated that 73 percent of the deaths involving patients 10 to 39 years of age involved resuscitation attempts, compared with only 33 percent for those 80 and over.

These studies all indicate that physicians consider expected quality of life in deciding whether to continue treatment. Crane (1975) found, however, that physicians were generally reluctant to withdraw all treatment on their own initiative. There was much less acceptance of positive euthanasia, reflecting a strong norm against direct killing. In the study referred to earlier, Williams (1973b) found that only 18 percent of a sample of physicians approved of positive euthanasia.

The public appears to be moving toward greater acceptance of the concept of euthanasia. In 1950 and 1973, Gallup polls asked national samples: "When a person has a disease that cannot be cured, do you think doctors should be allowed by law to end the patient's life by some painless means if the patient and his family request it?" Acceptance of this voluntary elective death increased from 36 percent in 1950 to 53 percent in 1973 (Ostheimer and Ritt, 1976). As with physicians, the public is more accepting of passive than active euthanasia: a 1973 Harris poll found that 62 percent thought physicians should "let him die," but only 37 percent agreed that they should "put him out of his misery" (Ostheimer and Ritt, 1976).

Although older people are less anxious and fearful about death, they are also less likely to agree that patients or their families should be allowed to discontinue treatment in terminal cases (Ostheimer and Ritt, 1976; Haug, 1978). This may simply reflect educational differences, since education is strongly related to attitudes favorable to elective death. It also seems to reflect a more general stance about patient-physician interaction. Haug, in a study conducted in one metropolitan area, found that the best predictor of favorable attitudes toward elective death was the general belief that people have a right to make their own health decisions without relying on a physician's advice. Such beliefs may well reflect cohort differences in the "godlike" qualities attributed to physicians.

There are many unresolved issues surrounding elective death and euthanasia (Bok, 1975). How much suffering legitimates euthanasia? Must the patient be terminal, and if so, how close to death? The problems are less severe when the individual is conscious and competent to make his or her own decisions, though every care should be taken to insure that the decision is not based on emotional or financial burdens to others, the person is fully informed and provided with options, and elective death is not the only alternative to dehumanized suffering. The most difficult decisions involve those who have no voice: deformed newborns, the senile aged, and the comatose. Decisions must be based on the individual case. Since these decisions are not strictly medical decisions, they should not be left solely to the medical community. Culliton (1976) describes two hospitals which have set up committees (referred to by some as "God Squads") of physicians, nurses, psychiatrists, lawyers, and patients, to decide about the withdrawal of treatment. At one hospital, patients are classified according to their probability of survival, as follows:

Class A—"maximum therapeutic effort without reservation"
Class B—same as Class A, but with "daily evaluation"

Class C—"selective limitation of therapeutic measures" (e.g., no resuscitation, no antibiotics in case of pneumonia)

Class D—"all therapy can be discontinued" (with brain death, or where no chance exists of regaining "cognitive and salient life")

Physicians at this hospital retain full authority, however, and may reject the classification. At the other hospital described by Culliton, patients or their families must consent to the withdrawal of treatment.

Culliton notes that policies set up by such committees protect physicians by supporting the medical "reasonableness" of their decisions. There is also a need, however, to more generally define and limit the criteria to be used in supporting or ending lives. Legislators are naturally reluctant to take a firm stand on as complicated a moral issue as euthanasia, but legislation could be directed toward defining the situations in which it might be permissible and procedures for determining and carrying out actions, and could provide legal protection for the persons involved, especially patients and physicians.

The intrusion of social criteria into medical decision making is in part a function of the fact that *resources are limited*—we cannot do everything for everyone. The unfortunate truth is that the huge expenses incurred in keeping some people alive takes resources away from such things as medical research and preventive medicine, and may indirectly contribute to the death of others (Fuchs, 1974). This problem is well-illustrated in the excruciating decisions involved in organ transplants (Fox and Swazey, 1974). Organs for transplant are scarce—how do we decide who receives a heart or a kidney, and what are our priorities? Do we spend money on organ transplants and kidney dialysis to benefit a relative few or consign these people to death and spend our health resources on prevention and outreach? How many visiting nurses are not funded for the sake of one heart transplant? These life-and-death issues, including but not limited to elective death and euthanasia, are exceedingly difficult, and in some ways distasteful, but they cannot be ignored.

Summary

The "mortality revolution" accompanying modernization has brought increased life expectancy and shifts in the major causes of death, and death is increasingly confined to the aged. The typical location of death has also shifted from home to institutions. These changes affect the social structure. High-mortality societies are characterized by stress on the extended family, reduced importance of children, high fertility, arranged marriages, little career planning, and an emphasis on religion. Modern people are more insulated from death, as the aged die in special institutions. There is less need for elaborate cultural rituals, and funerals are criticized as being irrelevant. But these changes may have made death more difficult for individuals.

Cultural views on death display wide variation, both what "being dead" is presumed to be like and the ultimate meaning attributed to death. Four personifications of death have been described: the Macabre, the Gentle Comforter, the Gay Deceiver, and the Automaton (which may be the most modern view). In some ways we deny death, attempting to achieve some magical or symbolic feeling of immortality. Many fears may be attached to death, though the greatest concerns appear to be the grief of others, the pain of dying, and the ending of projects and experiences. Other evidence suggests a relative acceptance of death. Probably both denial and acceptance exist, reflecting both the "naturalness" of death and an inability to truly comprehend our own nonexistence.

Death conceptions change over the life cycle. Children only gradually perceive the finality and inevitability of death, though even very young children have perceptions of death. Middle age is often a time of personally relevant deaths, and a sense of impending death is considered important to the psychology of old age. The aged think more about death, but their attitudes appear to be more accepting than those of younger people. They also appear less likely to reorganize their lives in the face of death. Age peers can provide support in achieving an accepting approach to death.

The dying typically face withdrawal by others, sometimes amounting to "social death." Hospitals and other "dying institutions" seek to minimize the disruptiveness of death through isolation and routinization, which is reflected in staff predictions of the dying trajectory. Medical staff typically receive little preparation for caring for the dying, and their responses may reflect their own fears and insecurities. Death implies failure and is often dealt with by avoidance or detachment.

The dying typically have some awareness of their condition, but may engage in "mutual pretense" to protect others. Unfortunately, because it is often difficult to break through this shared denial, the social and emotional needs of the dying are too often unmet. The dying tend to exhibit many reactions—anxiety, depression, anger— but they are not typically overwhelmed by fear. Personality plays a role in shaping these reactions. There do not appear to be universal stages to the dying process, and, although many achieve acceptance, there are a variety of reactions to impending death.

Those who care for the dying should strive to achieve an "appropriate death." Such care is exemplified by the environment at St. Christopher's Hospice.

The bereaved also have important needs which must be met. There are many complex reactions to bereavement, and adjustment problems may continue for a year or more following the loss. Bereavement appears to be much more difficult when death is sudden or unexpected. It has been argued that the bereaved receive little support in modern societies, making their "grief work" more difficult.

The modern funeral has been criticized as irrelevant and exploitative, and the claim of funeral directors that they are professional "grief specialists" has been challenged. But most people seem to approve of traditional funerals, and some type of ceremony appears to be beneficial to the bereaved. To some extent, funeral directors and clergy are in competition, and the role of the clergy appears to be declining in importance.

Changes in the nature and location of death, and in medical technology for "combatting" death, have created new issues and given increased relevance to a concern over "death with dignity." One development has been the concept of "brain death" to replace traditional criteria of death. Debate over the definition of death involves social and ethical judgments about the nature of life. These issues are also reflected in debates about elective death and euthanasia. Proponents of euthanasia stress relief of suffering, human dignity, and the importance of quality of life. Opponents cite the uncertainty of medical knowledge and the danger of cheapening life. Passive euthanasia has been an accepted part of medical practice for some time, and the public is increasingly supportive. But active euthanasia has little support among physicians or lay persons. The whole area of elective death exists in a state of legal limbo, and there is a need to more clearly define the responsibilities of the actors, such as physicians, and the criteria which should be used.

References

Ad Hoc Committee of the Harvard Medical School to Examine the Definition of Brain Death
    1968   "A definition of irreversible coma." Journal of the American Medical Association 205: 337–40.
Becker, Ernest
    1973   The Denial of Death. New York: The Free Press.
Behnke, John and Sissela Bok (eds.)
    1975   The Dilemmas of Euthanasia. Garden City, N.Y.: Anchor Books.

Bell, Bill
    1975   "The experimental manipulation of death attitudes: A
            preliminary investigation." Omega 6: 199–205.
Benoliel, Jeanne
    1977   "Nurses and the human experience of dying." In Herman
            Feifel (ed.). New Meanings of Death. New York:
            McGraw-Hill.
Binger, C. M., et al.
    1969   "Childhood leukemia: Emotional impact on patient and
            family." New England Journal of Medicine 280: 414–18.
Blauner, Robert
    1966   "Death and social structure." Psychiatry 29: 378–94.
Bluebond-Langner, Myra
    1977   "Meanings of death to children." In Herman Feifel (ed.).
            New Meanings of Death. New York: McGraw-Hill.
Bok, Sissela
    1975   "Euthanasia and the care of the dying." In John Behnke and
            Sissela Bok (eds.). The Dilemmas of Euthanasia. Garden
            City, N.Y.: Anchor Books.
Bowers, M., et al.
    1964   Counseling the Dying. New York: Thomas Nelson &
            Sons.
Butler, Robert
    1975   Why Survive?: Being Old in America. New York:
            Harper & Row.
Cantor, Norman
    1975   "Law and the termination of an incompetent patient's life-
            preserving care." In John Behnke and Sissela Bok (eds.).
            The Dilemmas of Euthanasia. Garden City, N.Y.:
            Anchor Books.
Charmaz, Kathy
    1976   "A symbolic interactionist critique of Kübler-Ross' stages of
            dying." Paper presented at Annual Meeting of American
            Sociological Association, New York.
Coombs, Robert and Pauline Powers
    1976   "Socialization for death: The physician's role." In Lyn
            Lofland (ed.). Toward a Sociology of Death and Dying.
            Beverly Hills, Calif.: Sage.
Crane, Diana
    1975   The Sanctity of Social Life: Physicians' Treatment of Crit-
            ically Ill Patients. New York: Russell Sage Foundation.
Culliton, Barbara
    1976   "Helping the dying die: Two Harvard hospitals go public
            with policies." Science 193: 1105–06.
Dempsey, David
    1975   The Way We Die. New York: McGraw-Hill.
Devins, Gerald and Robert Diamond
    1977   "The determination of death." Omega 7: 277–96.

Diggory, James and Doreen Rothman
  1961   "Values destroyed by death." Journal of Abnormal and
         Social Psychology 63: 205–10.
Duff, Raymond and A. G. M. Campbell
  1973   "Moral and ethical dilemmas in the special-care nursery."
         New England Journal of Medicine 289: 890–94.
Dumont, Richard and Dennis Foss
  1972   The American View of Death: Acceptance or Denial?
         Cambridge, Mass.: Schenkman.
Easson, William
  1977   "Accidents and trauma." In E. Mansell Pattison (ed.). The
         Experience of Dying. Englewood Cliffs, N.J.: Prentice-Hall.
Fletcher, Joseph
  1968   "Elective death." In E. Fuller Torrey (ed.). Ethical Issues
         in Medicine. Boston: Little, Brown.
  1973   "Ethics and euthanasia." In Robert Williams (ed.). To Live
         and To Die: When, Why, and How. New York:
         Springer-Verlag.
Fox, Renee and Judith Swazey
  1974   The Courage to Fail: A Social View of Organ Transplants
         and Dialysis. Chicago: University of Chicago Press.
Fuchs, Victor
  1974   Who Shall Live?: Health, Economics, and Social Choice.
         New York: Basic Books.
Fulton, Robert
  1961   "The clergyman and the funeral director: A study in role
         conflict." Social Forces 39: 317–23.
  1965   "The sacred and the secular: Attitudes of the American
         public toward death, funerals, and funeral directors." In
         Robert Fulton (ed.). Death and Identity. New York:
         John Wiley.
  1976   "The traditional funeral and contemporary society." In
         Vanderlyn Pine et al. (eds.). Acute Grief and the Funeral.
         Springfield, Ill.: Charles C Thomas.
Gerber, Irwin, et al.
  1975   "Anticipatory grief and aged widows and widowers." Journal
         of Gerontology 30: 225–29.
Glaser, Barney and Anselm Strauss
  1966   Awareness of Dying. Chicago: Aldine.
  1968   Time for Dying. Chicago: Aldine.
Glick, Ira, Robert Weiss, and C. Murray Parkes
  1974   The First Year of Bereavement. New York:
         Wiley-Interscience.
Goldscheider, Calvin
  1971   Population, Modernization, and Social Structure. Boston:
         Little, Brown.
Gorer, Geoffrey
  1965   Death, Grief and Mourning. New York: Doubleday.

Gubrium, Jaber
    1975   Living and Dying at Murray Manor. New York: St. Martin's.
Gustafson, Elizabeth
    1972   "Dying: The career of the nursing home patient." Journal of
           Health and Social Behavior 13: 226–35.
Haug, Marie
    1978   "Aging and the right to terminate medical treatment."
           Journal of Gerontology 33: 586–91.
Hausman, C. Stewart
    1976   "Who are we—what are we—why we do what we do." In
           Vanderlyn Pine et al. (eds.). Acute Grief and the Funeral.
           Springfield, Ill.: Charles C Thomas.
Heffernan, Robert and Charles Maynard
    1977   "Living and dying with dignity: The rise of old age and
           dying as social problems." In Armand Mauss and Julie
           Wolfe (eds.). This Land of Promises: The Rise and Fall of
           Social Problems in America. Philadelphia: J. B. Lippincott.
Hinton, John
    1972   Dying. Baltimore: Penguin Books.
    1975   "The influence of previous personality on reactions to having
           terminal cancer." Omega 6: 95–112.
Hochschild, Arlie
    1973   The Unexpected Community. Englewood Cliffs, N.J.:
           Prentice-Hall.
Ingram, Donald and John Barry
    1977   "National statistics on deaths in nursing homes: Interpreta-
           tions and implications." The Gerontologist 17: 303–08.
Institute of Society, Ethics and the Life Sciences
    1972   "Refinements in criteria for the determination of death: An
           appraisal." Journal of the American Medical Association
           221: 48–53.
Jaffe, Lois and Arthur Jaffe
    1977   "Terminal candor and the coda syndrome: A tandem view
           of fatal illness." In Herman Feifel (ed.). New Meanings of
           Death. New York: McGraw- Hill.
Jeffers, Frances, Claude Nichols, and Carl Eisdorfer
    1961   "Attitudes of older persons toward death: A preliminary
           study." Journal of Gerontology 16: 53–56.
Kalish, Richard
    1969   "Experiences of persons reprieved from death." In A.
           Kutscher (ed.). Death and Bereavement. Springfield, Ill.:
           Charles C Thomas.
    1970   "The onset of the dying process." Omega 1: 57–69.
    1976   "Death and dying in a social context." In Robert Binstock
           and Ethel Shanas (eds.). Handbook of Aging and the Social
           Sciences. New York: Van Nostrand Reinhold.
    1977   "Dying and preparation for death: A view of families." In
           Herman Feifel (ed.). New Meanings of Death. New York:
           McGraw-Hill.

Kalish, Richard and David Reynolds
  1976   Death and Ethnicity: A Psychocultural Study. Los Angeles: University of Southern California Press.
Kastenbaum, Robert
  1977a Death, Society, and Human Experience. St. Louis: C. V. Mosby.
  1977b "Death and development through the life span." In Herman Feifel (ed.). New Meanings of Death. New York: McGraw-Hill.
Kastenbaum, Robert and Ruth Aisenberg
  1976   The Psychology of Death: Concise Edition. New York: Springer.
Kelly, Orville
  1977   "Make today count." In Herman Feifel (ed.). New Meanings of Death. New York: McGraw-Hill.
Khleif, Baheej
  1976   "The sociology of the mortuary: Religion, sex, age and variables." In Vanderlyn Pine et al. (eds.). Acute Grief and the Funeral. Springfield, Ill.: Charles C Thomas.
Knutson, Andie
  1970   "Cultural beliefs on life and death." In Orville Brim et al. (eds.). The Dying Patient. New York: Russell Sage
Kübler-Ross, Elisabeth
  1969   On Death and Dying. New York: MacMillan.
Lerner, Monroe
  1970   "When, why, and where people die." In Orville Brim et al. (eds.). The Dying Patient. New York: Russell Sage Foundation.
Leviton, Daniel
  1977   "Death education." In Herman Feifel (ed.). New Meanings of Death. New York: McGraw-Hill.
Lieberman, Morton
  1965   "Psychological correlates of impending death: Some preliminary observations." Journal of Gerontology 20: 181–90.
Lifton, Robert
  1967   Death in Life: Survivors of Hiroshima. New York: Random House.
  1977   "The sense of immortality: On death and the continuity of life." In Herman Feifel (ed.). New Meanings of Death. New York: McGraw-Hill.
Lifton, Robert and Eric Olson
  1974   Living and Dying. New York: Praeger.
Lindemann, Erich
  1944   "Symptomatology and management of acute grief." American Journal of Psychiatry 101: 141–48.
Liston, Edward
  1973   "Education on death and dying: A survey of American medical schools." Journal of Medical Education 48: 577–78.

Mandelbaum, David
1959   "Social uses of funeral rites." In Herman Feifel (ed.).
       The Meaning of Death. New York: McGraw-Hill.
Mannes, Marya
1973   Last Rights. New York: William Morrow.
Mant, A. Keith
1968   "Definition of death." In Arnold Toynbee et al. (eds.).
       Man's Concern with Death. New York: McGraw-Hill.
Marcuse, Herbert
1959   "The ideology of death." In Herman Feifel (ed.). The
       Meaning of Death. New York: McGraw-Hill.
Marshall, Victor
1975a "Age and awareness of finitude in developmental
       gerontology." Omega 6: 113–29.
1975b "Socialization for impending death in a retirement village."
       American Journal of Sociology 80: 1124–44.
1976   "Organizational features of terminal status passage in
       residential facilities for the aged." In Lyn Lofland (ed.).
       Toward a Sociology of Death and Dying. Beverly Hills,
       Calif.: Sage.
Mauksch, Hans
1975   "The organizational context of dying." In Elisabeth Kübler-
       Ross (ed.). Death: The Final Stage of Growth. Englewood
       Cliffs, N.J.: Prentice-Hall.
Meyers, David
1975   "The legal aspects of voluntary medical euthanasia." In John
       Behnke and Sissela Bok (eds.). The Dilemmas of
       Euthanasia. Garden City, N.Y.: Anchor Books.
Mitford, Jessica
1963   The American Way of Death. New York: Simon & Schuster.
Nagy, Maria
1948   "The child's theories concerning death." Journal of Genetic
       Psychology 73: 3–27.
Ostheimer, John and Leonard Ritt
1976   "Life and death: Current public attitudes." In Nancy
       Ostheimer and John Ostheimer (eds.). Life or Death—Who
       Controls? New York: Springer.
Ostheimer, Nancy and John Ostheimer (eds.)
1976   Life or Death—Who Controls? New York: Springer.
Parkes, C. Murray
1970   " 'Seeking' and 'finding' a lost object." Social Science and
       Medicine 4: 187–201.
1973   Bereavement. London: Tavistock.
Phillips, D. and K. Feldman
1973   "A dip in deaths before ceremonial occasions: Some new
       relationships between social integration and mortality."
       American Sociological Review 38: 678–96.

Pine, Vanderlyn
  1975   Caretaker of the Dead: The American Funeral Director.
         New York: Irvington.
  1976   "Social meanings of the funeral." In Vanderlyn Pine et al.
         (eds.). Acute Grief and the Funeral. Springfield, Ill.:
         Charles C Thomas.
Pine, Vanderlyn, et al.
  1976   Acute Grief and the Funeral. Springfield, Ill.:
         Charles C Thomas.
Pressey, Sidney
  1977   "Any rights as to my dying?" The Gerontologist 17: 296.
Raether, Howard and Robert Slater
  1977   "Immediate postdeath activities in the United States."
         In Herman Feifel (ed.). New Meanings of Death.
         New York: McGraw-Hill.
Rea, M. Priscilla, Shirley Greenspoon, and Bernard Spilka
  1975   "Physicians and the terminal patient: Some selected
         attitudes and behavior." Omega 6: 291–302.
Reiser, Stanley
  1975   "The dilemma of euthanasia in modern history: The English
         and American experience." In John Behnke and Sissela Bok
         (eds.). The Dilemmas of Euthanasia. Garden City, N.Y.:
         Anchor Books.
Riley, John
  1970   "What people think about death." In Orville Brim et al.
         (eds.). The Dying Patient. New York: Russell Sage
         Foundation.
Riley, Matilda and Anne Foner
  1968   Aging and Society. Volume I: An Inventory of Research
         Findings. New York: Russell Sage Foundation.
Russell, O. Ruth
  1975   Freedom to Die: Moral and Legal Aspects of Euthanasia.
         New York: Human Sciences Press.
Saunders, Cicely
  1977   "Dying they live: St. Christopher's Hospice." In Herman
         Feifel (ed.). New Meanings of Death. New York:
         McGraw-Hill.
Schneidman, Edwin
  1971   "You and death." Psychology Today 5 (6): 43.
Schulz, Richard and David Aderman
  1974   "Clinical research and the stages of dying."
         Omega 5: 137–43.
  1976   "How the medical staff copes with dying patients: A critical
         review." Omega 7: 11–21.
Sudnow, David
  1967   Passing On: The Social Organization of Dying. Englewood
         Cliffs, N.J.: Prentice-Hall.

Swanson, Thomas and Marcia Swanson
  1977   "Acute uncertainty: The intensive care unit." In E. Mansell
          Pattison (ed.). The Experience of Dying. Englewood Cliffs,
          N.J.: Prentice-Hall.
Toynbee, Arnold, et al.
  1968   Man's Concern with Death. New York: McGraw-Hill.
Veatch, Robert
  1972   "Brain death: Welcome definition . . . or dangerous
          judgement." Hastings Center Report 2 (5).
Volkhart, Edmund and Stanley Michael
  1957   "Bereavement and mental health." In A. Leighton,
          J. Clausen, and R. Wilson (eds.). Explorations in Social
          Psychiatry. New York: Basic Books.
Waechter, Eugenia
  1971   "Children's awareness of fatal illness." American Journal
          of Nursing 71: 1168–72.
Wass, Hannelore and Martha Scott
  1977   "Aging without death??" The Gerontologist 17: 377–80.
Weisman, Avery
  1972   On Dying and Denying. New York: Behavioral Publications.
Weisman, Avery and Robert Kastenbaum
  1968   "The psychological autopsy: A study of the terminal phase
          of life." Community Mental Health Journal Monograph
          No. 4.
Weisman, Avery and J. William Worden
  1975   "Psychosocial analysis of cancer deaths." Omega 6:61–75.
Williams, Robert
  1973b   "Propagation, modification, and termination of life: Contra-
          ception, abortion, suicide, euthanasia." In Robert Williams
          (ed.). To Live and to Die: When, Why, and How. New
          York: Springer-Verlag.
Wood, Juanita
  1975   "The structure of concern: The ministry in death-related
          situations." In Lyn Lofland (ed.). Toward a Sociology of
          Death and Dying. Beverly Hills, Calif.: Sage.
  1976   "Control by definition: The minister as death worker."
          Paper presented at Annual Meeting of Pacific Sociological
          Association.

13

The Future of the Aging Experience

~~~~~~~~~~~~~~~~~~~~~~~~~~~~~~~~~~~~~

We have seen many examples of the complexity of the aging experience, both for those undergoing it and for those who wish to study it. We need to avoid seemingly "simple" explanations and assessments of the nature of aging and of the aged. Such issues as retirement, widowhood, political activism require a certain tolerance of ambiguity on the part of social gerontologists. Rather than encountering a "typical old person," we find many different old persons, of different ages, generations, sexes, and races. Instead of either "the golden years" or "gloom and misfortune," we find that aging entails a complicated mix of pleasure and pain. Recognition of this variability and complexity is absolutely essential to an accurate portrayal of the aging experience. This is true if our goal is the scientific study of aging and its effects or to develop expectations of what our own old age will be like.

The necessity of an accurate portrayal of the aging experience leads us to a consideration of what aging will be like in the future. We have seen that the nature of aging is shaped in important ways by the context within which it occurs. To the extent that the future world differs from present and past worlds, the aging experience will also be different. In addition, the aged of the future will literally be different people, with different historical and cohort backgrounds. Before proceeding to the future, however, let us return briefly to the key concepts and themes of this book.

The Nature of Age Differences

There has never been any doubt that age differences exist in behaviors, attitudes, values, and other personal characteristics, though we should be wary of exaggerating those differences. Age differences result from two processes: aging effects and cohort effects.

Aging effects are changes which take place in the individual as he or she moves through the life cycle. That such effects should occur is not surprising, given the changes in social situations encountered by people as they age, as well as the biological effects of aging. Thus, it may be true that political attitudes, such as conservatism or alienation, are affected by age, as age determines other positions and needs. Similarly, length of commitment to various roles, including work career and marriage roles, is likely to affect attitudes and behaviors concerning those roles. Other studies suggest that perceived closeness to death has psychological consequences. These aging effects may be either intrinsic, giving them a certain universality and inevitability, or reactive, meaning that they are shaped by their context. It appears, for example, that disengagement by the elderly may be a response to their position in modern societies.

Other age differences reflect the socialization and historical experiences of different cohorts. As cohorts vary in work experiences, socialization regarding family and religion, or experiences with political activism, to name but a few examples, age differences will arise. Historical events have complex effects. Many cohorts may react differently to the same historical events because of their different positions in the life cycle, or there may be variations in response within a single cohort. Elder (1974) notes this complexity in understanding the varying effects of the Depression of the 1930s on children of different ages and parents, men and women, and different social classes (see Chapter 1).

Intrinsic aging effects lend continuity to the aging experience. But reactive aging effects and cohort effects both imply that aging may be quite different in the future, as new cohorts of older people encounter new social contexts for aging. Thus, general social change creates new problems and issues for aging individuals. Modernization has brought many changes in the positions and status of older people.

Aging and Age Stratification

The importance of the social context in shaping the aging experience is embodied in the model of age stratification discussed in Chapter 3. Societies structure the positions and roles of individuals according to their age, thereby creating a variety of age differences and age inequalities. Allocation according to age occurs both formally and informally, and is evident in the typical timing of marriage and family decisions, work career events, education, and so on. A model of age stratification helps us understand cross-cultural differences in the relative position of age groups, and suggests the possibility of age conflict over the allocation of roles and their associated rewards. This model also helps us understand the types of developmental issues which may arise as people age and the difficulties they may encounter in transferring into expected old age roles.

The age stratification system for any society is neither unchanging nor simple, however. As changes occur in the encompassing social structure, age stratification will also be modified, and with it the nature of the aging experience. This can be seem in some of the consequences of modernization discussed in Chapter 3. Nor does the age stratification system exist in isolation. Roles are stratified according to criteria other than age, including sex, race, and social class. While age stratification implies that age has a "leveling" effect, it is clear that the aging experience differs for men and women, blacks and whites, middle class and working class.

The development of a model of age stratification is an important contribution to social gerontology, but it is only a useful framework for organizing our thinking about the nature of aging in any society. Its utility is more clear-cut in such areas as the analysis of cross-cultural differences and age-based political conflict than in areas such as family relationships. Much more work is needed to flesh out all the ramifications of this model. How do age norms and expectations develop and change? How do these norms differ within subgroups of the population or across cultures, and how are they translated or internalized by individuals? How, and under what conditions, are individuals socialized for their positions in the age stratification system? How aware are individuals of the nature of age stratification, and how does this awareness affect activism and consciousness based on age? These are just some of the questions which need to be explored.

Aging and Symbolic Interactionism

A second underlying theme of the book is based on the premises of symbolic interactionism. Individuals are conscious actors in their worlds who behave and adapt to situations and events on the basis of their own perceptions and meanings for these situations and events, which arise from social interactions with others.

The symbolic interactionist perspective has important implications for the study of aging. Most basically, it means that the aging experience is shaped by the *meanings* individuals attach to "old age": their expectations, stereotypes, fears, desires. This provides a link to the larger culture and age stratification, as they define old age in a particular society. The age stratification of roles and experiences shapes individuals' perceptions of the world, but each individual also encounters a unique blend of experiences and interactions, which further shape the meanings of aging and old age. This is one reason for variation in the aging experience by sex, race, ethnicity, social class, religion, and place of residence. In order to truly understand the aging experience, we must be able to take the point of view of the person who is aging. We have long since passed the point where we can accept simple conclusions about the nature of aging in any society.

The importance of a symbolic interactionist perspective also becomes apparent when we recognize the tremendous potential for change in the social and symbolic worlds of the aging. Role losses, residential mobility, health problems, and other age-related changes pull the elderly from familiar groups. They are alienated from past worlds and identities and at the same time granted the potential for new worlds and new identities, which creates the possibility of satisfying personal change and growth, but also may result in stress, marginality, and unhappiness.

Such an approach suggests that "successful aging" is a highly ephemeral concept. Successful adaptation to aging is in the "eye" of the aging person, linked to previously successful styles of living. But aging may cut the individual off from important parts of the personal past and limit the possibility of continuity. Thus, adaptation to aging represents an interaction among previous patterns of living, changes brought by aging, and new contexts within which the aging individual must live and adapt.

The "Missing Link" in Social Gerontology

The need to study the *processes* by which people adapt to their own aging experience constitutes perhaps our biggest knowledge gap in social gerontology. Age stratification, and other approaches to the social context of aging, inform us of the likely problems and tasks in the transitions to old age. And we have many studies of the consequences of these transitions for older individuals. But we have little understanding of the processes by which these consequences are arrived at—of the adaptations made over time by individuals within social contexts. What are the first few days, months, or years of retirement (or widowhood, leisure, grandparenting) like? Suppose the aged do disengage from their social surroundings. How does this occur? What influences their choices? How do their views of themselves and the world change over time?

We have seen that the roles of modern older people are quite vague, compared with older people in earlier societies. But discussions of rolelessness and alienation notwithstanding, the ability to "make" one's own roles is not such a bad thing, since it implies less social "oppression," and though little *formal* socialization occurs, this does not mean that *no* socialization occurs.

At the most basic level, we need to understand how the aged come to view their own old age in particular ways, and knowledge about the general status of the aged in society or public stereotypes of aging are of limited utility. There is ample evidence that attitudes toward particular types of people are often poor predictors of actual behavior toward them (Deutscher, 1973). What are the real sources of older people's images of aging? How do these sources relate to the general context of their aging? How do these images lead the aged to choose their own patterns of aging? These are the questions which remain to be addressed. They constitute the marriage of age stratification and symbolic interactionism, pointing to a more complete *understanding* of the aging experience.

Aging in the Future

Social forecasting, based on extrapolation from current trends, is always a risky business since we cannot be sure that such trends will not be stopped or accelerated by unforeseen future events. Even more difficult are attempts to predict major alterations in the structure of society in 50 or 100 years. Nevertheless, forecasting must take place if we are to rationally and self-consciously set policies affecting future generations. This is all too clear in current debates over environmental policy, the "energy crisis," genetic engineering, and many other issues. Decisions made now, however gropingly, will affect the world of the future, and the failure to make decisions, to set long-term policies, is itself a decision, probably carrying even greater risks.

Forecasting the future may also help us to shape and choose from alternative futures. The alternatives we are presented with often seem highly conflicting. Some "futurists" paint a glowing portrait of Utopia, with glistening new technologies and an end to poverty and scarcity. Kahn and Wiener (1969), for example, have speculated on technical innovations likely to occur by the year 2000. Their list includes such things as permanent undersea colonies, large-scale desalinization of sea water, programmed dreams, genetic control of plants and animals, and drugs to improve memory and learning. An optimistic belief in the inevitability of progress has declined in recent years, however, as each day seems to heighten our awareness of a new "crisis." Some express a concern over a totalitarian "brave new world" of genetic engineering, neurosurgery, environmental manipulation, and electronic monitoring of individual behavior. Others paint a Doomsday portrait of the future, in which energy and food sources are depleted, and "rich" and "poor" nations are locked in mortal struggle.

The inevitability of progress is suspect, but so is the inevitability of global chaos. Beyond that, all predictions are speculative and debatable. Perhaps the best we can do is assess the "normal, expectable future" (Neugarten, 1975b), and on that basis attempt to shape the future in beneficial ways.

The Future Aged

Demographic forecasting about the nature and characteristics of older people 50 or 75 years from now involves relatively fewer risks, though we are faced with the indeterminacy of future birth rates and uncertain possibilities of mortality reduction. The number of older people in the United States will certainly rise, probably to 30 million or more people 65 and over (compared with 21 million currently). Their proportion of the population will also increase, perhaps going as high as 15 percent. These trends will be most evident in the decade 2020 to 2030, when most members of the post-World War II "baby boom" enter old age. This decade has been pinpointed as the critical period in the financing crisis of Social Security.

A number of predictions about the characteristics of these future older cohorts have been made (for example, see Neugarten, 1975a; Palmore, 1976). They will be better educated, with higher occupational status and income than present older people. Though mortality rates are likely to show only slow declines, with no dramatic changes in life expectancy, older people in the future will probably be in better health, assuming more effective forms of public health and health care systems. Past trends toward independent households in urban areas are not likely to be reversed, though Golant (1975) suggests that there may be some shifts in residential concentration of the elderly. The economic prosperity of sunbelt states will continue to encourage planned retirement centers, but these will also be increasingly prevalent in the fringes of northern metropolitan areas. Such communities will still hold only a small minority, however. The aged will continue to reside largely in metropolitan areas, though their numbers in the suburbs should increase as suburbs themselves mature.

Many of these predictions suggest that the objective status of the aged will rise in the future. But what of their status relative to the rest of the population? The theories of modernization we have examined link it to declining status of the aged, and an analysis of trends from 1940 to 1969 seemed to support this view in the United States (Palmore and Whittington, 1971). However, in analyzing more recent trends, Palmore (1976) found gains for the aged, compared with younger groups, in health, income, occupational status, and educational attainment. This suggests a "bottoming out" of the status decline associated with modernization, as younger cohorts advance more slowly than at first, and both government and private programs (such as Supplemental Security Income, Medicare, and private pensions) more adequately address the needs of older people. As one indication of these trends, the proportion of the older population living in poverty was cut in half between 1959 and 1974 (Table 2.15 in Chapter 2).

Cohort change may also mean that some of the difficulties now associated with aging may be transitory. For example, the proportion of the aged who are foreign-born or rural-born has been declining rapidly (Uhlenberg, 1977). Thus, older cohorts of the future are much less likely to encounter the additional "culture shock" of moving from one society to another or from rural to urban residence. Uhlenberg also notes that in the future, successive cohorts of the aged will be more similar to each other than they presently are, so that we can direct our attention to developing more stable mechanisms for enhancing the quality of their lives.

These changes in the status of older people suggest some possible changes in the activities and life styles of future aged. Basically, they indicate a lessening of the minority-group status of the aged, as the extent of age differences declines. Perhaps this also means that age stratification will become less important as a differentiating principle in future societies. More affluent older people, faced with increased free time, will engage in a greater variety of leisure life styles, perhaps with greater emphasis on service roles (Havighurst, 1975). They are likely to be less accepting of inadequate services and disadvantages based on age. Their higher status, combined with a greater history of activism, have led many to expect greater political awareness and activism by future older cohorts. Neugarten (1975b) suggests this is most likely for the "young-old" (ages 55 to 75), who are retiring earlier, are relatively healthy and affluent, and seek a wider range of options for community involvement. We are already witnessing a trend toward greater political activism, but the likely extent and effectiveness of this activism is much less clear and it will be undermined as the deprived status of the aged as a minority group declines.

The age structure of a population also has consequences for the society itself. What effects might increasing proportions of older people in the future have on the larger society? There are many speculative possibilities. Aging of the population may bring a natural lessening of the crime problem, since crime is especially prevalent between 15 and 30 (Wilson, 1975). This may be accompanied by declining emphasis on youth and a youth culture. Some have suggested cultural stagnation under the increased influence of a conservative, cautious older population, but such fears are exaggerated, since there is no inevitable link between old age and conservatism. We may see greater stability, however, and less importance attributed to generation gaps. The social problems created by rapid growth of the older population should also subside after about 2020, as low fertility, limited impact of further mortality changes, and low levels of immigration mean little additional growth in the relative size of the older population (Uhlenberg, 1977).

One concern is the cost of caring for increasing numbers of the aged. It is true that the old-age dependency ratio will rise, and programs such as Social Security will become increasingly burdensome. But there is little reason to expect that an older population will create vast crises in financing services. There will be declining pressure to support children and adolescents, as their share of the population declines. In 1900, for example, the overall dependency ratio was 94 dependents per 100 persons of working age, of which 86 were young and only 8 were old; by 1970, this ratio was about the same (91), but only 72 were young and 19 were old (Anderson, 1977). In the next century, the old-age dependency ratio will continue to rise, but the overall dependency ratio will decline. In addition, since future older people are likely to be more affluent and healthy, they will have less need for services.

One intriguing question related to the size of this dependency ratio and the quality of life for the aged is whether there will be significant changes in life expectancy in the future. Longevity is extended in two ways (Hayflick, 1977). The first is through the elimination of major causes of death, which accounts for the increased average life expectancy in modern societies. Even now, elimination of cardiovascular diseases and cancer would probably add about 20 years to life expectancy. While total elimination of disease is not likely in the near future, it was the consensus of a panel of specialists in biological and medical aspects of aging that life expectancy would increase by five to ten years by the year 2000, primarily through advances in disease control (Neugarten and Havighurst, 1977).

The second mechanism for extending longevity is alteration of the biological "clock" which results in physiological decline and increased vulnerability to disease as organisms age. Hayflick notes that the upper limit of the human life span (about 100 years) has apparently not changed over the course of recorded history, though increasing numbers survive toward this upper limit. Laboratory experiments with nonhuman species do indicate that life processes can be extended beyond normal ranges—for example, by cooling body temperature, manipulating immune systems, and sharply reducing caloric intake in diets (Goddard, 1977). Such research has received low priority for funding, however. The panel of experts mentioned above could reach no consensus that the "essential mechanisms of the biology of aging" were likely to be well-understood by the year 2000, though a sizable group did consider this likely (Neugarten and Havighurst, 1977). It is possible that the future will bring extensions to the life span itself, in addition to greater average life expectancy.

The issues discussed here lead us to considering the future of programs and policies affecting the aged. Before doing so, however, we should think about the nature of society in the future.

The Post-Industrial Society

Daniel Bell (1973) has presented the most prominent, and hotly debated, view of the future of modern societies—what he refers to as the *post-industrial society*. Whether or not this view of the future is accurate in its details, discussions of post-industrial society point to some key issues relevant to the future of aging. Bell predicts a shift from a goods-producing to a service economy, with rising preeminence of the professional and technical occupational classes. He notes, for example, that the number of scientists and engineers doubled from 1960 to 1975. The professional and technical class is expected to be the largest occupational group in the United States by the year 2000. They will be working in an economy based on services and information, continuing the recent tremendous growth in government employment.

Modern societies are characterized by enormously rapid change, altering the complexity and scale of the problems which confront us. This is illustrated by the tremendous growth of knowledge. It has been estimated that the scientific and technical literature increases by 60 million pages each year (Toffler, 1971). Bell expects that those who control "theoretical" knowledge will be the new elites of the post-industrial society. Scientists will play enhanced roles as both advisors and advocates within an increasingly centralized system of decision making and policy formulation.

Policy making will increasingly stress logical, rational, and technical assessment of choices and their consequences. These trends toward centralized decision making controlled by a new "meritocracy" may lead to some conflicts. As the government increases its role in all areas of social life, problems in protecting privacy will be exacerbated. There is already growing concern over the dangers of society as "big brother" (Rule, 1974). The centralization of decision making in the hands of technical experts also runs counter to current demands for more widespread participation by people in the decisions which affect their lives.

Bell's work opens up many issues for contention, but many of his ideas have little direct relevance for our concerns in this book. There are two aspects of post-industrial society which do have critical importance for the future of the aging experience, however: (1) post-industrial values, as they will affect life style, and (2) the nature of policy making in the post-industrial society and related issues concerning the setting of goals and priorities.

Post-Industrial Values

One reason for the apparent decline in status for the aged in modern industrial societies concerns the dominant values of such societies—achievement, productivity, independence—and the inability of the elderly to fulfill these values in the roles available to them. One study cited in Chapter 3 (Clark, 1967) went so far as to suggest a cultural discontinuity between the successful values of middle age (achievement, acquisition, control, progress) and those of old age (congeniality, conservation, harmoniousness, continuity). Some analysts of the post-industrial society have suggested, however, that there will be a greater questioning of the key values of industrial society, particularly the work ethic and the emphasis on economic growth.

Daniel Bell (1973) points to a growing contradiction between the social structure, with its emphasis on rationalization, linear progress, and technical mastery of nature, and the culture, with its growing emphasis on consumption and the quality of life. Values of frugality, dedication to work, and delayed gratification are being challenged by emerging cultural values of personal liberation and the acting out of impulses and desires. It is argued that industrial societies overemphasize material considerations and impersonal modes of functioning and the post-industrial society will see greater emphasis on the quality and meaning of life, human relationships, and a cultivation of satisfying social experiences (Rapoport and Rapoport, 1975). Trist (1976) suggests that the following shifts in cultural values will occur in post-industrial society: from achievement to self-actualization, from self-control to self-expression, from independence to interdependence, and from endurance of distress to capacity for joy.

Such value shifts may already be underway. There appears to be increased questioning of traditional forms of work, education, and family and sex roles, as in the loss of the central importance of work in the lives of many people, making retirement and leisure less of an identity crisis than many thought they would be. If these value shifts do occur, they have extremely important implications for the future of the aging experience. The post-industrial society may offer positive rewards for disengagement for both young and old, as an emphasis on leisure and self-actualization grows stronger. Thus, as values of achievement and independence become less important, the relative status of the aged should improve. Indeed, as the group with the greatest freedom of time and action, future older people, particularly the "young-old," may be best able to take advantage of an emerging emphasis on self-expression and self-actualization. Such changes would require revisions in some of our conceptual approaches to old age. For example, problems of rolelessness and minority-group status of the aged would be less important.

The aged—indeed, all of us—could benefit from a "loosening up" of life (Butler, 1975), in which we are no longer locked into life-long "careers" by decisions made early in life. In the post-industrial society, we may see new, more flexible approaches to the life course, as resourcefulness in the use of time is "disinhibited." New concepts of work may emerge, including redistribution of the work week and opportunities for periodic sabbaticals and career change at all occupational levels (Neugarten, 1975b; Butler, 1975). There may be a loosening up of marriage, as already indicated by trends in premarital cohabitation, rising divorce rates, increased remarriage by older people, and more general changes in the character of sex roles (Somerville, 1972; Butler, 1975). Butler also suggests that we may see institutionalization of the concept of education "for life" throughout the life cycle. Though these changes point to "identity crises" throughout the life cycle, as major decisions and changes are no longer confined to adolescence and old age, Butler rightly points out that this is healthy, unfreezing roles and allowing us to rebel against aspects of our lives which no longer "fit." These changes would also bring a blurring of age distinctions. As change is built into all parts of the life course, the aging in particular will be faced with less discontinuity compared with other groups. As was true of the rising relative status of the aged in the future, this means that age stratification assumes less importance, and the aged become less distinct from other age groups.

Many of the current concepts and debates within social gerontology center on discontinuity and failure of socialization for the "roleless role" of old age. Changes in cultural values and the flexibility of life styles in post-industrial society would force us to rethink many of our approaches to the problems of aging. And current older people may represent a unique sociological group. After all, a life expectancy of 80 years is a comparatively new phenomenon, and Shanas (1975) points out that recent cohorts of older people have, in a sense, been pioneers in the unexplored territory of widespread advanced age. They have perhaps failed to make intelligent use of extended life expectancy, still patterning their life careers (work, education, family, leisure) on the basis of decisions made in the teens and twenties.

> One would think that a man who had little chance of living beyond thirty-five would want to cram all the important stages of his life into a brief period. Conversely, one might expect that if given twice the time in which to live out his life cycle, an individual might plan and space out the major events in his life, such as education, marriage, birth of his children, beginning of his work career, and so on—to gain the optimal advantage of all this additional time. But, in reality, little intelligent use is being made of the extension of life expectancy in terms of the spacing of key events in the life cycle. (Browning, 1969:22)

We are now encountering cohorts of people who expect to live to an advanced age and who may have a greater sensitivity to the life cycle and the nature of aging. Rising interest in courses in social gerontology itself suggests that the problems of socialization to old age may be less pronounced in the future, as people prepare their life styles for an expanded life course.

It may be that flexibility of life style will lead people in the future to encounter social and psychological difficulties. Alvin Toffler, in *Future Shock* (1971), suggests that we may be overwhelmed by the pace of change, so that novelty would bring stress and personal disorganization.

> Caught in the turbulent flow of change, called upon to make significant, rapid-fire life decisions, he feels not simply intellectual bewilderment, but disorientation at the level of personal values. As the pace of change quickens, this confusion is tinged with self-doubt, anxiety and fear. He grows tense, tires easily. He may fall ill. As the pressures relentlessly mount, tension shades into

irritability, anger, and sometimes, senseless violence. Little events trigger enormous responses; large events bring inadequate responses. (Toffler, 1971:363)

Others point to a loss of "community" created by a highly mobile society characterized by competition (Slater, 1970; Packard, 1972). Yet these visions of the future do not seem sufficiently persuasive. Most people do seem to adapt reasonably well to uncertainty and change, and whether particular adaptations are "bizarre" depends on the beholder. On a smaller scale, the aged seem to have adapted satisfactorily to the ambiguity of old age. And most people do seem to carve out some place of their own, some community, in the midst of growing change. To take widely varying examples, a sense of community has been found in central cities (Suttles, 1972), racially integrated middle-class neighborhoods (Hunter, 1975), and old-age apartment buildings (Hochschild, 1973). Thus, rapid change and flexibility do not appear to psychologically or socially disable most people.

Flexible life styles and age sensitivity are not inevitable, however. Current trends represent only a very tentative beginning. These visions of post-industrial culture imply major restructuring and redirection of social institutions, as well as of individual character and motivation. Their realization requires opportunities provided by the social structure, in the form of flexible work arrangements, encouragement of life-cycle education, and expansion of alternative community roles. If these opportunities lag behind shifts in cultural values, as Bell (1973) implies they currently are, dislocations and dissatisfaction will emerge throughout the life cycle. And our options and resources in the future will also necessarily be constrained. Heilbroner (1974) has argued that our mounting environmental and energy problems create a necessity to limit growth, rather than optimistically seeking as much economic and technological "progress" as possible. This may prove costly for life style and the quality of life and require some reduction of traditional personal liberties in the face of mounting social and environmental problems. Bell (1973) also agrees that future growth may have to be limited, as we increasingly question our ability to "master" nature. Limited resources and diminishing returns, partly a consequence of the post-industrial shift from a production to a service economy, will make "relative scarcity" and the relative costs of alternative policies critical political issues in post-industrial society. This suggests that options for loosening up life may not always be available and leads us to a consideration of policy making in the future.

Policy Formulation in Post-Industrial Society

The future post-industrial society will be faced with even more rapid change and complex issues than now. The diffusion of innovations throughout the society and increasing interdependency of all segments of society alter the scale of policy issues. Few issues are still local, whether concerning the economy, crime, the environment, or energy, and decentralized political structures are increasingly inadequate for confronting these issues. Bell (1973) argues that problems are increasingly communal rather than individual or interest group concerns. In addition, decisions made about one aspect of society, such as the economy, have complex effects on other aspects, such as the environment.

All of these trends argue for greater societal guidance based on technical knowledge and analysis, to outline constraints, detail procedures, and assess the consequences of choices (Bell, 1973; Lakoff, 1976). For example, Bell notes the increased reliance on such techniques as "systems analysis" and "cost-effectiveness." The government will play an increased role in setting policy, based on centralized, rational planning and conscious definition of goals and priorities. There will be less emphasis on government's role as simply the arbiter among competing interest groups, and less reliance on the private, unregulated market.

If this view of the future is correct, it bodes well for the elderly. Those of us who are "scientific types" place great value on rationality and are always frustrated by the failure of policy makers to pursue carefully analyzed objectives. Programs for the aged have consistently suffered from fragmentation and lack of long-term objectives, particularly such programs as Medicare, which constitute stop-gap responses to a crisis atmosphere. Centralized policy, informed by technical knowledge, implies greater comprehensiveness and accuracy in meeting the needs of older people. Lakoff (1976) also notes the rise in collectivist ideologies— "socialism" or "social liberalism"—in which the state plays a greater role in insuring social justice for disadvantaged groups, including the aged.

And yet doubts linger. Can the future really be so promisingly rational? This question arose in a recent exchange between Peterson and associates (1976) and Cohen (1976). The former foresee a shift in political philosophy in post-industrial society, toward more liberal policies, protection of individual rights, and improvement in the quality of life and social justice. They expect a clear national policy for aging to be developed. Cohen, however, suggests that existing power relationships and the national style of piecemeal policy formulation are not easily changed and there is little evidence that future policies will be more comprehensive or coordinated. Indeed, he argues that we already have a national policy on aging, embodied in Title I of the Older Americans Act of 1965, but it has never been implemented.

We are faced, therefore, with alternative futures: one of rational, comprehensive policies or one of more interest-group competition and "irrationality" in response to problems. A mixture of the two futures is likely to be found in post-industrial society. Policies must increasingly be centralized, with greater long-term planning informed by available knowledge, if society is to avoid chaos. But the world can never be this rational, and conflicts will inevitably arise. Scientists and technicians will play expanded roles, but their power and control will remain limited and incomplete. Interest groups will still compete for resources in the political arena, and the aged are likely to continue to be disadvantaged in this competition. Although they may be more activist on their own behalf in the future, other groups will also make demands on the system. Resources are always limited, and will perhaps be especially so in the future, and we are already encountering a fiscal crisis in the ability of government to meet social needs. One must question the extent of continuing commitment to meeting the needs of the elderly, as there is a growing contradiction between expanding demand for governmental services and rising rebellion over the costs and centralized control associated with those services. It is noteworthy in this regard that Social Security, historically a political "sacred cow," is coming under increasing criticism.

As always, we are faced with complicated prospects for the future. The claims of the aged are not based on a special status conferred by age, as in many primitive societies, but on the general ethical ideal of social justice (Lakoff, 1976). Many other groups are making claims on the basis of social justice, and there is little reason to expect major improvement in the political position of the aged. The welfare of older people should improve, at least in the sense of eliminating their gravest problems: lessening of dire poverty, greater availability of basic medical care, expanded low-income housing, and the like. It is unlikely, however, that future social policy will assure them of a comfortable or prosperous life. This will still be determined by individual resources and the ability of the aged to benefit from programs designed for the general welfare of the population, such as national health insurance.

Policy and Planning for the Aged

It is not especially difficult to outline policy needs for the older population. Indeed, the United States has already outlined the basic requirements of policy for the aged in the Older Americans Act of 1965, which listed the following ten "Objectives for Older Americans":

1. An adequate income
2. The best possible physical and mental health
3. Suitable housing
4. Full restorative services
5. Opportunity for employment without age discrimination
6. Retirement in health, honor, and dignity
7. Pursuit of meaningful activity
8. Efficient community services when needed
9. Immediate benefit from proven research knowledge
10. Freedom, independence, and the free exercise of individual initiative

No one could argue with these laudable goals; yet we have seen ample evidence of failure to meet them. Too many older people continue to suffer from inadequate income, substandard housing, job discrimination, lack of medical care, and restricted opportunities to exercise personal choice in life styles.

The task before us is to implement programs which truly address these goals. Partly this means expansion of existing programs: more home health services, medical insurance which eliminates income inequities, expansion of low-income housing, and so on. Partly it means the development of new programs, some of which are now in their infancy. Butler (1975) has suggested such programs as a National Senior Service Corps to expand the social and community roles available to the elderly and nonprofit "social utilities" to replace commercial nursing homes. Tobin (1975) has predicted that the future will see expanded community-based organizations as alternatives to institutions, smaller long-term care institutions facilitated by such technical advances as telemetric monitoring, and increased establishment of terminal care centers or hospices. To be effective, any new programs must build into a *system* of comprehensive community and institutional services. Services for the aged have too long suffered from fragmentation and a diffusion of responsibility. There is still a crying need for consideration of long-term objectives and consequences of the programs we develop.

Perhaps the most critical need in policy directed at the aged is the encouragement of flexibility and the exercise of personal options. In contrast with preindustrial societies, age stratification in modern societies has largely restricted the roles and opportunities of older persons. A post-industrial society would best benefit the aging experience by loosening up these restrictions through support of increased options in work, leisure, service roles, and other aspects of life style. Specific services and programs should avoid the specter of a "therapeutic state" which structures people's lives for them. Rather, we should structure programs to support people of all ages in their efforts to adapt to their situations in their own chosen ways. In other words, we should support the "right to be different" (Kittrie, 1971). Robert Kahn (1975) recognizes this need in his call for future policies of "minimal intervention."

> Intervention can be harmful as well as helpful. Although resources for intervention should be available when needed, it is best to follow a policy of *minimal intervention;* that is, intervention that is least disruptive of usual functioning in the usual setting. Thus, it would be more sensible to provide care in the home or day-care center than in the hospital; in the storefront rather than in the clinic; in the neighborhood rather than downtown; for brief rather than for long periods; with neighborhood personnel rather than with explicit medical or social agency professionals. Minimal intervention as a positive concept must be differentiated from neglect. It must also be differentiated from "maximal-minimal" intervention, in which the person is removed from his community, then placed in an institution that provides no psychological or social compensatory measures. (Kahn, 1975: 29)

One aspect of Bell's vision of post-industrial society is particularly relevant for policy directed at the aged—the need for rational, informed approaches to increasingly complex problems. Aging policy suffers from inadequate attention to both short- and long-term consequences. Intervention must be based on carefully evaluated knowledge. This knowledge must begin with the causes of the problems to be addressed by policies and the recognition that there may be multiple causes. Some of these causes cannot be easily manipulated through conscious policies; thus, we must address ourselves to those areas in which intervention can have some impact. When intervention does occur, it should involve conscious outlining of the *theory* upon which it is based, the *objectives* we hope to achieve, and the *particular population* for whom it is relevant, and there should be careful assessment of both the *implementation* of programs (the processes by which they operate) and their *impact* (Estes and Freeman, 1976).

Unfortunately, knowledge about how to best address the problems encountered by individuals as they age is not advanced. Because of this, Lakoff (1976) has rightly suggested that we need to encourage a variety of "social experiments," rather than pre-

maturely settling on any single set of policies. We have noted that
it is a matter of debate whether policy formulation in the future
will be any more rational or informed than it has been in the past.
One can only hope that policy makers choose intelligently among
the alternative futures which face us.

The Future of Social Gerontology

The portrait painted of a scientific-technical meritocracy in post-
industrial society implies an expanded importance of social
gerontology and social gerontologists in shaping the aging experience. How well will this role be filled? The scientific study of
aging has made enormous progress during the past 30 years, and yet
as a field it is still in its infancy. This is frustrating in some respects,
as there are many gaps in our understanding of this part of the
life cycle, but there is also something exciting about a field undergoing intellectual ferment.

Many of the older paradigms of social gerontology—disengagement theory, notions about the retirement crisis—are being replaced by frameworks emphasizing age stratification and developmental processes. These newer approaches are far from complete;
at this point, they constitute *sensitizing perspectives*, rather than
coherent, testable theories. Tremendous changes are occurring in
the study of specific substantive areas, such as retirement, widowhood, death and dying, housing, and politics, and many new
"middle-range" theories are emerging to help understand these
aspects of the aging experience. In addition, there is increasing
recognition that the study of aging in any society must be informed by broader frameworks; one cannot understand aging as a
developmental period without looking at the whole of the life
cycle, retirement without looking at work, widowhood without
looking at marriage. Events affecting society also affect the nature
of the aging experience in that society. Thus, social gerontology
must continue to look to more "general" disciplines—such as
sociology, psychology, economics, political science—to accomplish
a true understanding of the processes of social and psychological
aging. And as societies change in the future, as we perhaps enter
a post-industrial society, many of our present concepts and theories
about aging will have to be reevaluated, and in some cases discarded, as we try to understand the aging experience for different
types of people in a different type of society.

There are some clear general research needs. In an assessment
of articles on psychological gerontology, Seltzer (1975) notes that
there has been little attention paid to ethnic and racial differences
or problems of reliability and validity of measurement. Although

findings are often repetitious, there is little cumulative impact, and studies are often not comparable because of differences in sampling and measurement. An assessment of work in social gerontology would undoubtedly find the same problems. More attention needs to be paid to coherent lines of research which conform to rigorous requirements of scientific research. The study of aging also requires its own particular research strategies. Most notably, there is a need for greater emphasis on longitudinal and cohort studies of the life cycle and comparative cross-national research, to investigate continuities and variations in the aging experience in different cohorts and cultures.

Sampling has been a particular problem in social gerontology. It is admittedly difficult—both costly and time-consuming—to get a truly representative sample of the older population. Researchers must often settle for available samples from nursing homes or senior centers, which obviously present biased views of the aging experience, and there is a tremendous gap in knowledge about racial and ethnic subgroups of the aged. Even sex differences have often been ignored. For example, we know relatively little about the reactions of older women to retirement, or of older men to widowhood. The national census is the one source of generalized data about the older population, but it has many flaws for both researcher and practitioner: the "right questions" are often not asked, many characteristics are not broken down by age or subgroups of the aged, sampling biases still exist, and so on. Kendig and Warren (1976) note, for example, that there are far fewer analyses for older people than for blacks, though they constitute roughly equal proportions of the population.

Valid study of the aging experience and effective comprehensive programs to meet the needs of the aged both require accurate information. Hopefully, both the census and gerontological research will better provide this in the future. There are some hopeful signs. Recognizing that one general census cannot adequately fill information needs, an increasing number of special censuses are being undertaken, to provide data about such areas as housing, crime victimization, and health. This coincides with rising interest in the development of *social indicators* to inform decision makers about policy needs and provide one way to measure progress in dealing with social problems.

Social indicators—statistics, statistical series, and all other forms of evidence—are summary measures that enable policy and decision makers to assess various social aspects of an ongoing society and to evaluate specific programs and determine their impact. Social indicators help experts and lay persons alike to better

understand their own and other societies with respect to values
and goals and the nature of social change. (Miller, 1977:267)

Such indicators are currently being refined to measure such diverse
characteristics of the society as crime, health, privacy, and even
the "quality of life."

Social gerontology seems to be enjoying better funding support
than many research areas. In 1975, the National Institute on Aging
(NIA) was established within the National Institutes of Health,
with a mandate "to conduct and support biomedical, social, and
behavioral research and training related to the aging process and
the diseases and other special problems and needs of the aged"
(Murphy, 1976:696). The NIA carries on its own intramural research programs, at the Gerontology Research Center in Baltimore,
as well as funding external research and training. There has also
been a recognition of the need for more training of researchers in
the area of aging. From 1934 to 1971, for example, less than 0.5
percent of all doctoral dissertations in "life sciences" in the United
States dealt with topics related to aging (Butler, 1977). The NIA
now supports approximately 100 scientists yearly through pre- and
postdoctoral fellowships, but this only begins to address the training needs in gerontology, not only for researchers, but for analysts
and practitioners as well.

Research has also received support from other governmental
agencies, such as the Administration on Aging, the National Institute of Mental Health, and the Veteran's Administration, and
from private sources, such as the Russell Sage Foundation and the
NRTA-AARP Andrus Foundation. Future research will be increasingly dependent upon support from the federal government.
While there seems to be a commitment to aging currently, the
continuing level of that commitment and commitment to programs
directed at the aged is uncertain. Without this commitment, however, the research needs we have been discussing cannot be met.

It has been suggested that the post-industrial society will be
faced with problems of increasing complexity and scale and that
there will be a greater need for informed policy formulation. This
has important implications for the future of social gerontology.
The complexity of issues in the study of aging require interdisciplinary approaches, and this will be even more true in the
future. That is why the emergence of interdisciplinary programs
for research and training in gerontology at many universities is a
very encouraging trend. Indeed, these institutes are apparently
achieving preeminence in the research literature on aging (Rasch,
1976).

The complexity of aging and the explosion of interest in this area are creating their own problems of information coordination. Some very useful bibliographies are in existence: for example, Nathan Shock's "Current Publications in Gerontology," published bimonthly in the *Journal of Gerontology,* and a series of bibliographies on specific topics published by the Andrus Gerontology Center, at the University of Southern California. But there is a growing need for comprehensive information systems to meet the needs of both researchers and policy makers (Miller and Cutler, 1976).

The need for policies based on the best available knowledge also requires a continuing dialogue among researchers, planners, and practitioners. Such dialogues encounter difficulties in any area, and gerontology is no exception. Research may lack relevance for policy needs and programs, and discipline boundaries and language barriers further hinder the translation of research into practice (Urban and Watson, 1974). Such barriers must be overcome, however, if we are to achieve rational, comprehensive programs to meet the needs of older people.

Some Final Comments

The aging experience is neither "good" nor "bad." As with all aspects of life, old age is a complicated mix of benefits and costs, problems and potentialities. This book has attempted to provide an appreciation of this complexity. Those who study aging and all of us who age can better accomplish both tasks when we have an accurate picture of what can be expected. Accuracy is the goal of all scientific endeavor, since it is the root of understanding.

The reader will have an opportunity to shape the aging experience in three ways. Some who read this book may choose a career in social gerontology. There is a tremendous need for researchers, social workers, planners, housing managers, physicians, nurses, teachers, program directors, and other professionals in the various fields associated with aging. As citizens, our impact on society and its future affects the context within which the aging experience takes place. Finally, all of us will shape our own aging experiences, in light of our own life styles and patterns of living. It is hoped that this book has contributed in some way to all three of these endeavors.

References

Anderson, Odin
    1977   "Reflections on the sick aged and the helping systems." In
            Bernice Neugarten and Robert Havighurst (eds.). Social
            Policy, Social Ethics, and the Aging Society. Washington,
            D.C.: U.S. Government Printing Office.

Bell, Daniel
   1973   The Coming of Post-Industrial Society. New York:
          Basic Books.
Browning, Harvey
   1969   "The timing of our lives." Transaction/Society 6: 22–27.
Butler, Robert
   1975   Why Survive?: Being Old in America. New York: Harper &
          Row.
   1977   "Trends in training in research gerontology." Educational
          Gerontology 2: 111–13.
Clark, Margaret
   1967   "The anthropology of aging: A new area for studies of
          culture and personality." The Gerontologist 7: 55–64.
Cohen, Elias
   1976   "Comment: Editor's Note." The Gerontologist 16: 270–75.
Deutscher, Irwin
   1973   What We Say/What We Do. Glenview, Ill.: Scott,
          Foresman.
Elder, Glen, Jr.
   1974   Children of the Great Depression. Chicago: University of
          Chicago Press.
Estes, C. L. and Howard Freeman
   1976   "Strategies of design and research for intervention." In
          Robert Binstock and Ethel Shanas (eds.). Handbook of
          Aging and the Social Sciences. New York: Van Nostrand
          Reinhold.
Goddard, James
   1977   "Extension of the life span: A national goal?" In Bernice
          Neugarten and Robert Havighurst (eds.). Extending the
          Human Life Span: Social Policy and Social Ethics.
          Washington, D.C.: U.S. Government Printing Office.
Golant, Stephen
   1975   "Residential concentrations of the future elderly." In
          Bernice Neugarten (ed.). Aging in the Year 2000: A Look
          at the Future. The Gerontologist 15 (1-Part II): 16–23.
Havighurst, Robert
   1975   "The future aged. The use of time and money." In Bernice
          Neugarten (ed.). Aging in the Year 2000: A Look at the
          Future. The Gerontologist 15 (1-Part II): 10–15.
Hayflick, Leonard
   1977   "Perspectives on human longevity." In Bernice Neugarten
          and Robert Havighurst (eds.). Extending the Human Life
          Span: Social Policy and Social Ethics. Washington, D.C.:
          U.S. Government Printing Office.
Heilbroner, Robert
   1974   An Inquiry into the Human Prospect. New York:
          W. W. Norton.

Hochschild, Arlie
  1973 The Unexpected Community. Englewood Cliffs, N.J.:
        Prentice-Hall.
Hunter, Albert
  1975 "The loss of community: An empirical test through replica-
        tion." American Sociological Review 40: 537–52.
Kahn, Herman and Anthony Wiener
  1969 "The next thirty-three years: A framework for speculation."
        In Daniel Bell (ed.). Toward the Year 2000: Work in
        Progress. Boston: Beacon Press.
Kahn, Robert
  1975 "The mental health system and the future aged." In
        Bernice Neugarten (ed.). Aging in the Year 2000: A Look
        at the Future. The Gerontologist 15 (1-Part II): 24–31.
Kendig, Harold, Jr. and Robert Warren
  1976 "The adequacy of census data in planning and advocacy for
        the elderly." The Gerontologist 16: 392–96.
Kittrie, Nicholas
  1971 The Right to Be Different. Baltimore, M.D.: Johns Hopkins
        Press.
Lakoff, Sanford
  1976 "The future of social intervention." In Robert Binstock
        and Ethel Shanas (eds.). Handbook of Aging and the Social
        Sciences. New York: Van Nostrand Reinhold.
Miller, Delbert
  1977 Handbook of Research Design and Social Measurement.
        New York: David McKay.
Miller, Emily and Neal Cutler
  1976 "Toward a comprehensive information system in gerontology:
        A survey of problems, resources, and potential solutions."
        The Gerontologist 16: 198–206.
Murphy, Donald
  1976 "Report from the National Institute on Aging: The
        research grant support mechanism." Journal of Gerontology
        31: 696–704.
Neugarten, Bernice
  1975a (ed.) Aging in the Year 2000: A Look at the Future. The
        Gerontologist 15 (1-Part II).
  1975b "The future and the young-old." In Bernice Neugarten
        (ed.). Aging in the Year 2000: A Look at the Future. The
        Gerontologist 15 (1-Part II): 4–9.
Neugarten, Bernice and Robert Havighurst (eds.)
  1977 Extending the Human Life Span: Social Policy and Social
        Ethics. Washington, D.C.: U.S. Government Printing
        Office.
Packard, Vance
  1972 A Nation of Strangers. New York: David McKay.

Palmore, Erdman
  1976   "The future status of the aged." The Gerontologist 16:
          297–302.
Palmore, Erdman and Frank Whittington
  1971   "Trends in the relative status of the aged." Social Forces
          50: 84–91.
Peterson, David, Chuck Powell, and Lawrie Robertson
  1976   "Aging in America: Toward the year 2000." The Gerontol-
          ogist 16: 264–70.
Rapoport, Rhona and Robert Rapoport
  1975   Leisure and the Family Life Cycle. London: Routledge and
          Kegan Paul.
Rasch, John
  1976   "Institutional origins of articles in *The Gerontologist*:
          1961–1975." The Gerontologist 16: 276–79.
Rule, James
  1974   Private Lives and Public Surveillance: Social Control in
          the Computer Age. New York: Schocken Books.
Seltzer, Mildred
  1975   "The quality of research is strained." The Gerontologist
          15: 503–07.
Shanas, Ethel
  1975   "Discussion." In Bernice Neugarten (ed.). Aging in the
          Year 2000: A Look at the Future. The Gerontologist 15
          (1-Part II): 38.
Slater, Philip
  1970   The Pursuit of Loneliness: American Culture at the
          Breaking Point. Boston: Beacon Press.
Somerville, Rose
  1972   "The future of family relationships." The Family
          Coordinator 487–98.
Suttles, Gerald
  1972   The Social Construction of Communities. Chicago:
          University of Chicago Press.
Tobin, Sheldon
  1975   "Social and health services for the future aged." In Bernice
          Neugarten (ed.). Aging in the Year 2000: A Look at the
          Future. The Gerontologist 15 (1-Part II): 32–37.
Toffler, Alvin
  1971   Future Shock. New York: Bantam Books.
Trist, Eric
  1976   "Toward a postindustrial culture." In Robert Dubin (ed.).
          Handbook of Work, Organization, and Society. Chicago:
          Rand McNally.
Uhlenberg, Peter
  1977   "Changing structure of the older population of the USA
          during the twentieth century." The Gerontologist 17:
          197–202.

Urban, Hugh and Wayne Watson
  1974 "Response to bridging the gap: Alternative approaches."
        The Gerontologist 14: 530–33.
Wilson, James
  1975 Thinking about Crime. New York: Basic Books.

INDEX

79 80 81 82 9 8 7 6 5 4 3 2 1